Pro .NET Memory Management

For Better Code, Performance, and Scalability

Konrad Kokosa

Pro .NET Memory Management

Konrad Kokosa
Warsaw, Poland

ISBN-13 (pbk): 978-1-4842-4026-7   ISBN-13 (electronic): 978-1-4842-4027-4
https://doi.org/10.1007/978-1-4842-4027-4

Library of Congress Control Number: 2018962862

Managing Director, Apress Media LLC: Welmoed Spahr
Acquisitions Editor: Joan Murray
Development Editor: Laura Berendson
Coordinating Editor: Nancy Chen

Cover designed by eStudioCalamar

Cover image designed by Freepik (www.freepik.com)

Distributed to the book trade worldwide by Springer Science+Business Media New York, 233 Spring Street, 6th Floor, New York, NY 10013. Phone 1-800-SPRINGER, fax (201) 348-4505, e-mail orders-ny@springer-sbm.com, or visit www.springeronline.com. Apress Media, LLC is a California LLC and the sole member (owner) is Springer Science + Business Media Finance Inc (SSBM Finance Inc). SSBM Finance Inc is a **Delaware** corporation.

For information on translations, please e-mail rights@apress.com, or visit http://www.apress.com/rights-permissions.

Apress titles may be purchased in bulk for academic, corporate, or promotional use. eBook versions and licenses are also available for most titles. For more information, reference our Print and eBook Bulk Sales web page at http://www.apress.com/bulk-sales.

Any source code or other supplementary material referenced by the author in this book is available to readers on GitHub via the book's product page, located at www.apress.com/9781484240267. For more detailed information, please visit http://www.apress.com/source-code.

Printed on acid-free paper

To my beloved wife, Justyna, without whom nothing really valuable would happen in my life.

Table of Contents

About the Author

Konrad Kokosa is an experienced software designer and developer with a specific interest in Microsoft technologies, while looking with curiosity at everything else. He has been programming for over a dozen years, solving performance problems and architectural puzzles in the .NET world, and designing and speeding up .NET applications. He is an independent consultant, blogger at `http://tooslowexception.com`, meetup and conference speaker, and fan of Twitter (@konradkokosa). He also shares his passion as a trainer in the area of .NET, especially regarding application performance, coding good practices, and diagnostics. He is the founder of the Warsaw Web Performance group. He is a Microsoft MVP in the Visual Studio and Development Tools category. He is the co-founder of the Dotnetos.org initiative of three .NET fans organizing tours and conferences about .NET performance.

About the Technical Reviewers

Damien Foggon is a developer, writer, and technical reviewer in cutting-edge technologies and has contributed to more than 50 books on .NET, C#, Visual Basic, and ASP.NET. He is the co-founder of the Newcastle based user-group NEBytes (online at `http://www.nebytes.net`), is a multiple MCPD in .NET 2.0 onward, and can be found online at `http://blog.fasm.co.uk`.

Maoni Stephens is the architect and main developer for the .NET GC in Microsoft. Her blog is at `https://blogs.msdn.microsoft.com/maoni/`.

Acknowledgments

First of all, I would like to thank my wife very, very much. Without her support this book would never have been created. Starting to work on this book, I did not imagine how much time not spent together we would have to sacrifice while writing it. Thank you for all the patience, support, and encouragement you have given to me during this time!

Secondly, I would like to thank Maoni Stephens for such extensive, accurate, and invaluable remarks when reviewing the first versions of this book. Without a shadow of a doubt I can say that thanks to her, this book is better. And the fact that the lead .NET GC developer helped me in writing this book is for me a reward in itself! Many thanks go also to other .NET team members that helped in reviewing some parts of the book, organized also with great help from Maoni (ordered by the amount of work they contributed): Stephen Toub, Jared Parsons, Lee Culver, Josh Free, and Omar Tawfik. I would like also to thank Mark Probst from Xamarin; he reviewed notes about Mono runtime. And special thanks go to Patrick Dussud, "the father of .NET GC," for taking time to review the history of CLR creation.

Thirdly, I would like to thank Damien Foggon, technical reviewer from Apress, who put so much work into a meticulous review of all chapters. His experience in publishing and writing was invaluable to make this book clearer and more consistent. Not once or twice, I was surprised by the accuracy of Damian's comments and suggestions!

I would obviously like to thank everyone at Apress, without whom this book wouldn't have been published in the first place. Special thanks go to Laura Berendson (Development Editor), Nancy Chen (Coordinating Editor), and Joan Murray (Senior Editor) for all the support and patience in extending the deadline again and again. I know there was a time when the date of delivery of the final version was taboo between us! I would also like to thank Gwenan Spearing, with whom I started working on the book, but I did not manage to finish it before she left the Apress team.

I would like to thank a great .NET community in Poland and all around the world, for inspirations from so many great presentations given, articles and posts written by you, for all encouragement and support, and for endless questions about "how a book goes?" Such thanks especially go to (alphabetically): Maciej Aniserowicz, Arkadiusz Benedykt, Sebastian Gębski, Michał Grzegorzewski, Jakub Gutkowski, Paweł Klimczyk,

ACKNOWLEDGMENTS

Szymon Kulec, Paweł Łukasik, Alicja Musiał, Łukasz Olbromski, Łukasz Pyrzyk, Bartek Sokół, Sebastian Solnica, Paweł Sroczyński, Jarek Stadnicki, Piotr Stapp, Michał Śliwoń, Szymon Warda, and Artur Wincenciak, all MVP guys (Azure guys, looking at you!), and many more; and I sincerely apologize for those omitted, big thank you to everyone who feels like receiving such thanks. It is simply not possible to list all of you here. You've inspired me and encouraged me.

I'd like to thank all experienced writers that found time to give me advice about book writing, including Ted Neward (`http://blogs.tedneward.com/`) and Jon Skeet (`https://codeblog.jonskeet.uk`) - although I bet they do not remember those conversations! Andrzej Krzywda (`http://andrzejonsoftware.blogspot.com`) and Gynvael Coldwind (`https://gynvael.coldwind.pl`) also gave me a lot of very valuable advices on writing and publishing a book.

Next, I'd like to thank all the great tools and libraries creators that I've used during this book writing: Andrey Shchekin, a creator of SharpLab (`https://sharplab.io`); Andrey Akinshin, a creator of BenchmarkDotNet (`https://benchmarkdotnet.org`); and Adam Sitnik, the main maintainer of it; Sergey Teplyakov, a creator of ObjectLayoutInspector (`https://github.com/SergeyTeplyakov/ObjectLayoutInspector`); 0xd4d, an anonymous creator of dnSpy (`https://github.com/0xd4d/dnSpy`); Sasha Goldshtein, creator of many useful auxiliary tools (`https://github.com/goldshtn`); and creators of such great tools like PerfView and WinDbg (and all its .NET-related extensions).

I'd also like to thank my former employee, Bank Millennium, who helped and supported me in starting to write this book. Our path has parted, but I will always remember that it was there that my writing, blogging, and speaking adventure began. Many thanks go also collectively to my former colleagues from there, for the same amount of encouragement and motivation by the "how a book goes?" question.

I'd like to thank all anonymous Twitter users that answered my book-related surveys, giving me directions about what is - and what is not - interesting, useful, and valuable for our .NET family.

And the last, but not least, I would collectively thank all my family and friends that missed me during my work on this book.

Foreword

When I joined the Common Language Runtime (the runtime for .NET) team more than a decade ago, little did I know this component called the Garbage Collector was going to become something I would spend most of my waking moments thinking about later in my life. Among the first few people I worked with on the team was Patrick Dussud, who had been both the architect and dev for the CLR GC since its inception. After observing my work for months, he passed the torch, and I became the second dedicated GC dev for CLR.

And so my GC journey began. I soon discovered how fascinating the world of garbage collection was - I was amazed by the complex and extensive challenges in a GC and loved coming up with efficient solutions for them. As the CLR was used in more scenarios by more users, and memory being one of the most important performance aspects, new challenges in the memory management space kept coming up. When I first started, it was not common to see a GC heap that was even 200mb; today a 20GB heap is not uncommon at all. Some of the largest workloads in the world are running on CLR. How to handle memory better for them is no doubt an exciting problem.

In 2015 we open sourced CoreCLR. When this was announced, the community asked whether the GC source would be excluded in the CoreCLR repo - a fair question as our GC included many innovative mechanisms and policies. The answer was a resounding no, and it was the same GC code we used in CLR. This clearly attracted some curious minds. A year later I was delighted to learn that one of our customers was planning to write a book specifically about our GC. When a technology evangelist from our Polish office asked me if I would be available to review Konrad's book, of course I said yes!

As I received chapters from Konrad, it was clear to me that he studied our GC code with great diligence. I was very impressed with the amount of detail covered. Sure, you can build CoreCLR and step through the GC code yourself. But this book will definitely make that easier for you. And since an important class of readers of this book is GC users, Konrad included a lot of material to better understand the GC behavior and coding patterns to use the GC more efficiently. There is also fundamental information on memory at the beginning of the book and discussions of memory usage in various libraries toward the end. I thought it was a perfect balance of GC introduction, internals, and usage.

If you use .NET and care about memory performance, or if you are just curious about the .NET GC and want to understand its inner workings, this is the book to get. I hope you will have as much enjoyment reading it as I did reviewing it.

Maoni Stephens

July 2018

Introduction

In computer science, memory has been always there - from the punch cards, through magnetic tapes to the nowadays, sophisticated DRAM chips. And it will be always there, probably in the form of sci-fi holographic chips or even much more amazing things that we are now not able to imagine. Of course, the memory was there not without a reason. It is well known that computer programs are said to be algorithms and data structures joined together. I like this sentence very much. Probably everyone has at least once heard about the *Algorithms + Data Structures = Programs* book written by Niklaus Wirth (Prentice Hall, 1976), where this great sentence was coined.

From the very beginning of the software engineering field, memory management was a topic known by its importance. From the first computer machines, engineers had to think about the storage of algorithms (program code) and data structures (program data). It was always important how and where those data are loaded and stored for later use.

In this aspect, software engineering and memory management have been always inherently related, as much as software engineering and algorithms are. And I believe it always will be like that. Memory is a limited resource, and it always will be. Hence, at some point or degree, memory will always be kept in the minds of future developers. If a resource is limited, there always can be some kind of bug or misuse that leads to starvation of this resource. Memory is not an exception here.

Having said that, there is for sure one thing that is constantly changing regarding memory management - the quantity. First developers, or we should name them engineers, were aware of every single bit of their programs. Then they had kilobytes of memory. From each and every decade, those numbers are growing and today we are living in times of gigabytes, while terabytes and petabytes are kindly knocking into the door waiting for their turn. As the memory size grows, the access times decrease, making it possible to process all this data in a satisfying time. But even though we can say memory is fast, simple memory-management algorithms that try to process all gigabytes of data without any optimizations and more sophisticated tunings would not be feasible. This is mostly because memory access times are improving slower than the processing power of CPUs utilizing them. Special care must be taken to not introduce bottlenecks of memory access, limiting the power of today's CPUs.

This makes memory management not only of crucial importance, but also a really fascinating part of computer science. Automatic memory management makes it even better. It is not as easy as saying "let the unused objects be freed." What, how, and when - those simple aspects of memory management make it continuously an ongoing process of improving the old and inventing new algorithms. Countless scientific papers and PhD theses are considering how to automatically manage memory in the most optimal way. Events like the International Symposium on Memory Management (ISMM) shows every year how much is done in this field, regarding garbage collection; dynamic allocation; and interactions with runtimes, compilers, and operating systems. And then academic research slightly changes into commercialized and open sourced products we use in everyday work.

.NET is a perfect example of a managed environment where all such sophistication is hidden underneath, available to developers as a pleasant, ready-to-use platform. And indeed, we can use it without any awareness of the underlying complexity, which is a great .NET achievement in general. However, the more performance aware our program is, the less possible it is to avoid gaining any knowledge about how and why things work underneath. Moreover, personally I believe it is just fun to know how things we use every day work!

I've written this book in a way that I would have loved to read many years ago - when I started my journey into the .NET performance and diagnostic area. Thus, this book does not start from a typical introduction about the heap and the stack or description of multiple generations. Instead, I start from the very fundamentals behind memory management in general. In other words, I've tried to write this book in a way that will let you sense this very interesting topic, not only showing "here is a .NET Garbage Collector and it does this and that." Providing information not only what, but also how, and more importantly - why - should truly help you understand what is behind the scene of .NET memory management. Hence, everything you will read in regard to this topic in the future should be more understandable to you. I try to enlighten you with knowledge a little more general than just related to .NET, especially in the first two chapters. This leads to deeper understanding of the topic, which quite often may be also applied to other software engineering tasks (thanks to an understanding of algorithms, data structures, and simply good engineering stuff).

I wanted to write this book in a manner pleasant for every .NET developer. No matter how experienced you are, you should find something interesting here. While we start from the basics, junior programmers quickly will have an opportunity to get deeper into

.NET internals. More advanced programmers will find many implementation details more interesting. And above all, regardless of experience, everyone should be able to benefit from the presented practical examples of code and problem diagnoses.

Thus, knowledge from this book should help you to write better code - more performance and memory aware, utilizing related features without fear but with full understanding. This also leads to better performance and scalability of your applications - the more memory oriented your code is, the less exposed it is for resource bottlenecks and utilization of them not optimally. I hope you will find the "For Better Code, Performance, and Scalability" subtitle justified after reading this book.

I also hope all this makes this book more general and long lasting than just a simple description of the current state of the .NET framework and its internals. No matter how future .NET frameworks will evolve, I believe most of the knowledge in this book will be actually true for a long time. Even if some implementation details will change, you should be able to easily understand them because of the knowledge from this book. Just because underlying principles won't change so fast. I wish you a pleasant journey through the huge and entertaining topic of automatic memory management!

Having said that, I would like also to emphasize a few things that are not particularly present in this book. The subject of memory management, although it seems very specialized and narrow at the first glance, is surprisingly wide. While I touch a lot of topics, they are sometimes presented not as detailed as I would like, for lack of space. Even with such limitations, the book is around 1104 pages long! Those omitted topics include, for example, comprehensive references to other managed environments (like Java, Python, or Ruby). I also apologize to F# fans for so few references to this language. There were not enough pages for a solid description simply, and I did not want to publish anything not being comprehensive. I would also have liked to put much more attention to the Linux environment, but this is so fresh and uncovered by the tools topic that at the time of writing, I only give you some proposals in Chapter 3 (and omitting the macOs world completely for the same reasons). Obviously, I've also omitted a large part of other, not directly memory-related part of performance in .NET - like multithreading topics.

Secondly, although I've done my best to present practical applications of the topics and techniques discussed, this is not always possible without doing so in a completely exhausting way. Practical applications are simply too many. I rather expect from a reader reading comprehensively, rethinking the topic, and applying the knowledge gained in their regular work. Understand how something works and you will be able to use it!

This especially includes so-called scenarios. Please note that all scenarios included in this book are for illustrative purposes. Their code has been distilled to the bare minimum to easier show the root cause of one single problem. There may be various other reasons behind the observed misbehaving (like many ways how managed memory leaks may be noticed). Scenarios were prepared in a way to help illustrate such problems with a single example cause as it is obviously not possible to include all probable reasons in a single book. Moreover, in real-world scenarios, your investigation will be cluttered with a lot of noisy data and false investigation paths. There is often no single way of solving the described issues and yet many ways how you can find the root cause during problems analysis. This makes such troubleshooting a mix of a pure engineering task with a little of an art backed by your intuition. Please note also that scenarios sometimes reference to each other to not repeat themselves again and again with the same steps, figures, and descriptions.

I especially refrained from mentioning various technology-specific cases and sources of problems in this book. They are simply... too much technology specific. If I was writing this book 10 years ago, I would probably have had to list various typical scenarios of memory leaks in ASP.NET WebForms and WinForms. A few years ago? ASP.NET MVC, WPF, WCF, WF,... Now? ASP.NET Core, EF Core, Azure Functions, what else? I hope you get the point. Such knowledge is becoming obsolete too soon. The book stuffed with examples of WCF memory leaks would hardly interest anyone today. I am a huge fan of saying: "Give a man a fish; you have fed him for today. Teach a man to fish; and you have fed him for a lifetime." Thus, all the knowledge in this book, all the scenarios, are teaching you how to fish. All problems, regardless of underlying specific technology, may be diagnosed in the same way, if enough knowledge and understanding are being applied.

All this also makes reading this book quite demanding, as it is sometimes full of details and maybe a little overwhelming amount of information. Despite everything, I encourage you to read in-depth and slow, resisting the temptation of only a skimming reading. For example, to take full advantage of this book, one should carefully study the code shown and presented figures (and not just look at them, stating that they are obvious, so they may be easily omitted).

We are living in a great time of open sourced CoreCLR runtime. This moves CLR runtime understanding possibilities to a whole new level. There is no guessing, no mysteries. Everything is in code, may be read, and understood. Thus, my investigations of how things work are heavily based on CoreCLR's code of its GC (which is shared with .NET Framework as well). I've spent countless days and weeks analyzing this huge amount of good engineering work. I think it is great, and I believe there are people who would also like to study famous gc.cpp file, with a size of several tens of thousands of lines of code. It has a very steep learning curve, however. To help you with that, I often leave some clues where to start CoreCLR code study with respect to described topics. Feel free to get an even deeper understanding from the gc.cpp points I suggest!

After reading this book you should be able to:

- Write performance and memory-aware code in .NET. While presented examples are in C#, I believe with the understanding and toolbox you gain here, you will be able to apply this also to F# or VB.NET.

- Diagnose typical problems related to .NET memory management. As most techniques are based on ETW/LLTng data and SOS extension, they are applicable both on Windows and Linux (with much more advanced tooling available on Windows).

- Understand how CLR works in the memory management area. I've put quite a lot of attention to explain not only how things work but also why.

- Read with the full understanding of many interesting C# and CLR runtime issues on GitHub and even participate with your own thoughts.

- Read the code of the GC in CoreCLR (especially gc.cpp) file with enough understanding to make further investigations and studies.

- Read with the full understanding of information about GCs and memory management in different environments like Java, Python, or Go.

As to the content of the book itself, it presents as follows. Chapter 1 is a very general theoretical introduction to memory management, without almost any reference to .NET in particular. Chapter 2 is similarly a general introduction to memory management on the hardware and operating system level. Both chapters may be treated as an important, yet optional introduction. They give a helpful, broader look at the topic, useful in the rest of the book. While I obviously and strongly encourage you to read them, you may omit them if you are in a hurry or interested only in the most practical, .NET-related topics. A note to advanced readers - even if you think topics from those two first chapters are well known to you, please read them. I've tried to include there not only obvious information, which you may find interesting.

Chapter 3 is solely dedicated to measurements and various tools (among which some are very often used later in the book). It is a reading that contains mainly a list of tools and how to use them. If you are interested mostly in the theoretical part of the book, you may only skim through it briefly. On the other hand, if you plan to use the knowledge of this book intensively in the diagnosis of problems, you will probably come back to this chapter often.

Chapter 4 is the first one where we start talking about .NET intensively, while still in a general way allowing us to understand some relevant internals like .NET type system (including value type versus reference type), string interning, or static data. If you are really in a hurry, you may wish to start reading from there. Chapter 5 described the first truly memory-related topic - how memory is organized in .NET applications, introducing the concept of Small and Large Object Heap, as well as segments. Chapter 6 is going further into memory-related internals, dedicated solely to allocating memory. Quite surprisingly, quite a big chapter may be dedicated to such a theoretically simple topic. An important and big part of this chapter is the description of various sources of allocations, in the context of avoiding them.

Chapters from 7 to 10 are core parts describing how the GC works in .NET, with practical examples and considerations resulting from such knowledge. To not overwhelm with too much information provided at the same time, those chapters are describing the simplest flavor of the GC - so-called Workstation Non-Concurrent one. On the other hand, Chapter 11 is dedicated to describing all other flavors with comprehensive considerations that one can choose. Chapter 12 concludes the GC part of the book, describing three important mechanisms: finalization, disposable objects, and weak references.

The three last chapters constitute the "advanced" part of the book, in the sense of explaining how things work beyond the core part of .NET memory management. Chapter 13 explains, for example, the topic of managed pointers and goes deeper into structs (including recently added ref structs). Chapter 14 puts a lot of attention to types and techniques gaining more and more popularity recently, like `Span<T>` and `Memory<T>` types. There is also a smart section dedicated to the not-so-well known topic of data-oriented design and, few words about incoming C# features (like nullable reference types and pipelines). Chapter 15, the last one, describes various ways how we can control and monitor the GC from code, including GC class API, CLR Hosting, or ClrMD library.

Most of the listings from this book are available at the accompanying GitHub repository at `https://github.com/Apress/pro-.net-memory`. It is organized into chapters and most of them contain two solutions: one for conducted benchmarks and one for other listings. Please note that while included projects contain listings, there is often more code for you to look at. If you want to use or experiment with a particular listing, the easiest way will be just to search for its number and play around with it and its usage. But I also encourage you to just look around in projects for particular topics for better understanding.

There are not so many important conventions I would like to mention here. The most relevant one is to differentiate two main concepts used throughout the rest of the book:

- Garbage collection (GC) - the generally understood process of reclaiming no-longer needed memory.

- The Garbage Collector (the GC) - the specific mechanism realizing garbage collection, most obviously in the context of the .NET GC.

This book is also pretty self-contained and does not refer to many other materials or books. Obviously, there is a lot of great knowledge out there, and I would need to refer to various sources many times. Instead, let me just list the suggested books and articles of my choice as a complementary source of knowledge:

- *Pro .NET Performance* book written by Sasha Goldshtein, Dima Zurbalev, and Ido Flatow (Apress, 2012.

- *CLR via C#* book written by Jeffrey Richter (Microsoft Press, 2012).

- *Writing High-Performance .NET Code* by Ben Watson (Ben Watson, 2014).

- *Advanced .NET Debugging* by Mario Hewardt (Addison-Wesley Professional, 2009).

- *.NET IL Assembler* by Serge Lidin (Microsoft Press, 2012)

- *Shared Source CLI Essentials* by David Stutz (O'Reilly Media, 2003).

- "Book Of The Runtime" open source documentation developed in parallel to the runtime itself, available at `https://github.com/dotnet/coreclr/blob/master/Documentation/botr/README.md`.

There is also a huge amount of knowledge from various online blogs and articles. But instead of flooding those pages with a list of them, let me just redirect you to a great `https://github.com/adamsitnik/awesome-dot-net-performance` repository maintained by Adam Sitnik.

CHAPTER 1

Basic Concepts

Let's start from a simple, yet very important question. When you should care about .NET memory management if it is all automated? Should you care at all? As you probably expect by the fact that I wrote such a book - I strongly encourage you to remember about memory in every developer's situation. This is just a matter of our professionalism. A consequence of how we conduct our work. Are we trying to make our best or just make? If we take care of the quality of our work, we should worry not only about our piece of work to be just working. We should be worried about how is it working. Is it optimal in terms of CPU and memory usage? Is it maintainable, testable, opened for extension but closed for modification? Is our code SOLID? I believe all those questions distinguish beginners from more advanced, experienced programmers. The former are mainly interested in getting the job done and do not care much about the above-mentioned, nonfunctional aspects of their work. The latter are experienced enough to have enough "mental processing power" to consider the quality of their work. I believe everyone wants to be like that. But this is, of course, not a trivial thing. Writing an elegant code, without any bugs, with each possible nonfunctional requirement fulfilled is really hard.

But should such a desire for the mastery be the only prerequisite for gaining deeper knowledge about .NET memory management? Memory corruptions revealing as `AccessViolationException` are extremely rare.[1] The uncontrolled increase in memory usage can also appear so. Do we have anything to be worried about then? As .NET runtime has a sophisticated Microsoft implementation, luckily we do not have to think about memory aspects a lot. But, on the other hand, when being involved in analyzing performance problems of big .NET-based applications, memory consumption problems were always high on the list of issues. Does it cause trouble in the long-term

---

[1] `AccessViolationException` or other heap corruption can often be triggered by the automatic memory management, not because it is the cause, but because it is the heaviest memory-related component in the environment. Thus, it has the biggest possibility to reveal any inconsistent memory states.

1

© Konrad Kokosa 2018
K. Kokosa, *Pro .NET Memory Management*, https://doi.org/10.1007/978-1-4842-4027-4_1

view if we have a memory leak after days of continuous running? On the Internet we can find a funny meme about a memory leak that was not fixed in the software of some particular combat missile, because the memory was enough before the missile reached its destination. Is our system such a one-time missile? Do we realize whether automated memory management introduces a big overhead for our application or not? Maybe we could use only two servers instead of ten? And further, we are not memory free even in the times of server-less cloud computing. One of the examples can be Azure Functions, which are billed based on a measure called "gigabyte seconds" (GB-s). It is calculated by multiplying the average memory size in gigabytes by the time in seconds it takes to execute a particular function. Memory consumption directly translates into money we spent.

In each case, we begin to realize that we have no idea where to start looking for the real cause and valuable measurements. This is the place where we begin to understand that it is worthwhile to understand internal mechanisms of our applications and the underlying runtime.

In order to deeply understand memory management in .NET, it is best to start from scratch. No matter whether you are a novice programmer or very advanced one. I would recommend that together we went through the theoretical introduction in this chapter. This will establish a common level of knowledge and understanding of concepts, which will be used through the rest of the book. For this not to be simply boring theory, sometimes I refer to specific technologies. We will have a chance to get a little history of software development. It fits well in the development of concepts related to memory management. We will notice also some little interesting facts, which I hope will prove to be interesting for you also. Knowing history is always one of the best ways to get the broader perspective of the topic.

But do not be afraid. This is not a historical book. I will not describe biographies of all engineers involved in developing garbage collection algorithms since 1950. Ancient history background won't be necessary either. But still, I hope you will find it interesting to know how this topic evolved and where we are now in the history timeline. This will also allow us to compare the .NET approach to the many other languages and runtimes you might hear about from time to time.

Memory-Related Terms

Before we begin, it is useful to take a look at some very important definitions, without which it is difficult to imagine discussing the topic of memory:

- *bit* - it is the smallest unit of information used in computer technology. It represents two possible states, usually meaning numerical values 0 and 1 or logic values true and false. We briefly mention how modern computers store single bits in Chapter 2. To represent bigger numerical values, a combination of multiple bits needs to be used to encode it as a binary number explained below. When specifying the data size, bits are specified with the lowercase letter b.

- *binary number* - integer numerical value represented as a sequence of bits. Each successive bit determines the contribution of the successive power of 2 in the sum of the given value. For example, to represent the number 5 we can use three successive bits with values 1, 0, and 1 because 1x1 + 0x2 + 1x4 equals 5. An n-bit binary number can represent a maximum value of $2^n - 1$. There is also often an additional bit dedicated to represent the sign of the value to encode both positive and negative numbers. There are also other, more complex ways to encode numeric values in a binary form, especially for floating-point numbers.

- *binary code* - instead of numerical values, a sequence of bits can represent a specified set of different data - like characters of text. Each bits sequence is assigned to specific data. The most basic one and the most popular for many years was ASCII code, which uses 7-bit binary code to represent text and other characters. There are other important binary codes like *opcodes* encoding instructions telling the computer what it should do.

- *byte* - historically it was a sequence of bits for encoding a single character of text using specified binary code. The most common byte size is 8-bit long, although it depends on the computer architecture and may vary between different ones. Because of this ambiguity, there is a more precise *octet* term, which means exactly an 8-bit long data unit. Nevertheless, it is the de facto standard to understand the byte as an 8-bit length value, and as such it has become an unquestionable standard for defining data sizes. It is currently unlikely to meet anything different than the standard one architecture with 8-bit long bytes. Hence, when specifying the data size, bytes are specified with the uppercase letter B.

By specifying the size of the data, we use the most common multiples (prefixes) determining their order of magnitude. It is a cause of constant confusion and misunderstanding, which is worth it at this point to explain. Overwhelmingly popular terms such as kilo, mega, and giga mean multiplication of thousands. One *kilo* is 1000 (and we denote it as lowercase letter k), one *mega* is 1 million (uppercase letter M), and so on. On the other hand, sometimes a popular approach is to express orders of magnitude in successive multiplications of 1024. In such cases, we talk about one *kibi*, which is 1024 (denoted as Ki), one *mebi* is 1024*1024 (denoted as Mi), one *gibi* (Gi) is 1024*1024*1024, and so on. This introduces common ambiguity. When someone talks about 1 "gigabyte," they may be thinking about 1 billion of bytes (1 GB) or 1024^3 of bytes (1 GiB) depending on the context. In practice, very few care about the precise use of those prefixes. It is absolutely common to specify the size of memory modules in computers nowadays as gigabytes (GB) when they are truly gibibytes (GiB) or the opposite in case of hard drives storage. Even JEDEC Standard 100B.01 "Terms, Definitions, and Letter Symbols for Microcomputers, Microprocessors, and Memory Integrated Circuits" refers to common usage of K, M, and G as multiplications of 1024 without explicitly deprecating it. In such situations, we are just left to common sense in understanding those prefixes from the context.

Currently we are very used to the terms such as RAM or persistent storage installed in our computers. Even smart watches are now equipped with 8 GiB of RAM. We can easily forget that the first computers were not equipped with such luxuries. You could say that they were not equipped with anything. A look at the short history of computer development will allow us to look differently on the memory itself. Let's start from the beginning.

We should bear in mind that it is very disputable which device can be named as "the very first computer." Likewise, it is very hard to name the one and only "inventor of the computer." This is just a matter of definition what "computer" really is. So instead of starting endless discussions what and who was first, let's just look at some of the oldest machines and what they offered to programmers, although the word *programmer* was to be coined a lot of years later. At the beginning, they were called *coders* or *operators*.

It should be emphasized that machines that may be defined as the first computers were not fully electronic, but electromechanical. For this reason, they were very slow and despite the impressive size offered very little. The first of these programmable electromechanical computers was designed in Germany by Konrad Zuse, named the Z3 computer. It weighed one ton! One addition took about one second and single multiplication took three seconds! Built from 2,000 electromechanical relays, it offered an arithmetical unit capable of add, subtract, multiply, divide, and square root operations only. Arithmetical units included also two 22-bit memory storages used for calculations. It offered also 64 general-purpose memory cells, each 22 bits long. Nowadays we could say it offered 176 bytes of internal memory for data!

The data was typed via a special keyboard, and the program was read during calculation from punched celluloid film. The possibility of storing a program into internal computer memory was to be implemented a few years later, and we will come back to it shortly, although Zuse was fully aware of this idea. In the context of the book you are reading, more important is the question of access to the Z3's memory. Programming the Z3, we had at our disposal only nine instructions! One of them allow you to load the value of one of the 64 memory cells to the memory storage of the arithmetic unit. Another was to save the value back. And that's all when it comes to "memory management" in this very first computer. Although Z3 was ahead of his time in many ways, for political reasons and the outbreak of World War II, its impact on the development of computers has become negligible. Zuse had been developing its line of computers for many years after the war, and its latest version of the Z22 computer was built in 1955.

During the war and shortly after, the main centers of development of computer science were the United States and the United Kingdom. One of the first computers built in the United States was the Harvard Mark I developed by IBM in collaboration with Harvard University called the Automatic Sequence Controlled Calculator. It was also electromechanical, like the Z3 mentioned before. It was enormous in size, measuring 8 feet high, 51 feet long, and 3 feet deep. And it weighed 5 tons! It is called the biggest calculating machine ever. Built a few years, the first programs launched at the end of the Second World War, in 1944. It served the Navy, but also John von Neumann, during his work in the Manhattan Project, on the first atomic bomb. Regarding its size, it offered only 72 memory slots for 23-digit numbers with sign. Such a slot was called an *accumulator* - a dedicated small memory place where intermediate arithmetic and logic results are stored. Translated into measures today, we could say that this 5-ton machine provided access to 72 memory slots each 78-bit long (we need 78 bits to represent quite a big 23-digit number); therefore, it offered memory of 702 bytes! The programs were then de facto a series of mathematical calculations operating on those 72 memory slots. Those were the first-generation programming languages (denoted as 1GL) or machine languages where programs were stored on punched tape, which was physically fed into the machine as needed or operated by front panel switches. It could proceed with only three additions or subtractions per second. Single multiplication took 20 seconds and calculation of sin(x) took one minute! Just like in the Z3, memory management did not exist in this machine at all - you could only read or write the value to one of the mentioned memory cells.

What is interesting for us that from this computer the *Harvard architecture* term has originated (see Figure 1-1). In accordance with this architecture, the storage of program and storage of data are physically separated. Such data is being processed by some kind of electronic or electromechanical device (like Central Processing Unit). Such a device is often also responsible for controlling Input/Output devices like punch card readers, keyboards, or displaying devices. Although Z3 or Mark I computers used this architecture because of its simplicity, it is not completely forgotten nowadays. As we will see in Chapter 2, it is used today in almost every computer as the *modified Harvard architecture*. And we will even see its influence on programs that we write on a daily basis.

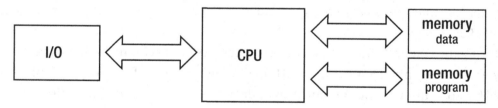

Figure 1-1. *Harvard architecture diagram*

The much better-known computer ENIAC, completed in 1946, was already an electronic device based on vacuum tubes. It offered thousands of times better mathematical operations speed than the Mark I. However, in terms of memory it looked still very unattractive. It offered only 20 10-digits signed accumulators, and there was no internal memory to store programs. Simply put, due to World War II, the priority was to build machines as fast as possible, for military purposes, not to build something sophisticated.

But academics like Konrad Zuse, Alan Turing, and John von Neumann were investigating the idea of using an internal computer's memory to store the program altogether with its data. This would allow a much easier programming (and especially, reprogramming) than coding via punched cards or mechanical switches. John von Neumann wrote in 1945 an influential paper named "First Draft of a Report on the EDVAC" in which he described architecture named the *von Neumann architecture*. It should be stated that it was not solely von Neumann's concept as he was inspired by other academics of his time.

The *von Neumann architecture* showed in Figure 1-2 is a simplified Harvard architecture in which there is a single memory unit for storing both the data and the program. It for sure reminds you of a current computer and this is not without a reason. From a high-level point of view, this is exactly how modern computers are still being constructed where von Neumann and Harvard architecture meets in a modified Harvard architecture.

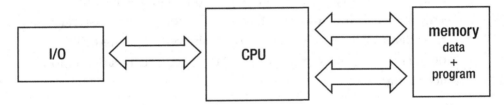

Figure 1-2. *Von Neumann architecture diagram*

The Manchester Small-Scale Experimental Machine (SSEM, nicknamed "Baby") built in 1948 and the Cambridge's EDSAC built in 1949 were the world's first computers that stored program instructions and data in the same space and hence incorporated the von Neumann architecture. "Baby" was much more modern and innovative because it was the first computer using a new kind of storage - the Williams tubes, based on cathode ray tubes (CRT). Williams tubes can be seen as the very first Random Access Memory (RAM) explained below. The SSEM had a memory of 32 memory cells, each 32-bits long. So, we can say that the first computer with RAM had 128 bytes of it! This is the journey we are taking, from 128 bytes in 1949 to a typical 16 gibibytes in 2018. Nevertheless, Williams tubes become a standard at the turn of the 1940s and 1950s, when a lot of other computers where built.

This leads us historically to a perfect moment that we may explain all the basic concepts of computer architecture. All are gathered below and shown in Figure 1-3:

- *memory* - responsible for storing data and the program itself. The way in which memory is implemented has evolved over time in a significant way, starting from the above-mentioned punch cards, through magnetic types and cathode ray tubes, until currently used transistors. Memory can be further divided into two main subcategories:

  - *Random Access Memory (RAM)* - allows us to read data at the same access time irrespective of the memory region we access. In practice, as we will see in Chapter 2, modern memory fulfills this condition only approximately for technological reasons.

  - *Non-uniform access memory* - opposite of RAM, the time required to access memory depends on its location on physical storage. This obviously includes punch cards, magnetic types, classical hard disks, CDs and DVDs, and so on where storage media has to be positioned (for example, rotated) to the correct position before accessing.

- *address* - represents a specific location within the entire memory area. It is typically expressed in term of bytes as a single byte is the smallest possible, addressing granularity on many platforms.

- *arithmetic and logic unit* (*ALU*) - responsible for performing operations like addition and subtraction. This is the core of the computer, where most of the work is being done. Nowadays computers include more than one ALU, allowing for parallelization of computation.

- *control unit* - decodes program instructions (opcodes) read from memory. Based on the internal instruction's description, it knows which arithmetical or logical operation should be performed and on which data.

- *register* - memory location quickly accessible from ALU and/or Control Unit (which we can collectively refer to as *execution units*), usually contained in it. Accumulators mentioned before are a special, simplified kind of registers. Registers are extremely fast in terms of access time, and there is in fact no place for data closer to the execution units than them.

- *word* - fixed-size basic unit of data used in particular computer design. It is reflected in many design areas like the size of most registers, the maximum address, or the largest block of data transferred in a single operation. Most commonly it is being expressed in the number of bits (referred to as the *word size* or *word length*). Most computers today are 32-bit or 64-bit so they have 32-bit and 64-bit words length respectively, 32-bit or 64-bit long registers, and so on.

Von Neumann architecture incarnated in SSEM or EDSAC machines leads as to the term of *stored-program computers* that is obvious nowadays, but it was not at the beginning of the computer era. In such a design, program code to be executed is stored in the memory so it can be accessed like normal data - including such useful operations like modifying it and overwriting with a new program code.

A control unit stores an additional register, called *instruction pointer (IP) or program counter (PC)*, to point to a currently executing instruction. Normal program execution is as simple as incrementing the address stored in PC to the succeeding instructions. Things like loops or jumps are as easy as changing the value of the instruction pointer to the other address, designating where we want to move the program execution.

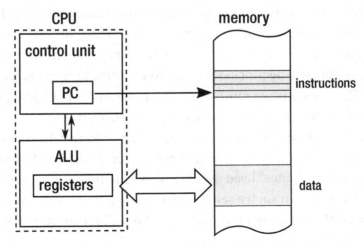

Figure 1-3. *Stored-program computer diagram - memory + instruction pointer*

The first computers were programmed using a binary code that directly described the executed instructions. However, with the increasing complexity of programs, this solution has become increasingly burdensome. A new programming language (denoted as second-generation programming languages - 2GL) has been designed describing the code in a more accessible way by means of the so-called *assembly code*. This is a textual and very concise description of the individual instructions executed by the processor. However, it was much more convenient than direct binary encoding. Then even higher-level languages have been designed (3GL), such as well-known C, C ++, or Pascal.

What is interesting to us is that all these languages must be transformed from text to binary form and then put into the computer memory. The process of such a transformation is called a *compilation*, and the tool that runs it is called a *compiler*. In the case of assembly code, we are rather naming it *assembling* by the *assembler* tool. In the end, the result is a program in a binary code format that may be later executed - a sequence of opcodes and their arguments (operands).

Equipped with this basic knowledge, we can now begin our journey in the memory management topic.

The Static Allocation

Most of the very first programming languages did allow only *static memory allocation* - the amount and the exact location of memory needed had to be known during compilation time, before even executing the program. With the fixed and predefined sizes, memory management was trivial. All major "ancient times" programming languages, starting from machine or assembly code to the first versions of FORTRAN and ALGOL had such limited possibilities. But they have many drawbacks also. Static memory allocations can easily lead to inefficient memory usage- not knowing in advance how many data will be processed, how do we know how much memory we should allocate? This makes programs limited and not flexible. In general, such a program should be compiled again to process bigger data volumes.

In the very first computers, all allocations were static because the memory cells used (accumulator, registers, or RAM memory cells) were determined during program encoding. So, defined "variables" lived over the whole lifetime of the program. Nowadays we still use static allocation in such a sense when creating static global variables and the like, stored in a special data segment of a program. We will see in later chapters where they are stored in the case of .NET programs.

The Register Machine

So far, we have seen examples of machines that were using registers (or accumulators as a special case) to operate on Arithmetic Logic Units (ALUs). Machine that constitute such a design is called *the register machine*. It is because while executing programs on such a computer, we are in fact making calculations on registers. If we want to add, divide, or do anything else, we must load proper data from memory into proper registers. Then we call specific instructions to invoke proper operations on them and then another one to store the result from one of the registers into memory.

Let's suppose we want to write a program that calculates an expression s=x+(2*y)+z in a computer with two registers - named A and B. Let's assume also that s, x, y, and z are addresses to memory with some values stored there. We assume also some low-level pseudo-assembly code with instructions like Load, Add, Multiply. Such a theoretical machine can be programmed with the following simple program (see Listing 1-1).

Listing 1-1. Pseudo-code of a sample program realizing s=x+(2*y)+z calculation on the simple, two-register register machine. Comments shows register's state after executing each instruction.

```
Load      A, y       // A = y
Multiply  A, 2       // A = A * 2 = 2 * y
Load      B, x       // B = x
Add       A, B       // A = A + B = x + 2 * y
Load      B, z       // B = z
Add       A, B       // A = A + B = x + 2 * y + z
Store     s, A       // s = A
```

If this code reminds you of x86 or any other assembly code you have ever learned - this is not a coincidence! This is because most modern computers are kind of complex register machines. All Intel and AMD CPUs we use in our computers operate in such a way. When writing x86/x64-based assembly code, we operate on general-purpose registers like eax, ebx, ecx, etc. There are, of course, many more instructions, other specialized registers, etc. But the concept behind it is the same.

Note   Could one imagine a machine with an instruction set that allows us to execute an operation directly on memory, without a need to load data into registers? Following our pseudo-assembly language, it could look much more succinct and higher level, because there are no additional load/store instructions from memory to registers and their opposites:

```
Multiply        s, y, 2      // s = 2 * y
Add             s, x         // s = s + x = 2 * y + x
Add             s, z         // s = s + z = 2 * y + x + z
```

Yes, there were such machines like IBM System/360, but nowadays I am not aware of any production-used computer of such kind.

The Stack

Conceptually, the stack is a data structure that can be simply described as "last in, first out" (LIFO) list. It allows two main operations: adding some data on the top of it ("*push*") and returning some data from top of it ("*pop*") illustrated in Figure 1-4.

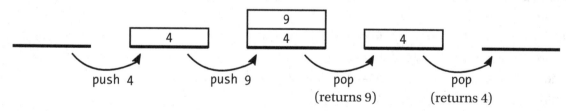

Figure 1-4. *Pop and push stack operations. This is a conceptual drawing only, not related to any particular memory model and implementation.*

Stack from the very beginning become inherently related with computer programming, mainly because of the concept of the subroutine. Today's .NET heavily uses a "call stack" and "stack" concepts, so let's look how it all started. The original meaning of the stack as a data structure is still valid (for example, there is a Stack<T> collection available in .NET), but let's now look how it evolved into a more general meaning of the computer memory organization.

The very first computers we were talking about earlier allowed only sequential program execution, reading each instruction one after another from the punch card or film. But the idea to write some parts of programs (*subroutines*) that could be reused from different points of the whole program was obviously very tempting. The possibility to call different parts of the program required, of course, the code to be addressable as we need somehow to point to what other part of the program we want to call. The very first approach was used by the famous Grace Hooper in the A-0 system- called the first compiler. She encoded a set of different programs on the tape, giving each a succeeding number to allow the computer to find it. Then "a program" consists of a sequence of numbers (programs' indexes) and its parameters. Although it is indeed calling subroutines, it is obviously a very limited way. A program could only call subroutines each after another, and no nested calls were allowed.

Nested calls require a little more complicated approach because computers must remember somehow where to continue with execution (where to return) after executing a specific subroutine. The return address stored in one of the accumulators was the very first approach invented by David Wheeler on the EDSAC machine (a method called "*Wheeler jump*"). But in his simplified approach, *recursive* calls were not possible, which means calling the same subroutine from itself.

A first mention of the stack concept as we know it today in the context of computer architecture was probably mentioned by Alan Turing in his report describing Automatic Computer Engine (ACE) written in the early 1940s. It described a concept of the von Neumann-like machine, which was in fact a stored-program computer. Besides a lot of many other implementation details, he described two instructions - BURY and UNBURY - operating on the main memory and accumulators:

- When calling a subroutine (BURY), the address of the currently executing instruction, incremented by one to point to the next (returning) instruction, was stored in the memory. And another temporary storage, serving as a stack pointer, was incremented by 1.

- When returning from the subroutine (UNBURY), the opposite action was taken.

This constituted the very first implementation of the stack in terms of the LIFO-organized place for the subroutines return addresses. This is a solution still used in modern computers, and besides that it has obviously evolved considerably since then, the foundations are still the same.

The stack is a very important aspect of memory management because when programming in .NET, a lot of our data may be placed there. Let's take a closer look at the stack and its use in function calls. We will use an example program from Listing 1-2 written in C-like pseudo-code that calls two functions - main calls fun1 (passing two arguments a and b), which has two local variables x and y. Then function fun1 at some moment calls function fun2 (passing single argument n), which has a single local variable z.

Listing 1-2. Pseudo-code of a program calling function inside another function

```
void main()
{
    ...
    fun1(2, 3);
    ...
}

int fun1(int a, int b)
{
    int x, y;
    ...
    fun2(a+b);
}

int fun2(int n)
{
    int z;
    ...
}
```

At first, imagine a continuous memory area, designed to handle the stack, drawn in such a way that subsequent memory cells have addresses growing up (see left part of Figure 1-5a) and also a second memory region where your program code resides (see right part of Figure 1-5a) organized the same way. As a code of functions does not have to lie next to each other, main, fun1, and fun2 code blocks have been drawn separated. The execution of the program from Listing 1-2 can be described in the following steps:

1.   Just before calling fun1 inside main (see Figure 1-5a). Obviously as the program is already running, some stack region is already created (grayed part of stack region at Figure 5a). Stack pointer (SP) keeps an address indicating the current boundary of the stack. Program counter (PC) points somewhere inside the main function (we marked this as address A1), just before the instruction to call fun1.

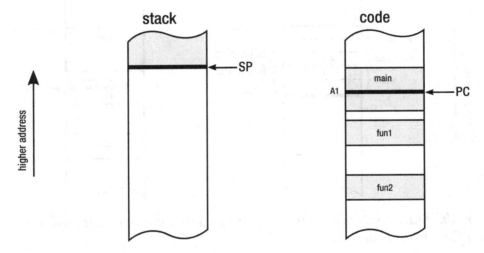

Figure 1-5a. *Stack and code memory regions - at the moment before calling function fun1 from Listing 1-2*

2.   After calling fun1 inside main (see Figure 1-5b). When function is called, stack is being extended by moving SP to contain necessary information. This additional space includes:

•   Arguments - all function arguments can be saved on stack. In our sample, arguments a and b were stored there.

•   Return address - to have a possibility to continue main function execution after executing fun1, the next instruction's address just after the function call is saved on stack. In our case we denoted it as A1+1 address (pointing to the next instruction after instruction under A1 address).

15

- Local variables - a place for all local variables, which can be saved also on stack. In our sample variables x and y were stored there.

Such a structure placed on stack when a subroutine is being called is named an *activation frame*. In a typical implementation the stack pointer is decremented by an appropriate offset to point to the place where a new activation frame can start. That is why it is often said that the stack grows downward.

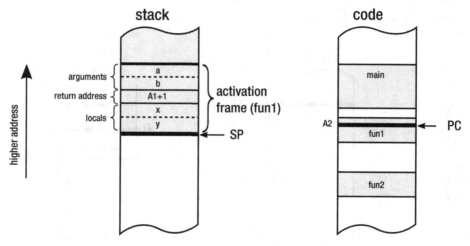

Figure 1-5b. *Stack and code memory regions - at the moment after calling function fun1 from Listing 1-2*

3. After calling fun2 inside fun1 (see Figure 1-5c). The same pattern of creating a new activation frame is being repeated. This time it contains a memory region for argument n, return address A2+1, and z local variable.

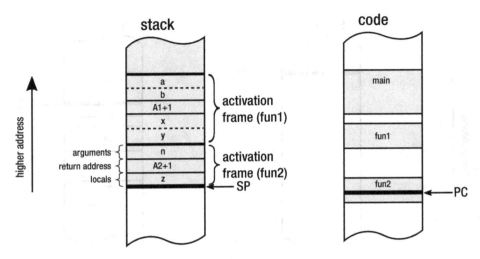

Figure 1-5c. *Stack and code memory regions - at the moment after calling function fun2 from fun1*

An activation frame is also called more generally as *stack frame*, meaning any structured data saved on a stack for specific purposes.

As we see, subsequent nested subroutines' calls just repeat this pattern adding a single activation frame per each call. The more nested the subroutine calls, the more activation frames on the stack will be. This of course makes calling infinite nested calls impossible as it would require a memory for an infinite number of activation frames.[2] If you ever encountered StackOverflowException, this is the case. You have called so many nested subroutines that the memory limit for the stack has been hit.

Bear in mind that mechanism presented here is merely exemplary and very general. Actual implementations may vary between architectures and operating systems. We will look closely how activation frames and stack is being used by .NET in the later chapters.

When a subroutine ends, its activation frame is being discarded just by incrementing stack pointer with the size of the current activation farm, while saved return address is used to accordingly set PC to continue execution of the calling function. In other words, what was inside stack frame (local variables, parameters) is no longer needed so incrementing stack pointer is just enough to "free" memory used so far. Those data will be simply overwritten in next stack usage (see Figure 1-6).

---

[2]There is one interesting exception called tail calls, not described here for its lack of brevity.

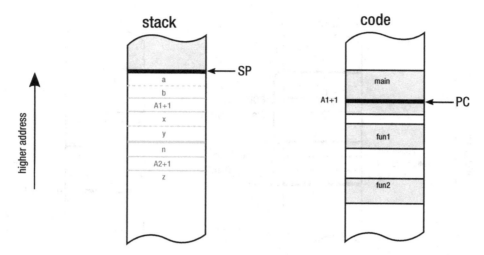

Figure 1-6. *Stack and code memory regions - after returning from function fun1 both activation frames are discarded*

Regarding implementation, both SP and PC are typically stored in the dedicated registers. At this point the size of the address itself, the observed memory areas and registers are not particularly important.

A stack in modern computers is supported both by the hardware (by providing dedicated registers for stack pointers) and by the software (by operating system abstraction of thread and its part of the memory designated as a stack).

It is worth noticing that one can imagine a lot of different stack implementations from the hardware architecture point of view. The stack can be stored on a dedicated memory block inside the CPU or on a dedicated chip. It can also reuse a general computer's memory. The latter is exactly the case in most modern architectures, where a stack is just a fixed-size region of a process memory. There can even be implementations with multiple stacks architecture. In such an exemplary case, the stack for return addresses could be separated from the stack with data- parameters and local variables. This can be beneficial for performance reasons because it allows for simultaneous access to two separated stacks. It allows for additional tunings of CPU pipelining and other low-level mechanisms. Nevertheless, with the current personal computers, the stack is just a part of the main memory.

FORTRAN can be seen as the very first broadly used high-level, general-purpose programming language. But since 1954, when it was defined, only static allocation was possible. All arrays had to have sizes defined during compile time and all allocations were stack based. ALGOL was another very important language that more or less directly inspired a myriad of other languages (like C/C++, Pascal, Basic, and through Simula and Smalltalk - all modern object-oriented languages like Python or Ruby). ALGOL 60 had only stack allocation - together with dynamic arrays (with a size specified by variable). Alan Perlis, a notable member of the team that created ALGOL, said:

> *Algol 60 would have been impossible to adequately process in a reasonable way without the concept of stacks. Though we had stacks before, only in Algol 60 did stacks come to take a central place in the design of processors.*

While the family of ALGOL and FORTRAN languages was mainly used by the scientific society, there was another stream of development for business-oriented programming languages starting from "A-0," FLOW-MATIC, through COMTRANS to more widely known COBOL (Common Business Language). All of them were lacking explicit memory management, operating mainly on primitive data types like numbers and strings.

The Stack Machine

Before we move on to other memory concepts, let's stay for a while with a stack-related context - so-called *stack machines*. In contrast to the registry machine, in the stack machine all instructions are operating on the dedicated, *expression stack* (or *evaluation stack*). Please bear in mind that this stack does not have to be the same stack that we were talking about before. Hence, such a machine could have both an additional "*expression stack*" and a general-purpose stack. There can be no registers at all. In such a machine, by default, instructions are taking arguments from the top of the expression stack - as many as they require. The result is also stored on the top of the stack. In such cases, they are called *pure stack machines*, opposite to impure implementations when operations can access values not only from the top of the stack but also deeper.

How exactly does operation on the expression stack looks? For example, hypothetical Multiply instruction (without any argument) will pop two values from the top of the evaluation stack, multiply them, and put back the result on the evaluation stack (see Figure 1-7).

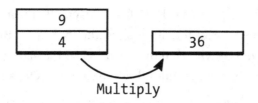

Multiply

Figure 1-7. *Hypothetical Multiply instruction in stack machine - pops two elements from the stack and pushes the result of multiplying them*

Let's back to the sample s=x+(2*y)+z expression from the register machine example and rewrite it in the stack machine manner (see Listing 1-3).

Listing 1-3. Pseudo-code of the simple stack machine realizing s=x+(2*y)+z calculation. Comments show evaluation stack state.

```
                  // empty stack
Push 2            // [2] - single stack element of value 2
Push y            // [2][y] - two stack elements of value 2 and y
Multiply          // [2*y]
Push x            // [2*y][x]
Add               // [2*y+x]
Push z            // [2*y+x][z]
Add               // [2*y+x+z]
Pop 1             // [] (with side effect of writing a value under 1)
```

This concept leads to very clear and understandable code. Main advantages can be described as follows:

- There is no problem regarding how and where to store temporary values - whether they should be registers, stack, or main memory. Conceptually this is easier than trying to manage all those possible targets optimally. Thus, it simplifies implementation.

- Opcodes can be shorter in terms of required memory as there are many no-operand or single-operand instructions. This allows efficient binary encoding of the instructions and hence produces dense binary code. So even the number of instructions can be bigger than in the registry-based approach because of more load/store operations; this is still beneficial.

This was an important advantage in the early times of computers when memory was very expensive and limited. This can be also beneficial today in case of downloadable code for smartphones or web applications. Dense binary encoding of instructions implies also better CPU cache usage.

Despite its advantages, the stack machine concept was rarely implemented in the hardware itself. One notable exception was the Burroughs machines like B5000, which included hardware implementation of the stack. Nowadays there is probably no widely used machine that could be described as the stack machine. One notable exception is x87 floating-point unit (inside x86 compatible CPUs), which was designed as a stack machine, and because of backward compatibility it is still programmed as such even today.

So why mention these kind of machines at all? Because such architecture is a great way of designing platform-independent virtual machines or execution engines. Sun's Java Virtual Machine and .NET runtime are perfect examples of stack machines. They are executed underneath by well-known register machines of x86 or ARM architecture, but it doesn't change the fact they realize stack machine logic. We will see this clearly when describing .NET's Intermediate Language (IL) in Chapter 4. Why have .NET runtime and JVM (Java Virtual Machine) been designed that way? As always, there is some mix of engineering and historical reasons. Stack machine code is of higher level and abstracts away actual underlying hardware better. Microsoft's runtime or Sun's JVM could be written as registry machine, but then, how many registers would be necessary? As they are only virtual, the best answer is - an infinite number of registers. Then we need a way of handling and reusing them. What would an optimal, abstract registry-based machine look like?

If we leave such problems away by letting something else (Java or .NET runtime, in this case) to make specific platform optimizations, it will translate either registry-based or stack-based mechanisms into specific registry-based architecture. But stack-based machines are conceptually simpler. Virtual stack machine (the one that is not executed by a real, hardware stack machine) can provide good platform independence while still producing high-performant code. Putting it together with the mentioned better code density makes a good choice for a platform to be run on a wide range of devices. That was probably the reason why Sun decided to choose that path when Java was invented for small devices like set-top boxes. Microsoft, while designing .NET, followed that path either. The stack machines concept is simply elegant, simple, and it just works. This makes implementing a virtual machine a nicer engineering task!

On the other hand, registry-based virtual machines' designs are much closer to the design of the real hardware they are running at. This is very helpful in terms of possible optimizations. Advocates of this approach say that much better performance can be achieved, especially in interpreted runtimes. The interpreter has much less time to proceed with any advanced optimizations so the more that the interpreted code is similar to the machine code, the better it is. Additionally, operating on the most frequently used set of registers provides a great cache locality of reference.[3]

As always, when making a decision, you need to make some compromises. The dispute between advocates of both approaches is long and unresolved. Nevertheless, the fact is that currently the .NET execution engine is implemented as a stack machine, although it is not completely pure - we will notice this in Chapter 4. We will see also how the evaluation stack is being mapped to the underlying hardware consisting of registers and memory.

Note   Are all virtual machines and execution engines stack machines? Absolutely not! One notable exception is Dalvik, which was a virtual machine in Google's Android until the 4.4 version, which was a registry-based JVM implementation. It was an interpreter of intermediate "Dalvik bytecode." But then JIT (Just in Time compilation explained in Chapter 4) was introduced in Dalvik's successor - Android Runtime (ART). Other examples include BEAM - a virtual machine for Erlang/Elixir, Chakra - JavaScript execution engine in IE9, Parrot (Perl 6 virtual machine) and Lua VM (Lua virtual machine). No one can therefore say that this kind of machine is not popular.

The Pointer

So far we have introduced only two memory concepts: static allocation and stack allocation (as a part of stack frame). The concept of a *pointer* is very general and could be spotted from the very beginning of the computing era - like previously shown concept

---

[3]Note: we will look at the importance of memory access patterns in the context of cache usage in Chapter 2.

of instruction pointer (program counter) or stack pointer. Specific registers dedicated to memory addressing like *index registers* can be also seen as pointers.[4]

PL/I was a language proposed by IBM in about 1965, intended to be a general proposition for both scientific and business worlds. Although its goal was not quite achieved, it is an important element of history because it was the first language that introduced the concept of pointers and memory allocation. In fact, Harold Lawson, involved in PL/I language development, was awarded by IEEE in 2000 "for inventing the pointer variable and introducing this concept into PL/I, thus providing for the first time, the capability to flexibly treat linked lists in a general-purpose high level language." That was exactly the need behind the pointer invention - to perform list processing and operate on other more or less complex data structures. The pointer concept was then used during the development of the C language, which evolved from the language B (and predecessors or BCPL and CPL). Only as late as the FORTRAN 90 version, a successor of FORTRAN 77, defined in 1991, introduced dynamic memory allocation (via allocate/ deallocate subroutines), POINTER attribute, pointer assignment, and the NULLIFY statement.

Pointers are variables in which we store the address of the position in memory. Simply put, it allows us to reference other places in memory by its address. Pointer size is related to word length mentioned before, and it results from the architecture of the computer. Thus nowadays, we typically deal with 32- or 64 bit-wide pointers. As it is just some small region of memory, it can be placed on the stack (for example, as a local variable or function argument) or CPU register. Figure 1-8 shows a typical situation where one of the local variables (stored within function activation frame) is a pointer to another memory region with the address Addr.

---

[4]In the context of the memory addressing, an important enhancement was an index register introduced in the Manchester Mark 1 machine, the successor of "Baby." An index register allowed us to reference memory indirectly, by adding its value to the other register. Hence, less instructions were required to operate on continuous memory regions like arrays.

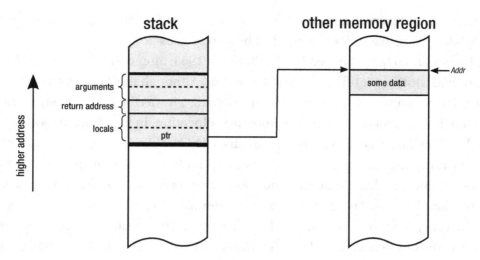

Figure 1-8. *Local variable of a function being a pointer* ptr *pointing to the memory under address* Addr

The simple idea of pointers allows us to build sophisticated data structures like linked lists or trees because data structures in memory can reference each other, creating more complex structures (see Figure 1-9).

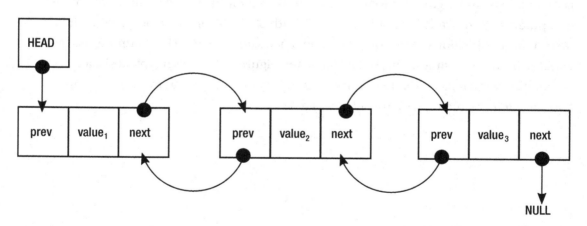

Figure 1-9. *Pointers used to build double-linked list structure when each element points its previous and next elements*

Moreover, pointers can provide so-called *pointer arithmetic*. They can be added or subtracted to the reference relative part of memory. For example, the increment operator increases the value of the pointer by the value of the size of the pointed object, not by single byte as one could expect.

Pointers in high-level languages like Java or C# are often not available or must be explicitly enabled, and it makes such code unsafe. Why that is will be clearer when talking about manual memory management using pointers in the next subchapter.

The Heap

Eventually, we reach the most important concept in the context of the .NET memory management. *The heap* (less known also as *the Free Store*) is an area of memory used for dynamically allocated objects. The free store is a better name because it does not suggest any internal structure but rather a purpose. In fact, one might rightly ask what is the relationship between the heap data structure and the heap itself. The truth is - there is none. While the stack is well organized (it is based on LIFO data structure concept), the heap is just more like a "black box" that can be asked for providing memory, no matter where it will come from. Hence "the pool" or mentioned "free store" would be probably a better name. The heap name was probably used from the beginning in a traditional English sense meaning "messy place" - especially the opposite of well-ordered, stack space. Historically ALGOL 68 introduced heap allocation but this standard was not widely adopted. But this is where this name probably come from. Fact is, the true historical origin of this name is now rather unclear.

The heap is a memory mechanism able to provide a continuous block of memory with a specified size. This operation is called *dynamic memory allocation* because both the size and the actual location of the memory need not be known at compile time. Since the location of the memory is not known at compile time, dynamically allocated memory must be referenced by a pointer. Hence pointer and heap concepts are inherently related.

An address returned by some "allocate me X bytes of memory" function should be obviously remembered in some pointer for future reference to a created memory block. It can be stored on a stack (see Figure 1-10), on the heap itself, or anywhere else.

```
PTR ptr = allocate(10);
```

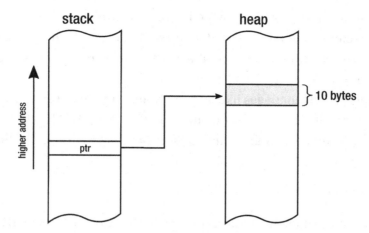

Figure 1-10. *Stack with pointer ptr and 10-bytes wide block on the heap*

The reverse operation of an allocation operation is called a *deallocation*, when the given block of memory is returned to the pool of memory for future use. How exactly heap is allocating a space with a given size is an implementation detail. There are many "allocators" possible, and we will learn about some of them soon.

By allocating and deallocating many blocks, we may end up with a situation where there is not enough free space for a given object, although in total there is enough free space on heap. Such situation is called heap *fragmentation* and may lead to significant inefficiency in memory usage. Figure 1-11 illustrates such problem, when there is not enough free continuous space for object X. There are many different strategies used by allocators to manage space as optimally as possible to avoid fragmentation (or make good use of it).

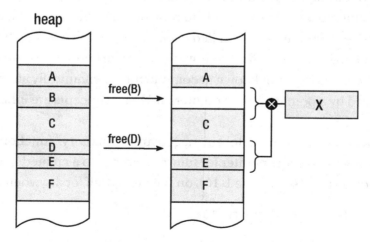

Figure 1-11. *Fragmentation - after deleting objects B and D, there is no enough space for new object X although in total there is enough free space for it*

It is also worth noting that whether there is a single heap or multiple heap instances within a single process is yet another implementation detail (we will see it when discussing .NET more deeply).

Let's make a short summary of the stack and the heap differences in Table 1-1.

Table 1-1. *Comparison of the Stack and the Heap Features*

Property	The Stack	The Heap
Lifetime	Scope of local variables (pushed on entry, popped on exit)	Explicit (by allocate and optional free)
Scope	Local (thread[5])	Global (anyone who has a pointer)
Access	Local variable, function arguments	Pointer
Access time	Fast (probably cached memory region in the CPU)	Slower (may be even temporarily saved to hard drive)
Allocation	Move stack pointer	Different possible strategies
Allocation time	Very fast (pushing stack pointer further)	Slower (depends on allocation strategy)
Freeing	Move stack pointer	Different possible strategies
Usage	Subroutine parameters, local variables, activation frames, not big compile-time size known data (arrays)	Everything
Capacity	Limited (typically few MB per thread)	Unlimited (to extent of hard drive space)
Variable size	No	Yes[6]
Fragmentation	No	Likely
Main threats	Stack overflow	Memory leak (forgetting to free allocated memory), fragmentation

---

[5]This is not entirely true as you can pass a pointer to the stack variable to other threads. However, it is definitely abnormal usage.

[6]Due to the dynamic nature of the heap, there are functions allowing us to resize (reallocate) a given block of memory.

Besides their differences, most commonly both the stack and heap are located at opposite ends of the process's address space. We will return to a detailed stack and heap layout inside the process address space when considering low-level memory management in Chapter 2. Nevertheless, one should remember it is still just an implementation detail. By providing abstractions of value and reference types (which will be introduced in Chapter 4), we should not care where they are created.

Now let's now move forward to the discussion over manual versus automatic memory management. As Ellis and Stroustrup write in *The Annotated C++ Reference Manual*:

> *C programmers think memory management is too important to be left to the computer. Lisp programmers think memory management is too important to be left to the user.*

Manual Memory Management

Until now what we have been seeing was a "manual memory management." What it means, in particular, is that a developer is responsible for explicitly allocating memory, and then when it is no longer needed, she should deallocate it. This is real manual work. It's exactly like a manual gear in most European cars. I am from Europe and we are just used to manually changing the transition. We must think whether it is a good time to change it now, or we should wait a few seconds until the engine speed is high enough. This has one big advantage - we have complete, full control over the car. We are responsible whether an engine is used optimally or not. And as humans are still much more adaptive to changing conditions, good drivers can make it better than an automatic gear. Of course, there is one big disadvantage. Instead of thinking about our main goal - getting from place A to place B, we have to additionally think about changing gears - hundreds, thousands of times during a long trip. This is both time consuming and tiresome. I know some people will say that it is fun and giving control to the automatic gear is boring. I can even agree with them. But still, I quite like how this automotive metaphor relates the memory management.

When we are talking about explicit memory allocation and deallocation, it is exactly like having a manual gear. Instead of thinking about our main goal, which is probably some kind of a business goal of our code, we must think also about how to manage memory of our program. This moves us back from the main goal and takes our valuable attention. Instead of thinking about algorithms, business logic, and domains, we are obliged to think also about when and how much memory I will need. For how long? And who will be responsible for freeing it? Does it sound like business logic? Of course not. The question whether it is good or is not another story.

The well-known C language was designed by Dennis Ritchie somewhere around the early 1970s and had become one of the most widely used programming languages in the world. The history how C evolved from ALGOL through intermediate languages CPL, BCPL, and B is interesting on its own, but in our context, it is important that altogether with Pascal (being a direct ancestor of ALGOL), they were the two most popular languages with explicit memory management at the time. Regarding C, without a doubt, I can say that a compiler of it has been written for any hardware architecture ever created. I will not be surprised if alien spaceships had their own C compiler on board (probably implementing TCP/IP stack as an example of another widely used standard). The relevance of this language on other programming languages is huge and not to imagine. Let's pause for a moment and take a deeper look into it in the context of memory management. This will allow us to list some of the characteristics of the manual memory management.

Let's look at simple example code written in C at Listing 1-4.

Listing 1-4. Sample C program showing manual memory management

```c
#include <stdio.h>

void printReport(int* data)
{
    printf("Report: %d\n", *data);
}

int main(void) {
    int *ptr;
    ptr = (int*)malloc(sizeof(int));
    if (ptr == 0)
    {
        printf("ERROR: Out of memory\n");
        return 1;
    }
```

```
    *ptr = 25;
    printReport(ptr);
    free(ptr);
    ptr = NULL;
    return 0;
}
```

This is, of course, a little exaggerated example but thanks to it we can illustrate the problem clearly. We can notice that this simple code has in fact only one simple business goal: printing "a report." For simplicity, this report consists only of a single integer, but you can image it is a more complex structure containing pointers to other data structures and so on. This simple business goal looks over-helmed by a lot of "ceremony code" taking care of nothing more than memory. This is a manual memory management in its essence.

Summarizing the above piece of code, besides business writing logic, a developer must:

- allocate a proper amount of memory for the required data using `malloc` function.

- cast returned generic (`void*`) pointer to proper pointer type (`int*`) to indicate we are pointing to the numerical value (`int` type in case of C).

- remember the pointer to the allocated region of memory in local pointer variable `ptr`.

- check whether it succeeded in allocating such amount of memory (returned address will be 0 in case of failure).

- dereference the pointer (access memory under its address) to store some data (numerical value of 25).

- pass the pointer to other function `printReport`, that dereferences it for its own purpose.

- free allocated memory when it is no longer needed using `free` function.

- to be assured we should mark the pointer with a special NULL value (which is a way of telling this pointer points to nothing and in fact corresponds to value of 0[7]).

As we see, there are a lot of things to be kept in mind by us when we must manage memory manually. Moreover, each of the above steps can be mistakenly used or forgotten, which can lead to bunch of serious problems. Going through each of those steps, let's see what bad things can happen:

- We should know exactly how much memory we need. It is as simple as sizeof(int) in our example, but what if we dealt with much more complex, nested data structures? One can easily imagine a situation in which we allocate too little memory because of some minor error in manual calculations of the required size. Later, when we want to write or read from such a memory region, we will probably end up with *Segmentation Fault* error - trying to access memory that has not been allocated by us or allocated for another purpose. On the other hand, by a similar mistake we can allocate way too much memory, which will lead us to memory inefficiency.

- Casting can be always error prone and can introduce really hard to diagnose bugs if we accidentally introduce a type mismatch. We would be trying to interpret a pointer of some type as it was a completely different type, which easily leads to danger access violations.

- Remembering the address is an easy thing. But what if we forget to do that? We will have a bunch of memory allocated and no way to free it - we've just forgotten its address! This is a direct path to the memory leak problem, as unfreeable memory can grow in time endlessly. Moreover, a pointer can be stored in something more complicated than a local variable. What if we forget a pointer to a complex graph of objects because we freed some structure containing it?

- A single check whether we were able to allocate the desired amount of memory is not cumbersome. But doing it a hundred times in each

---

[7]The implementation details of the NULL value in case of .NET will be explained in Chapter 10.

and every function for sure will be. We are probably going to decide to omit those checks, but this may lead us to undefined behavior in many points of our application, trying to access memory that was not successfully allocated in the first place.

- Dereferencing pointers is always dangerous. No one ever knows what is at the address pointed by them. Is there still a valid object, or maybe it has been freed already? Is this pointer valid in the first place? Does it point to the proper user-memory address space? Full control over a pointer in languages like C leads to such worries. Manual control over pointers leads to serious security concerns - it is only the programmer who must take care about not exposing data beyond regions that should be available according to the current memory and type model.

- Passing the pointer between functions and threads only multiplicates worries from the previous points in the multithreaded environment.

- We must remember to free the allocated memory. If we omit this step, we get memory leak. In an example as simple as the one above, it is of course really hard to forget about calling free function. But it is much more problematic in more sophisticated code bases, when ownership of data structures is not so obvious and where pointers to those structures are passed here and there. There is also yet another risk - no one can stop us from freeing memory that has been already freed. Yet it is another occasion to undefined behavior and a likely cause of segmentation fault.

- Last but not least, we should mark our pointer as NULL (or 0 or whatever we can name it) to note that it no longer points to a valid object. Otherwise it is called a *dangling pointer,* which sooner or later will lead to Segmentation Fault or other undefined behavior because it can be dereferenced by someone who believes it represents still valid data.

As we can see from the developer perspective, explicit memory allocation and deallocation can become really cumbersome. It is a very powerful feature, which for sure has its perfect applications. Where extreme performance matters and the developer must be 100% sure what is going under the hood - this approach can be found useful.

But "with great power comes great responsibility" so this is a two-edged sword. And as software engineering evolved, so languages were becoming more and more advanced in terms of helping the developer to escape from all those worries.

Going further, the C language direct successor, C++, has not changed a lot in this field either. However, C++ is worth devoting a few moments to because is so popular and introduces other broadly used concepts. As we all know, it is the language with manual memory management. Translating the previous example into C ++, we get the code as in Listing 1-5.

Listing 1-5. Sample C++ program showing manual memory management

```cpp
#include <iostream>
void printReport(int* data)
{
    std::cout << "Report: " << *data << "\n";
}

int main()
{
    try
    {
        int* ptr;
        ptr = new int();
        *ptr = 25;
        printReport(ptr);
        delete ptr;
        ptr = 0;
        return 0;
    }
    catch (std::bad_alloc& ba)
    {
        std::cout << "ERROR: Out of memory\n";
        return 1;
    }
}
```

In the context of our considerations we can spot some significant improvements:

- The new operator takes care to allocate enough memory, knowing how much it needs, thanks to the support of the compiler (which suggests proper type size).

- We need not cast the obtained pointer to the appropriate type. This removes some type safety concerns we were considering previously.

- Error handling is also improved as we are not obliged to check allocation success manually, because an exception will be thrown in case of a problem.

Still, we do see a lot of ceremony code in this example. There is also a new concern introduced. What if `printReport()` function will throw an exception? Without proper error handling, we can easily omit `delete` operator and introduce a memory leak. Fixing our sample code is easy, but it can be not so obvious in more complex applications as ownership of the data (who and on which layer should delete such pointers) may be not trivial.

All problems we saw in this chapter are additionally exaggerated in multithreaded environments, when pointers can be shared between multiple units of execution. Careful synchronization must be considered to not allow mixing invalid data. For example, what if one threads check whether a given pointer is valid (not NULL), while the other, just after that, will free memory pointed by it? Such situations can lead to intermittent and very hard to diagnose problems. In explicit memory management world, it is a developer responsibility to provide a suitable synchronization mechanism to avoid such situations.

The C++ example presented in Listing 1-5 is on purpose not aligned with the current memory usage patterns in this language. It should use some sort of RAII (Resource Acquisition Is Initialization) technique - where a resource (like memory) is represented by a local variable of type implementing some kind of memory ownership logic. An example of such will be presented later in Listing 1-10. Although, as we will see, such patterns help to solve some of the problems, they do not change a lot in our general discussion about manual and automatic memory management.

Automatic Memory Management

To overcome problems with manual memory management and provide the programmer a more pleasing way of handling it, different automatic memory management approaches have been proposed. It is interesting to know that as old as the second oldest high-level programming language - LISP - proposed about 1958 (just a few years after FORTRAN), have much to offer in this field. As in a mainly functional language heavily based on the processing of the lists - manual memory management would be very uncomfortable. A functional programming paradigm treats programs as an evaluation of combined functions and strongly avoids modification of data (mutation) and side effects. Allocating and deallocating memory is heavily mutable and has obvious side effects. Handling memory in such a way in functional code would clutter it a lot with imperative smell, while LISP was designed to be a highly declarative language. As LISP language creator said, "it was going to make everything absolutely ugly to have to explicitly erase lists." Hence, something more sophisticated had to be developed. The very first versions of LISP had a built-in `eralist` (erase list) function, but it was removed after automatic memory management had been introduced.

In general, LISP was a very innovative language, and the design of it have helped to invent many important computer science ideas, and automatic memory management was one of them. In fact, John McCarthy, one of the co-founders of Artificial Intelligence and the inventor of LISP, is also a father of the first garbage collection algorithms. Many of the ideas thought then are still valid and used in languages today. One can certainly say that automatic memory management was born in LISP. The first paper written by McCarthy in 1958 introduced the Mark and Sweep algorithm that we will investigate in depth in later chapters because it is still used in the .NET environment and many other places.

LISP, thanks to its expressiveness and conciseness, represents our sample program in a simple form shown in Listing 1-6.

Listing 1-6. Sample LISP program showing automated memory management

```
(defun printReport(data)
    (write-line (format nil "Report: ~a" data))
)

(prog
    ((ptr 25))
    (printReport ptr)
)
```

Thanks to automatic memory management, all the code clutter has gone, and we can clearly see the high-level description of the program business goal - printing "a report."

An interesting anecdote is one by John McCarthy in the paper on LISP design, "Recursive Functions of Symbolic Expressions and Their Computation by Machine, Part I." He described this mechanism succinctly but named it simply as "reclamation." Later, he annotated this part:

> *We already called this process "garbage collection," but I guess I chickened out of using it in the paper - or else the Research Laboratory of Electronics grammar ladies wouldn't let me.*

Besides its name, the idea was there and ready to implement. Currently the automatic memory management mechanism and *garbage collection* names are used interchangeably. We can define it as a mechanism that removes from the programmer the responsibility of manual memory management so that once created, objects are automatically destroyed (and the memory after them recovered) when no longer needed.

One of the main messages I would like to give in this book is the fact that even when memory management is fully automatic, it can cause problems. As a small confirmation, it is worth quoting a fun fact regarding first LISP's implementation of garbage collection. As McCarthy recalls in the book *History of Programming languages I*, during the very first public demonstration of LISP in one of MIT's Industrial Liaison Symposia, due to minor oversight, the Flexowriter (the electric typewriter of those times) started to print a lot of pages with an error message beginning with:

> *THE GARBAGE COLLECTOR HAS BEEN CALLED. SOME INTERESTING STATISTICS ARE AS FOLLOWS*

Due to this, the presentation had to be canceled while the audience was full of laughs. No one ever known it was due to garbage collector misuse, only John itself. And while it was rather a human than algorithmic error, still we can say garbage collectors make troubles from the very beginning!

Allocator, Mutator, and Collector

Mutators and other concepts we are going to familiarize with in this chapter are important terms in the automatic memory management academic research. Thanks to clear definitions, we can distinguish them later in academic and technical papers without ambiguity. One can say about, for example, an "overhead on Mutator" of specific algorithms. When considering various garbage collection designs, there will often be a discussion about the impact of the Collector on the Mutator and vice versa. Let's look closer at those terms.

The Mutator

Among the few basic concepts related to memory management, the most basic one and the pretty important one at the same time is an abstraction called *the Mutator*. In its simplest version, we can define a Mutator as an entity that is responsible for executing application code. Its name comes from the fact that Mutator mutates (changes) the state of the memory - objects are being allocated or modified and references between them are being changed. In other words, Mutator is a driving machine of all the changes in the application with respect to the memory. This name was coined (among others, in the same paper) by Edger Dijkstra in 1978 in the paper, "On-the-Fly Garbage Collection: An Exercise in Cooperation," where we can find detailed elaboration on this topic. An interesting side fact is that Dijkstra's proposition from this quite old paper is still being used, for example, by the Go language in 2015 and with good results.

I like the Mutator abstraction as it provides a nice and clean categorization of things inside a specific framework or runtime. We can define the Mutator as everything that has the possibility to modify memory, either by modifying existing objects or by creating new ones. Although it is not strict, additionally, we can extend it to everything that can read memory (as reading is a crucial operation for program execution). This leads us to an important observation. To be fully operable, Mutator needs to provide the running application three kind of operations:

- New(amount) - allocate a given amount of memory, which then will be used by a newly created object. Please note that at this abstraction level, we are not considering an object's type information, which may be or not be available from runtime. We are just providing the required size of the memory to be allocated.

- Write(address, value) - write a specified value under a given address. Here we also abstract whether we are considering an object field (in object-oriented programming), global variable, or any other kind of data organization.

- Read(address) - read a value from the specified address.

In the simplest world, where none of the garbage collection algorithms exists, those three operations have trivial implementation (written in C-like pseudo-code at Listing 1-7).

Listing 1-7. Three main Mutator's methods implementation without automated memory management

```
Mutator.New(amount)
{
    return Allocator.Allocate(amount);
}

Mutator.Write(address, value)
{
    *address = value;
}

Mutator.Read(address) : value
{
    return *address;
}
```

But in the world of automated garbage collection, those three operations are places when Mutator cooperates with the garbage collector (*Collector*) and allocation mechanism (*Allocator*). How this cooperation looks and how much it disturbs the simplicity of the above implementations is one of the most important design concerns. The most common enhancement we will meet in this book is adding a so-called *barrier* - either it will be a *read barrier* or a *write barrier*. A barrier is a way of augmenting an additional operation before or after particular operations. Barriers let us synchronize (directly or indirectly, synchronously or asynchronously) with the garbage collector mechanism to inform about the execution of the program and the memory usage. Three methods from Listing 1-7 are the injection points that every garbage collector may wish to plug in. We will return to some of the most common possible variations in the following chapters when describing different garbage collection algorithms.

In the everyday reality of developers, the most often implementation of the Mutator abstraction is a well-known *thread*. It suits out the definition perfectly - it is a single unit that runs code and mutates objects and references graphs between objects. This is perfectly intuitive for us, because the vast majority of the most popular runtimes uses this implementation. Among a lot of other functionalities, threads, via some additional layer, communicates with the operating system to allow operations New, Write, and Read.

Mutators do not have to be implemented as threads in the terms of the operating system threads. The popular example can be Erlang ecosystem with its processes - they are managed as super lightweight co-routines living in the runtime itself. They can be seen as so-called "green threads," but in the terms of Erlang VM it is better to call them "green processes" as the separation enforced by runtime is much stronger than between thread-like entities. This means they are entities managed on the runtime level, not the operating system level. Another common implementation of Mutator could be based on so-called *fibers*, lightweight units of execution implemented both in Linux and Windows.

The Allocator

Mutator has to be able to consume New operation, which we discussed in the previous point. When it comes to internals of those methods, sooner or later another very important concept must be mentioned - *the Allocator*. By simple means, Allocator is an entity responsible for managing dynamic memory allocation and deallocation. As we mentioned before, in ancient languages like ALGOL or FORTRAN, there was no Allocator, as there was no dynamic memory allocation at all.

Allocator must provide two main operations:

- `Allocator.Allocate(amount)` - allocates a specified amount of memory. This can be obviously extended by methods able to allocate memory for a specific type of object if type information is available for Allocator. As we have seen, this is internally used by `Mutator.New` operation.

- `Allocator.Deallocate(address)` - frees a memory under a given address to be available for future allocations. Please note that in case of automatic memory management, this method is internal and not exposed to the Mutator (and hence, no user code can call it explicitly).

The idea can appear to be really simple, not to say - trivial. But as we will see, it is not as easy as one would expect. There a lot of different aspects of Allocator design. And as always, in fact, all is about trade-offs, mainly between performance, implementation complexity (which leads directly to maintainability), and others. We will dig into the two most popular kinds of allocators: *sequential* and *free-list*. But as it is an implementation detail, it will be much better to learn about them in the specific context of the .NET in Chapter 4.

The Collector

While we defined a Mutator as an entity that is responsible for executing application code, we can similarly define *the Collector* as an entity that runs garbage collection (automatic memory reclaiming) code. In other words, we can see a Collector as a piece of software (code) or thread executing it, or both. It depends on the context.

How does Collector know which objects are no longer needed and can be deallocated? This is an impossible problem because it should in fact guess the future - is a specific object going to be used anymore? It depends on the code that will be executed, and this may furthermore depend on independent factors such as user actions, external data, and so on. An ideal Collector would know the *liveness* of the object - live objects are those which will be needed. In opposite - *dead* (or *garbage*) *objects* are not going to be used and can be destroyed. Obviously, therefore commonly Collector is called *Garbage Collector* or GC in short.

There is an interesting consequence of Mutator, Allocator, and Collector cooperation. Please note again that as there is no public `Allocator.Deallocate` method exposed, Mutator has no possibility to explicitly free memory obtained. Mutators can only ask to allocate more and more memory as there would be an infinite source of it. This indeed means that Garbage Collection mechanism is in fact a simulation of a computer with an infinite amount of memory. How this simulation works and how efficient it is become an implementation detail.

One can think of a special Garbage Collector that does not free allocated memory at all. It is being called *Null* or *Zero Garbage Collector*. It would work correctly only on computers with an infinite amount of memory, which unfortunately does not yet exist. But Null Garbage Collectors are not without any practical usage. It may be used for example for very short living programs where unbounded memory growth is acceptable. Maybe they will become more and more popular in the world of server-less, short-running single functions. An example draft of such Zero Garbage Collector for .NET is presented in Chapter 15.

Because knowing a liveness of an object is impossible,[8] Collector is based on a less strict property of the object - whether it is *reachable* by any Mutator. *Reachability* of an object means that there is a sequence of references (starting from any Mutator's accessible memory) between objects that eventually leads to that object (see Figure 1-12). Reachability obviously does not mean liveness of an object but it is the best approximate we can have. If an object is not reachable from any Mutator, it cannot be used anymore, so it is dead (garbage) and can be safety reclaimed. The opposite is obviously not truth. The reachable object can stay reachable forever (kept by some complex graph of references) but because of the execution conditions may be never accessed and as such it is dead. In fact, it is between liveness and reachability where most managed memory leaks reside.

---

[8]In Chapter 4 we will discuss escape analysis - a method for determining the true liveness of pointers for at least some special cases.

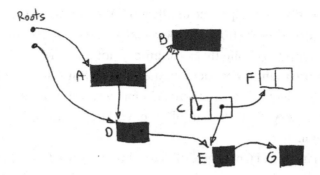

Figure 1-12. *Reachability - objects C amd F are not reachable because there is no path from roots (Mutator's locations) leading to them*

Mutator's starting points in terms of reachability are called *roots*. What they exactly are depends on specific Mutator implementation. But in most common cases, where a Mutator is simply a thread (represented by operating system-based native thread), roots can be:

- local variables and subroutine arguments - placed on stack or stored in registers.

- statically allocated objects (e.g., global variables) - placed on the heap.

- other internal data structures stored inside Collector itself.

Having knowledge about three major building blocks - Mutator, Allocator, and Collector - we could now move on to getting familiar with a plethora of different automatic memory management approaches. While it is tempting to provide a comprehensive list with detailed description of all of them, this is much more this book can cover. Instead, we will learn about some of the major, most popular approaches we can meet in today's languages.

Reference Counting

One of the two most popular methods of automatic memory management is called *Reference Counting*. The idea behind it is very simple. It is based on counting the number of references to an object. Every object has its own *reference counter*. When an object is being assigned to a variable or a field - the number of references to it is being increased. At the same time, the reference counter of the object to which this variable was previously indicated decreases.

The liveness of objects in the reference counting approach is being tracked by the number of objects referencing a referent. If the counter drops to zero, no one is referencing an object and thus it can be deallocated. But what if the counter does not drop to zero? This says nothing about the liveness of an object - it says only that someone is keeping a reference to it, not that it will use it. Thus, reference counting is yet another less strict way of guessing liveness of an object.

Coming back to our trivial Mutator example from Listing 1-7, in case of reference counting, it could be described as shown at Listing 1-8.

Listing 1-8. Pseudo-code describing simple reference counting algorithm

```
Mutator.New(amount)
{
    obj = Allocator.Allocate(amount);
    obj.counter = 0;
    return obj;
}

Mutator.Write(address, value)
{
    if (address != NULL)
        ReferenceCountingCollector.DecreaseCounter(address);
    *address = value;
    if (value != NULL)
        value.counter++;
}

ReferenceCountingCollector.DecreaseCounter(address)
{
    *address.counter--;
    if (*address.counter == 0)
        Allocator.Deallocate(address)
}
```

The reference counting behavior is illustrated by a simple program in Figure 1-13 and Listing 1-9. Three simple lines of code are rewritten in terms of Mutators' methods to show how references change.

Listing 1-9. Sample pseudo-code illustrating reference counting

```
o1 = new SomeObject();
o2 = new SomeObject();
o2 = o1;

// becomes:

addr1 = Mutator.New(SizeOf(SomeObject))   // addr1.counter = 0
Mutator.Write(&o1, addr1)                 // addr1.counter = 1
addr2 = Mutator.New(SizeOf(SomeObject))   // addr2.counter = 0
Mutator.Write(&o2, addr2)                 // addr2.counter = 1
Mutator.Write(&o2, &o1)                   // addr1.counter = 0; addr2.
                                          counter = 2
```

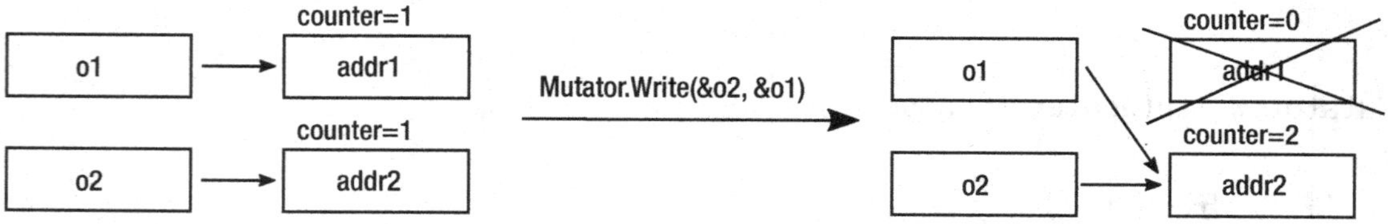

Figure 1-13. *Reference counting illustration of Listing 1-8*

As we see at Listing 1-9, a big overhead has been added to the `Mutator.Write` operation. It must check and modify counter data and take a deallocation action if the counter drops to zero. This becomes much more complicated in a multithreaded (where multiple Mutators are working in parallel) environment. In such a case, those operations should be thread-safe so synchronization adds its own additional overhead. `Mutator. Write` is a very common operation (introduced by any assignment), so an overhead in it introduces significant overhead for a whole program execution. Moreover, from an implementation point of view, it is not obvious where to store objects' counters. This can be a dedicated space or some kind of header kept as close to the object itself as possible. In both cases, it does not change the fact that each assignment generates additional memory writes, which are very undesirable. This may also lead to inefficient CPU cache usage, but this is a topic we will learn about more in the following chapter.

If we return to the reachability property mentioned before, one can say that reference counting is approximating liveness by local references and does not track a global state of an object graph of references. In particular, without any additional improvements, it can be mistaken by circular references. Such can be found in popular data structures like double-linked lists (see Figure 1-14). In such a case, the reference counter never drops to zero as the data structure with value1 and data structure with value2 points to each other.

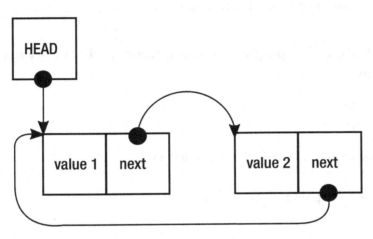

Figure 1-14. *Reference counting circular reference problem*

However, creating circular references can be made difficult on the language level, which is a win situation. In this case, the reference count algorithm may be used without much concern for memory leaks resulting from this problem.

One very big advantage and source of reference counting popularity is the fact it does not require any runtime support. It can be implemented as an additional mechanism for some specific types in the form of external library. It means that we can leave original `Mutator.New` and `Mutator.Write` intact and just introduce higher-level counterparts of such logic like classes with properly overloaded operators and constructors. For example, this is exactly the case with the most popular C++ implementations.

So-called *smart pointers* (also known as *intelligent pointers*) were introduced, which in a more sophisticated way manage the lifetime of objects they point to. From an implementation point of view, smart pointers in C++ are in fact just template classes that behave like normal pointers by appropriate operator overloading. In case of C++ we can use two kinds of them:

- unique_ptr that realizes unique ownership semantics (such as the pointer is a sole owner of an object that is going to be destroyed as soon as unique_ptr goes out of scope or another object is assigned to it).

- shared_ptr that realizes reference counting semantics.

Continuing with our sample code from Listing 1-5, using smart pointers we may result in the C++ code as presented in Listing 1-10.

Listing 1-10. Sample C++ program showing automated memory management with usage of smart pointers

```
#include <iostream>
#include <memory>

void printReport(std::shared_ptr<int> data)
{
    std::cout << "Report: " << *data << "\n";
}

int main()
{
    try
    {
        std::shared_ptr<int> ptr(new int());
        *ptr = 25;
        printReport(ptr);
        return 0;
    }
    catch (std::bad_alloc& ba)
    {
        std::cout << "ERROR: Out of memory\n";
        return 1;
    }
}
```

If we called `data.use_count()` method inside the `printReport` function, it would result in the value 2 because inside this function two different shared pointers point to the same object. On the other hand, after going out from `try` block scope, the use count will be 0 because no more smart pointers are pointing to our object.

Please note that code from Listing 1-10 is not aligned with C++ good practices. Passing a smart pointer just to read underlying data should be rather done by a constant reference (`const&`) than by a value, but this would not increase a reference count; hence it is not useful for our explanatory purposes.

We see big further improvement in such code because:

- We do not have to manually destroy an object using the `delete` operator.

- Exception handling is simplified because in case of any exception being thrown by a `printReport()` function, the smart pointer is just going out of the `try` region scope (and all enclosed scopes either) so it will be automatically destroyed. This is thanks to the *RAII* (*Resource Acquisition Is Initialization*) principle mentioned before, which takes care about the lifetime of the object based on the variable scope of the pointer it is represented by.

Shared and unique pointers can also be used as fields in the classes, which makes them quite powerful and useful tools.

The problem is smart pointers in C++ were introduced on the standard library level, not the language itself. Other libraries were introducing their own implementations, and it was sometimes problematic to make all them speaking with each other nicely. Qt has its `QtSharedPointer`, `wxWidgets` has `wxSharedPtr<T>` and so on. Without support of the compiler and the language it just must be like that. This is why automatic memory management is so crucial in the component-oriented[9] programming like .NET. When .NET was born, moving responsibility about memory management from developer to the runtime itself was one of the major, crucial design decisions. A common platform of how objects are created, managed, and reclaimed means each component will reuse it in the same way, and there is no coupling between components other than runtime itself.

---

[9]This consists of many smaller, interchangeable dependencies.

Regarding C++ it is interesting to note that Bjorne allowed more sophisticated GC in the C++ standard - it is not prohibited, it is just not yet implemented. Moreover, thanks to flexibility of the C++, although with the Memory Pool System, or the Boehm–Demers– Weiser collector, it is possible to use garbage collection as an extended library - we will introduce it shortly.

Other languages can incur smart pointers (incorporating reference counting) directly into their design and it is exactly the case with Rust - a modern, low-level programming language created by Mozilla. It enforces data safety on the compilation level by incorporating the concept of smart pointers (a few different kinds of them in fact) into the language. It strongly uses ownership semantics and the RAII principle, which allows to check at the compilation time whether there are no violations like dereferencing a dangling pointer. Another notable usage of reference counting is Automatic Reference Counting build into Swift language.

A brief summary of the drawbacks and advantages of reference counting is as follows: Advantages:

- Deterministic deallocation moment - we know that deallocation will happen when an object's reference counter will drop to zero. Therefore, as long as it is no longer needed, the memory will be reclaimed.

- Less memory constraint - as memory is reclaimed as fast as objects are no longer used, there is no overhead of memory consumed by the objects waiting to be collected.

- Can be implemented without any support from the runtime.

Disadvantages:

- Such a naive implementation as at Listing 1-8 introduces very big overhead on Mutator.

- Multithreading operations on reference counters require well- thought synchronization, which can introduce additional overhead.

- Without any additional enhancements, circular references cannot be reclaimed.

There are improvements to naive Reference Counting algorithms like *Deferred Reference Counting* or *Coalesced Reference Counting*, which eliminate some of these problems at the expense of some of the advantages (mainly immediate reclamation of memory). However, describing them here is far beyond the scope of this book.

Tracking Collector

Finding objects' reachability is hard because it is an object's global attribute (it depends on the whole object graph of the whole program), and the simple explicit call for freeing an object is very local. In this local context, we are not aware of the global context - are other objects using this object now? Reference Counting tries to overcome that by looking only at this local context with some additional information - the number of references to an object. But this obviously can lead to problems with circular references and has others drawbacks as we seen before.

Tracking Garbage Collector is based on knowledge of global context of an object's lifetime and can make a better decision whether it is good time to delete an object (reclaim memory). It is, in fact, such a popular approach that almost certainly when someone says something about Garbage Collector, he probably means Tracking Garbage Collector. We can encounter it in runtimes like .NET, different JVM implementations, and so on.

The core concept is that Tracking Garbage Collector finds true reachability of an object by starting from the Mutator's roots and recursively tracks the whole object's graph of a program. This is obviously not a trivial task because process memory can take several GB and tracking all interobject references in such big volumes of data can be difficult, especially while Mutators are running and changing all those references all the time. The most typical approach of Tracing Garbage Collector consists of two main steps:

- *Mark* - during this step Collector determines which objects in memory can be collected by finding their reachability.

- *Collect* - during this step Collector reclaims memory of objects that were found to not be longer reachable.

Implementation of this simple two-phase logic can be extended as is exactly the case in .NET that can be described as Mark-Plan-Sweep-Compact. We will see those internal workings in detail in the next chapters. For now, let's just look at the Mark and Collect steps in more general way as they also incur interesting issues.

Mark Phase

During the Mark step Collector determines which objects in memory should be collected by finding their reachability. Starting from Mutator's roots, Collector travels through the whole objects graph and marks those which were visited. Those objects that are not marked at the end of Mark phase are not reachable. Thanks to an object's marking, there is no problem with cyclic references. If during the graph's traversing we will get back to a previously visited object, we break further traversing because the object is already marked.

A few starting steps of such an algorithm are presented on Figure 1-15. Starting from the roots, we travel inside object's graph through interobjects references. It is an implementation detail whether we are visiting this graph in a depth-first or breadth-first manner. Figure 1-15 shows a depth-first approach, showing three possible states of each object:

- Not yet visited object, marked as a white box.

- Object remembered to be visited, marked as light gray box.

- Object already visited (marked as reachable), marked as dark gray. box

The first steps illustrated in Figure 1-15 may be described as follows (with each step describing the corresponding subfigure):

1. Initially all objects are not yet visited

2. An object A is added to be visited, as the first root.

3. As an object A has pointers (as fields) to objects B and D, they are added to be visited. Object A itself is at this stage marked as reachable.

4. Next object from "to visit" set is being visited - an object B. As it does not have any outgoing references, it is simply marked as reachable.

5. Next object from "to visit" set is being visited - an object D. It contains a single reference to object E so it is remembered to be visited. Object D itself is marked as reachable.

6. Object's E outgoing reference to object G is remembered to be visited. Object E is itself marked as reachable.

7. The last object from "to visit" set is being visited - an object G. It contains no references to it is simply marked as reachable. At this stage, there are no more objects to be visited so we have identified that objects C and F are not reachable (dead).

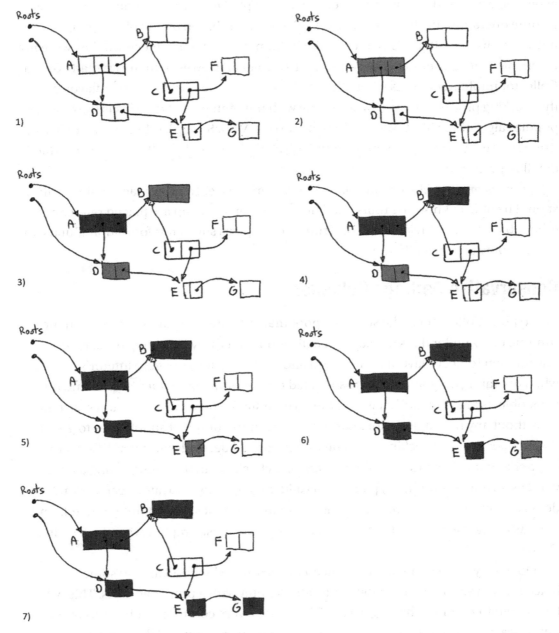

Figure 1-15. *A few first steps of Mark phase*

Obviously traversing such a graph is hard during normal Mutator's work as the graph is changing constantly due to normal program execution - creating new objects, variables, object's field assignments, and so on. Therefore, in some Garbage Collector implementations all Mutators are simply stopped for the duration of Mark phase. This allows for a safe and consistent traverse of the graph. Of course, as soon as the threads resume operation, the knowledge that Collector holds based on the object graph becomes obsolete. But this is not a problem for non-reachable objects - if they were not reachable before, they never become reachable again. However, there are many Garbage Collector implementations where the Mark phase is done in a concurrent flavor, so the marking process can be run alongside with the Mutator's code. This is the case for popular algorithms like CMS in JVM (Concurrent Mark Sweep), G1 in JVM, and in .NET itself. How exactly such concurrent marking is implemented in .NET will be described in detail in Chapter 11.

There is one not obvious problem with a Mark phase. To track reachability, Collector should be able to know the roots and know where on the heap are placed references to other objects. It is a trivial problem if runtime supports such an information. But it can be overcome also in a different way.

Conservative Garbage Collector

This type of Collector can be seen as a poor man's solution. It can be used when the runtime or compiler does not support collection directly by providing exact type information (object's layout in memory) and Collector does not get Mutator's support when operating on pointers. If the so-called *Conservative Collector* wants to find out what objects are reachable, it is scanning whole stack, static data areas and registers. As without any help it does not know what is a pointer or not, it simply tries to guess that. It does that by checking a several things (and all depends on specific Collector implementation), but the most important one check is whether interpreting a given word as an address (pointer) points to a valid, managed by Allocator heap region? If it does so, Collector *conservatively* (hence its name) assumes it is a pointer indeed. And it treats it as a reference to follow as in generic Mark phase graph traversing described above.

Obviously, Collector can be mistaken in guessing which will lead to some inaccuracy - random bits can look as a valid pointer with a proper address. This will lead to retain memory that is garbage. This is not a very common problem as most numerical values in memory are rather small (counters, financial data, indexes) so the only problem can be with dense binary data like bitmaps, floating-point numbers or certain blocks of IP addresses.[10] There are subtle algorithm's improvements that help to overcome that issue but we will not touch it here. Moreover, conservative reporting means you are not able to move objects around in memory. This is because you must update pointers to moved objects, which is obviously not possible if you are not sure whether something looking as a pointer is a pointer indeed.

So who may need such a Collector in the first place? Its main advantage is it can work without support of the runtime - in fact it just scans memory and so runtime support (reference tracking) is not needed. This is therefore, for example, convenient approach when developing a new runtime when full type information for GC is not yet developed. Without blocking of the work, the development of the rest of the system may take place. When providing the right type information is already implemented, you can simply turn off conservative tracking. Microsoft has used such an approach when developing some versions of their runtime.[11]

However, Conservative Collector requires the support of Allocator to overcome problems of the not-known object's memory layout. It can, for example, arrange the allocation of the objects in such a way that they are grouped into segments of equal size objects. Conservative scanning of such regions is possible because the object's boundaries are defined as simple multiplication of a particular segment object size.

In many languages Allocator can be replaced on the language (library) level, which leads to popularity of Conservative Garbage Collection as library. One of the most commonly used API-agnostic implementations for C and C++ is *Boehm–Demers–Weiser GC* (shortnamed *Boehm GC*).

It was used, for example, in Mono (open source CLR implementation) until version 2.8 (year 2010), which introduced the so-called *SGen* Garbage Collector - somehow mixed approach that still scans stack and registers conservatively but scanning the heap is being supported by the runtime type information.

---

[10]Boehm GC and other conservative GC lets you allocate a block or region with special flag (like `GC_MALLOC_ATOMIC` in Boehm's case) which indicates to the Collector that the block will not contain any pointers and should not be scanned. So we can use such block for storing dense binary data like bitmaps.

[11]An interesting fact is that .NET already contains conservative collector implementation inside, which is disabled by default.

Let's briefly summarize the main points regarding Conservative Garbage Collection:
Advantages:

- Easier for environments without support for garbage collection from ground up - for example, early runtime stages or unmanaged languages.

Disadvantages:

- Inaccuracy - everything that randomly looks like a valid pointer blocks memory from being reclaimed - although this is not a common situation and can be overcome by an improvement of the algorithm and additional flags.

- In a simple approach, objects cannot be moved (compacted) - because Collector is not sure what is a pointer indeed (and it cannot just update a value that it only assumes to be a pointer).

Precise Garbage Collector

In a so-called Precise Garbage Collector situation, this is much simpler because compiler and/or runtime provides a Collector full information about an object's memory layout. It can also support stack crawling (enumerating all objects roots on the stack). In such a case, there is no point in guessing. Starting from the well-defined roots, it just scans the memory object by object. Given a memory address pointing at the beginning of the object (or so-called interior pointer pointing inside an object and knowledge proper to interpret such a reference), Collector simply knows where the outgoing references (pointers) are placed, so it can recursively follow them during graph traversing.

.NET uses Precise Garbage Collector so we will see a lot more of its internals in the following chapters. In fact, entire chapters from 7 to 10 are dedicated to that purpose.

Collect Phase

After Tracking Garbage Collector has found reachable objects, it can reclaim memory from all the other dead objects. Collectors' Collect phase can be designed in many different ways due to many different aspects. It is impossible to describe all the possible combinations and variants in one short paragraph. But two major approaches can and should be distinguished, which various implementations are focused around.

Sweep

In this approach, dead objects are simply marked as a free space that can be later reused. This can be a very fast operation because (in exemplary implementation) only a single bit mark of a memory block must be changed. Such a situation is being shown in Figure 1-16 where no longer used objects C and F (following an example from Figure 1-15) become available space just by marking them as a free space.

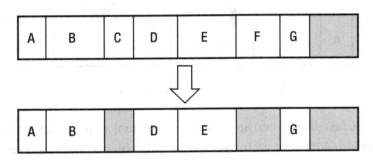

Figure 1-16. *Sweep collection - naive implementation*

Then, in naive implementation, during allocation the memory is being scanned for the gap size not less than the object's size to be created.

But nontrivial implementations may need to build data structures storing information about free blocks of memory for faster retrieval, typically in a form of a so-called *free-list* (shown in Figure 1-17). Moreover, those free-lists must be smart enough to merge adjacent free blocks of memory. Further optimization may lead to storing a set of free-lists for memory gaps of ranging size. In terms of implementation details, there are also different ways of how such a list can be scanned. Two of the most popular approaches are *best-fit* and *first-fit* methods. In the first-fit method, we stop free-list scan as fast as any suitable free memory block has been found. In the best-fit approach, we always scan all free-list entries trying to find the best match of the required size. The former is faster but may lead to bigger fragmentation, and the latter is exactly opposite.

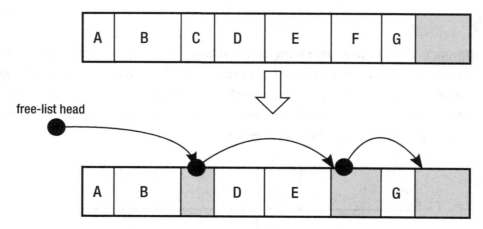

Figure 1-17. *Sweep collection - free-list implementation*

Although quite fast, the Sweep approach has one major drawback - it eventually leads to bigger or smaller memory fragmentation. As objects are being created and destroyed, more and more smaller or larger free gaps occur on the heap. This may lead to a situation when although there is enough free memory in total for a new object, as there is no single, continuous free space for it. We have seen such situation at Figure 1-11 when describing heap allocation in general.

Compact

In this approach, fragmentation is eliminated at the expense of lower performance because it requires moving around objects in memory. Objects are moved in a way that reduces the gap created after the deleted objects. Here two main different approaches can be further distinguished.

In a simpler way, from an implementation point of view, *Copying Compacting* all live (reachable) objects are copied to the different region of memory each time collections occurs (see Figure 1-18). Compacting is a simple consequence of copying each live object one after another, omitting those no longer needed. Obviously, this induces high memory traffic as all live objects have to be copied back and forth. It also puts a bigger memory overhead because we have to maintain twice more memory than normally would be needed.

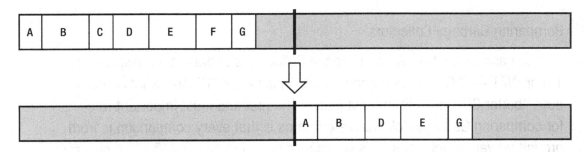

Figure 1-18. *Compact collection - copying implementation*

Due to these weaknesses, it would seem that the algorithm has no practical application. However, it may be used effectively. We just must remember to use it only for certain, small memory regions and not for the whole process memory. This is exactly the case in some JVM's implementation when copying compacting is being used for smaller memory regions.

In a more complex scenario, one can implement *In-Place Compacting*. The objects are moved toward each other so as to remove gaps between them (see Figure 1-19). This is the most intuitive solution and is exactly how we would move the Lego blocks. From an implementation point of view, it is not trivial but still doable. The main problem one can spot here is the question - how objects can be moved relative to each other without overwriting each other and without the use of any temporary buffer?

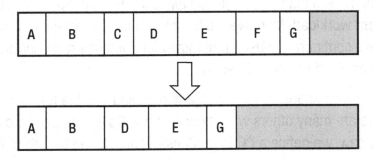

Figure 1-19. *Compact collection - in-place implementation*

As we will see in Chapter 9, .NET is using exactly this approach with a very clever data structure used for optimization, so we will find an answer to that question there.

Comparing Garbage Collectors

One can ask a question: Which Garbage Collector is better? Is it HotSpot Java 1.8 or .NET 4.6? Or maybe Python or Ruby has better GC? And what actually does "better GC" mean in the first place? The first and most important rule for comparing Garbage Collection algorithms is that every comparison is from ground up very ambiguous. This is because GC is extremely difficult to separate and compare between themselves as such. They are so fused with the runtime environment that it is virtually impossible to test them separately. Thus, it is difficult for any truly objective comparison. If we would like to compare performance of the different GC - we can use measures like Throughput, Latency, and Pause Time (we will see difference between those concepts in Chapter 3). But all those measures will be taken in the context of the whole runtime, not the sole GC only. A framework or runtime mechanism (for example, allocation patterns, internal object pooling, additional compilations, or any other hidden, internal mechanism) can be introduced so the noticeable overhead that the GC contribution to the overall performance will be negligible. Moreover, there are many fine-tunings in each and every GC that makes it performing better in a certain type of workloads. Some can be optimized to respond quickly in an interactive environment, others to process huge data sets. Others may try to dynamically change their characteristics to align with the current workload. Moreover, different GCs may behave differently because of the hardware configuration used (optimized for specific processor architectures, CPU core counts, or memory architecture).

Of course, we can compare GC for the algorithms used and the functionality provided. There are many others ways how Garbage Collectors can be categorized. As we already saw, we define a CG to be Conservative (Mono till 2.8) or Precise (.NET) or even a mix of it (Mono 2.8+). One implements the Sweep collection, the other Compact collection, and yet another both of them. Another important distinction is how GC partitions the memory. We will see in detail how a heap can be divided into smaller parts in Chapter 5. It may use Reference Counting in some parts or not at all completely. How is Allocator is implemented? Is it Parallel or Concurrent GC? (Chapter 11). With so many possible functional differences, it is really hard to say which combination is "better" - simply there is not one perfect solution.

A brief summary of the drawbacks and advantages of Tracking Garbage Collector is as follows:

Advantages:

- Complete transparency from the developer's perspective - a memory is just abstracted as would be infinite, without having to worry about freeing memory of no longer needed objects.

- No problems with circular references.

- No big overhead on Mutators.

Disadvantages:

- More complicated implementation.

- Non-deterministic freeing objects - they will be released after some time not being reachable.

- Stop the world needed for Mark phase - but only in a non-concurrent flavor.

- Bigger memory constraint - as objects are not reclaimed as fast after not being needed, more memory pressure can be introduced (more garbage lives for some period of time).

Mainly because of the first advantage, tracking GC is so popular in different runtimes and environments.

Small History

Having learned a solid dose of basic theoretical knowledge, let's now take a brief look at the history of automatic memory management in the context of different programming languages.

LISP is one of the longest living languages, with many appearing and disappearing dialects with the two most popular - Common LISP and Scheme. Nevertheless, without a doubt, the most popular is now dialect known as Clojure that compiles, among others, to Java Virtual Machine, Common Language Runtime (.NET), and JavaScript. This makes it very flexible and powerful, and of course this is nowadays an incarnation when the garbage collection and the LISP meet.

But not only functional language like LISP featured automated memory management at times when it was popular. Any language-related history should not ignore the influence of the other extremely influential language - Simula. Called the first fully object-oriented language, it introduced concepts of objects and classes, inheritance, polymorphism, and other fundamental pillars of OOP. All languages, beginning from Smalltalk, and then from C++, through Java and C#, to Python or Ruby, have been somehow inspired by this language. What is important, Simula 67 featured automatic memory management, which was first a combination of reference counting and tracking garbage collector but during the language development was replaced with the compacting garbage collector inspired by the LISP language. Altogether with its ancestor - Smalltalk - garbage collection had become a popular choice for language designers. The increasing complexity of the software pushed language designers to introduce more or less sophisticated ways to help the programmer with the memory management.

The popularity of the Web and the start of the Internet age in the 1990s has pushed software development to the need of higher-level programming. The times where C and C++ were the kings were passing by. Their low-level control over the system had no value in the context of web application programming and massive growth of the server-side applications. Along with the extremely rapid development of the Internet, it increased the complexity of web applications and the need to produce more code faster.

No one could tell the history of automatic memory management without a mention of the language and the Java platform. Planned by Sun Microsystem company as a "better C++," garbage collection mechanisms were one of the first and fundamental assumptions that the new platform should meet. Beginning from the 1990s, where the project started as an internal Oak language, it contained Mark and Sweep mechanisms. The very first publicly available Java 1.0a had been announced in 1994. With the explosion of the popularity of Java, awareness of the existence of garbage collection mechanisms was constantly growing. From that time, automatic memory management has become almost a "no-brainer" for all high-level language designers.

When Java was born, two other mainstream languages were coined - Python and Ruby. Both languages were equipped with automatic memory management for the same reasons mentioned before. Python prior to version 2.0 had only reference counting but then incorporated also more complex ways of taking care about cyclic references. Ruby provides a simpler mechanism based on the Mark and Sweep approach.

In our short historical stories, we cannot ignore JavaScript, which appeared in the same years as Java. And although the similarity to the name Java was more a marketing ploy than a real similarity, JavaScript has also been conceived as a high-level scripting language. There was no room for manual memory management. The aim was to allow operating an HTML content at a high level, without thinking over such aspects as memory usage. The JavaScript runtime environment was responsible for these tasks. In the context of more long-running usages of JavaScript - Single Page Applications and node.js back-end services - the importance of automatic garbage collections in JavaScript engines becomes more and more important. For example, a very popular V8 JavaScript engine, used by node.js, is using the Mark, Sweep, and Compact approach with its own additional optimizations.

As can thus be noted, even languages with automatic memory management have existed for 50 years, the real growth of their popularity occurred in the 1990s. This is the place where we can pass into the history of the most important and most interesting environment for us - history of the .NET Framework.

What's more important, Microsoft has developed at those times its own implementation of JavaScript called JScript. JScript is an important part of our story because it has created the foundation for solutions used to create the .NET. Of course, we are most interested in the topic of memory management. Actually, it all started with JScript written by four people over several weekends. One was Patrick Dussud, which we can undoubtedly name as the father of the garbage collector in .NET. He wrote a simple Conservative GC as a proof of concept.

Before starting work on the CLR, Patrick Dussud worked on the JVM. And yes, Microsoft at one point in time seriously considered its own implementation of the JVM, instead of creating something which we now know as the .NET runtime. So, inspired by the JVM and based on the already implemented JScript version he wrote another version, yet another Conservative GC. But the team, which in the future had partially formed a CLR, quickly found that JVM introduces uncomfortable limitations. First, the expectation for a newly created environment was strong support for the COM and unmanaged code. One of the objectives was to create an environment in which recompilation of the C++ program with a new flag of kind /CLR should make it possible to run it under a new environment. Moreover, a standardization was troublesome, and they were just probably scared of the resulting limitations. They even thought for a moment over the release of C ++ runtime with the garbage collection extension.

Afterward, after consulting with a friend (David Moon from the Symbolics company, dealing with generational garbage collectors) Patrick had made an educated decision to write "the best possible GC" from scratch and he implemented a prototype in Common

LISP. Why was this language chosen? It was the language he had been dealing with for many years and in which just worked well. In addition, he had experience in using "the best debugging tools" at that time for LISP. After writing the LISP version, he wrote a converter that transpiled[12] the code to C ++. And that is how an experimental Garbage Collector for the experimental implementation of the JVM has been created. When work on the CLR had been started, part of this experimental code was used in a project written from scratch in C++. It is therefore only a legend that the CLR's GC code has been completely converted from LISP.

Having already learned theoretical basics and some history, it is time to get to know the first of the many rules that will be introduced in this book.

Summary

We have covered a very wide range of material in this chapter. One could easily devote several separate books to the mentioned topics. Beginning with such basic concepts as bits and bytes, we learned the main types of computer architectures - Harvard and von Neumann. We have learned the basics of building computers, including definitions such as registry, address, and word. Learning concepts such as static or dynamic allocation, pointer, stack, or heap, we went on to discuss the most important concepts - automatic memory management also referred to as garbage collection. By the way, we met also inconveniences of manual memory management and the reasons to automate it. Fundamental to .NET implementations concepts such as tracing garbage collection and its phases Mark, Sweep, and Compact are only briefly discussed. We will look at them more closely in the corresponding chapters of this book. Everything we talked about was also covered with a bit of history and a broader context that allowed us to look at the subject from a wider perspective.

In the end, the knowledge we have gained here will allow us to better understand subsequent chapters. From chapter to chapter, we will be getting closer to the practical implementation issues of the .NET environment. However, without understanding the broader context presented in this chapter, it would have been an incomplete look. I now invite you to Chapter 2, where we will move from the theoretical foundations to the fundamentals of low-level computer and memory design.

---

[12]Transpilation is a source-to-source compilation.

Rule 1 - Educate Yourself

Applicability: As general as possible.

Justification: The most general rule in this book, it is applicable in a much broader scope than memory management alone. It means nothing less than that we should always set in expanding our knowledge to strive for being a professional. Knowledge does not come by itself. We have to earn it. It's a tedious, time-consuming, and laborious process. That is why we have to constantly motivate ourselves. Does such an obvious truth deserve a separate rule? I think so. In everyday life, we can easily forget about it. It seems to us that everyday tasks can teach us something. And certainly, to some extent, they do. But it is obvious, to get out of comfort zone, we need to follow a few steps. Consciously. And that means reaching out for a book, watching a web tutorial, reading an article. The possibilities are plentiful and it makes no sense to mention them here all. However, it is so fundamental that it must be on the list of rules of every professional. If you are not convinced of my words, get interested in the concept of Software Craftmanship and manifest available at `http://manifesto.softwarecraftsmanship.org`. I'm also a big fan of the concept of Mechanical Sympathy, which came up with the rally driver Jackie Stewart:

> *You don't have to be an engineer to be a racing driver, but you do have to have Mechanical Sympathy.*

This concept was then introduced into the IT world by Martin Thompson. What does it mean? Obviously, you do not need to be a mechanic to be a racing driver. But without some deeper knowledge about how a car works, what are its mechanics, how an engine works, what forces are influencing it - it is really hard to be a good racing driver. She should just "feel the car," to work with it in a harmony. She should feel Mechanical Sympathy. This is an exactly the case with us, programmers. Of course, we can just think about frameworks like .NET or JVM and stop there. But then we will be just like Sunday drivers, seeing a car from the perspective of a steering wheel and few pedals.

How to apply: In a such general rule, there is hardly one simple approach to take. You may read books about how a computer or your framework of choice works. You can use many online training services. You can watch or attend conferences and local user groups. You can start a blog and write about such topics because there is no better way to learn than to teach. There are so many possibilities, I will not even try to list them all. Just keep in mind the motto "educate yourself" and try to implement this rule in your life!

CHAPTER 2

Low-Level Memory Management

To understand how memory management works, we need to acquire a broader context. In the previous chapter we learned the theoretical basis for this topic. We could now go directly to the details of automatic memory management, how the Garbage Collector works, and where memory leaks may occur. But if we really want to "feel" the topic, it is worthwhile to spend a few more moments on the basic reminder of yet another aspect of this topic. This will allow us to better understand the various design decisions that were made by Garbage Collector creators in .NET (as well as other managed runtime environments). The creators of such mechanisms do not live in a vacuum and have to adapt to the state of being - limitations and mechanisms that govern computer hardware and operating systems. That's the aspect we're going to touch on now.

So I invite you to a chapter in which we will learn about those mechanisms and limitations. Of course, those topics are in themselves powerful enough that they can be devoted to a few large, separate books. We will focus only on some basics, more or less loosely related with memory management. To be honest, it is not easy to present such comprehensive subjects in a way that is not overwhelming and does not involve too many insignificant issues. And at the same time, I wanted to present it detailed enough so that the resulting influence on memory management in .NET is actually visible. I invite you to read!

Getting to know all of these details, even briefly, gives you the power to take on the complexity of a topic that is managing memory. Even if in the day-to-day management of memory, we associate it only with the call of the new operator, it is useful to be aware of how many mechanisms exist and on how many levels. Hardware, operating system, compiler – all these affect how it works and how .NET was written, although it is not always obvious. This knowledge is very consistent with the spirit of the Mechanical Sympathy presented in the previous chapter. I hope you will find it also just fun to know some of the little facts mentioned here.

65

© Konrad Kokosa 2018
K. Kokosa, *Pro .NET Memory Management*, https://doi.org/10.1007/978-1-4842-4027-4_2

Having said all that, please feel free to treat this chapter as the optional one. It provides a lot of theoretical information that, although helps a lot in the feeling memory management topic, is not necessary to understand the rest of the book. So if you are in a hurry or just want to move to more practical .NET internals and examples, feel free to skim this chapter or omit it completely (to return to it in a more relaxed time, hopefully).

Hardware

How does a modern computer work? It seems that any programmer for better or worse will be able to answer this question. If we studied computer science, something about this may be remembered from lectures. If we are self-taught, we probably read something here and there. And probably we recite the facts from memory, such as: a computer consists of a processor, which is the main processing unit - it executes programs. It has access to RAM (which is fast) and hard disks (which are slow). There is also a graphics card that is very important for gamers (and different kind of graphic designers), which is responsible for generating the image displayed on the monitor. Such a ten thousand foot look at the topic is not sufficient for our purposes. We need to get into the subject deeper. For the purposes of our deliberations, let me introduce the architecture of a modern computer, as in the diagram below in Figure 2-1.

The modern personal computers market is being dominated by PCs and Macs. I've modeled a schematic, generic computer architecture diagram based on them. If needed, I will mention hereinafter some possible nuances, such as those involving ARM processors or more sophisticated server machines.

Such main components of typical computer architecture can be listed as:

- *Processor* (CPU, central processing unit) - main unit, responsible for executing instructions. We have already seen it in Chapter 1. Here are components located such as the Arithmetic and Logical Units (ALUs), Floating-Point Units (FPUs), registers, and instruction *execution pipelines* - responsible for efficiently executing instructions divided into a set of smaller operations and executed (if possible) in parallel.

- *Front Side Bus* (FSB) - data bus that connects CPU with Northbridge.

- *Northbridge* - unit that contains mainly memory controller, responsible for controlling communication between memory and CPU.

- *RAM* (Random Access Memory) - main computer memory. It stores data and programs code as long as the power is on - hence it is also referred to as *Dynamic RAM* (DRAM) or *volatile memory*.

- *Memory Bus* - data bus that connects RAM with Northbridge.

- *Southbridge* - chip that handles all of a computer's I/O functions, such as USB, audio, serial, the system BIOS, the ISA bus, the interrupt controller, and the IDE channels -mass storage controllers such as PATA and/or SATA.

- *Storage I/O* - non-volatile memory that stores data, including popular HDD or SDD disks.

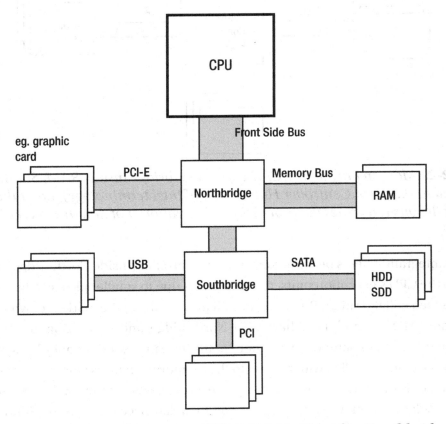

Figure 2-1. *Computer architecture - CPU, RAM, Northbridge, Southbridge, and others. The width of the bus illustrates the proportion of the amount of data transferred (very roughly).*

It is worth mentioning that formerly the CPU, Northbridge and Southbridge were separate chips but now they are closely integrated. From Intel's Nehalem and AMD's Zen microarchitectures, they include Northbridge inside (which is in such case often referred to as *uncore* or *System Agent*). This evolution of the architecture has been shown in Figure 2-2.

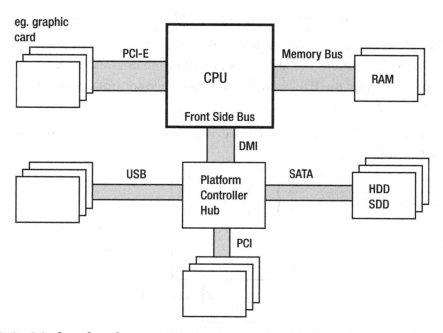

Figure 2-2. *Modern hardware - CPU with Northbridge inside, RAM, Southbridge (renamed to Platform Controller Hub in case of Intel terminology), and others. The width of the bus illustrates the proportion of the amount of data transferred (very roughly).*

Such integration helps because the memory controller (inside Northbridge), closely placed to the CPU's execution units, reduces delays due to smaller physical distances and enhanced collaboration. But there are still processors on the market (of which most popular are AMD FX family) that have CPU, Northbridge, and Southbridge separated.

The main problem behind any memory management is a discrepancy between performance of today's CPU with respect to the memory and mass storage subsystems. The processor is much faster than memory so every access to the memory introduces unwanted delays. When the CPU needs to wait for a data access to memory (either read or write), we call it a *stall*. The more stalls occur, the worse for the CPU utilization as its power is just being wasted for waiting.

The typical current processor operates at a frequency of 3 GHz or above. Meanwhile, the memory works with an internal clock with frequencies of only 200–400 MHz. This makes the order of magnitude performance difference. It would be too expensive to build RAM chips working with a frequency of CPU. This is because of how modern RAMs are built - loading and unloading of internal capacitors takes time, which is very difficult to reduce.

You may be surprised to find that memory works with such low frequencies. In fact, in the computer stores we buy memory modules marked as having a popular clocking like 1600 or 2400 MHz, which are far closer to the CPU speed. Where do such numbers come from? As we will see, such specifications are only part of the more complex truth.

Memory module consist of *internal memory cells* (storing data) and additional buffers that help to overcome their low internal clock frequency limitations. Some additional tricks are used (see Figure 2-3). Most of them rely on multiplying the read of data:

- Sending data from the internal memory cell twice within a single clock cycle. To be accurate, it is both on the falling as well as the rising slope of the signal. Hence the name by far is the most popular memory of various generations - *Double Data Rate* (DDR). This technique is also referred to as *double-pumping*.

- Using internal buffering to make a few reads at once in one memory clock cycle. This allows you to multiply the amount of data provided seen outside compared to the amount that comes from the internal frequency. DDR2 memory interface doubles the external clock frequency while DDR3 and DDR4 quadruple it.

These techniques are currently used in DDR modules as opposed to the much simpler SDRAM (Synchronous DRAM) modules used in the past.

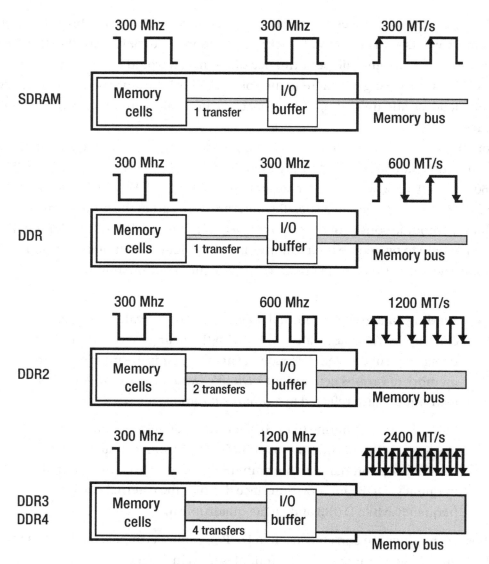

Figure 2-3. *SDRAM, DDR, DDR2, DDR3, DDR4 internals. An example of memory modules with 300 MHz internal clock. MT/s means "Mega transfers per second."*

Let's look at the typical DDR4 memory chip like 16 GB 2400 MHz (described in specifications as DDR4-2400, PC4-19200). In such case the internal DRAM array clock works at 300 MHz. The memory bus clock is quadrupled to 1200 MHz thanks to the internal I/O buffer. Additionally, as with each clock cycle there are two transfers (both slopes of the clock signal), and it results in a 2400 MT/s data rate (mega transfers per seconds). This is where the 2400 MHz specification comes from. Simply put, due to the nature of double-pumping in DDR memory, speed is typically specified as double of I/O clock frequency, which is then multiplication of the internal memory clock. Providing this value in MHz is just a marketing simplification. The second signature - PC4-19200 - comes the maximum theoretical performance of such memory - it is 2400 MT/s multiplied by 8 bytes (a single word 64-bit long is being transferred) gives the result of 19200 MB/s.

Let's look at example of my desktop PC in the context of the whole architecture. It is equipped with CPU Intel Core i7-4770K (Haswell generation) running at 3.5 GHz. Front Side Bus frequency is only 100 MHz. DDR3-1600 Memory (PC3-12800) used has 200 MHz internal memory clock, and due to the DDR3 mechanism the I/O bus clock is 800 MHz. This has been illustrated in Figure 2-4. We can confirm all of that using hardware diagnostic tools like CPU-Z (see Figure 2-5).

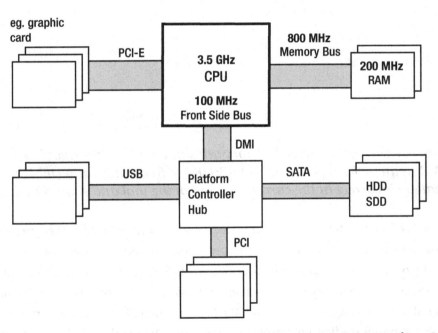

Figure 2-4. *Modern hardware architecture with sample clocking (Intel Core i7-4770K and DDR3-1600)*

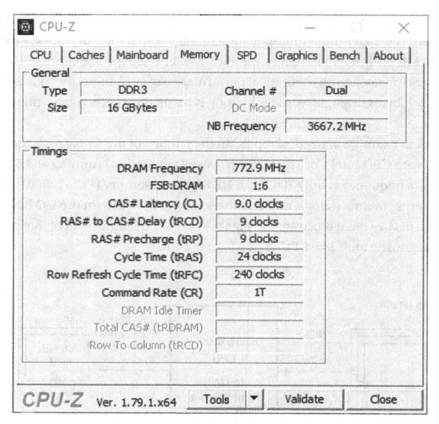

Figure 2-5. *CPU-Z screenshot - Memory tab showing Northbridge (NB) and DRAM frequencies together with FSB:DRAM frequency ratio (which is unfortunatelly incorrect in the current version of the tool and should be 1:8)*

Regardless of all the DDR memory improvements described here, CPUs are still faster than the memory they use. To overcome this problem, a similar approach on different levels is applied - by bringing some part of the data closer to the component with more performant (and more expensive) memory units. Such an approach is being referred to as *caching*.

In case of mass storage memory like HDD, data is usually being cached in RAM - or in a faster but smaller dedicated storage like a small SDD inside hybrid HDD drives dedicated for most frequently used data. In case of RAM, data is being cached inside CPU cache and we will see it shortly.

Of course there are more generic RAM optimizations including better hardware design, better memory controllers. and optimizing DMA (Direct Memory Access) for devices. However, we do not touch DMA in this book as it is not directly related with the program data and those regions are not managed by Garbage Collector.

Memory

A comprehensive book about memory should at least touch the topic of how memory is physically built nowadays. You may be surprised by some of the facts given in this section. They will, I hope, give you a better understanding of why modern computers have this and no other architecture.

There are currently two main types of memory found on personal computers, and they differ significantly both in terms of production and usage cost and performance:

- *Static Random Access Memory* (SRAM) - they provide very fast access but are quite complex, consisting of 4–6 transistors per cell (storing single bit). They hold data as long as power is on, and no refresh is needed. Because of high speed, they are used mainly in CPU caches.

- *Dynamic Random Access Memory* (DRAM) - very simple cell construction (much smaller than SRAM) consists of a single transistor and capacitor. Because of capacitor "leakage," a cell requires a constant refresh (which takes precious milliseconds and stales memory reads). A signal read from the capacitor has to be amplified also, which complicates things more. Reads and writes also take time and are not linear because of capacitor delays (there is some time required to wait to get a proper read or successful write).

Let's devote a few more words to DRAM technology because it is the basis of commonly used memory installed in our computers DIMM slots. As mentioned, a single DRAM cell consists of a transistor and a capacitor and stores a single bit of data. Such cells are grouped into *DRAM arrays*. The address to access a specific cell is being provided via so-called *address lines*.

It would be very complicated and costly to have each cell in the DRAM array have its own address. For example, in case of 32-bit addressing there would be 32-bit wide *address lines decoder* (component responsible for specific cell selection). The number of address lines influence overall cost of the system to a great extent - the more lines, the more pins and interconnections between the memory controller and memory (RAM) chips (modules). It would be too expensive and complicated, of course, even more so in the case of computers with 64-bit word. Because of that address lines are being reused as row and column lines (see Figure 2-6) and providing a full address is being split into two phases.

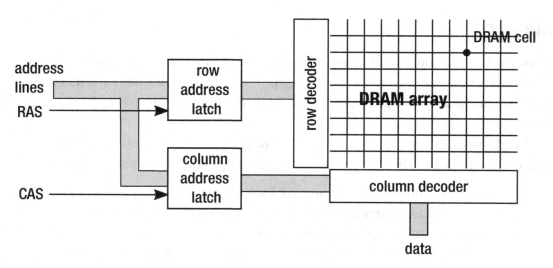

Figure 2-6. *DRAM chip example with DRAM array and the most important channels: address lines, RAS, and CAS*

Within a single array, the address (row) line selects the row and the column (data) line selects the column. A single bit from a particular cell is being read in the following process:

1. The number of the row is put on the address lines.

2. Interpretation is triggered by the Row Address Strobe (RAS) signal on a dedicated line.

3. The number of the column is put on the address lines.

4. Interpretation is triggered by the Column Address Strobe (CAS) signal.

5. Retrieve data - single bit (particular DRAM cell has been addressed).

DRAM modules we install in our computers consist of many such DRAM arrays organized in a way allowing us to access multiple bits (single word) in a single clock cycle.

The transition times between individual steps of obtaining this single bit strongly affects memory performance. These times can be familiar to you because they are an important factor in the specification of memory modules, which greatly affect their price by the way. So you are probably aware of DIMM modules timings like DDR3 9-9-9-24 numbers. All those timings are specified in clock cycles required to perform specific action. Subsequently they have the following meanings:

- tCL (CAS latency) - the time between a column address strobe (CAS) and beginning of the reply (receiving data).

- tRCD (RAS to CAS delay) - the minimal time between the row address strobe (RAS) and column address strobe (CAS) may occur.

- tRP (Row Precharge) - the time it takes to *precharge* a row before accessing it. The row cannot be used without prior preparation, which is calling precharging.

- tRAS (Row active delay) - minimum time the row has to be active to access information in it. This is typically at least the sum of the three above times.

Please note the importance of those times. If the row and column you are interested in have already been set, the readout is almost immediate. If you want to change the column, it will take tCL clock cycles. If we want to change the row, the situation is much worse. It must be first recharged (tRP cycles), followed by RAS and CAS delays (tCL and tRCD).

All these times are important for computer users expecting maximum performance. Players especially pay great attention to these parameters. What is enough for us to know is that while buying memory modules you should take care of the lowest possible timings you can afford if performance is a top priority for you.

However, we are interested in the impact of DRAM memory architecture and its timings on memory management. As you can see, the biggest is the cost of the row change - RAS signal timings and precharging. This is one of the many reasons why sequential memory access patterns are much faster than non-sequential ones. Reading data in a burst from a single row (changing column occasionally) is much faster than a need to change a row frequently. If the access pattern is completely random, most probably we will be hit by those row-changing timings on each and every memory access.

All of the information presented here has one goal - to make sure you have a deep reason to remember why non-sequential access to memory is so undesired. And as we will see, this is not the only reason why completely random access is the worst scenario.

CPU

Let's now go to the central processing unit topic. The processor is compatible with the so-called *Instruction Set Architecture* (ISA) - it defines, among others, the set of operations that can be executed (instructions), registers and their meaning, how memory is addressed, and so on. In this sense, ISA is a contract (interface) established between the processor manufacturer and its users - programs written under a given contract. This is the layer we see in programming, for example, in the assembly language of a given architecture. ISA IA-32 (32-bit i386, Pentium 32-bit processors) and AMD64 compliant (the vast majority of modern processors including Intel Core, AMD FX and Zen, etc.) are the most widely used in the world of the .NET ecosystem. Under ISA is the so-called *microarchitecture* of the processor that implements it. This allows us to improve microarchitecture without affecting the system and software, and so in a backwards compatible manner.

Note   There is a lot of confusion with the names of the 64-bit architecture standards, and you will often encounter the x86-64, EMT64T, Intel 64, or AMD64 interchangeably used. Despite the presence of producers' names and sometimes minor differences, we can safely assume for the purpose of this book that these are unambiguous names and can be used safely interchangeably.

As stated in the previous chapter, a key role in the operation of the CPU occupies registers because currently all computers are implemented as registry machines. In the context of data manipulation, access to registers is immediate in the sense that it takes place within a single processor cycle and does not introduce any additional delays. There is no space for your data closer to the CPU than just the processor registers. Of course, registers store data needed for the current instructions so they cannot be considered as a general-purpose memory. In fact, in general, the processor has more registers than is apparent from its ISA. This allows for various types of optimizations (like so-called *register renaming*). However, these are implementation details of microarchitecture and does not affect the mechanisms of memory management.

CPU Cache

As we mentioned earlier, to mitigate the performance gap between CPU and RAM, an indirect component is used to store a copy of the most used and most needed data - CPU cache. In a very general way this is illustrated in Figure 2-7.

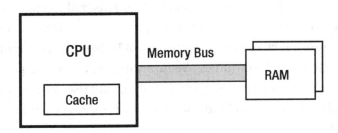

Figure 2-7. *CPU with cache and RAM relationship*

This cache is transparent from the ISA point of view. Neither the programmer (nor even the operating system) does not necessarily need to know about its existence. They do not have to manage it. In an ideal world, proper use and management of the cache should be the sole responsibility of the CPU.

Because as a cache we want to use as fast-as-possible memory, the previously mentioned SRAM chips are used. Due to the cost and the size (which takes up precious space in the processor) resulting from this technology, they obviously cannot have as large capacities as the main RAM. But depending on the assumed costs they can match the speed of the CPU or may be only one/two orders of magnitude slower.

Cache Hit and Miss

The idea behind a cache is trivial. When the instruction executed by the processor needs access to memory (whether it is write or read), it first looks at the cache to check whether the data we need is there already. If so, fantastic! We have just gained a very fast memory access and such a situation is referred to as *cache hit*. If the data is not in the cache (so-called *cache miss*), then it is being stored there after reading from RAM, which is obviously a much slower operation. *Cache hit ratio* and *cache miss ratio* are the very important indicators telling us whether our code uses the cache efficiently.

Data Locality

But why is such a cache helpful in the first place? Cache idea is based on the very important concept - *locality of data*. We can distinguish two kinds of locality:

- *temporal locality* - if we access some memory region, we will most probably access it again in the near future. This makes using a cache perfectly valid - we read some data from memory and we will probably reuse it later a few more times. Why is there a temporal locality? This is quite intuitive. We rarely use data once. In general, we load some data structures into variables and use those variables repeatedly. These are all kinds of counters, temporary data read from files, and so on.

- *spatial locality* - if we access some memory region, we will most probably access data from the close neighborhood. This type of locality can become our ally if we cache a little more surrounding data than we currently need. For example, if we need a few bytes from memory, let's read and cache them and a dozen or so more. This is also perfectly intuitive. We rarely use very isolated small areas of memory. We soon will find out the stack and heap are organized into segments so threads doing their job generally access similar areas of memory. Local variables or data structures are also generally placed close together.

Please note that the cache is beneficial if the above conditions actually apply. However, this is a double-edged weapon. If we write the program in a way that breaks data locality, the cache will become an unnecessary burden. We'll see about that later in the chapter.

Cache Implementation

In addition, as long as the compatibility with the ISA memory model is maintained, cache implementation details are theoretically unimportant. It should be just there to speed up memory access and that's it. However, this is a perfect example of *The Law of Leaky Abstractions* coined by Joel Spolsky:

> *All non-trivial abstractions, to some degree, are leaky*

What it means is that an abstraction that theoretically should hide the implementation details, unfortunately under certain circumstances exposes them outside. And it usually does so in an unpredictable and/or undesired way. How it does in case of a cache should be clear soon, but let just now dig into a little more implementation detail.

The most important and most influential fact is that the data between the RAM and the cache is transferred in blocks called *cache line*. Cache line has a fixed size and in the vast majority of today computers it is 64 bytes. It is very important to remember - you cannot read or write less data from memory than the cache line size, so 64 bytes. Even if you would want to read one single bit from memory, the whole block of a 64-bytes wide cache line will be populated. Such a design is utilizing better sequential DRAM access (remember the precharging and RAS delays described earlier in this chapter?).

As stated before, DRAM access is 64-bit wide (8 bytes), so eight transfers are required from RAM to populate such cache line. This requires quite a lot of CPU cycles so there are various techniques to accommodate that. One of them is *Critical Word First & Early Restart*. It makes the cache line not read word by word but starts with the word that is most needed. Imagine that in the worst case, such an 8-byte word could be at the end of the cache line so you would have to wait for all the previous seven transfers to access it. This technique first reads the most important word. Instructions waiting for this data can continue execution and the rest of the cache line will be filled asynchronously.

Note   How does a typical memory access pattern look? When someone wants to read data from memory, the corresponding cache line entry is created in the cache and 64 bytes of data are being read into it. When someone wants to write data in memory, the first step is exactly the same – the cache line is being filled in the cache if it is not there already. This cached data is modified in cache when someone writes data. Now one of two strategies can occur:

— *write-through* - after writing to the cache line, the modified data is saved immediately to the main memory. This is a simple approach to implement but creates a big overhead on the memory bus.

— *write-back* - after writing to the cache line it is marked dirty. Then, when there is no space in cache for other data, this dirty block is written to memory (and the modified dirty cache entry is deleted). The processor may write these blocks from time to time, as it deems appropriate (e.g., during idle times).

There is yet another one optimization technique called *write-combining*. It ensures that a given cache line from a given memory area is written in its entirety (rather than writing its individual words), again utilizing the fact of faster sequential access to memory.

Because of cache lines, each data stored in memory is aligned to 64-bytes boundaries. So in the worst-case scenario to read two successive bytes, two cache lines have to be consumed with a total size of 128 bytes. It will land into the cache but if no more data from this memory region will be needed, it will be waste of time. This is illustrated in Figure 2-8 when we want to read only 2 bytes under address A. Unfortunately address A is just one byte before the end of cache line-rounded boundary so in fact two whole cache lines have to be read.

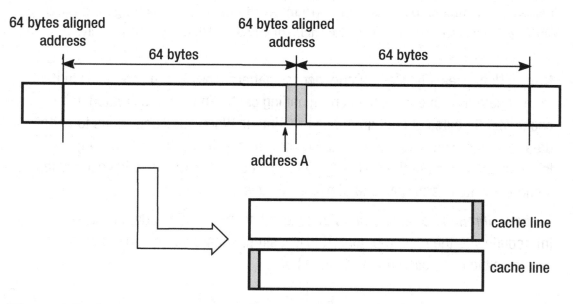

Figure 2-8. *Access to two successive bytes requires populating two cache lines because they were unfortunately located*

OK. Although it's really the tip of the iceberg, you can ask why we have to know such hardware implementation details? Does it really matter in a comfortable world of managed code? Let's continue our journey to find out.

A cost of non-sequential memory access patterns has been illustrated by sample code from Listing 2-1 and by results in Table 2-1. The sample program accesses the same two-dimensional array in two ways - row by row and column by column. Results are presented for three different environments: PC (Intel Core i7-4770K 3.5GHz), laptop (Intel Core i7-4712MQ 2.3GHz), and Raspberry Pi 2 board (ARM Cortex-A7 0.9GHz).

Listing 2-1. Column versus row indexing when accessing an array (5000x5000 array of ints)

```
int[,] tab = new int[n, m];
for (int i = 0; i < n; ++i)
{
    for (int j = 0; j < m; ++j)
    {
        tab[i, j] = 1;
    }
}

int[,] tab = new int[n, m];
for (int i = 0; i < n; ++i)
{
    for (int j = 0; j < m; ++j)
    {
        tab[j, i] = 1;
    }
}
```

Table 2-1. *Column versus Row Indexing results (n,m = 5000)*

Pattern	PC	Laptop	Raspberry Pi 2
By Rows	52 ms	127 ms	918 ms
By Columns	401 ms	413 ms	2001 ms

This example shows how unfavorable the non-sequential retrieval of data can be for performance. The sample program in the second version reads the data column after the column. As a result, we need to change the active line of DRAM cells every now and then. What's more, we use the cache very badly because we read only one byte of data by loading the entire cache line. And afterwards we immediately read under the other, distant address so another cache line must be populated. The difference in performance may be six times as you can see in Table 2-1! The CPU stalls very often to wait for memory access.

Figure 2-9 illustrates the difference between accessing elements by rows and by columns of some small array containing values from 1 to 40 (and illustration is assuming that four such values fit into a single cache line). Let's assume also for illustrative purposes that array access from Figure 2-9 happens on the CPU with a buffer for only four cache lines.[1] As we read memory row by row (left side of Figure 2-9), in fact we are reading successive integers within successive cache line-rounded memory regions:

- To read the first four elements (1,2,3,4), the first cache line is read and all those elements are used.

- To read the next four elements (5,6,7,8), the second cache line is read and again, all those elements are used.

- To read the next four elements (9,10,11,12), the third cache line is read. This access repeats through the entire array (and no cache line is needed to be read again).

The right side of Figure 2-9 show the second pattern, when we read only a single integer per each cache line and then move on to the another one:

- To read the first four elements, we read four cache lines but only one element from each of them is used (1 from first cache line, 9 from the second, and so on).

- To read the next element (33). one of the already cache lines must be purged because the buffer is already full. It most probably will be least accessed once (so containing 1,2,3,4 elements) and replaced with the new one (containing 33,34,35,36).

---

[1]In a real CPU, the "buffer" for cache lines is the entire CPU cache so it typically fits hundreds or thousands of 64-byte wide cache line-sized entries.

- To read the next element (2), again the least used data will be purged and the CPU will need to reload the first line (containing 1,2,3,4), unloaded just before.

- This access pattern repeats many times, requiring the cache line to be read four times.

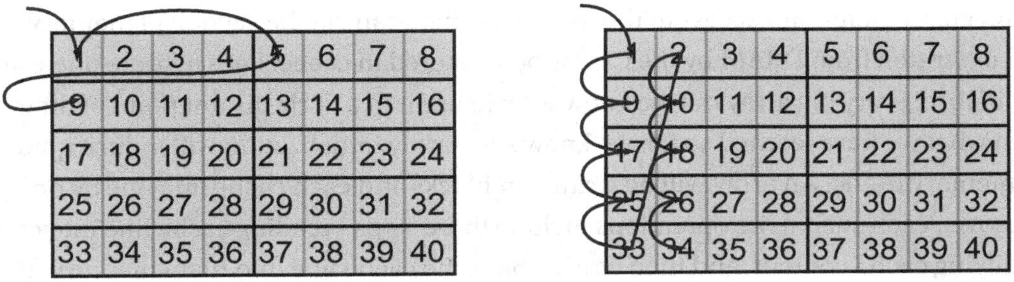

Figure 2-9. *By row versus by column access pattern - arrows show access triggering cache line invalidation (when accessing first 10 elements)*

Obviously, real CPUs have more than four cache-line buffers and the cache line fits more data than four integer values, so Figure 2-9 is a simplification for illustrative purposes. But exactly the same problem happens in the real-world scenarios and its results are clearly seen in Table 2-1.

As you can see, the entire .NET runtime environment and advanced memory management techniques used in it are not able to hide those CPU implementation details that are hitting us back. An unfavorable memory access pattern causes many times worse performance of our code. It will not be comforting that a similar test for Java and C/C++ would produce very similarly unfavorable results.

Data Alignment

There is yet one other very important aspect of accessing memory. Most CPU architectures are designed to access data that are properly aligned - meaning the starting address of such data is a multiplication of a given alignment specified in bytes. Each type has its own alignment and a data structure alignment depends on its field's alignment. A lot of care must be taken to not access unaligned data that may be a few times slower than a proper way. This is a responsibility of the compiler and a developer designing data structures. In case of CLR data structures, layout is mostly managed by the runtime itself. This is why we can spot a lot of code related to proper alignment handling in the Garbage Collector code. We will see in Chapter 13 how object memory layout looks and how it may be controlled, taking into consideration data alignment.

Non-temporal Access

What have been mentioned so far is the fact that in most common types of CPU architecture, there is no access to the memory other than via the cache. All memory read or written from DRAM by the CPU is being stored in cache. Let's assume one wants to initialize a very big array but we know we will use it in a fairly distant point of time. From what we have learned so far, we know such array initialization will induce quite big memory traffic. An array will be written in blocks and each cache line one by one. Moreover, each such write operations include three steps - reading cache line into cache, modifying cache content. and then writing back the cache line into main memory. We will populate cache lines only to write data back to main memory. Not only this is not optimal by itself, it also takes away cache from other programs.

We can avoid such cache traffic by using a so-called *non-temporal access* set of assembler instructions - MOVNTI, MOVNTQ, MOVNTDQ, etc. They allow the programmer to prevent caching of the data during the write to memory. They are exposed through _mm_ stream_* set of C/C++ functions so no assembler is required to use them. For example, _mm_stream_si128 executes MOVNTDQ instruction, which writes to memory a single quad-word (4 words of 4 bytes). An example of a fast array initialization using this technique is shown in Listing 2-2.

Listing 2-2. Example of low-level API in C++ to use non-temporal writes

```
#include <emmintrin.h>
void setbytes(char *p, int c)
{
  __m128i i = _mm_set_epi8(c, c, c, c, c, c, c, c, c, c, c, c, c, c, c, c);
// sets 16 signed 8-bit integer values
  _mm_stream_si128((__m128i *)&p[0], i);
  _mm_stream_si128((__m128i *)&p[16], i);
  _mm_stream_si128((__m128i *)&p[32], i);
  _mm_stream_si128((__m128i *)&p[48], i);
}
```

Why do we mention that at all? Currently there is no .NET support for non-temporal writes, although there are plans to use them in some parts of the runtime itself. And there are also some ideas to provide developers a way to hint the runtime to use non-temporal writes in their code (see Listing 2-3 showing an example of how it could look).

Listing 2-3. A possible implementation of future feature - asking runtime to use non-temporal write while storing data

```
public int[] Sum ( int[] op1, int[] op2 )
{
   var result = new int[op1.Length];
   Contract.Assume( Performance.NonTemporal(result) );
   result[i] = op1[i] + op2[i]
}
```

Besides, before it will be implemented on the JIT level, somebody may decide to use proper P/Invokes of _mm_stream_si128 inside C# in a very critical code performance, after obviously seriously deep thinking about it.

Note   There are also non-temporal access (NTA) load instructions MOVNTDQA exposed through _mm_stream_load_si128 functions.

Prefetching

Data locality is a great feature used by the cache mechanism automatically, as long as the programmer has not specifically tried to disrupt it. There is one additional mechanism that seeks to improve the cache utilization. It is about populating the cache with data that are likely to be needed in the nearest future – so-called prefetching. It can work in two different modes:

- Hardware driven - when the CPU notices a few cache misses with some certain pattern. Most CPUs track from 8 to 16 memory access patterns (to compensate a typical, multithreaded/multiprocess way of work). Note: Although we do not cover so-called memory pages yet, please bear in mind that hardware prefetching is *page limited*.

If not, it would trigger page miss, which would be big unnecessary overhead if the guess was not correct.

- Software driven - by explicit call from our code by using PREFETCHT0 instruction exposed through C/C++ _mm_prefetch () function.

Prefetch, like all other caching mechanisms, is a double-edged weapon. If we understand the memory access patterns in our code well, using prefetch can noticeably accelerate the performance of our program. On the other hand, it is very difficult to be sure that we really understand those memory access patterns, given the very broad context in which our code works - influenced by other threads in our program, other programs' threads, and threads in the operating system itself. There is a PREFETCHT0 instruction call contained in the .NET code but due to the fact that required PREFETCH identifier is not defined, prefetching is not used (see Listing 2-4).

Listing 2-4. Prefetching related parts of the .NET code shows it is disabled by default.

```
//#define PREFETCH
#ifdef PREFETCH
__declspec(naked) void __fastcall Prefetch(void* addr)
{
    __asm {
        PREFETCHT0 [ECX]
         ret
    };
}
#else //PREFETCH
inline void Prefetch (void* addr)
{
    UNREFERENCED_PARAMETER(addr);
}
#endif //PREFETCH
```

The prefetch call has been spread out through many places in CLR Garbage Collector code. But the use of PREFETCHT0 has been disabled in the .NET code probably for the reasons given earlier. Runtime is a very generic code, and it's hard to imagine a code snippet that can be found in it ensuring that, under all circumstances, the use of prefetch will be beneficial. This is therefore a safe-side selection.

Prefetching and cache-lined memory access obviously work against us if we won't try to lay out data in memory in a proper way. An example would be, if we designed a garbage collection algorithm in such a way that some very small, 1-byte diagnostic data is scattered all the way through memory in random places, an operation to gather this information will be very costly in terms of caching. We will have to fill cache through cache lines just to read single byte. And as we said, prefetching can make things even worse - "if you are reading those 64 bytes, let read twice more because you might be probably interested in it."

Algorithms that intensively operate on memory (and garbage collection is operating on memory in its essence) must be taking into consideration such CPU internals. Memory is just not a flat space where we can pick some single bytes or bits from here or there without penalty!

Hierarchical Cache

Returning to our architecture, due to performance requirements on the one hand and cost optimization on the other, the CPU design evolved today into a more complex *hierarchical cache*. The idea is simple. Instead of a single cache, let's create a few, with several different sizes and speeds. This allows you to create a very small and very fast *first-level cache* (called L1), then a bit bigger and a bit slower *cache level 2* (L2), and finally *the third-level cache* (L3). This enumeration in modern architecture ends on three levels. Such hierarchical cache of modern computers is shown in Figure 2-10. It is true that sometimes we can spot processors equipped with L4 cache, but it is a little different kind of memory and is designed mainly for integrated graphics cards inside those CPUs.

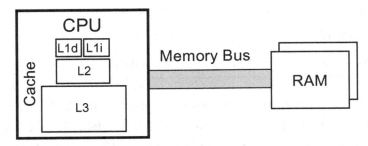

Figure 2-10. *CPU with hierarchical cache - first-level cache split into instruction (L1i) and data (L1d) cache and second (L2) and third (L3) level cache. The CPU is connected to DRAM via Memory Bus.*

The first-level cache is divided into two separate blocks. One is for data (labeled L1d) and the other one for instructions (labeled L1i). The instructions read from the memory and executed by the processor are also in fact data but interpreted appropriately. Data and code instructions at levels higher than L1 are actually treated identically, which should remind us of the Von Neumann architecture mentioned in Chapter 1. However, practice has shown that it is preferable to treat data and instructions separately for the lowest cache level. It is therefore the approach of the Harvard architecture. For this reason, the architecture of today's computers is referred to as *Modified Harvard Architecture*. This solution works well because of the strong independence of using memory regions for storing data and program code, but only at the lowest level.

Knowing that there are three main levels of cache, an obvious question arises - What are the typical differences in speed and size between them and the main memory? Memory at lower-cache levels can be fast enough that L1 and even L2 access may take up enough CPU cycles to be faster than the pipeline execution time (unless you have to wait for the exact address to be computed, which is also an expensive operation). So what do those timings look like?

At the moment, I am writing this chapter on a laptop with Intel Core i7-4712MQ CPU (Haswell generation) running at 2.30 GHz. Assuming one CPU cycle on my laptop takes approximately 0.4 ns (~1/2.30 GHz) and using Haswell i7 specification, the latency to access different memory levels can be seen as in Table 2-2.

Table 2-2. *Latency to Access Different Parts of Memory*

Operation	Latency
L1 cache	< 2.0 ns
L2 cache	4.8 ns
L3 cache	14.4 ns
Main memory	71.4 ns
HDD	150 000 ns

We can clearly see it is worth fighting for optimal cache usage. Latency can be as much as 5 times faster when the CPU has needed data available in an L3 cache rather than in RAM. With an L1 cache it is over 30 times better. That is why it is extremely important for the overall performance how the cache is utilized. How much data fits into the cache? It all depends on the specific CPU model but my i7-4770K specification pretty well reflects market standards. L1 cache has 64 KiB of data (split into 32 KiB for code and 32 KiB for data) while the L2 cache has 256 KiB. The L3 cache, always much bigger, is 8 MiB big.

Do those timings influence developers live, especially in the managed world of .NET? Let's look at the simple example showing the latency in accessing data depending on the amount of memory being processed. Using code from Listing 2-5, one can made a series of sequential readings (and therefore the most optimal). As the used structure has a 64 bytes size, the read is done with a 64-byte step and every time a new cache line needs to be loaded. Figure 2-11 shows average access times per single element of the tab array, depending how much memory this array took in total.

There is a clear deterioration of access time when the data size exceeds the cache size of each level. As benchmarks were performed on an Intel i7-4770K processor, the clearly visible performance degradation points are around 256 KiB and 8192 KiB, which correspond to L2 and L3 cache sizes. We can see that operating on small data sizes may be a few times faster than operating on data that does not fit the L3 cache.

Listing 2-5. Sequential read of succeeding cache lines

```
public struct OneLineStruct
{
    public long data1;
    public long data2;
    public long data3;
    public long data4;
    public long data5;
    public long data6;
    public long data7;
    public long data8;
}

public static long OneLineStructSequentialReadPattern(OneLineStruct[] tab)
{
    long sum = 0;
    int n = tab.Length;
    for (int i = 0; i < n; ++i)
```

```
    {
        unchecked { sum += tab[i].data1; }
    }
    return sum;
}
```

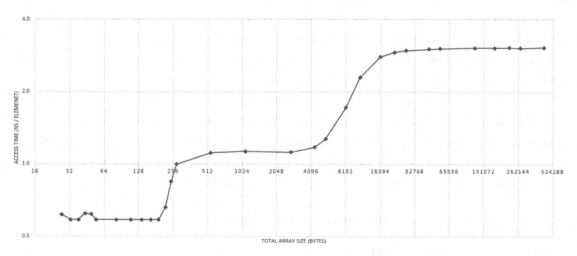

Figure 2-11. *Access time depending on the data size - Intel x86 architecture/ sequential read. Please note: both axes are logarithmic.*

Note   There is one interesting yet not so important topic in the context of cache - *the eviction strategies.* It's about how you get space for new data if it's missing at a given level. There are two possible approaches, sometimes mixed on the different levels:

— *Exclusive cache* - data is only on one level of cache. This method is most commonly used in AMD processors.

— *Inclusive cache* - where each cache line in a higher level (for example, L1d) is also present in a lower level (for example, L2).

Although interesting, this does not affect our thoughts on memory management. It should be assumed that CPU manufacturers are doing their best to ensure the most effective implementation of these mechanisms.

Multicore Hierarchical Cache

However, this is not the end of our journey through computer design. Contemporary CPUs have a majority of more than one core. In simplified terms, the *core* is what the individual, simplified processor is - it can execute code independently of other cores. In the past, each core performed exactly one thread. Thus, a quad-core processor could execute four threads simultaneously. At present, practically all processors have a *simultaneous multithreading mechanism* (SMT), allowing simultaneous execution of two threads within a single core. It is called Hyper-threading in case of Intel processors and full SMT support has been added into AMD Zen microarchitecture. The distribution of caches between individual cores in sample quad-code CPU is shown in Figure 2-12.

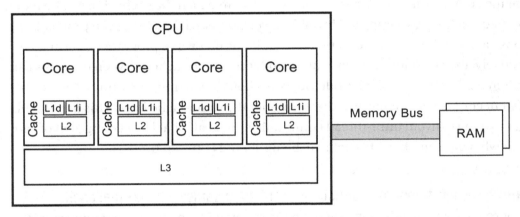

Figure 2-12. *Multiple Core CPU - each core owns its first-level cache split into instruction (L1i) and data (L1d) cache and second-level cache (L2). Third (L3) level cache is shared among cores. CPU is connected to DRAM via Memory Bus.*

As we can see, each of the cores has its own first- and second-level cache. The third-level cache is shared between them. How cores and L3 cache are interconnected is in fact an implementation detail. For example, in most modern Intel CPUs there is a bidirectional, extremely fast 32-byte wide bus that further connects them with the integrated GPU and System Agent. Note that for SMT processors, two threads running on the same core share L1 and L2 caches, so their actual usage is split in half unless care is provided that both threads have the biggest range of shared data. This obviously requires operating system support to deliberately assign threads to the cores based on their memory access patterns.

Because each thread can run on a separate processor and/or core, there is a consistency problem of cached data. Each core has its own version of the first- and second-level cache, and only the third level is being shared. This leads to the need to introduce an entire complex concept known as *cache coherency*. This mechanism describes how consistency of stored data is maintained, and it is being applied by *cache-coherency protocol* - a way of informing about data change between cores. One of the basic states is that the data in the local cache has been modified (maintained by some *dirty* or *modification flag*). Information about such change has to be broadcasted or updated as needed.

There are many extensions and advanced cache coherence protocols that are designed to provide efficient operations - in particular the very popular *MESI protocol*. Its name comes from the names of the four states in which the cache line can be found - modified, exclusive, shared, and invalid. Nevertheless, cache-coherency protocols can impose a big overhead on memory traffic and thus on overall program performance. Intuitively, the constant need for mutual updating of the cache between the cores can result in noticeable overhead. Code we write should try to minimize any access from different cores to the memory addresses under the same cache lines. This in particular means trying to avoid intra-thread communication at all or at least taking a lot of care about what data and how this data are being shared between threads.

Note   As non-temporal instructions mentioned earlier omit normal cache-coherency rules, using them should be in a pair with special sfence assembler instruction in order to make their results visible to other cores.

But again, is this knowledge useful in such high-level environments as .NET? Does Garbage Collector with its all knowledge and internal mechanisms hide such deep hardware implementation details? The answer to this question can be found in the following example.

Listing 2-6 shows multithreaded code that can simultaneously run a threadsCount number of threads accessing the same sharedData array. Each of the thread just increments a single element array without (theoretically) influencing other threads. In our example, there are two important parameters indicating how those elements are laid out within a shared array - whether there is a starting gap and how distant they are from each other (offset). As we will run this code for threadsCount=4 on a four-core machine, most probably each thread will have its own physical core assigned.

Listing 2-6. Possibility of False sharing between threads

```
const int offset = 1;
const int gap = 0;
public static int[] sharedData = new int[4 * offset + gap * offset];
public static long DoFalseSharingTest(int threadsCount, int size =
100_000_000)
{
    Thread[] workers = new Thread[threadsCount];
    for (int i = 0; i < threadsCount; ++i)
    {
        workers[i] = new Thread(new ParameterizedThreadStart(idx =>
        {
            int index = (int)idx + gap;
            for (int j = 0; j < size; ++j)
            {
                sharedData[index * offset] = sharedData[index * offset] +
1;
            }
        }));
    }
    for (int i = 0; i < threadsCount; ++i)
        workers[i].Start(i);
    for (int i = 0; i < threadsCount; ++i)
        workers[i].Join();
    return 0;
}
```

Table 2-3. *Benchmark Results of Code from Listing 2-6 Showing False Sharing Influence on Processing Time*

Version	PC	Laptop	Raspberry Pi 2
#1 (offset=1, gap=0)	5.0s	6.7s	29.0s
#2 (offset=16, gap=0)	2.4s	2.6s	13.8s
#3 (offset=16, gap=16)	0.7s	0.8s	12.1s

In Table 2-3 you can see significant differences in performance between various combinations of gap and offset. If we use an array in definitely the most intuitive and simple way, it means the gap is 0 and offset is 1. The layout and thread accesses are illustrated in Figure 2-13a. This unfortunately introduces a very big cache-coherency overhead. Each thread (core) has its own local copy of the same memory region (in its own cache line), so after each incrementation it has to invalidate the others' local copies. This forces cores to constantly invalidate their caches.

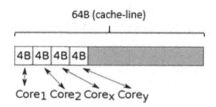

Figure 2-13a. *Version #1 with 1 byte offset and no gap - each thread access modifies the same cache line*

The obvious solution for this problem is to spread elements accessed by each thread to different cache lines. The simplest way is to create a much bigger array and use only every 16th element (16 times 4 bytes of single Int32 makes 64 bytes). This is a version when offset is 16 and gap is still 0 (see Figure 2-13b). As we can see in Table 2-3, the performance is much better but we can still do more.

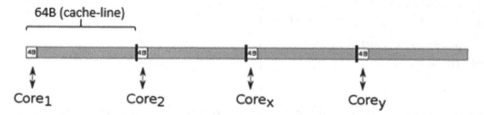

Figure 2-13b. *Version #2 with 16 byte offset and no gap - each thread access and modifies its own cache line*

There is still a single cache line constantly invalidated but it can be not so obvious at the first glance, leading to a problem referred to as *False sharing* - an unfortunate data access pattern in which theoretically not modified shared data is located within a cache line altered by some other thread, incurring its constant invalidation. As we will learn in the next chapter, each type in .NET has some additional header attached to its beginning. This in particular relates also to arrays. In case of arrays there is important data at the beginning of the object - the length of the array. What's more, when accessing array elements by an index operator, it internally checks whether it is not out of index. This means accessing the beginning of the array object to check the length of the array, every time we access any array element. Therefore, the first core is sharing the beginning of the object with other cores, constantly invalidating correspondent cache lines. To fix this we have to shift our elements by a single cache-line offset. This is a version when the offset is still 16 but the gap is also 16 (see Figure 2-13c).

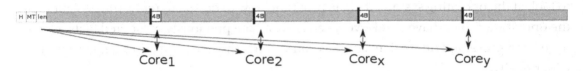

Figure 2-13c. *Version #3 with 16 bytes offset and 16 byte gap - each thread modifies its own cache line and reads shared cache line with the array header*

In this case each core has its own local copy of the first cache line for read only purposes. And it modifies their own cache lines with data. No cache-coherency protocol overhead is added. From Table 2-3 we can see this makes such code running even 7 times faster than with extensive false sharing!

Other architectures sometimes abandon the sequential consistency present in x86, which simplifies their design but makes programming difficult (explicit memory barriers are required). An example of such an architecture is applied to the 2006 PowerPC on Apple computers.

So far we have spent a lot of time understanding the caching of data. However, few pages ago it was mentioned that there is also a cache for program instructions (L1i). We do not look at it here for a few reasons. First of all, it is much less problematic in itself. Compilers can take good care of properly prepared code, and CPUs also do quite well in guessing code access patterns. As a result, this cache works well - the compiler and the nature of the program execution cause a good temporal and spatial locality that the CPU can use.[2] Moreover, instruction cache management does not fall into the area of memory management in .NET because it narrows it down to data management. The only obvious indication in this regard is the desire to generate the smallest code. Because it is cached at levels higher than L1, it consumes these resources. However, in fact it is difficult today to put this advice into practice - everything is done by the great compiler optimization, and the length of the code is rather due to business needs.

Operating System

We've spent quite a lot of time very close to the hardware so far. I initially also promised to look at the operating system. It is the best time now to do so. Actually, the designers of the operating system have to take very seriously all the previously presented facts, which have been presented only briefly. And as you will see shortly, it's still just a fragment of a wider reality.

Due to both operating system and hardware architecture, physical memory limits vary from 2 GB to 24 TB. And typical commodity hardware nowadays is equipped with from 4 to 8 GB of memory. If a given program had to use physical memory directly, it would need to manage all memory regions it creates and deletes. Such memory management logic would be not only complex, but also repeated in each and every program. Moreover, from a low-level programming perspective, it would be also cumbersome to use memory in such an approach. Each program would have to remember which regions of memory it uses so that programs do not interfere with each other. Allocators would need to cooperate with such region management to properly manage created and deleted objects. This is also quite dangerous from a security perspective - without any intermediate layer, a program could access not only its own memory regions.

Virtual Memory

Thus a very convenient abstraction has been introduced - a *virtual memory*. It moves memory management logic to the operating system, which provides a program a so-called *virtual address space*. In particular it means that each process thinks it is the only

---

[2]However, even in .NET we can still design method calls with L1i cache misses kept in mind. It mainly includes avoiding lot of virtual calls and favourites repetitive calls of the same method over a big set of data. We will see such example in Chapter 10.

one running in the system and that the whole memory is for its own purposes. Even more. Because address space is virtual, it can be larger than the physical memory. This allows it to extend physical DRAM memory with secondary storage like mass storage hard drives.

Note   Are there operating systems without virtual memory? For any commodity usage, no. But yes, there are some special purpose, mostly very small operating systems and frameworks targeted to embedded systems. One of the examples is (micro)Clinux kernel.

Here is where the *operating system memory manager* comes to play. It has two main responsibilities:

- Mapping virtual address space to physical memory - there is 32-bit-long virtual address on 32-bit machines and 64-bit long on 64-bit machines (although currently only lower 48 bits are used, which still allows an address of 128 TB of data; and both simplify the architecture and allows us to avoid unnecessary overhead).

- Moving some memory regions from DRAM memory to hard drives and back as they are requested or currently not needed. Obviously as the total used memory may be bigger than physical memory, sometimes some parts of it must be temporarily stored to slower media like HDD. A place where such data is stored is called *page file* or *swap file*.

The OS memory manager has also two main additional responsibilities: managing memory-mapped files and a copy-on-write memory mechanism. We do not touch them here, however, as they are irrelevant for our purposes.

The need to get rid of a piece of data from RAM and to save it on a temporary storage is obviously associated with a large decrease in performance. This process is defined in different systems as *swapping* or *paging* mainly for historical reasons. Windows has a dedicated file called a *page file* that stores data from memory, hence the term paging. For Linux, such data is stored on a dedicated partition, called *swap partition*. Hence the term swapping on Unix-like systems.

Virtual memory is implemented in CPU (with the help of *Memory Management Unit* - MMU) and used with cooperation with OS. Virtual memory management is organized in so-called *pages*. As it would be impractical to map virtual to physical space byte by byte, instead whole pages (continuous blocks of memory) are mapped. A page is therefore the basic building block for managing memory from the operating system point of view. A schematic illustration of virtual memory and physical memory is shown in Figure 2-14.

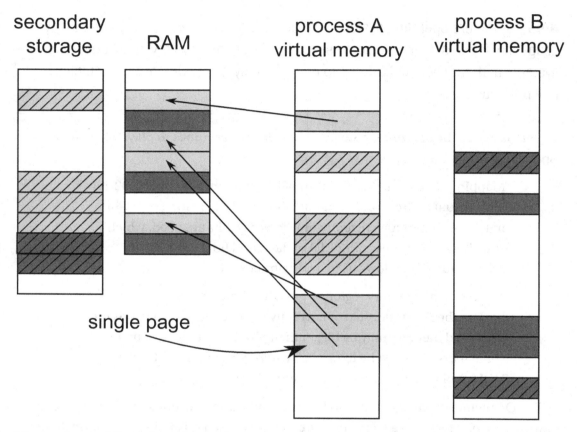

Figure 2-14. *Virtual to physical pages mapping. Each process (A is light gray and B is dark gray) sees its own virtual address space but physically their pages are stored both in RAM (solid-filled pages) and paged (swapped) to disk (dash-filled pages).*

There is also a *page directory* maintained by OS per each process that allows us to map a virtual address to a physical one. Simply put, page directory entries point to a page's physical starting addresses and other metadata like privileges. In old times there was a simple, one-level mapping where an address consisted of a *page selector* and *offset* within a page, which is illustrated in Figure 2-15.

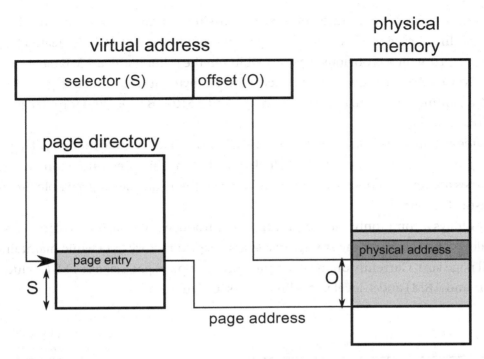

Figure 2-15. *One-level page directory - virtual address consists of selector (S) that choose single page entry from page directory and offset (O) within the page*

A one-level page directory has the main drawback of producing too big pages or too big of page directory size. A big page is a major problem because it would be a waste of resources – an operating system requires page alignment when allocating memory. So even for small data it would need to allocate a whole big page. On the other hand, too big of a page directory is also a problem as it is being stored in the main memory per each process so it would be a waste of memory. Let's see simple calculations of page size versus page directory size on both 32- and 64-bit machines (see Table 2-4).

Table 2-4. *Possible One-Level Page Directory Size on Different Machines*

| Page size | Offset size | 32 bit | | 64 bit (48-bit address) | |
		Selector size	Page directory size	Selector size	Page directory size
4 kB	12 b	20 b	4 MB	36 b	512 GB
4 MB	22 b	10 b	4 kB	26 b	512 MB

*Notes: Offset size has to be big enough to cover whole page size. Then Selector size is the remainder of the whole address. Page Directory Size is 2^selector * address size.*

So enormously big page directories are impossible to implement in case of 64-bit machines. In the case of 4 kB pages, each process should store 512 GB dedicated for a page directory, which is obviously not possible. On the other hand, a 4 MB page size is a huge overhead. Even if a process needed a few kilobytes, it would need to get from the system an entire 4MB-wide big memory page. And a 512 MB page directory size is still a lot.

Moreover, processes do not consume the whole available virtual memory. They tend to group used memory in logical blocks (stack, heap, binaries, and so on) so such directories are rather sparse with big holes between them, and storing a whole directory is a waste of resources.

Nowadays a commonly used approach is to introduce multiple levels of indexes. This allows us to compact the storage of a sparse page directory data while maintaining a small page size. Currently on most architectures, a typical page size is 4 kB (including x86, x64 and ARM) and 4-level page directory (see Figure 2-16).

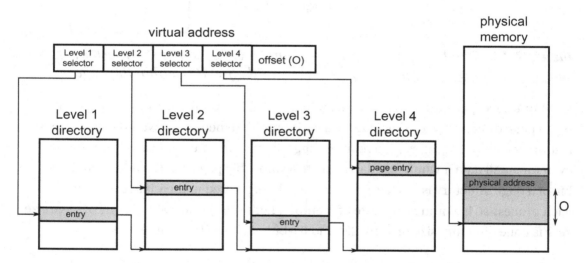

Figure 2-16. *Four-level page directory with 4kB page size - three level of pages selector allows it to represent much more sparse data*

When a virtual address is being translated into a physical address, it requires a *page directory walk*:

- Level 1 selector selects an entry within level 1 directory, which points to one of the level 2 directory entries.

- Level 2 selector selects an entry within specific level 2 directory entry, which points to one of the level 3 directory entries.

- Level 3 selector selects an entry within specific level 3 directory entry, which points to one of the level 4 directory entries.

- Eventually level 4 selector selects an entry within specific level 4 directory entry, which points directly to some page in the physical memory.

- Offset points to specific address within selected page.

Such translation requires traversing a tree but as we said, a page directory is kept in the main memory as all other data. This means it could be also cached through L1/L2/L3 caches. But still, it introduced an enormous overhead if each and every address translation (operation performed very often) would require access to those data (even using L1 cache). Thus, *Translation Look-Aside Buffers* (TLB) has been introduced, which cache the translation itself. The idea is simple - TLB works as a map where the selector is a key and the page's physical address start is a value. TLBs are built to be extremely fast so they are small in terms of storage. They are also multilevel as was the case with page directory structure. The result of the TLB miss (no virtual-to-physical translation already cached) is performing a full-page directory walk, which is costly as we mentioned.

Interesting note   As always with cache, TLB prefetching is tricky - if the CPU itself is to be the one who triggers prefetching (for example, because of branch prediction), it can induce unnecessary page directory walk (as the branch prediction could be invalid). Thus, rather software prefetching of TLBs is being used.

Are there any relevant to software development TLB optimizations? It can mainly mean one thing: reduce the number of pages in general to avoid many TLB misses. This will also allow us to keep page directory small, which is a way to increase chances it will stay in TLB for long time. However, we do not have influence on page management from the .NET perspective.

Interesting note   Typically, L1 operates on the virtual addresses because the cost of translation to the physical address would be much bigger than the fast cache access itself. This means when a page is being changed, all or some cache lines have to be invalidated. Thus, often page changes negatively impact cache performance also.

Large Pages

As it can be seen from previous descriptions, a virtual address translation can be costly and it would be great to avoid it as often as possible. The main approach would be to use a big page size. This would require less address translations as many addresses would fit into the same page, with already a TLB-cached translation. But as we stated, big pages are a waste of resources. There is one solution - so-called *large* (or *huge*) *pages*. With hardware support they allow us to create a large, continuous physical memory block consisting of many sequentially laid-off normal pages. These pages are typically two/three orders of magnitude bigger than a normal page. They can be useful in scenarios when a program requires random access throughout gigabytes of data. Database engines are examples of large pages consumers. A Windows operating system also maps its core kernel images and data with large pages. A large page is non-pageable (can't be moved to page file) and is supported both on Windows and Linux. Unfortunately, it is quite hard to allocate a large page because of fragmentation, and there may not be an adequate continuous range of physical memory.

Large pages are not currently used by the .NET runtime because it actually wants the pages to be smaller for the large percentage of possible scenarios. However, using large pages is on the list of things for consideration for the .NET GC but no timeline has been given yet. We can also try to use large pages when designing our custom CLR host, as presented in Chapter 15.

Virtual Memory Fragmentation

As always, when it comes to allocating and deallocating memory, the threat may be the fragmentation. We mentioned it in Chapter 1 while discussing the heap concept. In case of virtual memory, it means the operating system will not be able to allocate a continuous block of memory of a given size because there is not a big enough gap between used memory, although the total size of all free gaps can significantly exceed the required size.

This problem can be severe for 32-bit applications where virtual space may be too small for today's needs. Fragmentation can be particularly acute when the process allocates quite large segments of memory and works for quite a long time: exactly the kind of situation we may have, for example, to deal with in web-based .NET applications in a 32-bit version (hosted on IIS). To prevent fragmentation, it is the process who must properly manage memory (and for .NET process this process is the CLR itself). We will delve it into such details when describing garbage collection algorithms in Chapters 7-10 as it requires a bit deeper understanding of .NET itself.

General Memory Layout

Knowing the basic memory builder block, we can now go on to discuss memory at a higher level. The first question that arises is how a program looks in the memory. When describing a typical memory layout of a program, one can often spot a figure like the shown in Figure 2-17. It shows the structure of program memory written in C or C++ layout throughout all the virtual memory space. And that is why we are also interested in it. As we will see in the next chapters, CLR is written in C++, so managed programs perform in a similar environment.

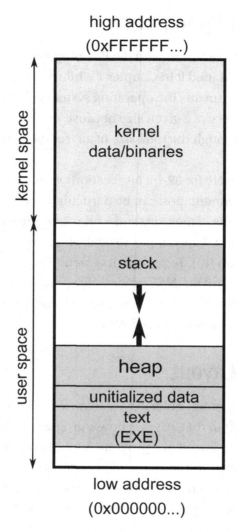

high address
(0xFFFFFF...)

kernel space

kernel
data/binaries

user space

stack

heap

unitialized data

text
(EXE)

low address
(0x000000...)

Figure 2-17. *Typical, generic process memory layout*

As can be easily seen, the virtual address space is divided into two areas:

- *Kernel space* - the upper range of addresses is occupied by the operating system itself. It is known as the kernel space, since it is the kernel that owns this area and only the kernel is allowed to operate on it.

- *User space* - the lower part of the address range is assigned to the process. This area is referred to as user space because it is the user process that has access to that area.

From our point of view, of course, the most interesting is user space, because this is the area of memory where a .NET program resides. Thanks to the existence of a virtual memory mechanism, each process sees the memory in that way -as if it were the only process in the system.

Regarding address space, when presenting schematic diagrams of a memory layout, the most common is a convention in which low addresses (starting at 0) are at the bottom and then are rising upward. Remember the stack and heap from Chapter 1? The usual convention is to draw a stack at high addresses and a heap underneath. The stack grows down, and the heap grows up. This may suggest that the stack could meet with the heap; but in reality, if only because of the imposed restrictions on the size, it never happens.

Here are the remaining memory segments description from Figure 2-17:

- The *data* segment includes both initialized and uninitialized global and static variables.

- The *text* segment containing the application binaries along with string literals. It is named as such for historical reasons because it contained, by definition, only read-only data.

Such a scheme is actually useful to realize the general layout of memory. But as soon as we see, reality is more complicated. And it is better described in the context of two major operating systems from the perspective of the .NET - Windows and Linux environments.

Windows Memory Management

The Microsoft Windows operating system is without a doubt the most popular .NET platform environment. So when we want to look at memory management in the context of the operating system, the obvious choice is to start from Microsoft Windows.

Because of the system design, the virtual address space is limited depending on the version of the system. A summary of these limitations is provided in Table 2-5.

Table 2-5. *Virtual Address Space-Size Limitations on Windows (User/Kernel)*

Process type	Windows (32-bit)	Windows 8/Server 2012	Windows 8.1+/Server 2012+
32-bit	2/2 GB	2/2 GB	2/2 GB
32-bit (*)	3/1 GB	4 GB/8 TB	4 GB/128 TB
64-bit	-	8/8 TB	128/128 TB

large address aware flag (also known as /3GB switch)

Note   There is a mechanism called Address Windowing Extensions (AWE) that allows us to allocate more physical memory than listed here and then map only parts of it into a virtual address space through an "AWE Window." This can be especially useful on a 32-bit environment to overcome a 2 or 3 GB limitation per process. However, this is not relevant for us because CLR does not use this mechanism.

Limitations of the size of virtual memory of a single process had become painful at the end of the reign of 32-bit systems. Limiting up to 2GB (or 3GB in extended mode) can be problematic in larger enterprise applications. The classic example is ASP.NET web application hosted on IIS at Windows Server 32-bit machines. If this limit was to be exhausted, there was no other choice than restarting the entire web application. This forced horizontal scaling across large web systems, creating multiple instances of servers that process less traffic, and consequently consuming less memory. Nowadays the world is dominated by 64-bit systems, and limiting virtual memory is no longer a problem. We have not yet seen the days when standard programs need tens of terabytes of RAM. But please note, however, that a 32-bit compiled program has a virtual memory limit of 4 GB even on 64-bit Windows Servers.

The memory management subsystem in Windows is exposed by two main layers:

- *Virtual API* - this is a low-level API that is operating on the page-granularity. You may have heard of the `VirtualAlloc` and `VirtualFree` functions that are examples of functions that belong to this layer.

- *Heap API* - higher-level API providing Allocator (recall it from Chapter 1) for allocations smaller than page size. This layer includes, among others, `HeapAlloc` and `HeapFree` functions.

Heap API (exposing Heap Manager) is being typically consumed by the C/C++ runtime implementation of memory management. You are probably familiar with the popular operators `new` and `delete` or `malloc` and `free` from C/C++. As CLR has its own Allocator implementation for creating .NET objects (which we will see in detail in Chapter 6), mostly Virtual API is being used by it. In a nutshell, the CLR asks the operating system for additional pages, and the appropriate allocation of objects within these pages is handled by itself. Heap API is also used by the CLR to create many smaller, internal data structures.

On Windows, it is important to understand the different memory categories associated with the process. It's not as trivial as it might seem. At the same time, without this knowledge it will be hard for us to understand one of the most important issues - how much memory the process we observe actually consumes?

In order to answer this question, we need additional knowledge about managing pages in Windows. Page can be in the four different states listed below:

- *Free* - not assigned yet to any process nor system itself.

- *Committed* (*private*) - assigned to a process. They are also called private pages because they can be used only by this particular process. When a committed page is being accessed for the first time by the process, it is being zero-initialized. Committed pages can be paged to disk and back.

- *Reserved* - reserved to a process. Memory reservation means obtaining a continuous range of virtual addresses without actually allocating memory. This allows us to reserve some space in advance, and only then actually commit some parts of it as they are needed. This does not consume memory physically and is only lightweight preparation of some internal data structures. Programs can also reserve and commit memory at once, when they know how big a block of memory they need at the moment.

- *Shareable* - reserved for a process but may be shared with other processes. This typically means binary images and memory-mapped files of system-wide libraries (DLLs) and resources (fonts, translations).

107

Moreover, private pages can be *locked,* which makes them remaining in physical memory (will not be moved to the page file) until explicitly unlocked or when the application ends. Locking can be beneficial for a performance-critical path in the program. We will see an example of utilizing page locking in a custom CLR host shown in Chapter 15.

Reserved and committed pages are managed by a process with the help of above-mentioned `VirtualAlloc`/`VirtualFree` and `VirtualLock`/`VirtualUnlock` method calls. It is also worth noticing that attempting to access free or reserved memory will result in an Access Violation Exception because this memory cannot be mapped to physical memory yet.

Note   Why did someone invent such a two-way process of obtaining memory? As mentioned earlier, a sequential memory access pattern is good for many reasons. A space consisting of a continuous sequence of pages prevents fragmentation and thus optimizes the use of TLBs and avoids page-directory walks. Continuous memory is, of course, also advantageous for cache utilization. It is therefore good to reserve some bigger space in advance, even if we do not need it now.

Armed with the knowledge of the page statuses, we can look at into what categories a Windows process memory is divided (Figure 2-18 graphically depicts the relationship between these indicators as overlapping sets):

- *Working set* - this is a part of virtual address space that currently resides in the physical memory. This means it can be further divided into:

  - *Private working set* - consists of committed (private) pages in the physical memory.

  - *Shareable working set* - consists of all shareable pages (no matter if they are actually shared or not).

  - *Shared working set* - consists of shareable pages that are actually shared with other processes.

- *Private bytes* - all committed (private) pages - both in the physical and paged memory.

- *Virtual bytes* - both committed (private) and reserved memory.

- *Paged bytes* - part of the virtual bytes that are stored in the page file.

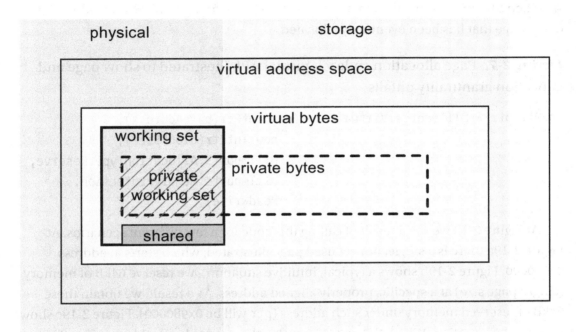

Figure 2-18. *Relationship between different memory sets withing a process on Windows*

Quite complicated, isn't it? Perhaps now we realize that the answer to the question of "how much memory actually takes up our .NET process" is not so obvious. Which of these indicators are we asking for? It is assumed that the most important indicator is the private working set because it shows what is the actual impact of our process on the consumption of the most important physical RAM. You will find out how to monitor these indicators in the next chapter. We will understand also what de facto is being displayed by Task Manager as a Memory column of a process.

Due to its internal structures, when Windows reserves a memory region for a process, it takes into account the following restriction - both the region start and its size has to be a multiple of the system page size (usually 4kB) and so-called *allocation granularity* (usually 64kB). This in fact means that each reserved region starts with an address being a multiplication of 64kB and has size being a multiplication of 64kB. If we want to allocate less, the reminder will be inaccessible (*unusable*). Thus proper alignment and size of the blocks are crucial in not wasting memory.

Let's illustrate it by an example. The simple code used for it is shown at Listing 2-7. It allocates virtual memory pages starting at the provided `baseAddress` and with a specified `blockSize` (specified in bytes). `VirtualAlloc` function returns an address `ptr` of the page that has been eventually allocated.

Listing 2-7. Page allocation code via Virtual API, illustrated to show page and allocation granurality pitfalls

```
IntPtr ptr = DllImports.VirtualAlloc(new IntPtr(baseAddress),
                                     new IntPtr(blockSize),
                                     DllImports.AllocationType.Reserve,
                                     DllImports.MemoryProtection.
                                     ReadWrite);
```

At Figure 2-19 we see a result of calling this code for a few different scenarios. At Figure 2-19a there is a single, not yet used page illustrated, which starts at address 0x9B0000. Figure 2-19b shows a typical, intuitive situation - we reserve 64kB of memory (single-page size) at a specific, properly aligned address. As a result, we obtain these 64kB of reserved memory under such address (`ptr` will be 0x9B0000). Figure 2-19c shows very similar situation. When 4kB was reserved with a proper base address, an entire allocation granularity block has been reserved but the rest of it (60 kB) is being marked as unusable. This memory has been wasted. There is no way to reuse it now. We can spot such situation in VMMap tool, which we will learn in the next chapter.

Figure 2-19d illustrates a situation when block size is not a multiplication of page size - it is being rounded up to the nearest multiplication. Thus even we wanted to allocate 6kB, 8kB is provided to us. The remaining 56kB are again unusable, obviously.

A similar situation illustrates Figure 2-19e where the base address is shifted by 17kB (0x9B4400) and we want to allocate 4kB. Hence, theoretically, only two pages are needed. But in such case `VirtualAlloc` still returns an allocation granularity-rounded start address of the entire block (0x9B0000), not the value that we provided as a base address

Taking all that into consideration, the worst case would be to reserve memory near the end of allocation granularity block, what was illustrated in Figure 2-19f. Here even we want to allocate only 8kB, a two 64 kB blocks are being consumed and almost half of this memory is unusable.

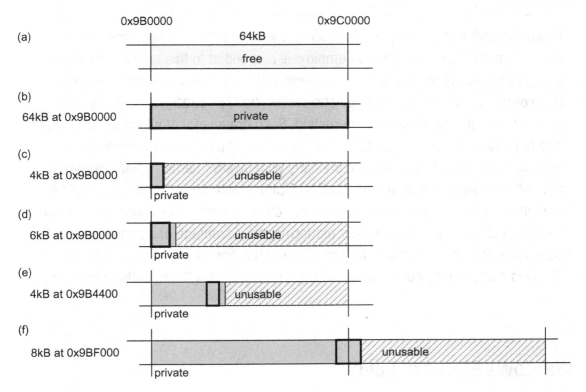

Figure 2-19. *From the top to bottom: (a) Free single page before any action, (b) Reserve 64 kB with base address 0x9B0000 (multiplication of 64kB), (c) Reserve 4 kB (single page) with base address 0x9B0000 (multiplication of 64kB), (d) Reserve 6 kB (over single page size) with base address 0x9B0000 (multiplication of 64kB), (e) Reserve 4 kB (single page) with base address unaligned by 2kB (0x9B0800), (f) Reserve 8 kB (two pages) with base address very unaligned by 2kB (0x9AF000)*

All this is to show us how important it is to care for correct page alignment. Although we do not manage memory at a Virtual API level on a daily basis, this knowledge can help us understand the concern for alignment in the CLR code. This knowledge will of course be necessary if we were to write such low-level code in the future.

A careful reader may ask why allocation granularity is 64kB while page size is 4kB? Raymond Chen, a Microsoft employee, responded to this question in 2003 [Why is address space allocation granularity 64K? - `https://blogs.msdn.microsoft.com/oldnewthing/20031008-00/?p=42223`]. And as usual in such cases, the answer is very interesting. Such granularity of allocation is mainly due to historical reasons. The kernel of the entire family of today's operating systems goes back to the roots of the early Windows NT kernel. It had supported a number of platforms, including the DEC Alpha architecture. And it was precisely this need for adapting to it that such a restriction was introduced. And since it was found not to be a nuisance to other platforms, the advantage of a common kernel base code was over the disadvantage of customization to one of the platforms. Detailed reasons why such a value on this platform you will find in the mentioned article.

Windows Memory Layout

Now let's look deeper into the processes running on Windows and executing .NET application. A process contains one default process heap (mostly used by internal Windows functions) and any number of optional heaps (created via Heap API). One example of such an optional heap is a heap created by Microsoft C runtime, consumed by C/C++ operators as mentioned before. There are three main heap types:

- *normal (NT) heap* - used by normal (non-Universal Windows Platform - UWP) apps. It provides basic functionality of managing memory blocks.

- *low-fragmentation heap* - an additional layer above normal heap functionality that manages allocations in varied-sized predefined blocks. This prevents fragmentation for small data and additionally, due to the internal OS optimizations makes this access slightly faster.

- *segment heap* - used by Universal Windows Platform apps, which provides more sophisticated allocators (including low-fragmentation allocator similar to mentioned above).

As mentioned in the case of general process memory layout, virtual address space is divided into two parts where upper addresses are occupied by the kernel and lower addresses are occupied by the user (program). This is shown in Figure 2-20 (32-bit on the left, 64-bit on the right). On 32-bit machines, depending on the large address flag, the user space is the lower 2 or 3 GB. On modern 64-bit CPUs that support 48-bit addressing, both user and kernel space have 128 TB of virtual memory available (8TB on previous versions - Windows 8 and Server 2012).

With some approximation, we can say that the typical user-space layout of the .NET program on Windows is as follows:

- Default heap mentioned earlier,

- Most images (exe, dlls) are located at high addresses,

- Thread stacks (referred to in the previous chapter) are mainly located at fairly low addresses but can be located anywhere. Each thread in the process has its own thread stack region. This includes CLR threads, which are using native system threads mechanism,

- GC heaps managed by the CLR to store .NET objects we create (they are regular pages in the Windows nomenclature, acquired by Virtual API),

- Various private CLR heaps managed by the CLR for its internal purposes. We will look at them in more detail in the following chapters,

- There is also of course quite a lot of free virtual address space, including huge blocks in the order of gigabytes and terabytes (depending on the architecture) somewhere in the middle of virtual address space.

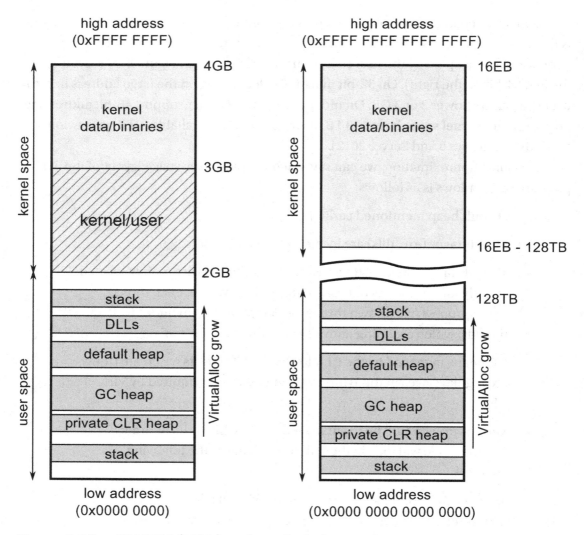

Figure 2-20. *x86/ARM (32bit) and x64 (64bit) virtual memory layout of process on Windows runing .NET managed code*

The initial thread stack size on Windows (both reserved and initially committed) is taken from the executable file (commonly known EXE file) header but can also be specified by methods like `CreateThread when creating threads manually by Windows API`.

How .NET runtime calculates the default size of the stack is quite complicated. The default value is 1 MB for typical 32-bit compilation and 4 MB for typical 64-bit compilation. Stack data are rather small and the call stack is typically rather shallow (hundreds of nested calls are rather uncommon). This makes 1 or 4 MB a good default value.

However, if you have ever encountered a StackOverflowException, you have just collided with this barrier. Even then, this is most probably due to our error of infinite recursion, which would obviously use an arbitrary large stack space. If we develop our program in a way that for some reason would like to store a lot of data on the stack, we can modify the header of the binary file. .NET executable is interpreted as a regular executable file, so this change will be reflected by the operating system. We will increase this stack size limit for such a purpose in Chapter 4.

Due to security reasons, *Address space layout randomization* (ASLR) mechanism was introduced, which makes all layouts shown at Figure 2-20 only schematic as all components (images, heaps, stacks) are placed randomly over the entire address space to not repeat any common pattern that could be used by the attacker.

I hope that such a birds-eye view will allow us to better understand the place of the CLR's memory in the context of the whole Windows ecosystem. We will refer to this knowledge once again when describing the CLR process layout in details.

Linux Memory Management

Until not so long ago, a chapter devoted to Linux in a book about .NET would find at most as a reference on the occasion of the Mono project. But times are changing. With the advent of the .NET Core environment, it is no longer possible to separate this platform from non-Windows systems. Moreover, you can anticipate the growing popularity of running .NET on non-Windows machines. We will devote a lot of attention to the CoreCLR, the runtime implementation of .NET Core. However, because Linux will be an alternative with growing popularity, we also need to look a little at this system. Because Linux uses the same hardware technology, including pages, MMU and TLB, much of the knowledge is covered by the descriptions in the previous subsections. Here we will focus only on the differences we are interested in. As more and more people will have to understand this new .NET environment, I believe it is very beneficial to understand at least some Linux basics also.

The popular and most-used Linux operating system distributions also use the concept of virtual memory. Their limits per process are also very similar and are summarized in Table 2-6.

Table 2-6. *Virtual Address Space-Size Limitations on Linux (User/Kernel)*

Process type	Linux 32-bit	Linux 64-bit
32-bit process	3/1, 2/2, 1/3 GB	-
64-bit process	-	128/128 TB*

*canonical 48-bit addressing

Like Windows, the basic builder block in Linux is the page, and it is also typically 4kB. The page can be in three different states listed below:

- *free* - not assigned yet to any process nor system itself.

- *allocated* - assigned to a process.

- *shared* - reserved for a process but may be shared with other processes. This typically means binary images and memory-mapped files of system-wide libraries and resources.

This makes a simpler and clearer view of the memory consumption by a process than in the case of the Windows operating system. As you can see, compared to Windows, the implicit page reservation stage is missing, while still it exists explicitly. Linux has built-in a *lazy allocation* mechanism that takes care of it. When one allocates memory on Linux, it is being treated as allocated but no physical resources are assigned (hence this is like a reservation on Windows). Actual resources assignment (consuming physical memory) will not take place until it is actually needed by accessing this particular region of memory. If you want to proactively prepare such pages in performance-critical scenarios, you can just "touch" them by memory access like reading at least one byte within them.

Knowing the possible page statuses, we can look at which categories a process memory on Linux is divided. There is quite a lot of confusion around this. Many Linux-based tools say slightly different things about this topic. Here is a most generic classification I was able to prepare. Process memory utilization can be measured with respect to the following terms:

- *virtual* (marked by some tools as vsz) - total size of the virtual address space reserved so far by the process. In popular "top" tool it is a VIRT column.

- *resident* (*Resident Set Size*, RSS) - space of pages that resides currently in the physical memory. Some resident pages can be shared among processes (those which are file backed or anonymous also). Therefore, this corresponds to "working set" measurement on Windows platform. In "top" tool this is referred to as a RES column. Further it can be split into:

  - *private resident pages* - those are all anonymous resident pages reserved for this process (indicated by MM_ANONPAGES kernel counter). That somehow correspond to the "private working set" measurement from Windows.

  - *shared resident pages* - those are both file backed (indicated by MM_FILEPAGES kernel counter) and anonymous resident pages of the process. Corresponding to "shared working set." In "top" this is referred to as SHR memory.

- *private* - all private pages of the process. In the "top" tool this is a DATA column. Please note this is an indicator of reserved memory and does not say how much of it has been already accessed ("touched") and thus has become resident. Corresponds to "private bytes" on Windows.

- swapped - part of the virtual memory that has been stored in the swap file.

Figure 2-21 graphically depicts the relationship between these indicators as overlapping sets.

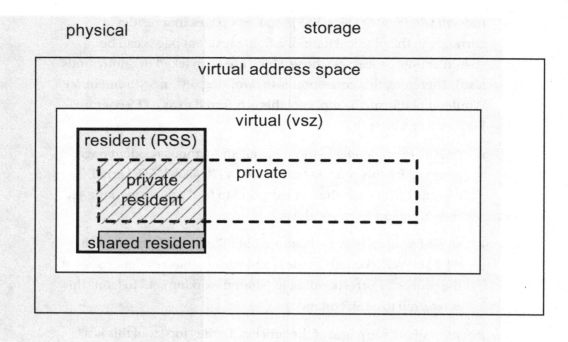

Figure 2-21. *Relationship between different memory sets within a process on Linux*

Pretty complicated. Just like with Windows, the answer to the question of what is consuming the memory of our .NET process is not trivial. The most sensible thing is to look at the "private resident pages" measurement because it shows the actual use of our valuable RAM resource by the process.

While on Windows, allocation granularity is 64kB; on Linux it is just page size bounded, which is 4kB in most cases.

Linux Memory Layout

The memory layout of the Linux process is very similar to that presented for Windows. For a 32-bit version, the user's space is 3GB and the kernel space is 1GB. This split point can be changed with the CONFIG_PAGE_OFFSET parameter configurable at kernel build time. For 64-bits, the split is made at a similar address like on Windows (see Figure 2-22).

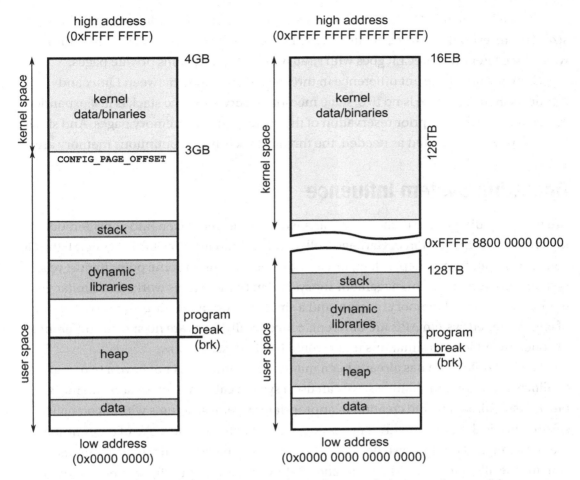

Figure 2-22. *x86/ARM (32bit) and x64 (64bit) virtual memory layout of process on Linux*

Similar to Windows, the system provides an API for operating on memory pages. It contains:

- mmap - to directly manipulate pages (including file maps, shared and normal ones, and anonymous mapping that is not related to any file but being used to store program data).

- brk/sbrk - this is the closest equivalent of the VirtualAlloc method. It allows us to set/increase so-called "program break," which in fact means increasing the heap size.

The well-known C/C++ allocators are using `mmap` or `brk` depending on the allocation size. This threshold can be configured by `mallopt` and the `M_MMAP_THRESHOLD` setting. As we will see later on, CoreCLR goes with `mmap` way with anonymous private pages.

There is one significant difference in thread stack handling between Linux and Windows. Because there is no two-stage memory reservation, the stack is just expanded as needed. There is no prior reservation of the corresponding memory pages. And since the next pages are created as needed, the thread stack is not a continuous memory area.

Operating System Influence

Are there any differences in memory management that were taken into consideration in the cross-platform version of Garbage Collector included in CoreCLR? In general, the GC code is very platform independent, but for obvious reasons, at some point it must reach system calls. A memory management subsystem in both systems works in a similar way - it is based on virtual memory, paging, and a similar way of allocating memory. Although, of course, called system APIs are different, conceptually there are no specific differences in code, except for two situations that I would like to describe now.

The first difference has already been mentioned. Linux does not have a two-step way to allocate memory. In Windows, we can use a system call to reserve a large memory block first. This will be the creation of appropriate system structures without actually seizing physical memory. Only if necessary, we make the second stage of committing memory range of our interest. Because Linux does not have this mechanism, memory can only be allocated without "reservation." However, a system API was needed imitating such a two-step way of work. A popular trick was used for this purpose. On Linux, "reservation" is made by allocating memory with access mode PROT_NONE, which de facto means no access to this memory. However, in such a reserved area, we can then allocate again specific subregions with normal rights, thus simulating "committing" memory.

The second difference is the so-called *memory write watch* mechanism. As we will see in later chapters, the Garbage Collector needs to track which memory areas (pages) have been modified. For this purpose, Windows provides a convenient API. By allocating a page, we can set `MEM_WRITE_WATCH` flag. Then, using the `GetWriteWatch` system call, we can retrieve a list of modified pages. While working on CoreCLR, it turned out that there was no reliable mechanism in the Linux system with a similar API. For this reason, this logic had to be moved to a write barrier (mechanism explained in details in Chapter 5), which is supported in runtime without operating system support.

NUMA and CPU Groups

There is one more important piece of memory management jigsaw puzzle worth mentioning in the context of the hardware and operating system. *Symmetric multiprocessing* (SMP) means a computer with multiple, identical CPUs that are connected to a shared main memory. They are controlled by a single operating system that may or may not treat all processors equally. As we know, each CPU has its own set of L1 and L2. In other words, each CPU has some dedicated local memory that is accessible much faster than the other regions. Threads and programs running on different CPUs will probably share some data, and this is by far not an optimal case because sharing data through CPUs interconnections induces significant delays. Here is where *non-uniform memory architecture* (NUMA) comes to play. It means that not all shared memory is the same from a performance perspective. And software (mostly operating system but optionally a program itself) should be *NUMA-aware* to prefer using those local memories over those more distant. Such a configuration is illustrated in Figure 2-23.

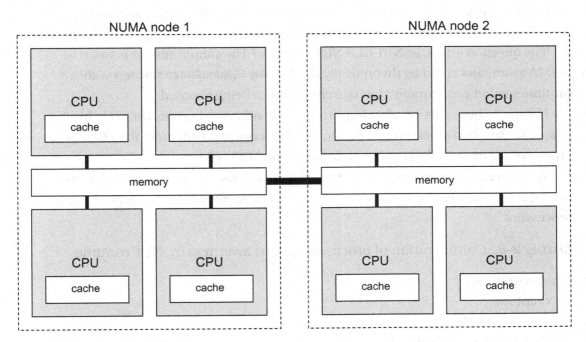

Figure 2-23. *Simple NUMA configuration consiting of eight processors grouped into two NUMA nodes*

Such additional overhead of accessing non-local memory is called *NUMA factor*. Because connecting each CPU peer to peer would be very expensive, CPU has typically connections to two or three other CPUs. In a bad scenario to access distant memory, a few hops between a processor has to be taken. The more CPUs, the NUMA factor is more relevant if not only local memory is being used. There are also systems with a somehow mixed approach where groups of processors have some shared memory and memory is non-uniform between those groups with a big NUMA factor between them. This is in fact the most common approach in a NUMA-aware system. CPUs are grouped into smaller systems called *NUMA nodes*. Each NUMA node has its own processors and memory with a small NUMA factor due to hardware organization. NUMA nodes are of course interconnected but transfers between them imply bigger overhead.

The main requirement of NUMA awareness of an operating system and program code is to stick with the process memory on DRAM local to the NUMA node containing the CPU executing it. But this may lead to an unbalanced state if some processes consume much more memory than others. In Linux it is possible to control NUMA-awareness behavior per process - whether it should stick with local memory only (good for small processes) or try to distribute it more evenly (big for huge processes). On Windows NUMA, awareness must be taken into account during program development.

The question arises, is .NET CLR NUMA-aware? The simple answer is yes, it is! NUMA awareness could be theoretically disabled by `GCNumaAware` settings within a runtime section configuration but currently it is not being exposed.

However, there are two other important application settings shown in Listing 2-8 related to so-called *processor groups*. On Windows systems with more than 64 logical processors, they are being grouped into mentioned CPU groups.

We can enable awareness of CPU groups in Windows-based .NET runtimes (see Listing 2-8), which is obviously important in environments with more than 64 logical processors.

Listing 2-8. Configuration of processor groups awerness in .NET runtime

```
<configuration>
   <runtime>
      <Thread_UseAllCpuGroups enabled="true"/>
      <GCCpuGroup enabled="true"/>
      <gcServer enabled="true"/>
   </runtime>
</configuration>
```

`GCCpuGroup` setting specifies whether Garbage Collector should support CPU groups by creating internal GC threads across all available groups and whether it takes all available cores into consideration when creating and managing heaps.

`Thread_UseAllCpuGroups` specify whether CLR should distribute normal managed threads (executing our code) across all CPU groups. Both options should be enabled simultaneously with the `gcServer` setting.

Summary

We have come a long way in this chapter. We have briefly identified the most important hardware and system memory management mechanisms. I hope that this knowledge, together with the theoretical introduction from the previous chapter, has allowed you to give you a much broader context: the context in which we are when it comes to memory management in .NET. I also hope that if you did not have it yet, you have gained some respect for the complexity of this topic. Yes, all we've talked about is the foundation of Garbage Collector in .NET! With each subsequent chapter, we will be moving further away from general hardware and theoretical statements. And we'll go deeper into the .NET environment.

Rule 2 - Random Access Should Be Avoided, Sequential Access Should Be Encouraged

Applicability: Mostly low-level, performance-oriented code.

Justification: Due to internal mechanisms on many levels, including RAM and processor cache designs, sequential access is definitely more optimal. DRAM requires far more CPU cycles to reach remote memory than its cache. The processor loads data in 64-byte blocks called cache lines. Each memory access less than 64 bytes is a waste of expensive resources. What's more, random access patterns make it unlikely that the cache prefetching mechanism will work. The processor has no chance of discovering any predictable pattern with the random access to memory. What is important, by randomness we do not mean total randomness, but rather the fact that it is not an ordered access that is compatible with any detectable pattern.

How to apply: Obviously, the opposite of random access is sequential access, so try always to use it. If you are operating on a large amount of data, you might want to consider packing them into arrays that are taking care of memory continuity. Iterating over double-linked lists can be an example of a typical, unstructured access. We will look closer at this aspect of memory access in Chapter 13 when describing so-called Data-oriented design.

Rule 3 - Improve Spatial and Temporal Data Locality

Applicability: Mostly low-level, performance-oriented code.

Justification: Spatial and temporal locality are the pillars of the cache. If present, the cache is used effectively and helps to achieve better performance. On the contrary. If we interfere with the temporal and spatial locality, we will lead to a significant decrease in productivity.

How to apply: Design your used data structures in such a way as to take care of your data's locality and to maximize their reusability in time. As we have seen in the examples given, distributed, random access to data is very unfavorable in terms of performance and can be several times slower. Sometimes, in very advanced and high-performance parts of the program, this means applying such non-intuitive changes as will be presented in Design-oriented design in Chapter 13. Sometimes it only comes down to ensuring that our data structures are reasonably small, preallocated, and used repeatedly.

Rule 4 - Consume More Advanced Possibilities

Applicability: Extremely low-level, performance-oriented code.

Justification: The .NET runtime environment is written in the most generic way. This is to ensure proper operation in a variety of possible scenarios. However, when writing our application, we know our needs perfectly. We may need to write extremely fast-performing fragments of memory-related code. If so, we may consider using some more advanced operating system-specific mechanisms. Such mechanisms will probably need about 0.0001% .NET developers in the world. If you are writing memory-related library like serializers, messaging buffers, or any kind of extremely fast event processor - maybe you can benefit by using some of the mentioned here low-level APIs of the system (like non-temporal memory access).

How to apply: This will require writing a really hard code. This code will be a pain to manage and probably no one will want to maintain it. Except you. Because it will use the low-level API of the operating system, it may also cause problems after updating or changing operating system versions. It is also very unlikely that you need such low-level memory management at all, because it will require extreme caution in coding. And it's very easy to make a mistake, which, instead of increasing performance, will drastically reduce it.

Read this book carefully. Then read carefully specific operating system books about its internals. And then try to use advanced mechanisms like large pages, non-temporal operations, and others mentioned in this chapter.

CHAPTER 3

Memory Measurements

Perhaps it is surprising to have a chapter with such a title almost at the beginning of
the book. We have not really said anything about .NET memory management yet,
and we are already looking at the tools associated with it? It is a deeply thought-out
decision. Firstly, using the tools described here, I will often illustrate the specific
concepts discussed later. Secondly, even though I'm trying to make this book be well
balanced, it has a very practical meaning. When discussing various topics, we will
touch on real problems and examples. With the tools outlined in this chapter, you can
see how these problems can be identified and diagnosed. So as long as we do not deal
only with the academic discussion of the Garbage Collector construction, the tools are
inseparable from the theory.

Without knowing what tools to use, we are quite clumsy. We do not know how to
check if our process has memory problems. We do not know how to make sure that
high CPU or memory consumption is associated with .NET memory management.
We do not know what is the possible cause of observed unwanted behavior, as for the
tools themselves. The truth is that there is no single, super universal Swiss Army knife.
Sometimes it is better to check one, sometimes another tool. To fully feel comfortable in
the topic of memory management, it is best to learn how to use each of them. At least if
we want to feel like being an expert in this field.

The range of tools described here will find a wide range of sophistication. At one
end, you can place such low-level tools as WinDbg. With its help we can proceed with
really deep analyses. Knowledge of dozens of magic commands that should be used in
the right order will allow us to investigate a lot. At the other end can be put commercial
products flattering with a convenient user interface. Here everything is pleasant and
easy, so we can get a lot of answers quickly. Even before asking. On the other hand, these
tools only allow what was provided by their creators. and customization is sometimes
very limited. Between these extremes, there are many other tools that are always a
compromise between versatility and ease of use. In my experience, these - let's call

© Konrad Kokosa 2018

K. Kokosa, *Pro .NET Memory Management*, https://doi.org/10.1007/978-1-4842-4027-4_3

them - high-level commercial programs are almost always enough. But this "almost" makes a big difference. From time to time. we encounter a problem that we will not solve easily within the analysis that those programs provide. In other words, if we deal with this topic seriously, sooner or later, your hands get dirty with grease from the engine.

You may be surprised by the lack of strong representation of static code analysis tools among those presented here. Almost all tools are based on runtime analysis. This is because it is not really that simple. The code can translate into many behaviors depending on the usage characteristics. Even the most inefficient memory management code fragment will not adversely affect the process if the operations associated with it are performed - like once per hour. Static code analysis can help, but it can also hurt. It can concentrate unnecessarily on irrelevant parts of the code.

Performance is more difficult than functionality or code quality, as we often do not know what "could" or "should" is. There are tools to help us show the violation of certain thresholds. But even then, without understanding the subject, we are not sure whether these thresholds apply in our application, in our specific circumstances. That is why although this chapter is extremely important, without the context of the entire book it would not be particularly practical.

The way we measure the behavior of .NET programs is radically different depending on the operating system we use. That is why the chapter is divided into two parts. Each one is dedicated to one of the two most popular solutions - Windows and Linux. Due to the very low popularity of using .Net on macOS, tools for this platform are not described in this book.

Importantly, this chapter is to present what are the different tools and the basics of how to use them. Their specific use and interpretation of the results will be provided later in the book. We do not yet have sufficient knowledge about the Garbage Collector to start using these tools to solve specific problems. Consider this chapter as a comprehensive list of tools that you can and should use. I encourage you to try them out while reading, at least a little. Thanks to this, you will gain a powerful dose of practical knowledge and familiarity with them. It will be useful in the next chapters. Obviously, there is a big chance that some or all of those tools are known to you. Feel free to skip their description, especially in the part showing basic steps in using them.

Please note also that this chapter suffers a little of the chicken and egg problem - it is impossible to show the practical side of many GC-related topics without using tools described here, while tools described here require often quite a good understanding of those GC-related topics. To not clutter the whole book with those tool descriptions introduced here and there, some basic usage is presented now, even if it mentions GC-related concepts. Therefore, do not be afraid if you do not understand every detail described here. I expect you will occasionally return to this chapter when using these tools in your regular work, with the full understanding gained from this book.

Measure Early

When we ask experts about performance optimization, frameworks developers, or simply professionals who have already seen many issues - what is the most important thing to take care of performance? - they all respond in the same way: *measure early*. Everyone probably heard the phrase that premature optimization is the root of all evil. First of all, it just does not pay off to spend hours or days optimizing code that will give us a really negligible return without compromising on either the economy or the hardware resources, or the shorter processing times of the application. And worse, it will surely translate into increased development costs. And probably unnecessarily complicated and thus unreadable code. The good rule is the opposite - instead of prematurely focusing on optimization, let's first measure whether we have any need at all. And since it's a book on memory management in .NET, it leads us to the next general rule - Measure GC Early - which I introduce at the end of this chapter.

Each measurement can be saddled with greater or lesser error. In addition, measuring may interfere with the observed process. We know these facts from physics and it's no different in the case of process parameters' measurements. Therefore, the answer to the question "how to measure" can be either very simple (if we do not go into details) or very complicated (if we take into consideration the precision). Different tools provide different precision and I will talk about it a little. However, the statistical discussions about the measurement errors are out of the scope of this book. Just be aware that certain inaccuracies can always happen as soon as we measure something.

Still, just because it is so important in the context of measurements, I want to highlight here a few major concepts and misconceptions. With these issues we will meet in the later part of this chapter as well as throughout the rest of the whole book. And most importantly, also in our daily work.

Overhead and Invasiveness

When it comes to different tools for measuring our application, it's always important to keep in mind the two following, most important concepts:

- *overhead* - it is hard to find a tool whose usage to measure an application does not make it slower or consume more resources in some way. We are talking then about the overhead of this tool and we usually express it by percentage. Certain tools can cause barely noticeable overheads at a few-percent level. This means, for example, that web application response times will be a few percent longer. Or these percentages will decrease the fluency of the animation in the desktop application. Such low-overhead tools can be used even on production environments. On the other hand, there are tools that by attaching to our application slow it down by orders of magnitude. In general, they provide a great deal of detailed information in return. However, due to the overhead they bring, they are only suitable for use on development environments or only single-developer stations.

- *invasiveness* - this concept is similar and is about how much the tool affects the functioning of the application as such. Does using the tool require running this application again? Do you need any additional permissions or installed extensions? Ideally a non-invasive solution can be turned on and off during application running without any effect on it. On the other hand, a completely invasive solution would require recompiling our application and re-deploying it to a given environment.

Sampling vs. Tracing

Another aspect of tool activity is how it collects diagnostic information. There are two main approaches:

- *tracing* - in this approach diagnostic data is collected on the occasion of specific, highlighted events (hence its other name - *event-based*). An example may be saving tracking data when opening or closing a file, at the moment of clicking the mouse, or starting the process of garbage collection. The undoubted advantage of this solution is the precision of the data, because they come from the moment of occurrence of the event and we may write all events of a given kind. However, if such events were very frequent, this would cause a very big overhead. Therefore, this kind of mechanism is not used for such frequent and low-level events as entering or returning from functions. Unless we can afford a very big overhead, for example, at a local developer station.

- *sampling* - in this approach, we agree to the loss of data precision and we only collect diagnostic data from time to time (hence its other name - *time-based*). This way we only try to sample the application state and the less frequently we do it, the less accurate the results we get from our measurements. A typical example of this approach is a periodical-saving functions call stacks on all processors, for example, every 1 ms. This allows you to statistically find out which functions are executing the longest. Although of course we can unfortunately lose information about functions that always run faster than 1 ms.

Call Tree

One of the most commonly used visualizations of application behavior is to build a *call tree*. In such a tree, each node represents one function. The children of such node represent other functions that this function has called. Each function has also some measurement attached, most likely total execution time. In fact, there is very often a pair of indicators related to each function (each element of a tree):

- *exclusive* - only measures the value of this particular function. In case of execution time, this will be the time spent only in this particular function.

- *inclusive* - measures the value of this particular function and the sum of all its descendants' measurements. In case of execution time, this will be the time spent in this function, all other functions called by it, all functions called by them and so on, and so forth, recursively.

131

In addition, the percentage of a given measure is often determined with respect to the entire range examined. This is known as *inclusive %* and *exclusive %* measurements. Let's look at an example in Figure 3-1 showing results from a hypothetical profiler.

We see here that function `main` has spent 100% inclusive time of the program - which was 3 seconds. This is the main function calling all other functions so this is an expected behavior. But only 22% of this time was spent in the `main` function itself; the rest was spent in other functions called by it. For example, 78% of time was spent in `SomeClass.Method1` function. Then, 66.7% of all time this function was devoted to calling another method called `SomeClass.HelperMethod`. Navigating through this call tree we will very quickly find out which application components are the slowest.

Please also note that such trees typically present aggregated data. In case of our example from Figure 3-1, it aggregates all mentioned method calls occurrences. So the `main` method was called only once, while the `HelperMethod` was called two thousand times (which explains why its aggregated inclusive time is so big). Therefore, analysis of such a tree involves searching for long-lasting methods or methods not necessarily slow but called many times.

Method name	Inclusive [ms]	Inclusive [%]	Exclusive [ms]	Exclusive [%]	Exclusive Counter
– main	3000	100.0	660	22%	1
– SomeClass.Method1	2340	78.0	50	1.7%	3
+ SomeClass.HelperMethod	2000	66.7	200	6.7%	2000
+ OtherClass.MethodA	360	12.0	10	3.3%	20
+ OtherClass.MethodB	120	4.0	10	3.3%	21

Figure 3-1. *Example of a call tree showing performance data*

The same idea can be used to visualize memory usage, where each node represents one particular type of object. Its children are other types whose instances of that type this object contains or refers to. Believe me, when analyzing the performance or memory consumption of your application, you will often be using these types of visualizations.

Objects Graphs

In the context of memory, we often use a graph representing relationships between objects in memory called an *object graph* or *reference graph*. An example of such a graph was seen in Figure 1-12 in the first chapter and is illustrated in Figure 3-2. In our example, it shows a set of objects with some referencing the other and only a single root. In general, such graphs for normal program sizes can be very large so their visualization is not easy; thus typically we analyze only a smart part of it. You can use them to show both aggregated information (how many instances of a given type have references to other types) or information about a particular instance (to which other object instances given objects have references).

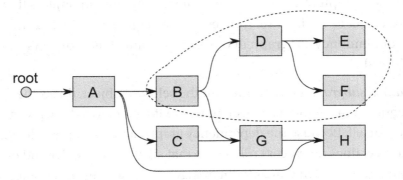

Figure 3-2. *Example of objects' graph. Retained subgraph of object B has been additionally marked.*

With object graphs, there are three important concepts that appear in the different tools you will have the opportunity to use:

- *shortest root path* - determined for the selected object, this is the shortest path of references from a particular object to some root. As the object graph can be complex and there may be multiple paths between the root (or even multiple roots) and the object, there is also obviously the shortest one. For illustration 3-2, the shortest root path for object H is the path root-A-H. There are also longer paths: root-A-C-G-H and root-A-B-G-H. The shortest path to the root may be important because it most often indicates the main and strongest relationships between objects and is a good indication what is the main reason that makes an object impossible to be considered unreachable (and thus removable). Other paths are most often created as a side effect of other complex dependencies. However, sometimes the shortest root path may be misleading as it is created by some (sometimes temporary) auxiliary references like caches. With such a situation we seem to be dealing in Figure 3-2 where object A probably holds the reference to object H for convenience (like caching), while H business owner is located among objects B, C, or G.

- *dependency subgraph* - determined for the selected object, this is the subgraph that contains the object itself and all objects that have direct or indirect references to it. At Figure 3-2, for example, the dependency subgraph of object B contains B and objects D, E, F, G, and H.

- *retained subgraph* - determined for the selected object, this is the subgraph that would have been removed if you removed the given object itself. Because the dependency graph can be complex, deleting an object does not necessarily mean that all objects that depend on it are removed. References to them may still be kept by other objects. The retained subgraph of object B from Figure 3-2 contains object B and objects D, E, and F.

Along with these concepts there are also different interpretations of how the object size is indicated in the tools:

- *shallow size* - the size of the object itself (all its fields including the size of references to other objects). This is obviously easy to calculate.

- *total size* - the sum of the shallow size of the object and all shallow sizes of objects to which it has direct or indirect references. In other words, it is the total size of all objects in the dependency subgraph. This is also easy to calculate because we just need to find an object's dependency subgraph and sum all the shallow sizes of included objects.

- *retained size* - total sum of all objects in the retention graph. In other words, retention size is the amount of memory that can be released after deletion of a given object. The more objects are shared by different references in the object graph, the retention size is smaller than total size. It is the hardest to count because it requires complex analysis of the entire graph of objects.

Whenever the tool we are using is talking about the size of the object, it is worth asking yourself which of the mentioned "sizes" is taken into consideration.

Statistics

Whenever we aggregate some measurements in different ways, we use statistical tools to a greater or lesser extent. If we do it unconsciously, this involves the risk of erroneous conclusions. For example, the most commonly used method of aggregating data is to calculate the *average*, which should give a sense of "typical value." But the average has two main disadvantages: its results do not point to any specific sample (did anyone see 2.43 children of the average family?). And it easily hides the true nature of the data distribution (as will soon be illustrated). Similar to other simple measures such as variance, those problems are perfectly illustrated by the so-called *Anscombe's quartet* (see Figure 3-3 taken from Wikipedia). Sometimes very different data sets may lead to statistically identical conclusions.

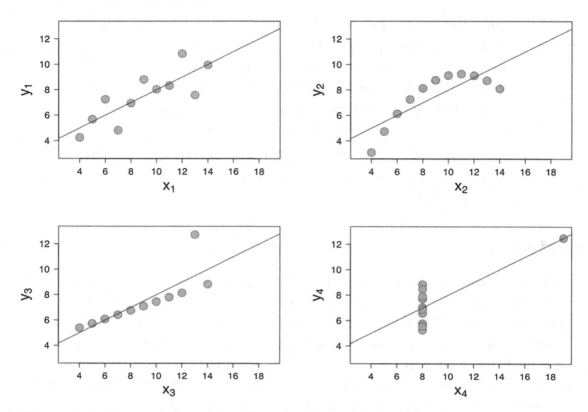

Figure 3-3. *Anscombe's quartet - four datasets with the same average and variance of x and y data. Source: Wikipedia*

The advantage and the cause for the popularity of the average is its intuitiveness and the fact that it can easily be calculated without storing individual samples - with each additional sample, we increase the sum and then divide it by the number of samples observed. Other aggregation methods require that all samples be kept up to date. This can create a lot of overhead for the tool.

What other methods of aggregation should you use? The most common include:

- *median* - the value separating the higher half and the lower half of the samples. It gives a better idea of the typical value because it is more resistant to very mismatched samples. Moreover, it indicates one of the real samples, not an artificially calculated one.

- *percentile* - the value below which a given percentage of samples fall. For example, the 95th percentile is the value below which 95% of the samples may be found. This is a great indicator of the data we are interested in, without taking into account very unusual measurements. I strongly encourage you to measure percentiles in the tools you use. Percentiles are also often business driven. For example, we want to make sure that 90% of response times of our application will not be slower than 1 second and 99% will not be slower than 4 seconds. Measuring 90th and 99th percentiles of response times will allow us to easily control this.

- *histogram* - graphical representation of the distribution of samples. It shows how many samples fall within specific ranges of values. It is the best possible measurement as it shows us the whole data distribution.

All those metrics are presented in Figure 3-4, showing an example histogram of the response time distribution - how many responses there were within each response time range (expressed in milliseconds). From the histogram we can clearly see that the most common response time is between 110 +/- 5 ms, and the more response time differs from this value, the less frequently it occurs. Moreover, we can say that:

- The average response time is 104.3 ms.

- 10% of all responses are shorter than 60 ms (10th Percentile).

- Median is 100 ms.

- 90% of all responses are shorter than 150 ms (90th Percentile).

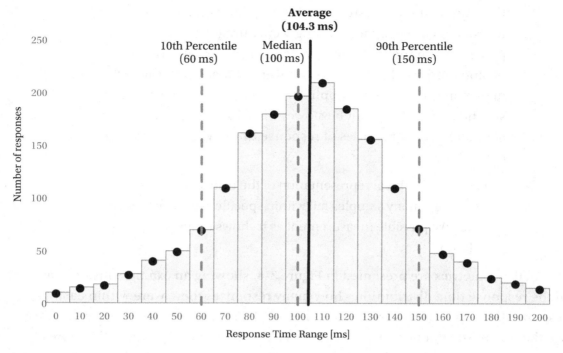

Figure 3-4. *Example of histogram with the values of median, 10th, and 90 percentile shown - normal distribution of data*

Distribution showed in Figure 3-4 is very similar to so-called *normal distribution,* often named also the *bell curve,* due to its characteristic shape. Many measurements will fall into this category, making interpretation of percentiles (and even an average) quite sensible.

However, be especially careful about the occurrence of so-called *bimodal* (and *multimodal* in general) distribution of data, which produces both the average and even the median and percentiles values that do not make a lot of sense (see Figure 3-5). Clearly, there are two types of responses measured (in fact, two different normal distributions), so making any aggregations on both of them is quite misleading. We would rather like to say that there are two categories of responses with medians around 40 and 150 ms (and should probably investigate why such bimodal response time happens in the first place).

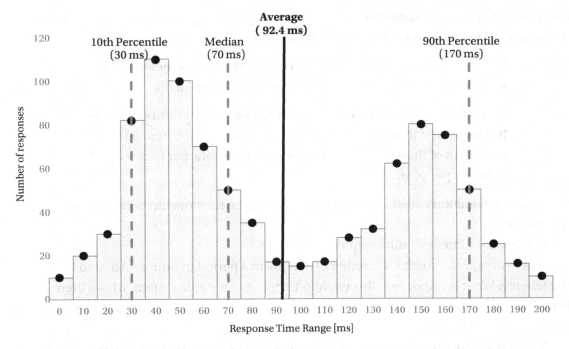

Figure 3-5. *Example of histogram with the values of median, 10th, and 90 percentile shown - bimodal distribution of data*

Fortunately, multimodal distribution may be easily, visually detected on a histogram; thus it makes it so crucial to have such data available when measuring something (or at least have an automatic indication that multimodal distribution has been detected).

The more measurements other than the average the tool offers, the better. Unfortunately, the vast majority still use only the average (with a very few showing any histograms). You need to be very careful when drawing conclusions. And it is best to try to use a tool that will also show us the distribution of results by means of percentiles or a histogram.

Latency vs. Throughput

Two title concepts are very important in the context of any performance analysis and optimization. Unfortunately, they are also sometimes misunderstood and mistakenly interpreted. Most often we think that one comes from the other and that they are completely dependent on each other. Therefore, it is worth giving them a few words of explanation. Let's start from their simple definitions:

- *latency* - time required to perform a given action. It is measured in some units of time - days, hours, milliseconds, and so on.

- *throughput* - number of actions executed per specific amount of time. It is measured in actions (or whatever a single specific item is) per some unit of time - like bytes per second, iterations per millisecond, or books per year.

A simple equation called *Little's Law* designates the relationship between these indicators:

occupancy = latency * throughput

where *occupancy* means a number of actions in a period of time designated by the latency. What is important, this equation applies to a stable system, where there is no unnatural queuing or dynamic adaptation to load change (e.g., during startup or shutdown of the system).

These two concepts are most commonly encountered in the context of computer networks but for our purposes we will use a more useful context of web applications. The processing time of a single user request determines the latency. The number of user requests per unit of time determines the throughput. Occupancy will be the number of requests in our system during considered period of time.

Of course, lowering latency (for example, by using a more powerful CPU) makes us process more user requests per unit of time so it also raises throughput. On the other hand, we can increase throughput just by increasing the number of processed requests in parallel (for example, by using more CPU cores, etc.) without changing latency (see Figure 3-6). In general, in computer science it is easier to increase throughput (by any kind of parallelization) than to decrease latency (by introducing complexity in more sophisticated hardware or algorithm design).

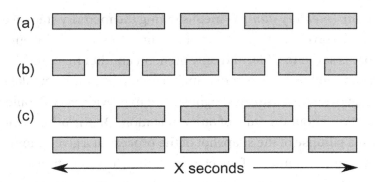

Figure 3-6. *Throughput vs. latency relationship: (a) with some base latency we are able to process 5 requests per X seconds, (b) with shortened latency we are able to process 7 requests per X seconds, (c) by doubling parallelization we doubled throughput to 10 requests per X seconds without changing latency*

Of course, increasing throughput is not possible indefinitely. And often after some threshold, further increasing throughput also negatively impacts latency as actions are not completely independent. Additional synchronization costs impacting latency may swallow the gain from increased throughput.

There is also a popular Amdahl's law derived from the fact that potential latency speedup is limited by the serial (not possible to parallelize) part of the program. So, for example, if 90% part of the program may be parallelized, there is still 10% that will run normally. Thus, the maximum potential speedup in such case is limited to at most 10 times.[1]

Memory Dumps, Tracing, Live Debugging

In order to analyze the state of our application, we have several standard approaches that differ in invasiveness:

- *monitoring* - usually means non-invasive application monitoring and the use of diagnostic information that it generates (either with the help of tracking or sampling). Sometimes it takes a more invasive form (such as a reboot of an application) but still allows you to observe it in action, even in a production environment.

---

[1]Please note that it extends to the whole application and underlying libraries, runtime, and other components, not only our code. So in case of an ASP.Net web application, even if all requests processing may be parallelized, there still may be some serial parts like session management, parts of the framework/hosting and, parts of the Garbage Collector executions.

- *core dump* (*memory dump*) - means saving the memory state of a process at a given moment. Most of the time, the state of the entire memory is saved to a file, and only then, on another machine, is being analyzed by various tools. Such a memory dump can take up a few gigabytes, but using the right skills can provide very detailed information about the state of our application. On the other hand, it is just a glimpse of the snapshot of the process at a given moment, and without the context of the change in time it is sometimes difficult to come to concrete conclusions. Therefore, two or more memory dumps are often performed and compared to each other. Invasiveness of taking a memory dump differs. Most often it causes the process to temporarily pause for some time. An important application of memory dumps is their automatic execution after application failure, which allows for later investigation of its cause (called *post-mortem analysis*) - hence we can spot also a *crash dump* name as a special case of memory dump. In practice, the concept of crash dump and memory dump are used interchangeably in the tools you will encounter.

- *live debugging* - the most invasive approach is to connect the debugger to the process and analyze the application step by step. This is the least common approach since the two previous ones are generally sufficient. Live debugging stops application entirely so it is possible only on development environment, if it is needed at all. Thanks to extensive monitoring and diagnostic tools, live debugging is rather uncommon in case of memory management solving.

Windows Environment

Let's get started by getting to know the tools on the native platform where .NET was born. It has been present here for about 15 years. The power of choice and level of refinement of tools on Windows are very good. We will begin by learning the low-level tools, free and built into the system. We devote the most time to them just because they will be used frequently later in the book. But for completeness, we'll finish with a review of commercial programs.

Overview

Windows monitoring and tracing infrastructure is quite mature, including context of the .NET environment. There are two main components available: metrics-driven *performance counters* providing time series of measurements and an event-driven mechanism called *Event Tracing for Windows (ETW)*. Those two tools cover almost all the monitoring and diagnostic needs. There is also a Windows Management Instrumentation mechanism, but it is not being used for our purposes at all (as it is more dedicated to, as its name suggests, management and administration).

When developing .NET, the choices were obvious in the field of the diagnostic mechanism used. Both a mature .NET Framework and its multiplatform counterpart .NET Core support both performance counters and ETW as diagnostic platform. More precisely:

- .NET application - can use `EventSource` class (from System. Diagnostics.Tracing namespace) to emit ETW events or obviously can use any other library to log directly into the files and many other possible targets.

- .NET framework - emits both Performance Counters and ETW data.

- Operating system API and kernel - also emits both Performance Counters and ETW data.

Now we will devote quite a lot of words to those two mechanisms and how to consume them in various tools.

VMMap

This great tool, part of Microsoft's Sysinternals tools suite, allows you to analyze process memory usage from the operating system point of view. It will be used by us in later chapters to see how .NET application consumes memory, with respect to organization described in Chapter 2 (pages that may be committed or reserved for various purposes).

It is a stand-alone tool not requiring any installation and may be downloaded from the a `https://docs.microsoft.com/en-us/sysinternals/downloads/vmmap` site. After unpacking and running it, we select process of our interest to immediately see its memory usage analysis (see Figure 3-7). VMMap detects pages used by the .NET Managed Heap as well as pages dedicated for stack or loaded binaries.

VMMap - Sysinternals: www.sysinternals.com   — □ ×

File   Edit   View   Tools   Options   Help

Process: dotnet.exe
PID: 19780

Committed: 82,228 K

Private Bytes: 8,480 K

Working Set: 14,360 K

Type	Size	Committed	Private	Total WS	Private WS	Shareable WS	Shared WS	Locked WS	Blocks	
Total	2,148,003,428 K	62,228 K	8,480 K	14,360 K	4,024 K	10,336 K	4,608 K		414	
Image	39,684 K	39,672 K	3,488 K	10,200 K	812 K	9,388 K	3,716 K		253	
Mapped File	4,148 K	4,148 K		420 K		420 K	420 K		3	
Shareable	2,147,509,292 K	33,352 K		576 K	56 K	520 K	464 K		66	2,147.
Heap	3,660 K	2,352 K	2,288 K	1,084 K	1,080 K	4 K	4 K		20	
Managed Heap	394,432 K	428 K	428 K	328 K	328 K				33	
Stack	9,216 K	156 K	156 K	76 K	76 K				18	
Private Data	39,184 K	612 K	612 K	188 K	164 K	4 K	4 K		21	
Page Table	1,508 K	1,508 K	1,508 K	1,508 K	1,508 K					
Unusable	2,104 K									
Free	135,290,951,488 K								31	133,143.

Address	Type	Size	Committed	Private	Total WS	Private WS	...	Protection	Details
⊞ 000001F622DA0000	Heap (Private Data)	64 K	8 K	8 K	8 K	8 K	2	Execute/Read/Write	Heap ID: 5 [COMPATABILITY]
000001F622DB0000	Free	192 K							
⊞ 000001F622DE0000	Heap (Private Data)	64 K	8 K	8 K	8 K	8 K	2	Read/Write	Heap ID: 4 [COMPATABILITY]
⊟ 000001F622DF0000	Managed Heap	393,216 K	272 K	272 K	172 K	172 K	4	Read/Write	GC
000001F622DF0000	Managed Heap	4 K	4 K	4 K	4 K	4 K		Read/Write	
000001F622DF1000	Managed Heap	24 bytes	24 bytes	24 bytes				Read/Write	Gen2
000001F622DF1018	Managed Heap	24 bytes	24 bytes	24 bytes				Read/Write	Gen1
000001F622DF1030	Managed Heap	195 K	195 K	195 K	152 K	152 K		Read/Write	Gen0
000001F622E22000	Managed Heap	261,944 K						Reserved	
000001F632DF0000	Managed Heap	72 K	72 K	72 K	16 K	16 K		Read/Write	Large Object Heap
000001F632E02000	Managed Heap	131,000 K						Reserved	
⊞ 000001F63A2F0000	Private Data	3,520 K	388 K	388 K	12 K	12 K	2	Read/Write	
⊞ 000001F63B150000	Heap (Private Data)	1,024 K	172 K	172 K	156 K	156 K	2	Read/Write	Heap ID: 1 [LOW FRAGMENTATION]
⊞ 000001F63B260000	Mapped File	3,292 K	3,292 K		112 K		1	Read	C:\Windows\Globalization\Sorting\Sor...
000001F63B597000	Unusable	36 K							
000001F63B5A0000	Free	133,143,009,4...							
⊞ 00007DF5FFBC0000	Shareable	2,147,483,648 K	28,504 K		264 K	56 K	50	Read	
00007FF5FFBC0000	Free	4,910,016 K							
⊞ 00007FF72B6B0000	Shareable	1,024 K	20 K		20 K		2	Read	
⊞ 00007FF72B7B0000	Shareable	140 K	140 K		76 K		1	Read	
00007FF72B7D3000	Unusable	52 K							
00007FF72B7E0000	Free	4,032 K							
⊞ 00007FF72BBD0000	Image (ASLR)	156 K	156 K	12 K	128 K	12 K	7	Execute/Read	C:\Program Files\dotnet\dotnet.exe

Timeline...   Heap Allocations...   Call Tree...   Trace...

Figure 3-7. *Sample VMMap view of simple .NET application (for example, Managed Heaps were properly detected)*

Performance Counters

One of the most commonly used tools for monitoring virtually every aspect of Windows is the so-called *Performance Counters* mechanism. This is a very lightweight mechanism that can be described in one sentence - processes can use it to share diagnostic data in a form of time series of numbers. The huge advantage of it is that it is a completely non-invasive mechanism and does not have a noticeable overhead. The disadvantage is precision - it is generating samples each single second, which may be not enough for specific purposes.

There are many different categories in which these data are published. Thanks to this we can get very comprehensive knowledge about the system. The general performance counters architecture is shown in Figure 3-8.

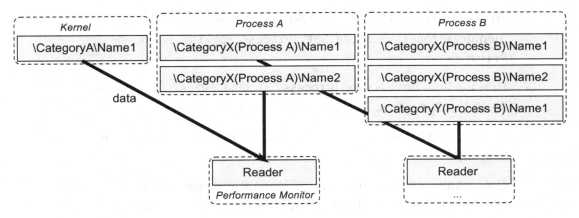

Figure 3-8. *Performance counters architecture*

In general, each process can decide to publish data under some specific Performance Counter and there can be multiple processes doing it. This mechanism works in user space rather than kernel level.

Each performance counter has several important attributes:

- category - defines what general scope of a given topic is the counter about;

- name - uniquely identifies counter within a given category;

- instance name - there may be multiple instances of the same counter in the system. By far the most common instances represent individual processes.

The combination that uniquely identifies the performance counter is written as "\<Category>(<Instance>)\<Name>". For example, the counter that indicates the CPU usage by the notepad process (notepad.exe) will be referred to as "\Process(notepad.exe)\% Processor Time".

What sample data can we get this way? I mention only a few of them to show the wealth of information provided:

- How the CPU usage spreads between the kernel and the programs (Processor/% Privileged Time, Processor/% User Time);

- To what extent the individual processes consume the CPU (Process/% Processor Time);

- To what extent and how the individual processes consume the memory (`Process/Working Set, Process/Working Set - Private`);

- How the hard drive is used (`Process/IO Read Bytes/sec`, `Process/IO Write Bytes/sec`, `Process/Page Faults/sec`);

- Is write/read to disk queued (`PhysicalDisk/Current Disk Queue Length`);

- How many exceptions does the .NET application generate? (`.NET CLR Exceptions/# of Exceps Thrown/sec`).

Of course, we are most interested in the `.NET CLR Memory` category where we find the following counters (spelling and capitalization unchanged):

- `# Bytes in all Heaps`

- `# GC Handles`

- `# Gen 0 Collections, # Gen 1 Collections, # Gen 2 Collections`

- `# Induced GC`

- `# of Pinned Objects`

- `# of Sink Blocks in use`

- `# Total committed Bytes, # Total reserved Bytes`

- `% Time in GC`

- `Allocated Bytes/sec`

- `Finalization Survivors`

- `Gen 0 heap size, Gen 1 heap size, Gen 2 heap size, Large Object Heap Size`

- `Gen 0 Promoted Bytes/Sec, Gen 1 Promoted Bytes/Sec`

- `Process ID`

- `Promoted Finalization-Memory from Gen 0`

- `Promoted Memory from Gen 0, Promoted Memory from Gen 1`

Note   Those performance counters names (as others in .NET CLR categories) are translated into the language of the operating system, so in your computer or server you may find it under different names and categories. This can be VERY annoying because in many translations, those names sound a bit odd. I suggest you switch to English for this and many other reasons as the default Windows language.

If the Garbage Collection topic is at least a little known to you, you probably guessed the meaning of most of the above counters. We will see them successively throughout the rest of the book. It is already enough to say that this is a complete set of data allowing for a very in-depth understanding of the state of our application.

Calculation of the counters is synchronized with the Garbage Collection life cycle. In particular, most measurements take place at the beginning or the end of the GC. In this sense, performance counters can provide very valuable and accurate information. However, there are some important remarks that should be mentioned in this context:

- The reading of the performance counter values is purely controlled by how often the tool we use samples it. If it samples often enough (like every second), the data will be completely accurate. However, if it samples rarely, the results may be very erroneous and misleading. For example, taking samples in such an unfortunate way that we will always hit full Garbage Collection (the one consuming the most resources), we will get false view about how much % time in GC is being spent. In other words, let's pay close attention to the way we sample data when we use performance counters. The best rule is to simply sample the data as often as possible.

- Performance counters data are only updated when specific events occur (mainly the mentioned GC start and end), and then their values remain unchanged. This may lead to misleading readings. Suppose, for example, that in our process full GC has recently occurred during which % Time in GC was at level of 50%. From this point on, the counter % Time in GC will indicate a high 50% value even if the observed process does not perform any work. As long as no new GC occurs, those values will not be updated. In other words, by observing counters, we should focus more on the changes than on current values. The observed value is just the last one that was sampled recently.

Microsoft, since .NET 4.0, prefers the use of ETW data (described in the following subchapter) instead of performance counters. However, the use of performance counters is much simpler than that of ETW and hence the high popularity of this mechanism. We will observe in detail the difference between measurements of performance counters and ETW in Chapter 5.

There may be many different consumers of data provided by performance counters. A lot of monitoring tools are using underneath performance counters because it is a very lightweight, no-waste way to get massive amounts of information. But one of the easiest tools, very often used, is the built-in *Windows Performance Monitor*. Run it with the perfmon.exe command or by searching on the Start menu.

Then select Performance ➤ Monitoring Tools ➤ Performance Monitor item on the left. In the graph that appears, in the context menu select Add Counters... option (see Figure 3-9).

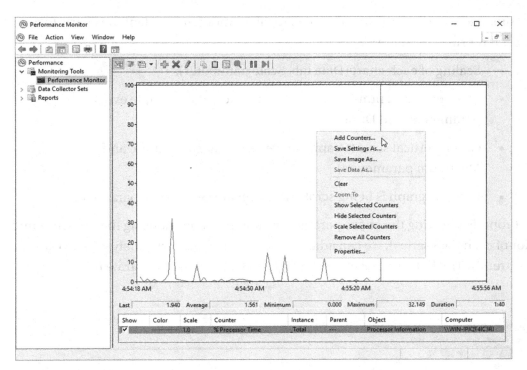

Figure 3-9. *Performance Monitor - overall view with Add Counters context option*

Use the dialog box to select the category of interest (.NET CLR Memory in our case) and specific counters and instances (see Figure 3-10).

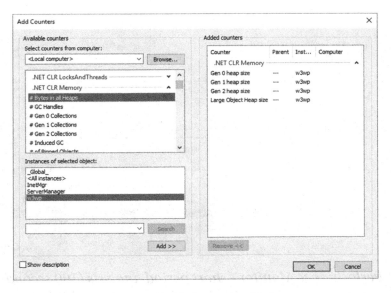

Figure 3-10. *Performance Monitor - Add Counters dialog*

After adding counters, we often need to take a moment to adapt the charts to our needs. It is primarily about:

- Scaling of each chart (Data tab, Scale parameter),

- Frequency and number of samples (General tab, Sample every parameters, and Duration),

- Graph vertical scale (Graph tab, Vertical scale Minimum, and Maximum parameters),

- How the graph is being scrolled (Graph tab, Scroll style parameter).

Properly selecting the above parameters (and possibly choosing the thickness and color of each data series), we can adjust the graph to short-term analysis or to observe daily trends. The following examples in Figures 3-11 and 3-12 illustrate this.

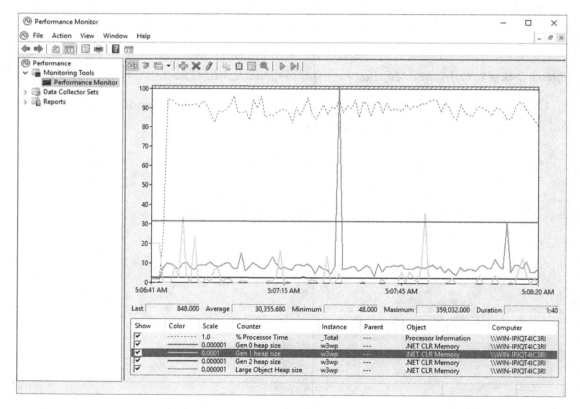

Figure 3-11. *Performance Monitor - short period analysis (100 seconds) with GC generation sizes visible*

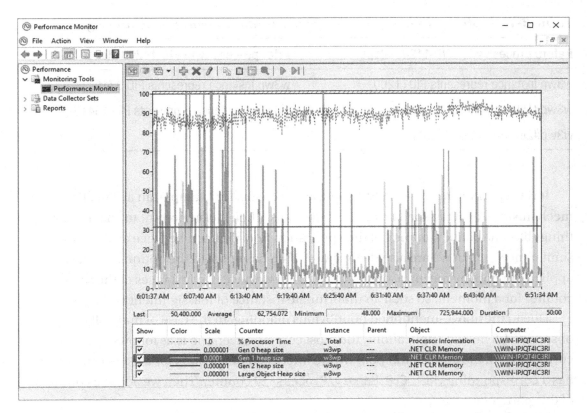

Figure 3-12. *Performance Monitor - long-term analysis (50 minutes) with GC generation sizes visible*

The performance counters mechanism has a certain annoying trait that we will have to learn to live with. As I mentioned, every process that publishes counters under the same name has a unique instance name. It corresponds to the name of the process. For example, a web application hosted on IIS will have a `\.NET CLR Memory(w3wp)\# Bytes in all Heaps` counter (because *application pool* process has name `w3wp.exe`). However, if there are several applications on the server hosted in different application pools, there will be several instances numbered sequentially, like `w3wp`, `w3wp#1`, `w3wp#2,` etc. How can we find out which instance corresponds to which application pool? Here will help us: `.NET CLR Memory/Process ID` counter. Thanks to it, we may find out what the PID of each instance process is. But be careful! The annoying part starts here – the assignment between a process and performance counter instance can change over time! If, for example, one of the application pools is stopped (due to inactivity or so), the remaining processes will override their instance assignment (see Table 3-1).

Table 3-1. *Problem with Application Pool Instances Dynamic Renaming*

Before process with PID 11200 stops	After process with PID 11200 stops
w3wp instance represents PID11200	w3wp instance represents PID 8710
w3wp#1instance has PID 8710	w3wp#1 instance represents PID 10410
w3wp#2instance has PID 10410	

It is very annoying, especially if you want to create, for example, an automatic mechanism to observe specific application pools. Then it is important to ensure that things like automatic stopping of the application pool do not take place at all. With a similar mechanism we are also dealing with if IIS has enabled the option to restart the application pool by means of overlapping. Then we have two instances of the same counter for a moment, so such an unfortunate instance of reassignment is certain.

Due to the above-mentioned nonobvious mapping, in the case of manually observing IIS hosted applications, the most common scenario is as follows: we check the current PID of the application pool we are interested in and look for a `w3wp` instance that has a corresponding `.NET CLR Memory/Process ID` counter. Then we add the counters of this particular instance.

It's actually all about what you can say about Performance Monitor. There are many other programs that consume performance counters, but let's just stop here. We will use Performance Monitor to illustrate Garbage Collection in action on Windows.

Event Tracing for Windows

Among the various diagnostic tools available, undoubtedly one of the most powerful is the mechanism called *Event Tracing for Windows (ETW)*. It seems to be, unfortunately, still a little underrated as per its capabilities. Perhaps this is due to the fact that this mechanism is developed gradually over the years and has yet to earn his rightful interest. It was present since Windows 2000 but with every new version of the system offers more and more. It has been extensively developed in Windows Vista and Windows Server 2003. In Windows 7, it introduces key logging capabilities of storing call stack per every event (see `https://msdn.microsoft.com/en-us/library/windows/desktop/dd392330`).

The power of the ETW mechanism is to provide vast amounts of information with very low overhead, which typically is smaller than few percent. Thanks to that it can be used in production systems without problems. It can be turned on or off while running our applications, without having to restart them. Many tools benefit from the ETW in fact. We may not even be aware of how much. For example, the well-known Event Log and its browser (`eventvwr.exe`) and Resource Monitor (`resmon.exe`) are built on this mechanism. They simply visualize events logged via ETW. However, to dispel doubts, the performance counters mechanism described in the previous section is not based on Event Tracing for Windows.

Before we go into the description of specific tools, it is good to get acquainted with the overall architecture of this solution. The ETW mechanism can distinguish certain concepts, which knowledge is very useful when using it. These are:

- *ETW event* - a single event that can be logged in the system.

- *ETW session* - central part of the whole mechanism. Conceptually it means, as the name suggests, an ongoing tracing session. Technically, this is a collection of system resources, such as in-memory buffers and threads for writing to disk (see Figure 3-13).

- *ETW provider* - each user or kernel mode element that can deliver events. There are many built-in system providers, grouped by certain categories, such as network providers, processes, etc. This also includes .NET runtime and our code as well (if we wish to publish our custom ETW events). Providers are identified by a global unique identifier (GUID).

- *ETW controller* - the process that is responsible for creating a session and connecting it to selected providers.

- *ETW consumer* - any tool that somehow consumes events data, storing them into so-called *Event Trace Log* (*ETL*) file or presenting in real time.

ETW Session is designed for the lowest possible overhead (see Figure 3-13). From the point of view of the process, this is just a quick action involving a non-blocking write to the queue (in-memory buffer) maintained at the kernel level. And when the application continues normal operation, the dedicated kernel thread processes those queues and writes events to specific targets - usually to the file or to some another in-memory buffer (to conduct real-time analysis).

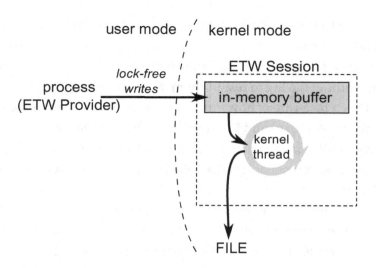

Figure 3-13. *Event Tracking for Windows internals*

Conceptually, the same provider can provide information to several sessions (see Figure 3-14). Conversely, a session can receive information from multiple providers. ETW's characteristic feature is to operate on the level of the providers rather than processes. In order to gather information from one or more providers, with the help of controller we create a new session to which we attach them. Since the session starts, all processes in the system that implement that provider will log events to our session. So it can be said that it is gathering events for the whole machine, not a specific process. Filtering of data for the processes we are interested in is only at the analysis level, in the consumer program.

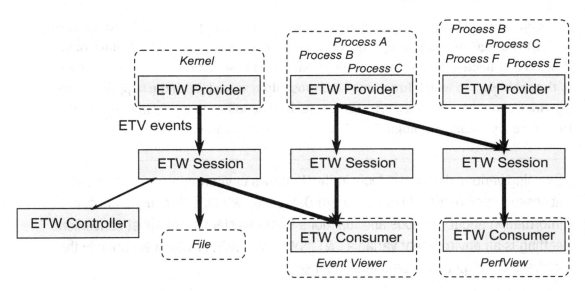

Figure 3-14. *Event Tracing for Windows (ETW) building blocks, illustrating various configuration possibilities. Please note that a process may have a role of multiple ETW providers; thus some processes are listed multiple times.*

Holding events in buffers outside the application process also has another advantage - the application crash will not cause the loss of diagnostic data. Of course, when logging a large number of events, access to the disk can become the bottleneck and create overhead for the entire machine. However, we will encounter this situation only when we choose too many intensively used providers for our session. Another threat could be the exhaustion of disk space, but there is a solution. You can write data to a file in circular-buffer mode, where we do not have to worry about disk overflow. Data will be overwritten cyclically in a fixed size buffer. The most typical scenario is to run session storing data in a circular-buffer and wait for a specific scenario to happen. Only then we close the session and save data from buffer to the file.

From Windows 7 it is possible to collect a stack trace associated with kernel and user events. The payload of such special events (paired with the source events) are the hexadecimal addresses on the stack frames, which are decoded only after, at the analysis phase. This applies, however, to native code (that is, also the CLR code), but no managed code prior to Windows 8. The stack trace of dynamic code generated by the 64-bit JIT in this case will not be decoded (it will be, however, for 32-bit code). This problem was fixed in Windows 8, where the ETW framework in the kernel was changed to recognize 64-bit JIT frames and traverse them without issues.

A built-in CPU-sampling ETW event allows us, for example, to track problems with high CPU usage. At every sampling event (generated each 1 ms), the call stack of all threads is collected from all processes. Thanks to that, statistically, we can see the cause of the problem - in which functions CPU most often stayed. With the support from OS providers, you can also track sync issues (such as deadlocks). It is being used by the Concurrency Visualizer plugin for Visual Studio, for example.

By using various diagnostic tools in the Windows environment, we often need access to symbol files (PDB - Program Database), which allows us to decode information about methods and functions from call stacks. The most convenient setting is an environment variable _NT_SYMBOL_PATH in which we specify the address of the public Microsoft symbol server:

`srv*C:\Symbols*https://msdl.microsoft.com/download/symbols`

This will allow us to obtain PDB files of the Windows operating system and CLR libraries. Also, in the path, we set up a local folder where files will be cached once downloaded.

There is a special *NT Kernel Logger session* that can be used only with kernel-level providers and not with user mode. The base kernel group logs, for example, the start and end of the process. There is, for example, the Microsoft-Windows-TCPIP user provider, which logs its events from the tcpip.sys kernel-mode driver.

Most often, with the session using the user-mode providers, additionally the NT Kernel Logger session is started. It provides information about running / destroying processes and threads. The results are then combined together during the analysis phase.

The operating system provides a lot of interesting information, such as process and thread management, networking, I/O operations, etc. But what interests us the most is that CLR is also an ETW provider, and this mechanism allows us to learn a lot about runtime in the context of our application.

We can use build-in `logman.exe` utility to find all .NET-related providers in the system (see Listing 3-1).

Listing 3-1. Using `logman` utility to list all .NET-related ETW providers

```
> logman query providers | findstr DotNET
```
Microsoft-Windows-DotNETRuntime	{E13C0D23-CCBC-4E12-931B-D9CC2EEE27E4}
Microsoft-Windows-DotNETRuntimeRundown	{A669021C-C450-4609-A035-5AF59AF4DF18}

We can also use it to find out what providers are available in the context of a particular process. For example, if we ask about the ASP.NET WebAPI hosted on IIS, we will get a list as in Listing 3-2 (the result presents only several of many listed providers).

Listing 3-2. Using `logman` utility to list all ETW providers of specified ASP.NET process

```
> logman query providers -pid 6228
```

Provider	GUID
.NET Common Language Runtime	**{E13C0D23-CCBC-4E12-931B-D9CC2EEE27E4}**
ASP.NET Events	{AFF081FE-0247-4275-9C4E-021F3DC1DA35}
IIS: WWW Global	{D55D3BC9-CBA9-44DF-827E-132D3A4596C2}
IIS: WWW Isapi Extension	{A1C2040E-8840-4C31-BA11-9871031A19EA}
IIS: WWW Server	{3A2A4E84-4C21-4981-AE10-3FDA0D9B0F83}
Microsoft-Windows-Application Server-Applications	{C651F5F6-1C0D-492E-8AE1-B4EFD7C9D503}
Microsoft-Windows-Application-Experience	{EEF54E71-0661-422D-9A98-82FD4940B820}
Microsoft-Windows-DotNETRuntimeRundown	**{A669021C-C450-4609-A035-5AF59AF4DF18}**

157

```
Microsoft-Windows-IIS                          {DE4649C9-15E8-4FEA-9D85-
                                               1CDDA520C334}

Microsoft-Windows-IIS-Configuration            {DC0B8E51-4863-407A-BC3C-
                                               1B479B2978AC}
```

...

If we ask about the console application running on CoreCLR then we will get a slightly different set of providers (see Listing 3-3).

Listing 3-3. Using logman utilit to list all ETW providers of console .NET Core process

> **logman query providers -pid 8528**

```
Provider                                  GUID
--------------------------------------------------------------------------
----

.NET Common Language Runtime              {E13C0D23-CCBC-4E12-931B-
                                          D9CC2EEE27E4}

Microsoft-Windows-AsynchronousCausality   {19A4C69A-28EB-4D4B-8D94-
                                          5F19055A1B5C}

Microsoft-Windows-COM-Perf                {B8D6861B-D20F-4EEC-BBAE-
                                          87E0DD80602B}

Microsoft-Windows-Crypto-BCrypt           {C7E089AC-BA2A-11E0-9AF7-
                                          68384824019B}

Microsoft-Windows-Crypto-RSAEnh           {152FDB2B-6E9D-4B60-B317-
                                          815D5F174C4A}

Microsoft-Windows-DotNETRuntimeRundown    {A669021C-C450-4609-A035-
                                          5AF59AF4DF18}

Microsoft-Windows-Networking-Correlation  {83ED54F0-4D48-4E45-B16E-
                                          726FFD1FA4AF}

Microsoft-Windows-Shell-Core              {30336ED4-E327-447C-9DE0-
                                          51B652C86108}

Microsoft-Windows-User-Diagnostic         {305FC87B-002A-5E26-D297-
                                          60223012CA9C}

Microsoft-Windows-WinRT-Error             {A86F8471-C31D-4FBC-A035-
                                          665D06047B03}
```

{012616AB-FF6D-4503-A6F0-EFFD0523ACE6}   {012616AB-FF6D-4503-A6F0-
                                                EFFD0523ACE6}

{05F95EFE-7F75-49C7-A994-60A55CC09571}   {05F95EFE-7F75-49C7-A994-
                                                60A55CC09571}

...

As we can see, apart from many different providers, we also find those .NET-related
ones. They have the same GUID both for the WebAPI .NET Framework and console
CoreCLR application. You will also note that there are two names for the same provider
used interchangeably: `Microsoft-Windows-DotNETRuntime` is also being called `.NET
Common Language Runtime`.

Each ETW event emitted within a given provider has several important attributes:

- `Id` - unique identifier of the event,

- `Version` - used for events versioning,

- `Keyword` - it can be used to assign an event to one or several meanings
  (keywords) because this field is actually a bit mask,

- `Level` - the logging level,

- `Opcode` - it means a specific action (stage) within a given event. The
  most commonly used built-in values are the `Start` and `End` opcodes,

- `Task` - it is used to group events within the provider into certain
  functionalities.

With the `logman` tool we can also learn the details of a particular provider. For the
main .NET ETW provider, we will get information as in Listing 3-4.

Listing 3-4. Getting details about .NET ETW providers

```
> logman query providers ".NET Common Language Runtime"

Provider                              GUID
-------------------------------------------------------------------

.NET Common Language Runtime          {E13C0D23-CCBC-4E12-931B-
                                      D9CC2EEE27E4}
```

```
Value                   Keyword                 Description
------------------------------------------------------------------------
0x0000000000000001      GCKeyword               GC
0x0000000000000002      GCHandleKeyword         GCHandle
0x0000000000000004      FusionKeyword           Binder
0x0000000000000008      LoaderKeyword           Loader
0x0000000000000010      JitKeyword              Jit
0x0000000000000020      NGenKeyword             NGen
0x0000000000000040      StartEnumerationKeyword StartEnumeration
0x0000000000000080      EndEnumerationKeyword   StopEnumeration
0x0000000000000400      SecurityKeyword         Security
0x0000000000000800      AppDomainResourceManagementKeyword
                        AppDomainResourceManagement
0x0000000000001000      JitTracingKeyword       JitTracing
0x0000000000002000      InteropKeyword          Interop
0x0000000000004000      ContentionKeyword       Contention
0x0000000000008000      ExceptionKeyword        Exception
0x0000000000010000      ThreadingKeyword        Threading
0x0000000000020000      JittedMethodILToNativeMapKeyword
                        JittedMethodILToNativeMap
0x0000000000040000      OverrideAndSuppressNGenEventsKeyword
                        OverrideAndSuppressNGenEvents
0x0000000000080000      TypeKeyword             Type
0x0000000000100000      GCHeapDumpKeyword       GCHeapDump
0x0000000000200000      GCSampledObjectAllocationHighKeyword
                        GCSampledObjectAllocationHigh
0x0000000000400000      GCHeapSurvivalAndMovementKeyword
                        GCHeapSurvivalAndMovement
0x0000000000800000      GCHeapCollectKeyword GCHeapCollect
0x0000000001000000      GCHeapAndTypeNamesKeyword GCHeapAndTypeNames
0x0000000002000000      GCSampledObjectAllocationLowKeyword
                        GCSampledObjectAllocationLow
0x0000000020000000      PerfTrackKeyword        PerfTrack
0x0000000040000000      StackKeyword            Stack
0x0000000080000000      ThreadTransferKeyword ThreadTransfer
```

```
0x0000000100000000    DebuggerKeyword      Debugger
0x0000000200000000    MonitoringKeyword    Monitoring

Value                 Level                Description
--------------------------------------------------------------------------------
0x00                  win:LogAlways        Log Always
0x02                  win:Error            Error
0x04                  win:Informational    Information
0x05                  win:Verbose          Verbose
...
```

For a list of events generated by .NET providers, for example, you can use the MSDN documentation at https://msdn.microsoft.com/en-us/library/dd264810(v=vs.110). aspx. However, it is not always up to date. Therefore, it is best to reach the source, which means the manifest file of the given provider. The *ETW manifest file* defines strongly typed event information generated by the given provider. This allows the consumer to correctly interpret the recorded session data. The manifest files are different for each .NET runtime environment. And so you can find it under different locations:

- In case of CoreCLR under- .\coreclr\src\vm\ClrEtwAll.man;

- In case of .NET Framework 4.0 and further under c:\Windows\ Microsoft.NET\Framework64\v4.0.30319\CLR-ETW.man;

- In case of .NET Framework 2.0 and earlier, it is not available as the first versions did not support ETW.

When we look at this file, we will see complete information about Microsoft-Windows-DotNETRuntime and Microsoft-Windows-DotNETRuntimeRundown providers. Fragments of this file are presented in Listing 3-5.

Listing 3-5. Fragments of ETW manifest file of .NET ETW providers

```
<instrumentationManifest xmlns="http://schemas.microsoft.com/win/2004/08/
events">
  <instrumentation xmlns:xs="http://www.w3.org/2001/XMLSchema"
xmlns:xsi="http://www.w3.org/2001/XMLSchema-instance" xmlns:win="http://
manifests.microsoft.com/win/2004/08/windows/events">
    <events xmlns="http://schemas.microsoft.com/win/2004/08/events">
      <!--CLR Runtime Publisher-->
```

```
<provider name="Microsoft-Windows-DotNETRuntime" guid="{e13c0d23-
ccbc-4e12-931b-d9cc2eee27e4}" symbol="MICROSOFT_WINDOWS_
DOTNETRUNTIME_PROVIDER" resourceFileName="%WINDIR%\Microsoft.NET\
Framework64\v4.0.30319\clretwrc.dll" messageFileName="%WINDIR%\
Microsoft.NET\Framework64\v4.0.30319\clretwrc.dll">
  <!--Keywords-->
  <keywords>
    <keyword name="GCKeyword" mask="0x1" message="$(string.
    RuntimePublisher.GCKeywordMessage)" symbol="CLR_GC_KEYWORD"/>
    <keyword name="GCHandleKeyword" mask="0x2" message="$(string.
    RuntimePublisher.GCHandleKeywordMessage)" symbol="CLR_GCHANDLE_
    KEYWORD"/>
      ...
  </keywords>
  <!--Tasks-->
  <tasks>
    <task name="GarbageCollection" symbol="CLR_GC_
    TASK" value="1" eventGUID="{044973cd-251f-4dff-a3e9-
    9d6307286b05}" message="$(string.RuntimePublisher.
    GarbageCollectionTaskMessage)">
      <opcodes>
        <!-- These opcode use to be 4 through 9 but we added 128 to
        them to avoid using the reserved range 0-10 -->
        <opcode name="GCRestartEEEnd" message="$(string.
        RuntimePublisher.GCRestartEEEndOpcodeMessage)" symbol="CLR_
        GC_RESTARTEEEND_OPCODE" value="132"> </opcode>
        <opcode name="GCHeapStats" message="$(string.
        RuntimePublisher.GCHeapStatsOpcodeMessage)" symbol="CLR_GC_
        HEAPSTATS_OPCODE" value="133"> </opcode>
          ...
      </opcodes>
    </task>
    <task name="WorkerThreadCreation" symbol="CLR_
    WORKERTHREADCREATE_TASK" value="2" eventGUID="{cfc4ba53-fb42-
    4757-8b70-5f5d51fee2f4}" message="$(string.RuntimePublisher.
    WorkerThreadCreationTaskMessage)">
```

```xml
        <opcodes>
        </opcodes>
      </task>
      ...
  </tasks>
  <!--Maps-->
  <maps>
    <!-- ValueMaps -->
    <valueMap name="GCSegmentTypeMap">
      <map value="0x0" message="$(string.RuntimePublisher.GCSegment.
      SmallObjectHeapMapMessage)"/>
      <map value="0x1" message="$(string.RuntimePublisher.GCSegment.
      LargeObjectHeapMapMessage)"/>
      <map value="0x2" message="$(string.RuntimePublisher.GCSegment.
      ReadOnlyHeapMapMessage)"/>
    </valueMap>
    ...
  </maps>
  <!--Templates-->
  <templates>
    <template tid="GCStart">
      <data name="Count" inType="win:UInt32"
      outType="xs:unsignedInt"/>
      <data name="Reason" inType="win:UInt32" map="GCReasonMap"/>
      <UserData>
        <GCStart xmlns="myNs">
          <Count> %1 </Count>
          <Reason> %2 </Reason>
        </GCStart>
      </UserData>
    </template>
    ...
  </templates>
  <events>
```

```
<!-- CLR GC events, value reserved from 0 to 39 and 200 to 239 -->
<!-- Note the opcode's for GC events do include 0 to 9 for
backward compatibility, even though they don't mean what those
predefined opcodes are supposed to mean -->
<event value="1" version="0" level="win:Informational"
template="GCStart" keywords="GCKeyword" opcode="win:Start"
task="GarbageCollection" symbol="GCStart" message="$(string.
RuntimePublisher.GCStartEventMessage)"/>
<event value="1" version="1" level="win:Informational"
template="GCStart_V1" keywords="GCKeyword" opcode="win:Start"
task="GarbageCollection" symbol="GCStart_V1" message="$(string.
RuntimePublisher.GCStart_V1EventMessage)"/>
...
      </events>
   </provider>
```

As you can see, this is a real mine of knowledge if we want to use the ETW in the context of .NET. Let's take a brief look at the events generated by both providers. We will return to all of these events through the following chapters of this book so you will have a full understanding of each of them. Here, however, we will pay attention to the most interesting of them. This will allow you to see how rich is the information provided by the ETW mechanism.

Looking at the generated events alone can lead to some interesting questions. For example, what is the ReadOnlyHeapMapMessage segment of type GCSegmentTypeMap? We will answer to this question in Chapter 5.

We are mostly interested in the Microsoft-Windows-DotNETRuntime provider, offering events grouped into 29 various Tasks (as in the ETW nomenclature, a Task's event attribute corresponds to its functional category). To get an idea of the richness of the information provided, these include (in parentheses the number of events of a given Task is shown): AppDomainResourceManagement (5),

CLRAuthenticodeVerification CLRILStub (2), CLRLoader (18), CLRMethod
(25), CLRPerfTrack (1), CLRRuntimeInformation (1), CLRStack (1),
CLRStrongNameVerification (4), Contention (3), Exception (3), ExceptionCatch
(2), ExceptionFilter (2), ExceptionFinally (2), GarbageCollection (58),
IOThreadCreation (4), IOThreadRetirement (4), Thread (2), ThreadPool (5),
ThreadPoolWorkerThread (3) and Type (1).

As we can see, the most numerous group is Garbage Collector's task - it contains
58 various events! Actually, there are 44 distinct ones, because some occur in several
versions. What do we find there? Very interesting stuff! A few selected events along with
the description and data that they contain, you will find in Table 3-2.

Table 3-2. *Example ETW Events Related to the GC*

Event	Data
GCStart_V2	ClientSequenceNumber(win:UInt64), ClrInstanceID(win:UInt16), Count(win:UInt32), Depth(win:UInt32), Reason(GCReasonMap), Type(GCTypeMap)
	Informs about beginning of the Garbage Collection, providing the reason and the generation triggering it (as Depth field).
GCEnd_V1	ClrInstanceID(win:UInt16), Count(win:UInt32), Depth(win:UInt32) Informs about the end of the Garbage Collection.
GCCreateSegment_V1	Address(win:UInt64), ClrInstanceID(win:UInt16), Size(win:UInt64), Type(GCSegmentTypeMap)
	Informs about creation of new memory segments, providing information about its size and type.
GCSuspendEEBegin_V1	ClrInstanceID(win:UInt16), Count(win:UInt32), Reason(GCSuspendEEReasonMap)
	Informs about beginning of the suspending runtime required by some parts of Garbage Collection.
GCSuspendEEEnd_V1	ClrInstanceID(win:UInt16)
	Informs about the end of the runtime suspending process. From now most of the threads are suspended.

(continued)

Table 3-2. (*continued*)

Event	Data
GCAllocationTick_V3	Address(win:Pointer), AllocationAmount(win:UInt32), Alloc ationAmount64(win:UInt64), AllocationKind(GCAllocationK indMap), ClrInstanceID(win:UInt16), HeapIndex(win:UInt32), TypeID(win:Pointer), TypeName(win:UnicodeString) Very interesting periodic sampling event (emitted after each 100kB of allocations) informs about allocation statistics.
GCHeapStats_V1	ClrInstanceID(win:UInt16), FinalizationPromotedCou nt(win:UInt64), FinalizationPromotedSize(win:UInt64), GCHandleCount(win:UInt32), GenerationSize0(win:UInt64), GenerationSize1(win:UInt64), GenerationSize2(win:UInt64), GenerationSize3(win:UInt64), PinnedObjectCount(win:UInt32), SinkBlockCount(win:UInt32), TotalPromotedSize0(win:UInt64), TotalPromotedSize1(win:UInt64), TotalPromotedSize2(win:UI nt64), TotalPromotedSize3(win:UInt64) Yet another one very interesting event provides rich information about the heap statistics in general, including generation sizes.

If we consider that each event has a precise timestamp and may contain a call stack, we are presented with a vision of the powerful diagnostics we can create on this basis. And that's why it is used by many different tools. Some of them will be revealed in the following subsections.

Do not be afraid if you do not understand descriptions of ETW events given in Table 3-2. It is obvious that some knowledge about the GC is needed to properly understand them. We will come back to many ETW events (including those from Table 3-2) in the following chapters.

The NT Kernel Logger session also provides much valuable information, including events like: Windows Kernel\ProcessStart, Windows Kernel\ProcessEnd - when process start and ends, Windows Kernel\ImageLoad - when dynamic library is being loaded, Windows Kernel\TcpIpRecv - when TCP/IP packets are being received, Windows Kernel\ThreadCSwitch - when a thread gets or loses access to the CPU. There are obviously many others, but listing only a small part of them here does not make any sense. Please refer to the NT Kernel Logger Trace Session documentation on MSDN for further details.

Windows Performance Toolkit

The Windows Performance Toolkit is a set of diagnostic tools in a Windows environment. What we are most interested in is their ability for collecting and analyzing ETW data. Prior to Windows 8, the main tool for this purpose was the rather cumbersome xperf program. Moreover, it is still present in the files installed with the WPT. It was used to set up and run ETW sessions as well as to analyze them later. In the ETW nomenclature, therefore, it had the function of both the ETW controller and ETW consumer. We can often meet him in many older ETW-related articles and blog posts. Due to the fact that it is a very flexible tool, it is still occasionally used to manage ETW sessions from the command line. However, since Windows 8, the Windows Performance Toolkit has introduced two new tools:

- Windows Performance Recorder - being an ETW controller
- Windows Performance Analyzer - being an ETW consumer

And these two programs within the Windows Performance Toolkit are most commonly used today. We will take a brief look at the basics of using these programs.

Note   Windows Performance Toolkit can be installed in two ways. Both rely on installing one of the two bigger packages - the Windows Assessment and Deployment Kit or the Windows SDK.

Windows Performance Recorder

Windows Performance Recorder from the point of view of the user is a simple dialog acting as ETW controller (see Figure 3-15). What events from which providers will be recorded is being configured by profiles. There are many built-in profiles visible in Figure 3-15, preinstalled with the tool.

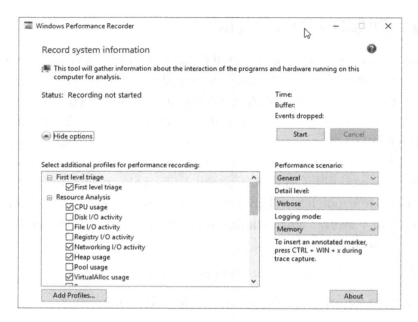

Figure 3-15. *Windows Performance Recorder dialog box*

Two more important options are available:

- Level of detail of recorded data - we are most interested in the Verbose level. In addition to the time of occurrence of events, it also says to record additional diagnostic information.

- Logging mode - we most often use the Memory mode, which records events to a temporary cyclic buffer in memory. This ensures that we never exceed the size of buffer and will not severely impact the entire operating system and other applications by creating too huge of files or memory buffers.

What exactly is included in the profile is not visible from the user interface. But we can see it in command-line version of the program. A list of built-in profiles, visible in the GUI, can be obtained using the profiles command switch (see Listing 3-6).

Listing 3-6. Using wpr command line version to list all profiles names

> **wpr -profiles**

Then we can ask for details of an individual profile using the profiledetails command switch. Thanks to that we can see what providers and keywords are enabled for .NET Activity profile (see Listing 3-7).

Listing 3-7. Using `wpr` command-line version to list a given profile configuration (some providers listed only by Guid were removed from the output for brevity)

```
> wpr -profiledetails DotNet
System Keywords: CSwitch, DiskIO, DiskIOInit, HardFaults, Loader,
MemoryInfo, MemoryInfoWS, NetworkTrace, ProcessCounter, ProcessThread,
SampledProfile
System Stacks: CSwitch, DiskFlushInit, DiskReadInit, DiskWriteInit,
FileCreate, FileRead, FileWrite, ImageLoad, ImageUnload, ProcessCreate,
SampledProfile, ReadyThread
Providers
...
Microsoft-Windows-DotNETRuntime: 0x4007ccbd: 0x05
Microsoft-Windows-IIS: : 0xffI
```

In case of .NET runtime, the provider-selected keyword mask has a value of 0x4007ccbd. We can use values from Listing 3-4 to decode it into a list of selected keywords. We can easily notice that in fact not all possible keywords have been selected (including several related to the Garbage Collector).

There are also built-in profiles for Windows Heap and VirtualAllocations. To have a full picture when doing CLR analysis, one can decide to select all those three profiles.

With the "Add profile" button, you can add manually defined profiles. This is the only way to connect to the only set of providers we are interested in and fine-tune used keywords. You can find the "Pro .NET Memory Management with stacks" sample profile at this book's accompanying GitHub repository (`NetMemoryManagement.wprp file`), which enables all .NET events along with call stacks recording (but please be warned that in such configuration tracing overhead will slow down .NET applications, mainly due to the stack collection).

Windows Performance Analyzer

Windows Performance Analyzer is a powerful ETW consumer. Very advanced analysis can be made there. At the same time, it is one of the main tools for the convenient visualization of ETW data. The first contact with this tool can be a bit overwhelming. The interface was designed in a very generic way. And it's really up to the user how to adapt it. As a result, it is hard to get started, and it is hard at first glance to see the dormant power of this tool.

The exact description of using Windows Performance Analyzer interface is beyond the scope of this book. Because it is so powerful, describing all its capabilities could take another small book. We will concentrate here on some of the most useful scenarios from our point of view. We will use the example of an open source, load test program called SuperBenchmarker written in .NET 4.5 available on GitHub at `https://github.com/aliostad/SuperBenchmarker`. During the load test, it generates a systematic load on a target web application, so it is well suited for experiments. The book is accompanied by a `WPA-Tutorial.zip` file containing an example of a recorded scenario `WPA-Tutorial.ETL` taken during load test with the following parameters:

```
.\sb.exe -u http://localhost/LeakWebApi/values/concatenated/100 -c 10 -n
100000 -y 100
```

This means 10 concurrent calls being made with 100 milliseconds gap between them and total of 100,000 calls will be made. Our LeakWebApi is a very simple ASP.NET MVC Web API project hosted on IIS. Due to the nature of ETW, there are many others processes recorded obviously, but we will concentrate on two of them: `sb.exe` itself and `w3wp.exe` hosting mentioned Web API project. The file was created with Windows Performance Recorder using profiles: CPU usage, Heap usage, VirtualAlloc usage, and our custom ".NET Memory Management with stacks." If you want to do the following exercises, unzip `WPA-Tutorial.zip` now to the folder of your choice.

Let's now go through some of possible scenarios of using the Windows Performance Analyzer. Please remember about the great flexibility of this tool. Therefore, if you follow the exercises described below and some result looks different than on the presented screenshots, double-check your view configuration - in particular, the visibility and order of columns in tables.

Opening File and Configuration

After launching the program, we will see an empty window with the Getting Started tab. Open the recording file by selecting File ➤ Open ... from the menu.

When you open the file, on the left we will see a new Graph Explorer panel with several graph groups - depending on what data was recorded. In case of our WPA-Tutorial.etl file there should be five groups of graphs:

- System Activity - broad data associated with the operation of the system, processes, and threads. Here is also a very important Generic Events chart, which we will look at in a moment.

- Computation – CPU-related data.

- Storage - data related to disks, including such precise data as used disk offsets.

- Memory - data related to memory.

- Power – power-related data, including CPU frequency and states.

Next to each group name is an expand button that allows you to navigate through the grouped graphs. Each of the visible graphs can be moved to the Analysis tab by dragging or double-clicking. You can add to it many different data, which will be placed one below the other. All the views added in the Analysis tab are synchronized (as well as the Graph Explorer itself). Therefore, for example, if you change the scale on the timeline on one of them, the change will be reflected on the others. This is similar to any kind of filtering or underlining of the currently investigated data.

Let's now create a first view that will allow us to learn the basics of program navigation in practice. From the Graph Explorer, expand the System Activity group. Let's drag to the workspace (or double-click) the Processes graph. It will appear in the Analysis tab. Then expand the Computation group and double-click the CPU Usage graph (Sampled). It should appear under the previously added. We should achieve the effect shown in Figure 3-16.

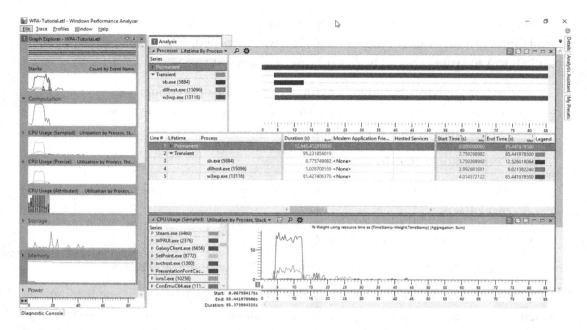

Figure 3-16. *A sample view with Processes and CPU Usage panels*

Quickly we may find out that a lot of elements have tooltips containing additional information. In the Processes pane, there are processes showed running at the time of recording. It is easy to find a block corresponding to the sb.exe process. Click it with your left mouse button. The time range of this process will be automatically highlighted on all other graphs. This is very helpful for navigation and referencing data to each other.

Sometimes data is more convenient to be analyzed in graphical or tabular form. Hence, in the upper right corner of each panel three buttons are placed: show only the chart, show only the table, and show both information (by default Display graph and table option is selected). Now select the "Display graph only" option for both display panels.

From the Graph Explorer add the Stacks panel from the System Activity group and set it to "Display table only." The stacks panel contains grouped information about all collected stack traces.

We can now take a closer look at the w3wp.exe process. First, from the graph, select the time range corresponding to the load test by right-clicking on the sb.exe block in the Processes panel and select Zoom. Having such a chosen time range, we can filter out data to only the web application process we are interested in. Thus, select the w3wp. exe process from the list in Stacks panel and select the "Filter to selection" option in its context menu. Next, expand (in Stacks panel) w3wp.exe in Process column, Thread: CSwitch in Event Name column, CLR in Stack Tag column and [Root] under Stack (Frame Tags) for JIT. After expanding several nodes starting with element [Root], we probably notice that there is a lack of information about the functions invoked (see Figure 3-17). Most of them are specified only with the name of the module and the question mark. This is due to missing symbols (PDBs). We will now take care of their configuration.

Line #	ig	Stack (Frame Tags)	Count	Count
38		| | iiscore.dll!?		526
39		▼ | | |- webengine4.dll!?		451
40		| | | webengine4.dll!?		451
41		| | | webengine4.dll!?		451
42		| | | webengine4.dll!?		451
43		| | | CLR\Other		451
44		▼ | | | |- KernelBase.dll!?		336
45		| | | | ntdll.dll!?		336
46		| | | | ntoskrnl.exe!?		336
47		| | | | ntoskrnl.exe!?		336
48		| | | | ntoskrnl.exe!?		336
49		| | | | ntoskrnl.exe!?		336

Figure 3-17. *Missing symbols resulting in incomplete stack trace information*

To configure the symbols used by the Windows Performance Analyzer, select Trace ➤ Configure Symbol Paths. In this pane we configure the directories where the PDBs are searched for. It is best to have at least the two following sources set:

- If we set the environment variable _NT_SYMBOL_PATH in the previous section, it will be added here by default.

- The path to the symbol files of our application (also provided along with the WPA-Tutorial.etl file).

In the Symcache tab of the same window, you should also deliberately set up a directory where local copies of the prepared symbols will be stored. After completing the above configuration, we can close the Configure Symbols window. When you select Trace ➤ Load symbols from the menu, "Loading symbols" information will appear. Downloading and loading (even if they are already cached) all the needed symbols can take quite a few minutes so please be patient.

After that operation we will have complete stack trace information. We can see this by using the "Quick search" in the panel Stacks (visible as a small magnifier). Use it and type "LeakWebApi" to find calls from within our test application (see Figure 3-18).

Line #	Stack (Frame Tags)	Count	Count
62	| | | | | | | | | | | | System.Web.Http.DLL!System.Web.Http.Controllers.ApiControllerActionInvoker::InvokeActionAsyn...		153
63	| | | | | | | | | | | | System.Web.Http.DLL!System.Web.Http.Controllers.ApiControllerActionInvoker::InvokeUsingResult...		153
64	| | | | | | | | | | | | mscorlib.dll!System.Runtime.CompilerServices.AsyncTaskMethodBuilder`1[System.__Canon]::Start 0...		153
65	| | | | | | | | | | | | System.Web.Http.DLL!System.Web.Http.Controllers.ApiControllerActionInvoker+<InvokeUsingRes...		153
66	| | | | | | | | | | | | System.Web.Http.DLL!System.Web.Http.Controllers.ReflectedHttpActionDescriptor::ExecuteAsync 0...		153
67	| | | | | | | | | | | | System.Web.Http.DLL!System.Web.Http.Controllers.ReflectedHttpActionDescriptor+ActionExecutor...		153
68	| | | | | | | | | | | | Anonymously Hosted DynamicMethods Assembly!dynamicClass::lambda_method 0x0		153
69	| | | | | | | | | | | | LeakWebApi.DLL!LeakWebApi.Controllers.ValuesController::GetConcatenated 0x0		153
70	| | | | | | | | | | | | mscorlib.ni.dll!System.String.Concat(System.String, System.String)$##600053A		153
71	▷ | | | | | | | | | | | | |- mscorlib.ni.dll!System.String.FillStringChecked(System.String, Int32, System.String)$##60004D6		130
72	▷ | | | | | | | | | | | |- CLR\Other		23

Figure 3-18. *Complete stack trace information with symbols loaded*

Generic Events

Quite a lot of events are interpreted in a special way in WPA, and in this way dedicated panels such as Processes or CPU Usage are created. However, it is not possible, of course, to prepare such views for any possible event recorded by ETW. For this purpose, a dedicated panel called Generic Events was created with a view of all registered events. Let's add it to our view by selecting it from the System Activity group. By default we will see all events grouped by the process. We can filter out all except those coming from the sb.exe process by selecting "Filter to selection" from its context menu.[2] By expanding Microsoft-Windows-DotNETRuntime in Provider Name column and then Garbage Collection task and win:Start opcode, we can create a view from Figure 3-19 (after appropriately zooming in an interesting time region). Please note that to get such view proper ordering of columns must be set, starting from Process, through Provider Name, Task Name, and Opcode Name.

---

[2]If you do not see a Process column, please add it and place it as a second column in the Generic Events panel.

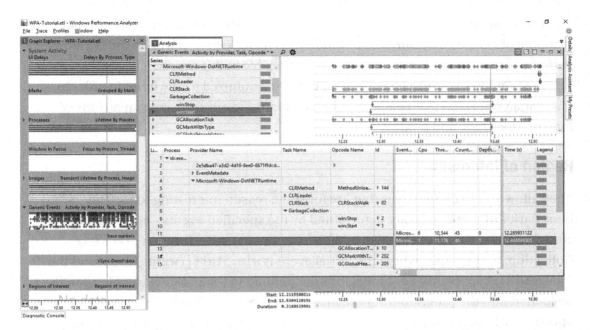

***Figure 3-19.** Generic Events view for process `sb.exe` and Microsoft-Windows-DotNETRuntime-related events*

We have set up a view in which we focus on the `sb.exe` process (second column), Microsoft-Windows-DotNETRuntime provider (third column) provider, and the GarbageCollection task (fourth column). We see, for example, that during almost 0.5 seconds of the selected fragment, there are two GarbageCollection/Start events.

Moreover, we can see the data associated with each of these events. To do this we need to expand the group (in our case by expanding the last grouped item in column Id) and scroll the view accordingly to show columns behind the yellow marker. Example of such a prepared view for GCStart and GCEnd events is shown at Figure 3-20.

Line #	Process	Provider Name	Task Name	Opcode Name	Id	Cpu	ThreadId	Count (Field 1)	Depth (Field 2)	Reason (Field...	Type (Field 4)	ClrInsta...
1	▾ sb.exe (5884)											
2		Microsoft-Windows-Networking-Correla... ▸										
3		▾ Microsoft-Windows-DotNETRuntime										
4			CLRStack	CLRStackWalk	▸ 82							
5			▾ GarbageCollection									
6				win:Stop	▾ 2							
7						6	10,544	45	0	8		
8						1	11,176	46	1	8		
9				win:Start	▾ 1							
10						6	10,544	45	0	AllocSmall	NonConcurrentGC	8
11						1	11,176	46	1	AllocSmall	NonConcurrentGC	8
12				Triggered	▸ 35							
13				PinObjectAtGCTime	▸ 33							

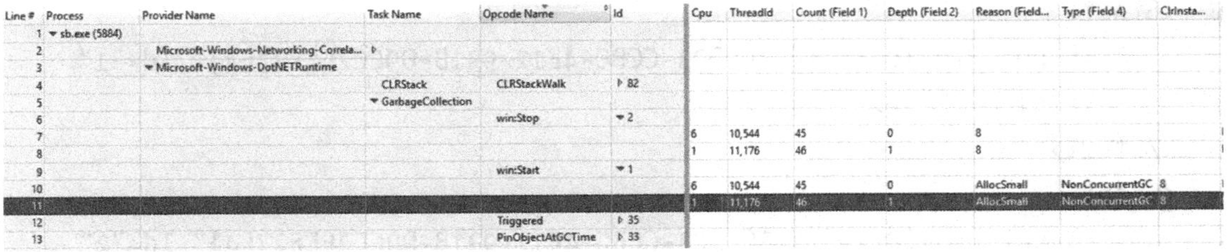

***Figure 3-20.** Garbage Collection start and stop events visible in Generic Events table view*

Adjusting the view by setting columns visibility and ordering altogether with desired grouping of items is the main task of which you will have to deal with in the Windows Performance Analyzer. Fortunately, it is really flexible in this aspect.

The Windows Performance Analyzer can be customized a little more in order to make analysis easier. This can be very helpful thanks to our own, custom *regions of interest*, *stack tags*, and *profiles*.

Region of Interests

They allow you to define areas that are for some reason interesting to us. The boundaries of these areas are determined by the specified events - opening and closing events. This is the ideal mechanism to illustrate the duration of Garbage Collection, for example, where the initial event is win:Start (with Id 1), and the final is win:Stop (with Id 2). Regions are defined in a separate file, which can then be loaded into the program from the menu Trace ➤ Trace Properties. In the tab that appears we load the regions files with the Add ... button in the Regions of Interest Definitions section. Afterwards, the Regions of Interests panel will become available in the Graph Explorer.

We need to create such files ourselves or search for interesting ones on the Internet. You can also use the ones that have been prepared for this book (located at the accompanying GitHub repository): roi_dotnetfinalization.xml and roi_dotnetgc. xml. Such files consist of region definitions expressed in terms of a starting and stopping event (see Listing 3-8).

Listing 3-8. Example of region of interest file definition

```
<Region Guid="{4fbb5999-8f4e-4900-9482-000000000001}"
          Name="DotNETRuntime-GarbageCollection-GC"
          FriendlyName="Garbage Collection">
    <Start>
        <Event Provider="{E13C0D23-CCBC-4E12-931B-D9CC2EEE27E4}" Id="1"
        Version="2" />
    </Start>
    <Stop>
        <Event Provider="{E13C0D23-CCBC-4E12-931B-D9CC2EEE27E4}" Id="2"
        Version="1" />
    </Stop>
```

```
<Match>
    <Event TID="true" PID="true" >
    </Event>
    <Parent PID="true" />
</Match>
<Naming>
    <PayloadBased NameField="ClrInstanceID" />
</Naming>
</Region>
```

As you can see, we need to have some knowledge to define regions: what events will be generated by the provider that we are interested in and how to pair them.

Based on Garbage Collector's events, we can designate the following regions:

- Garbage Collection (events GCStart and GCEnd);

- Suspending runtime (events GCSuspendEEBegin and GCSuspendEEEnd);

- Restarting runtime (events GCRestartEEBegin and GCRestartEEEnd);

- Finalization (events GCFinalizersBegin and GCFinalizersEnd).

This allows you to visualize and collect statistics (number and duration of occurrences) as in Figure 3-21. Please note that the appropriate zoom was set to produce such a view, as well as proper ungrouping of items in the left list (named Series).

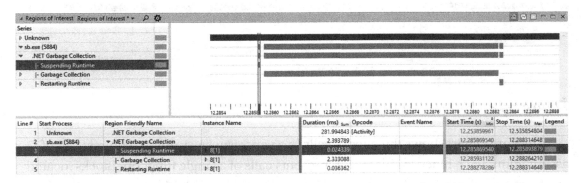

Figure 3-21. *View at Garbage Collection cycle with help of custom Region of interest*

Flame Charts

Performance analysis is possible using the mechanisms already outlined - among others by grouping calls in the Stacks panel. There is another very convenient mechanism – so-called flame charts. The "Flame by Process, Stack" view of CPU Usage (Sampled) panel is available in the Computation group. I encourage you to use it as part of our sample ETL file. By using the following steps, you should be able to get a view shown in Figure 3-22.

- While in the table part of the CPU Usage panel, use Find in Column... option from the context menu and try to find LeakWebApi text. If symbols are loaded, it should point you to the GetContatenated method of our WebAPI controller.

- Select its parent method (which should be lambda_method) and use Filter To Selection from its context menu. This should zoom in the view to a single method call.

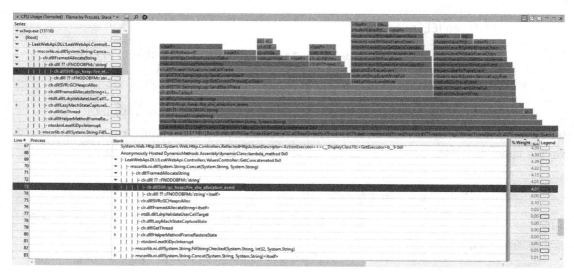

Figure 3-22. *Flame charts example*

The flame chart shows the piles of calls in a very visual way, but it requires a bit of assimilation. Each block visible on it represents calls of a single function. Blocks located on top of each other represent one function calling the other. In this way, the chart grows upward. The higher the function, the deeper the call stack. The width of a block is proportional to the total duration of a particular function call (and all its subcalls). This way we can quickly figure out which functions were associated with a long execution.

For example, in Figure 3-22, we see that the vast majority of the time spent by the WebAPI method `GetConcatened` is because of `System.String.Concat` calls, which then in the vast majority spends time in the `SVR::gc_heap::fire_etw_allocation_event` calls. This is tangible proof that connecting an ETW session to our application caused a lot of overhead. This is related to the option of writing a call stack at each CLR event - we can see that by going further into the method calls made by `fire_etw_allocation_event`. A lot of time is spent in `clr.dll!ETW::SamplingLog::GetCurrentThreadsCallStack` method. This is because getting a call stack per each frequent allocation event is not necessarily a good idea. However, it is completely fine for our learning purposes.

Stack Tags

As we have seen, ETW events can be logged together with a stack trace at their occurrence. The Windows Performance Analyzer lets you view this information using the Stack column. However, for a broader analysis than from the stack trace alone, more valuable is the aggregated information. One such mechanism of aggregation is so-called *Stack Tags*. They allow you to group called methods with respect to the given patterns. This way all events with a stack trace matching the pattern will be marked with the provided Stack Tag.

Default Stack Tags are located in `C:\Program Files (x86)\Windows Kits\10\Windows Performance Toolkit\Catalog\default.stacktags` file, including those related to the CLR and GC in particular. Thanks to that, when using Stack Tag column, we will see stacks grouped into CLR and GC nodes (instead of listing all methods inside).

Custom Graphs

From the Windows Performance Toolkit version for Windows 10, there is a way to draw your own graphs based on event loads. In other words, we can draw graphs where the Y-axis will come from one of the selected event fields. The X-axis will then automatically be the time of the event. The only requirement is that the selected field has an integer value.

Unfortunately, this restriction is very unfavorable for us. The vast majority of events that are interesting from the Garbage Collector's field are given in a hexadecimal format. This applies to various sizes, memory usage, and so on, and so forth. This makes the mechanism at this moment not very useful and we will simply not use it.

Profiles

Because configuration of all panels can be time consuming, the Windows Performance Analyzer provides the ability to save current views by using profiles. We can now save the current view using the Profiles ➤ Export... option. We load them with the Profiles ➤ Apply option. In addition to configuring the views themselves (including the order and layout of the columns), the profile may also define, among others, the file defining Region of Interests.

PerfView

The Windows Performance Toolkit was primarily designed for Windows and driver developers. Thanks to its high customizability, we can adapt it to the .NET environment, as we did in the previous subchapter. However, there is another ETW-based tool that was originally designed to help analyze .NET performance problems - PerfView. Its creator and patron is Vance Morrison, .NET Runtime Performance architect, and this tool is used by the .NET team to take care of the performance of the framework itself and managed code in general. So we obviously should be interested in it also. What's more, all the performance and CLR internals geeks were pleased to hear recently that PerfView has become a fully open source product available on GitHub.

In terms of ETW nomenclature PerfView is both a controller and a consumer (providing an extensive analysing capabilities). It is written as a very non-intrusive tool. It does not require any installation. It consists of just a single executable file - `perfview.exe`. This makes it easy to use on any computer, including production servers. So to start working with PerfView we have two options:

- The first one is to download the ZIP file from `https://www.microsoft.com/en-us/download/details.aspx?id=28567`, extract it, and simply run wherever you want.

- The second one is to compile the program from sources available on GitHub: `https://github.com/Microsoft/perfview`.

Just to notice, this tool can also be controlled from the command line and PowerShell, which enables automation and is especially useful in production analysis (prepared command line may be passed to a system administrator to be executed on restricted environment).

While the startup is simple, the first contact with this tool may scare you off. This program deserves the title of the most powerful, yet the most at first-glance overwhelming tool ever. The interface is not very intuitive and pretty, so it is not clear even where to start. Fortunately, it has very extensive help. Each option and GUI element have a link to the documentation. Below you can find some basic usage scenarios, but I encourage you to visit the help section frequently. You will find there an extension and broad explanation of the topics covered here. Believe me, this tool is worth every minute spent on learning it.

Note   Much of the functionality in PerfView's ETW-based analysis is based on a library `TraceEvent`. We'll go back to it in Chapter 15 to briefly see its capabilities. While PerfView is mainly based on ETW, it has also a built-in the ETWCLrProfiler (based on so-called CLR Profiling API) that allows PerfView to intercept the .NET method calls (enable .NET Call in the Collect dialog to start using it).

As a lightweight tool for ETW analysis, consider also using the etrace tool created by Sasha Goldshtein and available at `https://github.com/goldshtn/etrace`. It allows you to control ETW sessions from the command line, with various filtering features available.

While the Windows Performance Analyzer is in a sense based on the concept of charts, Perfview focuses on the tabular view. Actually almost everything we can see in this program is put in tabular form. This can sometimes be misleading because, in the same way, the memory consumption, call stacks, and everything else is being analyzed.

After launching the program, we will see a window with extensive help. We can take three main actions at this time:

- Start collecting ETW data using the Collect ➤ Collect option.

- Begin the data analysis by typing the path to the directory into the text box below the menu and selecting the ETL file you are interested in.

- Perform a memory dump using the option Memory ➤ Take Heap Snapshot.

As with other tools, it is necessary to configure symbol paths, which can be done from File ➤ Set Symbol Path menu. It is best to have three sources set:

- The public Microsoft symbol server, the same as in the _NT_ SYMBOL_PATH environment variable.

- Path to the subdirectory with the NGEN image symbols next to the opened ETL file although this is not strictly necessary as PerfView is able to automatically re-create them.

- The path to the symbol files of our application.

Data Collection

Because PerfView is an ETW controller, it allows you to manage an ETW tracing session. After selecting the Collect option, we will see a new dialog box with a number of parameters (see Figure 3-23).

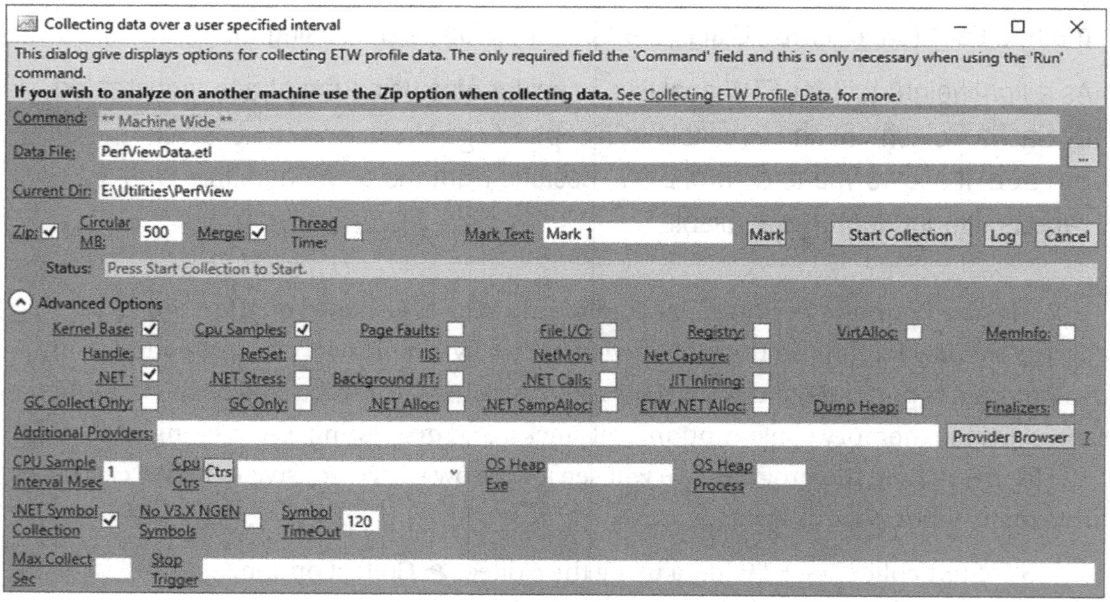

Figure 3-23. PerfView collection dialog with Advanced section expanded

By looking at the possible selection options, we will encounter quite a lot related to .NET. It is worth taking a moment to explain them, although they are also described in the program help. The most interesting options from our point of view are located under Advanced Options:

- .NET - enables the default events from .NET providers.

- .NET Stress - enabled events from .NET providers related to stress testing runtime itself. Those are rare events used rather internally by the CLR team.

- GC Collect Only - disables all other providers and enables only .NET provider with events associated with the GC process. This is a very lightweight option that allows you to collect basic GC-related diagnostic information for a long time.

- GC Only - similar to the above but additionally stack for sampling of allocations on the GC heap are enabled (every time 100 kB of objects were allocated).

- .NET Alloc - enables event with stack every time an object is allocated on the GC heap. This is a very costly option and can slow down the program several times. And we have recently seen this overhead, in fact, in Figure 3-21.

- .NET SampAlloc - enables event generated every time 10KB of objects are allocated on the GC heap. This is not based on built-in ETW events but using CLR Profiler API by injecting ETWClrProfiler library into the processes.

- ETW .NET Alloc - this enables events for allocations sampling but instead of injecting a Profiler API-based library, it is based on the `GCSampledObjectAllocationHigh` keyword available from .NET 4.5.3.

- Finalizers - enables events related to finalization process inside GC.

- Additional providers - this fields allows you to provide any additional providers you need. It can also be used to fine-tune providers that would anyway be enabled. For example, to enable stack capturing for CLR exceptions we can type `Microsoft-Windows-DotNETRuntime :ExceptionKeyword:Always:@StacksEnabled=true`. Extensive help about using this field is also provided.

- CPU Ctrs - this counter allows you to enable low-level CPU-related counters like branch mispredictions or cache misses. Keep in mind you will have disable Hyper-V virtualization to have access to those events.

Note: Apart from the discussed options for .NET, there are some general settings to keep in mind:

- Zip - packaging the files into an archive so that it is easy to transfer the whole thing for later analysis on another computer.

- Merge - merging the files into a single one but without creating a separate ZIP file.

You can omit those two options if you do not plan to send your analysis to another. However, it is extremely important to check the Merge option if you plan to do your analysis on a different machine than on the one the data has been collected. The merge option includes symbol-resolving preparation so if you omit it, most of the gathered data will be useless on another computer.

A very popular way of triggering ETW data collection is based on PerfView's command-line usage. This way, for example, you can ask the support team to easily gather data on the production environment, by providing them a single command to be executed. For example, the following command will trigger a lightweight session recording for GC-related events:`perfview /GCCollectOnly /nogui /accepteula /NoV2Rundown /NoNGENRundown /NoRundown /merge:true /zip:true collect`Using the command line we may also provide session stop triggers, like stopping session when GC happened longer than the specific number of milliseconds. Please run `perfview -?` for more help on the command line.

Data Analysis

Using the PerfView we can open files ETL recorded both by himself and every other ETW tool. After opening the sample ETL file, we will see the view as in Figure 3-24. On the left side, all the prepared analyses are available - depending on which providers and what events were selected during the session recording.

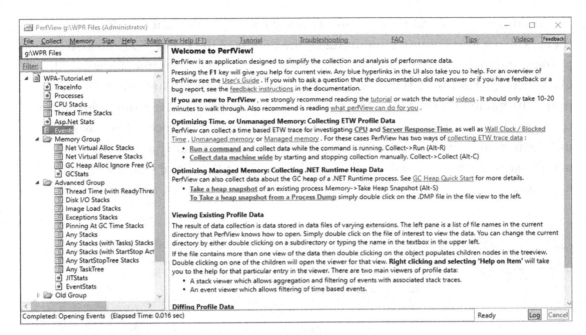

Figure 3-24. *Sample ETL file opened in PerfView*

One of the most basic views is a Generic Events panel, allowing you to view instances of all recorded events. When you open it and enter the GC in the Filter field, we will see all GC-related DotNetRuntime events (see Figure 3-25).

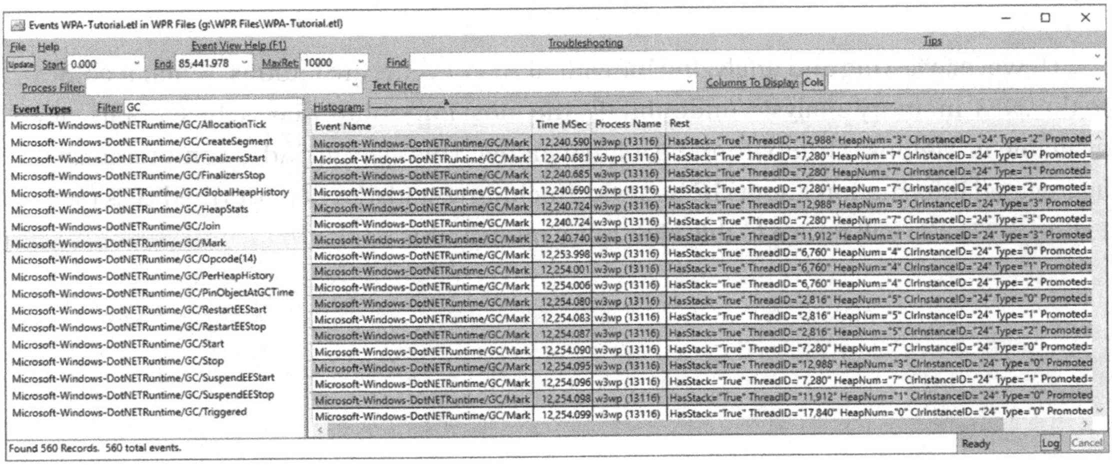

Figure 3-25. *PerfView - events related to GC shown in Events panel*

Aa you can see, in addition to the standard columns associated with the event, there is also a Rest column containing all the details of the event. You can also select particular data from events by clicking the Cols button. For example, filter out all events except Microsoft-Windows-DotNETRuntime/GC/HeapStats event by typing part of its name into the Filter field (like GC/HeapStats). Then, use the Cols button to select all the GenerationSize fields. In addition, fill in the Process Filter with a unique part of the process that we are interested in. We should have created a table of GC statistics (see Figure 3-26) that can be pasted to Excel and visualized, for example.

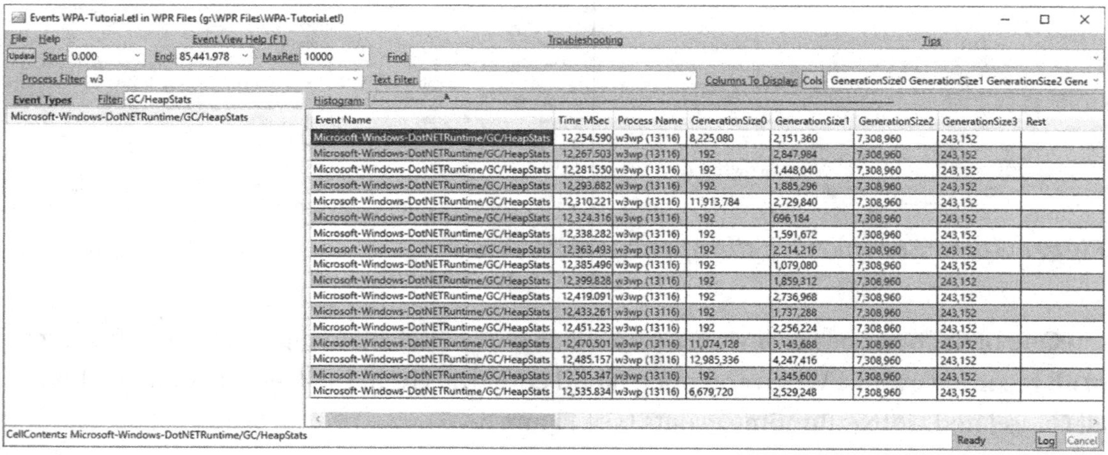

Figure 3-26. *PerfView - customized view of events related to GC*

However, viewing and analyzing individual ETW events are tedious. When it comes to the .NET memory analysis, undoubtedly the most important view is the GCStats view available in Memory Group from the main window. This view includes comprehensive aggregated information about GC behavior, including statistics of performed GCs (see Figure 3-27). We will return to this view quite often in this book.

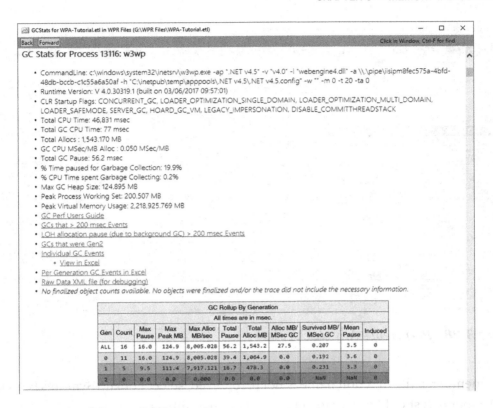

Figure 3-27. *PerfView - GCStats view*

Additionally, as you could see in the Rest column in Figure 3-25, the selected events have the `HasTrack = "True"` attribute. If you want to see the stack trace of the event, select one of them and select Open Any Stacks from its context menu (but be careful, you must do it in the context of Time MSec column). This will open another very popular PerfView's call-tree view (see Figure 3-28).

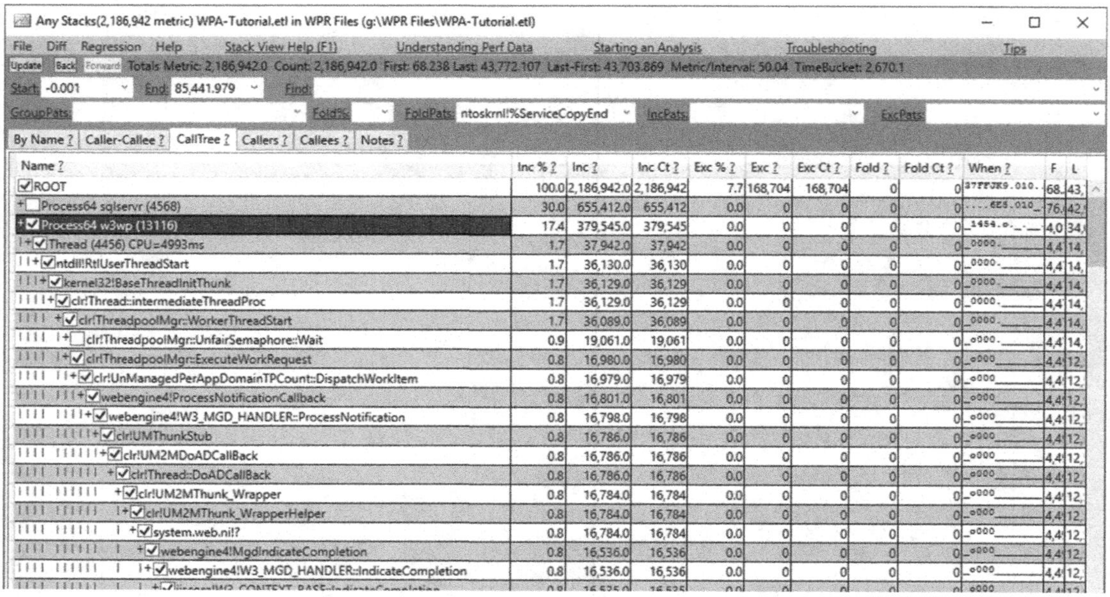

Figure 3-28. *PerfView - Any stacks view*

Remember, if the function name is not recognized, select Lookup Symbols from the context menu. It should trigger reading appropriate symbols.

There are also many other, extremely useful views. We will use them many times. But now I encourage you just to look around, including such views as CPU Stacks, mentioned GC Stats, or Asp.Net Stats.

Memory Snapshots

When you select Take Heap Snapshot from the menu, we will see a Collecting Memory Data window. It is good to immediately use the Filter field to find the processes we are interested in. Once you have selected the process and clicked on the Dump GC Heap, you will need to wait a few or dozen seconds to get the results (see Figure 3-29).

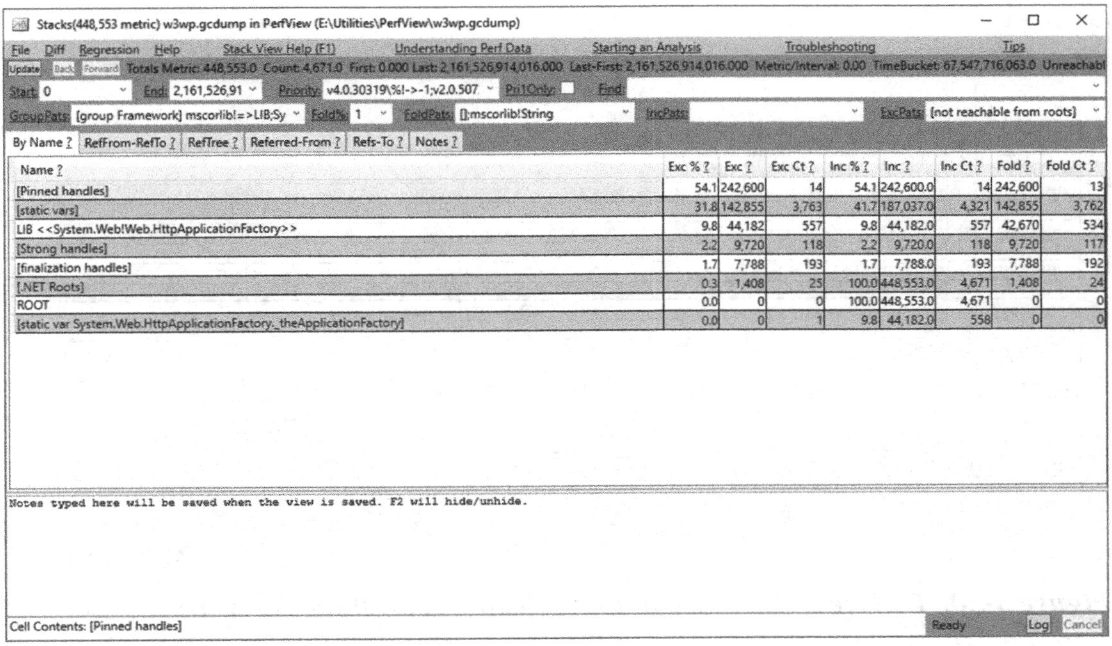

Figure 3-29. *PerfView - Memory snapshot view*

Note   Memory snapshot is not a typical memory dump - it does not contain all the memory of the process. It is a view of the process state, storing a preprocessed objects graph but without an object's content and ignoring all unmanaged memory regions.

The resulting window will show the table we already see, but this time it does not represent the call tree, but the reference tree in which nodes are object types or category of types. For example, initially visible "By Name" tab shows a summary of all the types found in the memory dump. We can further investigate a given entry by choosing Memory ➤ View Objects (or Alt + O) from the context menu. Let's do this for "[static vars]" entry to see a list of all static variables in the memory dump (see Figure 3-30).

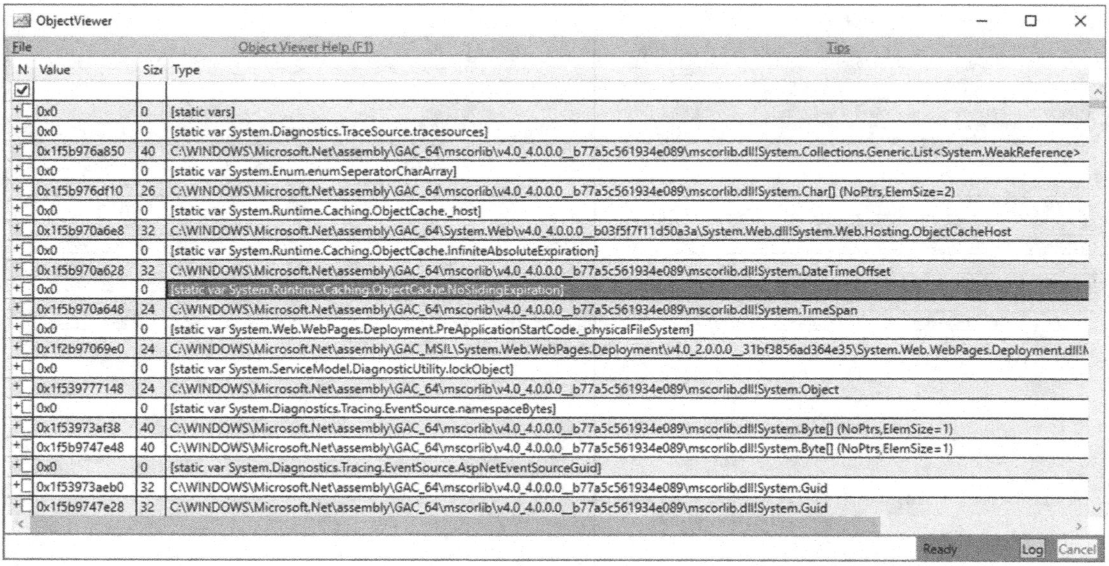

Figure 3-30. *PerfView - Memory snapshot listing of all static variables*

We see here pairs of lines one by one - where the given static variable was declared and an object it is assigned to. If we expand this object, we can investigate it further by navigating through all its children (fields).

There is one more important memory snapshots function - comparing them. This allows us to keep track of trends in our program and, for example, to quickly identify the cause of memory leaks. To compare two snapshots (created exactly as before), open them both, and from the Diff menu choose the option to compare to the second file. We will see Diff Stacks, which will display data in a similar way to a single snapshot but with an important difference that columns values will indicate the difference between the two files (see Figure 3-31).

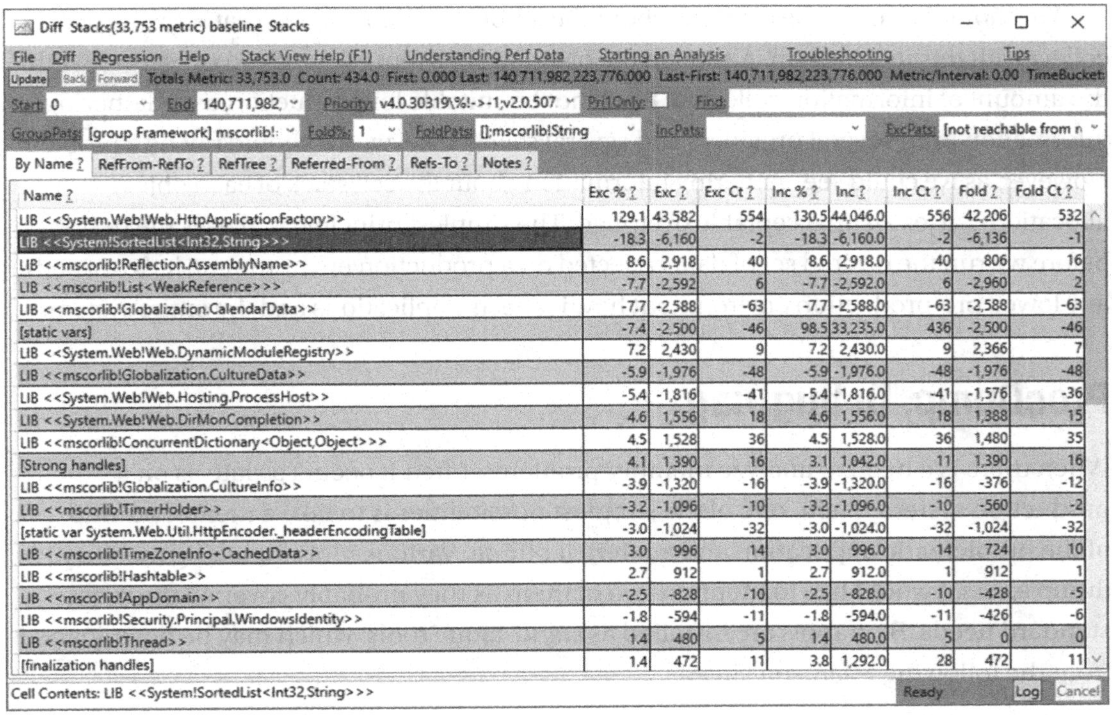

Figure 3-31. *PerfView - Memory snapshot difference*

Please note that there is Freeze option disabled by default in the Collecting Memory Data dialog. It controls whether we want to stop the entire process for the time of making heap snapshot. Is it obviously very intrusive, but also very precise approach. On production environment you will most probably be interested in disabling Freeze option, which unfortunately may produce more or less inconsistent data (as the snapshot is being made during normal application work).

The real power of PerfView is its low overhead and the ability to analyze production environments. We can use it for continuous performance monitoring or production troubleshooting. It can provide us a tremendous amount of data, and most of the performance or memory-related problems should be possible to diagnose using this tool. The only drawback is quite a steep learning curve to get used with its user interface and all possibilities hidden here or there thorough all available options.

We should of course be cautious about the amount of information that we want to collect with this mechanism. Although the overhead of a tool is low, if you exaggerate with the amount of information collected, it will not be suitable for production use. Gathering information from several providers and several selected keywords should not be a problem. However, as we could see, gathering information about the call stack of each object allocation causes an unacceptable overhead. The simplest principle is always the best - before we run the desired set of data collected on a production environment, let's test at the any lower, pre-production environment how it affects applications and the entire system.

ProcDump, DebugDiag

When there is a need to analyze memory problems, often it occurs as late as on a production system. Then, one of the simplest possibilities is to take a memory dump of the problematic application and analyze it offline. Various tools for taking memory dump exists. I would like to mention two of them as they probably cover all the most standard needs. Both tools are installed as stand-alone tools, which may be downloaded from the following Microsoft sites:

- ProcDump - `https://docs.microsoft.com/en-us/sysinternals/downloads/procdump`

- DebugDiag - `https://blogs.msdn.microsoft.com/debugdiag/`

ProcDump is a command-line tool that allows us to take a memory dump just by a single command ad hoc:

```
procdump -ma <process_pid>
```

However, there are numerous additional options, such as taking a memory dump when memory usage or a CPU exceeds a given threshold, as well as any other given performance counter value. There is also the possibility to take a few memory dumps periodically, etc. Look at ProcDump's comprehensive command-line help for a list of all available options.

DebugDiag is a GUI-based tool that allows you to do similar things but in a more UI-oriented way. It has a slightly wider range of functionality, such as taking a dump when the response times of a given HTTP address exceeds the specified threshold. The DebugDiag Analysis tool is part of this software and is used to generate automatic reports of taken memory dumps. This allows you to quickly and easily view the report for the most obvious problems.

You can also consider using a great Minidumper tool created by Sasha Goldshtein and available at `https://github.com/goldshtn/minidumper`. It has a great capability of saving a minimal amount of memory necessary for .NET memory analysis (so excluding a lot of overhead in the form of executable and DLL files, unmanaged memory regions, and so on, and so forth). Such "mini dump" may be then analyzed as any other memory dump but may be even a few times smaller than a regular one. Therefore, it may be especially useful in making memory dumps of huge processes.

WinDbg

Among the various tools we know about in this chapter, WinDbg is undoubtedly the most low level. We can do almost everything in it: starting with debugging .NET applications, through native Windows applications, and debugging the kernel itself. Universality with a bit of rigidity is the power of this tool. It allows you to go down really deep and show things at the level of individual bits. The severity of this tool allows for a fairly quick analysis of some cases, for example, without the overhead of nice drawings presenting results of multiple analyses available in other tools. Thanks to that, from my practice, I sometimes prefer to use WinDbg rather than wait for more advanced tools to process the data in their own way.

Luckily there is a new, completely refreshed new version of WinDbg available since mid-2017. which makes the user interface slightly more pleasant and customizable.

Currently there are two ways of installing WinDbg - as a part of Windows Driver Kit (WDK) or Windows Software Development Kit (for older version) or from Windows Store (newest version). When installing SDK, you can simply deselect any components other than Debugging Tools for the Windows component, which includes WinDbg. After installation of the old edition, there will be two versions of this tool - one for 32-bit and one for 64-bit analysis. Which one we should use depends what we want to debug - whether it is a 32- or 64-bit process or memory dump. The newest edition installed from the Windows Store comes in a single, universal version (but at the time of this writing it is available only in preview version).

WinDbg can be a great tool for experiments helping to understand the .NET runtime. We can attach to our managed program and we can debug it (and the runtime itself) as we are used to from Visual Studio. But in the context of daily work, if we need to use WinDbg, we will probably use it to analyze a previously made memory dump. Hereinafter we will use the new WinDbg edition.

193

Note   WinDbg is in fact a quite simple wrapper about the DbgEng library, which is responsible for the debugging platform on Windows. Its true power in the context of .NET analysis lies within extensions made especially for .NET, listed below.

When running WinDbg, we will see a window (see Figure 3-32) in which we can perform a few different operations:

- Use any of the recent activities again - which is particularly useful when attaching to or running the same process again and again;

- Launch or attach to the process - by selecting Attach to process option, a list of all running processes will be displayed;

- Opening dump file.

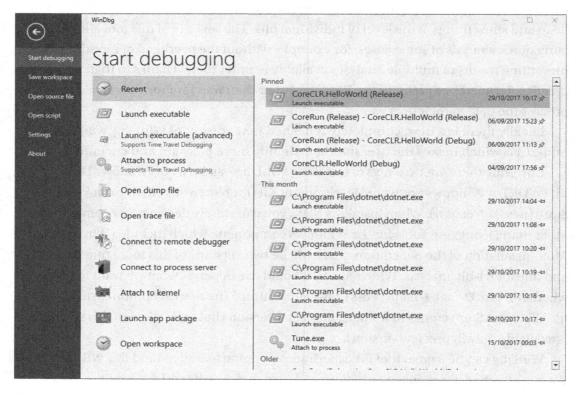

Figure 3-32. *WinDbg main window*

There are other options available like using time debugging (currently not available for managed code) or remotely connecting to another debugger, etc.

By default, WinDbg works as a native debugger so it does not understand .NET-related structures and concepts. We have to use WinDbg extensions that will provide him with such knowledge. There are many possible extensions, among which the most popular ones are:

- SOS - this is a basic, yet very powerful extension that comes with the .NET runtime itself. The name is an abbreviation of *Son of the Strike*. This is due to the fact that it is the successor of the debugging tool called Strike used during the .NET framework development.

- SOSEX - this is an extension of SOS (hence its name), which can be freely downloaded from its author, Steve Johnson's page: `http://www.stevestechspot.com/default.aspx`. It adds more powerful functionality when it comes to debug managed code and memory dumps.

- NetExt (from Rodney Viana, available at `https://github.com/rodneyviana/netext`) and MEX (Managed-code Debugging Extension, available at `https://www.microsoft.com/en-us/download/details.aspx?id=53304`) - yet two other extensions that allow us to do more sophisticated things than the two above.

To load an extension, we should use `.load <path to file>` command., for example, `.load g:\Tools\Sosex\64bit\sosex.dll`. In case of .NET built in SOS, you can also manually type an `sos.dll` extension path like that. Or you can use the convenient `.loadby` method, which allows you to locate path according to the second argument location. This means you can load `sos.dll` from the same path where `clr.dll` (main .NET runtime library) is located:

```
> .loadby sos clr
```

You can check whether this command succeeded by issuing the `!sos.help` command that prints all commands available in SOS. Just as a quick look, you can also check the `!threads` command. To load another two extensions, just use `!load <path to sosex.dll>` and for netext or mex accordingly. Remember to use the x86 or x64 version depending on which version your target application or memory dump is using. Then you can view the available commands using the `!sosex.help` and `!netext.help` commands.

There is yet another one helpful tool that can be used with WinDbg - command tree windows. As it is quite cumbersome to type all the commands again and again, you can create a file with a structured list of available commands. Then by using the `.cmdtree` `<file>` command, you can create dedicated windows with all those commands available just by simple clicking.

Note   It is also possible to take the memory dump of an operating system kernel itself by connecting to a remote machine or by analyzing the system crash dump. We will not need that for our purposes, but just keep in mind how powerful WinDbg is.

Additionally, to WinDbg, you may consider using the msos tool created by Sasha Goldshtein and available at `https://github.com/goldshtn/msos`, described as a "command-line environment a-la WinDbg for executing SOS commands without having SOS available." We can think of it as a command-line wrapper around SOS functionalities, without a need for installing WinDbg and searching for proper SOS extensions. Besides that, it adds some additional features like interpreting arbitrary dynamic queries over heap objects and classes.

Disassemblers and Decompilers

Although not directly related to the topic of memory management, sometimes it may be useful to understand the fragment of not your application – the one we only have in the binary version. As we will soon see, .NET binary code is fairly transparent. There are tools that let you see the code of other programs in a convenient way. One of the best, which I will use, is the free and open source dnSpy tool created on GitHub by the 0xd4d user and available at `https://github.com/0xd4d/dnSpy`. It is not only a tool that allows us to see code but we can also debug it and modify it. We will use it to show both the .NET standard library code itself and the programs compiled for that framework.

There are others popular tools like ILSpy, JetBrains dotPeek, and Redgate .NET Reflector, but dnSpy will be particularly useful due to the editing capabilities and will be just enough for our purposes.

BenchmarkDotNet

We often need to measure the performance of certain pieces of code. This will be particularly useful in this book because we will compare the effects of different optimization techniques. It would be ideal if with the measurement of the performance of the code itself (its execution time), it was possible to measure also the amount of memory needed.

The BenchmarkDotNet library is exactly that and even more powerful. With it we can test the performance of each method. We can conveniently compare their performance with each other, for example, with respect to various parameters. We can test against various .NET versions, JIT and GC configurations, and so on, and so forth.

What's more, this library takes care of avoiding any mistakes we might make ourselves, by writing similar micro-benchmarks. It has well-thought out stages of each test, such as warming up or cooling. Tests are carried out in many iterations. All measurements are processed statistically. Percentiles are calculated and multimodal distribution of data is also being detected (including visually presenting a simplified histogram). As a result, we get a powerful yet very easy-to-use tool.

The preparation of a simple test is illustrated in Listing 3-9. It really comes down to the attributes of the class and method we are interested in. As previously mentioned, we can also test with respect to some additional parameters provided (like N in our example benchmark).

Listing 3-9. Example of BenchmarkDotNet test

```
[BenchmarkDotNet.Attributes.Jobs.ShortRunJob]
[MemoryDiagnoser]
public class TailCallTest
{
    [Params(5, 10, 20)]
    public int N { get; set; }
    [Benchmark]
    public long FibonacciRecursive()
    {
        return FibonacciRecursiveHelper(N);
    }
}
```

```
private long FibonacciRecursiveHelper(long n)
{
    if (n < 3)
        return 1;
    return FibonacciRecursiveHelper(n - 2) + FibonacciRecursiveHelper
    (n - 1);
}
}
```

Execution of the test presented in Listing 3-9 is as simple as calling BenchmarkRunner. Run<TailCallTest>() in our program. The result of this test (see Figure 3-33) shows the average execution time of each method for each parameter and for two different JIT (Just In Time) compilers, resulting in rich statistical data about the results.

```
C:\WINDOWS\system32\cmd.exe                                                       —  □  ×

TailCallTest.FibonacciRecursive: RyuJitX64(Jit=RyuJit, Platform=X64) [N=20]
Runtime = .NET Framework 4.7.1 (CLR 4.0.30319.42000), 64bit RyuJIT-v4.7.2650.0; GC = Concurrent Workstation
Mean = 26.0061 us, StdErr = 0.0101 us (0.04%); N = 15, StdDev = 0.0393 us
Min = 25.9578 us, Q1 = 25.9718 us, Median = 25.9977 us, Q3 = 26.0399 us, Max = 26.0894 us
IQR = 0.0681 us, LowerFence = 25.8696 us, UpperFence = 26.1421 us
ConfidenceInterval = [25.9640 us; 26.0481 us] (CI 99.9%), Margin = 0.0420 us (0.16% of Mean)
Skewness = 0.59, Kurtosis = 2.05, MValue = 2
-------------------- Histogram --------------------
[25.944 us ; 26.103 us) | @@@@@@@@@@@@@@@
---------------------------------------------------


Total time: 00:01:55 (115.4 sec)

// * Summary *

BenchmarkDotNet=v0.10.14, OS=Windows 10.0.16299.431 (1709/FallCreatorsUpdate/Redstone3)
Intel Core i7-4770K CPU 3.50GHz (Haswell), 1 CPU, 8 logical and 4 physical cores
Frequency=3410069 Hz, Resolution=293.2492 ns, Timer=TSC
  [Host]      : .NET Framework 4.7.1 (CLR 4.0.30319.42000), 64bit RyuJIT-v4.7.2650.0
  LegacyJitX64 : .NET Framework 4.7.1 (CLR 4.0.30319.42000), 64bit LegacyJIT/clrjit-v4.7.2650.0;compatjit-v4.7.2650.0
  RyuJitX64   : .NET Framework 4.7.1 (CLR 4.0.30319.42000), 64bit RyuJIT-v4.7.2650.0

Platform=X64  Runtime=Clr

            Method |          Job |       Jit | N |        Mean |      Error |      StdDev | Allocated |
------------------ |------------- |---------- |---|-------------:|-----------:|------------:|----------:|
FibonacciRecursive | LegacyJitX64 | LegacyJit | 5 |    14.34 ns |  0.0685 ns |   0.0641 ns |       0 B |
FibonacciRecursive |    RyuJitX64 |    RyuJit | 5 |    17.16 ns |  0.0472 ns |   0.0441 ns |       0 B |
FibonacciRecursive | LegacyJitX64 | LegacyJit | 10 |   150.48 ns |  0.5388 ns |   0.5040 ns |       0 B |
FibonacciRecursive |    RyuJitX64 |    RyuJit | 10 |   206.75 ns |  1.2223 ns |   1.1433 ns |       0 B |
FibonacciRecursive | LegacyJitX64 | LegacyJit | 20 | 18,696.92 ns | 13.4930 ns |  11.2673 ns |       0 B |
FibonacciRecursive |    RyuJitX64 |    RyuJit | 20 | 26,006.05 ns | 42.0062 ns |  39.2926 ns |       0 B |
```

Figure 3-33. *Results of example BenchmarkDotNet test*

You can also extend the library by additional loggers, analyzers, diagnosers, and so on. Two are especially interesting for us. GC and Memory Allocation Diagnoser (MemoryDiagnoser) analyze how many garbage collections occurred and how many allocations have been made during the test. There is also the Hardware Counters Diagnoser (`HardwareCounters`), which is available only on Windows and can provide us deep insight into hardware-related statistics like CPU cache misses.

Commercial Tools

The tools discussed so far are all free. Although they offer powerful capabilities, sometimes their use is quite cumbersome. On the other hand, commercial programs are from the very beginning written for a pleasant user interface in mind. Below you will find a short list of possible tools to use. I cannot assure you that this list is complete. From the time of writing a book to its publication, many things may change. The tools I'm referring to have simply been used while working on the book and my own many years of experience.

Your mileage may vary when using those tools. I encourage you to try each of them during and after reading this book. You will decide which one suits you the most. They are very convenient to use, especially in the hands of an expert who understands the topic pretty well (which I hope you will become after reading this book).

There is no point in concentrating in this book for only one of those tools (which one should I choose then?). Instead, I put much more effort on free, open source alternatives.

Visual Studio

It is hard to imagine a .NET developer who has never used Visual Studio. It really is a powerful and robust programming tool. In addition to commonly known functionalities, it also provides options for monitoring and memory analysis:

- Opening memory dump files and analyzing them for the use of objects (see Figure 3-34) including statistics, individual object instances, and references between them.

- Live profiling is also possible. We are of course interested in the Memory Usage tool, but there are also CPU Usage and GPU Usage tools (see Figure 3-35). While using it we get a preview of the current memory consumption and the occurrences of GC. At any time, we can also take a snapshot that will give us insight into the statistics of managed objects.

Visual Studio does not have such extensive diagnostic options as other commercial programs listed here. However, its great advantage is undoubtedly the fact that with high probability, you already use this tool.

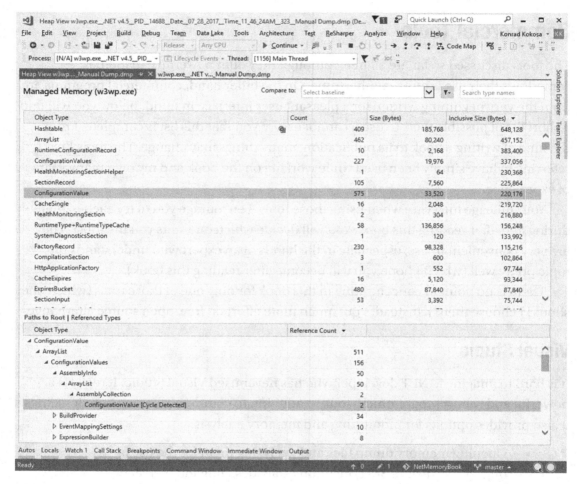

Figure 3-34. *Visual Studio snapshot view*

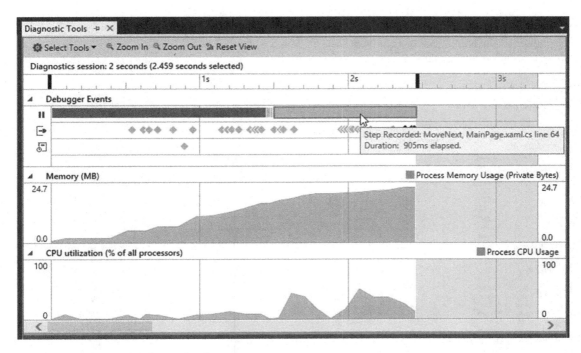

Figure 3-35. Visual Studio live view

Scitech .NET Memory Profiler

Scitech's tool is one of the available dedicated tools for analyzing .NET. It provides very powerful options for viewing the status of objects, including a breakdown by the different generations, objects' reachability, and so on. You can use it to display very complex reference graphs.

In each of the views, you can use a variety of filters, allowing you to greatly narrow down your research. As an example, we may find all interned strings (which we will know about in Chapter 4) in Generation 2 with only two clicks. The interface has been very well thought out and we will easily start working with the program. The application in many places prompts us (with the help of icons and tooltips) about possible problems and issues such as a large number of duplicate strings or a number of pinned instances. At the same time, the interface is not too simplistic, allowing for in-depth analysis of the situation with our chosen approach (see Figures 3-36 and 3-37).

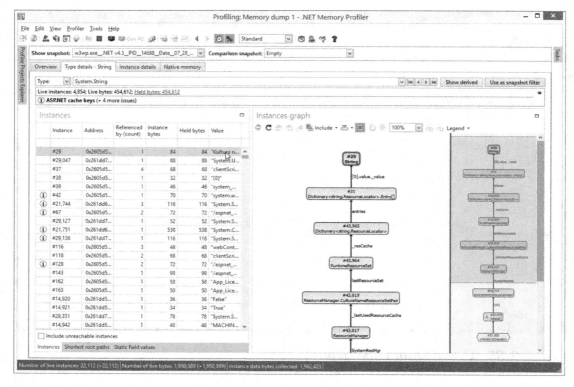

Figure 3-36. *.NET Memory Profiler snapshot view with reference graphs*

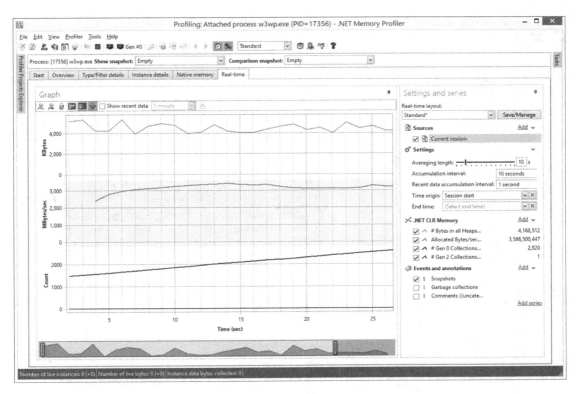

Figure 3-37. *.NET Memory Profiler snapshot live view*

With the program, we can use the .NET Memory Profiler API to study memory usage or detect memory leaks. The free command-line NmpCore program allows you to perform diagnostic sessions, including production environments. We can analyze them later in .NET Memory Profiler.

JetBrains DotMemory

JetBrains is known by a lot of people from .NET world, thanks to their ReSharper tool. However, the company also has excellent products for CPU (dotTrace) and memory (dotMemory) profiling. Of course, we are interested in the second one. dotMemory is designed for both live application profiling and also offers the possibility of memory dumps analysis. It is possible to remotely profile applications on another machine, which can be useful in environments higher than development.

Compared to the .NET Memory Profiler, the dotMemory interface is clearly simplified (which may be an advantage, though). Many possible analyses are being suggested in the interface itself, giving the results even before we ask (see Figures 3-38 and 3-39).

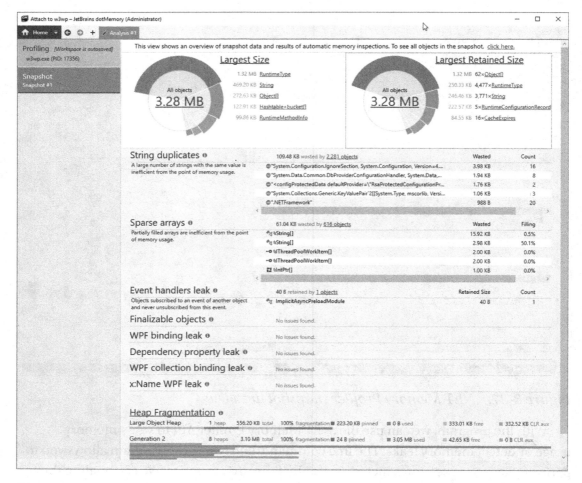

Figure 3-38. *JetBrains DotMemory snapshot view with reference graphs*

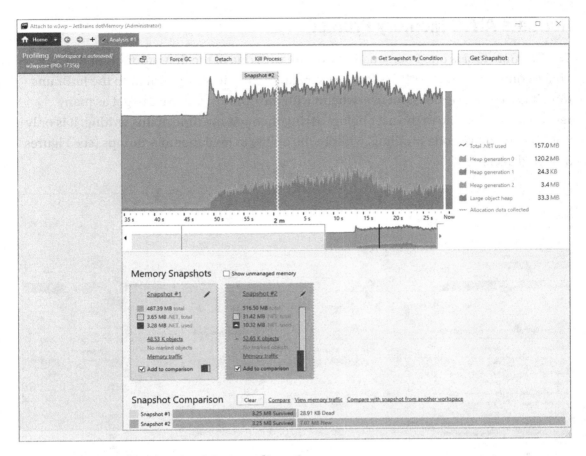

Figure 3-39. *JetBrains DotMemory live view*

DotMemory provides some interesting visualizations, including heap fragmentation. We will also quickly learn what objects have the largest retained size.

It is also worth mentioning two neighboring tools. The dotMemory Unit allows you to perform unit tests that take into account memory consumption. It can be included in Visual Studio as a part of unit testing framework or into your Continuous Integration process. The second tool is a Heap Allocations Viewer extension to the above-mentioned ReSharper Visual Studio extension. It supports static analysis of our code with respect to unwanted hidden allocations (we will talk about them in Chapter 5).

205

RedGate ANTS Memory Profiler

The RedGate tool is one I personally associate with one of the first products of this type I have come in contact with. As for the user experience, it is very similar to the JetBrains tool. It is easy to use, does not overwhelm with the options, and tries to get as many responses as possible to the user before asking them. At the time of this writing, it is only possible to do live code profiling, without the ability to load memory dumps (see Figures 3-40 and 3-41).

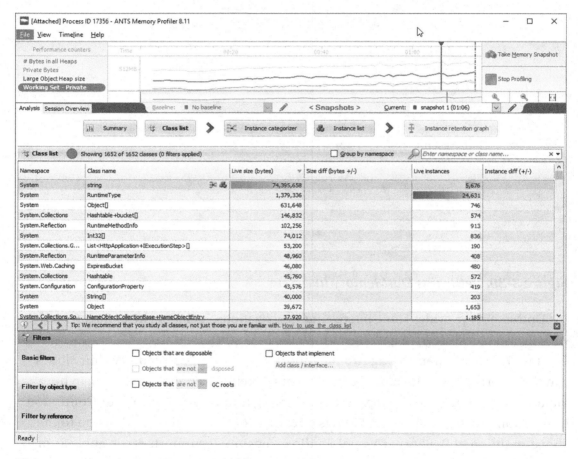

Figure 3-40. *ANTS Memory Profiler snapshot view*

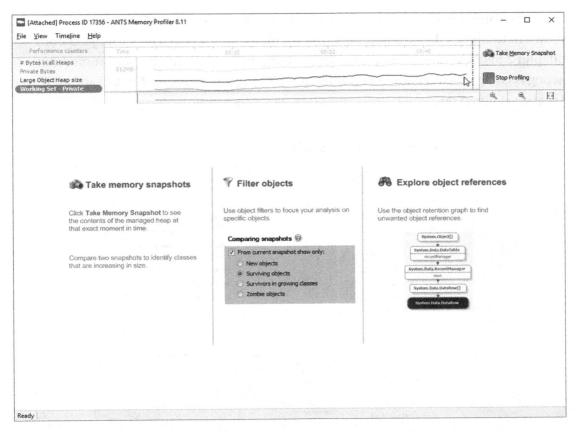

Figure 3-41. ANTS Memory Profiler live view

Intel VTune Amplifier and AMD CodeAnalyst Performance Analyzer

Beyond the typical code and memory profilers, there are tools dedicated for low-level hardware-based profiling of your code usually provided by the processor manufacturers. Two main options mentioned in the title are provided by AMD and Intel as commercial, paid tools. They offer a much deeper analysis beyond the classical profiling of the code that states which methods perform the longest. We can get information from hardware counters built into hardware (processor, graphics card) about its internal behavior - cache and memory utilization, pipeline stalls, and many more.

In the everyday work of the .NET developer we are rather not interested in going into such details. However, they may be very useful when fine-tuning your application, especially when we consider optimizing hot paths and tight loops executed millions of times.

In fact, only such low-level tools can point us clearly to problems like False Sharing shown in Chapter 2. Let's look at the results of the sample analysis for Listing 2-6 from Chapter 2 made in Intel VTune Amplifier (see Figure 3-42). It clearly states something wrong is going on - our code is highly memory bound and there are 100% Contested Accesses pointed out.

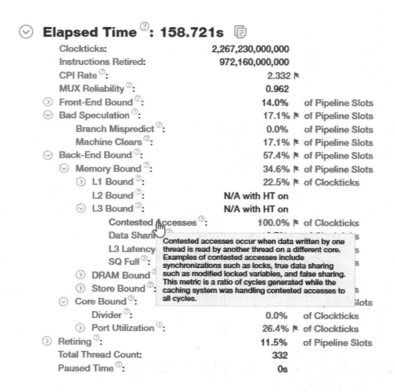

Figure 3-42. *Example results from Intel VTune Amplifier - summary view*

Because such tools track hardware counters on the lowest level, we can even figure out statistics per single line of program to find out the precise roots of the problems. In case of the program from Listing 2-6, such an analysis indeed points out to the source of contested access. Obviously, because underneath the .NET application, it is executed as native code (thanks to the JIT compiler explained in Chapter 4), VTune points us to concrete lines of JITted assembly code. With a good understanding of the JIT and Intel's assembly code in general, we can match those lines to concrete lines of our .NET code. For example, in case of our results, there are two problematic lines in particular (see Figure 3-43):

- Checking the size of the array (first highlighted line),

- Accessing old counter data (second highlighted line).

Address	Assembly	Clockticks	Locators			
			Back-End Bound			
			Memory Bound			
			L3 Bound			
			Contested Accesses	Data S...	L3 L...	SQ F...
0x7ff8cff94f36	Block 1:					
0x7ff8cff94f36	mov rdx, 0x1ffd91f2830	840,000,000	0.0%	0.0%	0.0%	0.0%
0x7ff8cff94f40	mov rdx, qword ptr [rdx]	1,610,000,000	0.0%	0.0%	0.0%	0.0%
0x7ff8cff94f43	mov rcx, rdx	6,930,000,000	0.0%	0.0%	0.0%	0.0%
0x7ff8cff94f46	mov r8d, dword ptr [rdx+0x8]	2,345,000,000		1.9%	34.6%	0.0%
0x7ff8cff94f4a	cmp esi, r8d	152,320,000, ...	0.0%	0.0%	0.0%	0.0%
0x7ff8cff94f4d	jnb 0x7ff8cff94f6a					
0x7ff8cff94f4f	Block 2:					
0x7ff8cff94f4f	mov edx, dword ptr [rdx+rax*4+0x10]	2,555,000,000		2.9%	0.0%	0.0%
0x7ff8cff94f53	inc edx	60,585,000,0 ...	0.0%	0.0%	0.0%	0.0%
0x7ff8cff94f55	mov dword ptr [rcx+rax*4+0x10], edx	5,950,000,000	0.0%	0.0%	0.0%	0.0%
0x7ff8cff94f59	inc edi	4,865,000,000	0.0%	0.0%	0.0%	0.0%
0x7ff8cff94f5b	cmp edi, 0x5f5e100	1,750,000,000	0.0%	0.0%	0.0%	0.0%
0x7ff8cff94f61	jl 0x7ff8cff94f36 <Block 1>	0	0.0%	0.0%	0.0%	0.0%

Figure 3-43. *Example results from Intel VTune Amplifier - assembly code view*

Therefore, obviously usage of such tools requires quite low-level knowledge about hardware used, the .NET runtime, and even the assembly language. It is also worth noticing that both tools are available for Windows and Linux.

Dynatrace and AppDynamics

Beyond many tools dedicated solely to .NET memory management, there are a bunch of higher-level tools for application performance monitoring in general. They provide a great insight into the application and are particularly well suited for production or pre-production environments. Because memory management is an important aspect of .NET applications, the tools that support this platform also provide convenient insight into the application memory usage.

Such so-called *Application Performance Management* (APM) tools from the two leading vendors listed in the title are excellent examples of this approach. Continuous monitoring of applications for problems and its impact on the end user is even more valuable than even the most sophisticated tools that work only on the local developer's computer. There is simply no confrontation with the reality and real traffic generated by users.

Linux Environment

Ideally, everything that was mentioned in the previous section should now be repeated in the context of the Linux operating system. However, the truth is that .NET on Linux is still very fresh in 2018. Initial production deployments are just beginning to emerge. Consequently, development on this platform is only beginning to show up. Because it is such a fresh field, there is a huge difference in knowledge and good practices establishment compared to the Windows environment. In Windows, many different tools are available, as we have seen: both free and commercial ones. In the case of Linux, the choice is virtually unremarkable. There are no standard procedures or even real experienced experts in the field. We are moving onto unspoiled terrain.

Overview

Linux rises up and develops as an extraordinary creation of countless contributors from the open source community. It was not designed and implemented by one company from the very beginning, as is the case with the Windows operating system. It is not surprising that there is a lack of strict standardization in some fields. One such aspect is monitoring and tracking applications that we are particularly interested in. There are many mechanisms available; some of them are slowly losing popularity, and others are just beginning to gain it. In this context, monitoring infrastructure in Linux becomes less homogeneous than in a Windows environment.

There is no widely accepted diagnostic tracing standard used in all distributions and the kernel of the system. When moving CoreCLR to the Linux environment, decisions must be made what mechanism will be used. It is being well documented in CoreCLR documentation at `https://github.com/dotnet/coreclr/blob/master/Documentation/coding-guidelines/cross-platform-performance-and-eventing.md`. For example, there were other mechanisms considered like SystemTap, DTrace4Linux, FTrace, and Extended Berkeley Packet Filter (eBPF).

Currently the following mechanisms are used on the different levels:

- .NET application - as in case of Windows, we can use EventSource library or obviously, any other library to log directly into the files and many other possible targets,

- .NET Core runtime - emits *LTTng* ("*Linux Tracing Toolkit Next Generation*") events,

- Operating system API and kernel itself - emits so-called *perf_events* data.

In the end, to have a good overview of the CoreCLR process on Linux, a combination of two mechanisms should be used:

- perf_events - it provides various data based on both hardware and software (including OS libraries and the kernel itself). This includes system-wide measurements like CPU sampling, context switches, memory usage.

- LTTng - event tracing on user mode side but with kernel-size modules and buffers. It provides strongly typed events and as such is very similar to the Event Tracing for Windows (ETW). Unfortunately, by default it does not support tracking stack traces (program has been recompiled to enable or disable them, which is not applicable for a general-purpose framework like CoreCLR). The same event names are used here as in the case of ETW events on Windows.

While perf_events is system-wide, the LTTng mechanism can be hooked up to individual processes.

Please find Table 3-3 that can help to understand the similarities and differences between the tracking mechanisms in Windows and Linux.

Table 3-3. *Tracking Mechanisms Comparison Between Linux and Windows*

Aspect	Windows	Linux
Static tracing		
Kernel-mode	ETW Kernel Logger	perf_events, BCC
User-mode	ETW ProvidersPerformance Counters	LTTng
Definition	ETW manifest	LTTng tracepoint definition
System-wide	Yes	No
Dynamic tracing		
	Not available	perf_events
		SystemTrap
		BCC

The most noticeable difference is the lack of a dynamic tracing mechanism in Windows. By dynamic tracing, we mean that you can enable or disable single-function call tracking in an application while it is running.

Perfcollect

The easiest way of getting tracing data is by using the official `perfcollect` bash script and then using Perfview on Windows to analyze this recorded data. This approach has some drawbacks. The main one is fairly limited analysis results available in PerfView - there is just a raw list of events available. The second, less burdensome one, is the need for Windows to... analyze Linux data.

To start monitoring your .NET Core application, follow official CoreCLR instructions at `https://github.com/dotnet/coreclr/blob/master/Documentation/project-docs/linux-performance-tracing.md`. It is not complicated. You should get `perfcollect` script from CoreCLR Github repository at `http://aka.ms/perfcollect`. Then you only need to execute `sudo ./perfcollect install,` which will install perf_event and LLTng tools on your Linux machine. Then, to start a tracing session you need to export two environment variables (the first enables generation of so-called *decoding maps*, needed to decode symbols from recorded traces, which will be stored in `/tmp/perf-PID.map`) as shown in Listing 3-10.

Listing 3-10. Setting environment variables needed for CoreCLR monitoring

```
> export COMPlus_PerfMapEnabled=1
> export COMPlus_EnableEventLog=1
> sudo ./perfcollect collect sampleTrace [-pid <PID>] [-threadtime]
```

After stopping the session, it will result in a ZIP file containing registered data. What exactly does the `perfcollect` script do? In short, it manages sessions and prepares the resulting file:

- It configures the LTTng session:

    - with the context consisting of procname, vpid (process ID), and vtid (thread ID)

    - with by default all events added from the groups `DotNetRuntime:*` and `DotNetRuntimePrivate:*` (a detailed list and available settings we can see in the script itself)

- It starts the LTTng session

- It starts the perf session to take CPU samples each 1 ms (at 999 Hz frequency)

- It prepares result the ZIP file with all necessary data:

    - `lttngTrace` subfolder contains recorded LTTng traces

    - main folder contains:

        – all `perf.map` files created during session

        – all symbol files generated for native images (AOT/NGEN) with the help of `crossgen` tool

        – all perf data and related logs

    - `debuginfo` subfolder - contains debuginfo (symbol files) for all other modules

After recording a session, we can also view it using the `perfcollect` script (see Listing 3-11).

Listing 3-11. Viewing perfcollect data

```
> sudo ./perfcollect view <tracefile>
> sudo ./perfcollect view <tracefile> -viewer lttng
```

The first command displays perf data as a call tree, and the second is just a textual listing of all LTTng events without any interpretation.

You can, of course, manually manage LTTng session (so what is scripted in `perfcollect`), to have better control over a created session and recorded events (see Listing 3-12).

Listing 3-12. Manually managing LTTng session

```
> lltng create sample_trace
> lltng add-context --userspace --type procname     // or vpid, vtid
> lltng enable-event --userspace --tracepoint DotNetRuntime:Exception*
> lltng enable-event --userspace --tracepoint DotNetRuntime:GC*
> lltng start
> lltng stop
> lltng destroy
```

Similarly, you can manually manage perf_events to create perf session (see Listing 3-13).

Listing 3-13. Manually managing perf session

```
> perf record -g -F 999 --pid=<PID> -e cpu-clock
```

This will start a session with call-graph recording (`-g` option) and sample at 999 Hz frequency, which in fact means each 1 ms (`-F 999` option).

Trace Compass

As this tool main page says: "Eclipse Trace Compass is an open source application for viewing and analyzing any type of logs or traces. Its goal is to provide views, graphs, metrics, and more to help extract useful information from traces, in a way that is more user-friendly and informative than huge text dumps."

Among the various supported formats, the most important for us is *CTF* format (*Common Trace Format*), in which events are generated by an LTTng mechanism used by CoreCLR. Trace Compass looks like a mix of PerfView and Windows Performance Analyzer tools - if you had contact with them, you might guess what I mean. It is powerful and allows us to make great things. But unfortunately, like the two mentioned programs, it has a very steep learning curve. Extensive configuration options make it hard to know where to start when you run it for the first time. If you are not interested in Linux diagnostics or if you just do not want to spend time to read a rather detailed description of Trace Compass adaptation to our needs, feel free to omit the rest of this subchapter for now.

Opening File

Assuming you get a `perfcollect` recording, please unzip it to some folder. The LTTng data we're interested in are in the `lttngTrace` subfolder, more specifically in the path that follows the schema `lttngTrace\auto-20170801-103533\ust\uid\1000\64-bit`. To open it in Trace Compass, select File ➤ Open Trace... and select metadata file. The default view we will see (see Figure 3-44) includes two main views: a list of all events (a "64-bit" bookmark for a sample file), and a histogram of event instances over time.

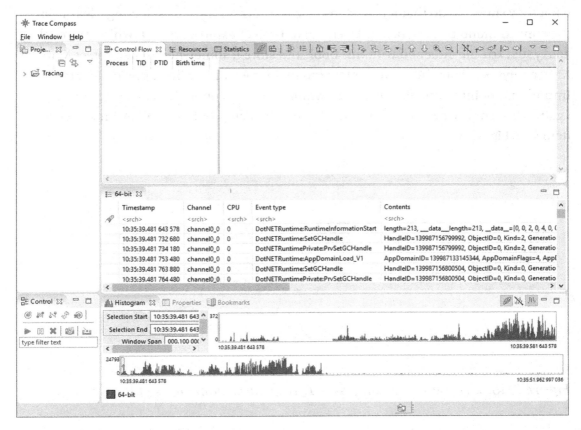

Figure 3-44. *Eclipse Trace Compass - The default view of LTTng trace*

We can take a moment to look at the events tab, where as you can see, along with each event there are also accompanying fields (including the generic `context._vpid` and `context._vtid`, respectively the process ID and the thread ID from which the event was generated). You can search and filter that view by manipulating the first row. On the other hand, the histogram can only help us to figure out the number of events in time and in that sense is not very helpful. We can close it, like other tabs: Control, Control Flow, Resources, Properties, and Bookmarks. After that we should end up only with Project Explorer, Statistics, and tracing tabs. Such a view, however, is not particularly useful, and this is where the complex customization process begins.

For this moment we will just open a file containing the ready-made analyses prepared for this book, and then one by one I will explain how they were created and what they show. To do that it is best to close the current trace by selecting Clear from the context menu under Tracing ➤ Traces in Project Explorer tab. Download `coreclr_analyses.xml` file attached with this book and store it somewhere. Then select Manage XML analyses... from the same context menu. In the window that appears, select Import and point to the file you just downloaded. Then open the same trace once again. Three new views should be visible under Tracing ➤ Traces ➤ 64-bit ➤ Views item (see Figure 3-45).

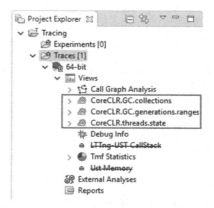

Figure 3-45. *Eclipse Trace Compass - Three new custom views of LTTng trace*

By expanding any of the new custom views, you will see additional possible views. You can double-click any of them to add it to the main view.

All these views are based on the Trace Compass feature called *Data driven analysis* http://archive.eclipse.org/tracecompass/doc/stable/org.eclipse. tracecompass.doc.user/Data-driven-analysis.html#Data_driven_analysis. It allows us to specify an interpretation of events sequences in a various way by providing dedicated XML files.

CoreCLR.GC.collections

Let's start from the simplest custom view. It is based on a simple pattern, matching Garbage Collection start and end events. Each such pair of starting and closing events generates a so-called "segment" in Trace Compass nomenclature, which is understood simply as a time interval with a name and possible attributes. Such analysis in Trace Compass is carried out with Finite State Machine (FSM) describing transitions of our interest (reactions to subsequent events) and related actions. Listing 3-14 shows a brief structure of such analysis (for simplicity I've removed the part matching the start and end of the same GC).

Listing 3-14. Fragments of CoreCLR.GC.collections custom analysis for Trace Compass

```xml
<pattern version="0" id="CoreCLR.GC.state">
    ...
    <patternHandler initial="gcsegments">
        <action id="gc_starting">
            <stateChange>
                <stateAttribute type="constant"
                value="#CurrentScenario" />
                <stateAttribute type="constant" value="Generation" />
                <stateValue type="eventField" value="Depth"/>
            </stateChange>
        </action>
        <action id="gc_ending">
            <segment>
                <segType>
                    <segName>
                        <stateValue type="query">
                            <stateAttribute type="constant"
                            value="#CurrentScenario" />
                            <stateAttribute type="constant"
                            value="Generation" />
                        </stateValue>
                    </segName>
                </segType>
```

```
            &lt;/segment&gt;
        </action>
        <fsm id="gcsegments" initial="state_before_gc">
            <state id="state_before_gc">
                <transition event="DotNETRuntime:GCStart_V2"
                target="state_during_gc" action="gc_starting"
                saveStoredFields="true" />
            </state>
            <state id="state_during_gc">
                <transition event="DotNETRuntime:GCEnd_V1"
                target="state_after_gc" action="gc_ending"
                cond="count_condition" saveStoredFields="true"
                clearStoredFields="true" />
            </state>
            <final id="state_after_gc" />
        </fsm>
    </patternHandler>
</pattern>
```

The name of each segment corresponds to the generation on which the GC was made (section segName in the above description). Therefore, views generated by this analysis include a list of all Garbage Collections per generation and their statistics (see Figures 3-46 and 3-47) - segment duration is being called latency.

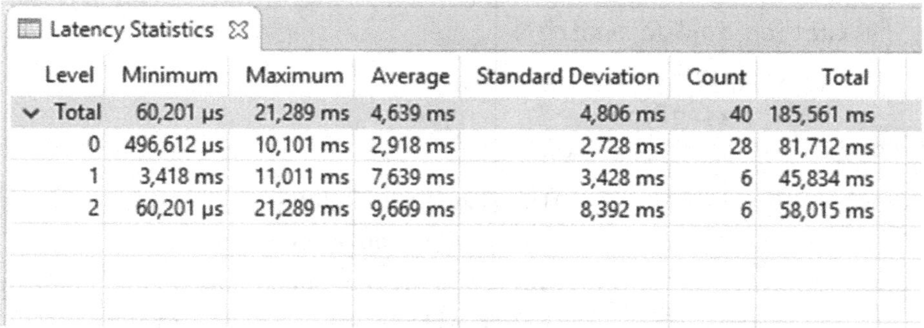

Latency Statistics

Level	Minimum	Maximum	Average	Standard Deviation	Count	Total
Total	60,201 µs	21,289 ms	4,639 ms	4,806 ms	40	185,561 ms
0	496,612 µs	10,101 ms	2,918 ms	2,728 ms	28	81,712 ms
1	3,418 ms	11,011 ms	7,639 ms	3,428 ms	6	45,834 ms
2	60,201 µs	21,289 ms	9,669 ms	8,392 ms	6	58,015 ms

Figure 3-46. *Eclipse Trace Compass - Statistics of all GCs during recorded trace - level indicates generation*

Latency Table ⊠				
Start Time	End Time	Duration	Name	Content
10:35:40.120 103 098	10:35:40.123 171 168	3 068 070	0	Type= 0, Reason= 0
10:35:40.232 678 765	10:35:40.241 342 762	8 663 997	1	Type= 0, Reason= 0
10:35:40.343 713 296	10:35:40.349 695 932	5 982 636	0	Type= 0, Reason= 0
10:35:40.680 964 283	10:35:40.688 450 054	7 485 771	0	Type= 0, Reason= 0
10:35:40.821 197 380	10:35:40.834 291 678	13 094 298	2	Type= 0, Reason= 0
10:35:40.919 630 424	10:35:40.921 618 469	1 988 045	0	Type= 0, Reason= 0
10:35:41.067 927 596	10:35:41.069 829 839	1 902 243	0	Type= 0, Reason= 0
10:35:41.985 780 706	10:35:41.990 064 403	4 283 697	0	Type= 0, Reason= 0
10:35:42.121 457 668	10:35:42.132 468 816	11 011 148	1	Type= 0, Reason= 0
10:35:42.273 567 798	10:35:42.283 668 626	10 100 828	0	Type= 0, Reason= 0
10:35:42.729 402 778	10:35:42.739 048 095	9 645 317	0	Type= 0, Reason= 0
10:35:42.862 408 377	10:35:42.883 697 457	21 289 080	2	Type= 0, Reason= 0
10:35:42 962 751 540	10:35:42 963 678 061	926 521	0	Type= 0 Reason= 0

Figure 3-47. Eclipse Trace Compass - List of all GCs during recorded trace - including additional parameters like Type and Reason

It means that in our sample trace, there were, for example, six GC on 2 generations and they took almost 10 ms in average. Type and Reason are additional recorded fields that come from GCStart_V2 event (not yet documented but those fields are also present in GCStart_V1 event (see https://docs.microsoft.com/en-us/dotnet/framework/performance/garbage-collection-etw-events#gcstartv1-event for details).

CoreCLR.threads.state

This is by far the most complex custom view made by me so far. It utilizes yet another powerful Trace Compass feature to create Gantt-like diagrams of XML-based data-driven analyses. You can open it by double-clicking CoreCLR.threads.state.view under CoreCLR.threads.state view. Just to show an overview of the underlying FSM, the beginning of its definition is presented in Listing 3-15.

Listing 3-15. Fragments of CoreCLR.threads.state custom analysis for Trace Compass.

```
<patternHandler initial="thread">
    <test id="thread_condition">
        <if>
```

```
        <condition>
            <stateValue type="eventField" value="context._vtid"/>
            <stateValue type="query">
                <stateAttribute type="constant"
                value="#CurrentScenario" />
                <stateAttribute type="constant" value="ThreadId" />
            </stateValue>
        </condition>
    </if>
</test>
...
<action id="on_thread_restarting_begin">
    <stateChange>
        <stateAttribute type="constant" value="#CurrentScenario" />
        <stateAttribute type="constant" value="Status" />
        <stateValue type="int" value="11"/>
    </stateChange>
</action>
...
<fsm id="thread" initial="state_before_thread" consuming="false">
    <state id="state_before_thread">
        <transition event="DotNETRuntime:ThreadCreated"
        target="state_normal_thread" action="on_thread_starting" />
    </state>
    <state id="state_normal_thread">
        <transition event="DotNETRuntime:ThreadTerminated"
        target="state_dead_thread" action="on_thread_ending"
        cond="thread_condition" />
        <transition event="DotNETRuntime:GCSuspendEEBegin_V1"
        target="state_suspending_thread" action="on_thread_suspending_
        begin" />
        <transition event="DotNETRuntimePrivate:BGCBegin"
        target="state_during_bgc_nonconcurrent" action="on_bgc_
        starting_nonconcurrent" cond="thread_condition" />
    </state>
    <state id="state_during_gc">
```

```
        <transition event="DotNETRuntime:GCEnd_V1" target="state_normal_
        thread" action="on_gc_ending" cond="gc_thread_condition" />
        <transition event="DotNETRuntimePrivate:BGCBegin"
        target="state_during_gc" action="on_bgc_starting_global"  />
    </state>
    ...
</patternHandler>
```

Such a fairly complex state machine responds to individual CoreCLR (mostly GC-related) events changing the state of one of the so-called "scenarios." In this case, scenario corresponds to s single thread, thanks to the `thread_condition` condition. In other words, the event most often changes the state of only one selected thread, assigned to a given scenario. This is not the case for some events like `GCSuspendEEBegin_V1`, which are impacting all current managed threads. The actions associated with each of these events (reactions) primarily change the `Status` field of a given scenario, which is simply a numerical value. Interpreted later by the `timeGraphView` component, as shown below in Listing 3-16.

Listing 3-16. Definition of timeGraphView showing CoreCLR.threads.state analysis results

```
<timeGraphView id="CoreCLR.threads.state.view">
    <head>
        <analysis id="CoreCLR.threads.state" />
        <label value="CoreCLR.threads.state.view" />
    </head>

    <definedValue name="USER THREAD" value="0" color="#CCCCCC"/>
    <definedValue name="GC THREAD" value="1" color="#D6F0FF"/>
    <definedValue name="FINALIZER THREAD" value="2" color="#118811"/>
    <definedValue name="THREADPOOL THREAD" value="4" color="#A0A0A0"/>
    <definedValue name="GCWORK" value="8" color="#0000FF"/>
    <definedValue name="SUSPENDING" value="9" color="#8C5656"/>
    <definedValue name="RESTARTING" value="11" color="#758C56"/>
    <definedValue name="GCPREPARE" value="12" color="#A38A8A"/>
    <definedValue name="BGCWORK NONCONCURRENT" value="16"
    color="#00A4FC"/>
```

```
<definedValue name="BGCWORK CONCURRENT" value="17"
color="#000099"/>

<entry path="scenarios/*">
    <display type="self" />
    <name type="self" />
    <entry path="*">
        <display type="constant" value="Status" />
        <name type="constant" value="ThreadId" />
    </entry>
</entry>
</timeGraphView>
```

This component visualizes each of the scenarios in a separate line, which gives us a separate line for each thread, colored according to the current state of the thread and name according to its ThreadID. This allows for a nice view of the application state (see Figure 3-48). And in particular, after zooming in, it shows us nice details of a single GC run (see Figure 3-49).

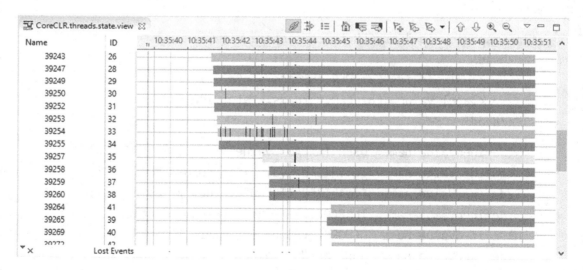

Figure 3-48. *Eclipse Trace Compass - Threads overall view*

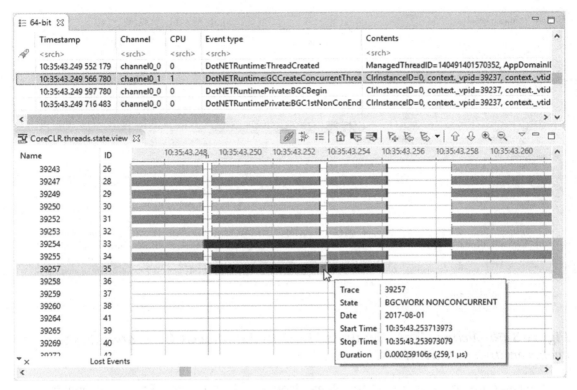

Figure 3-49. *Eclipse Trace Compass - Single background GC, creating concurrent GC thread*

In the above examples, we see details of a single generation 2 garbage collection run that triggered creation of the GC thread for non-concurrent parts of background GC (all those details are thoroughly explained in Chapter 11).

CoreCLR.GC.generations.ranges

The last option is to create so-called *XY graphs* (see http://archive.eclipse.org/ tracecompass/doc/stable/org.eclipse.tracecompass.doc.user/Data-driven- analysis.html#Defining_an_XML_XY_chart for details) based on data provided by events. Of course, it is especially tempting to visualize all kinds of measurable metrics such as size of generations and the like. There is one event especially useful here - GCGenerationRange, generated for each generation at the end of each GC run (see Figure 3-50).

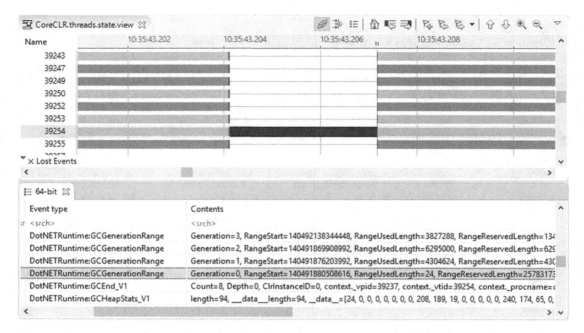

Figure 3-50. *Eclipse Trace Compass - DotNETRuntime:GCGenerationRange events emitted at the end of GC run*

We can consume its Generation, RangeUsedLength, and RangeReservedLength fields to visualize generations' sizes. Such analysis is based on a simpler mechanism and does not require creating s separate FSM. It is just event handler reacting on a particular event (see Listing 3-17).

Listing 3-17. Definition of CoreCLR.GC.generations.ranges custom analysis for Trace Compass and its corresponding view

```
<stateProvider version="0" id="CoreCLR.GC.statistics">
   <head>
      <traceType id="org.eclipse.linuxtools.lttng2.ust.tracetype" />
      <label value="CoreCLR.GC.generations.ranges" />
   </head>
   <eventHandler eventName="DotNETRuntime:GCGenerationRange">
      <stateChange>
         <stateAttribute type="constant" value="Generations" />
         <stateAttribute type="eventField" value="Generation" />
```

```
            <stateValue type="eventField" value="RangeUsedLength"
            forcedType="long"/>
        </stateChange>
    </eventHandler>
</stateProvider>

<xyView id="CoreCLR.GC.statistics.view">
    <head>
        <analysis id="CoreCLR.GC.statistics" />
        <label value="CoreCLR.GC.statistics.view" />
    </head>

    <entry path="Generations/*">
        <display type="self" />
    </entry>
</xyView>
```

We obtain graphical visualization of the size of generations over time, which can be very useful in analysis (see Figure 3-51).

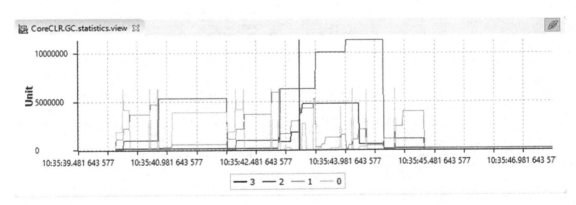

Figure 3-51. *Eclipse Trace Compass - XY visualization of generation sizes in time*

Note   There is yet another very interesting event `DotNETRuntime:`
`GCHeapStats_V1,` but unfortunately, currently its payload is interpreted as a byte array so it is not possible to consume it.

The Final Results

All this allows us to customize the Trace Compass for a fairly convenient analysis of the collected traces (see Figure 3-52). Of course, there is still a lot to do, but such an analysis will make some preliminary conclusions: how frequently and why GC runs occur and how memory consumption changes over time. Reviewing the list of events may allow you to get an idea of the details.

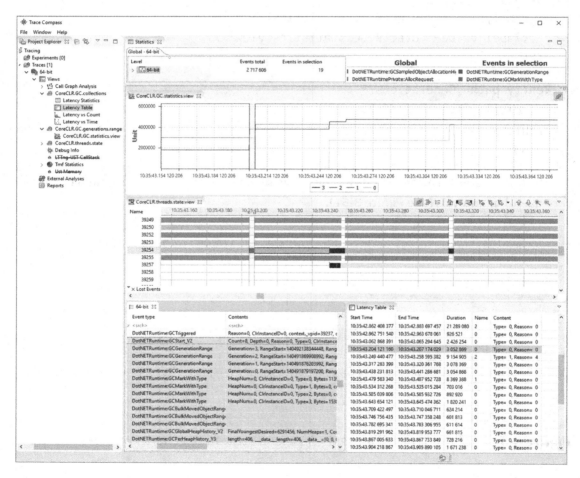

Figure 3-52. *Eclipse Trace Compass - CoreCLR analysis with all custom views altogether*

Memory Dumps

Taking the .NET Core application memory dump conceptually is no different than taking it for any other program running on Linux. To make a dump, execute the command gcore, one of the gdb (The GNU Project Debugger) tools (see Listing 3-18).

Listing 3-18. Taking a memory dump of process

```
$ gcore <PID>
```

It is just like using the already described Procdump on Windows.

When it comes to dump analysis, it is currently mostly based on using an SOS debugging extension - already mentioned as a very powerful extension that comes with the .NET Core runtime itself. To proceed with dump analysis, you have to use lldb debugger to open the dump file, load the SOS plugin and, additionally, tell the debugger where the CoreCLR runtime is placed - with the help of the setclrpath command (see Listing 3-19).

Listing 3-19. Loading memory dump and appropriate configuration into lldb

```
> lldb --core ./path.to.coreListing 3-20.
(lldb) plugin load /usr/share/dotnet/shared/Microsoft.NETCore.App/2.0.0/
libsosplugin.soListing 3-21.
(lldb) setclrpath /usr/share/dotnet/shared/Microsoft.NETCore.App/2.0.0
```

From now on we should be able to use any SOS command like in WinDbg.

Note   lldb is based on llvm and can be seen as just a completely new debugging environment not related to gdb at all.

Summary

In this extensive chapter we reviewed various tools that are useful in the context of .NET memory management analysis – both from the diagnostic side and from its monitoring side. Inevitably, it was only a brief review without going into the details of each service tool. Despite this, the chapter has grown to a substantial size. There are a lot of tools running on the Windows operating system and a little less operating on Linux. Most often these are not simple programs, and their manuals are the subject of separate, dedicated books. I highly recommend using these tools in your daily work and treating the list contained in this chapter as a starting point for further exploration. Download them and try them. Certainly, you will like some more than others.

Just as a little help, please find a brief summary of tools mentioned so far in Tables 3-4 and 3-5.

Table 3-4. *Summary of the .NET-Related Tools for Windows.*

Tool	Purpose	Pros and cons
Performance monitor	Performance counters viewer. Records and visualizes performance counter data.	+ easy to use + low overhead - may be sometimes misleading
Windows Performance Toolkit	Record and visually analyze ETW data. Focused mainly on Windows/drivers analysis.	+ very powerful + low overhead possible - steep learning curve
Perfview	Record and analyze ETW data with the help of many predefined views. Focused mainly on .NET related analysis.	+ very powerful for .NET + low overhead possible - steep learning curve
ProcDump, DebugDiag	Taking memory dump of a process. Either ad hoc or based on various metrics.	+ easy to use
WinDbg	Debugging both managed and native code. With the help of powerful extensions provides extensive analysis possibilities.	+ very low-level insight into process possible - very steep learning curve - may be too low level for many everyday purposes
dnSpy	Editing and debugging .NET assemblies even if source code is not available.	

(continued)

Table 3-4. (*continued*)

Tool	Purpose	Pros and cons
BenchmarkDotNet	Benchmarking library allowing us to benchmark .NET code with respect to execution time and resource utilization.	
Visual Studio (commercial)	Well-known, general purpose IDE. Includes debugging, profiling, and memory dump analysis capabilities.	+ well-known to .NET developers - profiling and dump analysis slightly limited in comparison to other dedicated, commercial tools
Scitech .NET Memory Profiler (commercial) JetBrains DotMemory (commercial) RedGate ANTS Memory Profiler (commercial)	Tools dedicated to .NET memory analysis.	+ easy-to-use user interface + many predefined analyses - paid tools
Intel VTune Amplifier and AMD CodeAnalyst Performance Analyzer	Hardware-level profiling of both native and managed code, including insight into cache utilization, CPU pipeline utilization, and much more.	+ very deep insight into hardware performance - may be too detailed for many typical scenarios - requires at least some basic hardware knowledge
Dynatrace & Appdynamics (commercial)	Continuous monitoring tools including collecting .NET-related data (depends on the tool).	+ deep insight into running applications - paid tools

Table 3-5. *Summary of the .NET-Related Tools for Linux*

Tool	Purpose	Pros and cons
Perfcollect	Script for collecting and simple viewing LLTng and perf data.	+ helps with configuring LLTng and perf sessions - very limited analysis
Trace Compass	Record and visually analyze LLTng data. Created for general purpose analysis, and can be tuned for .NET-related events.	+ quite powerful visualizations - a lot of customization required - steep learning curve
lldb	Native debugger with managed code debugging capabilities via sos extension.	+ very low-level insight into process possible - step learning curve
Intel VTune Amplifier and AMD CodeAnalyst Performance Analyzer	Refer to the Windows counterparts description.	

Some of the tools presented in this chapter will be used later in this book to show you the topics discussed. That is why it was so important for them to be presented before we could actually use them. We will have an opportunity to practice them in different circumstances later on. Since we have not introduced any details about GC in .NET yet, it was too early to address specific diagnostic issues in this chapter. There will be also some other small tools used later not mentioned here. It would be just too expansive to mention them all here.

The first three chapters you have just read are a general introduction to memory management. In Chapter 1 we learned about many theoretical concepts on this subject. In Chapter 2 we learned the hardware and system details of it. And now we are closing this extensive introduction by the third chapter about tools that can be used. And we're going to the right part, describing .NET itself, its internals, and common best practices. I invite you to read!

Rule 5 - Measure GC Early

Justification: Continuous monitoring of different metrics allows to answer to the question "whether we have a memory problem?" from the very beginning of our application existence. What's more, we can observe trends that will reveal the degradation of the performance of our process. Of course, this principle is general enough to apply not only in the GC context. Similarly, we should measure overall performance (e.g. response times) or synchronization problems (like number of context switches), etc.

How to apply: It is important to develop the habit of measuring GC parameters as early as possible, from first deployments in lower environments to continuous monitoring of production environments. Because it is more conceptual than practical advice, the answer to how to use it can be very broad. Undoubtedly, the goal should be, preferably automatic process of continuous monitoring of applications for memory usage and GC operation. The other rules listed in this book should be the starting point for creating this process. Thanks to them we will know what to measure and how to interpret the results. How this process will look to a large extent depends on what tools we use. In the case of Windows, most often measurements will be based, one way or another, on readings of relevant performance counters (section 3.2) or cyclic ETW event analysis (section 3.3). In the case of Linux, it will automate the analysis of the perf_events and LTTng data. Such automated checks can be integrated into our Continuous Integration and Delivery processes, such as after every build of a new product release. Absolutely the minimum approach should be to manually monitor the metrics selected after each production deployment and compare them with behavior against previous versions. What should we measure? Your mileage may vary. It all depends on the severity of our monitoring process. But I cannot imagine a well thought-out system that does not measure the following features of our applications:

- How much memory is in our process and does not grow out of control it in time;

- How often and how long the Garbage Collector is called and whether there is a noticeable overhead for the whole process.

CHAPTER 4

.NET Fundamentals

Although we are only in the fourth chapter, we have gone through quite a long journey about various aspects of memory management. They were discussed in general to make a more theoretical introduction to this topic. There were quite rare, specific references to .NET, which after all is what this book about. It's time to change that frequency. From this chapter to the end of the book, .NET will accompany us constantly. In this chapter we will look at it with a slightly broader perspective, we will learn some mechanisms behind it, and we will begin to delve into the topics related to how it manages memory. I strongly encourage you to acquire knowledge from the previous three chapters before continuing reading this one, but treat it as an optional approach. From now on, I will also assume some basic knowledge about assembly language for x86/x64 platforms as we are going into the .NET deeper and deeper. If you need some knowledge refresh, read, for example, an excellent book, *Modern X86 Assembly Language Programming*, by Daniel Kusswurm (Apress, 2014).

If the .NET Framework was a man, he would have gone to junior high school now, and in a few years slowly began preparing for the matriculation exam. In other words, it is a product developed and used for about 15 years now. During this period, both the rich collection of accompanying libraries and the runtime environment itself evolved significantly. All .NET developers have to know well the basic subjects - knowledge of the standard library and syntax of C# - the main programming language used in .NET environment (or others, like VB.NET constantly losing popularity and F# constantly gaining it). This is our "everyday bread." However, with the age, or as you like, with the experience, often comes the reflection that it is worth knowing more. So let's learn more a little!

© Konrad Kokosa 2018

K. Kokosa, *Pro .NET Memory Management*, https://doi.org/10.1007/978-1-4842-4027-4_4

Be aware that this book concentrates on memory management, only briefly mentioning other .NET-related topics. Thus, for example, do not expect detailed description of C# language features or approaching multithreading issues. There are many other great books and online materials dedicated solely to them.

.NET Versions

The .NET environment is not as homogeneous as it may seem at a first glance. It is most commonly associated with the most popular version of the .NET Framework, which runs from version 1.0, through versions like 2.0, 3.5, or 4.0, up to the current version 4.7.2. But when we talk about the .NET environment, you can really now have in mind a lot of the richness of its versions and implementations. An important approach that allowed such richness was standardization. From the very beginning, the whole .NET concept was based on the specification called *Common Language Infrastructure* (CLI). This fundamental technical standard (standardized as *ECMA 335* and *ISO/IEC 23271* in 2003) describes the concept of a code and runtime environment that allows it to be used on different machines without being recompiled. I will refer to it many times in this chapter as there is no better source of truth than that.

Describing all components of CLI, including all implementation variations and differences between them, is very tempting. However, we will mainly focus on how they affect the topic about which we are concerned. Now just let's take a look at the various .NET variations in the context of memory management and Garbage Collection:

- .NET Framework 1.0 - 4.7.2 - Developed since 2002, the commercial and most mature product known to us all. It has been here for years so that the core of Garbage Collector has been developed and improved from version to version. Over the years, the subject was treated as a black box, described more or less casually on the occasion of releasing the new .NET version. Because the .NET Framework's commercial runtime code is closed, how exactly these mechanisms work, we could mainly learn from the information provided by Microsoft itself. The information was quite detailed, allowing us to understand and diagnose memory problems in applications. But still developers remained a little unsatisfied, especially if you confront it with the openness of sources, for example, of Java.

- Shared Source CLI (also known as Rotor) - Released in 2002 (version 1.0) and 2006 (version 2.0) runtime implementation for educational and academic purposes. It has never been intended to run a production code. It let you know the numerous implementation details of the CLR. There is even a great book, *Shared Source CLI Essentials*, by David Stutz, Ted Neward, and Geoff Shilling (O'Reilly Media, 2003), which describes this version in detail. However, first of all, it did not fully implement a "mature" .NET 2.0 Framework. Secondly, the implementation of it was sometimes very different from the proper CLR, unfortunately, especially in the memory management area. Only a very simplified Garbage Collector has been implemented there.

- .NET Compact Framework - The "mobile" version of .NET since Windows CE/Mobile and Xbox 360 times. Its Garbage Collector was significantly different from the main version and much simplified, for example, it does not include the generation concept (which we will learn about in the next chapter). However, it is already a historical system and probably we do not have to worry about it anymore. But a lot of lessons have been learned during development of this framework, especially because of porting for platforms like various processors running Windows CE devices. Here is where the CoreCLR we know all started conceptually.

- Silverlight - A web browser plugin that allows you to run applications like normal window applications. Since Microsoft started building it in times of .NET 2.0, it was based on a runtime copy of that period. If you still use it, lots of information about the current .NET will also apply here. Except that this would have to be information about an older runtime version of .NET 2.0. This was a runtime ported to the OSX platform, which provided code base for the current CoreCLR (.NET Core) runtime.

- .NET Core (with its runtime called the CoreCLR) - The appearance of the open source version of. NET has changed a lot. From now on, there is a production-ready runtime code that we can study ourselves in depth. More importantly, the Garbage Collector code has been practically copied here from the commercial runtime code. It seems that .NET Core can slowly begin to overtake the functionality of the .NET Framework, whose changes will be successively "merged" back. .NET Core is also an officially supported cross-platform solution. It works on Windows as well as on Linux and MacOS.

- Windows Phone 7.x, Windows Phone 8.x, and Windows 10 Mobile - The older versions of the system were based on simple memory management known from the .NET Compact Framework 3.7. Windows Phone 8.x introduced significant enhancements of the internal .NET runtime, which was based on the mature .NET Framework 4.5 version, inheriting its Garbage Collector.

- .NET Native - A technology that allows CIL code to be compiled directly into machine code. It is based on a lightweight runtime called CoreRT (formerly MRT). They share the Garbage Collector code with .NET Core.

- .NET Micro Framework - A separate implementation for small devices, with open source code. The most popular application is the .NET Gadgeeter that contains its own, simplified version of Garbage Collector. Due to the niche and the hobby nature of this solution, we will not deal with it in this book.

- WinRT - A new way to expose the OS functionality to developers that is set up of APIs used to build Metro style apps available in JavaScript, C++, C#, and VB.NET languages and is to replace Win32. It is written in C++ and it is in fact not .NET implementation at all. But it is object oriented and it is based on .NET metadata format so it may look like a normal .NET library (especially when using from within .NET).

- Mono - A completely separate, cross-platform implementation of the CLI, with its own memory management. Getting to know it does not do much to understand the main theme of .NET. However, there are at least two very popular solutions based on this technology - Xamarin, the framework for writing mobile applications; and Unity3D, a popular game engine. Due to the popularity of those projects, we will sometimes look at Unity by the comparison.

A pretty positive picture emerges from the above list - the memory-management mechanism is very similar (not to say - almost identical) to all the major .NET platforms currently in use - the .NET Framework, the .NET Core, and the one used in .NET Native.

This book is full of explanations about the internal mechanisms of the Garbage Collector in .NET, based on the .NET Core 2.1 source code. As we mentioned, there is a great convergence of this implementation with the main variant of the .NET Framework and the mobile variation. As a result, relying on the source code for .NET Core is a very valuable and comprehensive form of information acquisition. Hereinafter, when showing .NET source code examples, I mean by default the .NET Core 2.1 source code, unless otherwise noted. I also refer to so-called "Book of the runtime" open source documentation developed in parallel to the runtime itself, available at `https://github.com/dotnet/coreclr/blob/master/Documentation/botr/README.md`. It contains much valuable information about the runtime implementation.

We should know some .NET internals to fully understand the memory-management topic. We will look at them now, however, by omitting much information that is not needed in this context. There are many other valuable sources in which you will find more information including the great *CLR via C#* book written by Jeffrey Richter (Microsoft Press, 2012); *Pro .NET Performance* written by Sasha Goldshtein (Apress, 2012); or *Writing High-Performance .NET Code* by Ben Watson (Ben Watson, 2014).

.NET Internals

When writing a program in C or C++, the compiler compiles it into an executable file. It can then be directly executed on the target machine, because apart from libraries that cooperate with the operating system, it contains a binary code directly executed by the processor.

On the other hand, the .NET runtime environment has a lot of important responsibilities, which, together, make the whole thing doing what it is supposed to do - executing application written by us. Unlike programs written in C or C++, when you write a program in C#, F#, or any other .NET-compatible language, it is compiled into the so-called *CIL* (*Common Intermediate Language*). This code is then used by the *Common Language Runtime* (*CLR*). CLR is the place when all the managed magic happens. Above the CLR, there is a more general concept of the whole .NET framework - including all standard libraries and the tooling (so we have various .NET framework versions that may or may not include runtime changes). CLR has several responsibilities, among which we can mainly distinguish:

- *Just-in-time compiler* (*JIT compiler*)- Its function is to transform the CIL code into machine code. This way of executing managed code is really a clever encapsulation of native-system mechanisms - like memory management includes the stack for threads and the heap and so on and so forth.

- type system - takes care of the type control and compatibility mechanisms. It consists of, among others, *Common Type System* (CTS) and Metadata (used by the Reflection mechanism).

- exception handling - It takes care of exception handling, both at the user-program level and the runtime itself. Also, both native mechanisms built into Windows SEH (*Structured Exceptions Handling*) mechanism and C++ exceptions are used here.

- memory management (commonly referred to as Garbage Collector) - this is a whole part of runtime that manages memory used by the runtime and our application. Obviously one of its main responsibilities is taking care of the automatic release of no longer needed objects.

We often split those responsibilities into two main units:

- Execution Engine - is taking care of most of the runtime responsibilities included above, like JIT compilation and exception handling. It is named in ECMA-335 as *Virtual Execution System* (VES) and described as *"responsible for loading and running programs written for the CLI. It provides the services needed to execute managed code and data using the metadata to connect separately generated modules together at runtime."*

- Garbage Collector - is taking care of memory management, objects allocation, and reclaiming no longer used memory regions. ECMA-335 describes it as *"the process by which memory for managed data is allocated and released."*

All these elements work together as in a well-folded machine full of large and small chunks. It is difficult to remove one of them and expect that the whole machine continues to work. And so it is with memory management. We can talk about memory-management mechanisms, but it is good to realize that other components work closely with it. The JIT compiler, for example, produces the lifetime information of variables that are then used by the Garbage Collector. Type systems provide the information necessary to make key decisions - for example, whether the type has a so-called finalizer. Exception handling must be written in a manner that is aware of the memory-reclaiming mechanisms - for example, to be stopped when the garbage collection takes place. A number of such functionalities of the various components within the CLR are very interesting, little facts.

We may often hear about *managed code* in the context of .NET. What it particularly means is that code executed by the runtime should be able to cooperate with it to provide responsibilities mentioned above. As ECMA-335 standard says:

managed code: Code that contains enough information to allow the CLI to provide a set of core services. For example, given an address for a method inside the code, the CLI must be able to locate the metadata describing that method. It must also be able to walk the stack, handle exceptions, and store and retrieve security information.

To summarize, let's look at the bird's-eye view of the .NET runtime executing our application (see Figure 4-1).

Figure 4-1. *Source code (text files) are being compiled into Common Intermediate Language (binary files). Then on a target machine with .NET runtime installed, it is being run by the runtime itself. It consist of two main units: Execution Engine (EE) and Garbage Collection (GC). EE is taking CIL from the binary files and transforms it in memory to the machine code.*

We can describe such process as consisting of the following steps:

- We write our code in the editor of our choice - Visual Studio, Visual Studio Code, or whatever else. As a result, we get a project containing a set of source files. Those are, simply put, text files with the source of our program written in C#, VB.NET, F#, or any other supported language.

- We compile our project with the help of a proper compiler - whether it is the Visual Studio built-in compiler (for .NET Framework projects) or .NET Core compiler. As a result, we get a set of files (assemblies) containing our code in the form of binary code representing instructions in Common Intermediate Language. This code represents our program as a set of low-level instruction operating on a "virtual" stack machine (see Chapter 1). There may be other assemblies containing libraries we use in our program. Such set of assemblies can be now distributed to other users as a ZIP package or via installer.

- We run application - this is obviously the most important part and can be subsequently split into the following steps:

  - for .NET Framework - executable file contains a bootstrap code that is loading the proper version of the .NET Runtime with the support of the Windows operating system.

  - for .NET Core - multiplatform solution does not depend on Windows cooperation. If we want to run managed assembly, we have to explicitly use a proper command like dotnet run in the catalog containing our program. This will bootstrap the runtime.

  - .NET runtime will load the currently needed part of the assembly CIL code from the file and pass it to the JIT compiler.

  - JIT compiler will compile CIL code to the machine code, optimized for the platform it is running at. It will additionally inject different calls to the Execution Engine providing cooperation between your code and .NET runtime.

  - From now on, your code is being executed like normal unmanaged code. The difference is that there is cooperation with the runtime mentioned above.

It is now probably a good time to explain some common misconceptions we may encounter related to the .NET environment:

- .NET is not a virtual machine in a common sense - .NET runtime does not create any isolated environment and is not simulating any particular architecture or machine. In fact, .NET runtime is reusing built-in system resources like the operating system memory management, including the heap and the stack, processes and threads, and so on and so forth. It is then building just some additional functionality on top of them (automated memory management and so on).

- There is no single .NET Runtime running on a machine - there is one binary distribution, but it is loaded and executed per each .NET application running. For example, garbage collection from process A does not influence directly garbage collection from process B. Obviously there is some sharing of resources on the hardware and operating system level, but in general each .NET runtime is not aware of any other managed application running their own .NET runtime instances. In fact, we can host a .NET runtime inside an unmanaged application (what is the case of SQL Server CLR capabilities). Even more, we can host multiple .NET runtimes in a single process, although there is a little practical usage of such behavior.

Sample Program in Depth

Let's now follow a step-by-step process of compiling and running a simple Hello world application (see Listing 4-1) to better understand some .NET internals. This will allow us to familiarize with some basic concepts needed later. Everyone ever learning C# probably recognizes this example whose only purpose is to display a short text on the console. We will use it as our playground run under .NET Core 2.1 runtime on Windows. Obviously, we are not going too deep here as we are mostly interested in memory-management stuff. If you are really interested in how .NET runtime loads itself, manage its types and similar topics, yet once again I recommend the great books introduced earlier.

Listing 4-1. Sample Hello World program written in C#

```
using System;

namespace HelloWorld
{
    class Program
    {
        static void Main(string[] args)
        {
            Console.WriteLine("Hello world!");
        }
    }
}
```

Sample code from Listing 4-1, when compiled by C# compiler (Roslyn in case of used here Visual Studio 2017), will produce a single DLL file, which in my case is called `CoreCLR.HelloWorld.dll`. This file contains all the data required to run such a program. We can see it in details, for example, by opening it in dnSpy tool. After doing that we are able to navigate through various decoded sections of the file (see Figure 4-2):

- metadata describing itself (in terms of a Windows or Linux binary file description) - called DOS and PE header in case of Windows binary file visible in Figure 4-2;

- metadata describing its .NET-related content - including all types declared in our assembly, their methods, and other properties (visible as Storage Stream #0 named #~);

- list of references to the other required files;

- binary stream of the declared types and their methods encoded as bytes representing Common Intermediate Language.

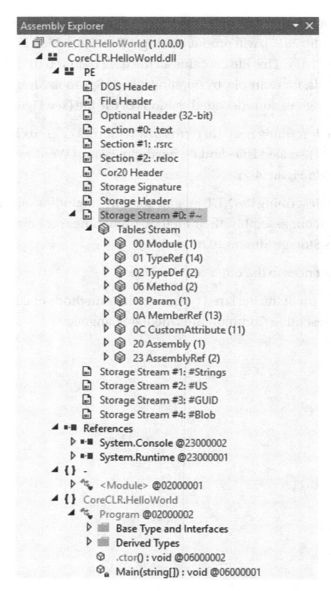

Figure 4-2. *Content of the CoreCLR.HelloWorld.dll binary file - the result of compiling the program from Listing 4-1*

Each method or type has its unique identifier called a *token*, and its location is identifiable within the file because of metadata streams mentioned above. Thanks to that, we can identify file regions containing each method body. For example, to see the Main method body, select it from the Assembly Explorer and use Show Method Body in Hex Editor option from its context menu (see Figure 4-3).

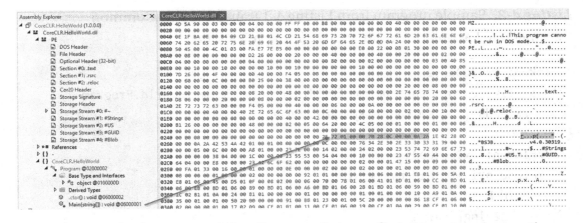

Figure 4-3. *A few bytes containing Common Intermediate Language instructions for the* `Program.Main` *method (arrow was added for clarity)*

Of course, looking at raw bytes, it is really hard to understand their meaning. But we can decode CIL of each method into a more readable form thanks to decompilation mentioned in Chapter 3. To do that, just select `Main` method in Assembly Explorer and select IL as the decompilation language from the dnSpy menu.

The result of the decompilation of `Program` type from CoreCLR.HelloWorld.dll is shown at Listing 4-2 (constructor has been removed for clarity). In comments we can see original bytecode for given instructions (for example, byte `2A` represents `ret` CIL instruction) so now we can fully understand `7201000070280C00000A2A` bytes highlighted in Figure 4-3.

If we look at the simple CIL code of the `Main` method (see Listing 4-2), we will see how it has been compiled into the stack machine code:

- `ldstr "Hello World!"` - reference to string literal is being pushed onto the evaluation stack;

- `call System.Console::WriteLine` - static method is called, taking first argument from the evaluation stack;

- `ret` - method returns (without a return value as there is nothing on evaluation stack).

Listing 4-2. Sample program from Listing 4-1 transpiled into Common
Intermediate Language. Output comes from dnSpy tool.

```
// Token: 0x02000002
.class private auto ansi beforefieldinit CoreCLR.HelloWorld.Program
    extends [System.Runtime]System.Object
{
    // Token: 0x06000001
    .method private hidebysig static
        void Main (
            string[] args
        ) cil managed
    {
        // Header Size: 1 byte
        // Code Size: 11 (0xB) bytes
        .maxstack 8
        .entrypoint

        /* 7201000070    */ IL_0000: ldstr      "Hello World!"
        /* 280C00000A    */ IL_0005: call       void [System.Console]System.
                                                 Console::WriteLine(string)

        /* 2A            */ IL_000A: ret
    } // end of method Program::Main
} // end of class CoreCLR.HelloWorld.Program
```

If you look closely at Listing 4-2 code, you can see a `.maxstack 8` instruction,
which seems to be related with the program execution. This is, however, not CIL
instruction. Such a metadata description can be consumed by various tools to
validate code safety. `maxstack` tells how many maximum bytes can be allocated
on the evaluation stack due to method execution. In case of `Main` method, eight
bytes are required for the string literal reference. A tool like PEVerfiy can use this
information to confront it with what method's CIL code wants to do. This makes
.NET code verifiable and secure as many kinds of buffer overruns are the most
dangerous threats in computer environments.

When considering a .NET stack machine, we should mention an important concept of *locations*. When considering storage of various values required for program execution, a few logical locations exists:

- local variables in a method;

- arguments of a method;

- instance field of another value;

- static field (inside class, interface or module);

- local memory pool;

- temporarily on the evaluation stack.

How each location is mapped into a particular computer architecture is the sole JIT compiler responsibility and we will dive into that a little while.

Note   There are few JIT compilation engines currently available in .NET's ecosystem:

- legacy x86 JIT used by the .NET Runtime (till version 4.5.2) and .NET Core 1.0/1.1 for x86 architecture (32-bit versions)

- legacy x64 JIT used by the .NET Runtime till version 4.5.2

- new RyuJIT used by the .NET Core 2.0 (and later) and .NET Framework 4.6 (and later) for both 32- and 64-bit compilations

- Mono JIT for x86 and x64 platforms

As replacing legacy ones is an ongoing work, I am concentrating here only on the new RyuJIT engine.

Now, we may use WinDbg if we want to see how our program has been translated into machine code by JIT in case of 64-bit Windows. Obviously, we need to run our application as it triggers bootstrapping the runtime and JIT compilation of the necessary methods.

Assuming we are using the newest WinDbg distributed as Universal Windows App, we may choose Launch executable (advanced) from the File panel and provide the following parameters (assuming our solution is located in C:\Projects):

- Executable: `C:\Program Files\dotnet\dotnet.exe`

- Arguments: `\CoreCLR.HelloWorld.dll`

- Start directory: `C:\Projects\CoreCLR.HelloWorld\bin\Release\` `netcoreapp2.1`

Many people prefer to launch WinDbg from the command line to debug programs. In our case, to start a debugging session, you can use this command: `windbgx C:\` `Program Files\dotnet\dotnet.exe C:\Projects\CoreCLR.HelloWorld\` `bin\x64\Release\netcoreapp2.1\CoreCLR.HelloWorld.dll`

After clicking OK, the Hello world application will start and its execution will immediately break. We now need to set a breakpoint that will stop the program just before terminating (after printing the Hello World! message). We may specify the following command:

```
bp coreclr!EEShutDown
```

Now hit Go and wait a moment until this breakpoint will be hit. After that we should load an SOS extension (mentioned in Chapter 3) and look for the `Main` method by using commands:

```
.loadby sos coreclr
!name2ee *!CoreCLR.HelloWorld.Program.Main
```

The second one should produce the following output - saying that JITted code for the `Main` method is located under address `00007ffbca3e06b0`:

```
Module:      00007ffbca284d78
Assembly:    CoreCLR.HelloWorld.dll
Token:       0000000006000001
MethodDesc:  00007ffbca285d30
Name:        CoreCLR.HelloWorld.Program.Main(System.String[])
JITTED Code Address: 00007ffbca3e06b0
```

We can use the !U 00007ffbca3b0480 command to see emitted assembly code and the results are presented at Listing 4-3. We see there the following steps of execution:

- sub rsp,28h - move stack pointer by 40 bytes;

- mov rcx,24D6CCA3068h - store address 24D6CCA3068h into rcx register (this is a handle to our "Hello World!" string literal, which is used here because of a string-interning mechanism explained later);

- mov rcx,qword ptr [rcx] - dereference the address stored in rcx register which points to a string with our string literal value;

- call 00007ffb`ca3b0330 - call static Console.WriteLine method passing text to be displayed in rcx register;

- nop, add rsp,28h and ret - end function call.

Listing 4-3. Machine code produced by JITting code from Listing 4-2

```
Normal JIT generated code
CoreCLR.HelloWorld.Program.Main(System.String[])
Begin 00007ffbca3b0480, size 1c
00007ffb`ca3b0480 4883ec28           sub      rsp,28h
00007ffb`ca3b0484 48b96830ca6c4d020000 mov rcx,24D6CCA3068h
00007ffb`ca3b048e 488b09             mov      rcx,qword ptr [rcx]
00007ffb`ca3b0491 e89afeffff         call     00007ffb`ca3b0330 (System.
Console.WriteLine(System.String), mdToken: 0000000006000083)
00007ffb`ca3b0496 90                 nop
00007ffb`ca3b0497 4883c428           add      rsp,28h
00007ffb`ca3b049b c3                 ret
```

This is how our simple C# program has been translated through CIL into executable code. The evaluation stack location used by ldstr and call CIL instructions has been consumed by the JIT compiler as a CPU register rcx. There is no the stack or the heap allocation from inside the Main method - but please keep in mind that there are already some allocations made from the runtime itself and the framework assemblies.

As there are many possible ways of utilizing registers and memory during functions calls, standardized ways of doing it exists called a *calling convention*. They define how to pass arguments and manage the stack during a method call and how they return a value. When illustrating assembly code in this book, I assume a *Microsoft x64 calling convention*. Simplified for our purposes, the set of rules states that:

- first four integer and pointer arguments are passed into registers RCX, RDX, R8 and R9;

- first four floating-point arguments are passed in XMM0 through XMM3 registers;

- additional arguments are pushed onto the stack;

- integer return values are returned in RAX if 64 bits or less.

Please note the Linux x64 calling conventions are different so please feel free to read about this if you need to.

I hope that this very short, yet possible, and slightly overwhelming journey shows you what .NET runtime is. In the end, all methods are JIT compiled into regular assembly code, utilizing optionally some "managed" parts of the runtime.

Assemblies and Application Domains

A basic unit of functionality in the .NET environment is called *assembly*.[1] It can be seen as a bunch of stored CIL code that may be executed by the .NET runtime. A program consists of at least one or more assemblies. For example, when we compiled code from Listing 4-1, we have produced a single assembly represented by CoreCLR.HelloWorld.dll file. Such program also uses various other assemblies, starting from a Basic Class Library (called mscorlib, including so important namespaces like System.IO, System.Collections. Generic) and so on and so forth. A complex .NET application may consist of many

---

[1]Please do not confuse it with assembly (machine) code. Those are two completely separate concepts just having the same name.

different assemblies containing our code. In terms of source project management, there is simple correspondence - one project in our solution is built into a single assembly. There is also a possibility to create dynamic assembly during program execution (often used to *emit* dynamically created code into such dynamic assembly), which is a functionality often used by various serializers.

In other words, an assembly may be seen as the unit of deployment for managed code, which typically corresponds one to one with some DLL or EXE file (such file is referred to as a *module*).

The .NET Framework provides a possibility to isolate different parts of the managed application code (assemblies) separating them into so-called *application domains* (commonly abbreviates as *AppDomains* from its BCL type name). Such separation may be desired because of security, reliability, or versioning needs. To execute code from assembly, we must load it to some application domain (the same applies to dynamically created assemblies).

There is a quite complicated yet well-documented relation between assemblies and AppDomains. Please refer to this great .NET Framework documentation: `https://docs.microsoft.com/en-us/dotnet/framework/app-domains/application-domains` for the details.

Keeping .NET Core small required cutting out some features and AppDomains were one of them. They were just too heavy for the functionality they provided and for the functionality they needed. Hence no AppDomain API has been exposed in .NET Core related to the application domain handling. However, the piece of code responsible for them is still available in CoreCLR as the runtime itself is using them internally. For developers, Microsoft suggests using plain old processes or shiny new containers for isolation of .NET Core applications. As for dynamic loading of assemblies, there is a new `AssemblyLoadContext` class you can look at.

AppDomains are in our interest because they affect the memory structure of the .NET process. In general, runtime can create a few different application domains:

- Shared Domain - all code shared between domains is loaded here. It includes Basic Class Library assemblies, types from `System` namespace, and so forth.

- System Domain - it used to be responsible for creating and initializing other domains as core runtime components are loaded here. It also keeps process-wide interned string literals (we will talk about interning later in this chapter).

- Default Domain (for example, called Domain 1) - user code is loaded to such a default domain.

- Dynamic domains - with the help of the runtime, .NET Framework application can create (and delete afterwards) as many additional AppDomains as it wishes. For example, via `AppDomain.CreateDomain` method (but as mentioned, .NET core is missing that functionality by design and it is unlikely it will be ever provided).

In case of a .NET Core there are no dynamically created domains obviously. There is Shared Domain responsibility for all shared code. And there is a single default AppDomain for all user code. System Domain is not physically visible in the process memory but its structures and logic are also included.

Collectible Assemblies

Assemblies we load contain a manifest describing what other assemblies they require. Standard CLR behavior consists of loading all required assemblies into the main application domain - the one that will live for the entire program execution. This is fine for most cases, but there are some in which we would like to have some more control about an assembly's lifetime:

- Scripting - if we allow it to execute user-defined scripts in our application (for example, compiled with the help of Roslyn API), it would be ideal to compile such script into some temporary assembly and delete it as soon as the script is no longer needed.

- Object-relational mapping (ORM) - we may wish to map some database data to .NET objects but do not necessarily need this for the entire application lifetime - especially if our application is specific enough to temporarily connect to a lot of different sources. Cleaning up created ORM data (separated into assemblies) would be a nice feature.

- Serializers - like above, we may need to serialize/deserialize many various entities (be it files or HTTP requests), so if we have done it a lot of times, it would be nice to clean created temporary assemblies no longer needed. Such assemblies are created by serializers for performance reasons - types dedicated for serialization of concrete data are created to omit any unnecessary "generic" way of handling it.

- Plugins - our application may provide extensibility capabilities by loading user-provided plugins. It would be obviously great to load them and unload as necessary.

In case of the .NET Framework, the unloading assembly is possible indirectly by unloading an entire application domain where it is loaded to. So, for example, a typical scenario of handling user-defined scripts would consist of creating a dynamic application domain, emitting an assembly with the compiled script, loading it into our temporary application domain, executing code, and eventually - unloading such application domain. In case of .NET Core, due to AppDomain's API unavailability, such scenarios are currently not available (at the time of this writing, with .NET Core 2.1).

While in the .NET Framework case, it is a perfectly working solution, it has its own caveats - especially the cost of the remoting communication between application domains.

Exactly because of mentioned overhead, most often, even in the need of creating dynamic assembly, they are simply loaded into the main application domain - even if it means they cannot be unloaded afterward (as it would require unloading the application itself). This is the case of popular XmlSerializer we can meet in .NET, which may lead to a memory leak described later in this chapter in Scenario 4-4.

Thus, an idea of more lightweight, collectible assemblies is present. A *Collectible assembly* is a dynamic assembly that can be unloaded, without unloading the application domain in which it lives. It makes perfect sense in all the above-mentioned scenarios. However, they are currently not available in both Microsoft .NET runtimes. Stay tuned to .NET Core announcements because a work about unloadable `AssemblyLoadContext` is ongoing.

In .NET Framework, collectible assemblies are implemented but only partially, in case of emitting code manually with the help of `Reflection.Emit`. As MSDN documentation says: "Reflection emit is the only mechanism that is supported for loading collectible assemblies. Assemblies that are loaded by any other form of assembly loading cannot be unloaded."

Process Memory Regions

As mentioned in Chapter 2 and shown in Figure 2-20, .NET runtime inside a process manages multiple memory regions. When we consider memory usage of the .NET process, we should take into consideration each of them. Let's look at these areas one by one to understand the anatomy of the .NET process. We will be using the excellent VMMap tool that shows us memory regions used in a process we are attached to. Memory regions shown hereinafter are from the moment just before exiting the application from Listing 4-1.

When we look inside the Hello World application, we will see memory regions as listed in Figure 4-4. To interpret such VMMap output, it is worth it to recall the description of virtual memory regions presented in Chapter 2. As we can see, the process has nearly 128 TB of free memory (which corresponds to 128 TB of virtual address space on 64-bit platform).

Type	Size	Committed	Private	Total WS	Private WS
Total	2,147,961,700 K	78,568 K	6,828 K	11,740 K	2,388 K
Image	37,924 K	37,908 K	3,436 K	9,236 K	772 K
Mapped File	4,064 K	4,064 K		388 K	
Shareable	2,147,508,516 K	33,140 K		512 K	20 K
Heap	3,828 K	2,344 K	2,280 K	1,084 K	1,080 K
Managed Heap	393,856 K	380 K	380 K	272 K	272 K
Stack	4,608 K	104 K	104 K	60 K	60 K
Private Data	7,000 K	592 K	592 K	152 K	148 K
Page Table	36 K	36 K	36 K	36 K	36 K
Unusable	1,868 K				
Free	135,290,991,744 K				

Figure 4-4. *Memory regions shown in VMMap tool for the running application from Listing 1.64-bit .NET Core 2.0 runtime*

Let's look at all of these items along with a brief description and meaning from the .NET perspective:

- *Shareable (around 2 GiB) - shareable memory* that we are not particularly interested in - only 32 MiB has been committed and only 20 KiB resides in the physical memory. Those regions are dedicated for system management purposes not related to .NET at all.

- *Mapped files* (around 4 MiB) - as mentioned in Chapter 2, those regions contain mapped files for things like fonts and localization files. Although they are consumed by the .NET runtime, consuming various localization APIs, those regions should not cause any problems in our applications.

Address	Type	Size	Committed	Private	Total WS	Private WS	Shareable WS	Shared WS	Lo...	Blocks	Protection	Details
00000289C-7990000	Mapped File	772 K	772 K		276 K		276 K	276 K		1 Read		C:\Windows\System32\locale.nls
00000289E1AD0000	Mapped File	3,292 K	3,292 K		112 K		112 K	112 K		1 Read		C:\Windows\Globalization\Sorting\SortDefault.nls

- *Images (around 37 MiB) - binary images* containing images of various binary files including .NET runtime itself and a library with our .NET assembly. Please note most of this space is shared and only 772 KiB are a private working set. Those are files read from the disk during application startup.

Address	Type	Size	Committed	Private	Total WS	Private WS	Shareable WS	Shared WS	Lo...	Blocks	Protection	Details
0000000029C3200000	Image (ASLR)	32 K	16 K		12 K	4 K	8 K	8 K		8	Read	F:\Github\Projects\.NetMemoryBook\Projects\CoreCLR.General.CoreCLR.ConsolePlayground.exe
00007FF6262A6000	Image (ASLR)	156 K	156 K	12 K	132 K	12 K	120 K	120 K		7	Execute/Read	C:\Program Files\dotnet\dotnet.exe
00007FFF42810000	Image (ASLR)	11,576 K	11,576 K	2,724 K	1,872 K	172 K	1,700 K	1,700 K		41	Execute/Copy on W...	C:\Program Files\dotnet\shared\Microsoft.NETCore.App\2.0.0\coreclr.dll
00007FFF48A0000	Image (ASLR)	5,420 K	5,420 K	104 K	1,816 K	88 K	1,728 K	1,724 K		14	Execute/Read/Write	C:\Program Files\dotnet\shared\Microsoft.NETCore.App\2.0.0\clrjit.dll
00007FFF4610000	Image (ASLR)	1,112 K	1,112 K	16 K	748 K	16 K	732 K	732 K		7	Execute/Read	C:\Program Files\dotnet\shared\Microsoft.NETCore.App\2.0.0\System.Console.dll
00007FFF6F4A0000	Image (ASLR)	156 K	156 K	4 K	88 K	4 K	84 K	84 K		6	Execute/Read	C:\Program Files\dotnet\shared\Microsoft.NETCore.App\2.0.0\System.Console.dll
00007FFF6F880000	Image (ASLR)	548 K	548 K	24 K	324 K	20 K	304 K	304 K		9	Execute/Read	C:\Program Files\dotnet\shared\Microsoft.NETCore.App\2.0.0\hostpolicy.dll
00007FFF6FAB0000	Image (ASLR)	324 K	324 K	12 K	260 K	12 K	248 K	248 K		7	Execute/Read	C:\Program Files\dotnet\host\fxr\2.0.0\hostfxr.dll
00007FFF74C80000	Image (ASLR)	76 K	76 K	4 K	36 K	4 K	32 K	32 K		4	Execute/Read	C:\Program Files\dotnet\shared\Microsoft.NETCore.App\2.0.0\System.Threading.dll
00007FFF79880000	Image (ASLR)	52 K	52 K	4 K	48 K	4 K	44 K	44 K		4	Execute/Read	C:\Program Files\dotnet\shared\Microsoft.NETCore.App\2.0.0\System.Runtime.dll
00007FFFA1770000	Image (ASLR)	40 K	40 K	4 K	28 K	8 K	20 K	20 K		5	Execute/Read	C:\Windows\System32\version.dll
00007FFFA4D10000	Image (ASLR)	172 K	172 K	4 K	64 K	8 K	56 K	56 K		5	Execute/Read	C:\Windows\System32\bcrypt.dll
00007FFFA4E30000	Image (ASLR)	60 K	60 K	4 K	52 K	12 K	40 K	40 K		5	Execute/Read	C:\Windows\System32\kernel.appcore.dll
00007FFFA4E50000	Image (ASLR)	424 K	424 K	4 K	84 K	8 K	76 K	76 K		6	Execute/Read	C:\Windows\System32\bcryptprimitives.dll
00007FFFA5F30000	Image (ASLR)	624 K	624 K	16 K	116 K	20 K	96 K	96 K		5	Execute/Read	C:\Windows\System32\msvcp_win.dll
00007FFFA5760000	Image (ASLR)	2,164 K	2,164 K	20 K	468 K	28 K	440 K	440 K		6	Execute/Read	C:\Windows\System32\KernelBase.dll
00007FFFA5B80000	Image (ASLR)	120 K	120 K	4 K	76 K	8 K	68 K	68 K		5	Execute/Read	C:\Windows\System32\win32u.dll
00007FFFA5C20000	Image (ASLR)	980 K	980 K	12 K	300 K	16 K	284 K	284 K		5	Execute/Read	C:\Windows\System32\ucrtbase.dll
00007FFFA5C70000	Image (ASLR)	1,536 K	1,536 K	16 K	152 K	28 K	124 K	124 K		6	Execute/Read	C:\Windows\System32\gdi32full.dll
00007FFFA5EF0000	Image (ASLR)	208 K	208 K	4 K	148 K	16 K	132 K	132 K		5	Execute/Read	C:\Windows\System32\gdi32.dll
00007FFFA64C0000	Image (ASLR)	648 K	648 K	20 K	108 K	28 K	80 K	80 K		8	Execute/Read	C:\Windows\System32\advapi32.dll
00007FFFA6570000	Image (ASLR)	688 K	688 K	4 K	256 K	20 K	236 K	236 K		5	Execute/Read	C:\Windows\System32\kernel32.dll
00007FFFA6530000	Image (ASLR)	1,156 K	1,156 K	8 K	96 K	20 K	76 K	76 K		4	Execute/Read	C:\Windows\System32\rpcrt4.dll
00007FFFA6760000	Image (ASLR)	1,428 K	1,428 K	8 K	148 K	24 K	124 K	124 K		5	Execute/Read	C:\Windows\System32\user32.dll
00007FFFA6930000	Image (ASLR)	764 K	764 K	12 K	104 K	24 K	80 K	80 K		5	Execute/Read	C:\Windows\System32\oleaut32.dll
00007FFFA69F0000	Image (ASLR)	194 K	194 K	4 K	52 K	16 K	40 K	40 K		5	Execute/Read	C:\Windows\System32\sechost.dll
00007FFFA6D40000	Image (ASLR)	632 K	632 K	32 K	160 K	24 K	136 K	136 K		5	Execute/Read	C:\Windows\System32\msvcrt.dll
00007FFFA6DE0000	Image (ASLR)	2,848 K	2,848 K	24 K	244 K	28 K	216 K	216 K		8	Execute/Read	C:\Windows\System32\combase.dll
00007FFFA70B0000	Image (ASLR)	328 K	328 K	4 K	96 K	16 K	80 K	80 K		5	Execute/Read	C:\Windows\System32\shlwapi.dll
00007FFFA7260000	Image (ASLR)	1,248 K	1,248 K	8 K	176 K	24 K	152 K	152 K		6	Execute/Read	C:\Windows\System32\ole32.dll
00007FFFA73F0000	Image (ASLR)	356 K	356 K	12 K	56 K	16 K	40 K	40 K		5	Execute/Read	C:\Windows\System32\sechost.dll
00007FFFA8960000	Image (ASLR)	1,864 K	1,864 K	36 K	916 K	48 K	868 K	860 K		7	Execute/Read	C:\Windows\System32\ntdll.dll

- *Stacks* (around 4.5 MiB) - there are three threads in our Hello World application so there are three stack regions dedicated for them.

Address	Type	Size	Committed	Private	Total WS	Private WS	Shareable WS	Shared WS	Lo...	Blocks	Protection	Details
000000DB27C00000	Thread Stack	1,536 K	72 K	72 K	52 K	52 K				3	Read/Write/Guard	Thread ID: 29128
000000DB28200000	Thread Stack	1,536 K	16 K	16 K	4 K	4 K				3	Read/Write/Guard	Thread ID: 29144
000000DB28380000	Thread Stack	1,536 K	16 K	16 K	4 K	4 K				3	Read/Write/Guard	Thread ID: 29148

- *Heap* and *Private Data* (around 9 MiB) - those are various native memory regions managed by the .NET runtime for its internal purposes. They mostly store things not relevant to us (and even not known without deep CoreCLR sources analysis). However, we may note that there are some fundamental data structures stored here used by Execution Engine and Garbage Collector like:

  - Mark list and card tables, which we will get familiar with in Chapters 5, 8, and 11.

  - String interning enrollment lives in those regions.

  - Please note also the two last memory regions are marked with Execute/Read/Write protection flags. Those are regions where the JIT compiler emits machine code when compiling CIL code. That's why they are marked with Execute flag as they have to be normally callable as any other program code. Those regions constitute in fact the core of our application executing code we wrote in C# or other .NET-compatible language. If by some reason our application is JITting a lot, we may observe constant growth of such Execute/Read/Write private memory regions.

- Various temporary memory regions needed during JIT compilation also will be visible here.

Address	Type	Size	Committed	Private	Total WS	Private WS	Shareable WS	Shared WS	Lo...	Blocks Protection	Details
000000007FFE0000	Private Data	64 K	4 K	4 K	4 K		4 K	4 K		2 Read	
000000DB27A00000	Private Data	2,048 K	28 K	28 K	28 K	28 K				5 Read/Write	Thread Environment Block ID: 29128
00000289C7980000	Private Data	8 K	8 K	8 K	8 K	8 K				1 Read/Write	
00000289C7D80000	Private Data	4 K	4 K	4 K	4 K	4 K				1 Read/Write	
00000289C7D90000	Private Data	4 K	4 K	4 K	4 K	4 K				1 Read/Write	
00000289C9340000	Private Data	64 K	8 K	8 K	8 K	8 K				2 Read/Write	
00000289C9350000	Private Data	4 K	4 K	4 K	4 K	4 K				1 Read/Write	
00000289C9360000	Private Data	4 K	4 K	4 K	4 K	4 K				1 Read/Write	
00000289C9370000	Private Data	64 K	64 K	64 K						1 Read/Write	
00000289C93A0000	Private Data	64 K	64 K	64 K	64 K	64 K				1 Read/Write	
00000289E1550000	Private Data	3,520 K	388 K	388 K	12 K	12 K				2 Read/Write	
00007FFEE8590000	Private Data	576 K								1 Reserved	
00007FFEE8690000	Private Data	256 K	4 K	4 K	4 K	4 K				2 Execute/Read/Write	
00007FFEE86E0000	Private Data	256 K	8 K	8 K	8 K	8 K				2 Execute/Read/Write	

- *Managed Heaps* (around 384 MiB) - the core part of the .NET memory management is the Managed Heap maintained by the Garbage Collector and other heaps used by the runtime. Since this is definitely the most important memory area for us, we look at it separately in a moment.

Address	Type	Size	Committed	Private	Total WS	Private WS	Shareable WS	Shared WS	Lo...	Blocks Protection	Details
00000289C9550000	Managed Heap	393,216 K	272 K	272 K	164 K	164 K				4 Read/Write	GC
00000289C9550000	Managed Heap	4 K	4 K	4 K	4 K	4 K				Read/Write	
00000289C9551000	Managed Heap	24 bytes	24 bytes	24 bytes						Read/Write	Gen2
00000289C9551018	Managed Heap	24 bytes	24 bytes	24 bytes						Read/Write	Gen1
00000289C9551030	Managed Heap	195 K	195 K	195 K	144 K	144 K				Read/Write	Gen0
00000289C9582000	Managed Heap	261,944 K								Reserved	
00000289D9550000	Managed Heap	72 K	72 K	72 K	16 K	16 K				Read/Write	Large Object Heap
00000289D9562000	Managed Heap	131,000 K								Reserved	
00007FFEE8570000	Managed Heap	64 K	24 K	24 K	24 K	24 K				8 Execute/Read/Write	Shared Domain
00007FFEE8570000	Managed Heap	8 K	8 K	8 K	8 K	8 K				Read/Write	Shared Domain Low Frequency Heap
00007FFEE8572000	Managed Heap	4 K								Reserved	
00007FFEE8573000	Managed Heap	4 K	4 K	4 K	4 K	4 K				Execute/Read/Write	
00007FFEE8574000	Managed Heap	8 K								Reserved	
00007FFEE8576000	Managed Heap	8 K	8 K	8 K	8 K	8 K				Read/Write	Shared Domain High Frequency Heap
00007FFEE8578000	Managed Heap	20 K								Reserved	
00007FFEE857C000	Managed Heap	4 K	4 K	4 K	4 K	4 K				Execute/Read/Write	Shared Domain Stub Heap
00007FFEE857E000	Managed Heap	8 K								Reserved	
00007FFEE8580000	Managed Heap	64 K	40 K	40 K	40 K	40 K				2 Read/Write	Domain 1
00007FFEE8580000	Managed Heap	12 K	12 K	12 K	12 K	12 K				Read/Write	Domain 1 Low Frequency Heap
00007FFEE8583000	Managed Heap	28 K	28 K	28 K	28 K	28 K				Read/Write	Domain 1 High Frequency Heap
00007FFEE858A000	Managed Heap	24 K								Reserved	
00007FFEE8620000	Managed Heap	448 K	20 K	20 K	20 K	20 K				10 Execute/Read/Write	Shared Domain Virtual Call Stub
00007FFEE8620000	Managed Heap	4 K	4 K	4 K	4 K	4 K				Read/Write	Shared Domain Virtual Call Stub Indcell Heap
00007FFEE8621000	Managed Heap	20 K								Reserved	
00007FFEE8626000	Managed Heap	4 K	4 K	4 K	4 K	4 K				Read/Write	Shared Domain Virtual Call Stub Cache Entry Heap
00007FFEE8627000	Managed Heap	20 K								Reserved	
00007FFEE862C000	Managed Heap	4 K	4 K	4 K	4 K	4 K				Execute/Read/Write	Shared Domain Virtual Call Stub Lookup Heap
00007FFEE862D000	Managed Heap	12 K								Reserved	
00007FFEE8630000	Managed Heap	4 K	4 K	4 K	4 K	4 K				Execute/Read/Write	Shared Domain Virtual Call Stub Dispatch Heap
00007FFEE8631000	Managed Heap	148 K								Reserved	
00007FFEE8656000	Managed Heap	4 K	4 K	4 K	4 K	4 K				Execute/Read/Write	Shared Domain Virtual Call Stub Resolve Heap
00007FFEE8657000	Managed Heap	228 K								Reserved	
00007FFEE86D0000	Managed Heap	64 K	24 K	24 K	24 K	24 K				2 Read/Write	Domain 1
00007FFEE86D0000	Managed Heap	24 K	24 K	24 K	24 K	24 K				Read/Write	Domain 1 Low Frequency Heap
00007FFEE86D6000	Managed Heap	40 K								Reserved	

- *Page Tables* (small 36 KiB region) - page table directory structures described in Chapter 2 lives there.

- *Unusable* (almost 2 MiB) - due to page allocation granularity also described in Chapter 2, some parts of memory have become unusable.

We can split a group denoted above as Managed Heaps further into the following categories:

- GC Heap - by far the most important heap for us, managed by the Garbage Collector. Most of the types our application creates go there and hence it is the most important place we should understand and the most probable source of any problems. All chapters from Chapter 5 to the end of the book will be describing how GC manages this heap. In terms of what we have learned so far, this is a Free Store managed by the Garbage Collector mechanism and its Allocator. Please note, however, how many interesting facts we have seen so far until we even reached this memory region! And many chapters will be dedicated to describing it in detail.

- Other domains heaps - each AppDomain has its own set of heaps so there can be heaps for Shared Domain, System Domain, Default Domain, and any other dynamically loaded domains. Each may have multiple subregions:

  - *High Frequency Heap* - used to store any data frequently accessed by the AppDomain for its internal purposes. As comments from CoreCLR states, those are "Heaps for allocating data that persists for the life of the AppDomain. Objects that are allocated frequently should be allocated into the HighFreq heap for better page management." Because of that, for example, a High Frequency Heap of Shared Domain contains the most frequently used type-related data like detailed methods and fields descriptions. Here is also where primitive static data lives.

  - *Low Frequency Heap* - contains less frequently used type-related data. In case of a type system they are, among others, EEClass and other data required for JITting, Reflection, and type-loading mechanism.

  - *Stub Heap* - As the documentations says, it "hosts stubs that facilitate code access security (CAS), COM wrapper calls, and P/Invoke."

- *Virtual Call Stub* - contains data structures and code used by a virtual stub dispatching (VSD) technique (using stubs for virtual method invocations instead of the traditional virtual method table) used for interface dispatch. They are subsequently divided into heaps of types Cache Entry Heap, Dispatch Heap, Indcell Heap, Lookup Heap, and Resolve Heap. All those include just various types of data required for VSD. Those heaps are pretty small (hundreds of kibibytes) even for thousands of interfaces in our applications.

- High Frequency Heap, Low Frequency Heap, Stub Hub, and various Virtual Call Stub Heaps are altogether called *Loader Heap* type because they are responsible for storing data required by a type system (and hence loading types). In contrary to what we may hear sometimes, there is no such thing as *Loader Heap* created as a memory region. It is just a concept of grouping mentioned regions altogether.

Note   Those heaps are by default really small, in the order of magnitude of a single page - typically about 64 KiB. We can see this in the CoreCLR default sizes definitions:

```
#define LOW_FREQUENCY_HEAP_RESERVE_SIZE      (3 * GetOsPageSize())
#define LOW_FREQUENCY_HEAP_COMMIT_SIZE       (1 * GetOsPageSize())

#define HIGH_FREQUENCY_HEAP_RESERVE_SIZE     (10 * GetOsPageSize())
#define HIGH_FREQUENCY_HEAP_COMMIT_SIZE      (1 * GetOsPageSize())

#define STUB_HEAP_RESERVE_SIZE               (3 * GetOsPageSize())
#define STUB_HEAP_COMMIT_SIZE                (1 * GetOsPageSize())
```

Remember that any type once loaded to a Loader Heap region will not be unloaded until the whole corresponding AppDomain is unloaded. If we constantly load a lot of types (for example, dynamically loading or generating assemblies), we can end up with big memory usage. Moreover, the default AppDomain will not be unloaded ever until the program stops.

As mentioned in Chapter 2, there is a possibility to change the default stack size of the program's threads. It is possible with the help of a `dumpbin` command-line program distributed with the Visual Studio. By issuing the following command, it appropriately edits the binary header of the provided executable file:

```
editbin DotNet.HelloWorld.exe /stack:8000000
```

In case of a .NET Framework-based executable (as above), it currently works but should be treated as an unsupported approach - there is no guarantee that in the future, .NET Framework will not ignore those values while creating threads. In case of .NET Core based builds, the executable is a runtime launcher itself, located most commonly at `C:\Program Files\dotnet\dotnet.exe`. We would need to edit this file with the help of `editbin` to change stack size of threads in .NET Core applications, which is obviously unacceptable in most cases. Thus, although manipulating stack size in the described way is possible, we should rather not rely on it at all.

Let's now move to one of the important parts of this book- our first scenario. As it always will be, it consists of some situation description, altogether with the description of how to approach analyzing and solving it.

Scenario 4-1. How Big Is My Program in Memory?

Problem: The customer for whom we are writing a .NET application asked us how much RAM it requires and what is its typical memory usage because she suspects it consumes too much. This caused consternation in the team because suddenly it turned out that no one knows the answer and even does not know how to properly measure it. Everybody suggests another tool and different way to interpret it. Let's assume we are Paint.NET (`https://www.getpaint.net/`) developers!

Answer: To properly answer our customer's question, we should understand how the operating system sees our process memory usage. It has been described briefly in Chapter 2 and you may probably notice there is no great consistency between various tools showing it. From the high-level point of view, we should concentrate on the following measurements:

- private working set - the most important measurement that indicates the amount of physical RAM memory occupied by the process. This obviously may be the main bottleneck so we should look here at first.

- private bytes (aka commit size) - indicates the amount of memory both in the physical RAM and paged to disk. We do not want excessive paging so if this size is much bigger than the private working set, we should start to be suspicious. Indefinite growth of the paging file is also dangerous as our hard drives do not have infinite storage obviously.

- virtual bytes - indicates all virtual bytes, both committed (private) and only reserved, regardless of its location. This measurement is the most abstract one because it does not incur a big consumption of physical resources except page tables directories (see Chapter 2). However, the size of the hundreds of gigabytes or simply constantly growing can arouse our anxiety.

On Windows, to measure those sizes we can simply use the Task Manager's Details tab, which shows them as Memory (private working set) and Commit size columns respectively (virtual bytes are not shown there) - see Figure 4-5.

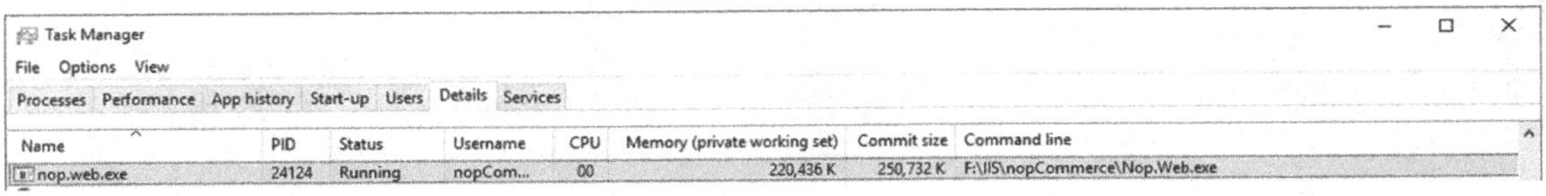

Name		PID	Status	Username	CPU	Memory (private working set)	Commit size	Command line
nop.web.exe		24124	Running	nopCom...	00	220,436 K	250,732 K	F:\IIS\nopCommerce\Nop.Web.exe

Figure 4-5. Window's Task Manager showing basic memory usage data

We may also use Performance Monitor tool (see Figure 4-6) to record them in time by adding \Process(processname)\Working Set - Private, \Process(processname)\ Private Bytes and \Process(processname)\Virtual Bytes counters respectively. Apart from absolute sizes, trends are of course equally important. On Linux you can use the top tool and corresponding columns described in Chapter 2.

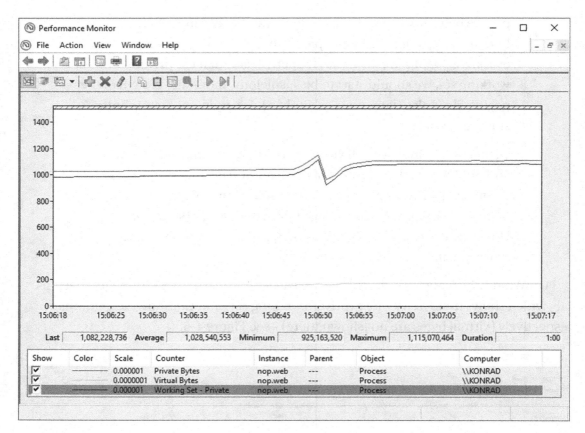

Figure 4-6. *Performance counters showing basic memory usage data*

You may also consider analyzing what is included in the measured process size by using VMMap tool on Windows (see Figure 4-4 where it was already presented). You will notice there what counts in into corresponding to the above measurement columns: Private WS, Private, and Size. Regarding memory types, of course, it is important to look at Managed Heap first. However, knowing what are parts of the .NET process, it is also worth looking at the other memory types. If you suspect a memory leak - observe all memory types' sizes in time and try to discover what is constantly growing. There may be memory leak both in your managed code or some unmanaged component used by you (even implicitly while you are not aware of it).

Scenario 4-2. My Program's Memory Usage Keeps Growing

Description: Our customer reports an OutOfMemory exception after a few days of continuous work with our Windows Service written in .NET. We have to investigate the reason and, of course, we have to do it quickly.

Answer: Given that we are not provided with the full memory dump of a process, we may start our investigation from observing a program's memory usage in time. We may start from using the Performance Monitor tool to watch a few most important counters (see Figure 4-7):

- `\Process(processname)\Working Set - Private`

- `\Process(processname)\Private Bytes`

- `\Process(processname)\Virtual Bytes`

- `\.NET CLR Memory(processname)\# Total committed Bytes` - counter to observe Managed Heap usage

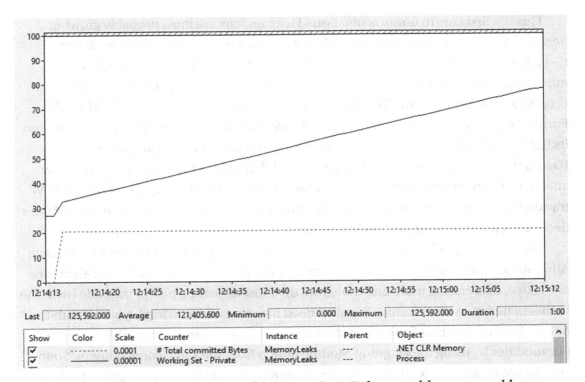

Figure 4-7. *Performance counters for Scenario 4-2 show stable managed heap size, but the private working set is constantly growing*

From what we see it is clear there is a memory leak - the process memory usage constantly grows. However, the Managed Heap size is very stable so this is probably an unmanaged memory leak not related to our .NET code (however, still it might be as we will see in scenario 4-3!). Knowing that, it is worth it to look inside a process with the help of a VMMap tool. As we may notice during short observation, the Heap memory type Private size is constantly growing. Our program slowly produces more and more around 16 MiB Heap memory regions (see Figure 4-8).

⊞ 00000293F6510000	Heap (Private Data)	1,024 K	1,020 K	1,020 K	204 K	204 K
⊞ 00000293F6610000	Heap (Private Data)	2,048 K	2,044 K	2,044 K	404 K	404 K
⊞ 00000293F6810000	Heap (Private Data)	4,096 K	4,092 K	4,092 K	796 K	796 K
⊞ 00000293F6C10000	Heap (Private Data)	8,192 K	8,164 K	8,164 K	1,588 K	1,588 K
⊞ 00000293F7410000	Heap (Private Data)	16,192 K	16,164 K	16,164 K	3,124 K	3,124 K
⊞ 00000293F83E0000	Heap (Private Data)	16,192 K	16,164 K	16,164 K	3,120 K	3,120 K
⊞ 00000293F93B0000	Heap (Private Data)	16,192 K	16,164 K	16,164 K	3,112 K	3,112 K
⊞ 00000293FA380000	Heap (Private Data)	16,192 K	16,164 K	16,164 K	3,124 K	3,124 K
⊞ 00000293FB350000	Heap (Private Data)	16,192 K	2,964 K	2,964 K	584 K	584 K

Figure 4-8. *VMMap view of Heap memory regions for Scenario 4-2. There are constantly growing and occasionally created Heap (Private Data) memory regions.*

This is a first clue in our investigation - Heap regions are most probably growing because of extensive usage of Heap API (like calling `malloc` in C or `new` operator in C++). Now we should find out what code is calling it. Doing that with the help of a memory dump of the process may be tedious because unmanaged memory analysis is very difficult (especially for .NET-based people not used to unmanaged world at all). Fortunately, there is a much simpler way to investigate it using the PerfView tool. Within its Collect dialog box, type the executable name into the OS Heap Exe field or process ID into the OS Heap Process field (keep in mind that only in the second case you may attach to already running process). Providing one of the OS Heap options enables ETW tracking of the Heap API usage. Start collection and wait the appropriate amount of time depending how fast your process is growing.

After stopping collection and all processing is ended, you should open Net OS Heap Alloc Stacks from the Memory Group folder. Gradually expand the individual elements of the tree, descending more and more into the most allocating part of the code (with the highest value in Inc % column). You may need for some nodes to load symbols with the help of Lookup Symbols from the context menu. It is also worth it to disable grouping of our modules by using the Ungroup Module option from the same context menu. Soon you should be able to clearly see the reason of over 90% of allocations (see Figure 4-9). This is the power of ETW in our hand!

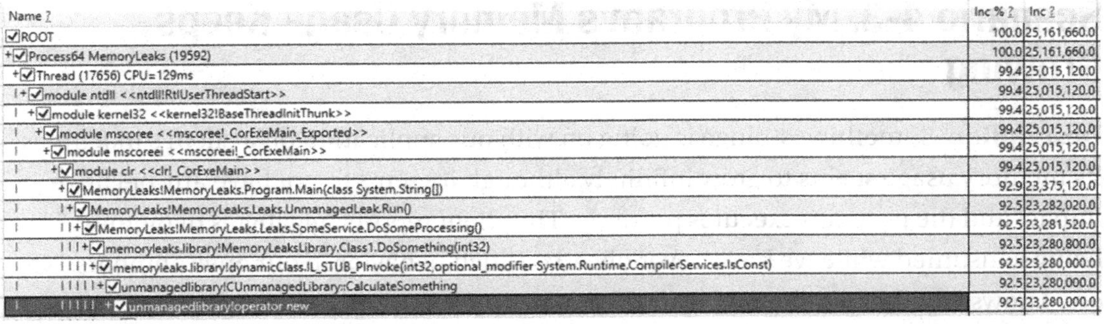

Name ?	Inc % ?	Inc ?
☑ROOT	100.0	25,161,660.0
+☑Process64 MemoryLeaks (19592)	100.0	25,161,660.0
+☑Thread (17656) CPU=129ms	99.4	25,015,120.0
│+☑module ntdll <<ntdll!RtlUserThreadStart>>	99.4	25,015,120.0
│ +☑module kernel32 <<kernel32!BaseThreadInitThunk>>	99.4	25,015,120.0
│ +☑module mscoree <<mscoree!_CorExeMain_Exported>>	99.4	25,015,120.0
│ +☑module mscoreei <<mscoreei!_CorExeMain>>	99.4	25,015,120.0
│ +☑module clr <<clr!_CorExeMain>>	99.4	25,015,120.0
│ +☑MemoryLeaks!MemoryLeaks.Program.Main(class System.String[])	92.9	23,375,120.0
│ │+☑MemoryLeaks!MemoryLeaks.Leaks.UnmanagedLeak.Run()	92.5	23,282,020.0
│ │ │+☑MemoryLeaks!MemoryLeaks.Leaks.SomeService.DoSomeProcessing()	92.5	23,281,520.0
│ │ │+☑memoryleaks.library!MemoryLeaksLibrary.Class1.DoSomething(int32)	92.5	23,280,800.0
│ │ │ │+☑memoryleaks.library!dynamicClass.IL_STUB_PInvoke(int32,optional_modifier System.Runtime.CompilerServices.IsConst)	92.5	23,280,000.0
│ │ │ │ │+☑unmanagedlibrary!CUnmanagedLibrary::CalculateSomething	92.5	23,280,000.0
│ │ │ │ │ +☑unmanagedlibrary!operator new	92.5	23,280,000.0

Figure 4-9. *PerfView analysis for Scenario 4-2. We see the aggregated call stack for* operator new.

We see that the reason behind most of allocations is the new operator used inside CUnmanagedLibrary::CalculateSomething method, which is called by other components of our .NET application. This is indeed the root cause of the problem, as the mentioned method has a specially prepared, indeed silly implementation (see Listing 4-4).

Listing 4-4. The reason behind memory leak in Scenario 1-2

```
int CUnmanagedLibrary::CalculateSomething(int size)
{
    int* buffer = new int[size];
    return 2 * size;
}
```

In real-world scenarios, there may be many other allocations sources so you will have to investigate them a little and make an educated guess, which may be the real trouble. Please note also that if we do not have symbol files for the unmanaged libraries consumed by our application, we will not see specific method and function names in Net Virtual Alloc Stacks view. It will however still point us to what component is making trouble so we may contact its producer or search for the solution online. It is also worth it to remember that ETW tracing for Heap API may introduce quite big overhead, so be cautious when enabling it, especially in production environments.

Scenario 4-3. My Program's Memory Usage Keeps Growing

Description: Something strange is going on with our application on a client's machines. Its memory usage seems to grow infinitely although it seems to not have any negative impact and the program executes properly. The client reports "gigabytes of memory" is being consumed while we have never observed such behavior in our environments. No one knows whether we should be afraid or not.

Analysis: We should again start our investigation from observing the program's memory usage in time. We may start from using the Performance Monitor tool to watch:

- `\Process(processname)\Working Set - Private`
- `\Process(processname)\Private Bytes`
- `\Process(processname)\Virtual Bytes`
- `\.NET CLR Memory(processname)\# Total committed Bytes`

We may soon notice that both managed heap usage and private working set sizes are stable. However, there is constant growth of private bytes - probably most of the allocated memory does not reside in physical RAM. Virtual bytes are also constantly growing indicating gigabytes of virtual memory "consumed"! When looking into the process with the help of a VMMap, we will see the reason behind it (see Figure 4-10). There is over 40 GB of virtual memory indeed. However, around 37 GB of it is marked as unusable! This indicates someone is allocating pages very inefficiently (recall Chapter 2). We can see it by looking at the memory regions list (see Figure 4-11) where there are many, many pages with unusable data.

Type	Size	Committed	Private	Total WS	Private WS
Total	40,117,824 K	2,615,052 K	2,558,776 K	89,832 K	80,228 K
Image	52,668 K	52,656 K	5,316 K	9,220 K	356 K
Mapped File	4,064 K	4,064 K		424 K	
Shareable	24,996 K	4,808 K		308 K	
Heap	2,988 K	2,000 K	1,936 K	376 K	372 K
Managed Heap	393,856 K	4,264 K	4,264 K	4,228 K	4,228 K
Stack	12,288 K	116 K	116 K	16 K	16 K
Private Data	2,478,796 K	2,471,944 K	2,471,944 K	60 K	56 K
Page Table	75,200 K	75,200 K	75,200 K	75,200 K	75,200 K
Unusable	37,072,968 K				
Free	137,398,910,784 K				

Figure 4-10. *VMMap view of a process for Scenario 4-3. There is a huge amout of virtual memory (Size) but most of it is Unusable.*

Address	Type	Size	Committed	Private
⊞ 0000019492DB0000	Private Data	4 K	4 K	4 K
0000019492DB1000	Unusable	60 K		
⊞ 0000019492DC0000	Private Data	4 K	4 K	4 K
0000019492DC1000	Unusable	60 K		
⊞ 0000019492DD0000	Private Data	4 K	4 K	4 K
0000019492DD1000	Unusable	60 K		
⊞ 0000019492DE0000	Private Data	4 K	4 K	4 K
0000019492DE1000	Unusable	60 K		
⊞ 0000019492DF0000	Private Data	4 K	4 K	4 K
0000019492DF1000	Unusable	60 K		
⊞ 0000019492E00000	Private Data	4 K	4 K	4 K
0000019492E01000	Unusable	60 K		
⊞ 0000019492E10000	Private Data	4 K	4 K	4 K
0000019492E11000	Unusable	60 K		
⊞ 0000019492E20000	Private Data	4 K	4 K	4 K
0000019492E21000	Unusable	60 K		
⊞ 0000019492E30000	Private Data	4 K	4 K	4 K
0000019492E31000	Unusable	60 K		

Figure 4-11. VMMap view of a Unusable regions for Scenario 4-3. There are many, many such regions interleaved with single page-sized Private Data.

Now we need to understand what part of our program is using pages in such an improper way. Again, we may use the PerfView tool. This time we are interested in the Virtual API (like calling `VirtualAlloc`) because Private Data memory type is used (not Heap type). Again, we may use the PerfView tool to investigate related ETW data. This time we should check the VirtAlloc option within the Collect dialog box and start collection while our problematic applications are running. Enabling this provider introduces smaller overhead than the Heap API used in Scenario 4-2.

After stopping collection and all processing ended, you should open the Net Virtual Alloc Stacks from the Memory Group folder. If the memory leak is significant you will probably find the root cause on the top of the presented list - in our case 94.1% of all allocations were done through `VirtualAlloc` call (see Figure 4-12)!

Name ?	Exc % ?	Exc ?
OTHER <<kernelbase!VirtualAlloc>>	70.4	15,859,710
OTHER <<ntdll!RtlUserThreadStart>>	13.1	2,953,216
OTHER <<mscorlib.ni!System.String.FormatHelper(System.IFormatProvider, System.String, System.ParamsArray)>>	9.9	2,232,320
OTHER <<mscorlib.ni!System.Console.WriteLine(System.String)>>	2.6	593,920

Figure 4-12. PerfView analysis for Scenario 4-3 show there is a lot of VirtualAlloc calls

If we double-click on it, a call tree will be presented. Expand nodes with the biggest allocation contribution. Optionally use symbol loading and grouping disabling through Lookup Symbols and Ungroup Module options from the context menu. In that way we should be able to find the most allocating source of the program. It is a MemoryLeaks. Leaks.UnusableLeak.Run() method from MemoryLeaks module in our case (see Figure 4-13).

Name ?	Inc % ?	Inc ?
☑OTHER <<kernelbase!VirtualAlloc>>	70.4	15,859,710.0
+☑memoryleaks!dynamicClass.IL_STUB_PInvoke(int,int,value class AllocationType,value class MemoryProtection)	70.4	15,859,710.0
+☑memoryleaks!MemoryLeaks.Leaks.UnusableLeak.Run()	70.4	15,859,710.0
+☑memoryleaks!MemoryLeaks.Program.Main(class System.String[])	70.4	15,859,710.0
+☑OTHER <<ntdll!RtlUserThreadStart>>	70.4	15,859,710.0
+☑Thread (31964) CPU=424ms (Startup Thread)	70.4	15,859,710.0
+☑Process64 MemoryLeaks (45900)	70.4	15,859,710.0
+☑ROOT	70.4	15,859,710.0

Figure 4-13. PerfView analysis for Scenario 4-3 shows the aggregated call stack for VirtualAlloc

And indeed, this method contains the VirtualAlloc interop call, which allocates only a single page (typically 4 KiB) while as we know, allocation granularity on Windows is 64 KiB (see Listing 4-5). Hence unusable 60 KiB of memory is wasted per each VirtualAlloc call.

Listing 4-5. Fragment of problematic code for Scenario 4-3

```
ulong block = (ulong)DllImports.VirtualAlloc(IntPtr.Zero, new
IntPtr(pageSize),
      DllImports.AllocationType.Commit,
      DllImports.MemoryProtection.ReadWrite);
```

In a real-world scenario some unmanaged library used by us my use VirtualAlloc in such inefficient way. By using ETW data for Virtual API we've managed to track down the source of it to the single method call.

Scenario 4-4. My Program's Memory Usage Keeps Growing

Description: Our customer is complaining about big memory usage of our application. It is constantly growing up to gigabytes and then crashes due to an OutOfMemory exception. We are sure we do not use any unmanaged components so we are convinced that the memory leak happens in C# code (although always keep in mind that libraries we use may internally use some unmanaged code so... always be cautious and remember about previously presented scenarios). The customer has sent us a couple of Task Manager screenshots showing that, indeed, all memory sizes are constantly growing.

Analysis: We start our analysis by typical Performance Counter monitoring of the process. We monitor for few hours the following counters:

- `\Process(processname)\Working Set - Private`
- `\Process(processname)\Private Bytes`
- `\Process(processname)\Virtual Bytes`
- `\.NET CLR Memory(processname)\# Total committed Bytes`

We are very surprised because it turns out that the managed heap size is stable. But indeed, all other observed sizes are actually growing, including the most problematic private working set. Instinctively we look inside the interior of the process using VMMap. We see after a few minutes of observation that Managed Heap's private working set is constantly growing so apparently our memory leak is related to .NET somehow. But why is it not reflected by used performance counters? Looking at the Managed Heap type list in VMMap, we notice something unusual (see Figure 4-14). The Managed Heap region marked as GC (the part which stores objects allocated by our application) grows very slowly. On the other hand, there are dozens of Domain 1, Domain 1 Low Frequency Heap, and Domain 1 High Frequency Heap memory regions! This means a lot of additional assemblies are being created, most probably because of dynamic assembly loading.

Address	Type	Size	Committed	Private	Total WS	Private WS	Shareable WS	Shared WS	Lo...	Blocks	Protection	Details
00000160D33E0000	Managed Heap	393,216 K	5,512 K	5,512 K	5,352 K	5,352 K				4	Read/Write	GC
00007FF88DD20000	Managed Heap	64 K	60 K	60 K	60 K	60 K				4	Execute/Read/Write	Shared Domain
00007FF88DD30000	Managed Heap	64 K	56 K	56 K	56 K	56 K				3	Execute/Read/Write	Domain 1
00007FF88DD40000	Managed Heap	576 K	48 K	48 K	48 K	48 K				8	Execute/Read/Write	Domain 1 Virtual Call Stub
00007FF88DDD0000	Managed Heap	448 K	20 K	20 K	20 K	20 K				10	Execute/Read/Write	Shared Domain Virtual Call Stub
00007FF88DEB0000	Managed Heap	64 K	64 K	64 K	64 K	64 K				1	Read/Write	Domain 1 Low Frequency Heap
00007FF88DE90000	Managed Heap	64 K	64 K	64 K	64 K	64 K				1	Read/Write	Domain 1 Low Frequency Heap
00007FF88DEA0000	Managed Heap	64 K	64 K	64 K	64 K	64 K				1	Read/Write	Domain 1 High Frequency Heap
00007FF88DEB0000	Managed Heap	64 K	64 K	64 K	64 K	64 K				1	Read/Write	Domain 1 Low Frequency Heap
00007FF88DEC0000	Managed Heap	64 K	64 K	64 K	64 K	64 K				1	Read/Write	Domain 1 Low Frequency Heap
00007FF88DED0000	Managed Heap	64 K	64 K	64 K	64 K	64 K				1	Read/Write	Domain 1 High Frequency Heap
00007FF88DEF0000	Managed Heap	64 K	60 K	60 K	60 K	60 K				2	Read/Write	Domain 1
00007FF88DF00000	Managed Heap	64 K	64 K	64 K	64 K	64 K				1	Read/Write	Domain 1 High Frequency Heap
00007FF88DF10000	Managed Heap	64 K	60 K	60 K	60 K	60 K				2	Read/Write	Domain 1
00007FF88DF20000	Managed Heap	64 K	60 K	60 K	60 K	60 K				2	Read/Write	Domain 1
00007FF88DF30000	Managed Heap	64 K	60 K	60 K	60 K	60 K				2	Read/Write	Domain 1
00007FF88DF40000	Managed Heap	64 K	60 K	60 K	60 K	60 K				2	Read/Write	Domain 1
00007FF88DF50000	Managed Heap	64 K	64 K	64 K	64 K	64 K				1	Read/Write	Domain 1 High Frequency Heap
00007FF88DF60000	Managed Heap	64 K	60 K	60 K	60 K	60 K				2	Read/Write	Domain 1
00007FF88DF70000	Managed Heap	64 K	60 K	60 K	60 K	60 K				2	Read/Write	Domain 1
00007FF88DF80000	Managed Heap	64 K	60 K	60 K	60 K	60 K				2	Read/Write	Domain 1
00007FF88DF90000	Managed Heap	64 K	60 K	60 K	60 K	60 K				2	Read/Write	Domain 1
00007FF88DFA0000	Managed Heap	64 K	64 K	64 K	64 K	64 K				1	Read/Write	Domain 1 High Frequency Heap
00007FF88DFB0000	Managed Heap	64 K	60 K	60 K	60 K	60 K				2	Read/Write	Domain 1
00007FF88DFC0000	Managed Heap	64 K	60 K	60 K	60 K	60 K				2	Read/Write	Domain 1
00007FF88DFD0000	Managed Heap	64 K	60 K	60 K	60 K	60 K				2	Read/Write	Domain 1
00007FF88DFE0000	Managed Heap	64 K	60 K	60 K	60 K	60 K				2	Read/Write	Domain 1
00007FF88DFF0000	Managed Heap	64 K	64 K	64 K	64 K	64 K				1	Read/Write	Domain 1 High Frequency Heap
00007FF88E000000	Managed Heap	64 K	60 K	60 K	60 K	60 K				2	Read/Write	Domain 1
00007FF88E010000	Managed Heap	64 K	60 K	60 K	60 K	60 K				2	Read/Write	Domain 1
00007FF88E020000	Managed Heap	64 K	60 K	60 K	60 K	60 K				2	Read/Write	Domain 1
00007FF88E030000	Managed Heap	64 K	60 K	60 K	60 K	60 K				2	Read/Write	Domain 1
00007FF88E040000	Managed Heap	64 K	64 K	64 K	64 K	64 K				1	Read/Write	Domain 1 High Frequency Heap
00007FF88E050000	Managed Heap	64 K	60 K	60 K	60 K	60 K				2	Read/Write	Domain 1
00007FF88E060000	Managed Heap	64 K	60 K	60 K	60 K	60 K				2	Read/Write	Domain 1
00007FF88E070000	Managed Heap	64 K	60 K	60 K	60 K	60 K				2	Read/Write	Domain 1
00007FF88E080000	Managed Heap	64 K	60 K	60 K	60 K	60 K				2	Read/Write	Domain 1
00007FF88E090000	Managed Heap	64 K	64 K	64 K	64 K	64 K				1	Read/Write	Domain 1 High Frequency Heap
00007FF88E0A0000	Managed Heap	64 K	60 K	60 K	60 K	60 K				2	Read/Write	Domain 1
00007FF88E0B0000	Managed Heap	64 K	60 K	60 K	60 K	60 K				2	Read/Write	Domain 1
00007FF88E0C0000	Managed Heap	64 K	64 K	64 K	64 K	64 K				1	Read/Write	Domain 1 Low Frequency Heap
00007FF88E0F0000	Managed Heap	64 K	60 K	60 K	60 K	60 K				2	Read/Write	Domain 1

Figure 4-14. *VMMap view of managed heaps for Scenario 4-4*

We confirm that by coming back to the Performance Monitor and adding the following additional counters:

- \.NET CLR Loading(processname)\Bytes in Loader Heap
- \.NET CLR Loading(processname)\Current Classes Loaded
- \.NET CLR Loading(processname)\Current Assemblies
- \.NET CLR Loading(processname)\Current appdomains

The first three counters are constantly growing, so apparently we've just found the root cause of the memory leak. Some part of our code is loading dozens of dynamic assemblies. Unfortunately, we will not be able to deeply analyze such kind of memory leak with the help of commercial tools like JetBrains dotMemory or .NET Memory Profiler (at least at the moment of the book writing). Even though such a leak is related to the .NET runtime, such memory growth is often seen under those tools as "unidentified" memory without the possibility to dig further into details. Again, ETW and PerfView comes to the rescue! This time we are interested in events related to assembly loading. We can enable tracking them by using an Additional Providers field from within the Collect dialog box. Type there Microsoft-Windows-DotNETRuntime:LoaderKeyword: Always:@StacksEnabled=true that means we are interested in loader-related events and we want to register stack calls during the event's occurrence. Start the collection and wait the appropriate amount of time (for example, during which loading of few new assemblies will be visible under Current Assemblies performance counter).

After stopping collection and all processing ended, you should open the Events list and find `Microsoft-Windows-DotNETRuntime/Loader/AssemblyLoad` events for our process (see Figure 4-15).

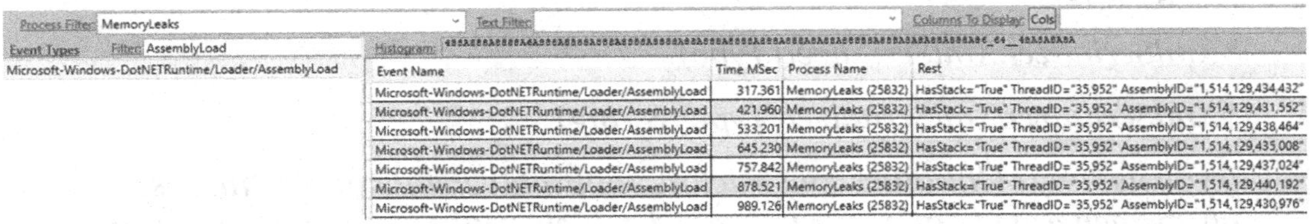

Event Name	Time MSec	Process Name	Rest
Microsoft-Windows-DotNETRuntime/Loader/AssemblyLoad	317.361	MemoryLeaks (25832)	HasStack="True" ThreadID="35,952" AssemblyID="1,514,129,434,432"
Microsoft-Windows-DotNETRuntime/Loader/AssemblyLoad	421.960	MemoryLeaks (25832)	HasStack="True" ThreadID="35,952" AssemblyID="1,514,129,431,552"
Microsoft-Windows-DotNETRuntime/Loader/AssemblyLoad	533.201	MemoryLeaks (25832)	HasStack="True" ThreadID="35,952" AssemblyID="1,514,129,438,464"
Microsoft-Windows-DotNETRuntime/Loader/AssemblyLoad	645.230	MemoryLeaks (25832)	HasStack="True" ThreadID="35,952" AssemblyID="1,514,129,435,008"
Microsoft-Windows-DotNETRuntime/Loader/AssemblyLoad	757.842	MemoryLeaks (25832)	HasStack="True" ThreadID="35,952" AssemblyID="1,514,129,437,024"
Microsoft-Windows-DotNETRuntime/Loader/AssemblyLoad	878.521	MemoryLeaks (25832)	HasStack="True" ThreadID="35,952" AssemblyID="1,514,129,440,192"
Microsoft-Windows-DotNETRuntime/Loader/AssemblyLoad	989.126	MemoryLeaks (25832)	HasStack="True" ThreadID="35,952" AssemblyID="1,514,129,430,976"

Figure 4-15. *PerfView event's view for Scenario 4-4. We see lot of AssemblyLoad events.*

Select one of them and select the Open Any Stacks context menu option for Time MSec column (stack will not be displayed if cell in any other column has been right-clicked). The stack trace of the event occurrence will be displayed. By grouping modules of not our interest (like `clr`, `mscoree,` or `mscoreei` .NET runtime modules) and ungrouping our own modules, we will clearly identify the source of dynamic assembly creation (see Figure 4-16). It is a `XmlSerializer` constructor called in our `XmlSerializerLeak.Run()` method.

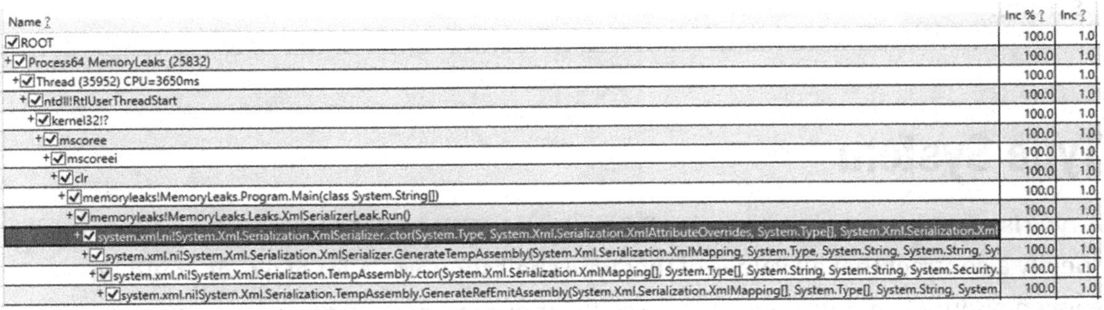

Figure 4-16. *PerfView stack trace view for a single AssemblyLoad events points to XmlSerializer constructor*

We have just found the problem! Indeed, MSDN documentation for XmlSerializer states that:

> *To increase performance, the XML serialization infrastructure dynamically generates assemblies to serialize and deserialize specified types. The infrastructure finds and reuses those assemblies. This behavior occurs only when using the following constructors:*
>
> * *XmlSerializer.XmlSerializer(Type)*
>
> * *XmlSerializer.XmlSerializer(Type, String)*
>
> *If you use any of the other constructors, multiple versions of the same assembly are generated and never unloaded, which results in a memory leak and poor performance. The easiest solution is to use one of the previously mentioned two constructors. Otherwise, you must cache the assemblies in a Hashtable, as shown in the following example.*

In our case, as it may be visible in Figure 4-16, one of the other, unfortunate constructors is being used that does not reuse generated assembly, hence the observed memory leak.

Note The cause of the problem may be similarly addressed in other situations related to dynamic assembly creation like calling AppDomain.CreateDomain without unloading it or by various script engines creating assemblies for compiled scripts.

Type System

A *type* is a fundamental concept in CLI, defined in ECMA 335 to "describe values and specify a contract that all values of that type shall support." A lot of words could be spoken about *Common Type System* itself. For our memory-management purposes it will be enough, however, to stay with the intuitive type definition we all have from the everyday work with C# or other language code. We will however later learn in depth about various type categories existing in .NET.

Each type in .NET is described by a data structure called a *MethodTable*. It contains a lot of information about the type, among which the most important in our perspective are:

- GCInfo - data structure for Garbage Collector purposes (and we will investigate it in next chapters obviously);

- flags - describing various type properties;

- basic instance size - indicates the size of the object;

- EEClass reference - stores "cold" data that are typically only needed by type loading, JITing or Reflection, including description of all methods, fields, and interfaces;

- description of all methods (including inherited ones) required to call them;

- static fields-related data - they include data related to primitive static fields (we will delve into static fields details later in this chapter).

Runtime uses address to the MethodTable (denoted as TypeHandle) whenever it has to gain information about the loaded type through it. We will see them a lot in the rest of the book as MethodTable is one of the fundamental building blocks of cooperation between the Execution Engine and the Garbage Collector.

Type Categories

Almost every article about .NET memory tells the same story - *"there are value types allocated on the stack and reference types allocated on the heap."* And *"classes are reference types while structs are value types."* They are so many popular job interview questions for .NET developers touching this topic. But this is by far not the most appropriate way of seeing a difference between *value types* and *reference types*. Why it is not quite correct? Because it describes the concept from the implementation point of view, not from the point that explains the true difference behind those two categories of types.

We will delve into implementation details later, but it is worth it to note that they are still only implementation details. And as all implementations behind some kind of abstractions, they are subject to change. What really matters is the abstraction they provide to the developer. So instead of taking the same implementation-driven approach, I would like you to present a rationale behind it. And only then we can reach the point when understanding the current implementation will be possible (and will be sensible also).

Let's start from the beginning, which is an ECMA 335 standard. Unfortunately, the definitions we need are a little blurry, and you can get lost in different meanings of words like type, value, value type, value of type, and so on, so forth. In general, it is worth remembering that this standard defines that "any value described by a type is called an *instance* of that type." In other words, we can say about *value* (or *instance*, interchangeably) of value type or reference type. Going further, those are defined as:

> *type, value: A type such that an instance of it directly contains all its data. (...) The values described by a value type are self-contained.*

> *type, reference: A type such that an instance of it contains a reference to its data. (...) A value described by a reference type denotes the location of another value.*

We can spot here the true difference in abstraction that those two kinds of types provide: instances (values) of value types contain all its data in place (they are, in fact, values itself), while reference types values only point to data located "somewhere" (they reference something). But this data-location abstraction implies a very significant consequence that relates to some fundamental topics:

Lifetime:

- Values of value types contain all its data - we can see it as a single, self-contained being. The data lives as long as the instance of the value type itself.

- Values of reference types denote the location of another value whose lifetime is not defined by the definition itself.

Sharing:

- Value type's value cannot be shared - if we would like to use it in other place (for example, although we are passing a bit of implementation details here, method argument, or another local variable), it will be copied byte by byte by default. We say then about *passing-by-value semantics*. And as a copy of the value is passed to another place, the lifetime of the original value does not change.

- Reference type's value can be shared - if we would like to use it in other place, *passing-by-reference semantics* will be used by default. Hence, after that, one more reference type instance denotes the same value location. We have to track somehow all references to know the value lifetime as discussed in Chapter 1.

Identity:

- Value types does not have an identity. Value types are identical if and only if the bit sequences of their data are the same.

- Reference types are identical if and only if their locations are the same.

Again, there is no single mention about heap or stack in this context at all. Keeping in mind those differences and definitions should clarify things a little, although you may need a while to get used to them. Next time when asked during job interview about where value types are stored, you may start from such an alternative, extended elaboration.

There is yet another type category we should know - *immutable types*. Immutable type is a type whose value cannot be changed after creation. No more and no less. They do say nothing about their value or reference semantics. In other words, both value type and reference type can be immutable. We can enforce immutability in object-oriented programming by simply not exposing any methods and properties that would lead to changing an object's value.

Type Storage

But one could insist on asking where is the place here that implies using stack or heap for those two, basic kinds of types? The answer is - there is none! This is an implementation detail taken during design of Microsoft .NET Framework CLI standard. Because it was for years overwhelmingly the most popular one, the "value types allocated on the stack and reference types allocated on the heap" story have been repeated again and again like a mantra without deep reflection. And since it is a very good design decision, it was repeated in different CLI implementations we have discussed earlier. Keep in mind, this sentence is not entirely true in the first place. As we will see in the following sections, there are exceptions to that rule. Different locations can be treated differently as to how to store the value. And this is exactly the case with CLI as we will soon see.

Nevertheless, we only can think about the storage of the value types and reference types when designing CLI implementation for a specific platform. We simply just need to know whether we have stack or heap available at all on that particular platform. As the vast majority of today's computers have both, the decision is simple. But then probably we have also CPU registers and no one is mentioning them in the "value types allocated on the..." mantra although it is the same level of implementation detail like using stack or heap.

The truth is that the storage implementation of one or another type may be located mostly in the JIT compiler design. This is a component that is designed for a specific platform on which it is running so we know what resources will be available there. x86/x64-based JIT has obviously both stack, heap, and registers at its disposal. However, such a decision on where to save a given type value can be left not only at the JIT compiler level. We can allow the compiler to influence this decision based on the analysis that it performs. And we can even expose somehow such a decision to the developer at the language level (exactly like in C++ where you can allocate objects both on the stack or on the heap).

There is an even simpler approach taken by Java, where there are no user-defined value types at all, hence no problem exists where to store them! A few built-in primitives (integers and so forth) are said to be value types there, but everything else is being allocated on the heap (not taking into consideration escape analysis described later). In case of .NET design, we could also decide to allocate all types instances on the heap, and it would be perfectly fine as long as the value type and reference type semantic would not be violated. When talking about memory location, the ECMA-335 standard gives complete freedom:

> *The four areas of the method state - incoming arguments array, local variables array, local memory pool and evaluation stack - are specified as if logically distinct areas. A conforming implementation of the CLI can map these areas into one contiguous array of memory, held as a conventional stack frame on the underlying target architecture, or use any other equivalent representation technique.*

Why these and no other implementation decisions were taken will be more practical to explain in the following sections, discussing separately the value and the reference types.

There is only single important remark left. When we know now that talking about stack and heap is an implementation detail, it can still be reasonable to do that. Unfortunately, there is a place where "as it should be" odds with the "as is practical." And this place is a performance and memory usage optimization. If we are writing our code in C# targeting x86/x64 or ARM computers, we know perfectly that heap, stack, and registers will be used by those types in certain scenarios. So as The Law of Leaky Abstractions mentioned in Chapter 2 says, value or reference type abstraction can leak here. And if we want, we can take advantage of it for performance reasons (what will be especially visible in Chapter 14, describing various more advanced optimization techniques).

Value Types

As previously said, value type "directly contains all its data". ECMA 335 defines value as:

> *A simple bit pattern for something like an integer or a float. Each value has a type that describes both the storage that it occupies and the meanings of the bits in its representation, and also the operations that can be performed on that representation. Values are intended for representing the simple types and non-objects in programming languages.*

We have two categories of value types in the Common Language Specification:

- *structs* - there are many built-in integral types (char, byte, integer, and so forth), floating-point types, and bool. And, of course, the user can define its own structs.

- *enumerations* - they are basically an extension of integral types, becoming a type that consists of a set of named constants. From the memory-management point of view, they are just integral types so we won't deal with them in this book at all as they are in fact structs also internally.

Value Types Storage

So what about *"value types are stored on stack"* part of the story? Regarding implementation, there is nothing stopping from storing all value types on the heap, irrespective of the location used. Except the fact that there is a better solution - using the stack or CPU register. As described in Chapter 1, the stack is quite a lightweight mechanism. We can "allocate" and "deallocate" objects there by simply creating a properly sized activation frame and dismissing it when no longer needed. As the stack seems to be so fast, we should use it all the time, right? The problem is it is not always possible, mainly because of the lifetime of the stack data versus desired lifetime of the value itself. It is the life span and value sharing that determines which mechanism we can use to store value type data.

Let's now consider each possible location of value type and what storage we can use there:

- local variables in a method - they have a very strict and well-defined lifetime, which is a lifetime of a method call (and all its subcalls). We could allocate all value-type local variables on the heap and then just deallocate them when the method ends. But we could also use stack here because we know there is only a single instance of the value (there is no sharing of it). So there is no risk that someone will try to use this value after the method ends or concurrently from another thread. It is then just perfectly fine to use a stack inside an activation frame as a storage for local value types. Additionally, CLI clearly says that "a managed pointer which references a local or parameter variable may cause the reference to outlive the variable, hence it is not verifiable." (we will return to managed pointers in Chapter 14).

- arguments of a method - they can be treated exactly as local variables here so again, we can use stack instead of a heap.

- instance field of reference type - their lifetime depends on the lifetime of the containing value. For sure it may live longer than the current or any other activation frame so a stack is not the right place for it. Hence, value types that are fields of reference types (like classes) will be allocated on the heap along with them.

- instance field of another value-type - here the situation is slightly complicated. If the containing value is on the stack, we would also use it. If it is on the heap already, we will use the heap for the field's value also.

- static field (inside class, interface or module) - here the situation is similar to using an instance field of reference type. The static field has a lifetime of the type in which it is defined. This means we could not use stack as a storage, as an activation frame may live much shorter.

- local memory pool - its lifetime is strictly related to the method's lifetime (ECMA says "the local memory pool is reclaimed on method exit"). This means we can without a problem use stack and that's why local memory pool is implemented as growth of the activation frame.

- temporarily on the evaluation stack - value on the evaluation stack has a lifetime strictly controlled by JIT. It perfectly knows why this value is needed and when it will be consumed. Hence, it has complete freedom whether it would like to use heap, stack, or register. From performance reasons it will obviously try to use CPU registers and the stack.

So that is how we come to the first part - "value types are stored on stack." As we see, the truer is the statement - "value types are stored on the stack when the value is a local variable or lives inside local memory pool. But are stored on the heap when they are a part of other objects on the heap, or are a static field. And they always can be stored inside CPU register as a part of evaluation stack processing." Slightly more complicated, isn't? And this is not still the whole truth because as we will see so-called *closures* capture local variables into a reference type context promoting it to being the heap allocated.

Structs

Structures are probably one of the most overlooked and underestimated elements of C#, existing from the very beginning of .NET at the same time. This seems to be due to the following reasons:

- It is difficult to understand the meaning of the existence of structures if we reduce them to formula "value types are stored on the stack."

- They introduce many limitations (no possibility to define a parameterless constructor, no inheritance is possible).

- Using only classes works very well enough and we do not feel the need to change anything in this regard.

- Knowing that they are realizing the copy-by-value semantics, we know that passing them as parameters to methods or assigning them between variables results in a poor performance of data copying (which is in general not true, as we will soon see).

- Their behavior is not always obvious, and in the absence of visible need for their use, it effectively discourages their use at all.

So why may we may need structs in our code? Here are the main advantages of using structs:

- They may be allocated on stack instead of the heap - and yes, this is where an implementation detail leaks and where we can benefit from a performance point of view. Allocation on the stack simply avoids overhead of managing such a type instance by the GC, which is always good.

- They are smaller - as structs stores only its data and not any additional kind of metadata, they need less memory than classes. And although memory is cheap, it may be beneficial when considering really large data volumes.

- They provide us better data locality - as structs are smaller, we can pack our data more densely in collections (as will be illustrated later). And this, as we've seen in Chapter 2, is always good from a cache utilization point of view.

- Access to them is faster - they contain data directly so no additional dereferencing is needed.

- They provide pass-by-value semantic out of the box - we may wish to create a type that is immutable and hence struct is a good candidate. But we may also use pass-by-reference semantic with them (as explained soon), combining advantages of both value and reference-type worlds.

We will look through those advantages in detail in the rest of the book, as using structs is one of the most common and effective memory and performance optimizations available. We will pay especially big attention to them in Chapters 13 and 14, when describing passing by reference with the help of in, out, and ref keywords (especially in the context of types like Span<T>). Before that we just need to continue our short, general introduction.

Structs in General

Struct can be seen just as a type describing a layout of a memory region together with methods we can invoke on its instances. Struct instances contain only its data (being aligned with value-type definition) so when we define a sample struct from Listing 4-6, it will have memory representation visible at Figure 4-17 (both for 32-bit and 64-bit architecture). It needs a place for four integers so it will occupy 16 bytes.

For 32-bit systems, the de facto standard is called *ILP32* - that is, `int`, `long` and pointer are all 32-bit wide long. For 64-bit systems there is a slight difference between Windows and Linux. The primary Unix standard is *LP64* - `long` and pointer are 64-bit (but `int` is still 32-bit). The Windows 64-bit standard is *LLP64* - specially defined "double-long" (`long long`) and pointer are 64-bit (but `long` and `int` are both 32-bit).

Listing 4-6. Sample struct definition

```
public struct SomeStruct
{
    public int Value1;
    public int Value2;
    public int Value3;
    public int Value4;
}
```

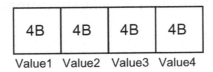

Value1 Value2 Value3 Value4

Figure 4-17. *Memory layout of struct from Listing 4-6*

Depending of the location used (and particular implementation), such a memory region could be used on the stack or the heap (or even just CPU register, as we will see). Current CLR implementations however do not allow us to use such memory layout directly on the managed heap. Objects on the managed heap must be self-descriptive reference types. Hence, when there is a need to store struct on the heap, so-called *boxing* happens. We will elaborate on boxing more in the section about it later in this chapter. We will also talk a little about how memory layout depends on the fields of a given type here and in Chapter 13 because it touches both structs and classes.

What is interesting for us now is using structs from the memory-management point of view. If a struct becomes boxed (its copy allocated on the heap), it is probably too late to take benefits from it. The real power of structs reveals when we are utilizing their non-boxed versions. In other words, we want to benefit from the fact that they are not heap allocated. As one of the core rules states, "Avoid allocation," structs are one of the mechanisms that can help us to achieve this. Moreover, due to many limitations structs have, like no inheritance, compiler and/or JIT compiler are able to infer a lot about how they are used. Inheritance, on the other hand, implies virtual calls and polymorphism and so it is much harder to infer the final look of the data usage.[2]

Structs Storage

Let's consider a sample class from Listing 4-7, which uses a struct defined in Listing 4-6. We see there a method Main that has one local variable sd storing an instance of a struct type SomeStruct. So here is what we can say about this structure based on the information you heard so far:

- sd instance is passed to Helper method by value, which probably means copying its data. Helper operates on its own copy of the data so modifying it would not change the original sd value.

- sd is a local value-type variable so it will be (most probably) allocated on the stack, not on the heap.

Listing 4-7. Sample code with method using struct from Listing 4-6

```
public class ExampleClass
{
  public int Main(int data)
  {
      SomeStruct sd = new SomeStruct();
```

---

[2]Although so-called *devirtualization*, meaning a way to discover during compilation which particular method will be called, is slowly being planned to be added to .NET at the time of this writing.

```
        sd.Value1 = data;
        return Helper(sd);
    }

    private int Helper(SomeStruct arg)
    {
        return arg.Value1;
    }
}
```

If we look at the CIL code of the Main method, for example, by using dnSpy as previously (see Listing 4-8), we will see how it has been compiled into the stack machine operating on the evaluation stack and what steps are executed step by step:

- ldloca.s 0 - address of the first local variable (with index 0) is pushed onto the evaluation stack.

- initobj Samples.SomeStruct - memory region under address taken (and removed) from the evaluation stack is initialized as SomeStruct (as MSDN states, initobj "initializes each field of the value type at a specified address to a null reference or a 0 of the appropriate primitive type").

- ldloca.s 0 - address of first local variable is pushed again onto the evaluation stack.

- ldarg.1 - second method's argument is pushed onto the evaluation stack (which is int data, the first argument is the class instance by default).

- stfld int32 Samples.SomeStruct::Value1 - store the value from the first element on the evaluation stack into SomeStruct.Value1 field at address under the second element on the evaluation stack. Both elements are removed from the evaluation stack.

- ldarg.0 - first method's argument (the class instance itself, known as this keyword in C#) is pushed onto the evaluation stack.

- `ldloc.0` - value of the first local variable is pushed onto the evaluation stack - here is the place where we can assume a whole 16-bytes of `SomeStruct` data are being copied and then accessed inside `Helper` method.

- `call instance int32 Samples.ExampleClass::Helper(valuetype Samples.SomeStruct)` - call `Helper` method, push the result onto the evaluation stack.

- `ret` - return from the method to the caller.

Listing 4-8. Method Main from Listing 4-7 compiled into Common Intermediate Language

```
.method public hidebysig instance int32 Main (int32 data) cil managed
{
    // Method begins at RVA 0x2048
    // Code size 24 (0x18)
    .maxstack 2
    .locals init (
        [0] valuetype Samples.SomeStruct
    )

    IL_0000: ldloca.s 0
    IL_0002: initobj Samples.SomeStruct
    IL_0008: ldloca.s 0
    IL_000a: ldarg.1
    IL_000b: stfld int32 Samples.SomeStruct::Value1
    IL_0010: ldarg.0
    IL_0011: ldloc.0
    IL_0012: call instance int32 Samples.ExampleClass::Helper(valuetype
            Samples.SomeStruct)
    IL_0017: ret
} // end of method ExampleClass::Main
```

Three different locations are used in code from Listing 4-8 - local variable, method arguments, and evaluation stack itself. What we can clearly see is that there is no heap allocation indeed (which uses `newobj` instruction as we will see in the counterpart example for class in Listing 4-13)! This is the optimization we desired. We can expect that there will be SomeStruct allocated on the stack and copied over into the Helper activation frame when calling it. This obviously implies that we should think deeply whether using struct is beneficial (but see below Note).

Copying struct data because of pass-by-value can outweigh performance improvement we gained by avoiding heap allocation. However, there are two aspects that still makes using structs seriously considerable when writing high-performance code:

- often small struct data may be nicely optimized by the JIT compiler to use only CPU registers and no stack at all (as is illustrated in the next paragraphs).

- popular workaround is based on passing struct data by reference, which is also possible (with the help of already mentioned ref, in and out keywords, explained in detail in this book also).

This all makes perfect sense and we could stop just here. However, it is really worth taking a moment to see how the code operating on such an abstract stack machine is transformed by the JIT compiler into the proper machine code. How are those three locations mapped into the heap, the stack, and CPU registers? This obviously depends on what JIT compiler we are talking about but let's just stick to the most popular combination of RyuJIT in .NET Framework on x64 platform. The result we see at Listing 4-9 is overwhelmingly positive. JIT was able to optimize the whole evaluation stack processing and noticed that single mov instruction is enough! What just this code does is:

- mov eax, edx - it moves second argument data (stored in edx register according to Microsoft x64 calling convention) to the register eax, which should contain the result at the method exit

- ret - return from the method

There is no call to the Helper method (it has been inlined), there is no struct data copying, and in fact there is no struct at all!

Listing 4-9. Method Main from Listing 4-7 after Just-In-Time compilation by RyuJIT x64

```
Samples.ExampleClass.Main(Int32)
0x00007FFA`5178BA40:      L0000: mov eax, edx
0x00007FFA`5178BA42:      L0002: ret
```

One could say that this is because the `Helper` method is so trivial. But the truth is the `SomeStruct` would not be probably stack allocated even if we made more complex processing inside the `Helper` method and using all its fields. This is just the level of sophistication that nowadays' JIT algorithms provide.

What I would like to provide to you is the conviction that the structures are efficient data containers, which due to their simplicity allow for far-reaching code optimizations. There is a lot of truth in the "local variables of structs are allocated on the stack" but as we see, things can be even better. Local variables can be just optimized to be handled by CPU registers without the need to touch the stack at all. Even if we expect that passing by value a struct data will incur memory copying, the JIT compiler may optimize it to simply CPU registers usage.

Optimizations seen in Listing 4-9 happen when we compile in the Release mode because then all possible optimizations are enabled. If we compiled a sample from Listing 4-7 in Debug mode, `Main` method would be JITted into a 41-line long assembly code containing stack copying of `SomeStruct` and the `Helper` method would not be inlined either (and it would take additional 25 lines of assembly code). So instead of 2 lines of assembly code in Release, we would get 66 lines in Debug mode!

There is still one very important remark to be mentioned. .NET runtime may treat and optimize structs differently depending on their size. For example, if we added yet another integer field to the `SomeStruct` from Listing 4-6, JIT would not optimize the `Main` method. Stack allocation and memory copying would indeed happed. This boundary of different struct treatment is yet another deep implementation detail but we can spot it around 24 bytes. It is then said to quite safely assume such optimizations are done for structs no bigger than 16 bytes although I believe 24 bytes will be still fine.

Memory copying in such cases is also optimized to its extent and tries to utilize processor capabilities as much as possible. For example, data on my Intel 4th generation Haswell processor is being copied with the help of the vmovdqu instruction. This *AVX (Advanced Vector Extensions)* assembly instruction moves values from an integer vector to an unaligned memory location back and forth. Still, if we care about high performance, care should be taken to avoid copying wherever possible.

Funny interesting fact. Maybe you already know it, but it is possible to assign new value to this field inside a struct's method. Although it may sound like curiosity from a language point of view, there is nothing unusual about memory management in such an example:

```
public struct SomeData
{
    public int Value1;
    public int Value2;
    public int Value3;
    public int Value4;

    public void Bizzarre()
    {
        this = new SomeData();
    }
}
```

As value types store their data in place, we can just treat such reassignment as a re-initialization of the struct's fields.

When you define your struct, it is most probably better to make it behave as immutable. When passing around your object between method calls and fields assignments, one may have the impression that modifying it will modify its original value. This, as we know, is not true with pass-by-value semantics realized by value types. It is better than to explicitly state that object should not be modified by making it immutable - for example, by making all its fields to have only getters and its methods not modifying data. It may help in avoiding unexpected behavior.

Reference Types

As we said, reference types are such that an instance of them contains a reference to its data. We have two main categories of reference types in Common Language Specification:

- *object type* - as ECMA 335 says, object is a "reference type of self-describing value" and "its type is explicitly stored in its representation." They include well-known classes and delegates. There are some built-in reference types, among which by far the most known is `Object` type.

- *pointer type* - it is a plain machine-specific address of a memory location (see Chapter 1). Pointers can be managed or unmanaged. Managed pointers will be thoroughly explained in Chapter 13 as they play an important part in implementing passing-by-reference semantics.

When talking about reference types, it is convenient to consider them as consisting of two entities (see Figure 4-18):

- *reference* - a value of the refence type is a reference to its data. This reference means in particular an address of data stored elsewhere. A reference itself can be seen as a value type because internally it is just a 32- or 64-bit wide address. References have copy-by-value semantics so when passed between locations, they are just copied.

- *reference type's data* - this is a memory region denoted by the reference. Standard does not define where this data should be stored. It is just stored elsewhere.

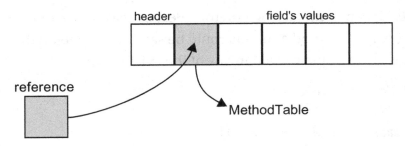

Figure 4-18. *Reference type shown schematically*

This reassembles Figure 1-10 from Chapter 1 describing pointers and the data they refer to. This is because references can be seen as a kind of pointers with additional safety provided by the runtime.

Considering possible storage for each location of reference type is simpler than for value types. As mentioned, because references can share data, the lifetime of them is not well-defined. In general cases, it is impossible to store reference types on the stack because their lifetime is probably much longer than an activation frame life (method call duration). Hence it is quite an obvious implementation decision where to store them and that is how we come to "reference types are stored on the heap" part of the story. Of course, the .NET runtime has a few heaps available at its own disposal so even this simple sentence is not entirely true.

Regarding the heap allocation possibilities for reference types - there is one exception. If we could know that a reference type instance has the same characteristic as a local value-type variable, we could allocate it on the stack as usually used for value types. This particularly means we should know whether a reference does not *escape* from its local scope (does not escape the stack or thread) and start to be shared among other references. A way of checking this is called *Escape Analysis* (see Listing 4-10). It has been successfully implemented in Java where it's especially beneficial because of their approach of allocating almost everything on the heap by default. At the time of this writing, .NET environment does not support Escape Analysis.[3]

---

[3]However, this feature is being developed as a and is likely to be included (at least, optionally) in .NET Core 3.0.

Listing 4-10. Escape Analysis for a method `Helper` may notice that local variable c does not "escape" method and thus could be safely allocated on the stack. Currently this is not implemented in any of the .NET runtimes.

```
private int Helper(SomeData data)
{
        SomeClass c = new SomeClass();
        c.Calculate(data);
        return c.Result;
}
```

Classes

Everyone using .NET-compatible language is using and declaring its own classes. Class is a user-defined reference type. They are full first-class citizens in CTS and a cornerstone of every C# application. They can contain fields, properties, methods, static fields and static methods, and so on so forth. Let's define a struct's counterpart from Listing 4-6 as a class to notice the difference between structs and classes (see Listing 4-11).

Listing 4-11. Sample class definition (a counterpart to the struct from Listing 4-6)

```
public class SomeClass
{
  public int Value1;
  public int Value2;
  public int Value3;
  public int Value4;
}
```

Because of how .NET memory management has been designed, each object on the heap has a strict memory layout consisting of the following parts (sizes vary depending on whether we are talking about a 32- or 64-bit runtime; see Figure 4-19):

- *object header* - place for "any addition information that we might need to attach to arbitrary objects" as the CoreCLR source says. This is often just zero but the most typical usage includes: information about lock taken on the object or cached value of the GetHashCode result. This field is used on a first-come, first-served basis. If the runtime will need it for lock-related information, the hash code will not be cached there and so on and so forth. This is also an important place used by the Garbage Collector during its internal workings.

- *method table reference* - as previously said, object's "type is explicitly stored in its representation," and this is exactly the MethodTable from an implementation point of view. This is also the place where all outgoing references to an object points - in other words, if a given object has some references to it, they will point to an address of its method table reference. That's why it is said that object header is located at a "negative index." The MethodTable reference entry is itself a pointer denoting a proper entry in the type's description data structures (from a High Frequency Heap of a domain containing this type).

- optional data placeholder if type has no fields- current Garbage Collector's design requires that each object has room for one more additional pointer-wide field. This field is reused for many purposes like the first field in the case of normal objects (like illustrated in Figure 4-19 by Value1 field) or the collection length in case of arrays. And it is also very important for GC as stated before and as we will see in Chapter 7.

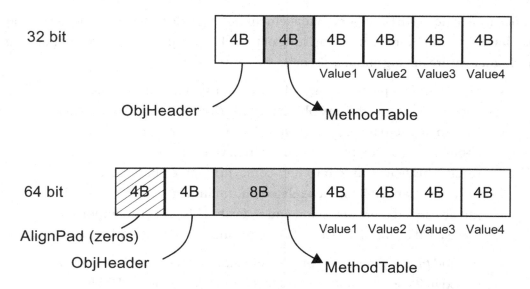

Figure 4-19. *Memory layout of class from Listing 4-11*

As a result, there is no possibility of an object's existence on the heap smaller than one that could accommodate these three fields (see Listing 4-12 from CoreCLR source). It means the smallest object (without no fields) on the heap will be 12 bytes in case of a 32-bit runtime:

- 4 bytes for an object header

- 4 bytes (pointer size) for method table reference

- 4 bytes (pointer size) for internal data placeholder

and 24 bytes in case of a 64-bit runtime:

- 8 bytes for an object header - within which in fact only 4 bytes are used and remaining 4 are just zero-filled alignment (because memory layout with 8-byte alignment is desired in 64-bit architecture)

- 8 bytes (pointer size) for method table reference

- 8 bytes (pointer size) for internal data placeholder

Listing 4-12. The minium size of the heap allocated object

```
// The generational GC requires that every object be at least 12 bytes in
size.
#define MIN_OBJECT_SIZE     (2*sizeof(BYTE*) + sizeof(ObjHeader))
```

We will benchmark this difference in section Types data locality, but the memory overhead is clear. A struct containing a single byte allocated on the stack will occupy only this single byte.[4] The class containing a single byte allocated on the heap will occupy 24 bytes of memory in case of a 64-bit runtime.

Let's consider now a sample class from Listing 4-13, which uses a class defined in Listing 4-11 as we did for the struct example. We see there a method Main, which has one local variable sd of class type SomeClass. So here's what we can say about this, based on the information you heard so far:

- Data referenced by sd local variable is passed to Helper method by reference, which means no data copying. The reference itself is being copied as it is just a single memory address. Helper operates on this shared reference. Modifying the underlying value would change the original sd value.

- Data represented by sd is a local reference-type variable so it will be allocated on the heap as long as no Escape Analysis will be introduced to .NET, which would notice it could be allocated on the stack safely.

Listing 4-13. Sample code with method using class from Listing 4-11

```
public class ExampleClass
{
    public int Main(int data)
    {
        SomeClass sd = new SomeClass();
        sd.Value1 = data;
        return Helper(sd);
    }
}
```

---

[4]Although memory alignment requirements may add some overhead. In Chapter 10 an object's memory layout is explained in detail, including alignment influence.

```
private int Helper(SomeClass arg)
{
    return arg.Value1;
}
}
```

Let's look now at the CIL code of the Main method (see Listing 4-14) generated from such code. The stack machine operating on the evaluation stack executes step by step the following instructions:

- `newobj instance void Samples.SomeClass::.ctor()` - Allocator is being called creating a new instance of SomeClass object and the reference to it is pushed onto the evaluation stack. We will go deeply what happens here inside Chapter 6.

- `stloc.0` - reference from the top of the evaluation stack is removed and stored into the first local variable location.

- `ldloc.0` - the value from the first local variable location is pushed onto the evaluation stack.

- `ldarg.1` - the value of the second argument (as always, remember that the first argument is this reference) is pushed onto the evaluation stack.

- `stfld int32 Samples.SomeClass::Value1` - the first element on the evaluation stack is stored under the field Value1 of object referenced by the second element on the evaluation stack (and both elements are removed from the evaluation stack afterward).

- `ldarg.0` - the value of the first argument (this reference) is again pushed onto the evaluation stack.

- `ldloc.0` - the value from the first local variable location (reference to the newly created SomeClass instance) is pushed onto the evaluation stack.

- `call instance int32 Samples.ExampleClass::Helper(class Samples.SomeClass)` - a method is called, and it takes two arguments from the evaluation stack (which we know by its definition).

- `ret` - return from the method.

Listing 4-14. Method `Main` from Listing 4-13 compiled into Common Intermediate Language

```
.method public hidebysig instance int32 Main (int32 message) cil managed
{
        .locals init ([0] class Samples.SomeClass)
        IL_0000: newobj instance void Samples.SomeClass::.ctor()
        IL_0005: stloc.0
        IL_0006: ldloc.0
        IL_0007: ldarg.1
        IL_0008: stfld int32 Samples.SomeClass::Value1
        IL_000d: ldarg.0
        IL_000e: ldloc.0
        IL_000f: call instance int32 Samples.ExampleClass::Helper(class
        Samples.SomeClass)
        IL_0014: ret
} // end of method ExampleClass::Main
```

We may see a little redundancy here in calling `stloc.0` and then calling the `ldloc.0` instruction immediately. Obviously, the compiler has to be written in a generalized way so we may sometimes meet such code that seems to be obviously optimizable.

Nevertheless, assembly code generated by the x64 .NET Framework JIT is very simple and well-optimized (see Listing 4-15). It mainly calls the internal Allocator function `JIT_TrialAllocSFastMP_InlineGetThread` inside .NET runtime. Still it is much more complicated than the two-line assembly generated for the struct usage from Listing 4-9!

Listing 4-15. Method Main from Listing 4-13 after Just-In-Time compilation in RyuJIT x64

```
Samples.ExampleClass.Main(Int32)
0x00007FFA`5176E5A0:      L0000: push rsi
0x00007FFA`5176E5A1:      L0001: sub rsp, 0x20
0x00007FFA`5176E5A5:      L0005: mov esi, edx
```

```
0x00007FFA`5176E5A7:      L0007: mov rcx, 0x7ffa5192f838
0x00007FFA`5176E5B1:      L0011: call clr.dll!JIT_TrialAllocSFastMP_
InlineGetThread+0x0
0x00007FFA`5176E5B6:      L0016: mov [rax+0x8], esi
0x00007FFA`5176E5B9:      L0019: mov eax, [rax+0x8]
0x00007FFA`5176E5BC:      L001c: add rsp, 0x20
0x00007FFA`5176E5C0:      L0020: pop rsi
0x00007FFA`5176E5C1:      L0021: ret
```

How does this difference translate into performance? We can run a simple benchmark comparing the Main method performance from Listings 4-7 and 4-13 (see Table 4-1). Because of object allocation, a method using a class is over four times slower and, obviously, allocates memory while the struct version does not.

Table 4-1. *Benchmark Results of Main Method Performance from Listings 4-7 and 4-13. BenchmarkDotNet Was Used on .NET Framework 4.7*

Method	Mean	Gen 0	Allocated
ConsumeStruct	0.6864 ns	-	0 B
ConsumeClass	3.3206 ns	0.0076	32 B

In C++ a syntax of class instantiation allows us to allocate on the stack (MyClass c) or on the heap (MyClass* c = new MyClass()). However, in the C++/CLI language when you create an instance of a reference type using stack semantics, the compiler does internally create the instance on the heap (using gcnew).

Strings

String is a well-known reference type that represents a sequence of characters. In other words, they represent some text. They are by far one of the most popular data types in a usual .NET program, even if we are not aware of it. That is because most of our programs nowadays, in fact, more or less, depend on text processing. Whether it will be data from database, REST, or SOAP web requests or XML files read from disk - we have to get it, make some processing, and emit results in, most probably, textual form. That is why when analyzing memory dumps of typical .NET applications (especially web based), strings will always be high on the list of existing object types.

String popularity is very typical, so by analyzing the memory consumption of the program and seeing a lot of strings there, do not assume right away that they are root of the problem. They may be but not necessarily. Only a thorough analysis of the relationship and comparison of memory dumps taken by some time interval can provide an answer.

Strings have special treatment in the .NET environment as they are immutable by default. Unlike in unmanaged languages like C or C++, we cannot change a string value once it has been created. That's why code from Listing 4-16 will end up with a compilation error `Property or indexer 'string.this[int]' cannot be assigned to -- it is read only`.

Listing 4-16. String immutability example

```
string s = "Hello world!";
s[6] = 'W';
```

Keep in mind that "strings are immutable so cannot be changed once created" sentence is not entirely truth. It is only Basic Class Library not exposing API that would allow us to modify a string's value (even via Reflection API). Immutability is however not enforced on the runtime level. String's content is just a continuous block of bytes interpreted as characters in provided encoding. Nothing could stop us to get a pointer to some of those bytes in unsafe mode and change them in place. This is however strictly not supported behavior, so you will be on your own analyzing any issues happening with such an approach taken.

Strings immutability introduces a lot of confusion in the first contact with the C# language. It is often illustrated by examples like in Listing 4-17. Greet method is creating a new string joining some string literals and method parameters. A beginner C# programmer may expect that using operator += she step-by-step modifies the result variable (like she is incrementing an integer value by using the same operator).

Listing 4-17. String concatenation and hidden temporary string creation example

```
public string Greet(string firstName, string secondName)
{
        string result = "Hello ";
        result += firstName;
        result += " ";
        result += secondName;
        result += "!";
        return result;
}
```

Sooner or later she learns that it is impossible because strings are immutable and code from Listing 4-17 creates a temporary strings line by line (see Listing 4-18). Thus, unintentionally we've created four temporary strings. Each of them has a very short lifetime because it will be consumed only as soon as by the following Concat call. And as we will see in later chapters, avoiding allocations is one of the most common ways of improving our code.

Listing 4-18. CIL version of method from Listing 4-17. We see here that each += operator has been changed into String::Concat method call which concats two strings from the top of evaluation stack and pushes the result on the evaluation stack.

```
.method public hidebysig instance string Write (string firstName, string
secondName) cil managed
{
        IL_0000: ldstr "Hello "
        IL_0005: ldarg.1
```

```
IL_0006: call string [mscorlib]System.String::Concat(string, string)
IL_000b: ldstr " "
IL_0010: call string [mscorlib]System.String::Concat(string, string)
IL_0015: ldarg.2
IL_0016: call string [mscorlib]System.String::Concat(string, string)
IL_001b: ldstr "!"
IL_0020: call string [mscorlib]System.String::Concat(string, string)
IL_0025: ret
}
```

What can be done to improve such code? A common solution is to use a StringBuilder type that provides mutable string behavior (see Listing 4-19). Internally StringBuilder stores text as a linked list of characters blocks (called chunks; see Figure 4-20). We can see StringBuilder as an entry point to the chain of internal buffers. The number and size of chunks will be dynamically adjusted while our text will grow. When we need a regular string at some time, we can call the ToString, which allocates a new string and copies data into it chunk by chunk.

Listing 4-19. String creation using "mutable string" type StringBuilder instead of string concatenation from Listing 4-17

```
public string Greet(string firstName, string secondName)
{
    StringBuilder sb = new StringBuilder();
    sb.Append("Hello ");
    sb.Append(firstName);
    sb.Append(" ");
    sb.Append(secondName);
    sb.Append("!");
    return sb.ToString();
}
```

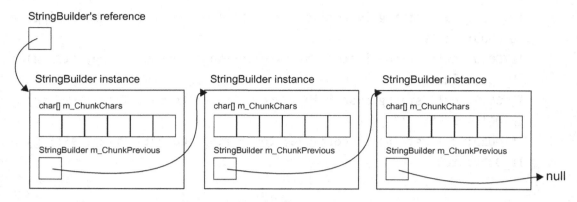

Figure 4-20. *StringBuilder internal data structure*

We should always consider using `StringBuilder` when we need complex string creation: for example, when aggregating data from collections.

Please note that for such simple cases like formatting a message with a few arguments, the most efficient way will be to just use `string.Format` or string interpolation built on top of it: `public string Greet(string firstName, string secondName) => $"Hello {firstName} {secondName}!";`

Popular helper methods like `string.Format` or `string.Join` internally use `StringBuilder`. They even go further and try to optimize more by using cached `StringBuilder` instances wrapped by a `StringBuilderCache` class (see Listing 4-20).

Listing 4-20. Example of `StringBuilder` usage inside `FormatHelper` method used by various `string.Format` overrides

```
private static String FormatHelper(IFormatProvider provider, String format,
ParamsArray args) {
    ...
    return StringBuilderCache.GetStringAndRelease(
        StringBuilderCache
            .Acquire(format.Length + args.Length * 8)
            .AppendFormatHelper(provider, format, args));
}
```

StringBuilderCache stores internally the ThreadStatic static StringBuilder instance (see Listing 4-21). Thus it can be safely reused without multithreading issues because its value is unique for each thread (thread static storage is explained in detail in Chapter 13).

Listing 4-21. Beginning of the StringBuilderCache class showing its internal structure

```
internal static class StringBuilderCache
{
    // The value 360 was chosen in discussion with performance experts as a
    compromise between using as litle memory (per thread) as possible and
    still covering a large part of short-lived StringBuilder creations on
    the startup path of VS designers.
    private const int MAX_BUILDER_SIZE = 360;

    [ThreadStatic]
    private static StringBuilder CachedInstance;
    ...
}
```

As there will be probably as many cached StringBuilder instances as threads in our application, the capacity of it has been balanced between usefulness versus memory overhead. Nevertheless, it shows us that it is always worth it to think about memory overhead when designing such commonly used APIs like string formatting.

The performance difference can be significant when using mutable StringBuilder versus concatenation of immutable strings. Table 4-2 shows benchmark results for three methods from Listing 4-22. It is comparing two mentioned approaches. Additionally, the third version uses StringBuilderCache, which although is not public, can be easily copy-pasted from the .NET Framework sources (https://referencesource.microsoft. com/#mscorlib/system/text/stringbuildercache.cs).

Listing 4-22. Three approaches to building complex string. First uses classic string concatenation, producing many temporary short-lived strings. Second uses StringBuilder and the third utilizes StringBuilder instance caching (acquiring cached instance big enough to contain produced text).

```
[Benchmark]
public static string StringConcatenation()
{
     string result = string.Empty;
     foreach (var num in Enumerable.Range(0, 64))
          result += string.Format("{0:D4}", num);
     return result;
}

[Benchmark]
public static string StringBuilder()
{
     StringBuilder sb = new StringBuilder();
     foreach (var num in Enumerable.Range(0, 64))
          sb.AppendFormat("{0:D4}", num);
     return sb.ToString();
}

[Benchmark]
public static string StringBuilderCached()
{
     StringBuilder sb = StringBuilderCache.Acquire(2 * 4 * 64);
     foreach (var num in Enumerable.Range(0, 64))
          sb.AppendFormat("{0:D4}", num);
     return StringBuilderCache.GetStringAndRelease(sb);
}
```

Table 4-2. *Benchmark Results of Three String Building Methods from Listing 4-22. BenchmarkDotNet Was Used on .NET Core 2.1.0.*

Method	Mean	Gen 0	Allocated
StringConcatenation	12.420 us	6.3477	26.75 KB
StringBuilder	7.708 us	1.7090	7.64 KB
StringBuilderCached	7.630 us	1.4648	6.57 KB

As we can clearly see from the results in Table 4-2, the memory consumption may be four times bigger if we are not aware of string concatenation caveats. It introduces a four-time bigger GC overhead also. This may be trivial in our test case but for large web application processing thousands of requests, it may make a real difference.

Two questions may arise when considering string design decisions:

- Why strings are immutable - if immutability introduces counterintuitive behavior and hidden allocations problems, why make a string immutable at all? The answer is quite simple - the use of immutability for such an overwhelmingly popular type is very beneficial because of the many advantages it gives us, at the expense of the few defects that it introduces. On the benefits side of this decision we can list:

- Safety - strings are widely used as important elements of other data structures. Possibility to change them "in place" might lead to many errors. Image things like keys in various dictionary-like structures. If one could change such a key's value, it would probably invalidate the internal representation of such a structure (often built upon different kinds of balancing trees). Strings are also passed to various APIs to specify credentials, file names and path, and so on and so forth. The possibility to change string content after it has been checked would be very dangerous.

- Concurrency - data are not going to change so there is no risk in sharing it between multiple threads. No need of locking, no risk of False Sharing.

- A main disadvantage includes:

  - Modifying operations will introduce additional instances of the string (like `Concat` seen above). This may be particularly painful for big text data. Image a few megabyte-long text stored in string and a single `Replace('a', 'b')` call on it. It will create a few new megabytes big string with possibly only a few characters changed.

- All this makes a perfectly good decision to treat string immutability as an opt-in option. If you really need to make some mutable operation on string, use `StringBuilder`. This forces the developer to expect that he/she will consider which approach he/she should use.

- If string is immutable, why is string not a struct? Value types are perfect candidates for being immutable - they store all their data in place and realize pass-by-value semantics so making them immutable seems natural. So why not make a string a struct? But think for a minute. Although value type may be a good immutable type, the opposite does not necessarily have to be true. Copying by value large strings would introduce quite big overhead, and it is much more efficient to pass them by reference.

Going further, if immutability is so good, why not make everything immutable by default?! This is in fact what most functional languages are doing. And F# in not an exception here. In F#, the type's mutability is an opt-out solution so it has to be explicitly declared (like by using `mutable` keyword).

String Interning

There is a mechanism inside the .NET runtime called *string interning*, which sometimes makes more confusion than it deserves. This is yet another one of those topics willingly repeated as a question during the job interview. String interning is an optimization technique for effective use of memory for repetitive texts. The same text is not repeatedly copied, but only one copy is kept in memory. But the issue is that this mechanism by default applies only to string literals and not to strings dynamically created during a normal application execution. As ECMA 335 says, *"by default, the CLI guarantees that the result of two ldstr instructions referring to two metadata tokens that have the same sequence of characters, return precisely the same string object (a process known as string interning)."* And we have seen already usage of ldstr instruction to load a string literal in Listing 4-18.

String interning is often illustrated by examples like in Listing 4-23. We see there two "Hello world!" string literals in different contexts but with the same value. Line 4 from the Main method would print True because runtime has interned "Hello world!" literal and both s1 and Global are referencing the same string instance.

String interning used by default only for string literals makes this mechanism not especially interesting for developers. It is rather an implementation detail of the runtime-optimizing memory usage for an obvious thing - to not duplicate the same hard-coded text again and again. It should be stressed once again - by default only string literals are interned. This case is also shown in Listing 4-23. Although string s3 has the same "Hello world!" value, line 5 shows that this is a different instance than the interned one. Thus, string s3 created dynamically is not interned (although both "Hello " and "world!" literals are).

Listing 4-23. String interning example with comments describing output

```
private static string Global = "Hello world!";
static void Main(string[] args)
{
    string s1 = "Hello world!";
    string s2 = "Hello ";
    string s3 = s2 + "world!";
    Console.WriteLine(string.ReferenceEquals(s1, Global));    // True
    Console.WriteLine(string.ReferenceEquals(s1, s3));        // False
    ...
```

Why are dynamically created strings not interned by default? Because it might introduce significant overhead. When trying to create a new string, the runtime should check whether it is not already interned. But such a check can be a noticeable cost if there is already a huge amount of interned strings. Such checks could possibly outweigh the benefit of not creating a new string in the first place.

However, we have the possibility to explicitly manage string interning, the static method string.IsInterned returns null if there is no interned string with a given value and interned string reference otherwise. Listing 4-24 shows the continuation of the Main method from Listing 4-23. In line 1, if we check using string.IsInterned method whether there is a string interned with the value of s3 variable (which is "Hello world!"), we get the interned reference - because indeed there is an interned "Hello world!" string literal. This allows us to use the interned string version if it exists and the original s3 instance would be eventually garbage collected as probably we will not be using it anymore.

We can even explicitly intern string by using string.Intern method (see line 8 in Listing 4-24). It will return us an interned string reference. In case in which there was no such value interned before, it will intern such reference and will return it to us as a string.Intern result. In other words, interning dynamically created string implies nothing more than just remembering it in some internal data structures. In our example, string.Intern call interns a reference message, so s6 and message references are equal.

Listing 4-24. Manual string interning example

```
string s4 = string.IsInterned(s3);
Console.WriteLine(s4);     // Hello world!
Console.WriteLine(string.ReferenceEquals(s4, Global)); // True
string message = args[0];
string s5 = string.IsInterned(message);
Console.WriteLine(s5);     // null
string s6 = string.Intern(message);
Console.WriteLine(string.ReferenceEquals(s6, message)); // True
```

This brings us gently to the next issue. There is quite a lot of confusion regarding the location of the interned strings. If the dynamically created message string from Listing 4-24 has been interned, where it is being stored? We can often read that interned strings are stored in a so-called String Intern Pool that resides in a Large Object Heap (LOH; we will learn about it in Chapter 5), a part of the Managed Heap. The problem is that LOH is designated for objects bigger than 85,000 bytes as we will soon learn. Our string is obviously smaller. Does it mean it is being moved there during interning to some kind of bigger buffer? We can also sometimes hear that interned strings are stored inside an executable file, but this is unlikely for our dynamically created message string, isn't it? The truth is slightly more complicated.

There are a few places in memory related to the string interning (illustrated in Figure 4-21). The core part is an internal *String Literal Map* that resides in a .NET framework itself (within a private unmanaged heap). It manages a hash table of strings grouped into buckets. Every interned string has its own entry there, and it contains a calculated hash and an address to an entry in the other structure - `LargeHeapHandleTable`. This handle table, which in fact resides in the Large Object Heap, contains nothing more than references to the string instances. But those string instances are "normal" strings living in the Managed Heap. Thus, we cannot say that interned strings live in some special String Intern Pool data structure. They are simply registered and maintained by string literal and handle table structures. The important difference is that those structures live as long as the .NET application so interned strings will be always referenced by them once registered. In GC terms, they will be always reachable and thus never garbage collected! As interned strings live in Managed Heap as any other objects - in Small Object Heap (SOH, if they are smaller than 85000 bytes) or LOH (if they are bigger than 85,000 bytes), they eventually will be promoted to generation 2 and stay there forever.

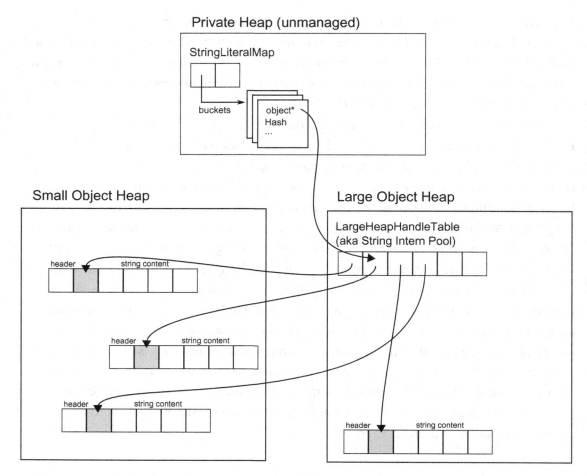

Figure 4-21. *String interning internals. All interned strings are in fact normal strings instances - kept in Small Object Heap or Large Object Heap depending on their size. References to them are being held by LargeHeapHandleTable located in Large Object Heap while information about those handles are stored in internal .NET runtime data structures.*

But what about string literals? Interestingly, their behavior is essentially the same. Let's assume we are using simple code like:

```
string s = "Hello world!";
```

When our source code is being compiled, all string literals (including "Hello world!") are stored into executable file in a so-called #US storage stream (the name comes from user strings abbreviation). The above line is being translated into one already known to us CIL instruction with an argument describing that it refers to #US stream (0x70000000) value under index 1 (0x00000001) - let's assume it is our "Hello world!" text there:

```
ldstr        0x70000001
```

During JIT compilation such instruction, following sequence of steps happens:

- String data are being read from #US stream under a given index.

- String Literal Map is being checked for such data. If it exists already, a proper handle address will be returned. If no entry exists for such data:

  - A new string is being allocated - as a normal string so it will be created in Generation 0 (or LOH if it is large enough)!

  - Data will be copied into that string from the stream.

  - A new handle in LargeHeapHandleTable will be created, pointing to the newly created string.

  - A new entry in String Literal Map will be created.

String interning has been exposed to the developer via the `string.Intern` method making it an opt-in setting. We can explicitly intern any string, including those dynamically created. This is the cause of most confusion. Why and when we can benefit from manual string interning? Let's consider string interning pros and cons.

String interning advantages:

- String deduplication - the obvious advantage and the rationale behind string interning is deduplication of the strings and thus avoiding unnecessary memory overhead. This makes perfect sense for strings literals as the runtime is taking care of it during JIT. When considering string deduplication for dynamically generated strings, things are not so obvious. We should analyze how many strings in our application are duplicated and what memory overhead it produces. It may just be not worth it to take into consideration the disadvantages mentioned below.

- Equality performance - string equality comparison may require comparing both strings byte by byte and thus can be quite slow, especially for bigger strings. However, string equality operators contain fast-path answers when the same reference is being compared (see Listing 4-25). Thus, if our code is based on comparing tons of often duplicated strings, we may benefit by such optimization.

String interning disadvantages:

- Immortality - as mentioned before, interned strings stay reachable until the runtime termination. Most probably the string we are interning will become soon unreachable and thus garbage collected. But by interning it we are just making it immortal and we should think twice if it is worth it. Instead of better memory usage, we may do just the opposite. It is like continuously keeping all strings we have ever seen in our application. All depends on their uniqueness.

- Creation of temporary string - we can only intern string already created. So for a short time, a non-interned string will exist, even if only for checking if there is no interned version available.

Listing 4-25. Beginning of the string equality comparison. If both strings represent the same reference, a very fast path is chosen.

```
public static bool Equals(String a, String b)
{
    if ((Object)a==(Object)b) {
        return true;
    }
    ...
```

If we are reading data from file, web request, and so forth, we are receiving strings instances. Those instances are not interned and if they are very often duplicated (like, for example, XML tags and attributes names), we may be tempted to intern them. But the question is - what is the lifetime of those strings? If they are just temporarily read into memory when doing input processing, they will be soon garbage collected. If we intern them, they will reside in memory forever while the same temporarily created string still will be generated by an underlying library most probably.[5] And as they are normal strings eventually promoted to generation 2, they will put additional pressure on garbage collection also.

Here we can come to the final conclusion - we may benefit by string interning mainly when considering a scenario in which we keep in memory for a long time a lot of duplicated strings. This is rather uncommon as most applications just process some burst of textual data and forget about them. Moreover, if we rely on comparing those overwhelmingly duplicated strings, it is an additional reason behind considering string interning.

Please note that when having good control over how your strings are instantiated, you have an option to implement string deduplication on your own. It requires you to have a convenient place that allows it, like a place where you receive byte stream data and want to deserialize it into a string. In such cases, we may write our custom deduplication in a way not creating temporary strings. Still, it will be mostly beneficial if there are big amounts of duplicated strings living in our application.

All this balance between pros and cons is illustrated in the following scenario.

Scenario 4-5. My Program's Memory Usage Is Too Big

Description: During application development, testers noticed that after a few hours of continuous work, the process is consuming gigabytes of memory. They let you know and you indeed easily reproduced this behavior on your local machine by using test automation tools.

Analysis: You have full control over the used environment so there are many possibilities to attack this problem. By looking at performance counters or VMMap output, you will easily confirm that the managed heap grows to gigabytes. In a development environment without a problem, we can attach to the process or analyze a memory dump with the help of various tools. Commercial tools will show us some predefined issues analysis pointing out that there is a huge amount of memory wasted because of duplicated strings (see Figure 4-22 from JetBrains dotMemory as an example).

---

[5]Because of not-so-obvious string interning benefits, even System libraries like XML or HTTP handling are not using interning by default.

This view shows an overview of snapshot data and results of automatic memory inspections.

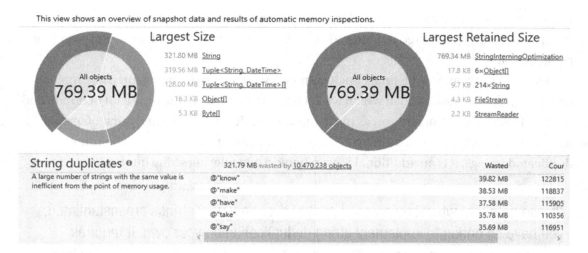

Figure 4-22. *String duplication analysis shown in JetBrains dotMemory tool for Scenario 4-5*

We can come to a similar conclusion with the help of PerfView tool. Within the Collect dialog box, we should check the .NET Alloc check box. This is a really expensive tracking operation and it is unlikely you should enable it on the production environment. However, we may agree to such overhead in the case of our local tests. Please not that in case of a .NET Alloc option, you should start the profiled application after collection starts. After stopping collection, open GC Heap Net Mem analysis from Memory Group. A list of mostly allocated types will be presented. In our example scenario, the string would be at the top of the list. If we double-click it, the aggregated stack of string allocations will be presented (see Figure 4-23). As we see in our simplified case, there is one main source of it - - System.IO.ReadLinesIterator.MoveNext() method.

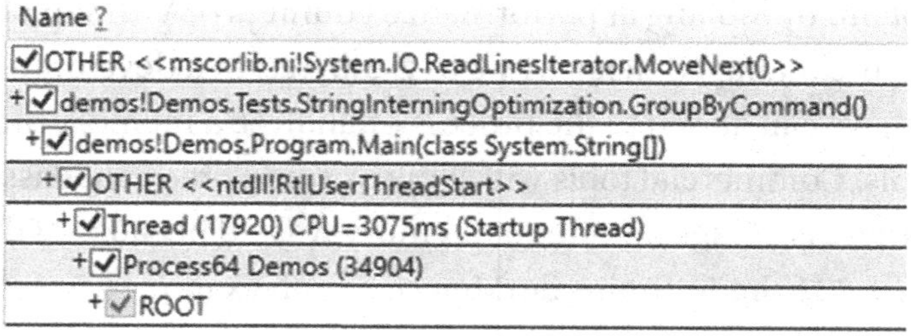

Figure 4-23. *PerfView graph for string allocation - used in Scenario 1-5*

If .NET Alloc introduces too much overhead, you can still track allocations by sampling with the help of .NET SampAlloc or even GC only option, which can often be sufficient (if problematic allocations stand out from the other allocations in our application).

If we look at the code indicated by the analysis - System.IO.ReadLinesIterator. MoveNext() (see Listing 4-26), we will see very simple file-parsing functionality that counts each unique line occurrence and stores all lines in a dictionary altogether with the occurrence timestamp. Obviously if there are many duplicated lines, there will be many duplicated strings in memory.

Listing 4-26. Very simple line-counting C# code used to illustrate possible string duplication

```
foreach (var line in File.ReadLines(file))
{
    bool counted = false;
    foreach (var key in counter.Keys)
    {
      if (key == line)
      {
          counter[key]++;
          counted = true;
          break;
      }
    }
    if (!counted)
    {
      counter.Add(line, 0);
    }
    list.Add(new Tuple<string, DateTime>(line, DateTime.Now));
}
```

We can change this code to use string interning. Just after a line has been read from file into string line, we may intern it (see Listing 4-27). New strings will be allocated for each line read from file, but their lifetime will be very short. We will add only interned strings to the dictionary. Those interned strings are stored for the whole application's lifetime so we will benefit from string deduplication. We may even gain an additional performance boost because now string comparison may use reference equality underneath for similar strings.

Listing 4-27. Code from Listing 4-26 changed to use explicit string interning

```
foreach (var line in File.ReadLines(file))
{
    var line2 = string.Intern(line);    // line lifetime ends here (except
                                         // first occurence when it will be
                                         // interned)
    bool counted = false;
    foreach (var key in counter.Keys)
    {
      if (key == line2) // should often use ReferenceEquals because of
                           comparing two interned string
      {
          counter[key]++;
          counted = true;
              break;
      }
    }
    if (!counted)
    {
      counter.Add(line2, 0); // adding interned string
    }
    list.Add(new Tuple<string, DateTime>(line2, DateTime.Now));
}
```

Such code will produce real benefits only if there are not so many unique strings that otherwise would be duplicated many times for a long time. If any of those conditions are not met, string interning will probably cause performance degradation instead of improvement.

Boxing and Unboxing

In .NET, conversion exists between value type and a reference type. As ECMA-335 says:

> *For every value type, the CTS defines a corresponding reference type called the boxed type. The reverse is not true: In general, reference types do not have a corresponding value type. The representation of a value of a boxed type (a boxed value) is a location where a value of the value type can be stored. A boxed type is an object type and a boxed value is an object.*
>
> *(...)*
>
> *All value types have an operation called box. Boxing a value of any value type produces its boxed value; i.e., a value of the corresponding boxed type containing a bitwise copy of the original value.*

As value type and reference type definitions do not mention the stack and the heap at all, so a boxing definition does not either. We can see boxing as a process of converting a value type instance into a reference type instance, hence converting those value's semantics.

Obviously, when we come to the implementation details, I've mentioned a few times already that in certain scenarios value-type instances (like struct) need to be allocated on the heap. And as we said, all objects on the managed heap need to have some additional corresponding data like the object header and MethodTable reference. Thus, when we want to allocate a value type on the heap, we need to wrap its value with those additional data. In other words, boxing is a two-step operation:

- allocates on the heap boxed type for the corresponding value type (a new reference type instance)

- copies data from value type instance to newly created reference type instance

We probably already have intuition that this is a not-so-efficient operation. We need to allocate an object and copy its data, which takes some precious clock cycles. What is worse, a boxed-type instance at some time will have to be garbage collected, which puts pressure on the GC.

Let's look at the typical boxing example from Listing 4-28. We see there that the value-type integer is being assigned to a reference object type. In such a case it must be boxed.

Listing 4-28. Implicit boxing example.

```
int i = 123;
object o = i;  // implicit boxing
```

A Common Intermediate Language code shown at Listing 4-29 illustrates how boxing looks from the perspective of the underlying stack machine. Box instruction is taking a value and pushes on the evaluation stack the result of boxing (which is a reference to a newly created reference-type instance).

Listing 4-29. CIL code generated for C# code from Listing 4-28

```
IL_0000: ldc.i4.s 123
IL_0002: box System.Int32
IL_0007: ret
```

This directly translates to the two-step operation mentioned above (see Listing 4-30). First, a boxed-type System.Int32 is allocated and then a value (in this case, single integer with value 123 so 0x7b in hexadecimal notation) is being copied into it.

Listing 4-30. Assembly mode generated from CIL code from Listing 4-29 (in Release x64 mode)

```
Samples.Echoer.Write(System.String)
0x00007FFB`7BE56180:    L0000: sub rsp, 0x28
0x00007FFB`7BE56184:    L0004: mov rcx, 0x7ffbd85e9288 ; (MT: System.Int32)
0x00007FFB`7BE5618E:    L000e: call clr!JIT_TrialAllocSFastMP_
                                InlineGetThread
0x00007FFB`7BE56193:    L0013: mov dword [rax+0x8], 0x7b
0x00007FFB`7BE5619A:    L001a: add rsp, 0x28
0x00007FFB`7BE5619E:    L001e: ret
```

One of the main memory-related rules in .NET world is - avoid boxing. A massive boxing code could indeed cause us performance problems. Unfortunately, most boxing is done implicitly so we may be even not aware of it. Thus, it is worth it to remember common places when such implicit boxing can occur:

- Value type is used where object (reference type) is expected - thus it needs to be boxed. Besides a little artificial example from Listing 4-28, we most often encounter this situation in the arguments of methods that accept a type object like various `string.Format`, `string.Concat`, and similar overrides:

```
int i = 123;
return string.Format("{0}", i);
```

We see in generated CIL code that boxing to `System.Int32` occurs:

```
IL_0003: ldstr "{0}"
IL_0000: ldc.i4.s 123
IL_0009: box [mscorlib]System.Int32
IL_000e: call string [mscorlib]System.String::Format(string,
object)
```

Unfortunately, there is nothing we can do here to avoid boxing. Even using more advanced syntax like string interpolation (`return $"{i}"` in our example) will introduce boxing as it uses `string.Format` underneath. We can call `ToString` on a value type during method call (`string.Format("{0}", i.ToString())`) to avoid boxing, but it will allocate a new string so the result will be in fact the same in terms of memory pressure. As a general rule, it is good to avoid methods taking objects as parameters, if possible. Before generics were introduced in .NET Framework 2.0, all collections types were storing its data as object references because they had to be flexible enough to store any possible data. Thus, many methods existed like `ArrayList.Add(Object value)` and so on, and so forth with much possible boxing to happen. Thanks to generic types, this problem no longer exists as a generic type or method will be compiled for a specific value type (like `List<T>` will become `List<int>`) and no boxing may be necessary.

- Value type instance is used as any interface type implemented by this
  value type. As the interface is a reference type, we also need boxing
  here. Assuming SomeStruct implements ISomeInterface interface
  with method GetMessage:

```
public string Main(string args)
{
  SomeStruct some;
  var message = Helper(some);
  return message;
}
  string Helper(ISomeInterface data)
{
  return data.GetMessage();
}
```

Again, implicit boxing is visible in the generated CIL code:

```
IL_0000: ldarg.0
IL_0001: ldloc.0
IL_0002: box Samples.SomeStruct
IL_0007: call instance string Samples.Program::Helper(class
Samples.ISomeInterface)
```

We can avoid boxing in such cases by introducing a generic method
that will expect a desired interface as a generic type parameter:

```
string Helper<T>(T data) where T : ISomeInterface
{
    return data.GetMessage();
}
```

Generic method will be compiled for this specific value type as an
argument, hence no boxing will be required:

```
IL_0000: ldarg.0
IL_0001: ldloc.0
IL_0002: call instance string Samples.Program::Helper<valuetype
Samples.SomeStruct>(!!0)
```

Let's look at the one of the most common sources of boxing, which comes from the fact of a value type being used as an interface - `foreach` instruction on `IEnumerable<T>` (see Listing 4-31). In such a case we are passing `List<int>` instance as an `IEnumerable<int>` to `Print` method. The `foreach` instruction underneath is operating on an enumerator concept - it is making `GetEnumerator()` call on the passed collection and then it calls `Current()` and `MoveNext()` on it sequentially. In the `Print` method, list collection is seen as `IEnumerable<int>` so `IEnumerable<int>.GetEnumerator()` will be called, which is expected to return `IEnumerator<int>`. `List<T>` implements `IEnumerable<int>` obviously but the important fact is that `GetEnumerator()` returns `Enumerator`, which is... struct. As this struct is being used as `IEnumerator<int>`, boxing happened once at the beginning of the `foreach` loop.

Listing 4-31. Hidden allocation because of boxing when using `foreach` statement

```
public int Main(string args)
{
    List<int> list = new List<int>() {1, 2, 3};
    Print(list);
    return list.Count;
}

public void Print(IEnumerable<int> list)
{
    foreach (var x in list)
    {
        Console.WriteLine(x);
    }
}
```

This obviously does not incur much overhead as a single boxing of `Enumerator` will be most probably outweighed by the operations made inside the `foreach` loop. As always in such problems, it can only hit us back if we are making tons of such `foreach` loops on the hot path executed. And as always, Measure Early whether it a problem in your application or not by investigating the number of `Enumerator` allocations. If you would like to avoid boxing, you may simply pass list as `List<int>` to `Print` method (making it `public void Print(List<int> list)`). In such a case, when `foreach` calls underneath

List<int>.GetEnumerator(), List<int>.Enumerator, a struct is expected and such local variable will be created for it. No need of boxing to happen. This is a place where good programming practices may conflict with code optimization. In general, it is good to design Print method to accept any IEnumerable<T> and do not tie it with concrete List<T> implementation. But this will incur boxing on the other hand so we have to choose between possible performance implications and good code practices.

The obvious questions may arise why common collections like List<T> have enumerators implemented as a struct in the first place if this implies such hidden boxing overhead? The answer is simple, and you may already guess it after all that has been said so far. The overwhelming majority of use cases is to use enumerators as local variables, so being value types, they can be cheaply and quickly allocated on the stack. This by far outweighs possible problems with boxing.

Boxing has its complementary operation called *unboxing*, which means converting a back-boxed reference-type value into a value type instance. This operation draws much less attention because it does not cause such significant memory overhead. First of all, we should do boxing first so if we do not do boxing, unboxing will not happen. Secondly, unboxing does not incur heap allocation. The value will be copied from the heap back to the stack so there is memory copying overhead. But as we already know, we are much less afraid of performance impact of the stack allocations so we are much less afraid of unboxing also.

There is a small, not-so-obvious caveat related to unboxing. As ECMA-335 says: "*All boxed types have an operation called unbox, which results in a managed pointer to the bit representation of the value.*" And in fact, there is a CIL unbox instruction that does exactly that - it pushes onto the evaluation stack the managed pointer to the data in the boxed instance. We can then say that unboxing in its pure form is neither copying nor allocating any data. But then such a pointer has to be used to obtain the actual value. This is what ldobj instruction is doing, it "*copies the value stored at address src to the stack.*" When the C# compiler wants to do unboxing, it emits unbox.any CIL instruction, which is equivalent to unbox followed by ldobj instructions.

There are many possible places where implicit boxing may occur and it is really hard to be aware of all of them all the time. What can we do to cope with this problem? For sure we can learn the most basic and common cases. But there are tools that can help us. There is a Heap Allocations Viewer extension for Visual Studio and Roslyn C# Heap Allocation Analyzer plugin for ReSharper that do exactly that. They show us any hidden allocations, including those coming from implicit boxing. I strongly encourage you to try these tools during everyday work. More examples of possible hidden allocation sources (including boxing) are also presented in Chapter 6, along with yet more scenarios of investigating them.

Passing by Reference

We have learned already, briefly, valuable types and reference types and passing-by value and passing-by reference semantics associated with them. There is yet another level of control above that. As mentioned already a few times, we can pass by reference any value, irrespective of whether it is a value type instance or reference-type instance.

Thus, let's take a look about those two respective contexts.

Pass-by-Reference Value-Type Instance

As pointed out many times, value types have pass-by-value semantics, so whenever we are assigning instances of value types, we are creating bitwise copy of its value. This is very often illustrated by an example similar to the one shown at Listing 4-32. We are using here the struct definition from Listing 4-6 defined earlier in this chapter. Helper method has a single value type argument. When we pass SomeStruct instance into it, a local copy inside Helper method is being created. Thus, modifying data.Value1 does not make sense - it will modify only this local copy and leave the original ss instance untouched. Main method will return 10.

Listing 4-32. Example of C# code passing struct by value

```
public int Main(int data)
{
    SomeStruct ss = new SomeStruct();
    ss.Value1 = 10;
    Helper(ss);
```

```
        return ss.Value1;
}

private void Helper(SomeStruct data)
{
        data.Value1 = 11;
}
```

We can change this behavior by passing the data instance by reference with the help of ref keyword (see Listing 4-33). In such a case we are using reference to the original value instance on the stack. Any modifications of it inside Helper method will be reflected in the original ss instance. Thus, Main method will return 11.

Listing 4-33. Example of C# code passing struct by reference

```
public int Main(int data)
{
        SomeStruct ss = new SomeStruct();
        ss.Value1 = 10;
        Helper(ref ss);
        return ss.Value1;
}

private void Helper(ref SomeStruct data)
{
        data.Value1 = 11;
}
```

Using structs (value types) as local variables and passing them by reference is a great optimization trick - not only that we cause no heap allocation, we also eliminate the overhead of possible data copying regardless of struct size.

Please remember the JIT compiler is so great in code optimization. In the case of Release build of program from Listing 4-33, the JIT compiler will notice that there is no need for struct even on the stack at all (as we have previously seen at Listing 4-9). Therefore, Main method in our example will be JITted to mov eax, 0xb and ret instructions!

Pass-by-Reference Reference-Type Instance

Here we may get a little bit lost as we are talking about passing by reference a reference-to-reference type. If you are familiar with C/C++ world, this would be something like using a pointer to the pointer.

Using the class definition from Listing 4-11 we can illustrate it by Listing 4-34. Here by reference is passed a reference to `SomeClass` reference-type instance. We can access it as usual inside `Helper` class (which however would be a little slower than by accessing normal reference as an additional pointer dereference is required here). But by having reference to the reference type, we can modify it and change it to point another reference type instance. In our sample Main method will return 11. If `SomeClass` was passed simply by reference, `Helper` code would overwrite locally passed reference by locally creating a new instance. But those changes would not be visible outside this method. You probably need a moment or two to get your head around it.

Listing 4-34. Example of C# code passing reference type by reference

```
public int Main(int data)
{
    SomeClass sc = new SomeClass();
    sc.Value1 = 10;
    Helper(ref sc);
    return sc.Value1;
}
private void Helper(ref SomeClass data)
{
    data = new SomeClass();
    data.Value1 = 11;
}
```

We will put quite a lot of attention to the passing-by reference in this book, in Chapter 14. This is a great and very interesting topic. It is also one of the most powerful optimization tricks used for performance tuning. If your job is to write a super-efficient library with the best possible performance, you should definitely focus on this kind of optimization. This is how commonly used solutions with the highest expected performance, such as the Roslyn compiler or the Kestrel server, are being optimized.

For now, let's just remember this mechanism as a great way of improving struct and class usage performance and hence a perfect tool for avoiding allocations in our code.

Passing-by reference is so important in terms of optimizing common code base of different libraries that it constantly gains more and more attention from creators of .NET and C# language. From C# 7.0 local reference variables and returning-by-reference capabilities have been added. From C# 7.1 and 7.2 there is the possibility to pass by read-only reference (by using `in` keyword instead of `ref`) to explicitly say that a reference is passed only for accessing data, without a possibility to modify it. We will look at all those possibilities in Chapter 14.

Types Data Locality

Due to no overhead from any additional data, structs are very compact. This is desirable for two reasons:

- It is always good to process less data - this obvious reason does not need any special comment. Even in the times when the memory is cheap, we can benefit from processing less - the time.

- It is always good to utilize cache to its extent - when we can load more objects into single cache line because they are smaller, we may gain a significant performance boost. As we saw in Chapter 2, it pays off if we lay out data in a way that helps to have as much as possible usable data into cache line. This is exactly where structs can help us.

Data structures build from structs provide more dense memory utilization because there is no overhead related with the reference types. What is even more important, arrays of structs constitute continuous regions of memory filled with its data, whereas in case of reference types, only references are laid out sequentially. Value they are referring to may be scattered through all the managed heaps, and we do not have control about it (see Figure 4-24).

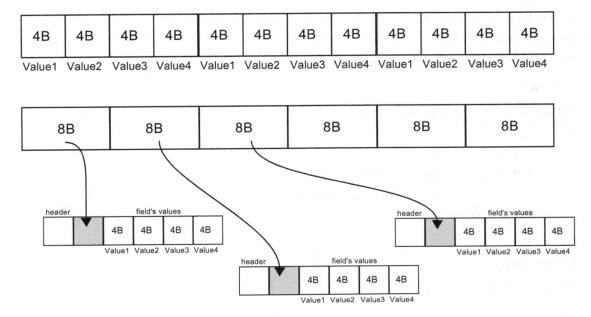

Figure 4-24. *Arrays of structs (at the top) constitute continuous regions of memory because value types store their data in place. Arrays of classes (at the bottom) are in fact only continuous arrays of references pointing to objects on the heap with undefined locations.*

Performance differences of such different data localities are presented with the help of a program from Listing 4-35. This program simply calculates the total sum off the first field in all array elements: once for arrays of structs and once for array of classes.

Listing 4-35. Benchmark showing performance difference in accessing array of structs versus array of classes

```
public struct SmallStruct
{
    public int Value1;
    public int Value2;
}

public class SmallClass
{
    public int Value1;
    public int Value2;
}
```

```
// both arrays are initialized with one million elements
private SmallClass[] classes;
private SmallStruct[] structs;

[Benchmark]
public int StructArrayAccess()
{
    int result = 0;
    for (int i = 0; i < items; i++)
        result += Helper1(structs, i);
    return result;
}

[Benchmark]
public int ClassArrayAccess()
{
    int result = 0;
    for (int i = 0; i < items; i++)
        result += Helper2(classes, i);
    return result;
}

public int Helper1(SmallStruct [] data, int index)
{
    return data[index].Value1;
}

public int Helper2(SmallClass [] data, int index)
{
    return data[index].Value1;
}
```

What may be interesting is that the only difference between those two approaches lies in the JIT-compiled code generated for each of the helper methods (see Listing 4-36). The difference is that struct's array access in Helper1 uses a single address dereference - it calculates the address in an array by multiplication by index times struct size. Then it stores value under this address in the result register. Helper2 has to dereference the address twice - first to get the reference to an object under a given index and second to get the value under this reference.

Listing 4-36. Fragments of assembly code generated after JITting Helper methods from Listing 4-35. In this case rdx register contains address of an array object and rax contains an index in this array.

```
Helper1(Samples.SomeStruct[], Int32)
...
0x00007FFA`526A0E8D:     L000d: mov eax, [rdx+rax*8+0x10]
...

Helper2(Samples.SomeClass[], Int32)
...
0x00007FFA`526A0E4D:     L000d: mov rax, [rdx+rax*8+0x10]
0x00007FFA`526A0E52:     L0012: mov eax, [rax+0x8]
...
```

Note The code for Helper methods will be in fact inlined into benchmarked methods, but they were presented in original form for clarity.

The result of both approaches is presented in Table 4-3. We can notice really big differences that obviously cannot be explained only by executing one more address dereference. The additional overhead comes from the fact of much worse data locality as class instances are not guaranteed to lie next to each other. Hence, more cache lines have to be loaded during such calculations.

Table 4-3. *Benchmark Results of Struct versus Class Array Access from Listing L1. BenchmarkDotNet Was Used on .NET Core 2.0.0.*

Method	Mean	Allocated
StructArrayAccess	618.7 us	0 B
ClassArrayAccess	1,816.5 us	0 B

Static Data

Static data may be seen as a kind of global variable in our program. And while global variables are not so welcome in good design practices, they still may be found useful. In case of C#, there is only one type of static data available - static fields. While VB.NET allows us to declare static variables in functions, they are simply a syntactic sugar around a regular static field (in case of usage in Shared function). Let's dig into static fields a little then.

Static Fields

Everyone programming in .NET perfectly understands static fields - their value is shared among all instances of a given type. We access them by using a type's name, globally from everywhere such type is accessible (see Listing 4-37). It makes perfect sense and probably does not need any more explanation.

Listing 4-37. Example of static field usage

```
public class C {
    public void Method1()
    {
        S.Value = 10;
    }
    public void Method2() {
        Console.WriteLine(S.Value);
    }
}

public class S
{
    public static int Value;
}
```

However, from a memory-management perspective, a few additional remarks should be added:

- Static data have per AppDomain scope - if we load the same assembly into multiple application domains, there will be multiple, same static data instances.

- Static data of types defined in an assembly lives as long as the AppDomain lives, where such assembly was loaded - thus, until assembly is unloaded, all static data and objects referenced by them will stay reachable (thus, not garbage collected).

- While they are implementation details, one may wish to be aware that:

  - Static primitive data (like numbers) are stored in a High Frequency Heap of the corresponding application domain (part of its Loader Heap).

  - Static reference type instances (objects) are living on the regular GC Heap - the difference to normal objects is that they are additionally referenced by the internal "statics table." Because such objects will obviously live long, they will eventually land in generation 2 and stay there.[6]

  - Static user-defined value type instances (structs) are also living inside the regular GC Heap in a boxed form.

---

[6]Unless it is large object, which will from the beginning live on a Large Object Heap.

Having said that, if you are interested how exactly statics are implemented in .NET, read the following section about its internals.

Static Data Internals

Each application domain in a .NET application is represented by a set of internal data structures (see Figure 4-25). For each module existing in loaded assemblies, the DomainLocalModule data structure is maintained. It contains two crucial regions from the internal static data point-of-view implementation:

- For fields of reference type and structs (in boxed form) - a reference pointing inside Object[] table where static references of a given module begins (m_pGCstatics in Figure 4-25). Such Object[] table is shared between all modules and assemblies loaded into the application domain.

- For fields of primitive types - its values, grouped by types where they are defined, including necessary padding because of memory alignment requirements (*statics blob* in Figure 4-25).

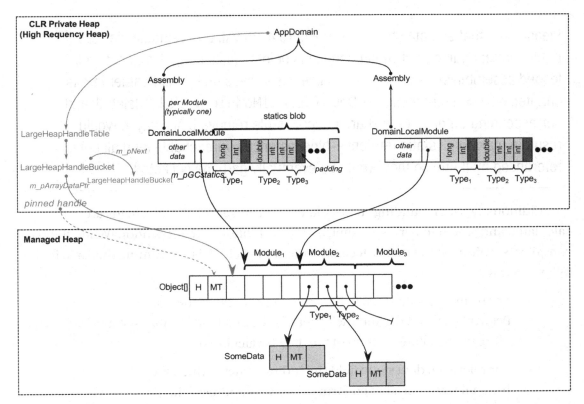

Figure 4-25. *Internals of static fields storage in .NET Core (from the perspective of single-application domain and two assemblies loaded into it). Places where static data is indeed stored are marked as gray (while every other visible structure may be seen as a supporting, auxiliary data). In case of .NET Framework, static blob is stored next to given type's MethodTable.*

The above-mentioned shared `Object[]` array is maintained by the internal `LargeHeapHandleTable` data structure (already mentioned in section about string interning, where it is also used) and it is allocated in a Large Object Heap (being also pinned, to make it safe to store addresses pointing into it). Such a handle table maintains arrays in buckets, so when the currently used array is filled, a new bucket and new corresponding array will be created (which may happen, for example, if a new generic type with static fields needs to be constructed).

Please note that all data structures in Figure 4-25 will be eventually deleted if the corresponding application domain is deleted (including all static data in loaded assemblies). In case of collectible assemblies mentioned earlier in this chapter, only corresponding the `DomainLocalModule` would be deleted, and corresponding entries in the shared handle table removed. Anyway, it would result in making all static reference-type instances unreachable (and all objects referenced by them) so they would be eventually garbage collected.

Additionally, when building static-related data, offsets of all static fields are calculated and stored in corresponding a MethodTable's field description. When the JIT compiler is emitting code that is accessing the static field, it is consuming this data in the following way:

- For primitive data static field - knowing address of the proper `DomainLocalModule` and the offset of accessed field within its statics blob, the absolute address of the data is calculated.

- For reference data static field (including structs, which are heap allocated in a boxed form) - knowing address (via `LargeHeapHandleTable` and its buckets) of the corresponding `Object[]` array and the offset of accessed field within it, the absolute address of the proper element of such array is calculated (which is a reference, pointing to the appropriate object).

Using as an example a few simple types defined in Listing 4-38, we can see in action using data structures shown in Figure 4-23.

Listing 4-38. Simple types used in the next code examples

```
public class ExampleClass
{
    public static int StaticPrimitive;
    public static S StaticStruct;
    public static R StaticObject = new R();
}
```

```
public class R
{
    public int Value;
}

public struct S
{
    public int Value;
}
```

When accessing a primitive static field (see Listing 4-39), assembly code emitted by the JIT compiler is indeed very simple (see Listing 4-40) - it consists only of reading a given value from the proper statics blob region. Thus, accessing primitive static data can be seen as a very fast operation without additional overhead (at least until we won't guard it with some thread safety like using locks).

Listing 4-39. Trivial example of accessing primitive static field

```
[MethodImpl(MethodImplOptions.NoInlining)]
public void Method1()
{
    Console.WriteLine(ExampleClass.StaticPrimitive);
}
```

Listing 4-40. JIT-compiled code from Listing 4-39 (only relevant part)

```
...
mov    ecx,dword ptr [00007ff9`3c8a4bd8] ; address in High Frequency Heap
(inside statics blob)
call   00007ff9`3c9c1380 (System.Console.WriteLine(Int32), mdToken:
000000000600007e)
...
```

Structs that are static fields are becoming heap allocated in a boxed form; thus they are treated as any other object. When accessing such a static field data (see Listing 4-41), assembly code emitted by the JIT is accessing the handle table to get an address of the heap-allocated struct instance on the GC Heap (see Listing 4-42). We should be aware of this additional overhead of handle dereference, because we could think that structs are stored in statics blob as primitive value types described above.

Listing 4-41. Trivial example of accessing user-defined value type static field data

```
[MethodImpl(MethodImplOptions.NoInlining)]
public void Method2()
{
    Console.WriteLine(ExampleClass.StaticStruct.Value);
}
```

Listing 4-42. JIT-compiled code from Listing 4-41

```
...
mov    rcx,19510002938h      ; addres in LOH (inside handle table)
mov    rcx,qword ptr [rcx]    ; dereference handle (rcx contains boxed
struct address)
mov    ecx,dword ptr [rcx+8]  ; access the first field of a boxed struct
call   00007ff9`3c9c2b60 (System.Console.WriteLine(Int32), mdToken:
000000000600007e)
...
```

Accessing the reference type static field data (see Listing 4-43) generates exactly the same code as seen previously: to access the handle table to get an address of the object (see Listing 4-44). Again, handle dereferencing overhead exists, but in case of reference data it is more expected.

Listing 4-43. Trivial example of accessing reference-type static field data

```
[MethodImpl(MethodImplOptions.NoInlining)]
public void Method3()
{
    Console.WriteLine(ExampleClass.StaticObject.Value);
}
```

Listing 4-44. JIT-compiled code from Listing 4-43

```
mov    rcx,19510002940h       ; addres in LOH (inside handle table)
mov    rcx,qword ptr [rcx]    ; dereference handle (rcx contains object address)
mov    ecx,dword ptr [rcx+8] ; access the first field of an object
call    00007ff9`3c9c2b60 (System.Console.WriteLine(Int32), mdToken:
000000000600007e)
```

Exactly the same code (with slightly different addresses, obviously) would be generated if `ExampleClass` was a struct. This is because the static field type is important, not the type in which such field is defined.

Summary

The first three chapters were merely .NET-related. We have learned some algorithmic and computer architecture basics. However, this chapter is a game changer. We started looking at .NET much more intensively. After starting with some basic historical background, we took a deep dive into .NET internals. We have devoted a few pages to learning the different areas of memory that are part of the .NET process. We have looked deeper at some of these areas, for example, having the opportunity to diagnose the problems related with them. This happened with the help of a new kind of information also introduced in this chapter - scenarios. They are intended to show you various problems and possible ways to analyze them. I hope this makes you feel that learning is not only theory but also very practical aspects of .NET memory management.

We've seen quite a lot of this topic already and have not even touched on Garbage Collector by itself. Some aspects mentioned in this chapter will even return to us from time to time in the rest of the book. However, it is not hard to notice that most of this chapter is dedicated to the type system and various aspects of different type categories in .NET. After learning about structs and classes quite a lot in this chapter, it is worth ending with a brief summary of their strengths and weaknesses summarized below.

Structs

- better data locality - they contain all its data in place and are stored without any additional overhead so cache utilization is much better

- may be allocated on stack - in certain scenarios, structs being local variables are allocated on the stack, which is much more lightweight and does not incur future GC-related overhead.

- may be overwhelmingly optimized - as we have seen in some scenarios, the struct concept just disappears from the generated machine code completely and whole processing is done via CPU registers.

- risk of unintentional boxing - when used carelessly, structs may be a source of boxing, which incurs hidden allocations.

- harder to understand - pass-by-value semantics and a few other various caveats may sometimes be less intuitive than well-known classes.

- most of the performance benefits are strongly implementation dependent - now they work but it is not guaranteed that in future the implementation details won't change.

Classes

- "just works" - classes are the basic building blocks and code we write using them just works. We are used to them very much and using them is an obvious choice.

- overhead of GC - allocating class instances incur heap allocations and those give GC additional work.

It is also high time we introduced some new Rules related to the material from this chapter. There are a few as the topics we touch are becoming more and more practical. Please note that the rule Avoid Hidden Allocation is highly related to string concatenation shown in this chapter, will be presented in Chapter 5.

Rule 6 - Measure Your Program

Justification: It is really hard to know whether your program consumes a lot of memory or not if you do not know how to measure it. The answer to the question - how big my program is - may be quite difficult. There are various metrics we can look at and without deeper understanding of them, we may simply get lost. We do not know how to compare different programs in terms of size. And we do not know how to ask our customer to check it.

How to apply: Using the knowledge gained in the second and fourth chapters, we can understand quite precisely what each program size means. When analyzing different memory-related issues, we should always start to investigate its size and how it changes in time. We should always start to look at the most troublesome size - the one that indicates how much physical RAM is being consumed. We should look at whole private and virtual also. Only knowing those measurements gives us context wide enough to proceed with further analysis.

Related scenarios: Scenario 4-1.

Rule 7 - Do Not Assume There Is No Memory Leak

Justification: It is tempting to assume that in a managed .NET environment there is no chance that memory leaks will occur. Memory is automatically reclaimed so why should we care? This is almost always true and it is a great engineering achievement of .NET runtime creators. However, there still exists many scenarios that may hit us back in the less-appropriate moment. And most probably they reveal some of the customer's production environment.

How to apply: Just don't do that. Measure You Program (Rule 6) and Measure GC Early (Rule 5). Keep your eyes open to suspicious trends, especially when one of the observed sizes start to grow infinitely.

Related scenarios: Scenarios 4-2, 4-3, and 4-4.

Rule 8 - Consider Using Struct

Justification: Using classes in object-oriented programming in C# is so popular that it is used by default and without any thinking. Classes "just work" so why should we care? However, structs were not invented without a reason. Add structs to your everyday developer's life toolbox. You do not need to start using them everywhere for now. Just try to consider them after knowledge you gained in Chapter 4 of this book.

How to apply: Read about structures. Learn their strengths and weaknesses. Understand pass-by-value and pass-by-reference semantics. Measure Early to find out whether it makes sense to put effort in optimizing this part of code you are looking at. If so, try to make use of some leaky implementation details of struct - the stack allocation, JIT optimization, and so on and so forth. And if you decide to use struct in your code, remember the possibility of passing them by reference - consider using ref parameters, local ref and ref return values. This can help you gain even more performance. Also, always remember a stack is precious resource - do not expect that you will be able to put a huge amount of data there.

Rule 9 - Consider Using String Interning

Justification: Strings are almost always one of the most common types in our program's memory. And storing in memory a lot of duplicated string is obviously inefficient. .NET runtimes take care of it in case of string literals. If we want to take care of it in case of dynamically generated strings (for example, loaded or received from external source like file or HTTP request), we may use string interning manually.

How to apply: Measure whether you indeed have a lot of duplicated strings. Consider their lifespan and uniqueness. Do you have a lot of duplicated strings living for minutes or hours inside your process? Or do you have only big bursts of temporary string during some input processing. String interning has its own drawback and it may be beneficial only in the first scenario. Remember that string once interned will live till the runtime termination. Thus, interning a string is a very risky decision and must be well-thought out.

Related scenarios: Scenario 4-5.

Rule 10 - Avoid Boxing

Justification: Boxing operation converts value type into a corresponding reference type. This introduces hidden allocation as the reference type will be allocated on the heap. Avoid Allocation (Rule 14) is one of the most important optimization approaches so we should avoid boxing whenever possible, especially since most happen without our knowledge as implicit boxing.

How to apply: Learn about typical implicit boxing scenarios and just try to avoid them. You can Measure GC Early (Rule 5) whether your program allocates a lot and boxing can turn out to be one of the reasons. You can help yourself in spotting implicit boxing by using the Heap Allocations Viewer extension for Visual Studio and Roslyn C# Heap Allocation Analyzer plugin for ReSharper.

CHAPTER 5

Memory Partitioning

We have already learned some basic memory-related facts about .NET internals in the previous chapter. We've looked inside process memory running managed code. As we have seen, there are many various memory segments inside it. Some of them are used internally by the .NET framework itself. Some of them are part of operating system cooperation. But there are also more important heaps for us denoted as the Managed Heap.

As it was explained in Chapter 4, some of them contain various data required for the Execution Engine, like types description. Those are `Domain` heaps, `Low Frequency` heaps, and `High Frequency` heaps. But among all those different heaps, there is yet the most important one that is for the sole Garbage Collector purposes (see Figure 5-1). Those are the memory segments that contain the Heap (or the Free Store) as defined in Chapter 1 from the CLI perspective. Let's agree that these memory areas will be called the Garbage Collector's Managed Heap (the GC Managed Heap or the GC Heap in short).

⊞ 0000008BF8900000	Private Data	2,048 K	52 K	52 K	52 K	52 K	3 Read/Write	Thread Environment Block ID: 18376
⊞ 0000008BF8A00000	Thread Stack	1,536 K	20 K	20 K	8 K	8 K	3 Read/Write/Guard	Thread ID: 17980
⊞ 0000008BF8B80000	Thread Stack	1,536 K	20 K	20 K	8 K	8 K	3 Read/Write/Guard	Thread ID: 2432
⊞ 0000008BF8D00000	Thread Stack	1,536 K	20 K	20 K	8 K	8 K	3 Read/Write/Guard	Thread ID: 14436
⊞ 0000008BF8E80000	Thread Stack	1,536 K	20 K	20 K	8 K	8 K	3 Read/Write/Guard	Thread ID: 19740
⊞ 0000008BF9000000	Thread Stack	1,536 K	20 K	20 K	8 K	8 K	3 Read/Write/Guard	Thread ID: 18712
0000008BF9180000	Free	1,992,407,552 K						
⊞ 0000026700000000	Managed Heap	393,216 K	336 K	336 K	224 K	224 K	4 Read/Write	GC
0000026718000000	Free	1,610,688 K						
⊞ 000002677A4F0000	Heap (Shareable)	64 K	64 K		4 K		1 Read/Write	Heap ID: 2 [COMPATABILITY]
⊞ 000002677A500000	Private Data	4 K	4 K	4 K	4 K	4 K	1 Read/Write	
000002677A501000	Unusable	60 K						
⊞ 000002677A510000	Shareable	88 K	88 K		88 K		1 Read	

Figure 5-1. *Among various heaps existing inside a process running .NET application, there is one type that is the most interesting for us - GC Heap containing all objects allocated by our program*

When our application is running, the .NET runtime Allocator is allocating objects inside the GC Heap. The Collector implemented in .NET runtime tracks the reachability of objects located in the GC Heap to reclaim memory of those which are no longer reachable.

339

© Konrad Kokosa 2018
K. Kokosa, *Pro .NET Memory Management*, https://doi.org/10.1007/978-1-4842-4027-4_5

As we have seen in the previous chapter, the misbehaving of any of those different heaps can indicate some problem. Nevertheless, from the .NET developer's point of view, the GC Heap is the place of the most interest. Thus, we can freely say that the rest of this book will focus on this area of memory.

Partitioning Strategies

GC Heap can grow to the size of many gigabytes. It might not be a problem from the Allocator perspective. But taking such possible big sizes into account, it is difficult to imagine that the Collector is able to treat so much data uniformly. It's difficult to handle gigabytes of data in a timely manner. When designing Garbage Collector as a whole, one of the most important parameters is the overhead it introduces. Among other things, for example, for how long it stops thread activity due to garbage collection. Or how much CPU it consumes. One would like to achieve less than millisecond pauses. However, due to the memory access latencies listed in Chapter 2, in the time of milliseconds we may read megabytes, not gigabytes of data. This is why one of the most important design decisions behind every Garbage Collector implementation is the *memory partitioning strategy*.

Simply put, we want to split the whole GC Heap into smaller parts to have the possibility to operate on them independently. If done wisely, it can tremendously speed up the Garbage Collector work because, as it turns out, there is in fact no need to treat all the data equally during program execution.

There are many different partitioning strategies possible. They are usually based on one of the properties of the existing object:

- Size - we can split GC Heap into parts of various object's sizes. For example, you may want to treat differently small objects from those really big ones. This may be especially important when the compacting collection is used. Copying big objects may introduce significant memory overhead, so we may decide to compact only areas of small objects and use sweep collection for larger ones.

- Lifetime - the life of the object is pretty important. Intuitively, it is worth treating objects that live very short differently from those that live most of the entire application lifetime. Obviously we do not know the future, but at least we can differentiate objects living long from those recently created. Memory areas for objects with different lifetimes are generally referred to as *generations* and called *"young"* / *"old"* or by consecutive numbers.

- Mutability - one of the most important properties of an object is its mutability. If an object cannot be changed once created (it is immutable), it may we worth it to treat it differently than mutable ones.

- Type - one may decide to treat differently some specific type of objects. Do we want to maintain a separate heap for strings, integers or any other special classes, interface implementations, or attributes? Your mileage may vary.

- Kind - objects can be classified in many different ways and partitioned in this respect. For example, does an object contain any pointers (outgoing references)? If not, we do not have to worry about them when compaction of other objects happened. Has an object been *pinned* (*pinning* will be described in detail in Chapter 7) so it will not be moved even during compacting collection? If yes, maybe it is worth it to move it to yet another memory partition to not introduce all overhead related to moving objects around those pinned instances.[1]

In case of both Microsoft's .NET implementation and Mono implementation, only the first two of these strategies were chosen. Their GCs do not particularly care about the type or mutability of an object, they simply manage the appropriate number of required bytes (like "give me N bytes for the new object"). However, as GC design is constantly evolving, no one knows if in the future, one of the additional strategies will not be implemented in either .NET's or Mono's GC.

Now just let's look in detail at both of these partitioning strategies. As always, most details will be related to Microsoft's implementation with only side notes related to Mono or any other runtime.

---

[1]This is, however, much more complex that it sounds. For example, objects in .NET are not created pinned - we can decide to pin and unpin them at any time afterward. Thus, such a separate region of currently pinned objects in case of CLR could be counterproductive, requiring copying the object back and forth during pin/unpin.

Size Partitioning

The first strategy is to treat differently objects of various sizes. As mentioned above, the main reason behind it is the memory copying overhead in case of compacting collection. Since there is no particular justification for dividing into several size ranges, a single threshold value was selected that defines the boundary between a small and a large object. GC Heap is then divided into two physically separated memory regions:

- *Small Object Heap* (SOH) - all objects smaller than 85,000 bytes are created here.

- *Large Object Heap* (LOH) - all objects equal or larger than 85,000 bytes are created here.

Most of the logic and code are shared between them, but obviously there are important differences. Please note this threshold is 85,000 bytes but people tend to understand it incorrectly as 85 times 1024 bytes as it would be 85 KiB (or 85 kB in common sense).

Because we separated in that way "small" and "large" objects, we can treat both heaps differently:

- Compacting collections may be used for SOH because for small objects, we are not so afraid of memory copying. As we will see in Chapter 7, both sweep and in-place compacting collection have been implemented in case of Microsoft's Small Object Heap. During the additional Plan phase, it is decided which one of them will be executed.

- Only a sweep collection is used in LOH because of the compacting (copying) cost of large objects (although a user may trigger LOH compaction explicitly).

Currently for Mono 5.4, the single threshold value is 8,000 bytes. All bigger objects are allocated in a region named in Mono as Large Object Store (LOS) and smaller objects are allocated in Nursery. Similar to Microsoft's .NET, small objects' space may be compacted while LOS is cleaned only by sweeping.

We may wonder why a threshold value of 85,000 bytes and not another has been selected. As we've seen it already a few times in this book and we will see many times in other places, there is often a mix of engineering and historical reasons. The simplest answer is that this value has been selected experimentally based on numerous tests conducted at the very beginning of .NET. There is a rumor that these tests were conducted mainly in the context of a SharePoint product, but this is completely unconfirmed. A bunch of various scenarios were selected including internal and external teams. Since then, there is simply no evidence that changing this value would provide any benefits.

You may also wonder what size 85,000 bytes threshold applies to. Obviously it considers the shallow size of an object - references are counted as references, not the size of the objects they refer to. For this reason, in LOH most often we may find... arrays. It is hard to imagine an object having so many large fields that its shallow size exceeds 85,000 bytes. Please also note that an object having a large array as a field is not large itself - this field is only a small reference to the array.

There is one notable implementation detail worth mentioning. SOH has different memory alignments on various platforms. In case of a 32-bit runtime, the alignment is 4 bytes. It means that all allocated objects are arranged in the way that their starting addresses are a multiplication of 4. In that way no unaligned memory access happens, which would always come with noticeable performance cost. In case of a 64-bit platform, the alignment in SOH is 8 bytes. LOH is different because the memory alignment there is always 8 bytes, regardless of the bitness of the framework. For a 64-bit platform it seems to be natural. However, why 8 bytes alignment in case of a 32-bit runtime, in opposite to 4-bytes alignment of SOH? It was mainly for arrays of doubles so their access is aligned (as will be explained soon). And since 8 bytes is very small compared to how big a large object is, LOH was 8-byte aligned without no worries.

Small Object Heap

A Small Object Heap is by far the most popular memory region because most of the objects we create are smaller than 85,000 bytes. Thus, typically the number of the objects allocated in SOH outnumbers the number of LOH-located objects in orders of magnitude. Since a large number of objects can cause problems (like traversing a large graph during the Mark phase), it is worth considering dividing this area into even smaller, separated pieces. Such a decision was made in the majority of known environments with automatically managed memory for separating objects in terms of their lifetime.

Because Small Object Heap organization is strictly related to lifetime partitioning, any further details of it are provided in the next point.

Large Object Heap

A Large Object Heap is sometimes called 3-th generation or is referenced by 3rd index (after 0, 1, and 2 for three generations residing in SOH as we will soon see). Although the idea behind is simple - store all objects equal or larger than 85,000 bytes

---

From the Collector point of view, large objects in LOH belong logically to generation 2 because they are collected only when generation 2 is being collected.

There is an assumption that large object allocations are rather infrequent because most programs do not need so many big data structures. This may be not true in some cases and may lead to performance degradation (see Rule 15 Avoid Excessive LOH Allocations in Chapter 6). In general, it is true that only objects bigger than 85,000 bytes are allocated inside a Large Object Heap. However, there are some little exceptions as to what is being placed there.

Large Object Heap - Arrays of Doubles

The most noteworthy exception of what we can find inside LOH applies to arrays of doubles in case of a 32-bit runtime environment (even when executed on 64-bit machine). Arrays of double are treated as "large objects" and thus allocated in LOH when they have equal or more than 1,000 elements (see Listing 5-1). As double is always 8-bytes long, it means that LOH contains around at least 8,000-byte big arrays, breaking the rule of containing only objects bigger than 85,000 bytes.

Listing 5-1. In case of 32-bit .NET runtime, arrays of doubles with equal or more than 1,000 elements are allocated in LOH so this sample program will print "0" and "3" respectively.

```
double[] array1 = new double[999];
Console.WriteLine(GC.GetGeneration(array1));      // prints 0
double[] array2 = new double[1000];
Console.WriteLine(GC.GetGeneration(array2));      // prints 3
```

Why has such a strange and quite specific exception been made? As mentioned before, in this case the reason is related to memory alignment, not to memory copying overhead. Double is 8-byted long. Unaligned access to double is very expensive (far more than for integral types). This is not a problem for a 64-bit environment, which always uses 8-byte alignment for both SOH and LOH. But it may be problematic for a 32-bit SOH with a 4-byte alignment.

Thus it is worth it to use LOH, which, as mentioned, always uses an 8-byte alignment. In this way, we avoid a large cost of unaligned access for bigger arrays. But why not always allocate arrays of doubles in LOH for 32-bit runtime then? Allocating in LOH has its own drawbacks - as it is not being compacted, a lot of smaller structures may introduce unwanted fragmentation. Choosing to allocate there only arrays above a certain size is in fact a compromise balancing between costs of unaligned access versus fragmentation. And again, a threshold of 1,000 was chosen experimentally.

We should still be aware of fragmentation caused by arrays of doubles when using a 32-bit framework. A lot of continuously created and reclaimed arrays of doubles bigger than one thousand elements may be, for example, created during some kind of signal processing. In such a situation, we should create a reusable buffer (pool) of arrays instead of constantly creating new ones. See Scenario 6-1 for further details.

Large Object Heap - Internal CLR Data

There are no other exceptions to Large Object Heap allocations of objects we allocate in our code and not being bigger than the given size threshold. However, LOH is also used by the .NET Framework internally to store some additional data. We have mentioned them twice in the previous Chapter 4, in the context of string interning and static fields. We refer here to the `LargeHeapHandleTable` structure. Let's now dedicate a few words to it.

LargeHeapHandleTable

`LargeHeapHandleTable` is a data structure maintained by the .NET runtime, which manages objects' arrays allocated in Large Object Heap for its internal purposes. Internally it is organized into buckets (see Figure 5-2 for an illustration of those data structured in CoreCLR). Each bucket represents a single `Object[]` array allocated in LOH. Those arrays are pinned so they will not be ever moved by the Garbage Collector. This is because various unmanaged parts of CLR may store pointers to the array's elements, so moving them would require a lot of work by updating those pointers.

Each bucket stores a pinned handle to the corresponding array. It also stores (for convenience) a direct pointer to the beginning of the array's data (`m_pArrayDataPtr`) and the current index of the not-yet-used array element (`m_currentPos`, as these arrays are created with some spare space in advance). If all array elements have been used, a new bucket will be created (which incurs creating a new `Object[]` array in Large Object Heap). Buckets inside a `LargeHeapHandleTable` are chained into a single-linked list (each bucket stores `m_pNext` pointer that points to the next bucket or null in case of being the last element).

As mentioned earlier, there are two main usages of LargeHeapHandleTable structure. As CoreCLR source code states:

```
// There are two locations you can find a LargeHeapHandleTable
// 1) there is one in every BaseDomain, it is used to keep track of the
//    static members in that domain
// 2) there is one in the System Domain that is used for the
//    GlobalStringLiteralMap
```

Those have been also illustrated in Figure 5-2. In other words, inside LOH there will be:

- one or more `Object[]` for global string literal map (aka String Intern pool) - managed by single `LargeHeapHandleTable` as it consists of at least a single bucket;

- one or more `Object[]` for each domain used for statics - managed by `LargeHeapHandleTable` in `BaseDomain`, as it consists of at least a single bucket.

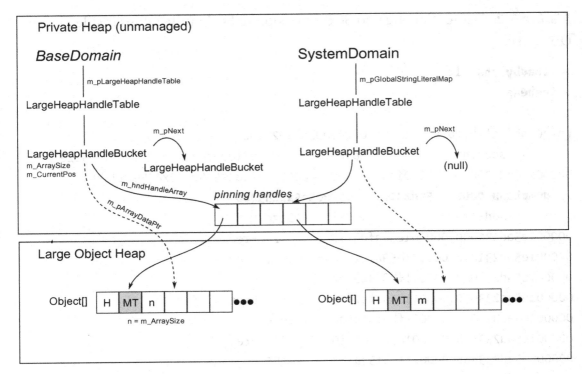

Figure 5-2. *LargeHeapHandleTable structure*

Even that SystemDomain is a domain in general, and it derives from BaseDomain so it contains m_pLargeHeapHandleTable, it is not being used by it - System Domain does not contain any managed module so there is no need for static members in it.

We can see handle table arrays by using WinDbg, for example. After attaching to the .NET process, we should load an SOS extension and list all GC-related memory regions by the eeheap command (see Listing 5-2). After learning the address range corresponding to LOH, use the dumpheap command to list all objects inside it. Results for the simple "Hello world" console program are also listed in Listing 5-2. As we can see, in such a pure program, there are only three Object[] arrays (column with value 00007ffb8f34a5b8 corresponds to MethodTable of Object[]).

Listing 5-2. Using WinDbg and SOS extension to list handle tables inside Large Object Heap

```
> .loadby sos clr
> !eeheap
...
Large object heap starts at 0x000001e5ad231000
        segment            begin          allocated              size
000001e5ad230000  000001e5ad231000  000001e5ad235480  0x4480(17536)
> !dumpheap 000001e5ad231000   000001e5ad235480
        Address                 MT      Size
000001e5ad231000 000001e59afc2ff0      24 Free
000001e5ad231018 000001e59afc2ff0      30 Free
000001e5ad231038 00007ffb8f34a5b8    8184
000001e5ad233030 000001e59afc2ff0      30 Free
000001e5ad233050 00007ffb8f34a5b8    1048
000001e5ad233468 000001e59afc2ff0      30 Free
000001e5ad233488 00007ffb8f34a5b8    8184
```

Those three arrays are:

- under 000001e5ad231038 address - handle table for Domain 1 (that contains most libraries and modules with our program itself),

- under 000001e5ad233050 address - string intern pool,

- under 000001e5ad233488 address - handle table for Shared Domain (which in case of simple console application may only contain System.Private.CoreLib.dll module).

If you wonder why there are also very small Free spaces visible at Listing 5-1, the answer is in Chapter 6 in the Large Object Heap Allocation section.

Unfortunately, currently there is no single way of knowing which array corresponds to which usage - we can investigate it mainly by looking at the content of each of them (by issuing `dumparray` command on each address).

Obviously a string intern pool will contain references to interned strings. The other two will contain mainly various static members of the used libraries and our code.

They will also contain strings that are created during resolving string literals of NGENed assemblies (and not using string interning due to `NoStringIntern` option).

There is yet one more usage of table handles - runtime uses them to store various Reflection-related data. If `GetType`, `typeof,` or any other Reflection API is used - underlying `RuntimeType` and other information is also saved via a handle in table handles. Thus we may also spot quite a lot of type-related objects referenced by those arrays.

It is rather unlikely that `LargeHeapHandleTable` will be a problem in our application. It would require creating a lot of static members (dynamically) or loading many dynamic AppDomains in general. Another possible reason would be interning a lot of strings. If you see a lot of big Object arrays in a Large Object Heap whose only root is a pinned handle - it may indicate you have just ended with one of such rare situations. However, as those arrays store only references, you will probably first notice a lot of those objects elsewhere in the first place.

Lifetime Partitioning

As mentioned earlier, due to the possible huge amounts of objects inside Small Object Heap, the decision was made to separate it into pieces regarding an object's lifetime. This concept is called *Generational Garbage Collection* because objects are divided into generations - with similar lifetimes defined in some specific manner. We can define lifetime in many possible ways, but let's stay with the two most obvious ones:

- absolute time - we can somehow relate object lifetime to real time. The simplest way would be to use the number of CPU clock ticks at the moment when the object has been created. This approach, however, comes with some drawbacks. How long should a "long life" last? And how about short? Is a second a long or short life? It is almost impossible to provide a generic answer because it depends on the specific program characteristics - how many objects it allocates, how often they should be garbage collected, and so on and so forth. We could create a self-learning mechanism to calculate thresholds between short- and long-living objects but it would be probably overcomplicated.

- relative time - instead of real time, we can relate an object's lifetime to some specific event, like garbage collection itself. In this way we are counting how many garbage collections the object has survived.

We may manage some internal counter that counts those survivals for each object. If it exceeds some given (or calculated) threshold, we treat such object as being "older."

We could even imagine less obvious ways of indicating an object's lifetime. For example, if Collector and Allocator are designed in a way that objects are never pushed back to the lower addresses, we can calculate the age of the object as the difference of its address in relation to another place in the memory.

It is interesting to note that many Garbage Collection descriptions almost always start from the fact that .NET has a Generational GC. But as we see, there is much more before we came to this implementation detail.

But why are Generational Garbage Collections applicable at all? Why does splitting and different treatment of objects due to their age make sense? This comes mainly from an observation called *generational hypothesis*. In fact, there are weaker (less general) and stronger (more general) versions of it, which put together are foundations of Generational GCs. They are kind of against intuition about human life:

- *weak generational hypothesis* (also known as *infant mortality*) - observation that most young objects live short. In other words, most of the objects that a program allocates become unused quickly. Those are all temporary objects represented by local variables, temporary (hidden) allocations, and all short-lived processing. This hypothesis is quite broadly confirmed by various computer science studies.

- *strong generational hypothesis* - observation that the longer an object lives, it most probably will live even longer. This would be various long-living objects like long caches, "managers," "helpers," object's pools, business workflows, and so forth. However, studies do not confirm this hypothesis completely as an object's lifetime characteristics seem to be much more complex that such a single sentence. There is even no universal definition of this hypothesis.

We can benefit knowing such distribution of objects regarding its age (see Figure 5-3). It is worth it to reclaim memory for young objects as fast as possible (by separating them into a "young" generation) if most of them die fast. And it is worth it to much less frequently reclaim memory for old objects (by separating them into an "old" generation) if they die rarely. We can, of course, also decide to create any number of "temporary," intermediate generations between them.

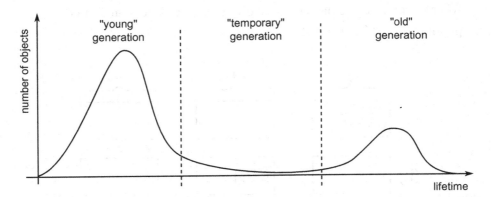

Figure 5-3. *Weak and strong generational hypothesis illustrated as a number of life (or reachable less precisely) objects regarding their age*

Having objects grouped into various generations, we can treat them separately. We can, for example, do garbage collection only on the youngest generation or only on the oldest one. We may also decide to collect all generations, which is typically referred to as a *full garbage collection.*

When an object reaches a certain lifetime threshold, it said to be *promoted* to the next generation. In other words, after promotion, we treat an object as belonging to the successive, older generation. What does exactly such a promotion mean and why does it vary significantly between various GC implementations?

One of the possibilities includes copying to some other region of memory. In such case it realizes copying of GC mentioned in Chapter 1 (Figure 1-18). Imagine generations' organization as in Figure 5-4 where we have three separate regions of memory for generations named 0, 1, and 2. The following example steps might be as follows:

- After a while of program execution, we have created objects A, B, and C - they are allocated in the youngest generation "0" (Figure 5-4a).

- After some time, GC happened - let's assume that object A turned out to be unreachable. Thus, only objects B and C are copied to generation "1" (Figure 5-4b).

- After some time, we have created object D - it has been allocated in generation "0" (Figure 5-4c).

- After some time, GC happened again - let's assume now B is no longer reachable. So, objects C and D have been copied to older generations (Figure 5-4d).

- After some time, we have created object E - it has been allocated in generation "0" (Figure 5-4e).

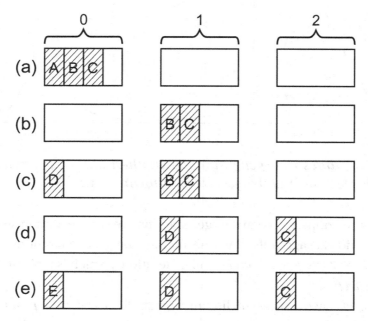

Figure 5-4. *Generations in case of copying GC, as separated memory regions. Promotion means copying an object to a different region.*

We can sometimes meet the claims that generations in Microsoft .NET work in such a rather intuitive way. It is very important to remember that this is not true. Microsoft's implementation of CLR has slightly different, more complex, yet a more efficient approach, thoroughly explained in Chapter 7.

In another approach, generations can be defined logically by addresses' boundaries. Promotion will be then just moving those boundaries, not the objects themselves (see Figure 5-5). This is a much faster approach than copying as moving such logical boundaries takes almost no time. Additionally, we may or may not compact survived objects (although it will be a lot more complex if we do). Imagine generations' organization as in Figure 5-5 where we have one continuous block of memory. The following example steps might be as follows:

- After a while of program execution, we have created objects A, B, and C - there is only a single, youngest generation "0" (Figure 5-5a). Boundaries of generations 1 and 2 are degraded to zero or very small sizes (it depends on specific implementation details).

- After some time GC happened - let's assume again object A turned out to be unreachable. Let's assume also that we are doing a simple sweep collection. Memory of object A has been reclaimed. And because now objects B and C should belong to older generation "1" we are moving its boundary after object C (Figure 5-5b), adjusting the boundary of generation "0" as well. No memory copying was needed.

- After some time we have created object D - it has been allocated in generation "0" (Figure 5-5c). But this has no drawbacks at all.

- After some time, sweeping GC happened again - let's assume again that B is no longer reachable so the memory of it has been reclaimed. We have to adjust generations' boundaries again. Object D now belongs to generation "1" and C to generation "2" (Figure 5-5d). Generation 0 boundary is also appropriately adjusted.

- After some time we have created object E - it has been allocated in generation "0" (Figure 5-5e).

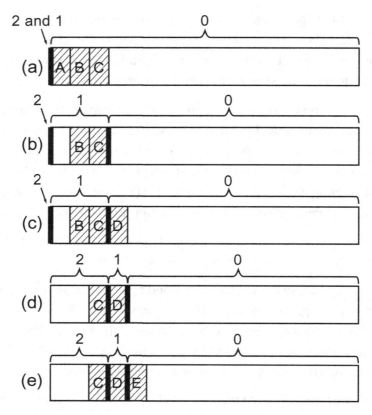

Figure 5-5. *Generation as logical boundaries inside single, continuous memory regions. Promotion is only a fact of belonging to a different generation due to the change of generations' boundaries.*

This is exactly how generations are handled in the case of Microsoft .NET runtimes. The decision has been made to create three generations named just after successive numbers, like in our previous examples. Hence, we have generation 0 ("young"), generation 1 ("temporary"), and generation 2 ("old"). The other decision is how lifetime boundaries between generations are being calculated. In case of Microsoft .NET runtimes, it is very simple - in general, an object is promoted into its older generation if it survives garbage collection.

There are exceptions to such a rule and we are calling it *demotion* (or simply not promoting). Why this may happen will be described in the next chapters as it is strongly related to various Collector and Allocator mechanisms.

In other words, when an object survives generation N, it is now belonging to generation N+1 (we say it has been promoted to generation N+1). It also means that just after two successive GCs, it may land in generation 2 and stay there until it won't be needed any longer.

Mono, as the main alternative to Microsoft .NET, has similar organization for small objects (smaller than 8,000 bytes as mentioned in LOH description above). It distinguishes only two generations - "young" is called Nursery and the "old" is called old space or just major heap. It also uses a simpler copying mechanism of promotion described above - when an object in Nursery survives garbage collection, it is copied to the old generation.

Generational garbage collection has one quite notable drawback, however. As generational hypotheses underlie its construction, failure to comply with them in our application can cause severe disadvantageous behavior. This leads to an important conclusion - in a healthy system consistent with the generational hypotheses, the older the generation is, the less often it should be garbage collected. We should strongly follow Rule 18 - Avoid Mid-Life Crisis described in Chapter 7.

However, we may be also very interested in the sizes of the generations. This is how in fact we can most easily confirm whether we have a memory leak in our application or not. The easiest way to observe generation sizes is by using Performance Counters or ETW mechanisms (see Table 5-1). They both measure the state of the heap just after garbage collection has happened. There are just two small caveats:

- Due to legacy reasons \.NET CLR Memory(processname)\Gen 0 heap size counter does not show true generation 0 size but something called its *allocation budget* (in simplest words - number of bytes to be allocated into a generation before a GC is triggered on that generation). Thus, looking at this counter may be misleading.

- We should remember that the highest possible sampling in the Performance Monitor is one second regardless of the fact that underlying data is refreshed more often. Therefore, if garbage collection takes place more than once per second, we will lose some measurements.

Table 5-1. *Basic Generation Sizes Measurements (Where* `Processname` *Is Obviously an Instance Name Corresponding to Your Process)*

Generation	ETW (GCHeapStats_V1 event)	Performance Counter (\.NET CLR Memory(processname))
0	GenerationSize0	Gen 0 heap size ("allocation budget")
1	GenerationSize1	Gen 1 heap size
2	GenerationSize2	Gen 1 heap size
3 (LOH)	GenerationSize2	Large Object Heap size

However, those caveats are not very annoying because the most often garbage collected generations 0 and 1 are generally quite small and do not cause any problems.

Scenario 5-1. Is My Program Healthy? Generation Sizes in Time

Description: We want to observe generations' sizes during web application execution. Ideally we would like to do it in a non-invasive way during load tests performed on our pre-production environment. This would give us some confidence that there are no memory leaks in our code. The application under test is plain nopCommerce 4.0 installation - a universal open source e-commerce platform written in ASP.NET (you may wish also to see Scenario 5-2 in which a similar test is performed under slightly different conditions).

Analysis: Let's skip the technical part of the load test preparation, assuming that the appropriate procedures and tools are just in place. Load test execution will be executing around 7 requests per second and last 170 minutes to create the opportunity to notice a memory leak if any exists. nopCommerce is being hosted on IIS via .NET Core Windows Server Hosting. It means although there is `w3wp.exe` process representing application pool, it only passes a request to the self-hosted .NET Core web application. In our case this process is named `Nop.Web.exe`.

First of all, we may wish to check overall memory usage of the application according to Scenario 4-1 from Chapter 4. This includes observing `Working Set - Private`, `Private Bytes,` and `Virtual Bytes` from `Process(Nop.Web)` counters altogether with `\.NET CLR Memory(Nop.Web)\# Total committed Bytes` counter.

Secondly, the easiest observation is to use the Performance Monitor tool to observe counters listed in Table 5-1. The results are showed in Figure 5-6 and a simple numerical summary is provided in Table 5-2. Please note that generations are drawn with different scales to visualize them clearly. As we may notice:

- generation 0 size (thin solid line) changes continuously between two values of 4,194,300 and 6,291,456 bytes. As mentioned earlier, those are not the real generation sizes but its allocation budgets. And although they are not real values, we can interpret them as a sign of a healthy state. The size of the generation is stable. If it grew with time, the illustrated counter would also grow (even it does show only size-related value).

- generation 1 size (dashed line) changes a lot due to its intermediate nature. As there is no upward trend visible, here also the measurement confirms the healthy state of an application.

- generation 2 size (thick solid line) shows a typical triangle pattern - objects are gathering in the oldest generation and from time to time they are garbage collected. It is typical to postpone full garbage collection until really needed so periodical gathering of oldest data is quite typical. In the case of web applications, the reachability of a large part of the objects is related to the lifetime of the user session and possible data caching. Thus, such a triangular pattern may be just normal. However, it is a small indication of possible problems, and we should treat it as a warning triggering further investigation. The next step should be observing this pattern in an even longer period in time and validate whether there is an increasing trend in the maximum generation 2 size. We should also observe `\.NET CLR Memory(Nop.Web)\% Time in GC` counter (see Scenario 7-1 for details) to check GC overhead on the whole process.

Please also note that both generations 0 and 1 in total are quite small so any changes here should not worry us much. This is a typical scenario as any memory leaks will be visible by a constant increase of the oldest generation (more and more long-living objects will be held).

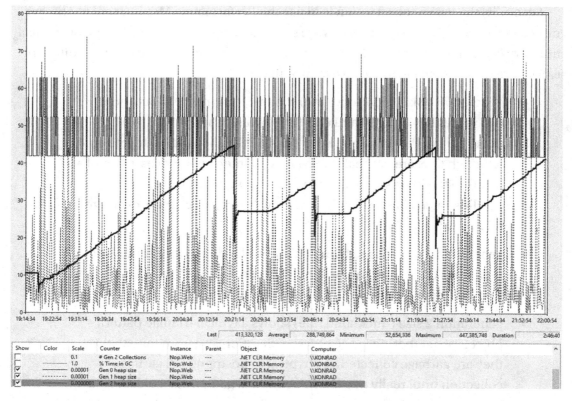

Figure 5-6. *Performance Monitor view of generation sizes during near 3-hour long load test of ASP.NET application*

Table 5-2. *Summary of Measurements Illustrated in Figure 5-6*

Generation	Min	Max
0	4,194,300	6,291,456
1	~18,268	7,384,704
2	52,654,336	447,385,748
LOH	0	38,826,368

It is also interesting to compare ETW data to those collected by performance counters. As previously said, the latter are sampled only every second while the former allows us to record each and every sample (GCHeapStats_V1 event emitted at the end of GC). Figures 5-7a, b, and c illustrate this difference in case of much smaller 20-second time spans (to make it more visible). ETW-based generation sizes were recorded by Perfview with a low-overhead GC Collect Only option selected. Data from GCHeapStats_V1 events was exported then to the CSV file. Performance counters data were collected by a Data Collector Set mechanism available in Performance Monitor, which allows to record a session to a file (including CSV text file format) instead of drawing it in real time. As we can see:

- Performance counter data are indeed sampled every second. Because the web site was heavy loaded during the test, garbage collections happen much more frequently. Therefore, there are many more ETW samples available.

- For generation 0 the difference between both data is huge (see Figure 5-7a). This is due to mentioned legacy reasons. If we really need to track generation 0 size in time, we should use ETW.

- For generation 1 it is clear that some performance counter samples correspond to ETW data (see Figure 5-7b). However, there is again much more happening in between. It is clearly seen how dynamic are changes of generation 1 size. This is, of course, knowledge that we do not necessarily need. One second-based sampling of performance counters may be just fine. In most applications GC will not occur so frequently so the difference may be even completely eliminated (if GC mostly occurs less often than every second). However, it is certainly worth being aware of this difference.

- For generation 2 we see almost complete adequacy of the data (see Figure 5-7c). This is because of much less frequent full garbage collections so almost no samples are lost in the case of performance counters.

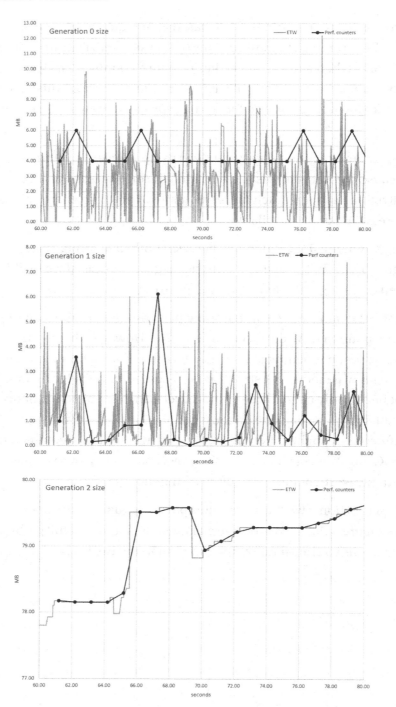

Figure 5-7. *Generation size charts created from CSV data exported from ETW and performance counters data*

The general verdict is positive. We can consider the application to be healthy. Long-running observation of appropriate performance counters did not show anything especially alarming. In the scenario, only a small region of ETW data was shown to visualize the difference in measurements between ETW and performance counters. Analysis of the whole ETW data also would not show anything alarming. However, further steps should be taken to measure overall GC overhead (see Scenario 7-1 from Chapter 7).

Remembered Sets

We have learned that objects in SOH are separated into generations, and thanks to that we may treat each of them separately. In particular it means we should be able to run garbage collection on each of the generations separately. We could garbage collect objects in the "young" generation only. Or in the "old" generation only. This is, however, an oversimplified point of view.

If we remember the general garbage collection mechanism described in Chapter 1, we may recall the Mark phase used by the Collector. Its responsibility is to find out reachability of the objects - starting from the roots and by a traversing objects graph. During this process GC is following outgoing references contained in visited objects. This works perfectly if we are visiting a whole objects graph, containing all objects in our application. But what if we want to garbage collect only a subset of it - like collecting only "young" generation? Let's imagine a situation illustrated in Figure 5-8. It shows a three-generational Garbage Collector in some moment in time:

- generation 0 contains objects A, B, C, and D. A is directly rooted (most probably it held by a local variable hold on stack) and it has a field referencing object B. C is only refenced by an object from an older generation. Object D has no references pointing to it (it is thus truly unreachable).

- generation 1 contains objects E, F, and G. E is directly rooted and it has a field referencing object C (from a younger generation). Object F has no references pointing to it (so this is yet another truly unreachable object). Object G has a reference from object D in the younger generation.

- generation 2 contains no objects to not clutter our explanation here - the mechanism remains the same, no matter if an "older" generation means generation 1 or 2.

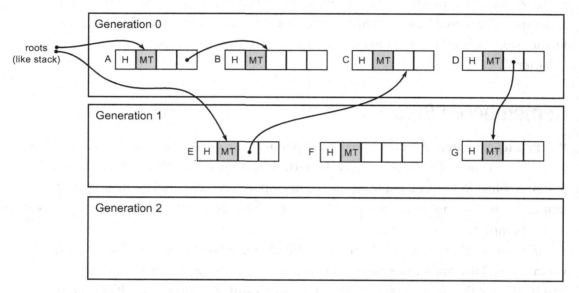

Figure 5-8. *Cross-generational references illustrated in a sample scenario with two generations*

Figure 5-8 shows us the most typical possible references that may occur in our applications. Cross-generational references showed there are perfectly valid:

- younger to older - recently created object may be created with a reference to already existing older object (like objects D and G).

- older to younger - object created some time before may be set to contain newly created object's reference (like objects E and C).

From the Mark phase perspective such *cross-generational references* need to be handled. We could of course traverse the whole objects graph to find the reachability of objects A, B, C, D, E, F, and G. But traversing the whole graph would obviously defeat the purpose of splitting objects into generations. So let's take a naive approach of marking only the "young" generation - which means traversing only objects in the young generation. To be more precise, we start from the roots and continue traversing until we meet objects from the generation other than the "young" generation. This obviously leads to wrong results.

Starting from the roots, we will mark as reachable only objects A and B. Object E, even it is rooted, will be ignored as it is located in an "old" generation. We will not visit object C as none of roots or other "young" objects are referencing it. We will simply not notice that object C is referenced by E. As a result, we will treat objects C and D as not reachable. Object D is indeed unreachable and may be removed. But object C would be garbage collected even it is still used by object E; we simply didn't notice that! This clearly shows that older to younger cross-generational references must be somehow handled. We must include them while considering objects' reachability in the younger generations if we want only young-generation collection.

To handle older to younger cross-generational references, a technique called *remembered sets* has been introduced. In general, a remembered set is a separately managed collection of references between separate sets of objects. In our case, it is a set of cross-generational collections remembering references from an older-to-younger generation. They are then simply investigated during the Mark phase.

In our sample scenario during young-generation garbage collection, we will traverse objects starting both from roots and from references stored in the remembered set - which includes E-to-C reference. This leads to desired proper results.

Please note that younger-to-older cross-generational references could be problematic only in case of collecting only old generation (without collecting younger ones at the same time). On the other hand, if we do only young-generation collection in our sample scenario, we may correctly garbage collect object D, even it is referencing something. We will just leave object G temporarily unreferenced. It will be marked as unreachable when doing older-generation garbage collection later. So both objects D and G will be eventually collected.

However, when trying to do old generation-only garbage collection, we encounter the same problem. We would not notice that G is being referenced by D. We should create another remembered set for young-to-old cross-generational references. As we will soon see, implementing remembered sets is not trivial so a simpler decision was made instead. As Microsoft's documentation says: "Collecting a generation means collecting objects in that generation and all its younger generations." This leads to some of the most important information regarding .NET memory management. Garbage collection in .NET may occur:

- for generation 0 only,

- for generations 0 and 1,

- for all generations 0, 1, and 2 and Large Object Heap (full garbage collection).

But how can a remembered set may be maintained? When we add or remove references to it? The common solution is to remember it when such reference is being created, which happens mainly during field assignment (see Listing 5-3). It may be triggered directly (in case of not private fields) or indirectly by property assignment or constructor and method calls.

Listing 5-3. Public field assignment as an example of creating older-to-younger cross-generational reference (assuming object e lives in older generation than object c)

```
E e = new E();
...
C c = new C();
e.SomeField = c;
```

The last line from Listing 5-3 would be a perfect place to remember a newly created reference in a remembered set. However, we should look at the problem in a more general way. Fields as defined in C# may be only one of the possible ways to hold references, resulting from the C# specification. However, we should not associate the remembered sets mechanism with one specific language. There may be other ways to store references in the future - be it in C# or in a new, not yet existing language.

Therefore, to implement this mechanism we should take advantage of a more low-level technique on the runtime level - the write barrier concept mentioned the Chapter 1. We may add appropriate write barrier code to the `Mutator.Write` operation (look at Listing 1-7 in Chapter 1). This operation is executed by a Mutator always when we want to store some value under a given address. Obviously this is a tremendously common operation so adding anything to it may introduce enormous overhead. When designing such a write barrier one must be extremely careful. It is beneficial for us that we need only to augment a Write operation by such a write barrier under certain conditions (representing storing a reference):

- value is a reference to a managed object,

- address is located in the Managed Heap and it represents some valid object's field,

- address is located inside generation older than generation where object referenced by value lives in.

As a result we may end up with a schematic implementation shown in Listing 5-4 that checks the above conditions and remembers the reference if it is appropriate. When executing the Mark phase, we should then include references stored in the RememberedSet along with the other roots.

Listing 5-4. A very simple, schematic pseudo-code of write barrier supporting remembered sets

```
Mutator.Write(address, value)
{
    *address = value;
    if (AreWriteBarrierConditionMeet(address, value))
    {
        RememberedSet.AddOrUpdate(address, value);
    }
}
```

This is a general concept illustrated how the .NET runtime could implement it. Obviously checking all those conditions every time would introduce tremendous overhead. If we think carefully about them, we may notice a lot of possible optimizations. Most of them come from the fact that these conditions can be checked in advance during Just-In-Time compilation. The JIT compiler perfectly knows from IL code whether we are storing a reference to a managed object into another managed object's field. During assembly code emitting, JIT can emit the proper version of the Mutator.Write, depending on whether the write barrier is needed or not. This is exactly an approach used by the .NET runtime.

If you are interested in getting more details, you may start by looking at CoreCLR code of method CodeGen::genCodeForTreeNode in case of GT_STOREIND operand. It calls CodeGen::genCodeForStoreInd that inside decides (by calling gcIsWriteBarrierCandidate) whether a write barrier is required or not. If the decision is positive, CodeGen::genGCWriteBarrier method is being called. This method emits assembly code of one of two helpers called CORINFO_HELP_ASSIGN_REF or CORINFO_HELP_CHECKED_ASSIGN_REF (the former is used when JIT compiler knows that it can optimize out checking whether target lives inside the Managed Heap; the former is used otherwise). Those two helpers correspond to the assembly code of functions JIT_WriteBarrier and JIT_CheckedWriteBarrier that you can find in .\src\vm\amd64\JitHelpers_Fast.asm file. Please note all this happens during JIT compilation and at runtime only JIT_WriteBarrier or JIT_CheckedWriteBarrier functions are being called (corresponding to two helpers mentioned above). Please also note this is a description in case of x64 runtime only. x86 handling of write barriers is similar but goes a different path, which is not described here for brevity.

Let's look deeper how a write barrier can be seen in our .NET applications. Let's start from the very simple lines of C# from Listing 5-5. It creates two objects and assigns the latter as a field of the former.

Listing 5-5. Sample code to illustrate write barriers in .NET

```
ClassA someClass = new ClassA();
ClassB otherClass = new ClassB();
someClass.FieldB = otherClass;
```

Code from Listing 5-5 may be compiled into CIL code shown at Listing 5-6 (it is slightly simplified without losing important details). We see there creating objects of type ClassA and ClassB. Both those instances are kept onto the evaluation stack. Then stfld instruction is being called, which stores a first value from the evaluation stack into a field (described by a token) of an object (second value from the evaluation stack).

Listing 5-6. Sample code from Listing 5-5 compiled into CIL

```
newobj CoreCLR.WriteBarrier.ClassA::.ctor
newobj CoreCLR.WriteBarrier.ClassB::.ctor
stfld CoreCLR.WriteBarrier.ClassA::FieldB
```

When doing JIT compilation, such code may be translated into an assembly code from Listing 5-7. We cannot say with certainty that it will look like this because we are already going down to a very low implementation level. How exactly this code will look depends on many factors, including runtime versions and so on, and so forth. However, it is general enough to help illustrate the issue. As you can see, stfld instruction has been translated into JIT_WriteBarrier function call (checked version is not used as JIT compiler knows that it is a managed object accessed here).

Listing 5-7. CIL code from Listing 5-6 after JIT compilation on x64 machine

```
; Those lines correspond to allocating memory for ClassA object and calling
its constructor
mov rcx,7FFCC4BA6600h (MT: CoreCLR.WriteBarrier.ClassA)
call    CoreCLR!JIT_TrialAllocSFastMP_InlineGetThread (00007ffd`241d2130)
mov     rdi,rax    ; rdi contains ClassA reference
mov     rcx,rdi
call    System_Private_CoreLib+0xc04060 (00007ffd`22e44060) (System.
Object..ctor(), mdToken: 0000000006000103)

; Those lines correspond to allocating memory for ClassB object and calling
its constructor
mov rcx,7FFCC4BA67B8h (MT: CoreCLR.WriteBarrier.ClassB)
call    CoreCLR!JIT_TrialAllocSFastMP_InlineGetThread (00007ffd`241d2130)
mov     rsi,rax    ; rsi contains ClassB reference
mov     rcx,rsi
```

```
call     System_Private_CoreLib+0xc04060 (00007ffd`22e44060) (System.
Object..ctor(), mdToken: 0000000006000103)

; Those lines are calling WriteBarrier, storing reference and using
remembered sets inside
lea      rcx,[rdi+8]     ; rcx contains address of FieldB field in ClassA
object
mov      rdx,rsi         ; rdx contains ClassB reference
call     CoreCLR!JIT_WriteBarrier (00007ffd`2403fae0)
```

We will look inside JIT_WriteBarrier function, but before that we have to learn about yet another important technique called card tables.

Card Tables

You may notice a serious caveat in an approach of storing every single reference in a remembered set. A remembered set is small in a such simple scenario like that illustrated in Figure 5-8 (in fact it contains only a single reference). But what about real-world applications with hundreds or thousands or even millions of objects referencing each other? Even worse, .NET has three generations so the number of possible cross-generational references is bigger. Additionally, changing references between objects is quite a common operation. Managing a remembered set as a naive collection of each and every single cross-generational reference would simply introduce too big of overhead.

As it often happens, in order to solve this problem, we must decide on some compromise. To reduce the overhead of collections management, individual references are not tracked so we lose accuracy. Instead, certain predefined areas of memory are tracked. They are managed by a technique called *card tables*.

To explain them let's go back in time a little bit from the moment in Figure 5-8 (see Figure 5-9a). We see there a moment before object E starts to hold cross-generational reference to object C. The idea behind card tables is quite simple - we split the older generation in constant-size regions (continuous regions of memory with a given number of bytes). In our exemplary case in Figure 5-9a, we see four such regions and a part of five. The first region happens to not contain any objects. The second region contains only a single object. The third region contains only part of some object (as it may happen that an object will live on the boundary of regions). The fourth region contains the remaining part of the same object and yet another part of other region, and so on, and so forth.

Each such region is represented by a single *card* entry in a card table data structure. At the beginning all cards are *clean* so the corresponding card entries have a flag set to "clean" (which may be indicated by a single bit value of 0). Clean card means there are no older-to-younger cross-generational references inside the corresponding memory region.

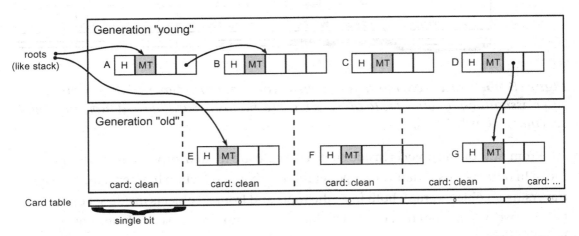

Figure 5-9a. *Card tables manage older-to-younger cross-generational references. A moment just before situation from Figure 5-8 has been illustrated. All cards are clean (no such reference exists).*

When somewhere in an application code we assign object C to the object's E field, we end up with situation illustrated in Figure 5-9b. We calculate the card for object E and mark the whole card as "dirty," commonly referred to as *set card* (like just by setting binary value to 1).

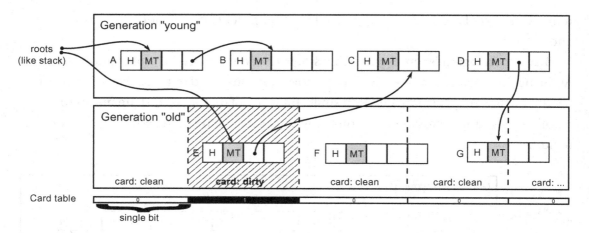

Figure 5-9b. *Card table manages older-to-younger cross-generational references. After assignment of object C to object's E,corresponding card in card table has been set (marked as "dirty").*

From now on, all objects inside such a set card are treated as possible, additional roots. In other words, when young-generation garbage collection happens, we will start traversing an objects graph both from the roots and from all objects inside set cards (in this way we will find out that C is reachable in our sample because E is being considered from set card).

The careful reader may ask, what if we were to change the last field of object F, which is in the fourth card, while object F starts within the third card? What card do we actually set then? Because the write barrier has to be as lightweight as possible, we simply set the fourth card (as it corresponds to the changed address). Later on, during the Mark phase, the object containing the starting address of the card (which is F in our case) will be found, thanks to the brick tables technique, described in Chapter 9.

This obviously comes with overhead. Even because of a single older-to-younger reference, we must visit all objects inside a card and follow their references. It is a trade-off between performance and accuracy. We may balance this trade-off by choosing s smaller or larger card size. If a card was so small that at most it contained only a single object, we would end up with a typical remembered set approach (each single reference would be tracked). If a card was so big that it covered a whole generation, we would end up with the approach of traversing the whole objects graph.

In case of .NET runtime, a single card corresponds to 256 bytes (on 64-bit) or 128 bytes (on 32-bit). Each such card is represented by a single bit flag. If any part of such 128- or 256-byte long region has a reference written to, it will be set. Those bits are grouped obviously into bytes so a single byte represents 8 times 256 bytes (2,048 bytes) memory region. Cards are grouped into 32 elements called a *card word*. This means the card word is a 4-byte-wide type DWORD (unsigned long). Thus, a single card word represents 8,192 bytes. This is being illustrated in Figure 5-10 (case for 64-bit platform).

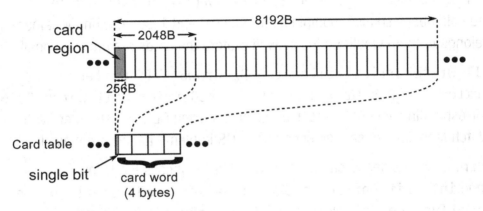

Figure 5-10. *Card tables organization in .NET runtime (64-bit version). Each single bit in card table represents 256 bytes of memory. Those bits are grouped into bytes (so each byte represents 2,048 bytes memory region). Bytes are grouped into card words representing 4 times bigger memory regions.*

With such knowledge we can now jump into the above-mentioned JIT_WriteBarrier function. What is interesting is that the memory region for JIT_WriteBarrier function is treated only as a placeholder for one of its more specific implementations. Those barriers may be changed at runtime, by copying over specific implementation into it (obviously it happens while program execution is suspended). This placeholder size is equal to the largest function implementation so any other can fit into it. We will look at the simplest version (see Listing 5-8), but they all differ very little so looking at one is completely sufficient (read below note for more details).

Different JIT_WriteBarrier implementations can be found in .\src\vm\
amd64\JitHelpers_FastWriteBarriers.asm file of CoreCLR source (in case
of amd64 implementations). It contains the following versions:

- JIT_WriteBarrier_PreGrow64 and JIT_WriteBarrier_PostGrow64 -
  those are used in workstation GC mode. The first is used when generations 0
  and 1 are located in their default locations. After some time, runtime may decide
  to move it to another place and then PostGrow version will be injected.

- JIT_WriteBarrier_SVR64 - used in server GC mode where there are
  multiple heaps so also multiple generations 0 and 1, so checking whether value
  belongs to them would be too slow, therefore the cards are unconditionally set.

- JIT_WriteBarrier_WriteWatch_PreGrow64, JIT_WriteBarrier_
  WriteWatch_PostGrow64 and JIT_WriteBarrier_WriteWatch_SVR64 -
  corresponding version of previous functions using CLR implemented Write
  Watch technique described soon (when OS implementation is not available).

When runtime decides to change the write barrier, it calls the following
method:int WriteBarrierManager::ChangeWriteBarrierTo(Write
BarrierType newWriteBarrier, bool isRuntimeSuspended)
{

```
    ...
    memcpy((PVOID)JIT_WriteBarrier,
    (LPVOID)GetCurrentWriteBarrierCode(), GetCurrentWriteBarrierSize());
    ...
```

}

Look at StompWriteBarrierResize and StompWriteBarrierEphemeral
methods in .\src\vm\amd64\JITInterfaceAMD64.cpp for more details.

As we can see at Listing 5-8, the write barrier code is in fact very simple:

- Argument stored in register rcx contains a destination address (address in our Mutator.Write sample) while register rdx contains a source reference (value in Mutator.Write sample).

- Line 3 is doing the main job of writing a memory under given address with a given value. We want to manipulate card table (set card) only if rdx does belong to young generation because runtime is interested only in older-to-younger cross-generational references (and it treats generations 0 and 1 as young, while generation 2 as old).

- Thus, lines from 6 to 14 are checking whether source reference belong to so-called *ephemeral region* (meaning both generations 0 and 1). If no, function ends. If yes, card table is being checked if it is not already set. Those are the most important lines for our considerations.

- Line 16 is storing an address to the card table (strange 0F0F0F0F0F0F0F0F0h constant is being replaced at runtime with proper value) into rax register.

- Line 17 is dividing a destination address (stored it rcx) by value of 2048.[2]

- Lines from 18 to 22 compare a byte inside card table to the value FFh and store it if not already set.

Listing 5-8. Implementation of the JIT_WriteBarrier_PostGrow64 function, with some original comments removed while others added

```
01. LEAF_ENTRY JIT_WriteBarrier_PostGrow64, _TEXT
02.         align 8
03.         mov    [rcx], rdx          ; store value from register rdx
                   under address rcx
04.         NOP_3_BYTE                 ; padding for alignment of constant
05. PATCH_LABEL JIT_WriteBarrier_PostGrow64_Patch_Label_Lower
06.         mov    rax, 0F0F0F0F0F0F0F0F0h ; 0F0F0F0F0F0F0F0F0h will be
                   patched at runtime with proper address
```

---

[2]shr rcx, 0Bh instruction shifts value in rcx by 0Bh bits - which means 11 bits. Shifting by n bits is equal to dividing by 2^n. 2^11 is equal to 2048

```
07.          cmp     rdx, rax              ; Check the lower ephemeral region
             bound (if rdx <                ;  rax, jump to Exit)
08.          jb      Exit
09.          nop                            ; padding for alignment of constant
10. PATCH_LABEL JIT_WriteBarrier_PostGrow64_Patch_Label_Upper
11.          mov     r8, 0F0F0F0F0F0F0F0F0h  ; 0F0F0F0F0F0F0F0F0h will be
                                              patched at runtime with
                                              proper address
12.          cmp     rdx, r8               ; Check the upper ephemeral
                                              region bound (if rdx >= r8,
                                              jump to Exit)
13.          jae     Exit
14.          nop                            ; padding for alignment of
                                              constant
15. PATCH_LABEL JIT_WriteBarrier_PostGrow64_Patch_Label_CardTable
16.          mov     rax, 0F0F0F0F0F0F0F0F0h ; 0F0F0F0F0F0F0F0F0h will be
                                              patched at runtime with
                                              proper card table address
17.          shr     rcx, 0Bh              ; Touch the card table entry,
                                              if not already dirty.
18.          cmp     byte ptr [rcx + rax], 0FFh
19.          jne     UpdateCardTable
20.          REPRET
21.     UpdateCardTable:
22.          mov     byte ptr [rcx + rax], 0FFh
23.          ret
24.     align 16
25.     Exit:
26.          REPRET
27. LEAF_END_MARKED JIT_WriteBarrier_PostGrow64, _TEXT
```

What is important is the fact that the whole byte representing eight cards is being set while we could set only a single bit in it. This is because of performance reasons. It is much more efficient to compare and store a whole byte (which is possible with single instruction, as we can see) than proceed with bit manipulation (which would require preparing and operating on appropriate bit masks).

Of course, this introduces some overhead. Instead of setting only a single card (256 byte-wide memory region), we are setting a byte that correspond to 2,048 bytes. This is yet another one example of compromise taken as a design decision.

Please note that current write barrier implementations, including the example from Listing 5-8, are only checking whether the source reference does belong to the young generation. It does not check whether the target address does belong to an older reference. Thus, the card table will be marked dirty also for young-to-young references. This is however acceptable because:

- during Mark phase, the card table may be checked only for the addresses belonging to older generations. Those related to young-to-young references will just be ignored.

- during runtime checking inside WriteBarrier whether rcx belongs to older generation would be too complicated. It is just faster to mark the card dirty than proceed with all required checks.

Card Bundles

The card tables technique optimizes remembered sets usage. Instead of tracking each and every cross-generational reference, we are tracking groups of them. As we have seen, in case of a .NET 64-bit framework, memory regions that are 256-bytes long are observed to be covered by a card. If any of the objects inside such a block has been modified to contain reference to the young generation, we should consider a whole block as dirty by setting a corresponding bit. Even more, due to low-level optimizations, we are marking the whole byte that corresponds to a 2,048-byte-long memory region. But there is still an optimization possibility.

Let's imagine we are running a typical web application on a server. Its memory usage may be around a few gigabytes. Let's assume that the older generation is 2GB big. Every byte in the card table is representing 2kB. Thus, we need a 1MB card table to cover the whole old generation. This may seem not so much at first glance. However, these bytes will have to be scanned at every collection of the younger generations (to find all possible older-to-younger references). Younger generation's collection should be extremely fast and it would be too much overhead to scan such a large card table -

even though it might take a few milliseconds. Those should be consumed by the whole garbage collection process, not only by scanning a card table. Moreover, the card table may be quite sparse - there are many non-set cards interleaved by set cards occasionally.

This is why one more level of observation has been added called *card bundles*. While a single card word was grouping multiple cards, a single card bundle word is grouping multiple card words. They have been designed to be much denser, to cover much bigger memory regions (see Figure 5-11). A single bit in a card bundle word represents 32 card words (they cover 256kB region). Thus, each byte represents 2MB, while whole a card bundle word consisting of four bytes covers 8 MB.

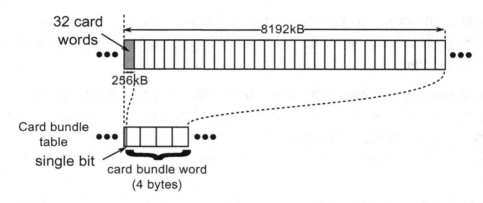

Figure 5.11. *Card bundle table organization in .NET runtime (64-bit version). Each single bit in card bundle table represents 32 card words (256 kB). Those bits are grouped into bytes (so each byte represents 2,048 kilobytes memory region). Bytes are grouped into card bundle words representing 4 times bigger memory regions (8MB).*

This allows a very fast (probably cached) scan of set cards. First, the card bundle table is being scanned to find dirty big regions and only inside them more precise scanning of the card table is being made. In our sample scenario with 2GB old generation, we would need only 1,024 bytes in the card bundle table to represent them. If any bit inside it is set, the corresponding 32 card words from the card table will be scanned to find set cards.

But what is making card bundles set ("dirty")? We have not seen any code in write barriers responsible for that. The underlying mechanism varies depending on the operating system.

In case of Windows, the operating system write-watching mechanism is being used mentioned in Chapter 1. When pages are being reserved by the Virtual API for the card table region, they are reserved with the special MEM_WRITE_WATCH flag. In such a case, when later a page is being modified (because write barrier set some card), it is being marked as dirty in a special Windows operating system structure. We can then ask for a list of such dirty pages by a WinAPI GetWriteWatch function. This function is called by .NET runtime at the beginning of the Mark phase inside gc_heap::update_card_table_ bundle() method. This method gets a list of all those dirty pages from the system and sets corresponding bits in the card bundle table.

In case of Linux, the .NET Core team could not find a reliable equivalent of operating system-based write watch mechanism. However, the advantages of a higher level of cards management are so important that it was decided to manually implement a replacement for this mechanism. This is why the write watch mechanism has been implemented in a write barrier in case of Linux. We can see it in write barriers code in .\src\amd64\jithelpers_fastwritebarriers.S file (see Listing Listing 5-9, which shows a significant part of one of the functions).

Listing 5-9. Part of the write barrier assembly code for Linux version of .NET runtime. It shows manual implementation of write watch mechanism managing card bundles.

```
#ifdef FEATURE_MANUALLY_MANAGED_CARD_BUNDLES
        NOP_6_BYTE // padding for alignment of constant
PATCH_LABEL JIT_WriteBarrier_PreGrow64_Patch_Label_CardBundleTable
        movabs  rax, 0xF0F0F0F0F0F0F0F0
        // Touch the card bundle, if not already dirty.
        // rdi is already shifted by 0xB, so shift by 0xA more
        shr     rdi, 0x0A
        cmp     byte ptr [rdi + rax], 0FFh
        .byte 0x75, 0x02
        // jne     UpdateCardBundle_PreGrow64
        REPRET
    UpdateCardBundle_PreGrow64:
        mov     byte ptr [rdi + rax], 0FFh
#endif
```

As we can see here also, the whole byte is being marked as dirty so card tables in the Linux-based .NET Core operate on 2MB granularity.

There is one more interesting topic to be discussed - handling of arrays by card tables. Imagine a large table of objects that resides in the older generation. This array is large enough to span over many cards and even card bundles. Let's also imagine that we assign a newly created object to one of the elements of this table. What will happen? Only a single corresponding byte in a card word will be made dirty as well as a corresponding bit in a card bundle word. However, how will this information be later consumed by a Mark process? Which elements of a table will be scanned? Only part of the corresponding card or maybe a whole array? The answer is simple - only the parts of the array that have set cards will be scanned.

We have learned a lot about remembered sets, card tables, and card bundles in .NET runtime. A lot of space has been devoted to this topic because it is one of the key mechanisms that allows GC to operate in .NET. On the other hand, this is one of the mechanisms described in less detail so far in the literature. One of the reasons for this is probably the fact that it is a deeply hidden implementation detail. It is highly optimized, which means it does not cause problems and does not have to be known in the general consciousness. However, I believe that there is no better place to explain and give you a chance to understand this topic than in the book on memory management in .NET. Knowing all that we have learned so far, we can also address the rule introduced at the end of the chapter - Avoid Unnecessary Heap References.

Physical Partitioning

We know already that managed memory is divided into two separate memory regions. Large Object Heap is a memory region for objects bigger than 85,000 bytes (and some additional exceptions). Small Object Heap contains smaller objects and is further divided into generations. We know also that all this lives in a memory region denoted as heap from an operating system perspective (as seen in Figure 5-1 at the beginning of this chapter). What is missing is how exactly GC Managed Heap is organized to contain both LOH and SOH with its generations. We will look at the physical organization of GC Heap at this point, putting all together what we have learned so far.

Physically, Managed Heap consists of a set of *heap segments*. A segment either belongs to the LOH or the SOH. And for SOH segments, if there are multiple of them, every segment is a generation 2 segment except one, which we call the ephemeral segment that holds objects from generations 0 and 1 (and optionally from generation 2). It is important to note also that Garbage Collector in Microsoft's implementation may be working in two significantly different modes:

- *Workstation* mode - it contains a single Managed Heap (so there will be a single SOH and LOH).

- *Server* mode - it contains multiple Managed Heaps (so there will be multiple SOHs and LOHs). By default, there are as many of them as the number of logical cores on the machine running .NET application.

We will go deep into many other differences between those two modes in the following chapters. For now, it is enough to note the difference regarding the number of managed heaps.

All these concepts are probably best explained by the example of creating individual elements during the start of .NET runtime. Figure 5-12 shows three stages of creating a managed heap in case of the simplest possible scenario (running in Workstation mode). More complex scenarios are described later.

In such a simple scenario the following steps happen:

- .NET runtime tries to allocate (reserve) a single, continuous block of memory (see Figure 5-12a) for the initial segments; it does this as an optimization so all the segments stay together. If there's no such virtual address space available, the segments will be discontinuous.

- It then needs to create two separate segments for SOH and LOH. They are created inside a newly reserved block by logically separating it into two pieces (see Figure 5-12b).

- Generations 0, 1, and 2 will be created inside the SOH segment by committing some specified amount of memory and LOH also will have some amount of memory committed (see Figure 5-12c).

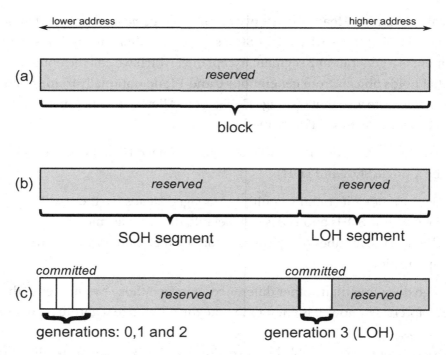

Figure 5-12. *Blocks and segments explained by an example of the simplest scenario - single block contains both SOH and LOH segments*

Segments are represented by `heap_segment` objects in .NET runtime, which we will look at more closely in the next and subsequent chapters. They are tracking information about memory addresses, how much memory has been already reserved and committed, and so on, so forth. As we will see in the next chapter, a heap segment is consumed from the lower address to the higher address. The more objects we allocate, the more memory must be committed inside a segment.

We can easily see the situation from Figure 5-12 in the real world by using the VMMap tool for a simple console application. If we expand GC Managed Heap block visible at Figure 5-1, we will notice the layout (see Figure 5-13) consistent with the one described above and illustrated in Figure 5-12c. We see there the following memory regions:

- around 260 KB dedicated for Gen0 (259 KB), Gen1 (24 bytes), and Gen2 (24 bytes),

- almost 256 MB reserved memory for the rest of SOH segment,

- 72 KB dedicated for Large Object Heap,

- almost 128 MB reserved for the rest of LOH segment.

⊟ 0000026700000000	Managed Heap	393,216 K	336 K	336 K	224 K	224 K	4 Read/Write	GC
0000026700000000	Managed Heap	4 K	4 K	4 K	4 K	4 K	Read/Write	
0000026700001000	Managed Heap	24 bytes	24 bytes	24 bytes			Read/Write	Gen2
0000026700001018	Managed Heap	24 bytes	24 bytes	24 bytes			Read/Write	Gen1
0000026700001030	Managed Heap	259 K	259 K	259 K	204 K	204 K	Read/Write	Gen0
0000026700042000	Managed Heap	261,880 K					Reserved	
0000026710000000	Managed Heap	72 K	72 K	72 K	16 K	16 K	Read/Write	Large Object Heap
0000026710012000	Managed Heap	131,000 K					Reserved	

Figure 5-13. *A single block inside simple console .NET application contains two segements (SOH and LOH) as visible in VMMap tool*

As already mentioned, the segment that contains generations 0 and 1 is called an *ephemeral segment*. This is an important distinction that appears in the implementation of GC in many places. Therefore, we will also come back to it many times in this book.

We can list all segments and generations information in WinDbg using an SOS extension by issuing an `eeheap` command (see Listing 5-10). Information about two separate segments is listed there corresponding to what we have seen at Figure 5-13. You may rightly notice that, in fact, generation starts at 0x1000 offset from the segment beginning. Why is that will be explained in subsequent Segments and heap anatomy section.

Listing 5-10. Segments and generations listed by eeheap command from WinDbg SOS extension. It shows the state of the same process as at Figure 5-13.

```
> !eeheap
Number of GC Heaps: 1
generation 0 starts at 0x0000026700001030
generation 1 starts at 0x0000026700001018
generation 2 starts at 0x0000026700001000
ephemeral segment allocation context: none
         segment              begin           allocated                 size
0000026700000000  0000026700001000  0000026700033b18  0x32b18(207640)
Large object heap starts at 0x0000026710001000
         segment              begin           allocated                 size
0000026710000000  0000026710001000  0000026710005480  0x4480(17536)
Total Size:               Size: 0x36f98 (225176) bytes.
---------------------------------
GC Heap Size:             Size: 0x36f98 (225176) bytes.
```

The default segment sizes depend on several factors. One of the most important is the GC mode of operation. The second is the bitness of the runtime environment. This is summarized in Table 5-3. For example, the console application showed in Figures 5-9 and 5-10 was executed on a 64-bit runtime working in Workstation mode. Thus, SOH segment was 256 MB big while LOH was 128 MB. As we can also see, in case of Server mode, default SOH segments sizes depend on the number of logical cores (the more cores, the smaller segment).

Table 5-3. *Default Segment Sizes for Various Conditions*

	Workstation		Server	
	32-bit	**64-bit**	**32-bit**	**64-bit**
SOH	16 MB	256 MB	64 MB (#CPU<=4)	4 GB (#CPU<=4)
			32 MB (#CPU<=8)	2 GB (#CPU<=8)
			16 MB (#CPU>8)	1 GB (#CPU>8)
LOH	16 MB	128 MB	32 MB	256 MB

Segments in Server mode are illustrated at Figure 5-14 by the VMMap view of the ASP.NET 4.5 application hosted on 8-core machine and 64-bit .NET runtime with Server mode enabled. As we can see, one single, huge, and continuous block has been reserved.

It contains eight SOH segments followed by eight LOH segments. Segments sizes correspond to the default sizes listed in Table 5-3 (2 GB for SOH and 256 MB for LOH).

We can now see why it is so important to know the difference between reserved and committed memory as described in Chapter 2. Although a managed heap in a web application from Figure 5-14 seems to consume huge 18 GB (reserved memory), obviously the real usage is only at the level of 8 MB (committed memory).

Address	Type	Size					Protection	
⊟ 000001A971E50000	Managed Heap	18,874,368 K	8,704 K	8,704 K	8,348 K	8,348 K	32 Read/Write	GC
000001A971E50000	Managed Heap	4 K	4 K	4 K	4 K	4 K	Read/Write	
000001A971E51000	Managed Heap	24 bytes	24 bytes	24 bytes			Read/Write	Gen2
000001A971E51018	Managed Heap	24 bytes	24 bytes	24 bytes			Read/Write	Gen1
000001A971E51030	Managed Heap	1,987 K	1,987 K	1,987 K	1,964 K	1,964 K	Read/Write	Gen0
000001A972042000	Managed Heap	2,095,160 K					Reserved	
000001A9F1E50000	Managed Heap	4 K	4 K	4 K	4 K	4 K	Read/Write	
000001A9F1E51000	Managed Heap	24 bytes	24 bytes	24 bytes			Read/Write	Gen2
000001A9F1E51018	Managed Heap	24 bytes	24 bytes	24 bytes			Read/Write	Gen1
000001A9F1E51030	Managed Heap	1,155 K	1,155 K	1,155 K	1,124 K	1,124 K	Read/Write	Gen0
000001A9F1F72000	Managed Heap	2,095,992 K					Reserved	
000001AA71E50000	Managed Heap	4 K	4 K	4 K	4 K	4 K	Read/Write	
000001AA71E51000	Managed Heap	24 bytes	24 bytes	24 bytes			Read/Write	Gen2
000001AA71E51018	Managed Heap	24 bytes	24 bytes	24 bytes			Read/Write	Gen1
000001AA71E51030	Managed Heap	1,475 K	1,475 K	1,475 K	1,428 K	1,428 K	Read/Write	Gen0
000001AA71FC2000	Managed Heap	2,095,672 K					Reserved	
000001AAF1E50000	Managed Heap	4 K	4 K	4 K	4 K	4 K	Read/Write	
000001AAF1E51000	Managed Heap	24 bytes	24 bytes	24 bytes			Read/Write	Gen2
000001AAF1E51018	Managed Heap	24 bytes	24 bytes	24 bytes			Read/Write	Gen1
000001AAF1E51030	Managed Heap	195 K	195 K	195 K	180 K	180 K	Read/Write	Gen0
000001AAF1E82000	Managed Heap	2,096,952 K					Reserved	
000001AB71E50000	Managed Heap	4 K	4 K	4 K	4 K	4 K	Read/Write	
000001AB71E51000	Managed Heap	24 bytes	24 bytes	24 bytes			Read/Write	Gen2
000001AB71E51018	Managed Heap	24 bytes	24 bytes	24 bytes			Read/Write	Gen1
000001AB71E51030	Managed Heap	1,027 K	1,027 K	1,027 K	1,012 K	1,012 K	Read/Write	Gen0
000001AB71F52000	Managed Heap	2,096,120 K					Reserved	
000001ABF1E50000	Managed Heap	4 K	4 K	4 K	4 K	4 K	Read/Write	
000001ABF1E51000	Managed Heap	24 bytes	24 bytes	24 bytes			Read/Write	Gen2
000001ABF1E51018	Managed Heap	24 bytes	24 bytes	24 bytes			Read/Write	Gen1
000001ABF1E51030	Managed Heap	771 K	771 K	771 K	716 K	716 K	Read/Write	Gen0
000001ABF1F12000	Managed Heap	2,096,376 K					Reserved	
000001AC71E50000	Managed Heap	4 K	4 K	4 K	4 K	4 K	Read/Write	
000001AC71E51000	Managed Heap	24 bytes	24 bytes	24 bytes			Read/Write	Gen2
000001AC71E51018	Managed Heap	24 bytes	24 bytes	24 bytes			Read/Write	Gen1
000001AC71E51030	Managed Heap	1,027 K	1,027 K	1,027 K	980 K	980 K	Read/Write	Gen0
000001AC71F52000	Managed Heap	2,096,120 K					Reserved	
000001ACF1E50000	Managed Heap	4 K	4 K	4 K	4 K	4 K	Read/Write	
000001ACF1E51000	Managed Heap	24 bytes	24 bytes	24 bytes			Read/Write	Gen2
000001ACF1E51018	Managed Heap	24 bytes	24 bytes	24 bytes			Read/Write	Gen1
000001ACF1E51030	Managed Heap	707 K	707 K	707 K	676 K	676 K	Read/Write	Gen0
000001ACF1F02000	Managed Heap	2,096,440 K					Reserved	
000001AD71E50000	Managed Heap	264 K	264 K	264 K	180 K	180 K	Read/Write	Large Object Heap
000001AD71E92000	Managed Heap	261,880 K					Reserved	
000001AD81E50000	Managed Heap	8 K	8 K	8 K	8 K	8 K	Read/Write	Large Object Heap
000001AD81E52000	Managed Heap	262,136 K					Reserved	
000001AD91E50000	Managed Heap	8 K	8 K	8 K	8 K	8 K	Read/Write	Large Object Heap
000001AD91E52000	Managed Heap	262,136 K					Reserved	
000001ADA1E50000	Managed Heap	8 K	8 K	8 K	8 K	8 K	Read/Write	Large Object Heap
000001ADA1E52000	Managed Heap	262,136 K					Reserved	
000001ADB1E50000	Managed Heap	8 K	8 K	8 K	8 K	8 K	Read/Write	Large Object Heap
000001ADB1E52000	Managed Heap	262,136 K					Reserved	
000001ADC1E50000	Managed Heap	8 K	8 K	8 K	8 K	8 K	Read/Write	Large Object Heap
000001ADC1E52000	Managed Heap	262,136 K					Reserved	
000001ADD1E50000	Managed Heap	8 K	8 K	8 K	8 K	8 K	Read/Write	Large Object Heap
000001ADD1E52000	Managed Heap	262,136 K					Reserved	
000001ADE1E50000	Managed Heap	8 K	8 K	8 K	8 K	8 K	Read/Write	Large Object Heap
000001ADE1E52000	Managed Heap	262,136 K					Reserved	

Figure 5-14. A huge, single block inside ASP.NET application contains eight segments (both SOH and LOH) as visible in VMMap tool. Application was hosted on a machine with eight logical cores (four physical cores and Hyper-Threading enabled) on a 64-bit runtime working in Server mode

Both scenarios shown so far have common property - all segments have been created inside a single continuous block. This is the most common initial scenario named an *all-at-once* allocation pattern (illustrated at Figures 5-15a and 5-16a). However, there are two other possible allocation patterns:

- *two-stage* - there are two separate blocks: for SOH and LOH segments separately (see Figures 5-15b and 5-16b);

- *each-block* - there is a separate block for each segment (see Figure 5-16c).

They may happen, for example, when .NET runtime was unable to reserve a single continuous block of virtual memory. If it happens, a two-stage pattern will be tried. If it fails, an even more granular each-block pattern will be chosen in case of Server mode.

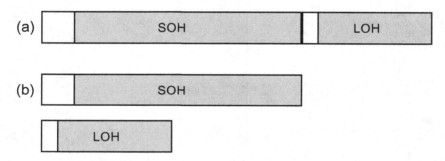

Figure 5-15. *Possible Workstation GC initial segments configuration: (a) all-at-once configuration, (b) two-stage configuration (the same as each-block configuration)*

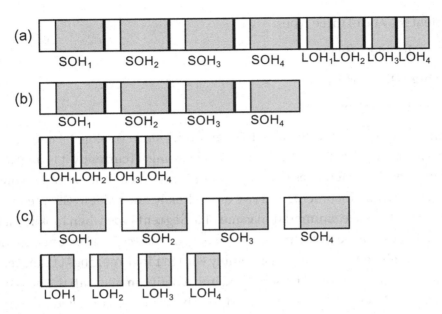

Figure 5-16. *Possible Server GC initial segments configuration (example of 4-core machine): (a) all-at-once configuration, (b) two-stage configuration, (c) each-block configuration*

When our application is running and allocating a lot of objects, the ephemeral segment or LOH may become full. In such case an additional segment may be allocated. We will see some typical ways of handling such situations in Chapter 6. Please also note that the segments configurations described here are the same for the Windows and Linux version of .NET Core.

In Mono (as the current 5.4 version state), physical organization of generations is slightly different:

- small objects are stored into two kinds of memory regions. A Nursery (representing young generation) is a continuous block of memory in the size of 4 MB. It does not change dynamically but may be set by configuration when Mono starts. Fast bump-pointer technique of allocation is used here. Old generation is organized into 16 kB blocks (but they are allocated in larger chunks to avoid fragmentation).

- large objects in Large Object Store are organized into 1 MB sections, while larger objects than that are directly allocated by a Virtual API and they are remembered as a single-linked list.

385

A segment may be of three types:

- Small Object Heap,

- Large Object Heap,

- Read-Only Heap.

The third option is deprecated in .NET Framework since version 3.5 and in .NET Core. However, other frameworks may still be using it (currently it is only .NET Native) so we may find references to it in various places - including CoreCLR source code, ETW events, and documentation (we even already noticed it in Chapter 3 as ReadOnlyHeapMapMessage enumeration value of GCSegmentType when looking at ETW events data). Read-only heap segments are used by the *object freezing* functionality, which may be enabled by marking an assembly with StringFreezingAttribute.

When such an assembly will be serialized into a native image with the help of Native Image Generator (Ngen.exe), all string literals will become pre-compiled (in managed form) into a generated image. The memory region within this image with such strings (or objects in general, although there is no API for handling them) may then be registered as a read-only segment and become usable immediately (as object is there already in a managed, allocated form).

Note the difference to string interning (described in Chapter 4), which requires regular string allocation at runtime. Additionally, as MSDN states: "Note that the common language runtime (CLR) cannot unload any native image that has a frozen string because any object in the heap might refer to the frozen string. Therefore, you should use the StringFreezingAttribute class only in cases where the native image that contains the frozen string is shared heavily."

Scenario 5-2. nopCommerce Memory Leak?

Description: We have just downloaded a plain installation of nopCommerce – open source e-commerce platform written in ASP.NET. As documentation states about hosted ZIP file: "download this package if you want to deploy a live site to a web server with the minimum required files." Installation is easy: "to use IIS, copy the contents of the extracted nopCommerce folder to an IIS virtual directory (or site root)." We want to validate nopCommerce performance, including memory usage patterns. We have prepared a simple load test scenario for JMeter 3.2 – a popular open source load testing tool. It executes three steps in a loop - visiting home page, one of the categories

("Computers"), and one of tags ("awesome"). We have added think times (pauses) between each request to simulate real users. Test will be performed for one hour.

Note: this scenario is quite long as it includes a few approaches to show you different ways you can take. Additionally, nopCommerce was chosen as a stable and well-proven technology. Certain mistakes have been made specifically to illustrate how to solve various problems. They should not be used to evaluate nopCommerce as a product.

Analysis: This scenario is similar to scenario 5-1 so we can start analysis in the same way. Therefore, we start from observing the following performance counters with the help of Performance Monitor (either in real time or via Data Collector Set):

- `\Process(Nop.Web)\Working Set - Private`

- `\Process(Nop.Web)\Private Bytes`

- `\Process(Nop.Web)\Virtual Bytes`

- `\.NET CLR Memory(Nop.Web)\# Total committed Bytes`

- `\.NET CLR Memory(Nop.Web)\Gen 0 heap size`

- `\.NET CLR Memory(Nop.Web)\Gen 1 heap size`

- `\.NET CLR Memory(Nop.Web)\Gen 2 heap size`

- `\.NET CLR Memory(Nop.Web)\Large Object Heap size`

We may quickly notice that the managed `# Total committed Bytes` are fast growing during the first 20 minutes of the test. Then suddenly the memory drops just to grow again very quickly. This pattern repeats again and again. Generation sizes recorded via Performance Monitor look as follows (see Figure 5-17):

- generation 0 size (long-dashed line) varies between 4,194,300 and 6,291,456 in a stable way. As we already know, this is not a real generation 0 size. However, "allocation budget" denoted by this measure is stable so we may assume there is no problem with generation 0.

- generation 1 size (short-dashed line) changes dynamically but is also stable. No growing trend can be spotted there so we can assume there are no problems either.

- generation 2 size (thin solid line) obviously stands out. It is responsible for a strange triangle pattern of memory consumption. This seems to be problematic as it reaches 1,314,381,592 bytes at maximum. We will have to dig deeper into it to find the root cause of the problem.

- Large Object Heap size (thick solid line) is growing very slowly. This may indicate the same problem but is unlikely the root cause of it. Please note this "memory leak" is not very burdensome. LOH grows up to around 38 MB (with small 46 MB peaks) after one hour of intensive work. This is hardly a problem compared to over 1 GB of generation 2 memory.

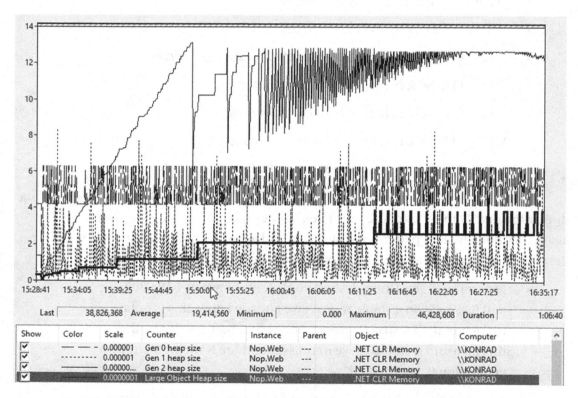

Figure 5-17. *Performance Monitor view of generation sizes during one-hour long load test of ASP.NET Core application*

If during the test we look at the state of the Nop.Web.exe process by VMMap tool, we come across the first clue. There are tons of Domain 1 Low and High Frequency heaps (see Figure 5-18a illustrating only a small part of them). As there are so many of them, it may indicate creating a lot of dynamic types, for example, via Reflection or by loading many assemblies. We may recall Scenario 4-4, which illustrated exactly such a problem with XmlSerializer.

⊞ 000000000B070000	Managed Heap	64 K	64 K	64 K	64 K	64 K	1 Read/Write	Domain 1 High Frequency Heap
⊞ 000000000B080000	Managed Heap	64 K	64 K	64 K	64 K	64 K	1 Read/Write	Domain 1 Low Frequency Heap
⊞ 000000000B0B0000	Managed Heap	64 K	64 K	64 K	64 K	64 K	1 Read/Write	Domain 1 High Frequency Heap
⊞ 000000000B0C0000	Managed Heap	64 K	64 K	64 K	64 K	64 K	1 Read/Write	Domain 1 High Frequency Heap
⊞ 000000000B0E0000	Managed Heap	64 K	64 K	64 K	64 K	64 K	1 Read/Write	Domain 1 Low Frequency Heap
⊞ 000000000B0F0000	Managed Heap	64 K	64 K	64 K	64 K	64 K	1 Read/Write	Domain 1 High Frequency Heap
⊞ 000000000B110000	Managed Heap	64 K	64 K	64 K	64 K	64 K	1 Read/Write	Domain 1 High Frequency Heap
⊞ 000000000B120000	Managed Heap	64 K	64 K	64 K	64 K	64 K	1 Read/Write	Domain 1 Low Frequency Heap
⊞ 000000000B130000	Managed Heap	64 K	64 K	64 K	64 K	64 K	1 Read/Write	Domain 1 High Frequency Heap
⊞ 000000000B150000	Managed Heap	64 K	64 K	64 K	64 K	64 K	1 Read/Write	Domain 1 Low Frequency Heap
⊞ 000000000B160000	Managed Heap	64 K	64 K	64 K	64 K	64 K	1 Read/Write	Domain 1 High Frequency Heap
⊞ 000000000B190000	Managed Heap	64 K	64 K	64 K	64 K	64 K	1 Read/Write	Domain 1 High Frequency Heap
⊞ 000000000B1A0000	Managed Heap	64 K	64 K	64 K	64 K	64 K	1 Read/Write	Domain 1 Low Frequency Heap
⊞ 000000000B230000	Managed Heap	64 K	64 K	64 K	64 K	64 K	1 Read/Write	Domain 1 High Frequency Heap
⊞ 000000000B240000	Managed Heap	64 K	64 K	64 K	64 K	64 K	1 Read/Write	Domain 1 Low Frequency Heap
⊞ 000000000B260000	Managed Heap	64 K	64 K	64 K	64 K	64 K	1 Read/Write	Domain 1 High Frequency Heap
⊞ 000000000B290000	Managed Heap	64 K	64 K	64 K	64 K	64 K	1 Read/Write	Domain 1 High Frequency Heap
⊞ 000000000B2A0000	Managed Heap	64 K	64 K	64 K	64 K	64 K	1 Read/Write	Domain 1 High Frequency Heap

Figure 5-18a. *Small part of VMMap view of the Nop.Web.exe process during test, showing a lot of Domain 1 Low and High Frequency heaps*

However, let us not jump to conclusions. As done in Scenario 4-4, we should confirm our suspicions by adding the following counters to our observation:

- \.NET CLR Loading(Nop.Web)\Bytes in Loader Heap

- \.NET CLR Loading(Nop.Web)\Current Classes Loaded

- \.NET CLR Loading(Nop.Web)\Current Assemblies

- \.NET CLR Loading(Nop.Web)\Current appdomains

We may be surprised that these counters do not change their value even within a few hours of testing. Our clue turned out to be false. In fact, even a large amount of Low and High Frequency heaps does not mean problems. If we look at them from time to time via VMMap, we will notice that their number does not change. We let ourselves be fooled. They are so many probably because of a lot of dynamically created types in a nopCommerce framework. Investigating it however does not make sense at this step.

Abandoning this trail, let's look at our main suspect - generation 2. Looking again at VMMap, we can sort Managed Heap regions by Details to have all GC Managed Heaps next to each other (see Figure 5-18b). Looking through them, we quickly see many segments containing only the second generation. What's more, we could pay attention to three more things:

- Addresses are short (the first half of them are zeroes) - so the process is using 32-bit .NET runtime, but we should know it from our deployment process.

- There is only a single segment with generation 0 and 1 (ephemeral segment) - this indicates most probably GC is running in Workstation mode.

- Segments containing generation 2 have size of 16 MB - according to Table 5-3 it may happen only on 32-bit Workstation GC, which confirms the two facts above.

Address	Type	Size	Committed	Private	Total WS	Private WS	...	Protection	Details
⊞ 000000000FB20000	Managed Heap	16,384 K	16,384 K	16,384 K	15,948 K	15,948 K	1	Read/Write	GC
⊟ 00000000122B0000	Managed Heap	16,384 K	16,384 K	16,384 K	16,372 K	16,372 K	1	Read/Write	GC
00000000122B0000	Managed Heap	16,384 K	16,384 K	16,384 K	16,372 K	16,372 K		Read/Write	Gen2
⊟ 00000000142F0000	Managed Heap	16,384 K	16,384 K	16,384 K	16,384 K	16,384 K	1	Read/Write	GC
00000000142F0000	Managed Heap	16,384 K	16,384 K	16,384 K	16,384 K	16,384 K		Read/Write	Gen2
⊟ 0000000016C90000	Managed Heap	16,384 K	16,384 K	16,384 K	16,384 K	16,384 K	1	Read/Write	GC
0000000016C90000	Managed Heap	16,384 K	16,384 K	16,384 K	16,384 K	16,384 K		Read/Write	Gen2
⊟ 0000000017C90000	Managed Heap	16,384 K	16,384 K	16,384 K	16,384 K	16,384 K	1	Read/Write	GC
0000000017C90000	Managed Heap	16,384 K	16,384 K	16,384 K	16,384 K	16,384 K		Read/Write	Gen2
⊟ 000000001A6E0000	Managed Heap	16,384 K	16,384 K	16,384 K	16,384 K	16,384 K	1	Read/Write	GC
000000001A6E0000	Managed Heap	16,384 K	16,384 K	16,384 K	16,384 K	16,384 K		Read/Write	Gen2
⊟ 000000001BCC0000	Managed Heap	16,384 K	16,384 K	16,384 K	16,384 K	16,384 K	1	Read/Write	GC
000000001BCC0000	Managed Heap	16,384 K	16,384 K	16,384 K	16,384 K	16,384 K		Read/Write	Gen2
⊟ 000000001D2C0000	Managed Heap	16,384 K	16,384 K	16,384 K	16,384 K	16,384 K	1	Read/Write	GC
000000001D2C0000	Managed Heap	16,384 K	16,384 K	16,384 K	16,384 K	16,384 K		Read/Write	Gen2
⊟ 000000001E2C0000	Managed Heap	16,384 K	16,384 K	16,384 K	16,384 K	16,384 K	1	Read/Write	GC
000000001E2C0000	Managed Heap	16,384 K	16,384 K	16,384 K	16,384 K	16,384 K		Read/Write	Gen2
⊞ 000000001F2C0000	Managed Heap	16,384 K	16,384 K	16,384 K	16,384 K	16,384 K	1	Read/Write	GC
⊞ 00000000202C0000	Managed Heap	16,384 K	16,384 K	16,384 K	16,384 K	16,384 K	1	Read/Write	GC
⊞ 00000000212C0000	Managed Heap	16,384 K	16,384 K	16,384 K	16,384 K	16,384 K	1	Read/Write	GC
⊞ 00000000224A0000	Managed Heap	16,384 K	16,384 K	16,384 K	16,384 K	16,384 K	1	Read/Write	GC
⊞ 00000000234A0000	Managed Heap	16,384 K	16,384 K	16,384 K	16,384 K	16,384 K	1	Read/Write	GC
⊞ 00000000244A0000	Managed Heap	16,384 K	16,384 K	16,384 K	16,384 K	16,384 K	1	Read/Write	GC

Figure 5-18b. *Small part of VMMap view of the Nop.Web.exe process during test, showing a lot of GC Managed Heaps containing generation 2*

The web application configured as running on 32-bit .NET runtime with Workstation GC mode may not be the most optimal setting. Even if it is quite an important finding we were not aware of so far, and it does not necessarily explain the observed memory leak. We should continue our investigation.[3]

---

[3]And by the way, there are other and better ways of checking GC's configuration of the running application. They are described in Chapter 8 (especially in dedicated Scenario 8-1).

VMMap tool usage is included in this scenario mainly to show the physical structure of the .NET application, to be aligned with the knowledge presented in this chapter. Additionally, it shows possible caveats if one decides to use it (like treating many high frequency heaps as a problem). It is good to have VMMap in your toolbox when solving problems. However, using VMMap is not a typical way that people would start an investigation for a problem like this. We should probably jump straight into WinDbg or PerfView after seeing presented performance counters.

At this point, we have to reach for other tools. The first choice may be WinDbg with SOS extension. A full memory dump of the Nop.Web.exe was taken by ProcDump tool. After loading it into WinDbg, we should load SOS by issuing .loadby sos clr command. Then we may issue two more commands: eeversion (prints .NET runtime information) and lmf (lists all loaded modules) - see Listing 5-11. As we can see, the process is using .NET Framework 4.7 and Workstation GC mode. It has loaded a 32-bit version of clr.dll (64-bit version is located under directory C:\Windows\Microsoft. NET\Framework64). This is the final confirmation of our previous findings.

Listing 5-11. Inside WinDbg with SOS loaded, commands eeversion, and lmf reveals that process is using 32-bit .NET Framework with Workstation GC mode

```
> !eeversion
4.7.2117.0 retail
Workstation mode
SOS Version: 4.7.2117.0 retail build
> lmf
...
72f70000 73656000   clr       C:\Windows\Microsoft.NET\Framework\v4.0.30319\
                              clr.dll
...
```

To start investigation of generation 2, we issue commands heapstat and eeheap (see Listing 5-12). As we may see, indeed generation 2 is huge (1,217,024,356 bytes) and it contains not so much free space (10,981,728 bytes). Fragmentation of it is probably not an issue. eeheap commands list a lot of segments details that we have seen previously in the VMMap tool.

Listing 5-12. Inside WinDbg with SOS loaded, commands heapstat, and eeheap reveals details about GC Managed Heap. eeheap command output has been stripped to show only a few relevant lines.

```
> !heapstat
Heap              Gen0           Gen1          Gen2          LOH
Heap0          9719400         280232    1217024356      38826368
Free space:                                           Percentage
Heap0          7042304            1152      10981728      12587408SOH:  1% LOH: 32%
> !eeheap
 segment      begin    allocated       size
024c0000   024c1000   034bffe4   0xffefe4(16773092)
0a070000   0a071000   0b06ffe0   0xffefe0(16773088)
0fb20000   0fb21000   10b1ffdc   0xffefdc(16773084)
122b0000   122b1000   132affe0   0xffefe0(16773088)
142f0000   142f1000   152effe0   0xffefe0(16773088)
...
41820000   41821000   4281ffec   0xffefec(16773100)
43820000   43821000   4410ea14   0x8eda14(9361940)
42820000   42821000   431aa510   0x989510(9999632)
```

Knowing the address range of segments, we may investigate its contents by the dumpheap command. Because the memory leak seems to be huge and objects live for a long time, let's investigate the content of one of the first segments (which most probably means one of the oldest ones). Listing 5-13 shows the result of the dumpheap command for statistical objects data in the fourth segment. A lot of the lines have been stripped for clarity and only a few last ones are shown. As we can see there is a huge number of objects from namespace Microsoft.Extensions.Caching.Memory. A particularly interesting class CacheEntry seems to indicate problems with caching.

Listing 5-13. Inside WinDbg with SOS loaded, dumpheap command shows statistical data of objects inside one of the segments (a lot of output's lines have been stripped for clarity)

```
> !dumpheap -stat 122b1000 132affe0
      MT     Count    TotalSize Class Name
...
04aa58e4    33795       946260 Microsoft.Extensions.Primitives.IChangeToken[]
0b542680    33808       946624 Microsoft.Extensions.Caching.Memory.
PostEvictionCallbackRegistration[]
089f26fc    33818      1082176 Microsoft.Extensions.Caching.Memory.
PostEvictionDelegate
71f91d64    34858      4327314 System.String
089e2b70    33786      4459752 Microsoft.Extensions.Caching.Memory.CacheEntry
Total 431540 objects
```

Now we can start a rather tedious process of investigating different instances of the CacheEntry object. Its MethodTable has an address 089e2b70 so we can modify dumpheap command to list only Microsoft.Extensions.Caching.Memory.CacheEntry instances inside the fourth segment (see Listing 5-14). The output will be a huge list of 33,786 instances, so only a few of the last lines are presented.

Listing 5-14. Inside WinDbg with SOS loaded, dumpheap command lists all objects inside specified segment with a given MethodTable

```
> !dumpheap -mt 089e2b70 122b1000 132affe0
 Address        MT     Size
...
132af460 089e2b70      132
132af64c 089e2b70      132
132af98c 089e2b70      132
132afd08 089e2b70      132
```

```
Statistics:
     MT      Count    TotalSize Class Name
089e2b70    33786       4459752 Microsoft.Extensions.Caching.Memory.CacheEntry
Total 33786 objects
```

We can investigate each instance with the help of DumpObj command, providing its address (see Listing 5-15). One of its fields has a name <Key>k__BackingField, which suggests we can inspect what is the key of the cache entry (see also Listing 5-15). It turns out to be Nop.pres.widget-79740-1-left_side_column_after_category_navigation-DefaultClean, which seems to be a data cached for some widget on a page.

Listing 5-15. Inside WinDbg with SOS loaded, DumpObj commands shows details of one of the instances listed in Listing 5-13

```
> !DumpObj 132afd08
Name:        Microsoft.Extensions.Caching.Memory.CacheEntry
MethodTable: 089e2b70
EEClass:     089c4f2c
Size:        132(0x84) bytes
File:        F:\IIS\nopCommerce\Microsoft.Extensions.Caching.Memory.dll
Fields:
...
71f81404   400000b      34 ...ffset, mscorlib]]  1 instance 132afd3c _
absoluteExpiration
...
71f92104   4000012      20         System.Object  0 instance 132afc18
<Key>k__BackingField
...
> !DumpObj 132afc18
Name:        System.String
...
String:      Nop.pres.widget-79740-1-left_side_column_after_category_
navigation-DefaultClean
```

Looking through all CacheEntry instances inside a segment in that way would be very tiresome and time consuming. Fortunately, we can use for this purpose the netext extension, mentioned in Chapter 3. Its wfrom command lets us write SQL-like

(or LINQ-like, if you wish) queries over objects. We can ask to list only _Key_k__
BackingField of objects with specified MethodTable, filtering them with respect to the
address of the segment we are interested in (see Listing 5-16).

Note   Netext slightly differently lists field's names so _Key_k__BackingField
is used instead of <Key>k__BackingField.

Listing 5-16. Inside WinDbg with netext loaded. Part of the wfrom command's
output is presented that selects _Key_k__BackingField from objects with
089e2b70 MethodTable and within a specified address range.

```
> !wfrom -mt 089e2b70 where (($addr() > 122b1000) && ($addr() < 132affe0))
select _Key_k__BackingField
...
_Key_k__BackingField: Nop.pres.widget-74954-1-mob_header_menu_after-
DefaultClean
_Key_k__BackingField: Nop.pres.widget-76130-1-header_menu_before-
DefaultClean
_Key_k__BackingField: Nop.pres.widget-75965-1-body_start_html_tag_after-
DefaultClean
_Key_k__BackingField: Nop.pres.widget-75369-1-searchbox_before_search_
button-DefaultClean
_Key_k__BackingField: Nop.pres.widget-75965-1-searchbox_before_search_
button-DefaultClean
_Key_k__BackingField: Nop.pres.widget-75867-1-header_selectors-DefaultClean
_Key_k__BackingField: Nop.pres.widget-75965-1-header_menu_before-
DefaultClean
_Key_k__BackingField: Nop.pres.widget-75573-1-body_start_html_tag_after-
DefaultClean
_Key_k__BackingField: Nop.pres.widget-75680-1-mob_header_menu_after-
DefaultClean
...
```

In the results, we will quickly see the obvious pattern. Actually almost all names start with `Nop.pres.widget`, followed by some numbers and (probably) the name of the widget. We should now be confident that the widget's data caching is somehow problematic. The question arises why there are so many cached similar entries. Why are there almost identical entries with only a first number difference? Immediately we may come to the question whether they are not cached for every request?

By looking at a few reference graphs with the help of the `gcroot` command, we may notice those entries are held by `MemoryCacheManager` inside `ProductTagService` or similar ones (see Listing 5-17).

Listing 5-17. Inside WinDbg with SOS loaded, `gcroot` command shows a references path of a sample `CacheEntry` instance. As this path is quite long, only a few relevant nodes are presented.

```
> !gcroot 132afd08
Thread 6d5c:
    0bc8f128 71ec99fa System.Threading.ExecutionContext.RunInternal(System.
Threading.ExecutionContext, System.Threading.ContextCallback, System.
Object, Boolean)
        ebp+4c: 0bc8f13c
            -> 0348777c System.Threading.Thread
            -> 025416d8 System.Runtime.Remoting.Contexts.Context
            -> 024c12e0 System.AppDomain
                ...
            -> 0ac5df50 Nop.Services.Catalog.ProductTagService
            -> 033dbacc Nop.Core.Caching.MemoryCacheManager
            -> 033db504 Microsoft.Extensions.Caching.Memory.MemoryCache
                ...
                -> 132afd08 Microsoft.Extensions.Caching.Memory.CacheEntry
```

This is the most difficult part of the puzzle to answer without access to the source code. Fortunately, most often we will analyze our own application so we will have access to its code that is well-known to us. In case of our scenario, it would turn out that the cache key includes a customer identifier that is taken from the cookie for anonymous users. But our test scenario in JMeter does not include HTTP Cookie Manager elements that manage cookies! In other words, each and every HTTP request was treated as issued by a new customer without a cookie set. There is certainly not a desired scenario that results from our error in the preparation of the load test script.

nopCommerce is open sourced so we may also quickly find the root cause of the problem:

- By searching for example name from a cache entry key (like `mob_header_menu_after` identifier), we will find the following line in `./src/Presentation/Nop.Web/Views/Shared/Components/TopMenu/Default.cshtml` file:

  `@await Component.InvokeAsync("Widget", new { widgetZone = "mob_header_menu_after" })`

- Widget component defined a file `./src/Presentation/Nop.Web/Components/Widget.cs` contains simple Invoke method calling widget factory:

  `var model = _widgetModelFactory.PrepareRenderWidgetModel(widgetZone, additionalData);`

- `WidgetModelFactory` method `PrepareRenderWidgetModel` is building `cacheKey` in the following way:

  ```
  var cacheKey = string.Format(ModelCacheEventConsumer.WIDGET_MODEL_KEY,
  _workContext.CurrentCustomer.Id,
  _storeContext.CurrentStore.Id,
  widgetZone,
  _themeContext.WorkingThemeName);
  ```

As we can see, widgets are using `CurrentCustomer.Id`, which is managed by a cookie in case of no logged users. If a cookie does not exist, a new integer value is used.

This scenario was to show that by understanding the concepts of generations and segments, we can notice a problem and use the low-level tools to find its cause. Of course, in situations you will encounter that causes of the problems can be very diverse. The mistakes made when configuring the load test will probably be one of the rarest. However, the exercise was not meant to show this one particular problem and its solution, but rather how to approach it. We could also use more pleasant tools like PerfView or any other commercial tool to analyze such a memory leak. Such an approach will be taken in later scenarios.

Scenario 5-3. Large Object Heap Waste?

Description: In our 64-bit workstation application, we are processing huge lists of objects - let it be some kind of "big data" process. But unfortunately, after some period of time, we are getting OutOfMemoryException and are unable to process all the data. Our process starts with a pre-processing stage - we are creating a list of large arrays of pre-processed objects. Each such block contains 10,000,000 references to objects located elsewhere. OutOfMemoryException occurs during allocating those arrays. We want to make processing possible so we start our investigation.

Analysis: It's worth starting by looking at the process by VMMap tool at the time just before when OutOfMemoryException occurs (see Figure 5-19). We see there indeed a huge amount of memory being consumed. Private Working Set of a process takes around 15 GB, which is almost all available physical memory (machine was equipped with 16 GB of RAM). Moreover, if we looked at the page file of the system, we would see that pagefile.sys takes almost 32 GB - the maximum possible value that has been set by the system administrator. This means there was no free memory left for more arrays and we just can do nothing about it (except changing system configuration by adding more RAM and/or extending maximum page file size).

However, one can notice alarming segments consumption. There is a huge amount of LOH segments and each and every one holds only around half of a size-committed region while the rest is only reserved. Why does this happen? If we look at Table 5-3, we recall that in the case of a 64-bit Workstation GC, LOH segments are 128 MB big. For our processing purposes we are creating arrays of 10,000,000 references. Each reference is 8-bytes long so a whole array requires around 76 MB of data. When a new array is being allocated, an existing LOH segment does not fit it as only around 52 MB is left in it. Thus, a new segment must be created for each and every new array we create. This results in "wasting" those 52 MB in each LOH segment (assuming our application does not intensively create smaller objects in LOH whose would fit in this additional space).

But a careful reader can see a certain mistake in our thinking. Remembering what has been said in Chapter 2, reserved virtual memory does not consume physical memory directly (only small reservation descriptors have to be remembered). If we look at Figure 5-19 carefully, we will notice that Reserved parts of LOH segments do not count into Committed nor Private bytes. It is hardly "wasting" a memory. Let's not be fooled by these measurements. In fact, we are really consuming all available memory and we cannot do anything about it (nothing else than allocating less arrays at once).

Type	Size	Committed	Private	Total WS	Private WS	Shareable WS	Shared WS	Locke
Total	2,217,056,684 K	41,533,868 K	41,461,692 K	13,515,100 K	13,513,696 K	1,404 K	584 K	
Image	39,656 K	39,644 K	3,908 K	1,600 K	248 K	1,352 K	556 K	
Mapped File	4,064 K	4,064 K						
Shareable	2,147,508,528 K	32,312 K		44 K		44 K	20 K	
Heap	9,296 K	3,400 K	3,335 K	400 K	396 K	4 K	4 K	
Managed Heap	68,682,368 K	40,707,112 K	40,707,112 K	13,364,264 K	13,364,264 K			
Stack	6,144 K	124 K	124 K	32 K	32 K			
Private Data	667,276 K	610,784 K	610,784 K	12,032 K	12,029 K	4 K	4 K	
Page Table	136,428 K	136,428 K	136,428 K	136,428 K	136,428 K			
Unusable	2,924 K							
Free	135,222,033,152 K							

Address	Type	Size	Committed	Private	Total WS	Private WS	...	Protection	Details
⊟ 00000248927B0000	Managed Heap	131,072 K	78,132 K	78,132 K	78,132 K	78,132 K		2 Read/Write	Large Object Heap
00000248927B0000	Managed Heap	78,132 K	78,132 K	78,132 K	78,132 K	78,132 K		Read/Write	Large Object Heap
00000248973FD000	Managed Heap	52,940 K						Reserved	
⊟ 00002489A7B0000	Managed Heap	131,072 K	78,132 K	78,132 K	78,132 K	78,132 K		2 Read/Write	Large Object Heap
00002489A7B0000	Managed Heap	78,132 K	78,132 K	78,132 K	78,132 K	78,132 K		Read/Write	Large Object Heap
00002489F3FD000	Managed Heap	52,940 K						Reserved	
⊟ 00000248A27B0000	Managed Heap	131,072 K	78,132 K	78,132 K	78,132 K	78,132 K		2 Read/Write	Large Object Heap
00000248A27B0000	Managed Heap	78,132 K	78,132 K	78,132 K	78,132 K	78,132 K		Read/Write	Large Object Heap
00000248A73FD000	Managed Heap	52,940 K						Reserved	
⊟ 00000248AA7B0000	Managed Heap	131,072 K	78,132 K	78,132 K	78,132 K	78,132 K		2 Read/Write	Large Object Heap
00000248AA7B0000	Managed Heap	78,132 K	78,132 K	78,132 K	78,132 K	78,132 K		Read/Write	Large Object Heap
00000248AF3FD000	Managed Heap	52,940 K						Reserved	
⊞ 00000248B27B0000	Managed Heap	131,072 K	78,132 K	78,132 K	78,132 K	78,132 K		2 Read/Write	Large Object Heap
⊞ 00000248BA7B0000	Managed Heap	131,072 K	78,132 K	78,132 K	78,132 K	78,132 K		2 Read/Write	Large Object Heap
⊞ 00000248C27B0000	Managed Heap	131,072 K	78,132 K	78,132 K	78,132 K	78,132 K		2 Read/Write	Large Object Heap
⊞ 00000248CA7B0000	Managed Heap	131,072 K	78,132 K	78,132 K	78,132 K	78,132 K		2 Read/Write	Large Object Heap
⊞ 00000248D27B0000	Managed Heap	131,072 K	78,132 K	78,132 K	78,132 K	78,132 K		2 Read/Write	Large Object Heap

Figure 5-19. *Part of VMMap view of the process a few moments before OutOfMemoryException happens*

However, such memory waste due to unusable reserved space within LOH segments is not a problem only in case of 64-bit configuration because we have plenty of virtual address space. It could be a severe problem on 32-bit .NET Runtime, where virtual address space is much more limited. If this is your case, you should consider splitting processed data into smaller arrays to better utilize single LOH segments and avoid fragmentation.

Segments and Heap Anatomy

As it will be explained later, a segment is the physical representation of a Managed Heap. Its internal structure is simple but it is worth it to get to know it (see Figure 5-20). As we have seen at Listing 5-10, the example program had an ephemeral segment with an address 0x0000026700000000 but it "begins" at address 0x0000026700001000. Those starting 4,096 bytes (0x1000 in hexadecimal) are dedicated to store segment information managed by the runtime. Objects are created in a subsequent address. Each SOH and LOH segment has the following structure:

- At the beginning *segment information* is stored (an instance of heap_ segment class). Although this class is only a dozen of bytes big, in most cases the whole page is being committed for this purpose. This is a performance optimization used in case of a runtime version that supports a popular background GC (explained in Chapter 11), which includes all publicly available runtimes at the time of this writing. The beginning of this structure (and whole segment itself) is listed as a segment address in previously seen eeheap command output.

- Objects are being allocated from the address named mem (in .NET source code). However, this address is listed as begin in case of an eeheap command. As we will see in Chapter 6, reserved memory of the segment is being committed in advance (not only for a single object), so there will be slightly more committed memory than required for current objects.

- Address where currently allocated objects end is named allocated.

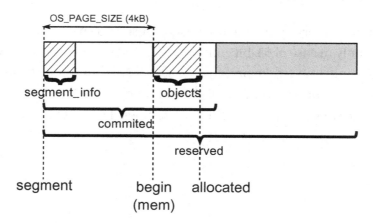

Figure 5-20. *Internal structure of heap segment*

Although it is not so useful for everyday work in .NET, when trying to analyze .NET Core code, it is worth knowing the relationship between several fundamental classes representing the entities described here. It will make it easier for you to start your own journey through the CoreCLR source code if you ever feel like it.

There are the following important classes representing core Garbage Collection functionality (see Figure 5-21):

- GCHeap - there is always one instance of this high-level API - it is used as an interface between Garbage Collector and Execution Engine (they both keep global instances g_pGCHeap and g_theGCHeap). It contains methods like Alloc and GarbageCollect. Additionally, in Server mode each Managed Heap is represented by an additional GCHeap instance. Thus, there will be one instance in Workstation mode and one plus number of cores instances in Server mode.

- gc_heap - low-level API of a single Managed Heap, used by GCHeap. It contains all the heavy work of GC, including methods like allocate, garbage_collect, make_gc_heap, make_heap_segment, and so on and so forth. In Server mode GCHeap instance operates on the corresponding gc_heap instance. In case of Workstation mode, all relevant gc_heap methods are static so there is no need for any instance at all. Thus, there will be no instances in Workstation mode or number of cores instances in Server mode.

- generation - represents single generation. It contains information about segments containing those generations, many allocation-related information, and other relevant data.

- heap_segment - represents single segment information as described before. All segments are chained into single-linked list so each segment may contain a pointer to the next segment.

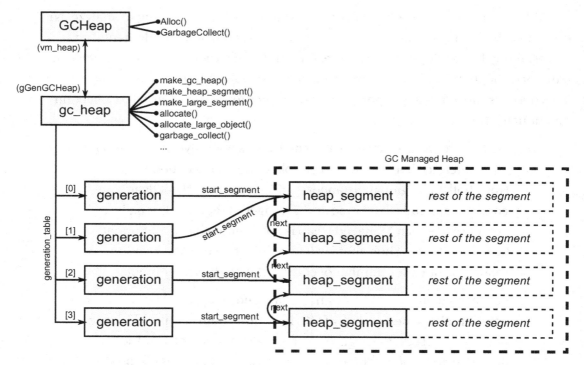

Figure 5-21. *Relationship between fundamental GC-related classes in .NET source code (based on .NET Core code). heap_segment instances are living in the managed heap, at the beginning of segments as explained earlier. All other data lives inside private heaps of the runtime.*

Knowing all the above, we may now understand, for example, the implementation of GC.GetGeneration method used earlier (see Listing 5-18).

Listing 5-18. Method in gc_heap class that is called when GC.GetGeneration method is executed

```
// return the generation number of an object.
// It is assumed that the object is valid.
// Note that this will return max_generation for a LOH object
int gc_heap::object_gennum (uint8_t* o)
```

```
{
    if (in_range_for_segment (o, ephemeral_heap_segment) &&
        (o >= generation_allocation_start (generation_of (max_
        generation-1))))
    {
        // in an ephemeral generation.
        for ( int i = 0; i < max_generation-1; i++)
        {
            if ((o >= generation_allocation_start (generation_of (i))))
                return i;
        }
        return max_generation-1;
    }
    else
    {
        return max_generation;
    }
}
```

Segments Reuse

During program execution, there may be more and more segments created to contain all allocated objects. The question arises whether segments are ever removed? The answer is positive. However, as often happens, the answer is more complicated than the simple "yes."

First of all, let's start by looking at the situations in which .NET runtime can decide to remove a segment. In fact, there is only one reason for that - the segment has become empty after garbage collection (it contains no objects at all). We will see when it happens when learning about garbage collection in detail.

Secondly, what does "remove a segment" mean at all? In the simplest manner it means calling VirtualFree (or Linux counterpart) on the whole reserved memory region of a segment. In that way we simply reclaim that memory and return it to the operating system. Let's imagine a situation as illustrated in Figure 5-22a. Our program has four segments. Generation 2 is quite big so it consumes two segments. As stated before, there is more memory committed (white regions) than needed for current objects (dashed regions) because memory is prepared in advance. After some time, compacting garbage collection may occur in which many objects in generation 2 have been removed (see Figure 5-22b). In fact, so much space has been reclaimed that one of the segments containing generation 2 has become empty (contains no objects). But the whole memory is still being committed at this moment. The simplest scenario is now just to free such memory (see Figure 5-22c).

Although it seems a perfectly sensible approach, it has an important disadvantage. Continual creating and removing segments may introduce a fragmentation problem. It may be especially severe in 32-bit applications where virtual memory space was not so big and particularly in case of long-running web applications. Those were the times of .NET 2.0 and ASP.NET 2.0 and that's why more intelligent handling of segments has been introduced called *VM Hoarding*. The idea behind it is quite simple. Instead of freeing an empty segment completely, we may store it (*hoard*) for later reuse (see Figure 5-22d). In such a case:

- whole segment's memory stays reserved;

- most of the segment's memory is decommitted (does not consume physical memory) - only small amount of the beginning memory stays committed, including segment info itself;

- segment is remembered in a list of reusable segments (`segment_standby_list` in case of CoreCLR) - when a new segment will be needed, this list will be first checked for reusage possibility. One of such segments may be then initialized as a new, valid segment.

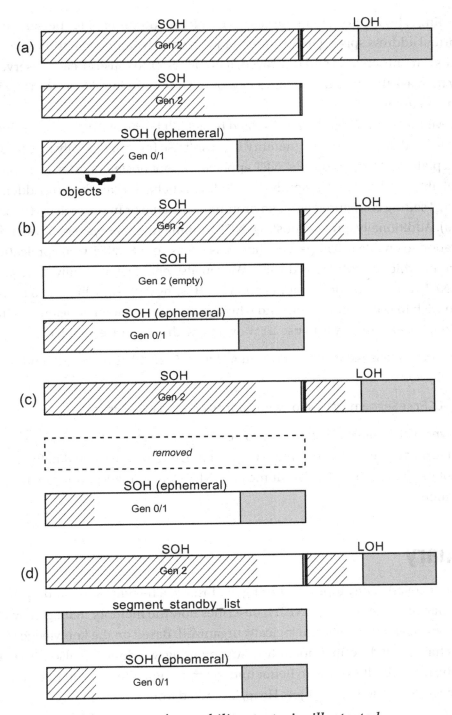

Figure 5-22. *Possible segments' reusability strategies illustrated*

Hoarding is less important in the case of 64-bit executions engines because of much bigger virtual address space. On the other hand, in very dynamic scenarios when there are many segments created and destroyed, it is still faster to reuse already reserved memory than ask the system to create a new one. Thus, even in a 64-bit scenario it may be worth it to use it.

However, segments hoarding is disabled by default because .NET runtime does not want to hold onto the virtual memory it doesn't use (even if it is only reserved). If you run a plain desktop or console .NET application (not hosted in external process), most probably VM hoarding is simply disabled. This behavior may be overridden by the GCRetainVM setting configured as an environment variable or in the registry (in case of Windows). Additionally, process hosting .NET runtime may use `System.GC.RetainVM` configuration to enable it. This is what happens in case of ASP.NET web applications hosted in IIS, which enables it by default. We can also enable it manually, if we are hosting .NET runtime inside our application via Hosting API (see Chapter 15 for details).

If you wish to track what, when, and why segments are created or destroyed in your application, the easiest way is to use ETW events (with stack trace enabled):

- `GCCreateSegment_V1` - shows an `Address`, `Size`, `ClrInstanceID` and `Type`

- `GCFreeSegment_V1` - shows an `Address` and `ClrInstanceID`

The `Type` listed above will contain two possible values: `SmallObjectHeap` or `LargeObjectHeap`. It could also contain `ReadOnlyHeap` value mentioned before, but this should not happen both in .NET Runtime and .NET Core as read-only segments are disabled there.

Summary

This chapter covers many topics that bring us closer to a better understanding of how memory management works in .NET. It describes how the memory managed by Garbage Collector has been physically and logically organized. Based on the knowledge from previous chapters, it describes not only how something was done but also tries to explain why. I hope that this allows you to better understand where the division into generations, Small Object Heap and Large Object Heap, is derived from.

This chapter describes in some detail the various aspects related to the organization of memory within Managed Heap. Some of those aspects are fundamental, and it is hard to understand .NET without being aware of them. Those include especially the concept of Generational Garbage Collection. Generations are a key concept that almost always appear in the context of memory management in .NET programs. Therefore, these topics should be considered very practical. On the other hand, topics with much less practical use are also described because it allows us to go much deeper into CLR internals and understand how some particular aspects of GC design have been implemented.

The chapter also contains three example scenarios for solving problems related to the topics discussed here. They allow you to look at the topic of generation or segments from a more practical side.

Rule 11 - Monitor Generation Sizes

Justification: Weak generational hypotheses are the foundation of Generation Garbage Collector implemented in .NET Runtime. A program, which due to uncommon (or erroneous) object creation patterns violates it, may incur serious problems to the GC performance.

How to apply: According to Rules 5 and 6 we should measure our program to check memory management behavior. One of the most important measures include how generations change their size in time. We should be aware (if not monitor continuously) how big are generations 0, 1, 2, and LOH. Two common misbehaviors should arouse our attention:

- One or more generations are constantly growing (even if it is spread over time and happens after a lot of memory garbage collections) - this may indicate a bigger or smaller memory leak.

- One or more generation changes in time very frequently - this may indicate a big memory traffic that triggers a costly GC process.

Obviously, generation sizes by themselves are not the only important measurement. One can imagine a generation 2 size that is stable but there is a lot of churn to it (meaning we are replacing a log of objects in it very often), so we are spending a lot of time spending generation 2 GCs. Thus, measuring CPU overhead (like % Time in GC counter) is at least as important as monitoring generation sizes.

Related scenarios: Scenarios 5-1, 5-2.

Rule 12 - Avoid Unnecessary Heap References

Justification: In Generational Garbage Collection, a special technique exists to track references between generations. This is called a Remembered Set technique in general. .NET runtime uses write barriers and card tables to realize such a technique. As described in this chapter, it has quite a sophisticated implementation, doing its best to provide as small of overhead as possible. However, the best intragenerational reference is a nonexisting one. We can help GC in reducing overhead by taking care of not introducing too many, sometimes unnecessary references.

How to apply: When constructing any long-running buffers or caches, a quite typical situation is to assign to them newly created objects. This may incur creating intrageneration reference (triggering card table mechanism). However, there may be cases when such a reference may be avoided: for example, when designing binary tree, instead of holding references to nodes:

```
class Node
{
    Data d;
    Node left;
    Node right;
};
```

You may store just an index to them and store nodes in an array:

```
class Node
{
    Data d;
    uint left_index;
    uint right_index;
};
```

Please bear in mind, however, that such a change incurs much more changes than just relieving a card table mechanism. For example, how will such arrays of nodes be allocated? How will such a change influence performance of traversing a graph, which now requires an additional array lookup per node? Only solid benchmarking can give as an answer whether applying this rule is beneficial or quite the opposite.

Rule 13 - Monitor Segments Usage

Justification: Segments are implementation details of how a Managed Garbage Collector heap is being organized. In most cases it is perfectly hidden so we should not be aware of it at all. However, as always, there are some exceptions. Segments itself and their layout may provide us some diagnostic clues when analyzing memory usage problems. They can even cause such problems rarely, especially in a tight 32-bit environment.

How to apply: It is sometimes good to look at our process under investigation with the help of appropriate WinDbg commands (or tools like VMMap). By analysis of segments created by the GC, we may gain some clues regarding possible issues. Knowing how generations are located in segments may be especially useful when doing low-level analysis in tools like WinDbg.

Related scenarios: Scenarios 5-2, 5-3.

CHAPTER 6

Memory Allocation

We have learned so far quite broad theoretical introduction about memory in general and low-level aspects of it in the first chapters. Starting from Chapter 4 we are learning more and more about the implementation of memory management in .NET. So far, we have learned mostly about some .NET internals (in Chapter 4) and how memory is being organized structurally (in Chapter 5). Based on the knowledge gained so far, in this chapter it is time to go to the most important topics in this book - the principles of operation and usage of Garbage Collector in .NET. As we are getting closer to the core topics, beside implementation details, expect also more and more practical knowledge both from diagnostics and from a code point of view.

We start with a mechanism without which the operation of any program would be impossible - allocating memory. This mechanism provides memory for objects that we create in our applications. And our programs need to create objects, no matter how hard we try. Simply running the simplest console application creates a lot of auxiliary objects even before the first line of our code is executed. Because of its crucial importance and heavy usage, as we shall see in this chapter, every effort has been made to make allocator in .NET as efficient as possible.

You may remember a brief mention of the concept of Allocator presented in Chapter 1 as "an entity responsible for managing dynamic memory allocation and deallocation." Method `Allocator.Allocate(amount)` has been defined there, which is responsible for providing a specified amount of memory. It is true that on this level of abstraction, Allocator especially does not care about the type of object, it just provides the right number of bytes (which will be then filled by runtime in a proper way).

Allocation Introduction

Obviously our abstract `Allocator.Allocate(amount)` is only the tip of the iceberg. This whole chapter is devoted to the details of the implementation of this single method and the practical tips resulting from it.

411

© Konrad Kokosa 2018
K. Kokosa, *Pro .NET Memory Management*, https://doi.org/10.1007/978-1-4842-4027-4_6

If we recall from Chapter 2, an operating system provides its own allocation mechanisms. Unmanaged environments like C/C++ are relying on them directly to acquire required memory. It is called Heap API (in case of Windows) or a combination of `mmap`/`sbrk` calls (in case of Linux). However, the .NET environment may benefit by introducing an additional layer between the operating system and executed program - which is .NET runtime. Most often managed environments like .NET preallocate continuous blocks of memory and implement their own allocation mechanism inside. This may be much faster than asking an operating system for more memory each time a new object is being created. Operating system calls may be costly and as we will see, much simpler mechanisms may be used.

As we know from the previous chapter, the GC Managed Heap consists of segments. This is exactly the place where the allocation of objects described in this chapter takes place. Although it was not clearly enough stated so far, you could probably notice it already - allocation of objects takes place:

- in generation 0 in case of Small Object Heap. It was illustrated by Figures 5-4 and 5-5 in the previous chapter. This happens physically is an ephemeral segment (containing generations 0 and 1).

- in Large Object Heap directly as it is not further partitioned into generations. This happens physically in one of the segments containing LOH.

As the Book Of The Runtime summarizes this: "Each time a large object is allocated, the whole large object heap is considered. Small object allocations only consider the ephemeral segment."

There are two popular ways how an allocator may be implemented. Both are used in .NET. They were already mentioned in Chapter 1 - *sequential allocation* and *free-list allocation*. Let's now dig into them one by one in the context of .NET implementation.

Bump Pointer Allocation

The allocator has segments at his disposal. The simplest and fastest way of allocating memory inside it is just to move some pointer indicating when the current memory "ends." This pointer is called an *allocation pointer*. If we moved it with a number of bytes corresponding to the size of the object we want to create - congratulations, we've just allocated memory for a given object! The idea is illustrated in Figure 6-1. Let's assume there are already some objects created (see Figure 6-1a). The allocation pointer points where those objects end. This is a place where a newly created object will be placed. When some memory for new object A is being requested, the pointer value becomes an address of this object. Then allocator just moves this pointer further by a specified number of bytes (see Figure 6-1b).

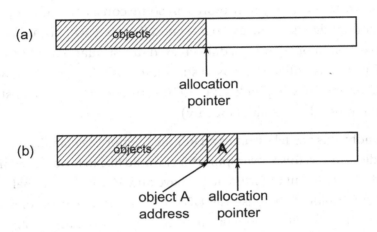

Figure 6-1. *Simple sequential allocator implementation*

Pseudo-code from Listing 6-1 illustrates this simple yet efficient technique. As we will later see, such implementation is one of the allocation possibilities inside CLR. Such a simple function can be written in an assembly code with just a few instructions, making it extremely efficient.

Listing 6-1. Simple bump pointer allocator implementation

```
Allocator.Allocate(amount)
{
    PTR result = alloc_ptr;
    alloc_ptr += amount;
    return result;
}
```

One may meet this kind of allocation also under the name *bump pointer allocation* as what it does is provide memory by "bumping" the allocation pointer from time to time. We can see two main properties of such an approach:

- Firstly, as its name states, this is a sequential algorithm - we just move always in one direction when allocating memory. This may lead to good data locality. If we create a bunch of objects in our program at once, they may represent some consistent and self-dependent data structures, so it is good that they will be laid near each other. In other words, data created in a similar period of time probably will later be used simultaneously (and as we may remember from Chapter 2, CPU architecture is making the best from temporal and spatial locality).

- Secondly, this model assumes an infinite memory availability. Needless to say, this is overoptimistic. I would like to have an infinite RAM in my PC, but unfortunately, I have only 16 GB. Does it make sequential allocation nonsense? Of course not, as we can do something with the left side of the pointer. For example, remove unused objects and compact holes left by them. This is where Garbage Collection comes into play obviously. Occasionally we may "rewind" the allocation pointer back after unused objects have been collected.

One can wonder what happens to the memory contents in the place where the object A is located. For the new object to be in a clean state, this memory must of course be zeroed (some individual fields of the object will be set by its constructor, but this is the role of the Execution Engine and not the Garbage Collector). This would require adding such a cleaning call to the `Allocate` method from Listing 6-1 (see Listing 6-2).

Listing 6-2. Simple sequential allocator implementation (with memory zeroing)

```
Allocator.Allocate(amount)
{
    PTR result = alloc_ptr;
    ZeroMemory(alloc_ptr, amount);
    alloc_ptr += amount;
    return result;
}
```

Zeroing memory introduces overhead though, which is not negligible in such an extremely important and common operation as creating new objects. Thus, to make allocation as fast as possible, it is worth it to prepare some amount of zeroed memory in advance. This would allow us to use code from Listing 6-1 as a fast path, falling back to zeroing memory from Listing 6-2 only as needed. Zeroing memory in advance makes also CPU cache usage more efficient because accessing it will "warm" the cache.

An additional pointer is introduced in a called *allocation limit*, which points where zeroed memory region ends. Such region is called an *allocation context* (see Figure 6-2). Allocation context is a place where fast, optimistic allocation happens by pointer bumping.

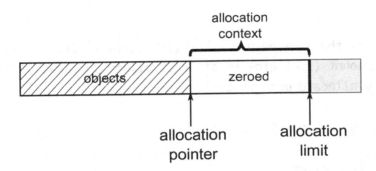

Figure 6-2. *Allocation context spans between allocation pointer and allocation limit. It contains ready-to-use zeroed memory.*

If there is not enough space in the allocation context for a required number of bytes, a fallback mechanism is being triggered (see Listing 6-3). This fallback mechanism may contain any level of sophistication. In case of CLR it contains quite a complicated state machine of possible actions as we will see in subchapters describing in detail allocation in Small and Large Object Heaps separately. One of the obvious possibilities is to grow the allocation context or get a new one to fit the required space. A typical amount of such growth is called *allocation quantum*. In other words, in a typical scenario, when there is no room in the allocation context, it will be enlarged by at least an allocation quantum (or more if more memory was requested).

Listing 6-3. More realistic bump pointer allocator with allocation context buffer containing already zeroed memory

```
Allocator.Allocate(amount)
{
   if (alloc_ptr + amount <= alloc_limit)
   {
      // This is the fast path - we have enough memory to bump the pointer
      PTR result = alloc_ptr;
      alloc_ptr += amount;
      return result;
   }
   else
   {
      // This is the slow path - allocation context will be changed to fit
         the amount (i.e. grow by at least allocation quantum bytes)
      if (!try_allocate_more_space())
      {
         throw OutOfMemoryException;
      }
      PTR result = alloc_ptr;
      alloc_ptr += amount;
      return result;
   }
}
```

As we remember from the previous chapter, GC already has one mechanism of memory preparation - two-stage building of segments. First, a large block of memory is reserved, and then, if necessary, subsequent pages are committed as needed. But when segments grow by committing more pages, not necessarily all those pages are instantly zeroed. In other words, allocation context may not consume all committed memory to its end (see Figure 6-3). It is a compromise between the profit from the preparation of memory and the cost of zeroing it. For example, in case of Small Object Heap, a default allocation quantum is 8 kB while the segment is grown by committing 16 pages at once (which is typically 64 kB).

While default allocation quantum size is 8 kB, it may be dynamically changed under certain circumstances. The current CLR implementation can set a value between 1,024 and 8,096 bytes depending on allocation's intensiveness and number of active contexts.

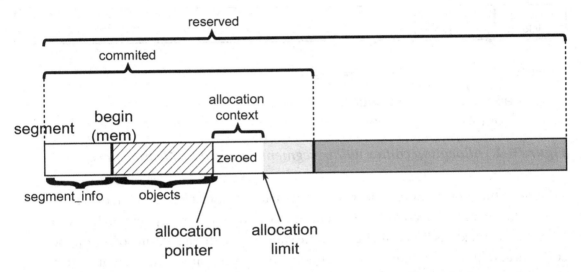

Figure 6-3. *Allocation contex within segment - created at the end of current allocations*

In this way an operating system is asked for committing pages much less frequently and only the allocation context is being grown. As we can see, there is quite a well-thought way of acquiring memory than just simple object by object allocation, which would be not effective at all.

Allocation context can be also placed in other places than just at the end of the segment. It may be spanned inside free space between existing objects (see Figure 6-4). In such a case, it will start with an allocation pointer set to the beginning of the free space and allocation limit pointing to its end.

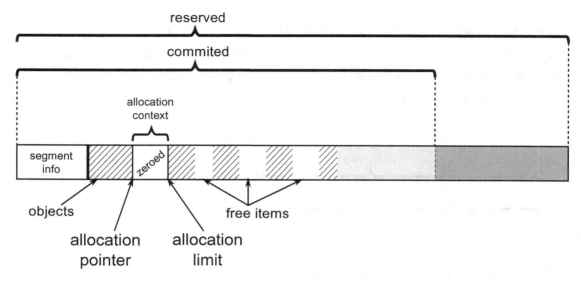

Figure 6-4. *Allocation contex within segment - created inside free space*

One of the most important facts is that allocation context has a *thread affinity*. It means that each managed thread (executing .NET code) in our application has its own allocation context. As Book Of The Runtime states: "The thread affinity of allocation contexts and quantums guarantee that there is only ever a single thread writing to a given allocation quantum. As a result, there is no need to lock for object allocations, as long as the current allocation context is not exhausted."

This is extremely important from a performance perspective. If allocation context was shared between threads, the `Allocate` method would introduce synchronization overhead. But as each thread has dedicated its own context, a simple bump pointer technique can be used without a worry that something else will modify the allocation pointer or limit inside it. This mechanism is based on *Thread-local storage* (TLS) to store allocation context per thread. And in general, we can meet this technique under the name *Thread Local Allocation Buffer*.

Note   On a machine with a single logic processor there will be only a single allocation context. Thus, access to it in such a case must be synchronized because different threads may access such a single, global allocation context. However, in such a case, synchronization is very cheap as only one thread can run at any given time.

Having multiple allocation contexts complicates our Figures 6-3 and 6-4 a little. There is no single context at the end of segment as it has been drawn in simplified form before. There are many managed threads in our application so a more typical scenario is when multiple allocation contexts live within a single segment (see Figure 6-5). As the program runs, some of them will be located at the end of segment and some will reuse free space between objects.

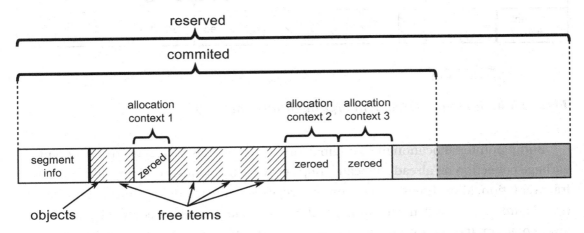

Figure 6-5. *Multiple allocation contexts within segment - each for one thread*

Allocation context lives within an ephemeral segment - the one which contains generation 0 and 1. Thus, Figure 6-5 shows ephemeral segment structure where "objects" part will be split into generations 1 and 0 (and 2 if it is small, for example, at the beginning of the program execution).

As we at this point pretty well touched .NET memory organization, it has been once again summarized in Figure 6-6. Remember - generations are just logical and moving boundaries inside a segment.

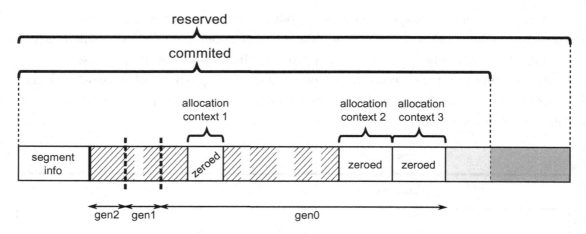

Figure 6-6. *Ephemeral segment organization summary*

Bump pointer allocation in its original form has one drawback. If we run sweeping garbage collection on already allocated objects, we will obviously end up with fragmentation. Many holes of free memory will exist to the left of the allocation pointer (see Figure 6-7a). A very naïve bump pointer technique (not one used in .NET) is not aware of them. It can only consume more and more memory. Obviously, no one would create a serious GC that sweeps the heap yet doesn't try to use the resulting free space to allocate something in. The simplest solution is that we can run compacting garbage collection so survived objects will be laid next to each other and whole allocation context will be pushed back (see Figure 6-7b). There is a much better solution than relying on compaction.

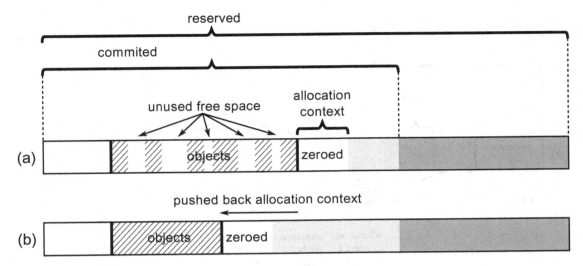

Figure 6-7. *Bump pointer allocation and fragmentation problem: (a) Sweeping Garbage Collection produces fragmentation and allocation context is not aware of free memory, (b) Compact Garbage Collection reclaims memory by pushing back allocation context but requires a lot of memory copying*

Fortunately, .NET implementation uses a smart combination of sequential allocation within allocation context but as we see in Figures 6-4 and 6-5, it may create allocation context inside free space (using fragmentation as a good thing). Once in a while GC may decide to compact and then allocation contexts will be reorganized in a natural way at the end of the segment (see Figure 6-8).

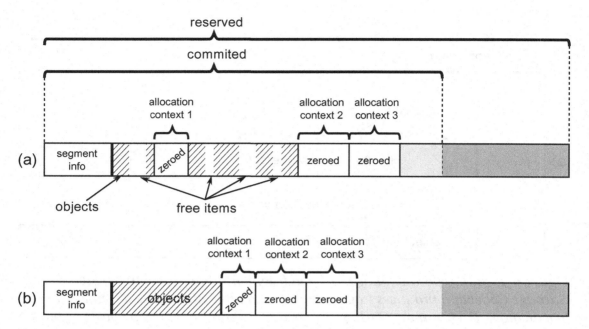

Figure 6-8. *Compacting Garbage Collector may reorganize all allocation contexts after its work – (a) initial situation with three allocation contexts scattered around the segment, (b) after compacting GC allocation segments will be reorganized optimally*

Free-List Allocation

The idea behind free-list allocation is trivial. When runtime asks GC to allocate a given number of bytes, it searches through a free list to find a free gap big enough to fit the specified number of bytes. As mentioned already in Chapter 1, two main strategies of free-list scanning may be taken:

- best-fit - to find free memory gap best suiting required space (which would be the smallest block bigger or equal than required size) to leave as small leftovers as possible. Naïve approach would require scanning the whole list of free items although a typical approach is based on buckets, as explained below.

- first-fit - scanning ends as fast as first suitable free memory gap has been found. This is fast in terms of required time but produces far than optimal results in terms of fragmentation.

Microsoft .NET implementation uses buckets to manage a set of free lists for various free gap sizes. In this way a fast scan may be used without compromising fragmentation optimization too much. By controlling the number of buckets (number of various size ranges of free gaps), a balance between performance and fragmentation reduction may be set. If there was a single bucket (all gaps regarding their size will land there), it would mean naïve first-fit approach. On the other hand, if there was a lot of buckets (with very detailed gap sizes granularity), it would mean a best-fit approach. As we will see, the number of baskets varies for each generation.

Free lists are maintained partially directly on the GC Heap due to the way free space is being represented. A free space between used objects is represented as it was an (almost) regular array. Thus, it has structure very similar to a normal object (see Figure 6-9). There is a special MethodTable representing such "free object." A number of the free space "elements" is stored after MethodTable pointer, as in the typical array. "Free object" array assumes one-byte element size so the number of elements simply becomes the size of the free space expressed in bytes. Additionally, instead of regular object header (which is unnecessary for "free object"), there is an element called "undo." It temporarily keeps an address of other free list items during list processing as we will see.

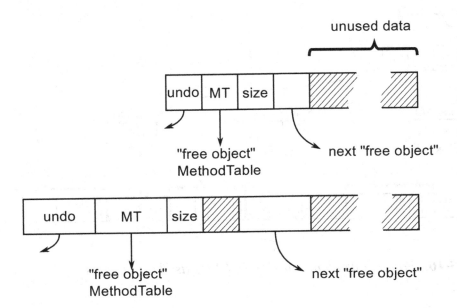

Figure 6-9. *"Free object" structure representing free space on GC Heap*

Note   If you are interested in CoreCLR code related to "free object," start from gc_heap::make_unused_array method, which prepares it. As you will see it uses static global pointer to g_pFreeObjectMethodTable as a new MT. Then it adds such gap to the free list by calling generation_ allocator(gen)->thread_item (gap_start, size). However, threading is done only for gaps larger than the double size of the minimum object size. This helps to ignore the list management overhead for such small items.

An allocator for each generation maintains a list of buckets (see Figure 6-10). The first bucket represents a free list of items with sizes lower than first_bucket_size. Each next bucket doubles this size and the last bucket is for largest sizes with no limit. Each bucket maintains a description of the corresponding free-item list, especially its head. However, as we see in Figure 6-10, the list itself is implemented as single-linked list between "free objects" on the GC Heap. This allows for fast traversal during list manipulation as at least some part of the heap is in cache already. Maintaining a separate list would be unnecessary here.

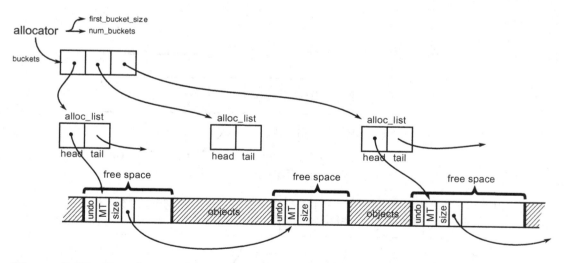

Figure 6-10. *Free-list implementation in CLR based on buckets*

You may be surprised by the fact that each generation has its own allocator because it was clearly stated that allocation of objects takes place either in SOH's generation 0 or in LOH. It is true, user allocations only happen in gen0 and LOH. But when GC promotes the survivors from one generation to the next one, it's also allocating into the next generation.

Each generation has its own configuration of the number and size of buckets. It has been summarized in Table 6-1. As we can see, both ephemeral generations are maintaining only a single bucket for all sizes. Generation 2 configuration varies between 32- and 64-bit runtimes. For example, in 64-bit runtime GC will maintain buckets for sizes smaller than 256 B, 512 B, 1 kB, 2 kB, 4 kB, 8 kB, and last one for bigger than 8 kB.

Table 6-1. *Free-List Buckets Configuration per Generation*

Region	First bucket size	Number of buckets
Generation 0	Int.Max	1
Generation 1	Int.Max	1
Generation 2	256 B (64-bit)	12
	128 B (32-bit)	12
LOH	64 kB	7

Allocation based on bucketed free lists is quite simple (see Listing 6-4). We have to start from the first appropriate bucket and try to find first the matching free item in the corresponding free-list. After allocating the needed amount of memory from the free item, a certain amount of free memory may still remain. If it is larger than the two minimum object sizes (that is, 48 bytes for the 64-bit platform), a new free item will be created from them and included in the list. If not, this small free memory region will be counted as unusable fragmentation.

Listing 6-4. Implementation of free-list allocation in pseudo-code

```
Allocator.Allocate(amount)
{
    foreach (bucket in buckets)
    {
```

```
    if (amount < bucket.BucketSize) // this will skip buckets with too
                                         small items
    {
        foreach (freeItem in bucket.FreeItemList)
        {
            if (size < freeItem.Size)
            {
                UnlinkItem(freeItem);
                ZeroMemory(freeItem.Start, amount);
                if (RemainingFreeSpaceBigEnough())
                    ThreadRemainingFreeSpace(freeItem, amount);
                return freeItem.Start;
            }
        }
    }
}
```

Please note that memory zeroing used in Listing 6-4 is needed only in case of user-allocated items (as they have to be created in a fresh, new state) but may be omitted in case of allocating in older generations during promotion (as it will be overwritten by the promoted object content). This is exactly how .NET implements it. Additionally, in case of generation 0 and 1, a free item is being discarded (becomes unusable fragmentation) if it fails to fit the required size. This means that in those two generations each free item will be checked only once. This is yet another compromise between the cost of maintaining a free list and the cost of allowing fragmentation. Two youngest generations are compacted often so the free list is built up often.

Undo element of "free object" mentioned earlier is used by Garbage Collector during the Plan phase when it decides to use one of the free items for allocation. To be precise, it is allocation in an older generation, used to find a place for a promoted object in an older generation if the GC wants to use a free item for this. In such case the GC "unlinks" the used free item from the free list by typical pointers manipulation as in single-linked lists (see Figure 6-11):

- The removed item address is stored in the previous item's "undo" (if there is previous item).

- The previous item "next" pointer is changed to the next available free item (the one that removed item pointed at).

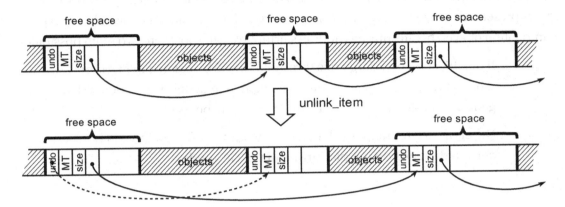

Figure 6-11. *Free-list item unlinking*

However, as it was said, this is done during the planning phase and later the GC may decide to do sweeping. Used free-list items have to be undone (because in case of sweeping older generation is left untouched so previously mentioned planned allocations need to be reversed). By using a free item's address stored in "undo," the original list can be restored. But we will learn about the planning, compacting, and sweeping stages relationship in much more detail in Chapter 7.

Creating New Object

Knowing two basic techniques of allocating memory for objects, we can now move on to the description how they are used together in case of .NET allocation. There are important differences between Small and Large Object Heap allocation so the description is divided into both areas.

When we create a new reference-type object (for example, by using new operator in C# - see Listing 6-5) it will be translated into CIL instruction newobj (see Listing 6-6).

Listing 6-5. Object creation example in C#

```
var obj = new SomeClass();
```

Listing 6-6. Object creation example in Common Intermediate Language

```
newobj instance void SomeClass::.ctor()
```

JIT compiler will emit the proper function call for newobj instruction depending on various conditions. The most typical case is to use one of the *allocation helpers*. The decision tree is presented in Figure 6-12. All decisions are based on conditions known during JIT compilation or even before, during runtime startup. We can spot there two main possibilities:

- If an object exceeds large size threshold (it will be created in LOH) or it has a finalizer (a special method explained in details in Chapter 12) - generic and slightly slower JIT_New helper will be used.

- Otherwise faster helper will be used - what specific version will be chosen depends on the platform and the GC mode.

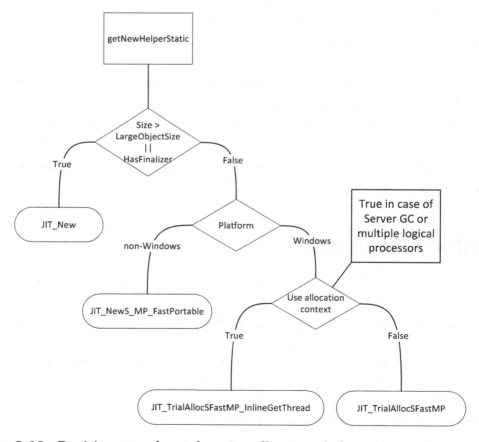

Figure 6-12. *Decision tree about choosing allocation helper during JIT compilation (function names comes from CoreCLR code)*

428

It is important to remember that this decision tree is being used during JIT compilation and the proper allocation helper will be emitted as a result. Thus, no overhead comes from it during normal program execution. One of the listed helpers will be just called later on.

Note   In case of creating arrays `newarr` CIL instruction will be emitted, which has its own various versions: for example, optimized for creating one-dimensional object arrays or one-dimensional value type arrays. However, as the allocation implementation underneath them is essentially the same, it was omitted here for brevity.

If you would like to dig more into the details of allocation in CoreCLR code, start from JIT compiler reaction on `CEE_NEWOBJ` opcode implemented in JIT importer (`importer.cpp:Compiler::impImportBlockCode`). It decides what to do - whether it is about creating an array, a string, a value type, or a reference type. For reference types other than strings and arrays, it calls `CEEInfo::getNewHelper`, which runs part of the decision tree from Figure 6-12. Slower and more generic helper is represented by `CORINFO_HELP_NEWFAST` constant and faster by `CORINFO_HELP_NEWSFAST`. What functions implement those helpers are decided during runtime startup in `InitJITHelpers1` method. It realizes the other part of the decision tree from Figure 6-12.

Small Object Heap Allocation

Allocation of small objects that land in a Small Object Heap is based mainly on bump pointer allocation. The goal is to allocate most of the objects with a bump pointer technique inside the allocation context as described earlier in this chapter. Only if it fails, would a slower path of allocation be executed (described later).

The fastest allocation helper in case of SOH realizes an allocation helper from Listing 6-3 in just a few lines of assembly code (see Listing 6-7). It will be used to allocate all objects in SOH that do not have a finalizer (based on the decision tree from Figure 6-12) in case of Server GC mode or in general, on a machine with multiple logical processors.

> A version for running on a single-processor machine is named JIT_
> TrialAllocSFastSP and contains a locking mechanism to allow safe access to
> a global, single synchronization context.

This is indeed very efficient code consisting of only a few assembly instructions doing comparison and addition. This is the reason why it is common to say that "allocations are cheap in .NET". As we see (with the help of comments), in a fast-path optimistic scenario it is indeed really fast to "allocate" a memory for an object - we are just increasing a value of an allocation pointer inside the already zeroed memory inside allocation context (of already Committed memory).

Listing 6-7. The fastest allocation helper

```
; As input, rcx contains MethodTable pointer
; As result, rax contains new object address
LEAF_ENTRY JIT_TrialAllocSFastMP_InlineGetThread, _TEXT
    ; Read object size into edx
    mov     edx, [rcx + OFFSET__MethodTable__m_BaseSize]
    ; m_BaseSize is guaranteed to be a multiple of 8.
    ; Read Thread Local Storage address into r11
    INLINE_GETTHREAD r11
    ; Read alloc_limit into r10
    mov     r10, [r11 + OFFSET__Thread__m_alloc_context__alloc_limit]
    ; Read alloct_ptr into rax
    mov     rax, [r11 + OFFSET__Thread__m_alloc_context__alloc_ptr]
    add     rdx, rax           ; rdx = alloc_ptr + size
    cmp     rdx, r10           ; is rdx smaller than alloc_limit
    ja      AllocFailed
    ; Update alloc_ptr in TLS
    mov     [r11 + OFFSET__Thread__m_alloc_context__alloc_ptr], rdx
    ; Store MT under alloc_ptr address (constituting new object)
    mov     [rax], rcx
    ret
```

```
AllocFailed:
    jmp     JIT_NEW             ; fast-path failed, jump to slow-path
LEAF_END JIT_TrialAllocSFastMP_InlineGetThread, _TEXT
```

If the current allocation context does not fit the required size, the fastest assembly-based allocator falls back to calling a more generic JIT_NEW helper (the same as used for objects with finalizer or in LOH). This more generic helper contains inside the slow-path allocation. It is the necessity of abandoning this fast path that makes the "allocation is cheap" phrase not always true. Slow path is realized as a quite complex state machine that tries to find a place with the required size.

How complex is the slow path? Figure 6-13 illustrates a state machine realizing it. It starts with a_state_start state when the fast allocation described above fails. This state unconditionally changes into a_state_try_fit, which calls gc_heap::soh_try_fit() method (see Figure 6-14). And so the whole story begins. There are many possible decisions, to name a few here are the most important:

- Slow-path starts from trying to use existing, unused space in ephemeral segment (see Figure 6-14 describing soh_try_fit method). It will:

    - Try to use free list to find a suitable free gap for a new allocation context (recall Figure 6-4).

    - Try to adjust allocation limit inside already Commited memory.

    - Try to Commit more memory from Reserved memory and adjust allocation limit inside.

- If all above fails, garbage collection will be triggered. Depending on conditions it may be called multiple times.

- If all above fails, allocator is not able to allocate requested memory, which is a critical situation so handling of OutOfMemoryException starts.

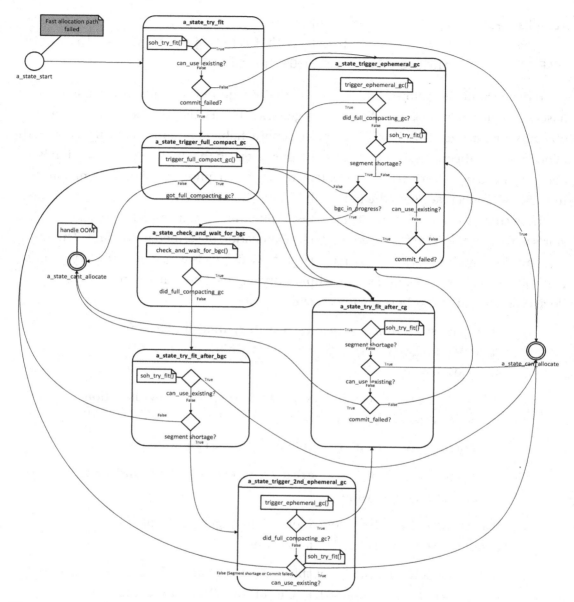

Figure 6-13. *Complex state machine of Small Object Heap slow-path allocation*

In case of Small Object Heap allocation, we may find slow-path code in CoreCLR's `gc_heap::allocate_small` method, with logic illustrated in Figure 6-13.

Triggering GC because of SOH allocation (thus, the most common one) is often referred to as AllocSmall reason in ETW data.

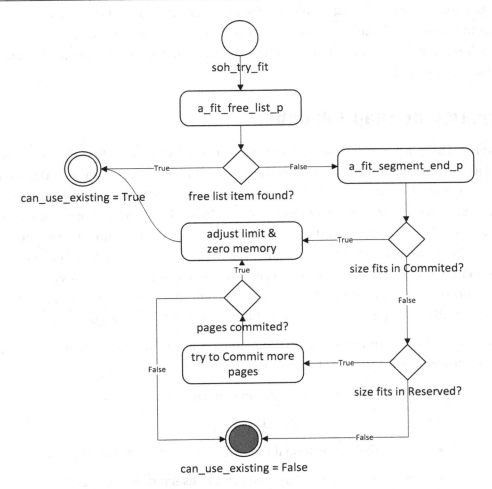

Figure 6-14. *Decision tree for* `soh_try_fit` *method*

Describing the whole state machine from Figure 6-13 is not particularly useful. Those are quite deep implementation details and may change until this book's publication (but I still encourage you to take a moment to analyze it on your own). However, it is good to note how complex a slow path may become comparing it to the fast-path allocation (like trying to fit in a free list item, triggering one or even multiple GCs). We should keep in mind though that the "allocation is cheap" sentence is true only to some extent. We should understand what allocations involve and use it carefully so we don't go and allocate objects unnecessarily or blindly use a heavy-allocating library without understanding what it does. As we see, even without triggering GC, slow path may be expensive. In absolutely performance-critical code the best rule about allocations is just to avoid them at all (which leads us to performance-related Rule 14 - Avoid Allocations).

Please also bear in mind that objects with finalizers are using more generic allocation helpers by default. And there is an additional overhead related to the finalization mechanism described in Chapter 12. This makes Rule 25- Avoid Finalizers - described there valid.

Large Object Heap Allocation

Allocation of large objects that land in Large Object Heap is based on free-list allocation, as well as a simplified bump pointer technique at the end of segment space (without using allocation context). Allocation context and related optimizations are not so important because the cost of clearing a large object is so dominant. Thus, it does not make sense to invest a lot of effort in optimizing things that are not going to make a noticeable difference. Instead, it better take care of possible fragmentation resulting from the fact that in LOH only Sweeping Garbage Collector is used (until we ask to compact it explicitly).

Therefore, there is no differentiation into a fast and slow path in the LOH allocator. It always takes the same path very similar to the SOH slow path (see Figure 6-15):

- It starts from trying to use existing, unused space (see Figure 6-16 describing `loh_try_fit` method). It will:
  - try to use free list to find a suitable free gap for an object

    In each segment containing LOH:
    - try to adjust allocation limit inside already Committed memory,
    - try to Commit more memory from Reserved memory and adjust allocation limit inside.
- If all above fails, garbage collection will be triggered. Depending on conditions it may be called multiple times.
- If all above fails, allocator is not able to allocate requested memory, which is a critical situation so handling of `OutOfMemoryException` starts.

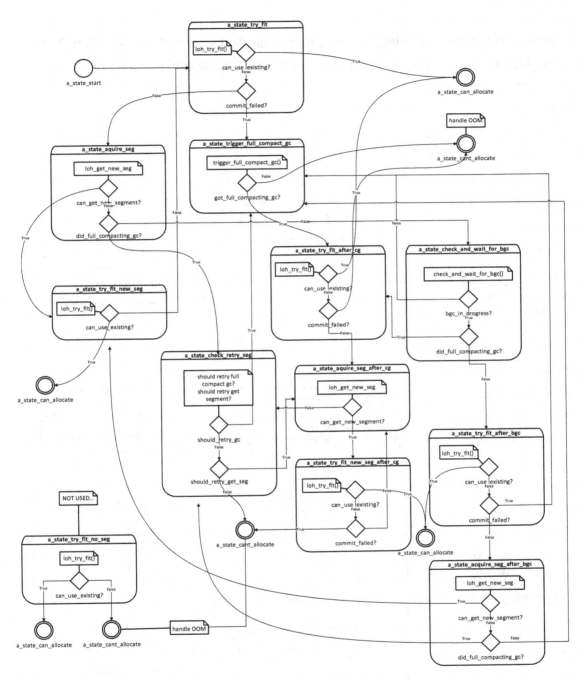

Figure 6-15. *Complex state machine of Large Object Heap allocation*

In case of Large Object Heap allocation, we may find slow-path code in CoreCLR's `gc_heap::allocate_large` method, with logic illustrated in Figure 6-16.

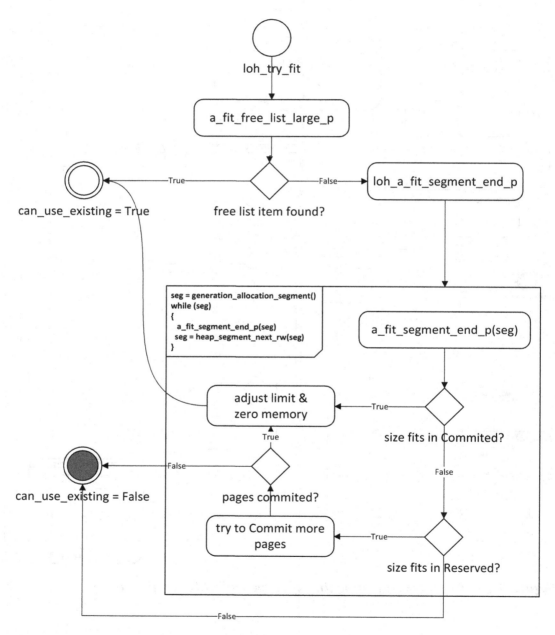

Figure 6-16. *Decision tree for* `loh_try_fit` *method*

As you can see, the state machine for LOH is even more complicated here than the one shown in Figure 6-13. As in that case, it is not particularly useful to describe exactly all possible transitions and behaviors here. Please note, however, that in LOH there is no allocation context used. However, Allocator still has to guarantee a clear object state after its creation so a memory for it must be zeroed. The cost of zeroing memory of large objects may be quite significant. Taking into account the latencies of memory access presented in Chapter 4 (Table 4-2), zeroing an object with a size of several megabytes can take tens of milliseconds. This can be a very long time for our application.

It is then important to remember that allocating objects in LOH is even more expensive than in SOH. And that even more we should avoid it, which leads us to Rule 15 - Avoid Excessive LOH Allocations. Creating a pool of reusable objects is the simplest solution to this problem.

Note   .NET GC is being constantly improved and often a new version of runtime introduces important improvements. For example, since .NET 4.5 (and hence since .NET Core 1.0), LOH allocator has been significantly improved to better utilize a free list with the help of described bucketed approach.

An interesting question may arise. What largest object can we create in .NET? What is the maximum object's size? From the very beginning of .NET it was 2 GB. Although we are rather not used to creating such big single objects, there may be scenarios where a bigger array is needed. Until .NET 4.5 there were no way to omit this limitation. Since version 4.5 a new gcAllowVeryLargeObjects setting was added (see Listing 6-8), which allows us to create objects with size fitting 64-bit signed long value (reduced by small yet not important value). While it enables arrays that are larger than 2 GB in size, it does not change other limits on object size or array size:

- The maximum number of elements in an array is UInt32.MaxValue (which is 2,147,483,591).

- The maximum index in any single dimension is 2,147,483,591 (0x7FFFFFC7) for byte arrays and arrays of single-byte structures, and 2,146,435,071 (0X7FEFFFFF) for other types.

- The maximum size for strings and other non-array objects is unchanged.

Listing 6-8. Configuration to enable gcAllowVeryLargeObjects settings (disabled by default)

```
<configuration>
  <runtime>
    <gcAllowVeryLargeObjects enabled="true" />
  </runtime>
</configuration>
```

Where will such a huge object be created? Certainly it will be allocated in one of the LOH segments as it is bigger than a large object size threshold. Most probably a whole new segment will be created for this purpose because it is unlikely there is one big enough already to fit our unimaginable big object. And remember - allocation of such a big object may take a few seconds due to memory access latency!

Heap Balancing

As mentioned a few times already, GC in Server Mode manages multiple heaps - one per each logical processor available to the runtime. As there are multiple managed heaps, it means that there are multiple ephemeral segments and multiple Large Object Heap segments. On the other hand, there are multiple managed threads running in our application. How do those two relate to each other? How is a heap assigned to the thread?

This requires an earlier answer to yet another question - how are heaps assigned to logical processors? In the discussion of this subject, we will need the knowledge from Chapter 4 on CPU cooperation with memory. Obviously, CLR wants to keep the managed heap as "close" to specific logical CPU (core) as possible (in terms of possible access times). And it obviously would like to avoid any synchronization overhead between them. As a consequence, the following design decisions were made:

- In case of OS supporting information about on which core current thread is being executed (which is true for Windows and probably most Linux and macOS versions) - each logical CPU is assigned to a subsequent managed heap and this assignment is never changed. This allows us to populate CPU caches accordingly during program execution and do not destroy it too often. On the other hand, managed heap is never shared between multiple cores to avoid cache coherency protocols overhead.[1]

- In case of OS not supporting such information - micro-benchmark is executed to empirically examine which heap has the best access times for a particular core.

- If machine uses NUMA groups (mentioned in Chapter 2), heaps assignment will stay inside single group.

If you are interested in how such a micro-benchmark is being executed, start from `heap_select::access_time` method.

When a managed thread starts to allocate, a heap is assigned to it - this one, which is assigned to the processor on which such thread is being executed. A typical situation between GC Managed Heaps, threads, and logical cores has been illustrated in Figure 6-17. Two logical processors are consuming managed memory built with an all-at-once strategy described in the previous chapter. First CPU has SOH_1 and LOH_1 segments assigned. Second CPU has SOH_2 and LOH_2 segments assigned (so no segments are shared between them). Note that processors simply use certain memory regions (isolated thanks to segment concept), but there is no magical mechanism in memory separating each of them by any kind of OS or hardware support. However, such isolation allows good cache utilization as each CPU operates on those segments often and exclusively.

Threads running on CPU #1 (marked as T_1 and T_2) have their allocation context inside SOH_1. Threads on second CPU (here single one, marked as T_3) utilize second heap and so on, so forth. In LOH allocation context does not exists so it was not illustrated.

---

[1]Sharing heaps between cores may happen, however, if for some reason we configured GC to have less managed heaps than logical processors.

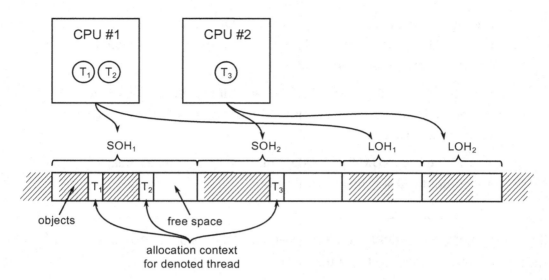

Figure 6-17. *Illustration of assigment between logical processors, threads, and GC Managed Heaps*

When a thread is created, the operating system decides on which logical processor will be executed. This is okay until all managed threads in our application allocate more or less the same amount of memory. However, there may be situations in which one or several threads start to allocate much more than others. This can lead to a state of *unbalanced heaps* illustrated in Figure 6-18. Thread 3 or 4 allocates much more memory than threads 1 and 2 (so there is much less space in SOH₂). This is an unwanted situation for two main reasons:

- There will be soon memory shortage in second SOH probably. It will trigger GC and eventually maybe new SOH segment will have to be created.

- CPU cache utilization is unbalanced.

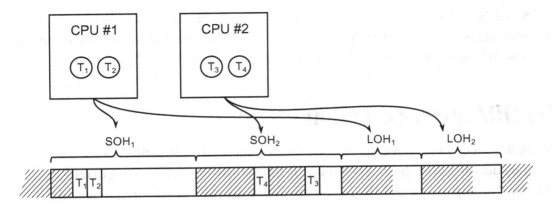

Figure 6-18. *Unbalanced heaps when several threads allocate much more than others*

GC periodically (when allocating) performs a heap balance check. If it will notice a heap unbalance, it will reassign a heap for most allocating thread. It means that its allocation context will be moved to the other heap. This obviously would violate the above-mentioned design patterns as thread executing on one logical core would use a heap assigned to another logical core. That's why GC will immediately ask operating system to move execution of such thread to the corresponding logical CPU. Currently, such behavior is supported only on Windows via `SetThreadIdealProcessor` function call (as other operating systems sometimes simply don't provide equivalent API). Thanks to that situation from Figure 6-18, it may be balanced into the situation shown in Figure 6-19.

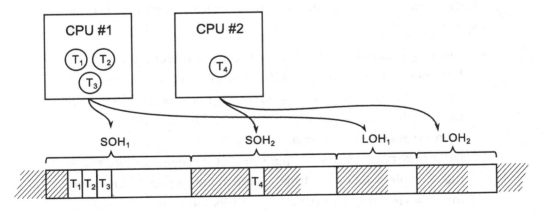

Figure 6-19. *Heap balancing situation from Figure 6-17*

Since .NET 4.5 LOH heaps are balanced, which introduced substantial improvements of allocation performance. The LOH heaps balance technique is the same as for SOH so it has been omitted here for brevity.

OutOfMemoryException

As we have seen in the allocator decision trees, sometimes a situation occurs when the final decision is the lack of possibility to allocate the desired amount of memory. It is good to stop at this topic for a moment to discuss the related, often repeated misunderstandings.

First of all, when can `OutOfMemoryException` happen? As it happens as a very last decision on the allocation paths described in Figures from 6-12 to 6-15, it means:

- The Garbage Collector has been already triggered. Maybe even more than once, including full compacting GC, so SOH fragmentation should not be a problem. There is a very little chance that your problem is so intermittent and volatile that triggering GC once more (adding to the GCs induced by allocator) could really help. For sure `OutOfMemoryException` does not happen because .NET runtime has forgotten to call GC to reclaim memory. On the other hand, if `OutOfMemoryException` happened during LOH allocation, you may consider explicitly triggering LOH compaction (as described in Chapter 7) and trigger GC once more time.

- Allocator failed to prepare memory region with a given size. This may happen because of two reasons:

  - Virtual memory is exhausted so allocator can't reserve large enough memory region (for example, to create a new segment). This may happen mainly because of virtual memory fragmentation, especially on 32-bit runtimes. Memory fragmentation confuses real memory usage so if `OutOfMemoryException` happens in such a scenario, there still may be quite a lot of free RAM visible in the system. Remember the tight virtual address space size limits shown in Table 2-5. A 32-bit runtime has only 2 or 3 GB virtual address space on its own disposal even on 64-bit systems with plenty of RAM installed!

- Physical backing store (meaning both RAM and page/swap file) is exhausted so allocator can't commit enough memory (for example, to grow already existing segment). Please note that operating system manages memory taking into consideration all processes in the system, not only your application. It may be a perfectly valid situation when there is still some free RAM visible, but your application's total memory consumption (both in RAM and on disk) is pushing the system to its limits so it declines the runtime to commit more memory.

I would like to highlight two important conclusions arising from the above facts:

- Triggering GC manually unlikely helps if you hit OutOfMemoryException (unless it happens while allocating a large object, when you may consider explicitly trigger LOH compaction).

- It is normal that you will notice some free RAM while OutOfMemoryException happens.

How will your application may be improved if you experience OutOfMemoryException? Consider taking one or more of the following steps:

- Allocate less objects - investigate your memory usage to cut off unnecessary allocations. As we will see later in this chapter, there are many sources of allocations and you may be even not aware of some of them.

- Use objects pooling - one of the solutions to allocate less objects is to reuse some pool of them. As we will see, there are ready-to-use pools you can utilize (and you can always write your own).

- Use VM Hoarding - as described in Chapter 5 (especially in case of 32-bit runtimes).

- Recompile to 64-bit - it may be as simple as that because most probably it will provide big enough virtual address space.

Scenario 6-1. Out of Memory

Description: One of the .NET Core processes intermittently crashes on the production environment with OutOfMemoryException exception. We are not able to reproduce this problem on other environments. It also happens so rarely that it is impossible to attach a more sophisticated monitoring tool. We would like to capture a full memory dump to analyze memory consumption, but it is impossible to predict when the OutOfMemoryException exception will come.

Analysis: The good news it is possible to automatically take a full memory dump when OutOfMemoryException occurs! This method works both on Windows in case of .NET Framework and .NET Core. The following steps must be taken:

- By using regedit tool - inside HKEY_LOCAL_MACHINE\SOFTWARE\ Microsoft\.NETFramework key, add (or set if exist already) a value with name GCBreakOnOOM, type REG_DWORD and value 0x2. This setting configures emitting Breakpoint Exception when OutOfMemoryException occurs. Such exception may be then consumed by DebugDiag.

- Configure DebugDiag rule accordingly:

  - add a new rule, select a Crash type rule.

  - select "A specific process" and select process of your interest.

  - under Advanced Settings, click on Exceptions, then select Add Exception.

  - from the list of exceptions select: 80000003 Breakpoint Exception.

  - from the Action Type list select: Full userdump and Action limit to 1.

  - click Save & Close button.

  - provide a name for the rule and location where the dump files will be saved.

  - choose Activate the rule now and click Finish.

- From now on your process is monitored and a full dump will be taken when OutOfMemoryException occurs.

- If this eventually happens, you have a set of possibilities how to analyze such a dump. You can start by opening it from within WinDbg. Start from loading the proper SOS extension. Then you may use analyzeoom command, which will print detailed information about OutOfMemoryException (see Listing 6-9).

Listing 6-9. Analyzing full memory dump with WinDbg - OutOfMemoryException information

```
> .loadby sos coreclr
> !analyzeoom
Managed OOM occurred after GC #4 (Requested to allocate 0 bytes)
Reason: Didn't have enough memory to allocate an LOH segment
Detail: LOH: Failed to reserve memory (50331648 bytes)
```

You may additionally investigate threads at the time of the dump to find one which triggered OOM - by using threads command followed by clrstack command (see Listing 6-10). This will point you directly to the problematic place in your code.

Listing 6-10. Analyzing full memory dump with WinDbg - threads

```
> !threads
ThreadCount:      3
UnstartedThread:  0
BackgroundThread: 2
PendingThread:    0
DeadThread:       0
Hosted Runtime:   no
```

								Lock
ID	OSID	ThreadOBJ	State	GC Mode	GC Alloc Context	Domain	
		Count	Apt	Exception				
0	1	3a5c	00a09c60	20020	Preemptive	0715D9C8:00000000	00a0c2e0
		0		Ukn	System.OutOfMemoryException 0715d954		
2	2	512c	00a9ba78	21220	Preemptive	00000000:00000000	00a0c2e0
		0		Ukn	(Finalizer)			
4	3	5660	00aa7758	21220	Preemptive	00000000:00000000	00a0c2e0
		0		Ukn				

```
> ~0s
> !clrstack
OS Thread Id: 0x3a5c (0)
Child SP       IP Call Site
0097ead8 73e008b2 [HelperMethodFrame: 0097ead8]
0097eb5c 06b404bf CoreCLR.LOHWaste.Program.Main(System.String[])
0097ecf0 0f8b926f [GCFrame: 0097ecf0]
0097f004 0f8b926f [GCFrame: 0097f004]
```

We can proceed with any other memory dump-based analysis mentioned in this book, including investigating segments and heaps. Bear in mind that code triggering OutOfMemoryException may not be a direct cause of the problem. It might just be only one of the threads that could unfortunately hit the moment when the allocator could not find a good place for a new object. However, the source of the memory congestion may be somewhere else. Therefore, it is worth taking a close look at the recorded memory dump for the most numerous objects, the largest objects, their distribution in generations, and so on and so forth.

Stack Allocation

So far, we have only touched on allocation of objects on the GC Managed Heap. This is obviously by far the most popular and commonly used approach. We have seen here how big an effort was put to make allocation on the heap as fast as possible. However, the allocation and deallocation on the stack is much faster by default as we remember from previous chapters. It is just only moving around stack pointer and it does not cause any overhead on the GC.

As said, value types may be allocated on the stack in certain circumstances. It is good news though that we may explicitly ask to allocate on the stack. Considering Rule 14 - Avoid Allocations on the Heap, it can be a very useful option.

To allocate on the stack explicitly in C# one should use stackalloc operator (see Listing 6-11). It returns a pointer to a requested memory region that will be located on the stack. Because a pointer type is used, such code must be used in unsafe code context (unless we use Span<T> type as showed later). The content of the newly allocated memory is undefined so we should not assume anything about it (like, for example, being zeroed).

Listing 6-11. Using `stackalloc` to allocate on the stack explicitly

```
static unsafe void Test(int t)
{
    SomeStruct* array = stackalloc SomeStruct[20];
}
```

`stackalloc` is a very rare creature in the C# code. This is mainly due to the unconsciousness and misunderstanding of programmers. We can use it, for example, if we want very high data processing efficiency and we do not want to allocate large tables on the heap. Profit of such a solution is twofold:

- As previously said, the deallocation of object thus created is as fast as the deallocation of any other object on the stack - there is no heap allocation helper, no slow-path possibility, no GC involved at all.

- Address of such object is implicitly pinned (will not move) because stack frames are never moved - we can safely pass the pointer to such data to the unmanaged code without introducing pinning overhead.

`stackalloc` operator is being translated into `localloc` CIL instruction (see Listing 6-12). Its description in ECMA standard says (with some parts stripped) that it "allocates size bytes from the local dynamic memory pool. When the current method returns, the local memory pool is available for reuse." Please note it does not say anything about the stack explicitly but more general "local memory pool" concept is used (mentioned already in Chapter 4). And as we have already seen in the Chapter 4, the ECMA standard tries to be technology agnostic and nowhere directly uses concepts of the stack or the heap.

Listing 6-12. Part of CIL code generated from Listing 6-11 shows how `stackalloc` operator has been translated into `localloc` instruction call

```
IL_0000: ldc.i4.s 10
IL_0002: conv.u
IL_0003: sizeof SomeStruct
IL_0009: mul.ovf.un
IL_000a: localloc
```

But what can be allocated on the stack that way? ECMA standard does not say anything about it regarding `localloc` instruction and promises only allocation of a specified number of bytes. As only what CIL guaranties is a block of memory, CLR is currently not able to use it in other way than just a container for simple data types. `stackalloc` operator definition from C# Language Specification describes those constraints in more details. It says that only an array of "unmanaged_type" may be used. An *unmanaged_type* is one of the following:

- primitive types - `sbyte`, `byte`, `short`, `ushort`, `int`, `uint`, `long`, `ulong`, `char`, `float`, `double`, `decimal`, or `bool`;

- any enum type;

- any pointer type;

- any user-defined struct that is not a constructed type [2] and contains fields of *unmanaged_types* only.

We should remember that there is no way to explicitly free memory allocated using `stackalloc`. It will be implicitly released when the method ends. We should remember about that when intensely using the stack because a large set of long-running methods may end with `StackOverflowException`.

`localloc` instruction is translated by JIT into a series of assembly `push` and `sub rsp, [size]` instructions to grow the stack frame accordingly. This growth is rounded to 8 and 16 bytes in case of 32 and 64-bit frameworks respectively. Thus, even if you `stackalloc` array of two integers, which normally may take 8 bytes, the stack frame will be expanded by 16 bytes (for 64-bit framework). This is because on x64 architecture stack need to be aligned on 16 bytes. If you are interested in more details, refer for example to documentation at `https://docs.microsoft.com/en-us/cpp/build/stack-allocation`

As mentioned before, we are not pushed to use unsafe code when working with `stackalloc`. Since C# 7.2 and .NET Core 2.1 there is a `Span<T>` type (very solicitously explained in Chapter 15) with support added to it so we can safely write code as from Listing 6-11.

---

[2]A generic type that includes type arguments.

Listing 6-13. Using `stackalloc` to allocate on the stack explicitly within safe code thanks to Span<T> support.

```
static void Test(int t)
{
        Span<SomeStruct> array = stackalloc SomeStruct[20];
}
```

Avoiding Allocations

Quite a lot has been said so far about allocations and their underlying mechanism. We are now fully aware that "allocations are cheap" in .NET is sometimes true, thanks to a bump pointer technique inside allocation contexts. But, there are a few remarks to this simple rule:

- Allocations are cheap as far as fast path is used. In some cases, in indeterministic points from the code perspective, allocation context has to be changed, which will trigger more complex (and thus, slower) allocation paths.

- Those more complex allocation paths from time to time will trigger Garbage Collection.

- Allocations of big objects in LOH is slower because it may be mainly dominated by zeroing memory costs.

- Allocating a lot of objects makes more work for Garbage Collection - this may be obvious but of great importance. If we allocate a lot of temporary objects, they will have to be cleaned. The more objects we create, there is also more chance we break a generational hypothesis about an object's lifetime.

Due to the above, one of the most effective methods of memory optimization in .NET is to avoid allocations or at least be aware of them. Little allocations mean little memory pressure put on GC, less costly memory accesses, less communication with the operating system. Thus, one of the main pieces of knowledge that a performance-aware .NET developer should gain is to know what are the sources of allocations and how they can be removed or minimized.

This section lists the most common sources of allocations and ways to overcome them. Please bear in mind, however, a very important remark - we should treat with full responsibility and awareness the topic of minimizing the allocations. There is such a popular and sometimes even overused sentence that "premature optimization is the root of all evil." Certainly, analyzing every line of the code in terms of the amount of allocations in each and every place of our program is unnecessary. It can paralyze our work without giving much in return. Does it matter that a line of code executed once per minute will allocate 200 bytes instead of 800 bytes? Probably not. It all depends on requirements put on your code. Thus, analyzing the allocations you do in the most performance-critical code paths is always a good place to start because reducing those will cause the most effect.

First of all, you should learn the most common sources of allocation to avoid obvious mistakes. Or at least be aware of how "heavy" for the memory is the code we are just writing. Knowing the context of the entire application and the requirements for this particular part, we will know if it is okay or not. Secondly, knowledge of the sources of the allocation will be useful when we implement (and we should!) Rule 2 - Measure GC Early. Only by the measurements we can avoid premature optimization of the wrong places of our code. Only by the measurements we will find out if there is a need to minimize the allocations at all. And we will be able to find out where in our code to concentrate our forces for this purpose.

Please find below a list of the most common sources of allocations. Some of them are obvious, some not so much. Along with information about their occurrence, information on whether and how to avoid them is given.

When showing certain mechanisms used by the C# compiler later in this chapter, it is good to see how it has transformed our original code. This allows us to better understand what is going underneath and to check if we are unsure. For this purpose, an excellent dnSpy tool was used again. I encourage you to experiment with it to better understand the topics described below. Play with the code, change it, decompile - see how it influences code that will be eventually executed by the runtime.

Explicit Allocations of Reference Types

Most cases of allocations are obvious - we are creating objects explicitly. This does not mean, however, that we should trivialize this source. We can consider whether in a given case we really need a reference type object that will be created on the heap. You can find below a set of different scenarios and solutions to them.

General Case - Consider Using Struct

We may tend to use classes just because we do not even think about alternatives. Most typical scenarios when instead we may use structs passing around small amounts of data via methods arguments and returns. Listing 4-7 from Chapter 4 illustrated such case and clearly showed how optimal code could be generated (see Listings 4-8 and 4-9) instead of just creating a small object on the heap. A benchmark from Table 4-1 presented big performance difference between those two approaches.

Thus, you may strongly consider using structs when passing around small data from and to methods if this data is local to those methods (is not stored inside any heap-based data). In fact, quite a lot of business logic meets these requirements - we get some data, process it locally, and return some result. Imagine example from Listing 6-14, which should return full names of all people employed with a given distance from a specified location. It shows typical usage of collection returned by external service (or repository). However, quite a lot of objects are created explicitly in this way:

- a list of `PersonDataClass` objects and `PersonDataClass` objects themselves

- employee object returned from external service

Listing 6-14. Example of simple business logic based solely on classes

```
[Benchmark]
public List<string> PeopleEmployeedWithinLocation_Classes(int amount,
LocationClass location)
{
    List<string> result = new List<string>();
    List<PersonDataClass> input = service.GetPersonsInBatchClasses(amount);
    DateTime now = DateTime.Now;
    for (int i = 0; i < input.Count; ++i)
```

```
    {
        PersonDataClass item = input[i];
        if (now.Subtract(item.BirthDate).TotalDays > 18 * 365)
        {
            var employee = service.GetEmployeeClass(item.EmployeeId);
            if (locationService.DistanceWithClass(location, employee.
            Address) < 10.0)
            {
                string name = string.Format("{0} {1}", item.Firstname,
                item.Lastname);
                result.Add(name);
            }
        }
    }
    return result;
}
internal List<PersonDataClass> GetPersonsInBatchClasses(int amount)
{
    List<PersonDataClass> result = new List<PersonDataClass>(amount);
    // Populate list from external source
    return result;
}
```

What if code from Listing 6-14 was rewritten to use structs where possible? In fact, data about persons and employees do not leak the PeopleEmployeedWithinLocation_ Classes method so it is safe to store them on stack using structs (see Listing 6-15). GetPersonsInBatch method may return an array of structs that produces better data locality and smaller overhead (as mentioned in Chapter 4). External services like GetEmployeeStruct method may return small structs instead of objects. They may also take value type arguments by reference(like DistanceWithStruct method) to explicitly avoid copying.

Listing 6-15. Example of simple business logic based on structs where possible

```
[Benchmark]
public List<string> PeopleEmployeedWithinLocation_Structs(int amount,
LocationStruct location)
```

```
{
    List<string> result = new List<string>();
    PersonDataStruct[] input = service.GetPersonsInBatchStructs(amount);
    DateTime now = DateTime.Now;
    for (int i = 0; i < input.Length; ++i)
    {
        ref PersonDataStruct item = ref input[i];
        if (now.Subtract(item.BirthDate).TotalDays > 18 * 365)
        {
            var employee = service.GetEmployeeStruct(item.EmployeeId);
            if (locationService.DistanceWithStruct(ref location, employee.
            Address) < 10.0)
            {
                string name = string.Format("{0} {1}", item.Firstname,
                item.Lastname);
                result.Add(name);
            }
        }
    }
    return result;
}
internal PersonDataStruct[] GetPersonsInBatchStructs(int amount)
{
    PersonDataStruct[] result = new PersonDataStruct[amount];
    // Populate list from external source
    return result;
}
```

Is code from Listing 6-15 a little "uglier" than from Listing 6-14? Probably a little, because of passing by reference (and ref local usage, explained in Chapter 14). However, this may be a matter of personal preference. Code from Listing 6-15 is still readable and self-descriptive. What we gain is a measurable difference in the number of allocated memory and thus, triggered GCs (see Table 6-2). The code based on structures allocates about half of what the code is based on objects. It can be a very significant difference if we call it very often!

Table 6-2. *DotNetBenchmark Results for Code from Listings 6-14 and 6-15 Assuming Amount of Value 1,000 (One Thousand Objects or Structures are Processed)*

Method	Mean	Gen 0	Allocated
PeopleEmployeedWithinLocation_Classes	348.8 us	15.1367	62.60 KB
PeopleEmployeedWithinLocation_Structs	344.7 us	9.2773	39.13 KB

Tuples - Use ValueTuple Instead

Quite often there is a need to return or pass as an argument a very simple data structure with only a few fields. If this type is used only once, we may be tempted to use a tuple or anonymous type instead of defining a class (see Listing 6-16). It is worth it to note however that both Tuple and anonymous types are reference types and thus, always created on the heap.

Listing 6-16. Tuples and anonymous types created for data used only once

```
var tuple1 = new Tuple<int, double>(0, 0.0);
var tuple2 = Tuple.Create(0, 0.0);
var tuple3 = new {A = 1, B = 0.0};
```

According to the previous point, we should consider using user-defined structs in such case. However, since C# 7.0, a new value type, has been introduced called a *value tuple* represented by ValueTuple structure (see Listing 6-17). This can be a great replacement for the previously used classes and in some scenarios, it relieves us of the need to create our own structures.

Listing 6-17. Value tuples introduced in C# 7.0

```
var tuple4 = (0, 0.0);
var tuple5 = (A: 0, B: 0.0);
tuple5.A = 3;
```

Typical use case includes returning multiple values from a method. Commonly we would use a Tuple (or custom class) to contain all results (see ProcessData1 method from Listing 6-18). However, we may use a perfectly valid value tuple struct containing just other structs (see ProcessData2 method from Listing 6-18).

Listing 6-18. Value tuples versus Tuple used to return multiple values from a
method

```
public static Tuple<ResultDesc, ResultData> ProcessData1(IEnumerable<
SomeClass> data)
{
    // Do some processing
    return new Tuple<ResultDesc, ResultData >(new ResultDesc() { ... }, new
    ResultData() { ... });
    // Or use:
    // return Tuple.Create(new ResultDesc() { ... }, new ResultData() {
    Average = 0.0, Sum = 10.0 });
}
public static (ResultDescStruct, ResultDataStruct) ProcessData2(IEnumerable
<SomeClass> data)
{
    // Do some processing
    return (new ResultDescStruct() { ... }, new ResultDataStruct() { ... });
}
public class ResultDesc
{
    public int Count;
}
public class ResultData
{
    public double Sum;
    public double Average;
}
public struct ResultDescStruct
{
    public int Count;
}
```

```
public struct ResultDataStruct
{
    public double Sum;
    public double Average;
}
```

This may significantly reduce overhead of returning multiple values from a method (see Table 6-3). Due to only structs usage, there are no allocations at all in case of ProcessData2! And the whole function becomes twice faster.

Table 6-3. *DotNetBenchmark Results for Code from Listing 6-18*

Method	Mean	Allocated
ProcessData1	11.326 ns	88 B
ProcessData2	5.207 ns	0 B

There is also a nice feature of value tuples called *deconstruction* that allows us to assign tuples returned from methods to tuples in place. It is also possible to use *discarding* of tuples elements to explicitly point out that some elements of the tuple do not interest us (see Figure 6-15). This may be useful in some scenarios as the compiler and JIT may use such information to further optimize underlying structure usage.

Listing 6-19. Deconstructing tuple with discarding

```
(ResultDescStruct desc, _) = ProcessData2(list);
```

There are planned and possible upcoming changes in ORMs to allow materializing database query results into value tuples and structs. This will make using them much more practical. Stay tuned to ORMs you use or vote for such changes on your own!

Small Temporary Local Data - Consider Using stackalloc

It has already been shown that the use of structures instead of objects can bring tangible benefits for local, temporary data. Instead of creating a list of objects, we can use an array of structures. However, remember that the array of structs is still allocated on the heap - the only thing we gain is a denser data packing. But we can go further and get rid of any heap allocations by using stackalloc.

Imagine a simple method that takes a list of objects, transforms it into some temporary list, and processes such list to calculate some statistics. The typical LINQ-based approach is presented in Listing 6-20 but hopefully you can extrapolate it to more complex cases. Such method allocates a lot – a list of many temporary objects.

Listing 6-20. Example of simple list processing based solely on classes

```
public double ProcessEnumerable(List<BigData> list)
{
    double avg = ProcessData1(list.Select(x => new DataClass()
        {
            Age = x.Age,
            Sex = Helper(x.Description) ? Sex.Female : Sex.Male
        }));
    _logger.Debug("Result: {0}", avg / _items);
    return avg;
}
public double ProcessData1(IEnumerable<DataClass> list)
{
    // Do some processing on list items
    return result;
}
public class BigData
{
    public string Description;
    public double Age;
}
```

We could use array of structs here as in the previous examples. Let's however use stackalloc instead together with Span<T> to avoid making code unsafe (see Listing 6-21).

Listing 6-21. Example of simple list processing based solely on structs and stackalloc

```
public double ProcessStackalloc(List<BigData> list)
{
    // Dangerous!
```

457

```
Span<DataStruct> data = stackalloc DataStruct[list.Count];
for (int i = 0; i < list.Count; ++i)
{
    data[i].Age = list[i].Age;
    data[i].Sex = Helper(list[i].Description) ? Sex.Female : Sex.Male;
}
double result = ProcessData2(new ReadOnlySpan<DataStruct>(data));
return result;
}

// Pass Span as read-only to explictly say it should not be modified
public double ProcessData2(ReadOnlySpan<DataStruct> list)
{
    // Do some processing on list[i] items
    return result;
}
```

New code version makes a huge difference (see Table 6-4). In fact, the improved version does not allocate at all and is about four times faster! This is for sure worth considering if such code was on our hot path.

Table 6-4. *DotNetBenchmark Results for Code from Listings 6-20 and 6-21 - Processing 100 Elements*

Method	Mean	Allocated
ProcessEnumerable	2,208.6 ns	3272 B
ProcessStackalloc	542.9 ns	0 B

However, please bear in mind that stackalloc should be rather used for small buffers (like not exceeding 1 kB). The main risk when using stackalloc approach is StackOverflowException, which may happen if there is not enough stack space left. StackOverflowException is one of those uncatchable exceptions that will kill your entire application without the possibility to mitigate it. Thus, it is risky to use too big of buffers. That's why the stack-allocating line in Listing 6-21 is commented as dangerous.

Allocating large data on the stack is even not so good from a performance perspective because populating a big memory region on a thread's stack will bring a lot of its memory pages into working set (incurring page faults). But those pages are not shared between other threads so it may be a wasteful approach.

If you decide to use `stackalloc` and want to be 100% sure that `StackOverflowException` will not happen, you may be tempted to use `RuntimeHelpers.TryEnsureSufficientExecutionStack()` or `RuntimeHelpers.EnsureSufficientExecutionStack()` methods. As documentation says, each of this method: "ensures that the remaining stack space is large enough to execute the average .NET Framework function." The current value is 128 kB and 64 kB for 64- and 32-bit environments respectively. In other words, if `RuntimeHelpers.TryEnsureSufficientExecutionStack()` returns true, it is probably safe to `stackalloc` buffer with size below 128 kB. I mean probably, because those values are implementation details and are not guaranteed - only space for "average .NET Framework function" is ensured, which probably does not include a large `stackalloc`. In other words, it is only safe to `stackalloc` really small buffers (mentioned before 1 kB size seems to be a good value).

Creating Arrays - Use ArrayPool

We have already seen in Table 6-2 is that operating on temporary arrays of structs instead of object's collections may be substantially beneficial. However, allocating array of structs each time as it is needed provides overhead - both in terms of performance and introduced memory traffic. It may be especially noticeable for large buffers. For such scenarios the best solution is to utilize objects pooling - reuse objects from pool of preallocated objects. For exactly that purpose an `ArrayPool` has been introduced (available in `System.Buffers` package) - a pool of reusable managed arrays.

It manages set of various-sized arrays of a given type, grouped into buckets. Those may be both reference and value types. Pooling arrays of a value typed object seems to be more efficient as we are pooling both the array and all their objects.

Each of 17 buckets in the default `ArrayPool` contains arrays twice as large as the previous ones, starting with the first containing 16-element arrays so it contains the following lengths: 16, 32, 64, 128, 256, 512, 1,024, 2,048, 4,096, 8,192, 16,384, 3,2768, 65,536, 131,072, 262,144, 524,288 and 1,04,8576. Please not that all those arrays are created on demand so there is no overzealous and rash allocation of so many arrays.

Such default pool of arrays is accessible as static `ArrayPool<T>.Shared` instance. When we need an array, we call `Rent` on it. And when it is no longer needed, we call `Return` to return it to the pool (see Listing 6-22).

Listing 6-22. Sample ArrayPool usage

```
var pool = ArrayPool<int>.Shared;
int[] buffer = pool.Rent(minLength);
try
{
    Consume(buffer);
}
finally
{
    pool.Return(buffer);
}
```

Please note that Rent method ensures returning an array with at least the specified length. Most probably it will be bigger because it will be rounded up to the nearest bucket size, not smaller than the requested size.

`ArrayPool<T>.Shared` returns an instance of `TlsOverPerCoreLockedStack sArrayPool<T>` class, which uses quite sophisticated caching techniques - there is a small per-thread cache of each array size and shared by all threads cache split into per-core stacks (hence its name). We will return to it for a minute when describing Thread Local Storage (TLS) in Chapter 13.

Let's now use `ArrayPool` by slightly changing `PeopleEmployeedWithinLocation_Structs` example from Listing 6-15. This time, instead of creating plain array each time, we are consuming a pooled array from default `ArrayPool` instance (see Listing 6-23).

Listing 6-23. Example of simple business logic based on structs and ArrayPool.

```
public List<string> PeopleEmployeedWithinLocation_ArrayPoolStructs(int
amount, LocationStruct location)
{
```

```
List<string> result = new List<string>();
PersonDataStruct[] input = service.GetDataArrayPoolStructs(amount);
DateTime now = DateTime.Now;
for (int i = 0; i < amount; ++i)
{
    ref PersonDataStruct item = ref input[i];
    if (now.Subtract(item.BirthDate).TotalDays > Constants.MaturityDays)
    {
        var employee = service.GetEmployeeStruct(item.EmployeeId);
        if (locationService.DistanceWithStruct(ref location, employee.
        Address) < Constants.DistanceOfInterest)
        {
            string name = string.Format("{0} {1}", item.Firstname, item.
            Lastname);
            result.Add(name);
        }
    }
}
    ArrayPool<InputDataStruct>.Shared.Return(input);
    return result;
}
internal PersonDataStruct[] GetDataArrayPoolStructs(int amount)
{
    PersonDataStruct[] result = ArrayPool<PersonDataStruct>.Shared.
    Rent(amount);
    // Populate array from external source
    return result;
}
```

Comparing code from Listing 6-23 to code from Listings 6-14 (using collection of objects) and 6-15 (using allocated array of structs) reveals how much we can gain from using ArrayPool (see Table 6-5). New code allocates only around 3.5% of what the standard code based on arrays (and triggers no GC during benchmark). This may be of great value when memory consumption is subject to strict restrictions. Remember that all those kilobytes that make this difference would need to be reclaimed by Garbage Collector!

Table 6-5. *DotNetBenchmark Results for Code from Listings 6-14 and 6-15 and 6-23 Assuming Amount of Value 1000 (One Thousand Objects or Structures Are Processed)*

Method	Mean	Gen 0	Allocated
PeopleEmployeedWithinLocation_Classes	348.8 us	15.1367	62.66 KB
PeopleEmployeedWithinLocation_Structs	344.7 us	9.2773	39.13 KB
PeopleEmployeedWithinLocation_ ArrayPoolStructs	343.4 us	-	1.35 KB

Such results as presented in Table 6-5 are interesting. But we should be aware that they can also be misleading - such synthetic benchmarks may not reflect well real-world behavior. For example, if you had hundreds of these operations in flight concurrently, only a small portion of them are going to actually succeed in getting an array from the pool; the rest will pay the cost of a pool lookup but end up still having to fall back to allocating the array, anyway. We should assume results from Table 6-5 as the best-case scenario, while not necessarily expecting such great memory usage improvement in a real-world, multithreaded application.

ArrayPool may be a default choice when your code needs to operate on large buffers frequently. Instead of allocating them over and over again, reuse them with the help of this class. More and more libraries are starting to support ArrayPool (and as mentioned already, .NET standard library also uses it extensively). As an example might serve the extremely popular Json.NET library. We can use it in a standard way by utilizing JsonTextReader or JsonTextWriter (see Listing 6-24). But since 8.0 version Json.NET supports using array pools for its internal working (see Listing 6-25), we can specify implementation of its IArrayPool interface, which is based on ArrayPool (see JsonArrayPool in Listing 6-25).

Listing 6-24. Example of standard usage of Json.NET library

```
public IList<int> ReadPlain()
{
    IList<int> value;

    JsonSerializer serializer = new JsonSerializer();
    using (JsonTextReader reader = new JsonTextReader(new
    StringReader(Input)))
    {
        value = serializer.Deserialize<IList<int>>(reader);
        return value;
    }
}
```

Listing 6-25. Example of ArrayPool usage in Json.NET library

```
public int[] ReadWithArrayPool()
{
    JsonSerializer serializer = new JsonSerializer();7
    using (JsonTextReader reader = new JsonTextReader(new
    StringReader(Input)))
    {
        // reader will get buffer from array pool
        reader.ArrayPool = JsonArrayPool.Instance;

        var value = serializer.Deserialize<int[]>(reader);
        return value;
    }
}
public class JsonArrayPool : IArrayPool<char>
{
    public static readonly JsonArrayPool Instance = new JsonArrayPool();

    public char[] Rent(int minimumLength)
    {
        // get char array from System.Buffers shared pool
        return ArrayPool<char>.Shared.Rent(minimumLength);
    }
```

```
public void Return(char[] array)
{
    // return char array to System.Buffers shared pool
    ArrayPool<char>.Shared.Return(array);
}
}
```

By providing ArrayPool to the Json.NET serializer, memory allocations may be significantly reduced (see Table 6-6). Please note this buffer is used internally by Json. NET to store an array of chars. Currently it is not possible to deserialize into buffered array (int[] in our example), which also would be very a desirable possibility.

Table 6-6. *DotNetBenchmark Results for Code from Listings 6-24 and 6-25*

Method	Mean	Allocated
ReadPlain	14.58 us	6.10 KB
ReadWithArrayPool	13.37 us	4.42 KB

One important remark. There is yet another ArrayPool<T> implementation that may be created with the help of ArrayPool<T>.Create(int maxArrayLength, int maxArraysPerBucket) method - called ConfigurableArrayPool<T>. It has a little simpler implementation based on buckets also, without usage of thread local storage. But, as you can see in Create method's signature, you can configure it to have a specified number of arrays in each bucket and the maximum cached array size (incurring number of buckets). The default maximum length of array in such pool is 1024*1024 (1 048 576) elements and by default there are 50 arrays in a bucket.

When using ArrayPool (whenever shared or created) it is worth it to monitor its usage with custom ETW provider named System.Buffers.ArrayPoolEventSource. For example, we can collect its data with the help of PerfView. When defining collection properties in the Collect dialog box type in Additional Providers field:

- *System.Buffers.ArrayPoolEventSource - if you want to collect only event's data

- *System.Buffers.ArrayPoolEventSource:::@StacksEnabled=true - if you want also to record stack traces of the events

In that way we will be able to see all array renting and allocations (see Figure 6-20). We should be particularly interested in the event `BufferAllocated` with the reason for `OverMaximumSize` and `PoolExhausted`. If they occur frequently, the current `ArrayPool` configuration probably does not suit your needs. In case of frequent `OverMaximumSize` probably our pool has too small of a maximum pool size set. In case of `PoolExhausted` maybe it is worth it to increase the number of arrays in a bucket. There is also `Pooled` reason for `BufferAllocated` event, used currently only by `ConfigurableArrayPool`, when a new array had to be allocated inside a bucket.

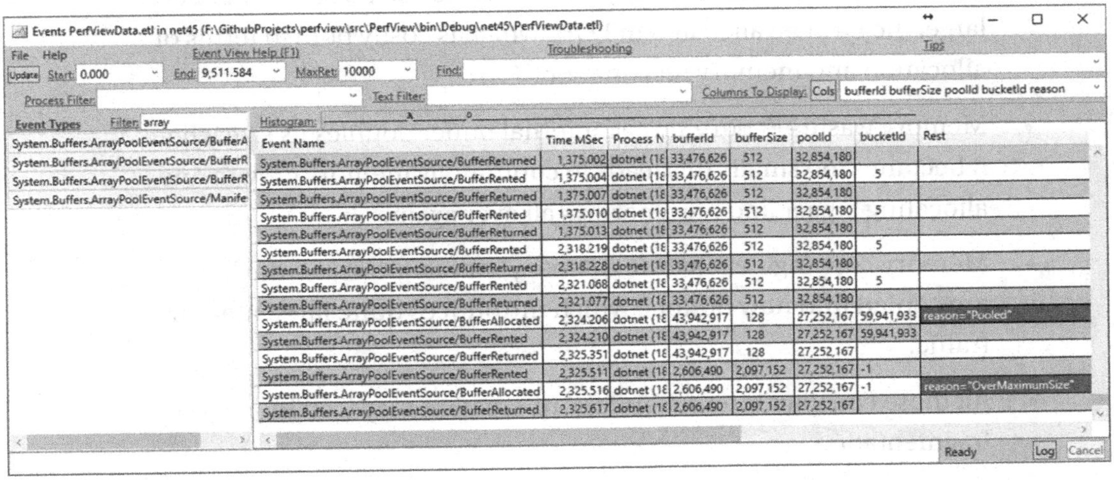

Figure 6-20. *ETW events generated by ArrayPool as seen by PerfView tool*

There is one caveat when using `ArrayPool`. Remember that pooled arrays will live forever - there is no "timing out" mechanism. This is ok if your arrays usage is quite constant and spread over time. If you, however, need only a single burst of allocations, you may grow your working set forever without much benefit. Please take into account such "reusage ratio" of your buffers when considering usage of `ArrayPool`.

Please note that `ArrayPool` is one of the mainstream improvements in .NET Core development (for example, it was significantly improved between .NET Core 2.0 and 2.1). While the overall description presented here will not change, implementation details may change in the next releases. One of the examples include the above-mentioned trimming mechanism, which may be include some day.

Creating Streams - Use RecyclableMemoryStream

If we use the System.IO.MemoryStream class extensively in our application, you should consider using the pool of these objects. Pooling for .NET MemoryStream objects has been implemented in Microsoft.IO.RecyclableMemoryStream package by RecyclableMemoryStream and RecylableMemoryStreamManager classes. As the comments in the code of these classes perfectly explain, intense use of MemoryStream is associated with the following undesirable effects:

- LOH allocations - since MemoryStream's internal buffers tend to be large, they will be allocated in LOH, which is costly both in terms of allocation and memory reclamation.

- Memory waste - MemoryStream internal buffer doubles its size when it becomes too small. This leads to continuous memory growth and allocating bigger and bigger arrays all over again.

- Memory copying - each time a MemoryStream grows, all the bytes are copied into new buffers, which introduces quite large memory traffic.

- All these constant internal buffers' re-creation may lead to fragmentation.

RecyclableMemoryStream was designed to overcome all those problems. It is worth citing here a good description in the comments to the class RecyclableMemoryStream: "The stream is implemented on top of a series of uniformly-sized blocks. As the stream's length grows, additional blocks are retrieved from the memory manager. It is these blocks that are pooled, not the stream object itself.

The biggest wrinkle in this implementation is when GetBuffer() is called. This requires a single contiguous buffer. If only a single block is in use, then that block is returned. If multiple blocks are in use, we retrieve a larger buffer from the memory manager. These large buffers are also pooled, split by size--they are multiples of a chunk size (1 MB by default)."

Example usage of standard MemoryStream to serialize an object has been presented in Listing 6-26. In addition to creating XmlWriter and DataContractSerializer (which should be cached), it also creates a new MemoryStream. It may lead to the above-mentioned problems if serialized objects are big and serialization happens often.

Listing 6-26. Example of XML serialization by using DataContractSerializer and MemoryStream

```
public string SerializeXmlWithMemoryStream(object obj)
{
    using (var ms = new MemoryStream())
    {
        using (var xw = XmlWriter.Create(ms, XmlWriterSettings))
        {
            var serializer = new DataContractSerializer(obj.GetType());
            // could be cached!
            serializer.WriteObject(xw, obj);
            xw.Flush();
            ms.Seek(0, SeekOrigin.Begin);
            var reader = new StreamReader(ms);
            return reader.ReadToEnd();
        }
    }
}
```

In case of high stream utilization RecyclableMemoryStream should be considered (see Listing 6-27). A RecyclableMemoryStreamManager needs to be created that can then provide pooled stream from its GetStream method. Such stream implements IDisposable in a way that memory used by it will be returned to the pool while disposing. A set of parameters may be passed when manager is created (Listing 6-27 shows default values):

- blockSize - size of each block that is pooled
- largeBufferMultiple - each large buffer will be a multiple of this value
- maximumBufferSize - buffers larger than this will not be pooled

Listing 6-27. Example of XML serialization by using DataContractSerializer and RecyclableMemoryStream

```
static RecyclableMemoryStreamManager manager =
        new RecyclableMemoryStreamManager(blockSize: 128 * 1024,
                                largeBufferMultiple: 1024 * 1024,
                                maximumBufferSize: 128 * 1024 * 1024);
```

467

```
public string SerializeXmlWithRecyclableMemoryStream<T>(T obj)
{
    using (var ms = manager.GetStream())
    {
        using (var xw = XmlWriter.Create(ms, XmlWriterSettings))
        {
            var serializer = new DataContractSerializer(obj.GetType()); //
            could be cached!
            serializer.WriteObject(xw, obj);
            xw.Flush();
            ms.Seek(0, SeekOrigin.Begin);
            var reader = new StreamReader(ms);
            return reader.ReadToEnd();
        }
    }
}
```

When using RecyclableMemoryStream it is worth it to monitor its usage with custom ETW provider named Microsoft-IO-RecyclableMemoryStream. We can collect its data with the help of PerfView. When defining collection properties in the Collect dialog box type in Additional Providers field:

- *Microsoft-IO-RecyclableMemoryStream - if you want to collect only event's data

- *Microsoft-IO-RecyclableMemoryStream:::
  @StacksEnabled=true - if you want also to record stack traces of the events

---

Note   During my experiments with RecyclableMemoryStream enabling ETW provider by its name was not working properly. I needed to refer to it by its Guide. Thus, you may also need to type B80CD4E4-890E-468D-9CBA-90EB7C82DFC7 instead of *Microsoft-IO-RecyclableMemoryStream as an Additional Provider.

RecyclableMemoryStream may provide quite detailed insight into its pool usage (see Figure 6-21). You may be especially interested in MemoryStreamOverCapacity event that informs about requesting a buffer larger than the provided maximum buffer size.

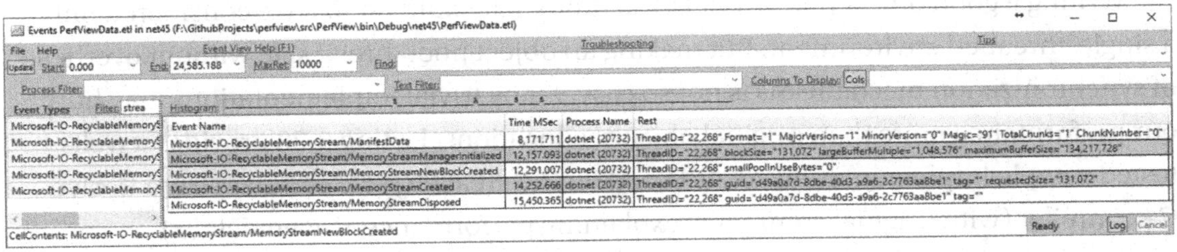

Figure 6-21. *ETW events generated by RecyclableMemoryStream as seen by PerfView tool*

Note   When using Streams intensively, you should also consider using System. IO.Pipelines API. It provides much more efficient and less allocating substitution of Streams. It is described in more detail in Chapter 14.

Creating a Lot of Objects - Use Object Pool

Like it is with collections, when using some type of object very extensively, you may consider using that object's pool. Please bear in mind however that if you allocate a lot of objects just to throw them away shortly, it still holds generational hypothesis. Hence, it might be just ok. Garbage Collector will clean them in generation 0 quickly. You should mainly consider object's pooling in one of the following scenarios:

- Objects are allocated on so an important and hot path, which each single CPU cycle counts - in this case avoiding object allocations (especially its slow path) by providing more stable mechanism may be beneficial. Properly written object pool should utilize CPU cache nicely so operating on pooled objects may be really fast.

- Objects are big enough to be worried about its allocation cost - in this case we may avoid memory zeroing overhead (especially for LOH objects). Additionally, to the allocation cost itself, we may be worried about object's initialization cost - if it's very complicated to initialize

fields of an object, we would not want to create new ones again and
again. Thus, we can benefit from reusing already initialized object (if
it is appropriate).

Writing a good object pool is not trivial though. It could be so if we considered only
a single-threaded environment. But making an object pool thread safe without overhead
of synchronization mechanisms is not so easy. Many trivial implementations may hurt
our performance more than original objects' allocations. Listing 6-28 provides a well-
tested sample implementation solely based on the great ObjectPool class from Roslyn
C# compiler (with original comments explaining performance-driven details).

Listing 6-28. ObjectPool implementation based on ObjectPool class from Roslyn
compiler

```
public class ObjectPool<T> where T : class
{
    private T firstItem;
    private readonly T[] items;
    private readonly Func<T> generator;

    public ObjectPool(Func<T> generator, int size)
    {
        this.generator = generator ?? throw new ArgumentNullException
        ("generator");
        this.items = new T[size - 1];
    }

    public T Rent()
    {
        // PERF: Examine the first element. If that fails, RentSlow will
            look at the remaining elements.
        // Note that the initial read is optimistically not synchronized.
            That is intentional.
        // We will interlock only when we have a candidate. in a worst case
            we may miss some recently returned objects. Not a big deal.
        T inst = firstItem;
        if (inst == null || inst != Interlocked.CompareExchange
        (ref firstItem, null, inst))
```

```
    {
        inst = RentSlow();
    }
    return inst;
}
public void Return(T item)
{
    if (firstItem == null)
    {
        // Intentionally not using interlocked here.
        // In a worst case scenario two objects may be stored into same
            slot.
        // It is very unlikely to happen and will only mean that one of
            the objects will get collected.
        firstItem = item;
    }
    else
    {
        ReturnSlow(item);
    }
}
private T RentSlow()
{
    for (int i = 0; i < items.Length; i++)
    {
        // Note that the initial read is optimistically not
            synchronized. That is intentional.
        // We will interlock only when we have a candidate. in a worst
            case we may miss some recently returned objects. Not a big
            deal.
        T inst = items[i];
        if (inst != null)
        {
            if (inst == Interlocked.CompareExchange(ref items[i],
                null, inst))
```

```
                {
                    return inst;
                }
            }
        }
        return generator();
    }
    private void ReturnSlow(T obj)
    {
        for (int i = 0; i < items.Length; i++)
        {
            if (items[i] == null)
            {
                // Intentionally not using interlocked here.
                // In a worst case scenario two objects may be stored into
                    same slot.
                // It is very unlikely to happen and will only mean that
                    one of the objects will get collected.
                items[i] = obj;
                break;
            }
        }
    }
}
```

Async Methods Returning Task - Use ValueTask

Since async was introduced in the C# 5.0, it has become almost a canonical way of programming. Actually, everywhere we see an asynchronous code. It is worth knowing how its use corresponds to the memory consumption. Take, for example, a simple asynchronous code for reading the entire contents of a file (see Listing 6-29). It first checks synchronously whether file exists and only if yes, it asynchronously awaits for the file operation to end.

Listing 6-29. An example of asynchronous method

```
public async Task<string> ReadFileAsync(string filename)
{
    if (!File.Exists(filename))
        return string.Empty;
    return await File.ReadAllTextAsync(filename);
}
```

Probably the majority of .NET programmers are already aware that applying the keyword `async` turns the method into a rather complicated state machine. This state machine is responsible for the proper processing of planned steps when subsequent asynchronous actions are completed. If we look at the code generated by the compiler on the basis of the `ReadFileAsync` method from Listing 6-29, we will see the code from Listing 6-30. The method has been transformed into a code starting the state machine represented by the enigmatically named object `Program.<ReadFil eAsync>d__14`. There are many good descriptions of this mechanism, so let us skip it here for brevity.

Listing 6-30. Method `ReadFileAsync` from Listing 6-29 after transformation made by the compiler

```
[AsyncStateMachine(typeof(Program.<ReadFileAsync>d__14))]
public Task<string> ReadFileAsync(string filename)
{
    Program.<ReadFileAsync>d__14 <ReadFileAsync>d__;
    <ReadFileAsync>d__.filename = filename;
    <ReadFileAsync>d__.<>t__builder = AsyncTaskMethodBuilder<string>.
    Create();
    <ReadFileAsync>d__.<>1__state = -1;
    AsyncTaskMethodBuilder<string> <>t__builder = <ReadFileAsync>d__.<>t__
    builder;
    <>t__builder.Start<Program.<ReadFileAsync>d__14>(ref <ReadFileAsync>d__);
    return <ReadFileAsync>d__.<>t__builder.Task;
}
```

From our point of view, the following facts are important (supported by the code from Listing 6-31):

- In compiler-generated code from Listing 6-30 all is a struct (including `Program.<ReadFileAsync>d__14` and `AsyncTaskMethodBuilder<string>`) - this is a great example of conscious use of structures where it would be tempting to use classes without thinking.

- `<ReadFileAsync>d__14` - compiler-generated structure representing state machine - will be boxed if asynchronous operation does not end instantly (which happens inside `AwaitUnsafeOnCompleted` visible in Listing 6-31)[3] - in such case "state" must escape current method because asynchronous operation may continue on different thread that it was initially started. Thus, it must land on the heap rather than stay on the stack. However, making `<ReadFileAsync>d__14` struct still makes sense because there may be common paths where such boxing will not occur (see case of `File.Exists` returning false in Listing 6-31).

- Compiler-generated structure representing state machine remembers (captures) all necessary local variables of the method (filename in our example) - we should be aware of this because in that way we may prolong their life significantly if state machine (`<ReadFileAsync>d__14`) gets heap allocated.

Listing 6-31. Struct representing a state machine for ReadFileAsync method from Listing 6-30

```
[CompilerGenerated]
[StructLayout(LayoutKind.Auto)]
private struct <ReadFileAsync>d__14 : IAsyncStateMachine
{
    void IAsyncStateMachine.MoveNext()
    {
        int num = this.<>1__state;
        string result;
        try
```

---

[3]This works differently starting in .NET Core 2.1. It's still moved to the heap, but as a strongly typed field on a class rather than being boxed

```
{
   TaskAwaiter<string> awaiter;
   if (num != 0)
   {
      if (!File.Exists(this.filename))
      {
         result = string.Empty;
         goto IL_A4;
      }
      awaiter = File.ReadAllTextAsync(this.filename,
      default(CancellationToken)).GetAwaiter();
      if (!awaiter.get_IsCompleted())
      {
         this.<>1__state = 0;
         this.<>u__1 = awaiter;
         this.<>t__builder.AwaitUnsafeOnCompleted<TaskAwaiter
         <string>, Program.<ReadFileAsync>d__14>(ref awaiter, ref
         this);
         return;
      }
   }
   else
   {
      awaiter = this.<>u__1;
      this.<>u__1 = default(TaskAwaiter<string>);
      this.<>1__state = -1;
   }
   result = awaiter.GetResult();
}
catch (Exception exception)
{
   this.<>1__state = -2;
   this.<>t__builder.SetException(exception);
   return;
}
```

```
    IL_A4:
    this.<>1__state = -2;
    this.<>t__builder.SetResult(result);
  }

}
```

In addition to the possible overhead resulting from a heap-allocating state machine, there is yet another caveat related to the async method. If we trace exactly what is happening in the code from Listing 6-31 for the case when the file does not exist, we see that after goto statement a SetResult is called on AsyncTaskMethodBuilder<string> struct. This is theoretically a very fast synchronous path without any asynchronous waiting overhead. However, mentioned SetResult method introduces allocation of the Task object to contain a result of the method (see Listing 6-32).

Listing 6-32. AsyncTaskMethodBuilder struct

```
public struct AsyncTaskMethodBuilder<TResult>
{
    public static AsyncTaskMethodBuilder<TResult> Create()
    {
        return default(AsyncTaskMethodBuilder<TResult>);
    }

    public void Start<TStateMachine>(ref TStateMachine stateMachine) where
    TStateMachine : IAsyncStateMachine
    {
        // ...
        stateMachine.MoveNext();
    }

    // ...

    public void SetResult(TResult result)
    {
        Task<TResult> task = this.m_task;
        if (task == null)
```

```
    {
        this.m_task = this.GetTaskForResult(result);
        return;
    }
    // ...
    }
    public Task<TResult> Task
    {
        get
        {
            Task<TResult> task = this.m_task;
            if (task == null)
            {
                task = (this.m_task = new Task<TResult>());
            }
            return task;
        }
    }
}
```

GetTaskForResult called inside SetResult will most probably allocate a new Task wrapping provided result, but with some exceptions made for performance reasons:

- for Task<bool> it returns one of the two cached objects (for true and false values),

- for Task<int> it returns cached object for values from -1 to 9 but will create a new Task for other values,

- for many numerical Task<T> it returns cached object for value 0,

- for reference types it returns cached task for value null,

- for other cases it creates a new Task.

It is not very efficient to allocate a Task object just to use it to pass the result value. If our async method is called very often and such a synchronous fast answer is common, we are introducing a lot of unnecessary allocations of the Task object. Exactly for that

477

purposes, a lightweight version of Task has been introduced called ValueTask. It is in fact a struct made as a discriminated union - a type that may take one of three possible values (see Listing 6-33):

- Ready-to-use result (if the operation completed successfully synchronously).

- A normal Task that may be awaited on

- It can also wrap an IValueTaskSource<T>, which can be implemented by arbitrary objects to be represented by ValueTask<T> (currently available only in .NET Core 2.1). These objects can then be pooled and reused to minimize allocation.

Listing 6-33. ValueTask introduced in C# 7.0 (version as in .NET Core 2.1)

```
public struct ValueTask<TResult>
{
    // null if _result has the result, otherwise a Task<TResult> or a
    IValueTaskSource<TResult>
    internal readonly object _obj;
    internal readonly TResult _result;
}
```

The corresponding AsyncValueTaskMethodBuilder<TResult> in its SetResult method sets the result (if it is already available) or just creates a Task in a normal way described above (if regular asynchronous path is to be taken). In that way we may avoid allocation completely in case of a synchronous answer of async method. This, in fact, requires nothing more than changing return type from Task<T> to ValueTask<T> (see Listing 6-34). The compiler will take care of the rest by using AsyncValueTaskMethodBuilder instead of AsyncTaskMethodBuilder.

Listing 6-34. An example of ValueTask usage

```
public async ValueTask<string> ReadFileAsync2(string filename)
{
    if (!File.Exists(filename))
        return string.Empty;
    return await File.ReadAllTextAsync(filename);
}
```

When consuming ValueTask-returning async methods, we may simply await it as any other regular async method. Only in the tightest of tight loops, on absolutely critical performance paths, we may additionally check whether it is already completed and use Result if so (see Listing 6-35). This will be solely based on structs so no allocation occurs. If task has not completed, then normal Task-driven path should be started.

Listing 6-35. Usage of an async method returning ValueTask

```
var valueTask = ReadFileAsync2();
if(valueTask.IsCompleted)
{
    return valueTask.Result;
}
else
{
    return await valueTask.AsTask();
}
```

There is yet another optimization possible. As already stated, in case of asynchronous path, Task must be still allocated. But if it is really frequently called on our performance-critical path, it would be great to remove this allocation also. For this reason, above-mentioned IValueTaskSource has been introduced. Since then we can create ValueTask that is wrapping instance of such interface implementation - which is beneficial if such instance is cached or pooled. In other words, asynchronous operation is then represented by such cached or pooled instance (see Listing 6-36). Therefore, there is no need for Task allocations at all.

Listing 6-36. An example of ValueTask usage backed by IValueTaskSource implementation

```
public ValueTask<string> ReadFileAsync3(string filename)
{
    if (!File.Exists(filename))
        return new ValueTask<string>("!");
    var cachedOp = pool.Rent();
    return cachedOp.RunAsync(filename, pool);
}
```

```
private ObjectPool<PooledValueTaskSource> pool =
    new ObjectPool<PooledValueTaskSource>(() => new
    PooledValueTaskSource (), 10);
```

When implementing `IValueTaskSource` interface, we must implement three following methods:

- `GetResult` - called only once, when the async state machine needs to obtain the result of the operation;

- `GetStatus` - called by the async state machine to check the status of the operation;

- `OnCompleted` - called by the async state machine when wrapping ValueTask has been awaited. We should remember here the continuation to be called when the operation completes (but if it already has been completed, we should call the continuation immediately);

Additionally, for convenience, such type should provide a method to start the operation and a method to react on the operation completion.

Having said that, we should be aware that implementing fully working, functional, and thread-safe `IValueTaskSource` is by far trivial. Including here whole `PooledValueTaskSource` implementation (used in Listing 6-36) altogether with all appropriate explanations is much more than this book can hold. It is also expected that only a few developers will in fact need to implement it. However, please refer to the accompanied source on Github to see the whole `PooledValueTaskSource` implementation (with extensive comments) and a dedicated blog post at `http://tooslowexception.com/implementing-custom-ivaluetasksource-async-without-allocations/`.

Please note we should not treat `ValueTask` as a default replacement of `Task` wherever we used it so far. Most often it is not worth the performance difference we could gain. However, such difference may pay off in very intensively used code when our async method often ends synchronously. There are also trade-offs to using a `ValueTask` instead of `Task`, greatly explained in the `ValueTask`'s API:

- "while a ValueTask<TResult> can help avoid an allocation in the case where the successful result is available synchronously, it also contains two fields whereas a Task<TResult> as a reference type is a single field. This means that a method call ends up returning two fields worth of data instead of one, which is more data to copy. It also means that if a method that returns one of these is awaited within an async method, the state machine for that async method will be larger due to needing to store the struct that's two fields instead of a single reference."

- "Further, for uses other than consuming the result of an asynchronous operation via await, ValueTask<TResult> can lead to a more convoluted programming model, which can in turn actually lead to more allocations. For example, consider a method that could return either a Task<TResult> with a cached task as a common result or a ValueTask<TResult>. If the consumer of the result wants to use it as a Task<TResult>, such as to use with in methods like Task.WhenAll and Task.WhenAny, the ValueTask<TResult> would first need to be converted into a Task<TResult> using AsTask, which leads to an allocation that would have been avoided if a cached Task<TResult> had been used in the first place."

Hidden Allocations

Besides being creating explicitly, many times objects are created implicitly by certain operations. This is often referred to as *hidden allocations* and a lot of effort is put into avoiding them. Of course, they are less pleasant in that sense; they do not stand out from our code directly until we know about them.

Delegate Allocation

Every time we create a new delegate (including popular Func and Action delegate), most probably we are incurring a hidden allocation. It may happen both in case of a delegate created from so-called method group (method referenced by name, see Listing 6-37) and created from a lambda expression (in this case lambda expression is turned into compiler-generated method; see Listing 6-38).

Listing 6-37. Delegate allocation from method group

```
Func<double> action = ProcessWithLogging; // hidden
Func<double> action = new Func<double>(this.ProcessWithLogging);
// explicit
```

Listing 6-38. Delegate allocation from lambda - hidden allocation

```
Func<double> action = () => ProcessWithLogging(); // hidden
Func<double> action = new Func<double>(this.<SomeMethod>b__31_0)();
//explicit
```

There is no way to avoid such allocations, but being aware of them we may more consciously write our code (for example, avoiding repeating delegate creation inside a loop).

There is an important optimization regarding lambda expressions. If they do not close (capture) any data - most likely C# compiler will generate code to cache such a delegate instance as a static field (so it will be allocated only once, at the first usage).

Boxing

Boxing has been described in Chapter 4. There are the two most-common sources of boxing mentioned there, so let just repeat them here shortly:

- A value type is used where object (reference type) is expected (see Listing 6-39) - this includes many obvious implicit conversions.

- Value type instance is used as an interface type implemented by this value type (see Listing 6-40).

Listing 6-39. Typical sources of boxing - common conversions

```
object obj = 0;    // Int32 struct boxed
FooBar(0); // 0 will be boxed
static void FooBar(object obj)
{
}
```

Listing 6-40. Typical sources of boxing - passing as an interface

```
// ValueTuple to ITuple
FooBar(new ValueTuple() {A = 1});

static void FooBar(ITuple tuple)
{
    // ValueTuple will be boxed
}
```

The first source of allocation may not always be avoidable. However, when an object is used as a way of telling that any object may be passed to a method (like FooBar in Listing 6-39), it is better to use generics instead (see Listing 6-41).

Listing 6-41. Avoiding boxing by using generic method

```
void FooBar<T>(T obj)
{
    // FooBar<Int32> will be called without boxing
}
```

The second source of allocation may be overcome by using generic method with generic constraint imposed (see Listing 6-42).

Listing 6-42. Avoiding boxing by using generic method with a constraint

```
void FooBar<T>(T tuple) where T : ITuple
{
    // ValueTuple will not be boxed
    Console.WriteLine($"# of elements: {tuple.Length}");
    Console.WriteLine($"Second to last element: {tuple[tuple.Length - 2]}");
}
```

There are three other less-known sources of boxing for value types:

- valueType.GetHashCode() and valueType.ToString() call when those virtual methods are not overridden in valueType,

- valueType.GetType() always boxes valueType,

- when creating a delegate from value type method, it will be boxed (see Listings 6-43 and 6-44).

483

Listing 6-43. Delegate allocation from value type method group

```
SomeStruct valueType;
Func<double> action2 = valueType.SomeMethod;
```

Listing 6-44. IL code from Listing 6-39

```
ldarg.1
box       CoreCLR.Program.SomeStruct
ldftn     instance float64 CoreCLR.Program.SomeStruct::SomeMethod()
newobj    instance void class [System.Runtime]System.Func`1<float64>::
          .ctor(object, native int)
callvirt  instance !0 class [System.Runtime]System.Func`1<float64>::Invoke()
```

Closures

Closures are mechanisms for managing the state of the calculations - "a function together with a referencing environment for the non-local variables of that function" (Wikipedia). To better understand them, let's use as an example a simple LINQ-based method using lambda expressions to filter and select values from a list (see Listing 6-45). If you are reading this chapter one by one, you probably already noticed two possible sources of allocations in the Closures method: two delegates may be created from lambda expressions as both Where and Select are expecting Func<> as parameters.[4]

Listing 6-45. An example of code using lambda expressions

```
private IEnumerable<string> Closures(int value)
{
    var filteredList = _list.Where(x => x > value);
    var result = filteredList.Select(x => x.ToString());
    return result;
}
```

---

[4]However, due to closures optimization mentioned before, most probably only a single delegate will be allocated per Closures method call, the one passed to Where. Lambda passed to Select doesn't close over any state, so the C# compiler generates code to cache such delegate. We can see it in Listing 6-46 as arg_43_1 field.

However, there is yet another important source of allocation. Code from Listing 6-45 will be translated into a more complex construct utilizing an additional `<>c__DisplayClass1_0` class (see Listing 6-46). This class implements mentioned closure. It contains both a function to be executed (under some internal name `<Closures>b__0`) and all variables required for execution (`value` in our case). Please note the following facts:

- Closure is implemented as a class so it incurs allocation - in our example `Program.<>c__DisplayClass1_0` will be allocated each time `Closures` method is executed.

- Local variables that are stored (captured) inside a closure are counting into the size of this closure on the heap - in our case, the value integer is captured. The more such variables, the bigger "closure class" becomes.

Listing 6-46. An example of code using lambda expressions after compiler transformation

```
private IEnumerable<string> Closures(int value)
{
    Program.<>c__DisplayClass1_0 <>c__DisplayClass1_ = new Program.<>
    c__DisplayClass1_0();
    <>c__DisplayClass1_.value = value;
    IEnumerable<int> arg_43_0 = this._list.Where(new Func<int, bool>(<>
    c__DisplayClass1_.<Closures>b__0));
    Func<int, string> arg_43_1;
    if ((arg_43_1 = Program.<>c.<>9__1_1) == null)
    {
        arg_43_1 = (Program.<>c.<>9__1_1 = new Func<int, string>(Program.<>
        c.<>9.<Closures>b__1_1));
    }
    return arg_43_0.Select(arg_43_1);
}

[CompilerGenerated]
private sealed class <>c__DisplayClass1_0
{
```

```
public <>c__DisplayClass1_0()
{
}

internal bool <Closures>b__0(int x)
{
    return x > this.value;
}
public int value;
}
```

We should be aware of closure allocations when trying to write low memory usage code - the less variables closure captures, the better. We can always check it, for example, by using dnSpy tool and looking at our decompiled code.

Listing 6-47 shows some additional insights about what and when is being captured. Be warned, however, that it is due to extensive compiler optimizations. There are so many rules and exceptions that sometimes all investigations about what and when are captured end with a conclusion - it's a magic (or more seriously, deep implementation detail of currently used optimizations). Please note that all examples from Listing 6-47 may contain hidden allocation of a delegate from a lambda expression.

Listing 6-47. Examples of different situations of closures capturing state

```
// There is no closure because nothing to be captured (this is not
   captured):
Func<double> action1 = () => InstanceMethodNotUsingThis();

// There is no closure because nothing to be captured (this still is not
   captured)
Func<double> action2 = () => InstanceMethodUsingThis();

// There is nothing to be captured
Func<double> action3 = () => StaticMethod();

// Captures ss
Func<double> action3 = () => StaticMethodUsingLocalVariable(ss);

// Closure captures ss and this (to call this.<>4__this.
ProcessSomeStruct(this.ss); inside)
```

```
// if ss argument was missing, nothing would be captured (this would not be
capture solely)
Func<double> action6 = () => InstanceMethodUsingLocalVariable(ss);
```

If we want to get rid of closures, we should produce code with lambda expressions not capturing any variables or without lambda expressions at all. Listing 6-48 shows an example of how the method from Listing 6-45 could be rewritten. Please note however this method now needs to allocate a list for results, which may be even less efficient than allocations made by the closure itself.

Listing 6-48. An example of code avoiding lambda expressions and closures

```
private IEnumerable<string> WithoutClosures(int value)
{
    List<string> result = new List<string>();
    foreach (int x in _list)
        if (x > value)
            result.Add(x.ToString());
    return result;
}
```

Local functions introduced in C# 7.0 are in fact similar to lambda expressions and may incur a need to allocate a closure. Rewriting code from Listing 6-45 into code using local functions, we get code with two local functions (see Listing 6-49). In this way, however, we do not avoid capturing a value variable.

Listing 6-49. Code from Listing 6-45 rewritten to use local functions

```
private IEnumerable<string> ClosuresWithLocalFunction(int value)
{
    bool WhereCondition(int x) => x > value;
    string SelectAction(int x) => x.ToString();

    var filteredList = _list.Where(WhereCondition);
    var result = filteredList.Select(SelectAction);
    return result;
}
```

Code generated by the compiler (see Listing 6-50) still contains a closure capturing it.

Listing 6-50. An example of code using local functions after compiler transformation

```
private IEnumerable<string> ClosuresWithLocalFunction(int value)
{
    Program.<>c__DisplayClass26_0 <>c__DisplayClass26_ = new Program.<>
    c__DisplayClass26_0();
    <>c__DisplayClass26_.value = value;
    return this._list.Where(new Func<int, bool>(<>c__DisplayClass26_.<Closur
    esWithLocalFunction>g__WhereCondition0)).Select(new Func<int, string>
    (Program.<>c.<>9.<ClosuresWithLocalFunction>g__SelectAction26_1));
}
```

Yield Return

In addition to async methods and closures, there is yet another mechanism that causes hidden allocations of auxiliary classes generated by the compiler - yield return mechanism. It is used for quick and convenient creation of iterator methods. All the heavy work of creating an iterator class that will hold iteration state is on the compiler side. For example, rewriting the method from Listing 6-45 using yield operator, we may easily get rid of lambda expressions (see Listing 6-51).

Listing 6-51. An example of code using yield operator

```
private IEnumerable<string> WithoutClosures(int value)
{
    foreach (int x in _list)
        if (x > value)
            yield return x.ToString();
}
```

However, it does not allow us to get rid of the allocation of a temporary object completely. It is created to represent the state of the iterator (Listing 6-52). As we can see, it also captures value variable and additionally, this reference. But taking into consideration that besides closures, code from Listing 6-45 allocates also enumerables used by Where and Select methods; this is still a less-allocating alternative.

Listing 6-52. An example of code using yield operator after compiler transformation

```
[IteratorStateMachine(typeof(Program.<WithoutClosures>d__26))]
private IEnumerable<string> WithoutClosures(int value)
{
    Program.<WithoutClosures>d__26 expr_07 = new Program.<WithoutClosures
    >d__26(-2);
    expr_07.<>4__this = this;
    expr_07.<>3__value = value;
    return expr_07;
}
```

Parameters Array

Since the old times of C# 2.0 it is possible to create a method with a variable number of parameters with the help of params keyword (see Listing 6-53). One should know that it is only syntactic sugar for a compiler. Underneath it is just an array of objects that is the last argument of a method.

Listing 6-53. An example of method taking variable number of parameters

```
public void MethodWithParams(string str, params object[] args)
{
    Console.WriteLine(str, args);
}
```

Thus, when passing arguments to a method with params, new object[] array is being allocated. There is a simple optimization in case of no parameters were passed (see Listing 6-54).

Listing 6-54. Usage of method with params

```
SomeClass sc;
MethodWithParams("Log {0}", sc); // Allocates new object[] with single
                                 element sc

int counter;
```

```
MethodWithParams("Counter {0}", counter); // Boxes integer and allocates
                                              new object[] with single
                                              element counter

p.MethodWithParams("Hello!");   // No allocation, uses static Array.
                                   Empty<object>()
```

To overcome this source of hidden allocations, many methods that expect various number of parameters provide overloads for typical, few parameters usage - in form of objects or generic method (see Listing 6-55).

Listing 6-55. An example of method's overload taking variable number of parameters

```
public void MethodWithParams(string str, object arg1)
{
    Console.WriteLine(str, arg1);
}
public void MethodWithParams(string str, object arg1, object arg2)
{
    Console.WriteLine(str, arg1, arg2);
}
public void GenericMethodWithParams<T1>(string str, T1 arg1)
{
    Console.WriteLine(str, arg1);
}
public void GenericMethodWithParams<T1,T2>(string str, T1 arg1, T2 arg2)
{
    Console.WriteLine(str, arg1, arg2);
}
```

String Concatenation

String concatenation and design decisions behind making a string class immutable were described in Chapter 4. Let's just remind for the completeness of typical examples causing the allocation of temporary strings (see Listing 6-56).

490

Listing 6-56. Example of most common string manipulations

```
// This will produce a temporary string "Hello " + otherString
string str = "Hello " + otherString + "!";
// This allocates str + "you are welcome" (previous str will become
garbage)
str += " you are welcome";
```

As mentioned in Chapter 4, for middle-sized string manipulations, it is better to use String.Format overrides as they use cached StringBuilder inside. For creating bigger texts by appending smaller strings, StringBuilder would be the best choice. But for the simplest scenarios when only two or three parts are concatenated, it is best to use simply the plus operator (as in the first line in Listing 6-56), which underneath uses an efficient string.Concat implementations (see Listing 6-57) directly manipulating string data (or use such Concat explicitly).

Listing 6-57. Efficient string.Concat implementation (FillStringChecked directly manipulates internal string data)

```
public static String Concat(String str0, String str1)
{
    if (IsNullOrEmpty(str0)) {
        if (IsNullOrEmpty(str1)) {
            return String.Empty;
        }
        return str1;
    }
    if (IsNullOrEmpty(str1)) {
        return str0;
    }
    int str0Length = str0.Length;
    String result = FastAllocateString(str0Length + str1.Length);
    FillStringChecked(result, 0,         str0);
    FillStringChecked(result, str0Length, str1);
    return result;
}
```

If your code formatting strings is on a hot path and you really want to avoid any allocations, consider using an external library like StringFormatter (`https://github.com/MikePopoloski/StringFormatter`). It is an allocation-free library with API very similar to `string.Format`. There are even more high-level libraries built on top of it like allocation-free logging library ZeroLog (`https://github.com/Abc-Arbitrage/ZeroLog`). Since .NET Core 2.1 you may also wish to use all the new `Span<T>`-related APIs for string manipulation (mentioned in Chapter 14).

Various Hidden Allocations Inside Libraries

Due to the many allocation sources (both explicit and hidden) that may occur, obviously using other libraries puts as a risk of allocations we are not aware of. It is impossible to describe here all possibilities as it would require an extremely extensive description of the most popular libraries we can use. For this reason, we will only look at the most-popular sources of this type of allocations.

System.Generics Collections

Some commonly used collections from `System.Generic` namespace may be seen as wrappers around an array. Let's take as an example overwhelmingly popular `List<T>` class (see Listing 6-58). Inside it just stores an array of elements with some predefined size (if no capacity was specified in its constructor). When `List` grows (for example by using `Add` method), this array may become too small - a new one will be created and all existing items copied.

Listing 6-58. Beginning of the `List<T>` implementation (from .NET Reference Source code)

```
public class List<T> : IList<T>, System.Collections.IList, IReadOnlyList<T>
{
    private const int _defaultCapacity = 4;
    private T[] _items;
    ...
```

Thus, a List<T> and collections like Stack<T>, SortedList<T>, or Queue<T> may need to resize underlying arrays multiple times while being populated. If you approximately know the resulting size in advance, it is always better to use construction overload with the capacity provided. In general, it is always a good practice to specify expected capacity if possible without worrying how it will be consumed by the collections - let's leave it to its operation, trusting that it will use this information optimally.

LINQ - Delegates

Using LINQ is elegant and pleasant. We may write complex data manipulations succinctly in a just few lines of code. However, LINQ is one of the most allocation-like mechanisms in C#. When using LINQ, there are many hidden sources of allocations (like already described in Closure section). One of the most common was already described - allocations of delegates. As LINQ methods are based on delegates, we create a lot of them when using it (see Listing 6-59).

Listing 6-59. An example of delegate allocation in LINQ query

```
// Alocates delegates for lambda
var linq = list.Where(x => x.X > 0);
```

However, as explained previously, when executed function does not need to capture anything, such delegates are cached internally. Thus, they will be allocated only once (see Listing 6-60), which is a nice compiler optimization.

Listing 6-60. An example of delegate allocation in LINQ query from Listing 6-59 after compiler transformation

```
Func<SomeClass, bool> arg_152_1;
if ((arg_152_1 = Program.<>c.<>9__0_0) == null)
{
      arg_152_1 = (Program.<>c.<>9__0_0 = new Func<SomeClass, bool>
      (Program.<>c.<>9.<Main>b__0_0));
}
arg_152_0.Where(arg_152_1);
```

493

LINQ - Anonymous Types Creation

When writing LINQ queries, there is a temptation to create temporary anonymous types that additionally adds to the already expensive bill of allocations. A contrived example from Listing 6-61 shows a simple LINQ query written in such way with an SQL-like query syntax.

Listing 6-61. An example of sinple LINQ query - with query syntax

```
public IEnumerable<Double> Main(List<SomeClass> list) {
    var linq = from x in list
        let s = x.X + x.Y
        select s;
    return linq;
}
```

We should be aware that the `let` statement is nothing else than creating an anonymous temporary object (see compiler-generated <Main>b__0_0 method Listing 6-62).

Listing 6-62. An example of simple LINQ query after compiler transformation

```
[CompilerGenerated]
private sealed class <>c
{
    internal <>f__AnonymousType0<SomeClass, double> <Main>b__0_0
    (SomeClass x)
    {
        return new <>f__AnonymousType0<SomeClass, double>(x, x.X + x.Y);
    }
    ...
}
public IEnumerable<double> Main(List<SomeClass> list)
{
    return list.Select(<>c.<>9__0_0 ?? (<>c.<>9__0_0 = <>c.<>9.<Main
                >b__0_0))
            .Select(<>c.<>9__0_1 ?? (<>c.<>9__0_1 = <>c.<>9.<Main
                >b__0_1));
}
```

We need those temporary types sometimes to write elegant LINQ queries. But we should always think about whether you really need them or whether we use them because it is just comfortable and looks nice. In our example, it is obviously redundant as we could return a sum directly (see Listing 6-63), which generates much simpler, non-allocating code (see Listing 6-64).

Listing 6-63. An example of sinple LINQ query - with method syntax

```
public IEnumerable<Double> Main(List<SomeClass> list) {
    var linq = list.Select(x => x.X + x.Y);
    return linq;
}
```

Listing 6-64. An example of LINQ query from Listing 6-63 after compiler transformation

```
[CompilerGenerated]
private sealed class <>c
{
    internal double <Main>b__0_0(SomeClass x)
    {
        return x.X + x.Y;
    }
    ...
}
public IEnumerable<double> Main(List<SomeClass> list)
{
    return list.Select(<>c.<>9__0_0 ?? (<>c.<>9__0_0 = <>c.<>9.<Main
                    >b__0_0));
}
```

LINQ - Enumerables

We may be not aware that LINQ methods are in fact building a chain of *enumerables* - a type responsible for enumerating collection's elements. Those enumerables must be obviously allocated. Even the simplest methods like static `Enumerable.Range` does that - allocating an *iterator*, one of the specific ways of implementing an enumerable (see Listing 6-65).

Listing 6-65. A simple example of hidden iterator allocation

```
// Allocates System.Linq.Enumerable/'<RangeIterator>d__111'
var range = Enumerable.Range(0, 100);
```

Popular methods like `Where` or `Select` are also allocating their iterators. For example, the `Where` method may allocate one of the following iterators:

- `WhereArrayIterator` - if it is called on an array

- `WhereListIterator` - if it is called on a `List`

- `WhereEnumerableIterator` - in other generic cases

Those iterators are around 48 bytes big because they contain data like a reference to the source collection, delegate for selection, thread ID, and so on and so forth. Allocating 48 bytes a few times inside a single method just because of LINQ usage may be, or may not be, a performance problem. As always, it depends on your performance criteria.

There are additional optimizations inside LINQ to combine iterators when possible, but unfortunately it does not help to avoid allocations. For example, when using popular `Where` and `Select` pair, a combined `WhereSelectArrayIterator` (or `WhereSelectListIterator` or `WhereSelectEnumerableIterator`) will be used but intermediate `WhereArrayIterator` (or corresponding ones) also will be created.

Let's take a sample of a trivial string filtering method (see Listing 6-66). It will allocate two different iterators:

- `WhereArrayIterator` - which is 48 bytes big, with very short lifetime as it will be soon replaced by the following one

- `WhereSelectArrayIterator` - which is 56 bytes big

Listing 6-66. A simple example of hidden iterator allocation

```
string[] FilterStrings(string[] inputs, int min, int max, int charIndex)
{
    var results = inputs.Where(x => x.Length >= min && x.Length <= max)
                  .Select(x => x.ToLower());
    return results.ToArray();
}
```

Additionally, it will allocate a delegate and the closure, which captures two integers (`min` and `max`).

You may have your cake and eat it, too, by using one of the libraries that take care of automatic rewriting LINQ queries into more procedural code. Two most popular ones are roslyn-linq-rewrite (`https://github.com/antiufo/roslyn-linq-rewrite`) and LinqOptimizer (`http://nessos.github.io/LinqOptimizer`).

Note   Nowadays, functional programming is becoming increasingly popular in the .NET environment, mainly due to the growing popularity of the F# language and a general return to interest in functional languages. One of the core principles of functional programming languages is the immutability of data. Functional languages such as F# rely on executing subsequent functions in such a way that they do not modify existing data but return new ones. This may of course raise some concerns about the performance. From C# world we know well that the immutability of string can create a series of temporary, unwanted objects. We see through the eyes of the imagination a lot of created objects and data copied between them. One could imagine that operating on data in F# is similar. In general, it requires to change a mindset quite significantly when working with immutable types and functional programming. When comparing its performance in typical mutating scenarios, immutable types may be much slower indeed. A typical example would be to benchmark how fast myriad objects may be added to a mutable List<T> and its immutable counterpart. Obviously, as immutable collections will most probably all over and over again create its own copy with new content added, it will be much slower operation (and by the way, functional language designers probably put a lot of effort to make such operations smarter than such dummy implementation, like reusing common part of data collections). This is however not how such collections should be compared. Immutability gives very important advantages, especially in the increasingly popular multithreaded world. Safe, lock-free access to the read-only data may be much more beneficial in highly contented scenarios (when a lot of threads are competing to access shared resource) than overhead produced by immutability itself. This makes immutable types a great choice for multithreaded and/or parallel processing. Due to its unchanging nature, immutable types may also greatly utilize CPU cache without cache coherency overhead. The same consideration applies to set of immutable collections available in C# in `System.Collections.Immutable` (like `ImmutableArray<T>`, `ImmutableList<T>` and so on so forth). This is thus a matter of choosing a right tool for your problem. Please only do not apply too much importance to benchmarks showing that overwhelming changes to the state of immutable collections are actually slow. Of course, it is, because they are not doing what they were designed for!

Scenario 6-2. Investigating Allocations

Description: After new version deployment of our ASP.NET Core web application, we noticed quite a big memory usage growth by observing `Working Set - Private`, `Private Bytes` and `Virtual Bytes` from `Process(dotnet)` counters altogether with `\.NET CLR Memory(dotnet)\# Total committed Bytes`. Developers can't point to a suspicious place in the changed code, which may be the source of the increased number of allocations. We want to help them by providing analysis of the newly deployed application.

Analysis: One of the best methods to investigate allocation is to use PerfView tool. You can choose between three different allocation sampling methods as described in Chapter 4. For the most accurate results you should try to use .NET Alloc method whenever possible. It utilizes .NET Profiling API injecting EtwCorProfiler library into a sampled process. Each and every allocation will be registered in that way. Obviously, this introduces a big overhead so should be used only on local or strictly controlled development environment. If it is not possible, consider using .NET SampAlloc, which uses the same technique but with less granularity. On the other hand, ETW-based ETW .NET Alloc should introduce quite low overhead so it may be safe to use it even on production environment. Please bear in mind, however, that those two last methods are sampling so only coarse results will be available.

PerfView .NET Alloc and .NET SampAlloc use CLR Profiling API to track allocation in the application. It uses `ICorProfilerCallback3::ObjectAllocated` callback called by runtime each time a new object is being allocated. To make it possible, JIT will disable fast-path allocation based on assembly code. Thus, only by this fact will the program under investigation be slightly slower.

Let's investigate memory allocations with the help of .NET Alloc method:

- Run PerfView.

- Use Collect with .NET Alloc option selected.

- Run web application you want to investigate - it is very important to do that after collection with .NET Alloc (or .NET SampAlloc) has been started.

- Navigate through the web site - most probably you will want to use those areas whose were influenced by the latest changes.

- Stop collection.

- In PerfView, select GC Heap Net Mem Stacks from Memory Group.

- Select dotnet.exe application.

We can choose between two main investigation paths from this point:

1. To gain high-level view of allocations:

   - On By Name tab, use sorting by declining Exc column - it will quickly show what are the most impactful sources of allocations (see Figure 6-22). Please note that many times Type <Unknown> will be one of the main contributors. Unfortunately, ETWClrProfiler is not always able to get type information from the runtime. In such cases it marks a type as <Unknown>.

Name ?	Exc % ?	Exc ?	Exc Ct ?	Inc % ?	Inc ?	Inc Ct ?
Type <Unknown>	98.7	24,549,600	405,260	98.7	24,549,600.0	405,260
Type System.Collections.Immutable.SortedInt32KeyNode`1	1.0	238,560	4,260	1.0	238,560.0	4,260
Type System.Collections.Immutable.ImmutableHashSet`1	0.1	19,760	494	0.1	19,760.0	494
Type <>c__DisplayClass42_0	0.1	16,160	505	0.1	16,160.0	505
Type ?[]	0.0	3,992	52	0.0	3,992.0	52
Type Microsoft.AspNetCore.Razor.Language.Extensions.DefaultTagHelperPropertyIntermediateNode	0.0	3,960	33	0.0	3,960.0	33
Type Microsoft.CodeAnalysis.CSharp.Syntax.CastExpressionSyntax	0.0	3,840	60	0.0	3,840.0	60
Type Microsoft.AspNetCore.Razor.Language.Extensions.PreallocatedTagHelperPropertyIntermediateN	0.0	3,600	30	0.0	3,600.0	30
Type Microsoft.AspNetCore.Razor.Language.Intermediate.TagHelperPropertyIntermediateNode	0.0	3,432	33	0.0	3,432.0	33
Type Microsoft.Net.Http.Headers.EntityTagHeaderValue[]	0.0	3,384	61	0.0	3,384.0	61
Type Microsoft.Net.Http.Headers.EntityTagHeaderValue	0.0	2,880	72	0.0	2,880.0	72
Type Microsoft.AspNetCore.Razor.Language.Extensions.PreallocatedTagHelperPropertyValueIntermed	0.0	2,016	21	0.0	2,016.0	21
Type <GetEnumerator>d__7	0.0	1,920	48	0.0	1,920.0	48

Figure 6-22. High-level view of allocations inside ASP.NET Core web application

The type itself, however, is not the only information because the aggregated sources (stack traces) of allocations may be equally useful. For example, to investigate sources of allocating those <Unknown> types, select Goto ➤ Goto Item in Callers from the found item context menu. Remember that during investigation:

- You can always try to load symbols for unnamed modules (ending with ?! like <<microsoft.codeanalysis.csharp!?>>) by using Lookup Symbols from context menu.

- You can group modules by using Grouping ➤ Group Module from context menu.

- By doing so we could, for example, group most allocating modules of <Unknown> type (see Figure 6-23).

Methods that call Type <Unknown>

Name ?	Inc % ?	Inc ?	Inc Ct ?
☑Type <Unknown>	98.7	24,549,600.0	405,260
+☑ntdll!NtTraceEvent	98.7	24,549,590.0	405,260
+☑ntdll!EtwpEventWriteFull	98.7	24,549,590.0	405,260
+☑ntdll!EtwEventWrite	98.7	24,549,590.0	405,260
+☑etwclrprofiler!Template_xxxx	98.7	24,549,590.0	405,260
+☑etwclrprofiler!CorProfilerTracer::ObjectAllocated	98.7	24,549,590.0	405,260
+☑coreclr!EEToProfInterfaceImpl::ObjectAllocated	98.7	24,549,590.0	405,260
+☑coreclr!ProfilerObjectAllocatedCallback	98.7	24,549,590.0	405,260
+☑coreclr!JIT_New	62.7	15,604,170.0	315,857
|+☐microsoft.codeanalysis.csharp	19.7	4,913,008.0	67,713
|+☐microsoft.aspnetcore.mvc.razor.extensions	19.1	4,743,088.0	115,424
|+☐system.linq	7.5	1,871,536.0	32,889
|+☐microsoft.aspnetcore.razor.language	5.9	1,465,576.0	42,897
|+☐system.private.corelib	3.2	796,712.0	19,524

Figure 6-23. Most common sources of <Unknown> type allocations

We should carry out a thorough analysis of frequently created objects. Unfortunately, this is quite a tedious task. To locate suspicious areas worth analysis, we can help ourselves by comparing heap snapshots taken by PerfView to identify the objects incurring the most memory traffic.

2. To investigate allocations made by a particular method:

- On By Name tab, select [No grouping] in GroupPats - to ungroup everything for more details.

500

- In Find type the name of your function - let it be
  HomeController.Contact.

- Click Goto ➤ Goto Item in Callees from the found item's context
  menu - you should see all allocations made by this method and
  all its callees (see Figure 6-24).

Methods that are called by CoreCLR.AspNetCore!CoreCLR.AspNetCore.Controllers.HomeController.Contact()

Name ?	Inc % ?	Inc ?	Inc Ct ?
☑CoreCLR.AspNetCore!CoreCLR.AspNetCore.Controllers.HomeController.Contact()	0.0	132.0	2
+☑system.private.corelib!System.Collections.Generic.Dictionary`2[System._Canon,System._Canon].set_Item(System._Canon, Sy	0.0	132.0	2
+☑system.private.corelib!System.Collections.Generic.Dictionary`2[System._Canon,System._Canon].TryInsert(System._Canon,	0.0	132.0	2
+☑system.private.corelib!System.Collections.Generic.Dictionary`2[System._Canon,System._Canon].Initialize(Int32)	0.0	132.0	2
+☑coreclr!JIT_NewArr1	0.0	132.0	2
+☐coreclr!AllocateArrayEx	0.0	96.0	1
+☐coreclr!??FastAllocatePrimitiveArray	0.0	36.0	1

Figure 6-24. *Allocations made by single method and all dependent method calls*

We can see that HomeController.Contact method allocates two arrays inside
System.Collections.Generic.Dictionary<>.Initialize method. Indeed Contact
method is trivial in our example as it only sets one item in ViewData dictionary (see
Listing 6-67). If we looked at Dictionary<TKey,TValue>.Initialize, we would see
that in fact it allocates two arrays - for buckets and entries. This is obviously only an
example of how detailed information we can get. During your investigations you will
be interested in allocations made by your code so it may be wise to group any other,
external modules.

Listing 6-67. HomeController.Contact method

```
public IActionResult Contact()
{
    ViewData["Message"] = "Your contact page.";
    return View();
}
```

Please note that in the case of Linux, diagnosis of allocations is not so easy and
pleasant. PerfView with its profiler will not help here. .NET Profiling API for Linux
is not so mature so there are no well-tested tools based on them. You can utilize
GCAllocationTick LTTng event to sample allocations - you will be able to get statistical
information about mostly allocated types of objects. Due to the LTTng mechanism you
will not get stack traces of the allocations in this way. They can be gotten by perf by

501

probing for the event-emitting function `EventXplatGCEnabledAllocationTick` inside libcoreclr.so. In that way, however, we achieve opposite - we may analyze stack traces but type information is missing. Currently there is no mechanism to join both pieces of that information together. There is also no good support for commercial programs at the moment for such diagnostics.

Scenario 6-3. Azure Functions

Description: Azure Functions are billed based on per-second resource consumption measured in Gigabyte-Seconds (GB-s) and number of executions. Functions pricing from Microsoft site says: "Memory used by a function is measured by rounding up to the nearest 128 MB, up to the maximum memory size of 1,536 MB, with execution time calculated by rounding up to the nearest 1 ms. The minimum execution time and memory for a single function execution is 100 ms and 128 MB respectively." It means each single function call will consume at least 0.0125 GB-s (100 ms times 128 MB which is 0.1 s times * 0.125 GB). Additionally, there is a free grant of 400,000 GB-s and 1 million of executions per month.

Taking such pricing into consideration, it seems clear that it is worth it to minimize memory usage as far as possible. If our Azure Function consumes memory inefficiently, we may exceed the free grant limit. We multiply the cost each time the memory usage exceeds another 128 MB. It is difficult currently to find a place in the .NET world where the use of memory so directly translates into the money spent by us.

Analysis: Azure through Application Insights provides a way of monitoring Azure Functions resource consumption. We can track their so-called Function Execution Units. They are measured in MB-ms (Megabyte-Milliseconds) currently so we need to scale them to get GB-s. By tracking Function Execution Units, we can monitor our costs, but unfortunately, they do not provide any deeper insight into functions memory usage. Thus, to analyze and optimize memory usage of our function, it is best to do it on development environment. Thanks to Azure Functions Core Tools, we can run Functions locally so the allocations investigation scenario would be as easy as in scenario 6-2. You only need to profile `func.exe` process (it is the name of Azure Function CLI executable hosting our functions).

> **Note**   If you would like to track the intensity of the allocation within your program, one of the simplest solutions is to use the `GC.GetAllocated BytesForCurrentThread` static method. In that way you get accurate information about how many bytes were allocated since the beginning of a current thread's lifetime.

Summary

This chapter covered in depth how objects are being created in .NET. We should be now fully aware that allocating an object may be really fast - but it may also trigger quite a complex logic of finding a place for it, including triggering Garbage Collector.

In the first part of the chapter, implementation details about allocator in .NET were presented. They reveal a big level of sophistication in making it as fast as possible. A lot of effort was made so that creating new objects was really fast so getting to know these details is very interesting and developing. It also allows us, in some respects, to look at how complicated is the topic in general and how well-implemented it is in .NET CLR.

The second part of this chapter is dominated by a practical review of one of the most important issues from the point of view of efficient memory management - avoiding allocation. Avoiding allocation is the obvious avoidance of its cost and the GC overhead. Therefore, one of the main performance optimizations in the .NET world is this topic. The presented list contains a rather extensive (though certainly not exhaustive) list of possible sources of allocation and (where possible) potential ways to avoid them.

The chapter also contains three example scenarios for solving problems related to the memory allocations. Besides the sections about avoiding allocations, they allow you to look at the topic of creating new objects from a more practical, diagnostic side.

Rule 14 - Avoid Allocations on the Heap in Performance Critical Code Paths

Justification: It is said - allocations are cheap in .NET. However, this chapter shows that it is not always entirely true. You should be aware of possible costs of allocations. Your performance context dictates whether they introduce significant cost or not.

Just remember that allocation means introducing possible memory traffic and communication with the operating system or triggering garbage collections. The more objects we allocate, the more work we put on GC. Thus, in very performance parts of code the best optimization solution is to avoid allocations.

How to apply: There are as many solutions how to avoid allocations as scenarios where allocations may happen. They have been thoroughly described in the section "Avoiding Allocations" in this chapter. Some allocations are explicit - we are fully aware of them. But still we may want to get rid of them by using object's pools or value types. Some allocations are hidden - various libraries and techniques may introduce them without our knowledge. To avoid them we obviously need to identify them. We may learn some of the most popular sources of hidden allocations so we will be able to quickly spot them in our code. Non-trivial ones should be traced via diagnostic tools.

Related scenarios: Scenarios 6-2, 6-3.

Rule 15 - Avoid Excessive LOH Allocations

Justification: While allocations are not always cheap in .NET, allocation of objects in Large Object Heap is even more often not cheap. Assumption that allocations in LOH are infrequent and the fact that they are big drives design decision to not preallocate space for them in advance. Thus, allocation of object in LOH may be dominated by the cost of zeroing its memory. If we are using really big objects frequently, it may be a good idea to manage some pool of reusable objects. It will introduce more stable memory usage and not only help with the allocation costs but also will relieve a little GC in its work.

How to apply: If we allocate big objects frequently, it is probably not possible to take a trivial optimization of not doing this at all. Using value types for this purpose is also rather not possible because of the stack space limits. The best solution here is to use one of the pooling mechanisms - see relevant parts of the "Avoiding Allocations" section in this chapter.

Rule 16 - Promote Allocations on the Stack When Appropriate

Justification: Classes are the fundamental data types in .NET. When we learn C#, classes accompany us from the very beginning. When we think - data structure - we immediately think - class. It is our default decision during development to create and use classes. On the other hand, structs are usually only some exotic thingy about which we learn at the beginning and then forget. They seem strange and incomprehensible to us. However, this does not have to be because they can provide really valuable features - like better memory locality, avoiding heap allocations at all, and great possible optimizations taken by the compiler and JIT.

How to apply: We should just learn about structs a little and try to add them to our everyday toolbox. When implementing a new feature, does our method need to utilize a class or maybe a simple structure will be just fine? Do we need a collection of objects? Maybe a small array of structures will be enough? Do not be afraid of struct copying - utilize more and more powerful C# possibilities to pass them by reference in various ways. Obviously, do not overengineer simple things. Do that only in a performance-driven parts of your code, executed often, and with a great impact on the perceived performance or resource utilization.

CHAPTER 7

Garbage Collection - Introduction

Welcome to the most important part of this book. Previous chapters have described quite broadly the subject of memory management. We have experienced some theoretical and hardware introduction. We also got to know a lot of details about the organization of memory in the .NET environment - how it is divided into segments and generations and how all this infrastructure works with the operating system. Much of this knowledge is valuable in itself, allowing us, for example, to diagnose problems with too many allocations or how to use different methods to avoid them.

However, it cannot be denied that when it comes to memory management, the .NET world is inherently related to its automatic memory reclamation. We have learned already about Allocator so we know how objects are being created. Now it's high time we learned how and when objects are being deleted and memory reclaimed after them, when no longer needed.

This and the following three chapters constitute a long story about how GC works in .NET. It has been split into four chapters to not overwhelm the reader with all that knowledge given at once. However, all four are inherently related to each other and to gain comprehensive knowledge should all be read.

Moreover, those chapters are based on knowledge from previous chapters. Therefore, if you do not read the book one by one, I still strongly recommend at least skimming previous chapters before reading this one (especially Chapters 5 and 6).

In this chapter we will find out in which situations GC can take place. We will find out exactly what stages are executed and delve into details of first steps. All this will be provided with comments and examples that allow you, besides the satisfaction of having such knowledge, to apply it also in practice.

© Konrad Kokosa 2018
K. Kokosa, *Pro .NET Memory Management*, https://doi.org/10.1007/978-1-4842-4027-4_7

High-Level View

Before going further, it is good to gain a 10,000-foot view of Garbage Collector implemented in Microsoft .NET runtime. The most important is the fact already mentioned in previous chapters: GC can operate in two main modes of operation:

- *Workstation* - it is designed to minimize delays introduced by the GC as seen from the managed threads perspective. In general, it can be summarized by a strategy that GC will happen more frequently so it will have less work to do, so perceived pauses will be shorter. This mode is especially useful for a desktop application where perceived latency is important for user experience - we would not like to freeze the whole application because a long-running GC happened.

- *Server* - it is designed to maximize application throughput. The strategy is that GC will be executed less frequently so it introduces longer pauses when it eventually happens. This also means that memory consumption will be higher - GC will allow memory to grow to higher values by rare collections. However, pauses and memory usage are not so important in favor of statistical resulting throughput - how many data were processed in a given amount of time.

There are important design differences between Workstation and Server GC modes. One of the most important ones is how many Managed Heaps exist. As mentioned in Chapter 5, in Workstation mode there is only a single Managed Heap while in Server mode, there may be many logical cores on the machine.

Additionally, each of the above modes may work in one of the sub-modes:

- *Non-concurrent* - in this mode GC is executed while all managed threads of our application are suspended.

- *Concurrent* - in this mode some parts of the GC are done while managed threads are working.

These two types of work modes give a total of four options of how GC can be configured in our application. Those combinations are described in detail in Chapter 11, altogether with the discussion when and where using each of them is most appropriate. For the simplicity of learning, in Chapters 7 to 10 only the simplest case is discussed - Non-concurrent Workstation mode. This allows us to understand the vast majority of GC aspects without going into cluttering details. In fact, other modes differ only in details so knowledge from this and the following three chapters is perfectly valid for all the others.

It is also worth recalling an important fact about the behavior of two areas of the Managed Heap:

- Small Object Heap may use Sweep or Compact collection - it's mainly an autonomous GC decision. We may ask the GC to select one if we wish to call GC manually.

- Large Object Heap uses only Sweep Collection by default - but we may ask for a single Compacting collection explicitly.

Hereinafter various CoreCLR source code internals will be presented for those who wish to investigate described topics on their own. When garbage collection starts in CoreCLR, several flags are representing selected options. One of the most important is `collection_mode` enumeration, which may have the following flags set:

- `collection_non_blocking` - non-blocking (concurrent) GC

- `collection_blocking` - blocking ("stop the world") GC

- `collection_optimized` - will proceed with GC only if it is needed (so-called *allocation budget* of specified generation is running out)

- `collection_compacting` - collection with Small Object Heap compaction

- `collection_gcstress` - internal CLR's stress testing mode

All those manual tunings and variations will be described later; let's now concentrate on the simplest Non-concurrent Workstation GC in detail.

GC Process in Example

I think it is at this point worth it to explicitly denounce certain facts that have so far been mentioned here and there. This will allow us to visualize a high-level view of the GC activity.

First of all, garbage collection happens in the context of a specific generation - which is commonly referred to as the *condemned generation*. A whole-generational GC technique benefits from the fact that we may decide to collect objects just from a single generation. As explained in Chapter 5, the decision was made to collect also all generations younger than the currently condemned generation. Additionally, objects in Large Object Heap are treated as being in generation 2. This leads to the following possible scenarios:

- generation 0 is condemned - only generation 0 is being collected,

- generation 1 is condemned - only generations 0 and 1 are being, collected,

- generation 2 is condemned - all three generations 0, 1, and 2 plus Large Object Heap are being collected. Such a situation is commonly named a *Full Garbage Collection* (hereinafter most of the time it will be referred to as the *full-GC*).

During its work the GC will check the reachability of objects (by marking) only in condemned and younger generations. Knowing this, each time GC has to decide whether it wants to carry out Sweep or Compact collection.

Let's now visualize all those possible cases in an illustration similar to Figure 5-5 from Chapter 5. Please, take some time to thoroughly understand the described example scenarios because they really form the very core of how GC works in .NET.

First of all, let's imagine an example situation that at some point in time .NET memory in our program looks as in Figure 7-1. Based on the knowledge from Chapter 5, we can recognize such typical layout - there is a single block of memory that contains SOH (ephemeral) and LOH segments. The SOH segment is further divided into generations 0, 1, and 2. All generations contain some objects and boundaries of generations have also been marked.

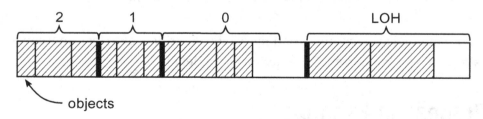

Figure 7-1. *Initial memory state used in the three following figures. Objects have been marked by dashed filling. Generation 0 has some free space at the end. SOH segment as well is not fully consumed by generations.*

Let's now consider an example when generation 0 is condemned (see Figure 7-2). In such case, Mark phase will only analyze reachability of objects in generation 0. Let's suppose only one object in generation 0 has been marked as reachable (see Figure 7-2a; marked objects are filled by dark gray). Now the GC must decide which collection technique to choose:

- Sweep Collection (see Figure 7-2b) - in such case all unreachable objects from generation 0 are considered as free space. Generation 1 boundary has been moved accordingly to contain promoted, reachable object (our single marked object has been promoted to generation 1). As is often the case with the Sweep Collection, note that this significantly increased fragmentation in generation 1 - there is now a large hole of the empty space in it.[1]

- Compact Collection (see Figure 7-2c) - in such case reachable objects in generation 0 are compacted and included by accordingly grown generation 1. There is no fragmentation obviously but the whole operation is more complex (requiring memory copying and updating references to moved objects).

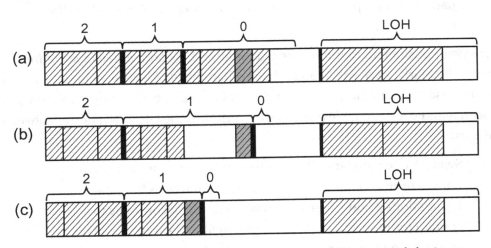

Figure 7-2. *Garbage Collection with generation 0 condemned –(a) objects marked as reachable, (b) Sweep Collection, (c) Compact Collection*

---

[1]As we know from a previous chapter, this free space is not unusable - it is being managed by a free-list allocator. But for generations 0 and 1 free-list items are checked only once and then discarded so this free space may quite fast become unusable; however, keep in mind gen0/1 collections also happen quite often so they get rebuilt often.

To summarize, after garbage collection with generation 0 being condemned:

- Only objects in generation 0 have been checked for reachability (marked).

- Generation 0 has become empty (with only really small space intentionally left) - this is the default behavior. All objects from the youngest generation are either collected or promoted to an older generation. As we will see later in this chapter, some exceptions may occur. For now, however, let's assume this simplest scenario.

- Reachable objects from generation 0 have been promoted to generation 1.

- Generation 1 has grown - both in case of Sweep (larger growth because of fragmentation) and Compact (smaller growth).

- Generation 2 and LOH have not changed. It was however analyzed to mark what they point to in generation 0 (using card tables described in Chapter 5).

Let's now consider an example when generation 1 is condemned (see Figure 7-3). In such case, the Mark phase will analyze the reachability of objects in generations 0 and 1. Again, suppose the same single object in generation 0 and two additional in generation 1 have been marked as reachable (see Figure 7-3a). Now the GC must choose between two techniques:

- Sweep Collection (see Figure 7-3b) - in such case all unreachable objects from generations 0 and 1 are considered as free space. Generations 2 and 1 boundaries were moved accordingly to contain promoted reachable objects. Again, this introduced big fragmentation (in our case in generation 1, but generation 2 could become fragmented too).

- Compact Collection (see Figure 7-3c) - in such case reachable objects in generations 0 and 1 are compacted and included by accordingly changed boundaries of generations 2 and 1.

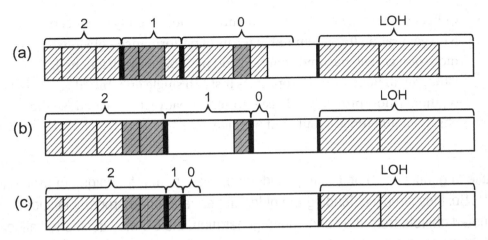

Figure 7-3. *Garbage Collection with generation 1 condemned -(a) objects marked as reachable, (b) Sweep Collection, (c) Compact Collection*

To summarize, after garbage collection with generation 1 being condemned:

- Only objects in generations 0 and 1 have been checked for reachability (marked).

- Generation 0 has become empty.

- Reachable objects from generation 0 have been promoted to generation 1.

- Reachable objects from generation 1 have been promoted to generation 2.

- Generation 1 may grow or shrink - depending on which collection technique has been chosen. This is interesting as theoretically generation 1 may grow when... generation 1 is being collected. This is of course due to fragmentation so GC is unlikely to decide to use Sweep in our example scenario. But still, this is theoretically and technically possible.

- Generation 2 has grown.

- LOH has not changed but it has been analyzed to mark what they point to in generations 0 and 1 (as well as generation 2).

- Collection with generation 1 condemned differs slightly to collection with generation 0 condemned in terms of performance - obviously more objects will become analyzed and possibly moved/touched. However, in both cases GC operates inside a single ephemeral segment (most probably at least partially already CPU-cached) so the observed difference should not be huge.

In case of generation 0 or 1 being condemned, yet another technique of promotion exists. Besides simply extending the older one generation to properly include promoted objects from the condemned generation, the GC may decide to "allocate them in the older generation" by using free space (managed by free list) in the older generation. This allows us to make use of fragmentation (reducing it at the same time) instead of blindly extending the generation region.

In case of an example similar to Figure 7-3, one of the objects could be allocated in the available free space:

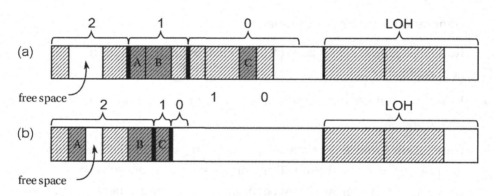

This technique obviously makes sense only in case of a compacting GC. In case of sweep collection, objects are not being moved so there is no possibility to place them into existing free space.

Let's now consider a last example, when generation 2 is condemned (see Figure 7-4). Such Full Collection incurs analyzing many more objects than the two previous ones. This is why care should be taken to not introduce too many unnecessary Full Collections as we will discuss later. In case of Full Collections, the Mark phase will analyze the whole Managed Heap - generations 0, 1, 2, and LOH. Certain objects have been marked for the example (see Figure 7-4a). The GC must choose now between two techniques:

- Sweep Collection (see Figure 7-4b) - all unreachable objects from all generations (including LOH) are considered as free space. All generation boundaries have been moved accordingly. Please note we introduced quite large fragmentation in generation 2, generation 1, and LOH.

- Compact Collection (see Figure 7-4c) - all objects inside SOH have been compacted (remember that LOH is not being compacted automatically). This is an optimal solution in terms of memory usage but obviously required the most work of copying many objects.

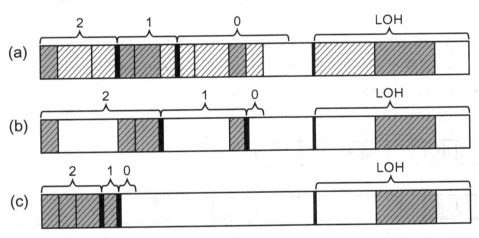

Figure 7-4. *Garbage Collection with generation 2 condemned (aka Full Collection) – (a) objects marked as reachable, (b) Sweep Collection, (c) Compact Collection*

To summarize, after garbage collection with generation 2 being condemned (aka Full-GC):

- All objects' reachability have been checked from all generations and the LOH.

- Generation 0 has become empty.

- Reachable objects from generation 0 and 1 have been promoted to generation 1 and 2 accordingly.

- Reachable objects in generation 2 stayed in generation 2.

- LOH has been also collected without compacting - we've introduced fragmentation, but this free space would be reused by free-list LOH's allocator.

A careful reader may notice that after each GC with generation 1 or 2 being condemned, generation 2 may grow inside our segment (if there are many long-living, non-reclaimable objects). Eventually there may be a moment when it is so big that generations 0 or 1 do not have enough room (see Figure 7-5a). In such case a simple Sweep or Compact collection is probably not enough. GC most probably will decide to use the Compact method with the following steps (see Figure 7-5b):

- Current ephemeral segments are changed into gen2-only segments - all reachable objects from generations 1 and 2 are being compacted there.

- A new ephemeral segment is created - all reachable objects from generation 0 are being compacted there (as generation 1 objects).

- LOH is treated with the Sweep collection as usual.

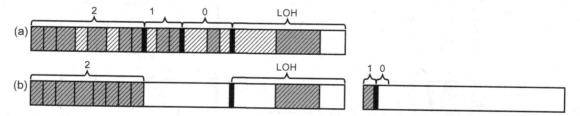

Figure 7-5. *Garbage Collection with generation 2 condemned (aka Full Collection) with big generation 2 - (a) objects marked as reachable, (b) Compact Collection with a new ephemeral segment created*

In this way generation 2 may grow "endlessly." If the same situation repeats in a new ephemeral segment, it will be turned into a gen2-only segment and three different scenarios may happen:

- A new ephemeral segment may be created by committing and reserving memory for a new segment - as in the case just described and illustrated in Figure 7-5.

- A new ephemeral segment may be created from the segment on the segment's standby list if any segments are on that list - we have seen a situation of building a segments standby list in Figure 5-22 (in Chapter 5) where segments' reusage was discussed. This requires VM hoarding to be enabled, which is not always the case.

- An already existing gen2-only segment with small gen2 may be reused as a new ephemeral segment (see Figure 7-6) - in this way even when VM hoarding is not enabled, a new segment does not need to be created. The old ephemeral segment will become s gen2-only segment in such s situation.

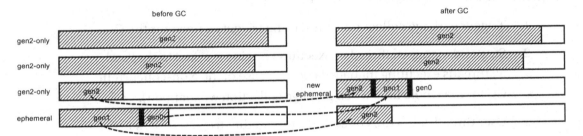

Figure 7-6. *Garbage Collection with generation 2 condemned (aka Full Collection) - Compact Collection with gen2-only segment reused as a new ephemeral segment*

Please note that turning the current ephemeral segment into a gen2-only segment (and making a new ephemeral segment by reusing some existing one or creating a completely new one) may be caused by extensive pinning - a lot of pinned objects living in ephemeral segments may make it hard to use (i.e., by fragmentation-hindering creation of allocation contexts) so the whole segment will be promoted to gen2. This is perfectly fine from the pinning requirements perspective, as addresses of pinned objects are not changed by that - only logically such region starts to represent generation 2.

It is worth reemphasizing this multiple times. A Full-GC includes marking all objects through all generations and LOH. They might span multiple segments and if a large amount of memory survives, this may be very costly. Moreover, during this process a gen2 segment may be reused or a new segment may be created. Thus, Full-GC performance overhead may be much, much bigger compared to the GC with generation 0 or 1 condemned that included operating only on a single, ephemeral segment most probably cached at some parts inside the CPU. Thus, the overhead difference between Full-GC and ephemeral GC (with generations 0 or 1 condemned) may be of orders of magnitude. A full-GC should be avoided as much as possible!

GC Process Steps

After the general introduction of what the effects of Garbage Collector work look like, let's look at what steps make up this process. From a high-level point of view, we can distinguish the following steps related to the GC work:

1. Trigger garbage collection - something triggers a need for the GC.

2. Suspend managed threads - Execution Engine is asked to suspend all threads executing managed code (in case of the Non-concurrent GC for the whole time when garbage collection will happen).

3. User thread starts the GC code - a thread that triggered GC starts to execute the Garbage Collector code.

4. Select generation to condemn - as the first step, the GC decides which generation should be condemned based on the various conditions.

5. Mark - the marking of reachable objects in the condemned and its younger generations are carried out.

6. Plan - the GC decides whether compacting is worth doing or maybe sweeping is just enough. Although this may not seem so at first glance, this step contains most of the calculations that are needed to complete the entire GC.

7. Sweep or compact - after a decision has been made, either a Sweep or Compact technique is used with the help of information gathered during Plan phase. If compaction was chosen, an additional relocate phase must be executed before, to update all addresses to the new ones.

8. Resume managed threads - Execution Engine is asked to resume all threads executing managed code.

Because mentioned GC steps really make up all the work it does, the rest of this chapter and Chapters 8 to 10 describe each of them thoroughly. You can treat them as a map that will carry us up to the end of them.

During those steps various diagnostic data are emitted immediately and some collected and emitted at the end of the process - using the well-known mechanisms of Performance Counters and ETW/LLTng events. Some of the data is available internally by SOS commands so we need to use WinDbg to access them. We will utilize those data and SOS commands in various scenarios in this chapter.

Scenario 7-1. Analyzing the GC Usage

Description: We want to observe usage of the GC during web application execution. We would like to do it in a non-invasive way during load tests performed on our pre-production environment. The application under test is plain nopCommerce 4.0 installation - a universal open source e-commerce platform written in ASP.NET Core - this is a continuation of scenario 5-1 from Chapter 5.

Analysis: Let's skip the technical part of the load test preparation, assuming that the appropriate procedures and tools are just in place. The load test was prepared and executed with the JMeter tool. It executes around 7 requests per second with a simple scenario (visiting home page, single product page, and single tag page). It is exactly the same JMeter test as used in scenario 5-1. However, this time only a 2-minute long analysis will be performed to quickly recognize the GC utilization. Self-hosted .NET web application will be monitored (process is named Nop.Web.exe).

First of all, we may wish to check the overall .NET memory and the GC usage of the application. This includes observing the following performance counters:

- \.NET CLR Memory(Nop.Web)\Gen 0 heap size (which actually is generation 0 allocation budget as explained in previous chapters)

- \.NET CLR Memory(Nop.Web)\Gen 1 heap size

- \.NET CLR Memory(Nop.Web)\Gen 2 heap size

- \.NET CLR Memory(Nop.Web)\Large Object Heap size

- \.NET CLR Memory(Nop.Web)\% Time in GC

The results of the first two minutes of the application run are shown in Figures 7-7 and 7-8. We can see quite stable generation sizes - the ephemeral ones are changing rapidly but not growing in time. The oldest one has stabilized at the value of 89,520,308 bytes. However, % time spent in GC is alarming. An average value of around 24% (clearly visible in Figure 7-8) means one-fourth of the process time is spent on garbage collection. This starts to be a significant overhead.

We can continue further analysis of this situation by analyzing ETW events in the PerfView. By selecting GC Collect Only option in the Collect dialog during our load test, GC keyword events from Microsoft-Windows-DotNETRuntime providers will be registered. After collection stops and processing ends, we will be able to investigate the GC usage thanks to the GCStats report available in the Memory Group folder.

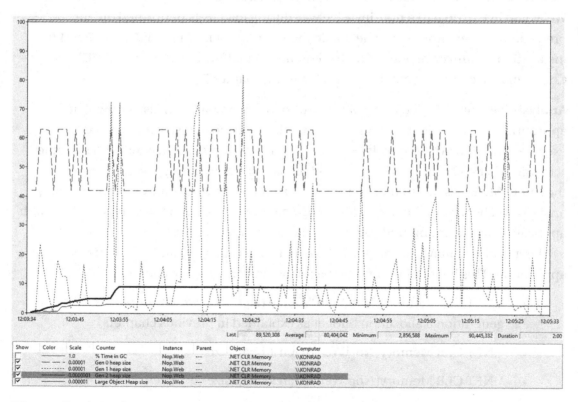

Figure 7-7. *Performance Monitor view of generation sizes during near 2-minute-long load test of ASP.NET Core application*

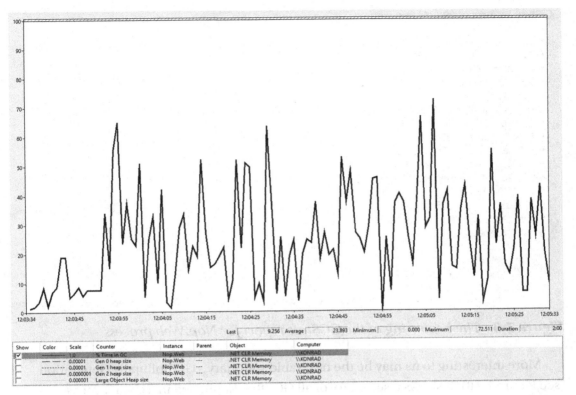

Figure 7-8. *Performance Monitor view of the GC utilization during near 2-minute- long load test of ASP.NET Core application*

GCStats report shows a comprehensive summary of GC-related events for all .NET runtime providers during session recording. At the beginning of the report all such providers are listed so we select Nop.Web process. At the beginning of such report, various diagnostic data are presented (see Figure 7-9). For example, CLR Startup Flags listed as None means used GC was a simple non-concurrent workstation GC.

GC Stats for Process 8724: nop.web

- CommandLine: F:\IIS\nopCommerce\Nop.Web.exe
- Runtime Version: V 4.0.30319.0
- CLR Startup Flags: None
- Total CPU Time: 0 msec
- Total GC CPU Time: 0 msec
- Total Allocs : 14,483.212 MB
- GC CPU MSec/MB Alloc : 0.000 MSec/MB
- Total GC Pause: 12,350.2 msec
- % Time paused for Garbage Collection: 10.2%
- % CPU Time spent Garbage Collecting: NaN%
- Max GC Heap Size: 86.492 MB
- GC Perf Users Guide
- GCs that > 200 msec Events
- LOH allocation pause (due to background GC) > 200 msec Events
- GCs that were Gen2
- Individual GC Events
    - View in Excel
- Per Generation GC Events in Excel
- Raw Data XML file (for debugging)
- *No finalized object counts available. No objects were finalized and/or the trace did not include the necessary information.*

Figure 7-9. *The beginning of the GCStats report for Nop.Web process*

More interesting to us may be the next table summary - GC Rollup by Generation (see Figure 7-10). It shows a summary of all GCs that happened in a given process duringww an ETW session time lasting 2 minutes. As we can see, there were a total of 3,016 garbage collections during that time (which makes about 25 GCs per second). Total pause time caused by GCs is over 12 seconds. For a 2minute-long test this makes around 10% of the time spent in the GC, while typical usage should not exceed a few percent at maximum. Please also note significantly slower gen2 GCs compared to the lower ones (Mean Pause column in Figure 7-10).

GC Rollup By Generation									
All times are in msec.									
Gen	Count	Max Pause	Max Peak MB	Max Alloc MB/sec	Total Pause	Total Alloc MB	Alloc MB/ MSec GC	Survived MB/ MSec GC	Mean Pause	Induced
ALL	3016	91.4	86.5	3,100.147	12,350.2	14,483.2	1.2	∞	4.1	0
0	1932	13.0	78.5	3,033.417	5,087.4	8,248.1	0.4	∞	2.6	0
1	1059	22.2	86.5	3,100.147	5,147.7	6,083.1	0.4	∞	4.9	0
2	25	91.4	84.2	2,264.039	2,115.1	152.0	0.1	∞	84.6	0

Figure 7-10. *GC Rollup by Generation table from the GCStats report for Nop.Web process*

What we can pay attention to is a very large number of indicated allocations. There is a total of over 12 GB of objects allocated! While, as we have seen in Figure 7-7, generation sizes remain quite stable, this obviously indicates allocating a huge amount of short-living, temporary data that fast becomes garbage.

Further analysis can be done with the help of great GC Events by a Time table from the same GCStats report (see Figure 7-11). It lists all GCs during the recorded session with various, extremely useful data. In case of a long session, the table is truncated (as in the figure presented), but you can always get the raw CSV data and see it, for example, in Excel.

GC Index	Pause Start	Trigger Reason	Gen	Suspend Msec	Pause MSec	% Pause Time	% GC	Gen0 Alloc MB	Gen0 Alloc Rate MB/sec	Peak MB	After MB	Ratio Peak/After	Promoted MB	Gen0 MB	Gen0 Survival Rate %	Gen0 Frag %	Gen1 MB	Gen1 Survival Rate %	Gen1 Frag %	Gen2 MB	Gen2 Survival Rate %	Gen2 Frag %	LOH MB	LOH Survival Rate %	LOH Frag %	Finalizable Surv MB	Pinned Obj
										2016 Beginning entries truncated, use View in Excel to view all...																	
2184	83,609.139	AllocSmall	1N	0.001	5.867	58.3	NaN	4.147	714.17	70.040	70.182	1.00	0.439	12.961	7	99.22	0.209	58	0.00	53.857	NaN	0.01	3.155	NaN	4.70	0.01	15
2185	83,645.298	AllocSmall	1N	0.012	4.875	13.9	NaN	4.155	136.47	70.182	70.312	1.00	0.503	12.897	8	99.20	0.273	62	0.00	53.987	NaN	0.01	3.155	NaN	4.70	0.02	16
2186	83,720.348	AllocSmall	1N	0.009	4.851	6.5	NaN	4.153	59.18	70.312	70.530	1.00	0.572	12.928	8	99.11	0.242	79	0.00	54.206	NaN	0.01	3.155	NaN	4.70	0.02	16
2187	83,733.031	AllocSmall	1N	0.004	4.631	37.1	NaN	4.148	529.28	70.530	61.478	1.15	0.878	3.277	16	98.71	0.682	65	0.00	54.364	NaN	0.01	3.155	NaN	4.70	0.00	12
2188	83,741.551	AllocSmall	0N	0.065	5.152	56.9	NaN	4.105	1,053.78	62.451	61.478	1.02	0.691	2.596	16	99.46	1.363	NaN	0.00	54.364	NaN	0.00	3.155	NaN	0.00	0.00	4
2189	83,751.447	AllocSmall	1N	0.126	8.001	62.7	NaN	8.214	1,728.88	67.284	59.627	1.13	2.095	0.000	11	0.00	0.921	86	0.00	55.551	NaN	0.01	3.155	NaN	4.70	0.00	0

Figure 7-11. GC Events by Time table from GCStats report for Nop.Web process

In the presented table fragment (as from the entire table, not presented here for obvious reasons), we can see some interesting facts:

- All GCs were triggered because of AllocSmall reason - that means GCs were triggered due to SOH allocation.

- Many GCs were triggered in a single second (see changes in Pause Start column) and allocations are quite big (see Gen0 Alloc MB column) - this confirms our suspicions stated before about allocating a lot.

At this stage we should investigate what is being allocated so often like in scenario 6-2 from Chapter 6.

We will come back to different columns from GC Events by Time table in this chapter in further scenarios. With the subsequent sections of this chapter, an increasing part of the GCStats report will became understandable. Ultimately, it should allow you to read it with full understanding.

Please note interesting information in the Gen column, which describes not only condemned generation but also the type of the GC:

- N - non-concurrent GC (blocking)

- B - Background GC

- F - Foreground GC (blocking collection of an ephemeral generations during Background GC)

- I - induced (manually triggered) blocking GC

- i - induced non-blocking GC

Profiling the GC

To roughly imagine the relative cost between these individual steps, look at Figure 7-12 with profiling data gathered, thanks to the ETW CPU profiling during a simple load test (the other one that presented in above scenario). Inc column shows a total time (in milliseconds) spent in each listed method (and all its callees). The application under the test was using Workstation GC. During the test, 627 garbage collections occurred (as noted from ETW report not shown here) that gives us an average pause time of 4.33 milliseconds per GC.

Methods that are called by clr!WKS::gc_heap::garbage_collect

Name ?	Inc % ?	Inc ?	Exc % ?	Exc ?
☑ clr!WKS::gc_heap::garbage_collect	6.1	2,717.8	0.0	0
+ ☑ clr!WKS::gc_heap::gc1	6.0	2,700.8	0.0	0
I + ☑ clr!WKS::gc_heap::plan_phase	3.1	1,408.8	0.6	282
I I + ☐ clr!WKS::gc_heap::relocate_phase	1.9	864.6	0.0	0
I I + ☐ clr!WKS::gc_heap::compact_phase	0.3	143.8	0.0	2
I + ☐ clr!WKS::gc_heap::mark_phase	2.9	1,276.4	0.0	0

Figure 7-12. Profiling data for the GC phases taken for an application with Workstation GC

The mark and plan steps have a relatively similar cost. The plan phase, due to the GC code structure, contains both compact and relocate phases. It may be surprising that relocation (updating addresses) takes more time than compaction itself (moving objects).

Do not pay too much attention to those numbers though. They can vary significantly depending on various conditions like ratio of survived objects, number of references between objects, or number of objects in total. If you are really interested, investigate them on your own, for your own specific scenario. This is as simple as using PerfView for the following two, simple steps:

- Collecting ETW session with CPU profiling enabled - by enabling CPU Samples option. You may also wish to change the sampling interval in CPU Sample Interval MSec from 1 to a lower value to get more precise results.

- Analyzing collected data from CPU Stacks view - you will most probably need to carry out the following simple changes (again clear all GroupPats and Folding):

    - locate `clr?!` or `coreclr?!` row (in case of full .NET or .NET Core respectively) and issue Lookup Symbols command on them.

    - find `garbage_collect` method and start investigation by issuing Goto Item in Callees command.

You can think about a few questions related to the nature of the GC activities - particularly, how the following conditions influence the overall GC cost (in terms of CPU usage and processing time):

- Big number of objects in general - the more objects, the more work the Plan phase has to do. It consists of scanning the whole Managed Heap object by object so it is natural that a large number of objects will affect the longer execution time of the Plan phase. The advantage is, however, strictly linear access to memory (object after object), so the overall cost is mitigated by cache mechanisms.

- Big number of survived objects - the more live objects, the more work the Mark phase has to do. It induces a lot of Managed Heap traversing, in unstructured (not especially cacheable) way. This overhead will be higher the more references between objects exist. Additionally, a big number of live objects, if the Compact phase is executed, means a lot of memory traffic and a costly need of updating many references. Plan phase is less sensitive to the number of live objects - it operates on "plugs" (explained thoroughly later in Chapter 9) of many live objects so the cost is alleviated.

The applications are simple and rather intuitive - the fewer objects we create the better. For example, it is better to create one large array in LOH and reuse its fragments (e.g., by using Span<T>) than create many smaller arrays.

Garbage Collection Performance Tuning Data

Before we start the journey through the subsequent stages of GC work, it is worth paying attention to the data that it manages. We often may hear about various "heuristics" or "internal tunings" used by GC for its internal work. This is exactly what we will look at in this section.

Data managed by GC may be split into two main groups: static and dynamic data. Both play very important roles in what and how GC is doing. Describing them in too much detail is not particularly sensible because they are a deeply hidden implementation detail. It is not guaranteed in any way that these data with such values will not be changed in subsequent versions of the framework.

On the other hand, those data are so important and so strongly affect the way GC operates, that it is impossible to omit them completely in the description of the entire process. It is also difficult to expect major changes in the functioning of at least the most important indicators in the near future. And we will focus on them in this section.

Static Data

Static data represents a configuration that is set at the beginning of the runtime start and it never changes later. It contains the following attributes for each generation:

- minimum size - minimum so-called allocation budget (a term explained thoroughly just a few paragraphs later),

- maximum size - maximum allocation budget,

- fragmentation limit and fragmentation ratio limit - used when deciding whether we should compact,

- limit and max limit - used to calculate growth of the generation allocation budget,

- time limit - time after which to collect generation (in some scenarios),

- time_clock - time after which to collect generation, in performance counts (see QueryPerformanceCounter),

- gc_clock - number of GCs after which to collect generation.

In case of CoreCLR, static data described here is represented by `static_data` struct defined in `.\src\gc\gcpriv.h` file. A static table `static_data_table` is then initialized in `.\src\gc\gc.cpp` file for two different latency modes. Some of the values are calculated at the runtime start in the `gc_heap::init_static_data` method.

Static data are tuned in respect to the GC latency level configuration (discussed in Chapter 11). Currently there are two modes that with respect to the static data differ mainly in terms of generation sizes:

- *balanced* - pauses are more predictable and more frequent, optimized for a balance between latency and memory footprint. This is a default setting.

- *memory footprint* - optimized for minimum memory footprint; pauses can be long and more frequent.

Static data values for both latency modes are presented in Tables 7-1 and 7-2 (with the assumption of running on a computer with 8 MB L3 cache). We can find interesting information there, for example:

- Generation 0 minimum allocation budget is strictly related to the CPU cache size - if we remember from Chapter 2 the importance of CPU cache utilization, this makes perfect sense. These settings ensure that the most commonly used generation 0 will consume a reasonable part of the CPU cache.

- Both ephemeral generations maximum allocation budgets are strictly related to the ephemeral segment size - if we remember physical memory organization from Chapter 5, this also makes perfect sense. These settings are especially important in Workstation and 32-bit Server mode because segments there are relatively small (refer to Table 5-3).

- Maximum allocation budget of generation 2 and Large Object Heap are limited only by the maximum address limit (SSIZE_T_MAX is half the size of word) - this also makes a perfect sense as all long-living objects are gathering in those two. Such space must be logically "unlimited" to handle any memory usage scenario. Obviously, those sizes are limited by physical resources (RAM and paging files, addressing limits).

Table 7-1. *Static GC Data - "Balanced" Mode (Assuming 8 MB LLC Cache)*

	Min alloc budget	max alloc budget	fragmentation limit	fragmentation burdenlimit	limit	max_ limit	time_ clock	gc_ clock
Gen0	1) 4/15 MB	2) 6-200 MB	40000	0.5	9.0	20.0	1,000 ms	1
Gen1	160 kB	3) at least 6 MB	80000	0.5	2.0	7.0	10,000 ms	10
Gen2	256 kB	SSIZE_T_ MAX	200000	0.25	1.2	1.8	100,000 ms	100
LOH	3MB	SSIZE_T_ MAX	0	0.0	1.25	4.5	0 ms	0

Table 7-2. *Static GC data - "Memory Footprint" Mode (Assuming 8 MB LLC Cache)*

	Min alloc budget	max alloc budget	fragmentation limit	fragmentation burdenlimit	limit	max_limit	time_ clock	gc_ clock
Gen0	1) 4/15 MB	2) 6-200 MB	40000	0.5	4) 9.0/20.0	4) 20.0/40.0	1,000 ms	1
Gen1	288 kB	3) at least 6 MB	80000	0.5	2.0	7.0	10,000 ms	10
Gen2	256 kB	SSIZE_T_ MAX	200000	0.25	1.2	1.8	100,000 ms	100
LOH	3MB	SSIZE_T_ MAX	0	0.0	1.25	4.5	0 ms	0

1. Minimum allocation budget is related to the CPU cache size (here assuming 8 MB), differently calculated for different chips (done by the hardware vendors). In general, a little smaller in case of Workstation mode (first number) than in Server mode (second number).

2. For Workstation GC with Concurrent version - 6 MB. For Server GC and Workstation GC with Non-concurrent version - half of the ephemeral segment size (refer to Table 5-3) but not less than 6 MB and no more than 200 MB.

3. For Workstation GC with Concurrent version - 6 MB. For Server GC and Workstation GC with Non-concurrent version - half of the ephemeral segment size (refer to Table 5-3) but not less than 6 MB.

4. Values for Workstation and Server GC respectively.

Those various limits, especially the minimum and maximum size of each generation, will be explained later in the chapter.

Garbage Collector during its work uses those data to make various decisions. We will return to them occasionally henceforth.

Dynamic Data

Dynamic data are representing the current state of the Managed Heap from a generation's perspective. They are updated during GCs to calculate data required for various decisions (including whether it should be compacting GC or not, whether generation is "full" and GC should be triggered, and so on, and so forth). Dynamic data contains a number of different attributes for each generation, the most important of which are:

- *allocation budget* (also referred to as "*desired allocation*") - the size the GC would like to spend on new allocations until the next GC,

- *new allocation* - the size of how much space is left for allocations until the next GC under the current allocation budget,

- *fragmentation* - total size consumed by free objects in that generation,

- *survived size* - total size taken by survived objects,

- *survived pinned size* - total size taken by survived pinned plugs (described in detail later in this chapter),

- *survived rate* - the ratio of the number of survived bytes divided by the total bytes,

- *current size* - total size of all objects after the GC happens (it doesn't include memory due to fragmentation),

- *GC "clock"* - the number of GCs that collected this generation,

- *time "clock"* - the time when the last GC collecting this generation started.

The *new allocation* attribute is essential for Allocator and the GC cooperation. It tracks how many allocations inside a generation have been made relative to its allocation budget - if it becomes negative, it means that the allocation budget has been exceeded and garbage collection will be triggered for that generation

This leads us to one of the most important attributes - the *allocation budget*. It represents a total size the GC would like to allow to be spent on allocations in a particular generation. As we remember from Chapter 6, user-code triggered allocations happen only in the generations 0 and LOH. However, the allocation budget is tracked for each generation. This apparent inconsistency is easy to explain if we realize that the promotion of objects between generations is regarded as their allocation in the older generation. As we will see in the Plan phase description, the GC uses internal allocator to find "places" for promoted objects (and we will also see that this sentence is a simplification used for brevity here). Both types of allocations consume the allocation budget.

The allocation budget is changed dynamically on each GC that collects that generation. Its new value is mostly based on the survival rate of that generation. If the survival rate is high (a lot of objects survived GC), the allocation budget is more aggressively increased with the expectation that there will be a better ratio of dead to live objects next time there is a GC for that generation. At the end of the GC it is recalculated on the basis of survival rate- the size of the survived object in respect to the total object size at GC beginning (i.e., not including fragmentation). Above a certain ratio threshold, the new allocation budget is always simply the maximum budget. And it may be set near to a minimum budget if the survival rate is low enough. The calculated value is sometimes additionally refined with a linear model that for boundary survival ratios mixes the current and previous allocation budget proportionally.

A general illustration of a function describing the new allocation budget in terms of the survival rate is illustrated in Figure 7-13. Steepness of the slope, the threshold from which the maximum size of the generation starts, and less important properties of such functions depend on the static parameters limit and max_limit presented in Tables 7-1 and 7-2. The smaller the values of these limits, the steeper the slope and the faster the maximum value is set.

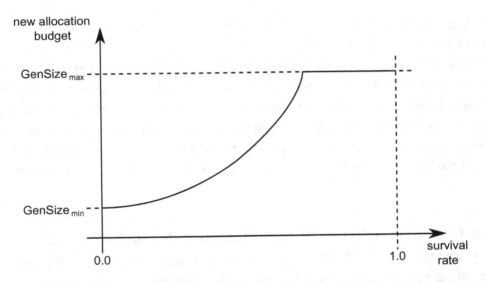

Figure 7-13. *An illustration of typical function describing relation between the survival rate and the resulting, new allocation budget*

For us, looking at values from Tables 7-1 and 7-2, it means that the younger generations respond much more dynamically to the survival rate than the older ones. Especially generation 0 "reacts" to it so sensitively that most often the new allocation budget becomes one of the boundary cases - the minimum or maximum generation size.

This is why when using ".NET Memory/Gen 0 heap size" performance counter, which is due to historical reasons, shows a generation 0 allocation budget and quite often stays in one of two possible values during the entire lifetime of the application. This is perfectly visible in Figures 5-6 and 5-7 from Chapter 5 or Figure 7-7, where "Gen 0 heap size" changes constantly between values of 4 MB and 6 MB. This in turn means that according to Tables 7-1 and 7-2, the GC was in Workstation GC with Concurrent version mode.

During runtime initialization, the allocation budget of each generation is set to the minimum budget from its static data (see Tables 7-1 and 7-2). How do the generation size and allocation budget relate to each other? The key is to understand that the allocation budget is a logical value. It represents the allocation limit in a given generation, which may be exhausted but may also change in the future due to changing conditions. Allocations in a given generation strive for the limit to be exhausted, but the limit itself may change. It may be seen that allocation budgets dynamically react to the survival ratios and as a result, generation sizes change dynamically in a way trying to be optimal.

Please note that in fact a popular question about "default generation sizes" is pretty unjustified. Generations are simply created empty; there is nothing like their default size. As objects are being allocated and promoted, they grow in size according to allocation budgets.

The relation between new allocations, the allocation budget, and generation size may be described in the simplest way by the current_generation_size method from CoreCLR sources (see Listing 7-1). At any time, the approximate generation data size (not including fragmentation) is its current data size plus the difference between the allocation budget and new allocation. At the end of GC the new allocation is set to the value of the allocation budget. While objects are allocated in generation 0 or LOH, new allocations of those generations are decreased accordingly. Hence, the allocation amount since the last GC is expressed in the difference of these two values.

Listing 7-1. Method to calculate current generation size (CoreCLR source code)

```
size_t gc_heap::current_generation_size (int gen_number)
{
    dynamic_data* dd = dynamic_data_of (gen_number);
    size_t gen_size = (dd_current_size (dd) + dd_desired_allocation (dd)
                        - dd_new_allocation (dd));

    return gen_size;
}
```

A careful reader may wonder how it is possible that a new allocation is updated with every object allocation. It was not mentioned in Chapter 6 at all. It is also difficult to expect that this would actually happen on the fast track of the allocation presented in Listing 6-7 or somewhere along the way. This is a fully justified suspicion. In fact, a new allocation is reduced only by the creation or growth of allocation contexts that are the units of memory that GC gives out.

If you are interested in understanding better how an allocation budget influences GC work, and how it relates to the generation size, please you are strongly invited to read comprehensive scenario 7-2 showing the first five GCs of a sample process.

Scenario 7-2. Understanding the Allocation Budget

Description: One wants to better understand the allocation budget concept, especially in terms of its relation to the generation size and overall influence on the GC job. This is not only useful during learning. Such a thorough analysis may be used when trying to understand what exactly triggers GC in your process.

Analysis: There is no better solution than a thorough debugging session analysis. A simple C# program from Listing 7-2 has been prepared. It allocates one million byte arrays in a loop and stores their references in an additional array, so everything is reachable (will survive the GC) during the entire lifetime of the application. Each individual byte array has a size of 25,024 bytes (25,000 bytes of the data plus 8 bytes for array length and 16 bytes for object metadata).

Listing 7-2. Sample program used in this scenario

```
1 static void Main(string[] args)
2 {
3     Console.ReadLine();
4     Console.WriteLine("Hello, Windows");
5     Console.WriteLine("Love from CoreCLR.");
6     GC.Collect();
7     Console.ReadLine();
8     const int LEN = 1_000_000;
9     byte[][] list = new byte[LEN][];
10    for (int i = 0; i < LEN; ++i)
11    {
12        list[i] = new byte[25000];
13        if (i % 100 == 0)
14        {
15            Console.WriteLine("Allocated 100 arrays");
16        }
17    }
18 }
```

Thanks to detailed debugging in Visual Studio and ETW logging, the first five garbage collections are comprehensively described in terms of the allocation budget, which allows us to better understand it.

The experiment focuses on the simplest variant of GC operation - Non-concurrent Workstation GC with "memory footprint" mode. The values of static data running on the author's machine are presented in Table 7-3 (calculated from Table 7-2). The maximum ephemeral generation sizes are 128 MB because in this configuration the size of the ephemeral segment is 256 MB (refer to Table 5-3 from Chapter 5).

Table 7-3. *Example Static GC Data - Non-concurrent Workstation GC in 64-bit,* *"Memory Footprint" Mode (Assuming 8 MB LLC Cache)*

	min_size	max_size	limit	max_limit
Gen0	4 MB	128 MB	9.0	20.0
Gen1	288 kB	128 MB	2.0	7.0
Gen2	256 kB	SSIZE_T_MAX	1.2	1.8
LOH	3 MB	SSIZE_T_MAX	1.25	4.5

To have full information provided in this scenario, a set of breakpoints were set during CoreCLR runtime debugging to print "new allocation" values for each generation. This step is obviously not required during normal problem analysis (which could be based only on ETW data described below).

The following information can be obtained from an ETW-based session analysis in PerfView by exporting data from GCStats report by Per Generation GC Events in the Excel option:

- generation sizes at the beginning of a GC (*Begin size*) - from columns Before0/1/2/3.

- allocation budgets (*Allocation budget*) - from columns Budget0/1/2/3. Additionally, the generation 0 budget is listed as FinalYoungestDesired field in Microsoft-Windows-DotNETRuntime/ GC/GlobalHeapHistory event and, as stated before, as .NET Memory/ Gen 0 heap size Performance Counter.

- promoted objects sizes (*Promoted size*) - from columns Surv0/1/2/3. Additionally, they may be read from Microsoft-Windows- DotNETRuntime/GC/HeapStats event.

- generation sizes at the end of a GC (*Final size*) - from columns After0/1/2/3.

Per Generation GC Events additionally list data about the GC start and stop, condemned generation, and fragmentation.

The following points provide a detailed description of internal GC workings during such experiment. Please note that in this scenario we are also using All GC Events table from the GCStats report in the PerfView, already presented in scenario 7-1.

Before GC

At the beginning of the application - before any object has been created - allocation budgets are set to the minimum budget (see Table 7-3). Thus, initial values are as follows (expressed in bytes):

	Gen0	Gen1	Gen2	LOH
Allocation budget:	4,194,304	294,912	262,144	3,145,728
New allocation:	4,194,304	294,912	262,144	3,145,728
Begin size:	24	24	24	24

As noted, new allocation values for each generation are also set to those values to reflect available space for allocations. Generations physically start empty at the beginning of the process; the size simply indicates an object of minimal size as the start of a generation

GC #1 - triggered by explicit GC.Collect() call

The first Garbage Collection in a sample program is explicitly triggered (see line 6 at Listing 7-2). The corresponding excerpt of the All GC Events table from the GCStats report in the PerfView looks as follows:

GCIndex	Trigger Reason	Gen	Gen0 Alloc [MB]	Promoted [MB]	Gen0 Survival Rate [%]	Gen1 [MB]	Gen1 Survival Rate [%]	LOH [MB]	LOH Survival Rate [%]
1	Induced	2NI	0.213	0.082	33	0.192	0	0.018	99

It confirms that induced a non-concurrent full-GC (2NI) has been triggered. Since the program start, 0.213 MB has been allocated in SOH and 0.018 MB in LOH. This in fact is reflected by the values of Begin size and New allocation at the beginning of GC:[2]

- New allocation of gen0 and LOH have been accordingly decreased, while gen1 and gen2 are left untouched.

---

[2]Note that those values are expressed in terms of allocation context changes, which are units of memory that GC gives out. Additionally, there may be little discrepancies between New allocation value (read at breakpoint in Visual Studio) and values from various ETW events - explained by rounding that appears in both sources.

- Begin size of gen0 and LOH have increased, while gen1 and gen2 are left untouched.

	Gen0	Gen1	Gen2	LOH
New allocation:	3,995,024	294,912	262,144	3,128,216
Begin size:	192,256	24	24	17,512

Each generation promotion size shows the following values:

	Gen0	Gen1	Gen2	LOH
Promoted size	64,088	0	0	17,440

It means that in generation 0, from a total 192,256 allocated, 64,088 bytes are reachable and will be promoted to generation 1 (around 33% survival rate, visible as Gen0 Survival Rate % in All GC Events table). Additionally, most of the LOH allocated objects will survive (17,440 from total 17,512 bytes, resulting in 99% survival rate).

At this stage, new allocation budgets will be calculated for the collected and all younger generations (that means for all generations in case of our full-GC) - mainly based on above-mentioned survival ratio. Because those ratios were zero for generations 1 and 2, those generations allocation budgets are set again to the minimum budgets. The generation 0 survival rate is high because it is common for the startup stage of the process - normally the CC tries to tune for a few percent or less survival ratio in the youngest generation. As a result, the new allocation budgets are as follows:

	Gen0	Gen1	Gen2	LOH
Allocation budget	4,194,304	294,912	262,144	3,145,728

New allocation values for each generation will be also set to be the same as the allocation budget.

And eventually, final generation sizes depend on objects physically promoted:

	Gen0	Gen1	Gen2	LOH
Final size	24	192,304[3]	24	17,536

GC #2 - triggered by allocation

Second and subsequent Garbage Collections happen because of a cyclic allocation of byte[] array. The corresponding excerpt of All GC Events table is as follows:

GCIndex	Trigger Reason	Gen	Gen0 Alloc [MB]	Promoted [MB]	Gen0 Survival Rate [%]	Gen1 [MB]	Gen1 Survival Rate [%]	LOH [MB]	LOH Survival Rate [%]
2	AllocSmall	2N	4.204	12.286	99	4.204	100	8.018	99

We see that since the last GC:

- 4.204 MB were allocated in generation 0 - because of allocating many byte arrays itself,

- around 8 MB in Large Object Heap - because of allocating byte[1_000_000][] array at Line 9, which is an array of one million 8-byte long references.

After such allocations happened, we may expect that:

- by allocating 4.204 MB, clearly generation 0 allocation budget should be exceeded (which was set to 4,194,304 bytes),

- 8 MB of LOH allocations also exceeds LOH allocation budget (which was set to 3 MB).

---

[3]Generation 1 is bigger than expected. It has size of 192,304 bytes while only 64,088 bytes are promoted from generation 0. This is due to the big fragmentation introduced after this GC. It could be noticed by the big Gen1 Frag % value of 66.69% in GC Events in Time table from the GCStats report in the PerfView. This obviously indicates that only Sweep collection was done, without compacting.

We can confirm that by looking at new, negative allocation values of gen0 and LOH at the beginning of GC:

	Gen0	Gen1	Gen2	LOH
New allocation:	-21,952	294,912	262,144	-4,854,328
Begin size:	4,204,064	64,040	0	8,017,472

The LOH budget was exceeded, elevating this GC to full-GC, even initially only generation 0 could be collected (thus, 2N generation value in events table above). Each generation promotion size shows the following values:

	Gen0	Gen1	Gen2	LOH
Promoted size	4,204,032	64,088	0	8,017,464

This leads to the following observations:

- generation 0 is fully promoted because all created byte arrays are reachable (references are kept by byte[ ][ ] array),

- generation 1 promotes data promoted to it in the previous step.

Regarding the allocation budget, we may notice the following changes:

	Gen0	Gen1	Gen2	LOH
Allocation budget	84,080,640	448,616	262,144	28,061,128

Current budget values may be explained as follows:

- generation 0 survival rate is now very close to 100%, hence generation allocation budget is increased significantly,

- generation 1 survival rate is also 100% (see Gen1 Survival Rate % in the events table), hence its budget is also increased,

- generation 2 allocation budget has not been changed because its initial data size is 0,

- LOH allocation budget has been increased by a factor of 3.5 (such multiplication factor is calculated by function similar to that Figure 7-13).

Eventually, final generation sizes depend on objects physically promoted:

	Gen0	Gen1	Gen2	LOH
Final size	24	4,204,088	192,328	8,017,592

It is good to stop and look around now for a while. After two successive GCs described so far, we ended up in the situation where:

- generation 0 allocation budget has grown to around 80MB because of a high survival rate - many objects survived collection of the youngest generation, so probably there may be even more and it is worth to extend it. Based on the new budget, we may expect the next GC after around 80MB of SOH allocations.

- generation 1 allocation budget is smaller than the actual generation size - this may happen as GC has not yet been able to accommodate a big rate of allocations/promotions. Further GCs will refine that either by stabilizing the allocation budget (in case if it was a single memory churn) or growing it constantly (in case if it was stable memory growth). This clearly shows the logic nature of allocation budgets and its good counterpart name - the desired allocation. It does not represent an actual generation size.

- generation 2 allocation budget has not been changed but big fragmentation has been "promoted" along with objects. It could be noticed by the big Gen2 Frag % value of 66.69% in GC Events in Time table.

- LOH allocation budget was increased to accommodate new large object allocations.

GC #3 - triggered by allocation

The third Garbage Collection happens because of further allocations of byte[ ] arrays. The excerpt of All GC Events table is as follows:

GCIndex	Trigger Reason	Gen	Gen0 Alloc [MB]	Promoted [MB]	Gen0 Survival Rate [%]	Gen1 [MB]	Gen1 Survival Rate [%]	LOH [MB]	LOH Survival Rate [%]
3	AllocSmall	0N	84.081	84.081	99	88.285	-	8.018	-

We see that since the last GC, as expected, around 84 MB were allocated in generation 0. That should consume its allocation budget. Only generation 0 is being collected (0N value in Gen column), which makes this the most typical, youngest-only GC triggered by SOH allocations.

We can confirm that by looking at a new, negative allocation value of gen0 at the beginning of GC:

	Gen0	Gen1	Gen2	LOH
New allocation:	-5,496	448,616	262,144	28,061,128
Begin size:	84,080,640	-	-	-

Each generation promotion size shows the following values:

	Gen0	Gen1	Gen2	LOH
Promoted size	84,080,640	-	-	-

It leads to an interesting situation in calculating new allocation budgets:

	Gen0	Gen1	Gen2	LOH
Allocation budget	134,217,728	-83,632,024	262,144	28,061,128

As we can see, the following changes has been made:

- According to the high survival rate, the new generation 0 allocation budget has been set to the maximum generation size (128 MB),

- Allocation budget of generation 1 has been decreased by the size of objects promoted from generation 0 - this makes its allocation budget exceeded, hence it is expected to be considered during the next GC.

Remember that the new allocation values for each generation will be also dynamically recomputed accordingly.

Eventually, final generation sizes present intuitive values according to the previous and promotion sizes - only gen0 and gen1 sizes have been changed:

	Gen0	Gen1	Gen2	LOH
Final size	24	88,284,752	192,328	8,017,592

GC #4 - triggered by allocation

The fourth GC happens also because of further allocations of byte[ ] arrays and exceeding generation 0 budget. The excerpt of All GC Events table is as follows:

GCIndex	Trigger Reason	Gen	Gen0 Alloc [MB]	Promoted [MB]	Gen0 Survival Rate [%]	Gen1 [MB]	Gen1 Survival Rate [%]	LOH [MB]	LOH Survival Rate [%]
4	AllocSmall	1N	134.229	222.513	99	134.229	99	8.018	-

We see that indeed 134.229 MB were allocated that should exceed the previously set gen0 allocation budget. However, as we remember, also generation 1 allocation budget should be exceeded due to promoted allocations from the previous GC. Thus, GC is elevated to generation 1 so instead of collecting only generation 0, also generation 1 will be included (see value 1N in Gen column).

We can confirm that by looking at negative new allocation values of both gen0 and gen1 at the beginning of GC (where gen1 value has been set in the previous GC):

	Gen0	Gen1	Gen2	LOH
New allocation:	-14,504	-83,632,024	262,144	28,061,128
Begin size:	134,228,736	88,284,672	-	-

Each generation promotion size shows the following values:

	Gen0	Gen1	Gen2	LOH
Promoted size	134,228,736	88,284,672	-	-

Because both generations 0 and 1 are collected, and they contain only reachable byte arrays, everything from them is being promoted (high 99% Gen0 and Gen1 Survival Rate).

Regarding the new allocation budgets, we may notice the following changes:

	Gen0	Gen1	Gen2	LOH
Allocation budget	134,217,728	134,217,728	-88,022,528	28,061,128

The following changes have been made to allocation budgets:

- The generation 0 allocation budget remains the same - despite the high survival rate, it cannot be changed to a higher value as it already hit maximum generation size.

- The generation 1 allocation budget has increased to the maximum generation size - this is a reaction to a high survival rate and big amount of promoted size.

- Allocation budget of generation 2 has been decreased by the size of objects promoted from generation 1 - this means the gen2 allocation budget is exceeded so it's expected to be considered for collection during the next GCs.

Final generation sizes present intuitive values according to the previous and promotion sizes - all SOH generation sizes have been changed:

	Gen0	Gen1	Gen2	LOH
Final size	24	134,228,760	88,477,048	8,017,592

GC #5 - triggered by allocation

A careful reader could expect now the GC triggered by SOH allocations exceeding the gen0 allocation budget, as usual. However, before that, another condition triggers GC. The excerpt of the All GC Events table is as follows:

GCIndex	Trigger Reason	Gen	Gen0 Alloc [MB]	Promoted [MB]	Gen0 Survival Rate [%]	Gen1 [MB]	Gen1 Survival Rate [%]	LOH [MB]	LOH Survival Rate [%]
5	OutOfSpaceSOH	2N	134.179	364.774	99	134.179	99	8.018	-

We can see there a new OutOfSpaceSOH reason that triggered the full-GC (2N Gen value). It could be easily explained when looking at internal GC data:

	Gen0	Gen1	Gen2	LOH
New allocation:	35,592	134,217,728	-88,022,528	28,061,128
Begin size:	134,178,688	134,228,736	88,348,760	8,017,440

Allocation budget is only exceeded for the generation 2 (due to promotions in the previous GC), but it is not the reason of triggering this GC. The true reason is the total size of both ephemeral generations (begin size) that exceeds the maximum ephemeral segment size (256 MB). In such a case GC is being triggered to collect at least ephemeral generations. And because of the generation 2 budget being exceeded, this GC is elevated to the full-GC one additionally.

Each generation promotion size shows the following values:

	Gen0	Gen1	Gen2	LOH
Promoted size	134,178,688	134,228,736	88,348,760	-

Because of high survival ratios, gen0 and gen1 allocation budgets remain at their maximums:

	Gen0	Gen1	Gen2	LOH
Allocation budget	134,217,728	134,217,728	178,062,152	28,061,128

Generation 2 allocation budget has been increased by a factor of 2 (such multiplication factor is calculated by function similar to that Figure 7-13) to align with its high survival rate.

At the end, generation sizes present as follows:

	Gen0	Gen1	Gen2	LOH
Final size	24	134,178,712	222,705,808	8,017,592

Those sizes are as expected. Generation 0 is empty, intermediate generation 1 is maximized, while generation 2 gathers all other SOH objects.

Subsequent GCs

Because memory usage of the sample program is constant, next GCs would repeat the pattern presented here. GCs would be called alternately for two reasons: AllocSmall (exceeding generation 0 budget) and OutOfSpaceSOH (exceeding total ephemeral segment size). The size of generation 2 would gradually increase, while the remaining ones would be at the same level.

Static data together with regularly updated dynamic data control the work of the GC. They control when the GC is triggered, what generation is condemned, and whether compaction or sweeping should be executed. It's good to have a general idea of what they are and how they affect the process.

Hopefully, the detailed description from scenario 7-2 illustrated the relation between those static and dynamic data, altogether with the influence of allocations. Generation sizes may be seen as dynamic values driven by the allocation budgets of corresponding generations, calculated from their survival rate. As a result, GC is constantly tuning generation sizes to accommodate current allocation and survival patterns, with respect to static data from Tables 7-1 and 7-2 (especially, influencing the look of the important function from Figure 7-13).

Remember that these are deep implementation details. It is not guaranteed that over the years these parameters will influence GC's work in an exactly way. In my opinion it is unlikely, however, that the concept of allocation budget will be changed dramatically.

In case of CoreCLR code, dynamic data described here is represented by `dynamic_data` class defined in `.\src\gc\gcpriv.h` file. You can easily map each attribute listed above to the corresponding fields of that class. Among others, the most important one is the allocation budget represented by `desired_allocation` field. At the end of GC it is calculated in `gc_heap::desired_new_allocation` method using various heuristics (mainly survivors rate-related like in Figure 7-13 and corrected by `gc_heap::linear_allocation_model` method - a linear correction between the previous and new value based on the generation's fullness). You may start further investigation on that field from `gc_heap::compute_new_dynamic_data` called at the end of GC.

Collection Triggers

The first question about the GC we may ask is - when can it actually occur? What triggers it? Before a concrete answer, it is worth it to understand the design decisions that were behind the implementation of GC - they have been very accessibly written in the Book Of The Runtime:

- GCs should occur often enough to avoid the Managed Heap containing a significant amount (by ratio or absolute count) of unused but allocated objects (garbage), and therefore use memory unnecessarily.

- GCs should happen as infrequently as possible to avoid using otherwise useful CPU time, even though frequent GCs would result in lower memory usage.

- A GC should be productive. If GC reclaims a small amount of memory, then the GC (including the associated CPU cycles) was wasted.

- Each GC should be fast. Many workloads have low-latency requirements.

- Managed code developers shouldn't need to know much about the GC to achieve good memory utilization (relative to their workload) – The GC should tune itself to satisfy different memory usage patterns.

Having those design decisions in mind, the answer sounds like this: GC should be called as rarely as possible, giving the best possible results. Of course, given the innumerable use cases and rapidly changing conditions, designing such a self-tuning GC is an extremely difficult challenge. However, realizing the above challenges posed by GC, it is quite easy to reject the idea of its cyclic call. However, it could be one of the first thoughts of an inexperienced .NET developer - maybe GC is called periodically, such as after a certain number of milliseconds? The answer is short - no, it isn't. It would not be productive just to call it and "see what happens next."

There are various reasons why a garbage collection may be started. The rest of this section we will look at them, grouped according to the main reasons behind these causes.

Various GC reasons are represented by an internal CoreCLR `gc_reason` enumeration. Start there if you want to investigate this topic on your own.

Allocation Trigger

As we have seen in Chapter 6, both Small and Large Object Heap Allocators may trigger Garbage Collection if it is unable to find a suitable space for an object being created. Depending on the conditions one or even two ephemeral GCs (with generation 0 or 1 condemned) as well as Full-GC may be triggered.

This is by far the most common reason of GC occurrence in our applications. There are four main reasons of this kind (names in parentheses denote names used in PerfView reports, as already seen):

- small object allocation (AllocSmall) - running out of budget on generation 0 during object allocation. This is the most common case, triggered in case of generation 0 allocation budget exceeding (as mentioned in Chapter 6).

- large object allocation (AllocLarge) - running out of budget on LOH during large object allocation.

- small object allocation on slow-path (OutOfSpaceSOH) - allocator is running out of space during the "slow-path" object allocation in SOH, even after some segment reorganizations and maybe even GCs already run, there is still no required free space. In 64-bit runtimes with large virtual memory space, it should be a rather uncommon reason. However, even on 64-bit runtime they may happen in the case of Workstation GC, as shown in scenario 7-2.

- large object allocation on slow-path (OutOfSpaceLOH) - allocator is running out of space during the "slow-path" object allocation in LOH. Similar to the OutOfSpaceSOH, it should be uncommon.

Of course, good memory management usually boils down to creating the smallest number of objects. That is why an allocation trigger is the most optimized source of GC - if there is no allocation, this type of trigger does not occur. There is no allocation, so there is no GC at all!

Explicit Trigger

In certain circumstances one may wish to ask for GC explicitly. Such Garbage Collections are often referred to as *induced*. They may be done in a few ways, thanks to the exposed API. The most common one is an explicit call to trigger GC via GC.Collect method call. It has several overrides with different level of control:

- GC.Collect() - ask for triggering full-GC, blocking but without forcing compaction;

- GC.Collect(int generation) - ask for triggering GC of specified generation, blocking but without forcing compaction;

- GC.Collect(int generation, System.GCCollectionMode mode) - ask for triggering blocking GC of specified generation and mode specifying whether it should be: Forced or Optimized (leaving decision to the GC itself);

- `GC.Collect(int generation, System.GCCollectionMode mode, bool blocking)` - ask for triggering GC of specified generation, explicitly blocking or not, and with mode specifying whether it should be: Forced or Optimized (leaving decision to GC);

- `GC.Collect(int generation, System.GCCollectionMode mode, bool blocking, bool compacting)` - ask for GC with all options specified explicitly.

As it will be later explained, GC contains a step to check a number of conditions to see which generation collection is the most productive. Hence, even if we provide a specific generation to `GC.Collect` call, while it is guaranteed that such generation will be indeed garbage collected (and all younger ones), even an older generation may be condemned - if current conditions incur that, for example, the older generation has exceeded its budget.

It may seem strange to call `GC.Collect(2, GCCollectionMode.Forced, blocking: false, compacting: true)` As we will learn in Chapter 11, non-blocking (concurrent) full-GCs are non-compacting, so such arguments seem to be contradicting. In such a case, indeed a triggered GC will be non-blocking and not-compacting or blocking and compacting (the decision is left to the GC).

Calling `GC.Collect` is rarely justified. This whole book is dedicated to the fact that the .NET GC is a complex and well-optimized thing. It keeps various statistics that support heuristic decisions on whether to make a garbage collection and if so, which generation will be the most productive to collect. By explicit calls to `GC.Collect` we disturb those heuristics.

Moreover, it is really difficult to find a justification for using this method. As we will see in Chapters 8 to 10, CLR makes its best to collect objects as fast as possible. Determining which objects are eligible for collections is based on marking. If an object is not garbage collected, it is because something still holds reference to it. Calling `GC.Collect` will not help here. Calling this also will not help in the situation like "probably CLR forgot to call the GC so I will remind him about it." GC is not being called if it is not productive. Thus, explicit `GC.Collect` call will also be non-productive. When you will see next time in someone's else code a `GC.Collect` call, it can mean two things: either the author of such code was unaware of the aforementioned remarks, or she is a smart one who has consciously used this method in this tiny fraction of the situations when it really gives something.

Let's consider the situations in which we would like to collect a memory of each generation:

- generation 0 - you believe there are many dead objects in the youngest generation and want to force collecting them. However, if you allocate some objects in your application, this generation is collected quite often anyway. And according to the CLR's settings (see Table 7-1), generation 0 would not grow to big sizes in the first place. Thus, most probably it is best just to leave GC to do its job. Due to self-tuning based on allocation and survivors' rate, it will collect generation 0 with optimized frequency. By explicit call we may only ruin those self-tunings.

- generation 1 - this generation is an intermediate one. It is hard to reason what, when, and for how long objects land there because it heavily depends on dynamic conditions of your application. Generation 1 is there to not promote young objects directly into ever-old generation 2 objects. It is there to give objects a chance to be collected before landing into generation 2. Allocation and survival rates tracked by GC are helping with that. By explicit call to collect generation 1, you are just throwing it all away. All still reachable objects will be promoted into generation 2, some of them probably prematurely and unnecessarily. And avoiding promotion to the oldest generation is one of the things we should consider really important. Explicitly triggering an ephemeral collection may be tempting though because it is quite fast and is the last resort before calling the full-blown full-GC. But I invite you to rethink your data structures in terms of shortening their lives instead.

- generation 2 - full-GC is much more expensive that others but it does its job - everything that could be collected will be collected. You may want to call it explicitly because you've noticed generation 2 is "big" or "constantly growing." Most probably it happens because of some roots that we are not aware of, not because the GC forget to do its job. In fact, the GC probably is already doing full garbage collections due to the memory pressure. Adding your own explicit calls does nothing more that adds additional overhead without possible positive effects. Instead of triggering GC, redesign your application to not generate so long-living objects end up in the oldest generation. Holding too big state, too long cached objects, or unnecessarily large database data are tunings you may consider as starting points of your optimizations.

And let's not forget that regardless of which generation we give as the argument of the GC.Collect call, it can end with full-GC anyway!

Having said that, what are the very few situations that may justify the use of GC.Collect? There are some that may be grouped into the following use cases:

- You know the nature of some intermittent behavior of your application that GC is unlikely to understand (but you will understand your application data life cycle) - like occasional batch processing that caused a large amount of allocations that ended up in generation 2. If such allocation churns are rare, later on GC may not decide to collect generation 2 for a long time. Thus, all that garbage created during batch processing will stay there, increasing total memory usage. It is not so bad (it does not incur GC overhead) but it makes your process staying big while you know that it could be not. Another example would be cleaning up memory before an expected huge allocation churn - like occasional batch processing mentioned before, loading a new level in a game and so on, and so forth. It may be also useful before turning an application into low-latency mode requiring as low GC (and runtime in general) overhead as possible.

All those scenarios are exactly the opposite of, for example, the steadily running web application that processes a stable number of requests. The GC then has good insight into the allocation and survival characteristics that will allow it to make better decisions than we would be able to.

- Proactive cleaning at consciously selected points in the program execution - similar to the first point, we can use the specificity of our application to be able to collect garbage in advance in moments that are not noticed by the user. A typical example is garbage collection while waiting for a user's input or displaying various kinds of loading screens. This is, however, a weaker reason than the first one. We should be really convinced about the meaningfulness of such calls. Are such calls productive or do we call "just in case"? Remember that they disrupt the work of GC tuning.

- Cleaning up due to benchmarking - any measurements require a carefully prepared environment. To make sure that the GC overhead will be repeatable, we should prepare a test environment to be in a consistent state before each benchmark. This requires cleaning up memory from everything that is possible to clean. Calling full-GCs before benchmarks is a common pattern.

- As special cases of unit and integration tests - for example, those that use WeakReference (an example is shown in Chapter 12) or are using third-party code suspected of producing memory leak. By calling GC. Collect explicitly before and after test (to clean everything that could be cleaned), we are creating repeatable test results.

As a solution to used third-party libraries' unfortunate memory usage characteristics - the behavior of the library in use may involve something similar to the first two reasons mentioned here. While we are not in control in such code, the only thing we can do (except changing library) is to clean garbage before and/or after its usage. Having said all that, still GC.Collect should be only an occasional call. Making it cyclic to overcome some problems means you are most probably just trying to sweep the whole problem under the rug. The typical, real problems are a mid-life crisis or ever-holding roots - those are not be solved by explicit GC calls.

There is one additional way of triggering GC almost explicitly by using GC.AddMemoryPressure (described in Chapter 15). By its call we inform GC that some managed objects are holding a specified amount of unmanaged memory. Because from a GC perspective such unmanaged data isn't tracked by the GC heap, GC can't take such data size into its decision regarding memory usage. If total unmanaged memory size set by GC.AddMemoryPressure calls exceeds dynamically tuned threshold, non-blocking GC of a generation based on internal heuristics will be triggered.

Current implementation starts with threshold of value 100,000 bytes (and will never drop below this value). It is then dynamically tuned based on the sizes passed via GC.AddMemoryPressure (increasing it by 10% or 8 times the specified size, depending which result is bigger) and GC.RemoveMemoryPressure calls. It also considers the ratio between each generation collection count. Although those are internal implementation details that most probably will change, it is worth noticing that memory pressure logic operates on its internal heuristics and do not relate to the ones managed by the core GC logic.

Scenario 7-3. Analyzing the Explicit GC Calls

Description: We are developing a desktop application written in WPF. Considering the above remarks, we want to check whether it triggers GC explicitly. Of course, having its source code, the simplest solution would be to search for GC.Collect calls. However, firstly, our application consists of various components and we do not have the source code for all of them. Secondly, the mere existence of a GC.Collect call does not say much about its real use - whether and how often it occurs. For example, we will look at the operation of the dnSpy application – a free, open source .NET debugger and assembly editor presented already in previous chapters.

Analysis: We will start the analysis of the program by checking if there are explicit GC triggers at all during its operation. The fastest and the easiest way is to use .\NET CLR Memory(dnSpy)\# Induced GC Performance Counter, which counts all GC calls of this type (see Figure 7-14). Clearly we see that indeed there are some induced GCs happening (six during a one-minute test). By observing this graph during the test, we may also quickly notice that they happen while opening new assemblies from the Assembly Explorer panel.

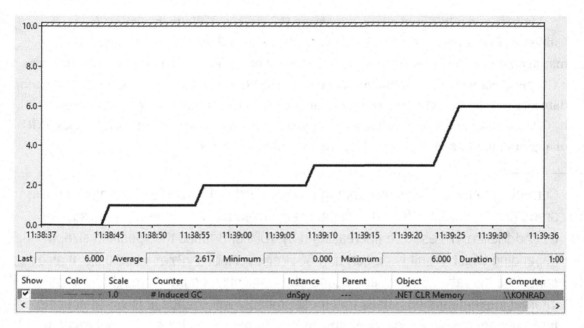

Figure 7-14. *Performance counter .\NET CLR Memory(dnSpy)\# Induced GC during the first minute of dnSpy application run*

After confirming that such calls are actually occurring, let's go to the analysis where it happens. For this purpose, we must again use the PerfView tool and GC analysis along with collecting the events stack traces. To do that we should type `Microsoft-Windows-DotNETRuntime:GCKeyword:Informational:@StacksEnabled=true` option into the Additional Providers field at the Collect dialog box.

After recording the session, open GCStats report from Memory Group. In the GC Rollup By Generation table of the dnSpy process, we will also find there a confirmation of induced GC calls (see column Induced from Figure 7-15).

GC Rollup By Generation										
All times are in msec.										
Gen	Count	Max Pause	Max Peak MB	Max Alloc MB/sec	Total Pause	Total Alloc MB	Alloc MB/ MSec GC	Survived MB/ MSec GC	Mean Pause	Induced
ALL	8	27.7	216.9	654.519	95.6	304.8	3.2	0.496	11.9	8
0	4	12.9	178.0	654.519	30.2	151.5	0.1	0.173	7.5	4
1	2	27.7	216.9	19.184	35.6	89.0	0.1	0.200	17.8	2
2	2	26.5	150.3	6.746	29.8	64.3	0.1	0.995	14.9	2

Figure 7-15. *GC Rollup By Generation table from GCStats report of dnSpy process*

Now open the Events panel from the recorded session and find `Microsoft-Windows-DotNETRuntime/GC/Triggered` events that are emitted when explicit GC calls happen. Because `StacksEnabled` option was turned on, we have corresponding stack trace of each event occurrence (see Figure 7-16).

Process Filter: dnSpy (10076)		Text Filter:			Columns To Display: Cols
Event Types Filter:		Histogram:			
Microsoft-Windows-DotNETRuntime/GC/Start		Event Name	Time MSec	Process Name	Rest
Microsoft-Windows-DotNETRuntime/GC/Stop		Microsoft-Windows-DotNETRuntime/GC/Triggered	7,775.846	dnSpy (10076)	HasStack="True" ThreadID="8,584" Reason="Induced" ClrInstanceID="9"
Microsoft-Windows-DotNETRuntime/GC/SuspendEEStart		Microsoft-Windows-DotNETRuntime/GC/Triggered	10,930.088	dnSpy (10076)	HasStack="True" ThreadID="4,544" Reason="InducedNotForced" ClrInstanceID="9"
Microsoft-Windows-DotNETRuntime/GC/SuspendEEStop		Microsoft-Windows-DotNETRuntime/GC/Triggered	13,538.767	dnSpy (10076)	HasStack="True" ThreadID="4,544" Reason="InducedNotForced" ClrInstanceID="9"
Microsoft-Windows-DotNETRuntime/GC/Triggered		Microsoft-Windows-DotNETRuntime/GC/Triggered	16,575.227	dnSpy (10076)	HasStack="True" ThreadID="4,544" Reason="InducedNotForced" ClrInstanceID="9"
Microsoft-Windows-DotNETRuntime/Loader/ModuleDCStop		Microsoft-Windows-DotNETRuntime/GC/Triggered	16,681.976	dnSpy (10076)	HasStack="True" ThreadID="4,544" Reason="InducedNotForced" ClrInstanceID="9"
Microsoft-Windows-DotNETRuntime/Method/DCStopCompl		Microsoft-Windows-DotNETRuntime/GC/Triggered	21,152.132	dnSpy (10076)	HasStack="True" ThreadID="4,544" Reason="InducedNotForced" ClrInstanceID="9"
Microsoft-Windows-DotNETRuntime/Method/DCStopVerbos		Microsoft-Windows-DotNETRuntime/GC/Triggered	21,597.239	dnSpy (10076)	HasStack="True" ThreadID="4,544" Reason="InducedNotForced" ClrInstanceID="9"
Microsoft-Windows-DotNETRuntime/Thread/Creating		Microsoft-Windows-DotNETRuntime/GC/Triggered	25,323.057	dnSpy (10076)	HasStack="True" ThreadID="4,544" Reason="InducedNotForced" ClrInstanceID="9"

Figure 7-16. *Events view filtered to the dnSpy process*

The following three values can appear in the Reason field:

- Induced - explicitly induced GC without preferences regarding compaction and blocking,

- InducedNotForced - explicitly induced GC that doesn't have to be blocking,

- InducedCompacting - explicitly induced GC that should be compacting (but only SOH, remember that LOH compaction is enabled explicitly by a different setting).

By selecting Open Any Stacks option from the context menu of values from Time MSec column, we will be able to see the exact stack trace of each explicit GC trigger.

`Microsoft-Windows-DotNETRuntime/GC/Start` event might seem to be a better place for an analysis start in this case. However, it is emitted from the place where the actual GC work begins. In our case, most of GCs are processed in background, on a dedicated thread. Stack trace of such event would always simply indicate the place on a dedicated GC thread where it got the signal to start its job.

From stack trace analysis we would be able to identify two main sources of explicit GC triggers (dnSpy tool is available on https://github.com/0xd4d/dnSpy that allows to show you exact code):

1. Cleaning memory after assembly decompilation (see Figure 7-17). After it happens, the temporary cache may contain no longer needed data. As fast as possible collection of them is triggered by an explicit GC.Collect call.

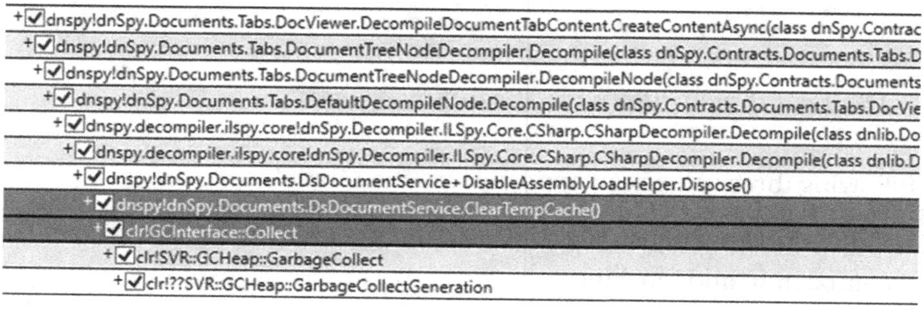

Figure 7-17. *Stack trace of the first kind of the explicit GC.Collect call*

The excerpt of corresponding code is shown in Listing 7-3. It represents an approach to wrap around resource-heavy object (DsDocumentService instance in our case) with the helper implementing IDisposable interface. Such a helper realizes a very simple reference-counting technique to track the usage of a wrapped object. If it is no longer used, an explicit clean of heavy resources is conducted.

Listing 7-3. Sample of the explicit GC call in dnSpy code

```
sealed class DsDocumentService : IDsDocumentService {
    int counter_DisableAssemblyLoad;
    // ...
    public IDisposable DisableAssemblyLoad() => new DisableAssemblyLoadHelper
    (this);
        sealed class DisableAssemblyLoadHelper : IDisposable
        {
```

```
        readonly DsDocumentService documentService;
        public DisableAssemblyLoadHelper(DsDocumentService document
        Service) {
            this.documentService = documentService;
            Interlocked.Increment(ref documentService.counter_Disable
            AssemblyLoad);
        }
        public void Dispose() {
            int value = Interlocked.Decrement(ref documentService.counter_
            DisableAssemblyLoad);
            if (value == 0)
                documentService.ClearTempCache();
        }
    }
    // ...
    void ClearTempCache() {
        bool collect;
        lock (tempCache) {
            collect = tempCache.Count > 0;
            tempCache.Clear();
        }
        if (collect) {
            GC.Collect();
            GC.WaitForPendingFinalizers();
        }
    }
    }
    // ...
}
```

The sample usage of such class is easy as presented in Listing 7-4.

Listing 7-4. Sample usage of code from Listing 7-3

```
using (context.DisableAssemblyLoad()) {
    // inside this block helper reference counter is incremented
    // context contains reference to the DsDocumentService instance
}
```

Code from Listing 7-3 is only one of the examples of how such defensive memory cleaning could be implemented. Instead of reference counting, one could simply call GC.Collect at some well-defined moment in time when an application notices that an assembly has been decompiled (like an event sent from UI). It may also be tempting to make DsDocumentService implement IDisposable directly and call GC.Collect from inside its Dispose method. This would, however, change the semantic of using DsDocumentService that not always might be appropriate. Another solution could be calling GC.Collect from inside DsDocumentService finalizer.

Manual memory cleaning presented here is an example of the first case of possible use cases listed above. The developer has decided to make the explicit GC call because it knows that intermittent, user input-related action requires cleaning a lot of temporary data.

2. Controlling unmanaged memory due to bitmaps usage (see Figure 7-18). As we can see, this time GC has been triggered internally by Windows Presentation Foundation (PresentationCore.dll is a part of WPF framework) because of loading an image.

```
+☑dnspy!dnSpy.Images.ImageService.GetImage(value class dnSpy.Contracts.Images.ImageReference,class dnS
 +☑dnspy!dnSpy.Images.ImageService.TryGetImage(class System.String,value class InternalImageOptions)
  +☑dnspy!dnSpy.Images.ImageService.TryLoadImage(class System.String,value class System.Windows.Size)
   +☑presentationcore.ni!System.Windows.Media.Imaging.BitmapDecoder.get_Frames()
    +☑presentationcore.ni!System.Windows.Media.Imaging.BitmapDecoder.SetupFrames(System.Windows.N
     +☑presentationcore.ni!System.Windows.Media.Imaging.BitmapFrameDecode.FinalizeCreation()
      +☑presentationcore.ni!System.Windows.Media.Imaging.BitmapFrameDecode.EnsureSource()
       +☑presentationcore.ni!System.Windows.Media.SafeMILHandle.UpdateEstimatedSize(Int64)
        +☑mscorlib.ni!System.GC.AddMemoryPressure(Int64)
         +☑clr!GCInterface::_AddMemoryPressure
          +☑clr!??GCInterface::AddMemoryPressure
           +☑clr!GCInterface::GarbageCollectModeAny
            +☑clr!SVR::GCHeap::GarbageCollect
```

Figure 7-18. *Stack trace of the second kind of the explicit GC.Collect call*

It turns out that this is a known issue. Bitmaps - represented by BitmapSource class in WPF - are small managed objects that hold image data as an unmanaged memory. This makes them small to the GC as unmanaged data is not included in object size. It could be done by making BitmapSource implementing IDisposable and calling GC.AddMemoryPressure and GC.RemoveMemoryPressure in its constructor and Dispose method respectively. Unfortunately, the design decision was the other.

Thus, as an internal WPF workaround, the bitmap data is held by an additional handle with reference counting, which deals with GC.AddMemoryPressure and GC.RemoveMemoryPressure calls (see Listing 7-5). As stated before, he AddMemoryPressure method may trigger GC if certain thresholds have been exceeded and that is exactly what we see in our scenario.

Listing 7-5. SafeMILHandleMemoryPressure class from the PresentationCore. dll (Windows Presentation Foundation)

```
namespace System.Windows.Media
{
    internal class SafeMILHandleMemoryPressure
    {
        [SecurityCritical]
        internal SafeMILHandleMemoryPressure(long gcPressure)
        {
            this._gcPressure = gcPressure;
            this._refCount = 0;
            GC.AddMemoryPressure(this._gcPressure);
        }

        internal void AddRef()
        {
            Interlocked.Increment(ref this._refCount);
        }

        [SecurityCritical]
        internal void Release()
        {
            if (Interlocked.Decrement(ref this._refCount) == 0)
            {
                GC.RemoveMemoryPressure(this._gcPressure);
                this._gcPressure = 0L;
            }
        }
```

```
    private long _gcPressure;
    private int _refCount;
  }
}
```

This example shows a similar reference-counting wrapper approach as for the previously shown assembly decompilation case. This time, however, the wrapper does not call the GC explicitly but only informs it about an additional, unmanaged memory pressure. It leaves the decision about triggering garbage collection to the GC itself.

Without this hack, GC would happen much less frequently than it should, leaving the application with a high memory usage for a long time. It is the more severe problem as more images are loaded. Most probably you will notice such induced GC calls in your own WPF applications. As long as they do not introduce big overhead (like big % Time in GC), this is fine. If it becomes severe, you can't obviously change the internal WPF code. As a workaround on an application level, one may create a pool of `WriteableBitmap` objects and reuse them accordingly.

Historically `SafeMILHandleMemoryPressure` managed its own set of counters to control memory usage and called `GC.Collect` to trigger full-GC explicitly when they were exceeded. It caused more problems than benefits, however. From .NET Framework 4.6.2, this logic has been transferred to the GC using a pair of `AddMemoryPressure`/`RemoveMemoryPressure` methods.

Note #2. If CLR is being hosted, there is yet another explicit GC trigger possible to use via `ICLRGCManager::Collect` method. It induces blocking the full-GC of a specified generation.

Low Memory Level System Trigger

Garbage collection may be triggered "externally." If an operating system notices it is running out of memory, it may broadcast "low memory notification" signal. Well-behaving applications may (but do not have to) listen to such a notification, trying to help or react to this situation. They may start reducing their working sets in the manner deemed appropriate by them. They may obviously also just ignore it if they consider it right.

.NET runtime is listening to such a signal. After receiving it, an ephemeral GC is triggered (but it may be turned into full-GC under high memory pressure). Additionally, GC becomes more aggressive during these collections. For example, it is more likely that full-GC will be executed. The benefits are mutual because reducing the pressure on memory helps all applications in the system (including our .NET-based).

Low memory notification mechanism is currently only supported on Windows. Internally it uses `CreateMemoryResourceNotification` WinApi function. Such notification is then observed by the Finalizer thread (it will be introduced in Chapter 11), which was chosen because it is guaranteed to run throughout entire lifetime of the application. After noticing the notification, GC is being called from the Finalizer thread. According to the comment in the internal `System.Runtime.Caching.PhysicalMemoryMonitor` class, that in turn is based on comments from internal Windows implementations, the low memory notification is signaled when 97–99% of physical memory is occupied (depending on the physical RAM amount installed in the system).

If we would like to check whether a low memory level notification triggers GC in our application, the easiest way is to record the ETW session and look in reports or `Microsoft-Windows-DotNETRuntime/GC/Start` for GCs with the following reasons:

- LowMemory - operating system has signaled low memory notification.

- InducedLowMemory - operating system has signaled low memory notification (and the runtime asked for blocking GC).

- LowMemoryHost - host has signaled low memory notification (this is currently not a used one).

Various Internal Triggers

There are various other places spread across both runtime and standard libraries that ask for GC internally. Such GCs are mostly marked as induced ones (like in case of explicit calls) because from GC perspective it does not matter whether it was being called from user, runtime, or managed library code.

The most common reasons of this type include:

- AppDomain unload - cleaning up AppDomain-related objects is a good reason to perform garbage collection. In this scenario a blocking, full-GC is triggered.

- Cleanup of Thread objects representing dead threads - in a long-running application various threads may be created and deleted. Each such thread is represented by a managed object. This scenario triggers non-blocking collection of generation that most dead Thread object lives, but not more often than the default period value of 30 minutes.

- Before starting NoGC region (see Chapter 15) - a region of code asked for not triggering GC may put some pressure on memory. Thus, it is good to make a proactive cleanup in advance. This scenario triggers blocking, full-GC to make sure every dead object will be collected.

There is also an internal mechanism used by .NET team called GC stress. It enables triggering GC much often for diagnostic reasons; mostly it's for discovering so-called *GC holes*, for example, things that are supposed to be reported to the GC but aren't.

In case of internal triggers listed here, most of them will be visible with reason Induced in ETW-based data. Additionally, the following reasons exist:

- Internal - internal reason used by the runtime in a stress test mode,

- Empty and PMFullGC - currently not used.

EE Suspension

During Garbage Collection work there are moments when threads executing application code should not be working because they could access and modify memory regions accessed by the GC itself. Depending on the GC mode those moments are shorter or longer. In a Non-concurrent mode whole the GC is executed while user threads are suspended. Even in Concurrent mode (described in Chapter 11) only some parts of the

GC are done while managed threads are working so even in such a case where there is a need to suspend managed threads for those parts.

The process of suspending all threads executing user code is called "*EE suspension*" (Execution Engine suspension meaning "*suspending the managed threads*"). In case of Non-concurrent GC mode, which is described here, GC asks the suspension service to suspend all managed threads at the beginning of its work and resume them when it finishes. Such an intrusive approach is often referred to as "stop the world" technique because from the application perspective the whole world is being paused for the time of Garbage Collection.

As Book Of The Runtime says: "The CLR must ensure that all managed threads are stopped (so they aren't modifying the heap) to safely and reliably find all managed objects. It only stops at safe point, when registers and stack locations can be inspected for live references."

Thus, a *safe point* is a code location where registers and stack locations can be inspected for live references. Implementation of safe points is not trivial. Suspension obviously must also be very efficient because suspending and resuming threads counts into the overall GC pause time. From the perspective of the .NET memory management, and thus our entire book, those implementation details are not so important though. Thread suspension is not a part of GC at all. However, it is good to at least familiarize yourself with the nomenclature used in this process, which can appear in various tools during the analysis of memory consumption (especially in WinDbg). Moreover, thread suspension logic is closely related to the local data liveness as we will soon see.

From the GC perspective, each managed thread may be in two distinct modes:

- *cooperative* - As CoreCLR source says in comments: "when a thread is in cooperative mode, it is basically saying that it is potentially modifying GC references, and so the runtime must Cooperate with it to get to a 'GC Safe' location where the GC references can be enumerated." This is the mode that threads are in most of the time when running managed code.

- *preemptive* - this mode means the suspension service does not need to care about it - it is guaranteed to be in a place where a GC can occur because it is executing code that does not access and manipulate GC references. Most of the time it just means such a thread knows how to suspend itself.

Having said that, EE suspension can be defined as forcing a situation when all managed threads are in preemptive mode. Transition from cooperative to preemptive mode may happen only at safe points. At every safe point a view of the thread's state is remembered - describing the layout of the stack and registers because they may contain references to objects (constituting roots of the object tree). Such data is called *GC info*. Treating all instructions in our application as safe points (making it possible to preempt thread at each instruction) would require storing GC info for each of them. That would consume quite large amounts of memory.

Thus, as often in such cases, a compromise has been introduced. Managed code might be JITed into two kinds of code:

- *partially interruptible* - the only safe points are during calls to other methods (including explicit GC pool calls checking whether a GC is pending.[4]). Number of instructions between method calls is an average .NET method is quite small. Thus, such approach provides good safe points density with a reasonable overhead of GC info storage. Generating partially interruptible code is preferred JIT compiler's choice.

- *fully interruptible* - every instruction of a method is treated as a safe point (whole code is preemptive) except prolog and epilog (small code fragments executed when the method starts and ends respectively). JIT compiler must somehow store GC info for every instruction but this makes fully interruptible code quickly suspendable. Because of the storage overhead, JIT compiler rather tries to avoid this approach. One of the typical scenarios when JIT chooses it are loops of unknown repetition size without any method calls inside (they do not guarantee a quick end that does not lead to blocking off GC). One of the other typical solutions to such a problem is injecting GC pool calls on back jumps of the loop. The doubtful efficiency of such redundant pooling calls seems to be low though.

---

[4]Such GC pool calls are spread around the runtime itself in various places and are also emitted by JIT for some scenarios. They are rare, however, because pooling is not such an efficient approach, and in an average method it is just enough to wait for the first method call that is also a safe point.

If you want to investigate more, search for FC_GC_POLL and FC_GC_POLL_RET macros inside CoreCLR code that realize above-mentioned GC pool calls.

As Book Of The Runtime says: "The JIT chooses whether to emit fully- or partially interruptible code based on heuristics to find the best trade-off between code quality, size of the GC info, and GC suspension latency."

During suspending the Execution Engine, it tries to orchestrate all threads currently running in cooperative mode by forcing them to move into preemptive mode at their safe points.[5] First of all, operating system API is called to suspend underlying native thread (SuspendThread function in case of Windows API) and then:

- For fully interruptible code this is easy. A thread is already at a safe point so it may be just left suspended.

- For partially interruptible code we might be lucky and suspend a thread during its safe point. In such case it may be left suspended as above. If a thread was suspended outside a safe point (which is more likely), the current stack frame's return address is being manipulated to a special stub that will "park" it in a safe point and the thread is resumed for a short while (it may also hit its own safe point during that time).

Resuming threads is much simpler than suspending. When a GC is finished, all the suspended threads will be woken up by signaling an event about a suspension end and they will resume their execution.

We may monitor GC suspension and thread resuming with the help of ETW events pairs GCSuspendEE_V1/GCSuspendEEEnd_V1 and GCRestartEEBegin_V1/GCRestartEEEnd_V1 accordingly.

---

[5]Please note that such description is simplified for brevity. If you are interested in very deep implementation details, please refer to the CLR Threading Overview section in the Book Of The Runtime and ample comments at the beginning of the .\src\vm\threads.h file in CoreCLR source code.

Scenario 7-4. Analyzing GC Suspension Times

Description: Developing our .NET application, we would like to check with curiosity how long GC suspension actually takes. We should not expect any problems here. Just pure curiosity on our part.

Analysis: Thanks to the ETW events mentioned before, it is easy to calculate GC suspension and resumption time. The easiest way is to look at GCStats report in PerfView. GC Events by Time table shows a nice summary of each event, including the suspension and GC execution time (see columns Suspend Msec and Pause MSec in Figure 7-19). As we may see, suspension takes a lot less time than the GC itself.

GC Index	Pause Start	Trigger Reason	Gen	Suspend Msec	Pause MSec	% Pause Time	% GC	Gen0 Alloc MB	Gen0 Alloc Rate MB/sec
4	3,877.501	AllocSmall	2N	0.006	4.822	32.7	NaN	4.194	422.62
33	4,929.946	AllocSmall	2N	0.006	13.602	27.8	NaN	6.291	177.97
72	6,241.174	AllocSmall	2B	0.011	2.851	7.6	NaN	0.000	0.00
92	7,748.723	AllocSmall	2B	0.012	1.096	8.0	NaN	0.000	0.00
109	10,513.568	AllocSmall	2B	0.020	7.109	7.4	NaN	0.000	0.00
230	21,402.063	AllocSmall	2B	0.021	1.940	12.7	NaN	0.000	0.00
275	22,536.014	AllocSmall	2B	0.249	5.347	55.4	NaN	0.000	0.00
306	23,672.918	AllocSmall	2B	0.085	2.890	10.1	NaN	0.000	0.00
321	24,249.275	AllocSmall	2B	0.017	3.835	9.0	NaN	0.000	0.00
375	25,915.426	AllocSmall	2B	0.099	3.191	33.2	NaN	0.000	0.00
487	28,916.898	AllocSmall	2B	0.529	7.109	50.3	NaN	0.000	0.00
506	29,400.041	AllocSmall	2B	0.581	6.658	37.0	NaN	0.000	0.00
628	33,148.673	AllocSmall	2B	0.255	3.313	40.2	NaN	0.000	0.00
668	34,169.166	AllocSmall	2B	0.153	2.612	23.5	NaN	0.000	0.00

Figure 7-19. *GC suspension and GC execution times from GC Events by Time table in PerfView's GCStat raport*

We should not observe noticeable suspending times during our application execution. It would most probably mean a bug in the runtime because we have no control over the GC suspension mechanism. For example, there was a bug in some rare conditions in .NET 2.0 that in certain scenarios (tight CPU-bound loops executing the same code and not hitting any safe point) caused the suspend time to be extended to a value of seconds. It has been fixed in .NET 4.0. In regular applications, we can observe longer suspensions (let's say, longer than 1 ms) in case of a long I/O operation or thread priorities messed up.

Unmanaged threads are not suspended and restarted. If you create a background native thread doing its work (like executing a timer callback), it will run independently from the EE suspensions. However, P/Invoke mechanism must block on a return from unmanaged code to managed code.

Generation to Condemn

When GC is triggered with a specific generation to be collected, GC can decide to condemn a generation that's older one than specified. Thus, if something (including your GC.Collect call) asked for collecting some particular generation, it may decide to collect an older generation - based on various heuristics it tracks internally. We have seen those data already in the section about static and dynamic GC data.

In this section an extensive list of possible reasons of changing condemned generation is provided. This allows you to better understand what and why GCs take place in our applications.

Let's take into account that the order of decisions presented here is important. Each subsequent decision (heuristics) can increase the condemned generation but not lower it. In other words, for example, if one of the checks decides to condemn generation 2 and some later check will like to decide to condemn generation 1, eventually the older one will be condemned (effectively ignoring suggestion of condemning generation 1).

Below is a comprehensive list of various decisions that may change the condemned generation (names in the parentheses are taken from PerfView's Condemned reasons for GCs table that is the best and only place when you can analyze this stage):

- Allocation budget has been exceeded (Generation Budget Exceeded) - the oldest generation that exceeded allocation budget will be condemned. This includes Large Object Heap in case of which generation 2 will be condemned (triggering full-GC) but only if background GC is not already running. Please note that, for example, it means older generation may be condemned because of its allocation budget even if originally only generation 0 budget violation was detected during object allocation. We have seen such a typical situation in scenario 7-2.

- Time-based tuning (Time Tuning) - it may be surprising but GC also cares about the appropriate proportions of collections of individual generations based on time dependencies and their counting. This is done however only in Workstation mode, not in Server mode, and only in case of Interactive or SustainedLowLatency latency modes. GC may decide to condemn a generation if enough time has elapsed since the last GC of that generation and the number of GCs of lower generation has exceeded a certain threshold. Threshold values have been already presented in Tables 7-1 and 7-2 in the clock_time and gc_time columns. It means in particular that:

  - generation 1 may be condemned if it was not collected since 10 seconds and 10 GCs,

  - generation 2 (triggering full-GC) may be condemned if it was not collected since 100 seconds and 100 GCs.

  This is to accommodate the fact that processes running in Workstation GC mode are less regular than those in Server GC mode so the GC wants a chance to notice the allocation/survival pattern sooner.

We can sometimes meet the so-called *Golden Rule* of GC that in a healthy application's proportions between a generation's collections count should be as 1:10:100 - clearly resulting from the time tuning described here. Please note, however, this only applies to Workstation GC and is considered no longer valid in general. The "Healthy" proportions of GCs the count are much more complex and dynamic than just such simple ratios.

- Low card table efficiency (Internal Tuning) - the card table has too many "generation faults." If we return to the information about card tables from Chapter 5, we will remind ourselves that they introduce a certain overhead. Each card represents continuous memory region where multiple objects may live. Each of such objects may contain references to other objects but only some of them will be truly cross-generational (will point to objects in the generations being collected). The ratio between these useful and all references is called card table efficiency. Low card table efficiency means unnecessary traversing through a lot of objects. Thus, if it drops below a certain threshold, it is worth it to condemn generation 1. This should group long-living objects into same generations, potentially removing most cross-generational references.

- Running out of space in the ephemeral segment (Ephemeral Low and Ephemeral Low with Very Fragmented Gen2) - there is a shortage of space in the segment containing generations 0 and 1 (more precisely, there is no space for the doubled size of minimum generation 0 in the segment's Reserved memory). In such case generation 1 will be condemned to free up ephemeral memory (with reason Ephemeral Low). Additionally, if there is a fragmentation in generation 2 big enough to fit (after compaction) generation 1, generation 2 will be condemned triggering full-GC (with reason Ephemeral Low with Very Fragmented Gen2). This in general means that if the ephemeral segment is running out of space, the GC is more aggressive in doing collections (meaning doing mainly more generation 1 collections) to avoid acquiring a new heap segment (or expanding current one).

- Ephemeral generation is too fragmented (Fragmented Ephemeral) - the ephemeral generation whose threshold of fragmentation has been exceeded will be condemned (that is, generation 0 or 1).

- Running out of space in the ephemeral segment requires expanding it (Expand Heap) - if there is no other way to fit growing ephemeral generations other than by expanding segment, generation 2 will be condemned (triggering full, blocking GC).

- Running out of space during allocation (Compacting Full-GC) - as a last resort before throwing `OutOfMemoryException` during Allocator's work, a full, blocking, and compacting GC will be triggered.

- Physical memory load in the system is more than 90% [6] or operating system has sent a low-memory notification (High Memory) - if generation 2 is heavily fragmented or it is already occupied in more than 10% of its allocation budget, condemn generation 2 (in many cases doing blocking GC). Please note, it means that the CLR may ignore a low-memory notification from the OS and does not trigger GC at all if it decides it is not worth doing it. In general, however, thanks to this point, system-wide memory pressure makes GC more aggressive if that's likely to yield free space. This is important to prevent unnecessary paging across the whole machine.

- Generation 2 is too fragmented (Fragmented Gen2) - the generation 2 threshold of fragmentation has been exceeded and it be condemned.

- Generation 2 or LOH is too small for doing background GC (Small Heap) - in such a case full, blocking GC will be triggered.

- In case of low-latency mode only generation 0 or 1 can be condemned (overriding any previous decisions).

Additionally, there is one special reason used in case of background GC (described in Chapter 11) to note starting an ephemeral GC before a background GC (Ephemeral Before BGC in PerfView).

---

[6]This is the value used in most cases. For powerful machines with many logical cores, this threshold may be bigger - up to 97%.

In some of the decisions described above, fragmentation threshold exceeding takes an important role. One can wonder what its value is. Each generation maintains its own threshold, consisting of two values taken from static generation data (see Tables 7-1 and 7-2):

- total memory size wasted because of unusable fragmentation - unusable fragmentation includes:

  - unused free space, not managed by the generation allocator - those include small gaps created during Sweeping (as we will see later) and space in ephemeral generations discarded after not successful fitting (as mentioned in Chapter 5, free-list items in these generations are checked only once and then released).

  - expected allocator efficiency - how well it has been possible to reuse free-list items so far.

- This value is represented by fragmentation_limit column in Tables 7-1 and 7-2 (see Table 7-4 for a summary).

Table 7-4. Fragmentation Thresholds for Generations

	Fragmentation limit	Fragmentation ratio
Gen0	40,000	75%
Gen1	80,000	75%
Gen2	200,000	50%

- fragmentation ratio - this is the ratio of the above total unusable fragmentation size to the size of the whole generation. This value is calculated from the fragmentation_burden_limit column in Tables 7-1 and 7-2 by doubling it, but not exceeding 75% (see Table 7-4 for a summary).

For example, generation 2 will be considered as too fragmented if the size of unusable fragmentation will exceed 200,000 bytes and it will be more than 50% of total generation size.

Scenario 7-5. Condemned Generations Analysis

Description: We want to understand the most common reasons of GCs in our application, altogether with the knowledge which and why generations were condemned. Such kind of analysis is very in-depth and will probably be necessary only in very specific cases (like, we see too many full-GCs happening and we want to understand why they are full-GCs).

Analysis: Currently there is no better tool to understand generations being condemned than analysis of GCStats report in PerfView. After recording even the simplest GC Collect Only session, it provides Condemned reasons for GCs table that pretty much explain everything (see Figure 7-20). This scenario is a follow-up of scenario 7-2 where the first five GCs were thoroughly analyzed. Now we can observe how they are described in PerfView. During analysis refer to the names from the list of various condemning decisions presented above.

Condemned reasons for GCs

This table gives a more detailed account of exactly why a GC decided to collect that generation. Hover over the column headings for more info.

GC Index	Initial Requested Generation	Final Generation	Generation Budget Exceeded	Time Tuning	Induced	Ephemeral Low	Expand Heap	Fragmented Ephemeral	Very Fragmented Ephemeral	Fragmented Gen2	High Memory	Compacting Full GC	Small Heap	Ephemeral Before BGC	Internal Tuning
1	2	2	0	0	Blocking	0	0	0	0	0	0	0	1	0	0
2	0	2	2	0	0	0	0	0	0	0	0	0	0	0	0
3	0	0	0	0	0	0	0	0	0	0	0	0	0	0	0
4	0	1	1	0	0	0	0	0	0	0	0	0	0	0	0
5	1	2	2	0	0	1	0	0	0	0	0	0	0	0	0
6	0	1	0	0	0	1	0	0	0	0	0	0	0	0	0
7	1	1	0	0	0	1	0	0	0	0	0	0	0	0	0
8	0	2	2	0	0	1	0	0	0	0	0	0	0	0	0
9	0	0	0	0	0	0	0	0	0	0	0	0	0	0	0
10	1	1	0	0	0	1	0	0	0	0	0	0	0	0	0

Figure 7-20. *Condemned reasons for GCs table from GCStats report in PerfView*

We can indeed see here confirmation of our analysis for the first five GCs from scenario 7-2:

- GC #1 is explicitly induced (value of Blocking in Induced column) as full-GC (value of 2 in Initial Requested Generation). And it is indeed executed as full-GC (value of 2 in Final Generation).

572

- GC #2 is initially requested for generation 0 (value of 0 in Initial Requested Generation) - because of this generation's allocation budget exceeding. However, it becomes full-GC because also generation 2 budget has been exceeded (value of 2 in Final Generation). As we know, it is in fact the LOH allocation budget being exceeded, but as already explained, it is being treated as gen2.

- GC #3 is initially requested for generation 0 and actually performed for it. There are no reasons for other generation condemnation.

- GC #4 is initially requested for generation 0 but due to generation 1 budget exceeding, finally generation 1 is condemned.

- GC #5 is initially requested for generation 1 - that happens in case of OutOfSpaceSOH reason (see value of 1 in Ephemeral Low column). However, due to generation 2 budget being exceeded, it becomes full-GC.

Careful analysis of Condemned reasons for GCs together with GC Events by Time tables may provide a great insight into your application GCs. However, this is q quite mundane and laborious task. You can view the Condemned reasons for GCs table and look for common patterns, frequently recurring reasons, and so on and so forth. Unfortunately, there is currently no tool that will try to summarize and analyze condemned reasons as a whole.

It is definitely worth paying special attention to the following columns that may indicate a problem in your code:

- Induced - explicit GC calls are rarely justified. If they occur frequently, we may wish to investigate why (refer to scenario 7-3).

- Fragmented Ephemeral and Fragmented Gen2 - if they occur frequently, they show problems with memory fragmentation. We probably should better understand the allocation patterns in our application (refer to scenario 5-2 and scenario 6-2).

If you would like to perform your own CoreCLR code analysis, carefully read `gc_heap::generation_to_condemn` method. All condemnation reasons described here are checked there one by one.

Summary

In this chapter we started to investigate deeply the heart of the .NET memory management - the Garbage Collector. We started here from the high-level view. An overall, generalized concept of GC work has been presented, including GC process in example and explained step by step. Then, all major phases of the GC were thoroughly described. While three subsequent chapters describe them in details, this one explained the three first:

- mechanisms that triggers garbage collection,

- how entire runtime cooperates to proceed with the EE suspension, that is - stopping all managed threads,

- how GC selects which generation should be collected.

Because those are such important topics, five practical scenarios were also presented here - including how to analyze the GC usage and finding explicit GC calls.

With all the knowledge from this chapter, we may proceed in explaining the next phases of the GC. The next chapter contains detailed explanation of the Mark phase.

CHAPTER 8

Garbage Collection - Mark Phase

In the previous chapter we have gained knowledge about some general GC topics, like when it is triggered and how it decides which generation should be collected. Let's now move into the details of implementation of the first main GC phase - Mark phase.

At this stage, GC decided which generations will be collected. It's time to investigate which objects may be reclaimed. As mentioned before, CLR implements a tracing Garbage Collector. It starts from various roots and recursively traverses a whole object's graph of the current program state. All those that are not reachable from any roots are considered dead (recall Figure 1-15).

In case of a Non-concurrent GC described in this chapter, at the beginning of this stage, all managed threads are suspended. Managed Heap is guaranteed to be not changing, and it remains the sole property of the GC. It can therefore start browsing safely in search of reachable objects.

Object Traversal and Marking

Despite the existence of many different roots, the mechanism of finding reachable objects remains common. Given a specific root address, a traversal routine performs the following steps:

- Translate it to the proper address of a managed object - in case of a so-called *interior pointer* (indicating not at the beginning but somewhere inside the managed object). It may be done efficiently thanks to the bricks table mechanism described later.

© Konrad Kokosa 2018
K. Kokosa, *Pro .NET Memory Management*, https://doi.org/10.1007/978-1-4842-4027-4_8

- Set pinning flag - if an object is pinned (which is known by the fact of traversal from the pinned handles table or flag reported to the GC), a proper single bit is set in the object's header.

- Start traversal through object's references - thanks to the type information (stored in a MethodTable), GC knows which offsets (fields) represent outgoing references. It starts visiting them in a depth-first manner by maintaining a collection of objects to be visited. This is called a *mark stack* because it is organized as a stack data structure with push and pop operations. During visiting an object:

  - already visited object is simply skipped.

  - not yet visited object is being marked - which is done by setting a bit in object's MethodTable pointer.[1]

  - its outgoing references are added to the mark stack collection.

Traversal ends when there are no more objects to visit on the mark stack.

Commonly, the typical approach to a depth-first graph traversal is based on recursive calls. However, they are hard to guarantee that no stack overflow will happen. It is easier and safer to replace the recursive-based technique with the iterative one - based on the heap allocated, stack-like collection (like mark stack used in CLR) that may be simply grown in case of exceeding its current size.

Please note, both pinned and marked flags are set during the Mark phase. Those flags are used and then unset during the Plan phase. During a normal object's lifetime (while managed threads are running), both the fact of pinning or marking is not presented in the object's header nor its MT pointer.

---

[1]It does not destroy the MT pointer because MethodTable data address is word-aligned (it is multiplication of 4 or 8 bytes) so at least the two lowest bits are unused (always set to zero). Getting a proper MT pointer from such a modified pointer requires only zeroing the two lowest bits - see GetMethodTable method in CoreCLR for reference.

If you are interested in details and want to study CoreCLR code, start from investigating GCHeap::Promote method. It calls the go_through_object_cl macro that triggers traversal through all objects' references. The main work is done in gc_heap::mark_object_simple1 method that realizes depth-first object graph traversal using an auxiliary stack-like collection called mark_stack_array (with mark_stack_bos and mark_stack_tos indexes pointing to the bottom and the top of the stack).

Knowing the overall structure of the marking process, let's now investigate in detail different GC roots that may exist in our application. Good understanding of them is one of the most useful pieces of knowledge related to the .NET memory management. Roots may be holding whole graphs of reachable objects, counting into the common problems:

- big memory usage - we may be unaware of the existence of certain roots that cause the reachability of a much larger number of objects than we would expect. The mere fact of the existence of a large number of objects can be an overhead for GC by itself.

- memory leak - even worse, roots may cause continuous growth of the object graph hold by them, leading to constantly increasing memory usage.

Local Variable Roots

Local variables are one of the most common roots. Some of them are very temporary (see Listing 8-1), while others live for the entire application lifetime (see Listing 8-2). We simply create local variables constantly here and there.

Listing 8-1. An example of very short-living local variable fullPath

```
public static void Delete(string path)
{
    string fullPath = Path.GetFullPath(path);
    FileSystem.Current.DeleteFile(fullPath);
}
```

Listing 8-2. An example of very long-living local variable `host` that lives for an entire self-hosted ASP.NET application lifetime

```
public static void Main(string[] args)
{
    var host = BuildWebHost(args);
    host.Run();
}
```

We often create them explicitly (like in Listings 8-1 and 8-2), but many times they are also created implicitly (see Listing 8-3).

Listing 8-3. An example of very long-living local variable host created implicitly (this code is in fact the same as in Listing 8-2)

```
public static void Main(string[] args)
{
    BuildWebHost(args).Run();
}
```

Local variable may represent a value type (like struct) or a reference to the reference type value [2] (please recall an important distinction between "reference" and "reference type data" discussed in Chapter 4). In this section a Garbage Collection of objects allocated on the heap are considered so we will look into details of local variables holding references (regardless of whether it is a typical reference type like class or boxed value type).

Local Variables Storage

When we assign a managed object reference to a local variable, we create a root like in Listing 8-4 where reference to a newly created object instance of type `SomeClass` has been assigned to a local variable `c`. Since then we should consider this instance to be reachable. Thus, assuming `c` is the only root, an object cannot be garbage collected until the method `Helper` ends because local variable `c` is used throughout the entire `Helper` method.

---

[2]Local variable may represent a primitive type (like numbers), but those are not in our interest here as they do not represent a heap-allocated object.

Listing 8-4. An example of local variable holding

```
private int Helper(SomeData data)
{
    SomeClass c = new SomeClass();
    c.Calculate(data);
    return c.Result;
}
```

In general, the situation from Listing 8-4 may be nicely illustrated by Figure 1-10 from Chapter 1. Maybe we are used to it and we would like to treat local variables as being stack allocated (because reference may be treated as value type). Thus, the situation from Listing 8-4 may be seen as follows: allocator creates an object instance on the Managed Heap while local variable `c` should be stored on the stack within `Helper`'s method activation frame. However, as we have seen already in Chapter 4, local variables may be enregistered (stored into CPU register) thanks to great JIT compiler optimizations. This leads to an important fact endlessly worth repeating - roots represented by local variables may be stored on the stack or in CPU registers. The JIT compiler makes its best to allocate registers and stack slots as efficiently as possible.

Stack Roots

Roots described above in this chapter are called *stack roots*. Fundamentals of Garbage Collection section in .NET Guide Docs are describing them as "stack variables provided by the just-in-time (JIT) compiler and stack walker." This description can be a bit confusing. As we know, it is really about the local variables in a method that is currently running and also local variables of all methods in the current call stack. It is the call stack that the term "stack roots" refers to. But please remember, such "stack roots" may be on the stack or in a CPU register.

When EE suspension is done, call stacks of all managed threads must be investigated to find all local variables because they may constitute what is referred to as stack roots. This is done by the mentioned *stack walker*. If a method from the current call stack has some local variables holding reference to the managed object - it is considered as live and starts such an object's graph traversal. However, it is not trivial to answer the question whether there are local variables at a given line of the method code (instruction address, to be precise) and whether they are a reference to an object or not.

As described in the section on suspension in Chapter 7, threads may be suspended at safe points - those include almost every instruction (in case of fully interruptible methods) or only other methods calls (in case of partially interruptible methods). This leads us to the conclusion that GC needs to store somehow the knowledge about live "stack roots" (both stack and register slots) for every safe point of a method. This is what GC info mentioned before really is.

Lexical Scope

In C# inseparable from the concept of a local variable is the related concept of its *lexical scope*. In the simplest words, it defines areas of code in which the given variable is visible - considering all nested code blocks, etc. Taking as an example code from Listing 8-5, there are three local variables defined:

- c1 - local variable that represents a reference to the managed object of type ClassOne. Lexical scope of c1 spans to entire LexicalScopeExample method - c1 is accessible in the entire method because it has been declared in the most outer scope of it;

- c2 - local variable that represents a reference to the managed object of type ClassTwo. Lexical scope of c2 is limited to the conditional block;

- data - local variable for primitive, integer type.

Listing 8-5. An example of two local variables with different lexical scopes

```
1 private int LexicalScopeExample(int value)
2 {
3     ClassOne c1 = new ClassOne();
4     if (c1.Check())
5     {
6         ClassTwo c2 = new ClassTwo();
7         int data = c2.CalculateSomething(value);
8         DoSomeLongRunningCall(data);
9         return 1;
10    }
11    return 0;
12 }
```

Let's now elaborate how reachability of objects created within a method relates to their lexical scope.

Live Stack Roots vs. Lexical Scope

When considering reachability of an object represented by a local variable, a very intuitive solution immediately comes to mind - it should be associated with the local variable lexical scope. Thus, taking Listing 8-5 as an example:

- Created instance of ClassOne should be reachable during entire method lifetime - since the creation (line 3) until the end of method (line 11). In other words, c1 local variable constitutes live stack root from line 3 until line 11;

- Created instance of ClassTwo may be reachable only within conditional block - since the creation (line 6) until the block end (line 9). In other words, c2 local variable constitutes live stack root from line 6 until line 9.

Taking such approach, GC Info of LexicalScopeExample method from Listing 8-5:

- For fully interruptible case could be imagined as in Listing 8-6 - each line has its own information (while obviously it would be created at an assembler level, let's now stick with C# lines of code for brevity).

- For partially interruptible case could be imagined as in Listing 8-7 - information is stored only at lines with method calls (including allocation/constructor).

Listing 8-6. A visualization of GC Info of LexicalScopeExample method from Listing 8-5-10 in fully interruptible case. Each line lists live stack roots.

```
1    No live slots
2    No live slots
3    Live slot of c1
4    Live slot of c1
5    Live slot of c1
6    Live slot of c1, live slot of c2
7    Live slot of c1, live slot of c2
```

```
8     Live slot of c1, live slot of c2
9     Live slot of c1, live slot of c2
10    Live slot of c1
11    Live slot of c1
12    No live slots
```

Listing 8-7. A visualization of GC Info of `LexicalScopeExample` method from Listing 8-5 in partially interruptible case. Each line lists live stack roots.

```
3     Live slot of c1
4     Live slot of c1
6     Live slot of c1, live slot of c2
7     Live slot of c1, live slot of c2
8     Live slot of c1, live slot of c2
```

GC info stores information about JITted, assembly code. Thus, it obviously does not operate on specific C# variable names, but on specific stack slots or CPU register slots. For example, the more realistic GC info representation of Listing 8-6 would look like in Listing 8-8 (assuming that JIT compiler has assigned register rax to local variable c1 and rbx to local variable c2).

Listing 8-8. A visualization of GC Info (at JITted assembly level) of `LexicalScopeExample` method from Listing 8-5 in fully interruptible case

```
1     No live slots
2     No live slots
3     Live slots: rax
4     Live slots: rax
5     Live slots: rax
6     Live slots: rax, rbx
7     Live slots: rax, rbx
8     Live slots: rax, rbx
9     Live slots: rax, rbx
10    Live slots: rax
11    Live slots: rax
12    No live slots
```

Imagine that due to GC, runtime has suspended a thread currently executing LexicalScopeExample method at line 7 (assuming the method has been JITted as fully interruptible). Thanks to the GC info presented in Listing 8-8, GC immediately knows that there are live stack roots in CPU registers rax and rbx. The marking process may be started with addresses stored in those registers.

Such an approach would be perfectly valid, leading to proper results. The reference local variable lexical scope obviously counts into the reachability of the reference type object. Similar, an even more relaxed approach is taken when compiling an application in Debug mode. JIT compiler extends the reachability of all local variables until the end of a method. This is very useful due to debugging purposes (like inspecting variable values). But more can be done in the Release mode to optimize memory usage.

Live Stack Roots with Eager Root Collection

Looking at the code from Listing 7-10 once again, we may notice that lexical scope is not the optimal representation of reachability. From the fact that due to its lexical scope a local variable may be used does not mean it is used indeed. What really matters is whether those variables are in fact used or not. Looking at LexicalScopeExample method from such perspective we notice that:

- Created instance of ClassOne is no longer used since line 5 - so despite lexical scope of variable c1, it constitutes live stack root only from line 3 until line 4,

- Created instance of ClassTwo is used only at lines 6 and 7 - so despite lexical scope of variable c2, it constitutes live stack root only at those lines.

In other words, the C# compiler may notice the real usage of each object (through local variables) and save this information. Then the JIT compiler will use it during slots allocation (shorter object lifetimes allows it to reuse valuable CPU registers) and while emitting GC info. This results in much more efficient generated GC info (see Listing 8-9).

Listing 8-9. A visualization of GC Info (at JITted assembly level) of
`LexicalScopeExample` method from Listing 8-5 in fully interruptible case using
eager root collectiont

```
1     No live slots
2     No live slots
3     Live slots: rax
4     Live slots: rax
5     No live slots
6     Live slots: rax
7     Live slots: rax
8     No live slots
9     No live slots
10    No live slots
11    No live slots
12    No live slots
```

With a new GC info, most of the time while the method is running, there are no live
stack roots. Each object is treated as unreachable from local variables when it is indeed
no longer needed. Such eagerness to collect an object as fast as possible is referred to as
eager root collection. This obviously is more efficient from a memory usage perspective
because it shortens an object's lifetime to the required minimum. This in turns also
allows it to use CPU registers more densely because they may be reused more often (like
reusing rax register in Listing 8-9). Generated GC info for partially interruptible methods
will be even shorter (see Listing 8-10).

Listing 8-10. A visualization of GC Info of `LexicalScopeExample` method from
Listing 8-5 in partially interruptible case using eager root collection

```
3     Live slots: rax
4     Live slots: rax
6     Live slots: rax
7     Live slots: rax
```

In all examples in this section, only CPU register slots were used. This is a typical scenario because JIT makes its best to use only blazingly fast CPU registers instead of stack slots. It may decide to use a stack slot in certain circumstances, but this will not change the mechanisms described here. Only a stack slot would be listed instead of a register name. Stack slots are represented as offsets to the `rsp` or `rbp` address (depending which one is used by a method). Thus, GC info also stores current `rsp` and `rbp` register values for each safe point. Moreover, JIT in x64 runtime is much more likely to consume registers because x64 platform added eight new general-purpose registers (named `r8` through `r15`).

When threads are suspended, their current context (including registers) is saved. So for example, when `LexicalScopeExample` happens to be suspended at line 6, based on the GC info, there will be one live stack root address taken from `rax` register (stored in the context). The same logic will be repeated for all methods on the call stacks by inspecting the call stack frame by frame (and restoring proper thread context thanks to information inside activation frames - like previous values of registers).

Eager root collection is used by JIT when our code is compiled in Release mode. It can sometimes lead to several surprising and even misleading behaviors. Most of the questions about such scenarios starts with "In Debug, my code does X. But in Release, it does Y... ."

First of all, setting a local variable to null to "inform" GC that we will no longer use a given object is not needed in most cases (see Listing 8-11). Even before long-running calls (to tell GC - hey, I am starting those very long-running calls so please note that this object is no longer used and may be collected). Thanks to an eager root collection technique, the compiler and JIT will perfectly notice the real scopes of our variables' usage. There is no need to tell them explicitly. Code from Listings 8-5 and 8-11 are perfectly identical in that respect. They produce the same GC Info and assembly code (JIT will optimize out those redundant null settings in the first place).

Listing 8-11. An example of unnecessary null setting

```
private int LexicalScopeExample(int value)
{
    ClassOne c1 = new ClassOne();
    if (c1.Check())
```

```
        {
            c1 = null;
            ClassTwo c2 = new ClassTwo();
            int data = c2.CalculateSomething(value);
            c2 = null;
            DoSomeLongRunningCall(data);
            return 1;
        }
        return 0;
}
```

There is one exception to that rule in case of so-called untracked variables (explained later), which are considered life for the entire method's lifetime. So in case of really, really crucial resources, you may wish to set a local variable to null to help out the JIT compiler.

Secondly, eager root collection may cause strange results when imposed on objects with methods causing side effects. We may expect particular object's lifetime based on its lexical scope, producing those side effects, while as we already know, the lifetime is not based on lexical scope. The typical scenarios here include using various timers, synchronization primitives (like Mutex), or system-wide resource access (like files).

Listing 8-12 shows a typical behavior that is hardly explainable without knowledge about eager root collection. Intuitively we expect Timer object lifetime to be corresponding to the local variable timer lexical scope. Thus, the presented program should print the current time endlessly until we do not hit any key. And this is a behavior we will observe in Debug build. However, in Release build, eager root collection comes into the play. As Timer object is not used since line 3, JIT compiler will emit GC Info about it. Timer object becomes unreachable after line 3! If GC will happen while Main method is executing code after that line, it will be collected (stopping printing current time). Depending how fast the GC will be processed, the timer may be able to print the current time a few times.

Listing 8-12. An example of unexpected Timer behavior due to early root collection

```
1 static void Main(string[] args)
2 {
3     Timer timer = new Timer((obj) => Console.WriteLine(DateTime.Now.
      ToString()), null, 0, 100);
4     Console.WriteLine("Hello World!");
5     GC.Collect(); // simulate GC happening here
6     Console.ReadLine();
7 }
```

Program result:

```
Hello World!
28/03/2018 14:29:01
```

Please note that in our example GC is called explicitly to produce repeatable results. In a real-world scenario such GC may happen due to allocations on other threads.

Moreover, eager root collection is so aggressive that an object may be treated as unreachable even while one of its methods is still running (if that method does not refer to this). Listing 8-13 shows a behavior simulating such scenario. While DoSomething method is running, GC occurs (again, for example purposes it is called explicitly). Additionally, SomeClass has a finalize method (finalization will be explained in detail in Chapter 12), which is executed when an object is being garbage collected.

Listing 8-13. An example of unexpected object behavior due to early root collection

```
static void Main(string[] args)
{
    SomeClass sc = new SomeClass();
    sc.DoSomething("Hello world!");
    Console.ReadKey();
}

class SomeClass
{
    public void DoSomething(string msg)
```

```
    {
        GC.Collect();
        Console.WriteLine(msg);
    }

    ~SomeClass()
    {
        Console.WriteLine("Killing...");
    }
}
```

Program result:

```
Killing...
Hello world!
```

Surprisingly enough, the program produces an output suggesting that an object died before its whole method had been executed. This is because DoSomething does not refer to this, so in fact, it does not require its own object instance!

Going further, in certain circumstances eager root collection may collect an object while one of its methods is still running and its code refers to this! Listing 8-14 shows a behavior simulating such a scenario. Even DoSomethingElse method refers to this, and SomeClass instance will be eagerly collected like in the previous example.

Listing 8-14. An example of unexpected object behavior due to early root collection

```
static void Main(string[] args)
{
    SomeClass sc = new SomeClass() { Field = new Random().Next() };
    sc.DoSomethingElse();
    Console.ReadKey();
}

class SomeClass
{
    public int Field;

    public void DoSomethingElse()
```

```
    {
        Console.WriteLine(this.Field.ToString());
        // further code
            Console.WriteLine("Am I dead?");
    }

    ~SomeClass()
    {
        Console.WriteLine("Killing...");
    }
}
```

Program result:

```
615323
Killing...
Am I dead?
```

How does it happen? It is possible due to method inlining. If JIT compiler decides to inline a method, it becomes a part of the calling method (see Listing 8-15). It may incur further optimizations. For example, DoSomethingElse used this.Field only at the beginning. After inlining into Main method, sc.Field reference will be the last one to the object and further code may be executed while the object is being collected.

Listing 8-15. An example of unexpected object behavior due to early root collection

```
static void Main(string[] args)
{
    SomeClass sc = new SomeClass() { Field = new Random().Next() };
    Console.WriteLine(sc.Field.ToString());
    // further code
        Console.WriteLine("Am I dead?");
    Console.ReadKey();
}
```

Please bear in mind that such optimizations are quite often as the JIT compiler is very aggressive at making the local variable lifetime as short as possible. In most cases the JIT compiler safely uses this technique because it does not change the program's logic. Any unexpected behaviors resulting from it should be very rare and related only to the above-mentioned objects with side effects related to their lifetime.

Sometimes for some reason we need to have better control over an object's lifetime. Coming back to Listing 8-12, we may really need a timer running for the whole lifetime of the application. For such scenarios the GC.KeepAlive method has been exposed (see Listing 8-16).

Listing 8-16. Fixing an example of unexpected Timer behavior due to early root collection (based on Listing 8-17)

```
static void Main(string[] args)
{
    Timer timer = new Timer((obj) => Console.WriteLine(DateTime.Now.
    ToString()), null, 0, 100);
    Console.WriteLine("Hello World!");
    GC.Collect(); // simulate GC happening here
    Console.ReadLine();
    GC.KeepAlive(timer);
}
```

GC.KeepAlive is a really simple trick to extend liveness of a stack root. Its implementation contains no code (see Listing 8-17) but is attributed with MethodImplOptions.NoInlining option. This makes KeepAlive no inlineable, which in turn forces the compiler to treat the passed argument as used (and thus reachable). So when GC.KeepAlive is used, resulting GC Info will extend liveness of the passed object until its occurrence.

Listing 8-17. Implementation of the GC.KeepAlive method in Base Class Library

```
[MethodImplAttribute(MethodImplOptions.NoInlining)] // disable
optimizations
public static void KeepAlive(Object obj)
{
}
```

Note   In most cases objects with such side effects (like Mutex or Timer) are implementing `IDisposable` interface. Thus, simple `timer.Dispose()` call at the end of Main method (or using clause) would extend its lifetime appropriately, without a need of using `GC.KeepAlive`. It is still worth keeping in mind eager collection caveats.

GC Info

Presented so far, visualizations of GC Info in Listings from 8-6 to 8-10 were only simplifications. In reality, GC Info is a very densely packed, binary piece of information. The actual implementation details of its storage are interesting but irrelevant for our purposes. The idea behind it remains the same as presented so far.

The only tool currently available allowing us to see it is WinDbg with SOS extension.

To see GC info in WinDbg running and either memory dump or process attached, find the method's MethodDesc you are interested in (see Listing 8-18).

Listing 8-18. Looking for a managed heap in WinDbg with SOS loaded

```
> .loadby sos coreclr
> !name2ee *!Scenarios.EagerRootCollection.LexicalScopeExample
...
Module:      00007ffea9944f30
Assembly:    Scenarios.dll
Token:       000000000600000d
MethodDesc:  00007ffea9948598
Name:        Scenarios.EagerRootCollection.LexicalScopeExample(Int32)
JITTED Code Address: 00007ffea9a63310
...
```

Then you can see detailed GC info with command `!gcinfo <MethodDesc>` (see Listing 8-19). Let's now analyze with its help the `LexicalScopeExample` method from Listing 8-5. Command output contains various general information about the selected method (like return type kind, whether it uses variable number of arguments, and so on, and so forth). More importantly to us, it also lists all safe points together with live stack roots in each of them (if any). With each safe point, an instruction offset inside a method is also provided.

Listing 8-19. !gcinfo command output for LexicalScopeExample method

```
> !gcinfo 00007ffea9948598
entry point 00007ffea9a63310
Normal JIT generated code
GC info 00007ffea9b29188
Pointer table:
Prolog size: 0
Security object: <none>
GS cookie: <none>
PSPSym: <none>
Generics inst context: <none>
PSP slot: <none>
GenericInst slot: <none>
Varargs: 0
Frame pointer: <none>
Wants Report Only Leaf: 0
Size of parameter area: 0
Return Kind: Scalar
Code size: 71
00000017 is a safepoint:
00000022 is a safepoint:
00000021 +rdi
0000002d is a safepoint:
00000040 is a safepoint:
0000004b is a safepoint:
0000004a +rdi
00000055 is a safepoint:
0000005c is a safepoint:
```

In case of `LexicalScopeExample` info showed in Listing 8-19, there are seven safe points generated. This is a way to find out that this method has been JITted as partially interruptible. In case of fully interruptible methods only stack root changes are stored without any safe points listed (as we will soon see). At Listing 8-19 only two safe points contain a single stack root (enregistered in `rdi` CPU register). Each safe point invalidates all other stack roots. Thus, from Listing 8-19 we can infer that:

- rdi register is live stack root from instruction offset 21 till instruction offset 2d,

- again rdi register is live stack root from instruction offset 4a till instruction offset 55.

Fully interruptible method may require significant storage (of quantity similar to the code itself). To make a good compromise between decoding time and storage efficiency, the main part of GC Info is stored internally as a chunk of bits representing stack roots' liveness changes through corresponding code regions. Additionally, initial state of that liveness is remembered for each chunk. Thus, to decode stack root liveness for a specific code offset, the proper chunk is being analyzed starting from initial liveness and then by applying described liveness changes offset by offset until the offset of interest is not being hit. WinDbg SOS extension does the same multiple times (for each valid instruction offset in a method) producing a nice summary seen in the presented listings.

However, such GC info without referring to code does not say much. Luckily, there is another command that interleaves JITted code with the GC info - !u -gcinfo <MethodDesc> (see Listing 8-20).

Listing 8-20. !u -gcinfo command output for LexicalScopeExample method

```
> !u -gcinfo 00007ffea9948598
Normal JIT generated code
Scenarios.EagerRootCollection.LexicalScopeExample(Int32)
Begin 00007ff81c5e3310, size 71
push    rdi
push    rsi
sub     rsp,28h
mov     esi,edx
mov     rcx,7FF81C69AD08h (MT: Scenarios.EagerRootCollection+ClassOne )
call    CoreCLR!JIT_New
0017 is a safepoint:
mov     rdi,rax
mov     rcx,rdi
```

```
call     System_Private_CoreLib+0xc890f0 (System.Object..ctor())
0022 is a safepoint:
0021 +rdi
mov      dword ptr [rdi+8],esi
mov      rcx,rdi
call     00007ff8`1c5e2bb8 (Scenarios.EagerRootCollection+ClassOne .Check())
002d is a safepoint:
test     eax,eax
je       00007ff8`1c5e3378
mov      rcx,7FF81C69AFE8h (MT: Scenarios.EagerRootCollection+ClassTwo )
call     CoreCLR!JIT_TrialAllocSFastMP_InlineGetThread
0040 is a safepoint:
mov      rdi,rax
mov      rcx,rdi
call     System_Private_CoreLib+0xc890f0 (System.Object..ctor())
004b is a safepoint:
004a +rdi
mov      rcx,rdi
mov      edx,esi
call     00007ff8`1c5e2be0 (Scenarios.EagerRootCollection+ClassTwo.
         CalculateSomething(Int32),)
0055 is a safepoint:
mov      ecx,eax
call     00007ff8`1c5e2d70 (Scenarios.EagerRootCollection.
         DoSomeLongRunningCall(Int32))
005c is a safepoint:
mov      eax,1
add      rsp,28h
pop      rsi
pop      rdi
ret
xor      eax,eax
add      rsp,28h
pop      rsi
pop      rdi
ret
```

Analysis of the result of the !u -gcinfo command confirms that safe points have been set only when calling methods. Those include both calling internal runtime methods (allocators) and calling other managed methods (including object constructors). GC info seen in Listing 8-20 is very similar to the one proposed in Listing 8-10. We see that:

- firstly, rdi register becomes live at offset 21 until the next safe point at offset 2d - this offset range covers holding a reference to ClassOne object from its construction untilcalling its Check method,

- secondly, rdi register becomes live again at offset 4a until the next safe point at offset 55 - this offset range covers holding a reference to ClassTwo object from its construction until calling its CalculateSomething method.

To see how GC info is shown in case of a partially interruptible method, we must write one. As mentioned before, its sole JIT responsibility is to choose between emitting fully or partially interruptible code. However, using non-trivial loops with a dynamic number of iterations makes generating a fully interruptible version more likely (see Listing 8-21).

Listing 8-21. An example of a method that probably will be JITted into fully interruptible code

```
private int RegisterMap(int value)
{
      int total = 0;
      SomeClass local = new SomeClass();
      for (int i = 0; i < value; ++i)
      {
            total += local.DoSomeStuff(i);
      }
      return total;
}

public int DoSomeStuff(int value)
{
      return value * value;
}
```

When looking at `RegisterMap` method under WinDbg with the help of `!u -gcinfo` command, we will indeed notice that fully interruptible code has been generated (see Listing 8-22). Please remember this decision is based on internal JIT heuristics and the result may vary between versions, runtimes, and other not named conditions. Thus, one may need to make a few approaches to modify `RegisterMap` in a way that will cause generating fully interruptible code.

Listing 8-22. !u -gcinfo command output for fully interruptible RegisterMap method

```
> !u -gcinfo 00007fff42c18518
Normal JIT generated code
Scenarios.EagerRootCollection.RegisterMap(Int32)
Begin 00007fff42d32f20, size 3d
push    rdi
push    rsi
sub     rsp,28h
mov     esi,edx
00000008 interruptible
xor     edi,edi
mov     rcx,7FFF42DEAAC8h (MT: Scenarios.EagerRootCollection+SomeClass)
call    CoreCLR!JIT_TrialAllocSFastMP_InlineGetThread
00000019 +rax
mov     rcx,rax
0000001c +rcx
call    System_Private_CoreLib+0xc890f0 (System.Object..ctor())
00000021 -rcx -rax
xor     eax,eax
test    esi,esi
jle     00007fff`42d32f54
mov     edx,eax
imul    edx,eax
add     edi,edx
inc     eax
cmp     eax,esi
jl      00007fff`42d32f47
```

```
mov     eax,edi
00000036 not interruptible
add     rsp,28h
pop     rsi
pop     rdi
ret
```

There are regions inside even fully interruptible code that is not interruptible (this includes function prolog and epilog by default), and this is in fact reflected with the presented output - interruptible code starts at offset 8 until offset 36. Instead of safe points around method calls, we notice various slot liveness changes (of registers rax and rcx in our example). In fact, all instructions within interruptible regions are safe points so there is no need to print it so. With the information already gained in this chapter and a little assembler knowledge, one can easily understand why so and no other GC info was generated. Please note, for example, that thanks to inlining DoSomeStuff method inside a loop, SomeClass object roots become dead even before that loop starts.

When using !gcinfo or !u -gcinfo commands, you may also encounter a so-called *untracked root*. Those represent an argument or local variable that contains a reference but whose lifetime information is not available at runtime. Untracked locations are assumed by the GC to be live during the entire method body (if they do not contain zero value obviously).

If you would like to investigate Mark phase from the stack root perspective, start from the gc_heap::mark_phase and its call to GCScan::GcScanRoots method. It calls Thread::StackWalkFrames with GCHeap::Promote callback for stack frames of the current call stack (for each managed thread). Analyzing Promote callback is a very good start to analyze marking in general.

Pinned Local Variables

A special type of local variable is a pinned local variable. It is created implicitly in C# and F# when using a fixed keyword (see Listing 8-23). VB.NET does not have it as it does not allow pointers at all.

597

Listing 8-23. C# example of fixing keyword usage

```
public class Program
{
    private List<byte[]> list = new List<byte[]>();
    public unsafe int Run()
    {
        // ...
        fixed (byte* array = list[7])
        {
            // ...
            Console.ReadLine();
        }
    }
}
```

If we look at the CIL code generated for the method Run from Listing 8-23, we will notice a special, pinned local variable - in our case the one with index 2 (see Listing 8-24). Such a pinned keyword is for exactly what it stated - such local variable content should not be moved by GC during its work.

Listing 8-24. Beginning of the CIL code from Listing 8-23

```
.method public final hidebysig newslot virtual
instance int32 Run () cil managed
{
    // Header Size: 12 bytes
    // Code Size: 166 (0xA6) bytes
    // LocalVarSig Token: 0x11000016 RID: 22
    .maxstack 4
    .locals init (
            [0] int32 i,
            [1] uint8[] bigArray,
            [2] uint8& pinned 'array',
            [3] uint8[],
            [4] int32 i)
```

```
// ...
// IL code
}
```

Information about pinned local variables is consumed by the JIT compiler and appropriate GCInfo is being generated. This time, along with the information about the root itself, the information is also preserved that it is pinned. We may notice it by looking at GCInfo emitted for Run method from Listing 8-24 (see Listing 8-25). A stack location under the address sp+20 (hence, relatively to the stack pointer at the beginning of the method execution) is noted as untracked and pinned. It means that content of such a stack address will be treated as pinned root during stack roots marking if the thread will be suspended within the Run method.

Listing 8-25. Fragments of method from Listing 8-24 disassembled (with GCInfo)

```
> !u -gcinfo 00007ff9fa9277d8
Normal JIT generated code
CoreCLR.CollectScenarios.Scenarios.SOHCompactionWithPinning.Run()
Begin 00007ff9faa43070, size 103
Untracked: +sp+20(pinned)(interior)
00007ff9`faa43070 57                push    rdi
00007ff9`faa43071 56                push    rsi
00007ff9`faa43072 4883ec28          sub     rsp,28h
00007ff9`faa43076 33c0              xor     eax,eax
00007ff9`faa43078 4889442420        mov     qword ptr [rsp+20h],rax
...
00007ff9`faa430bd 488b4e08          mov     rcx,qword ptr [rsi+8]
00007ff9`faa430c1 ba07000000        mov     edx,7
00007ff9`faa430c6 3909              cmp     dword ptr [rcx],ecx
00007ff9`faa430c8 e8830d155e        call    System.Collections.Generic.
                                            List`1.get_Item(Int32)
...
00007ff9`faa430eb 4883c010          add     rax,10h
00007ff9`faa430ef 4889442420        mov     qword ptr [rsp+20h],rax
```

Code in Listing 8-25 shows relevant fragments of the entire method. At the beginning of the method execution, sp+20 stack location is being zeroed. Later, get_Item method on generic List<T> is called and its result (reference to 7th element of the list, which is reference to byte array) is stored in rax register. A few instructions later, rax is modified accordingly to get an address of the array data within array object. And, in the last shown line, such address is saved on the stack under sp+20 address. If thread will be suspended after this line, GC will see this address and treat the whole object as pinned.

This is the reason why sp+20 root is also denoted as interior. Address at sp+20 location in fact points inside the array object (so it is called interior). It is later appropriately interpreted by the GC.

Such pinned roots will be visible for a short period of time - only during execution of the containing method. In fact, they will be marked as pinned only during GC execution - stack root scanning, based on the GCInfo, will mark them as pinned. And during the plan phase, the pinned bit will be cleared. This makes finding such sources of pinning not trivial. For example, when taking memory dumps, it is unlikely we will hit the middle of GC. In a memory dump taken during a normal application execution, simply they are not pinned at all.

Some tools may list sources of such pinning, however. With GCInfo for all methods executed on current threads and the status of all their local variables, one could check what variables would be pinned if the GC happened at the moment of memory dump. It would of course be approximate data because during GC the threads would stop in safe points, and not necessarily where they are at the moment of memory dump. Moreover, remember that memory dump is only a single snapshot of memory at a given moment in time. Such a single snapshot will not necessarily say a lot about local variable pinning in general. We should make a lot of such snapshots to get a better view.

Luckily, there is an ETW event called PinObjectAtGCTime emitted each time an object is being pinned. It is a great source of knowledge about every object being pinned, including local pinned variables.

In WinDbg we are able to list pinned handles, as soon will be presented. However, they are not the same as pinned local variables discussed here. This makes a difference you may observe in \.NET CLR Memory\# of Pinned Objects counter - it counts all pinned (not moved) objects at the GC time, while via WinDbg we can only list pinned handles. On the other hand, PerfView is clever enough to list both types of pinning roots from its Heap Snapshots. All this will be presented practically in scenario 9-2, including investigating `PinObjectAtGCTime` ETW events.

Stack Root Scanning

With all the description provided so far, it is easy to understand how GC Info helps to constitute stack roots. When all threads are suspended at their safe points, it can be decoded from GC info what live slots are there. Each such slot (either on stack or register) is being treated as root and starts marking traversal from it.

One can wonder how `goto` statement is being handled in the context of stack roots. It allows us to transfer the program control directly to a labeled statement - making an unconditional jump. It could disrupt the operation of the entire technique related to GC info described here - all of a sudden a thread could be executing a completely different set of data inside a completely different block of code. However, `goto` statement is not so powerful. As C# Language Specification says about labels (which are `goto` targets): "A label can be referenced from `goto` statements (§8.9.3) within the scope of the label. This means that `goto` statements can transfer control within blocks and out of blocks, but never into blocks." Thus, `goto` statement can't simply jump out of a method to a different method. It can't also jump into nested blocks, omitting code in between. In other words, `goto` statement is made safe. This is also useful for the GC Info mechanism. With the current limitations, executing `goto` statement is nothing else than changing the instruction pointer to a proper code inside a method.

Finalization Roots

Finalization is a mechanism used to add some behavior when an object is being collected. Most often it is used to make sure that unmanaged resources held by an object will be released. Because of its importance and some common caveats, finalization is described in detail in Chapter 12.

For now it will be enough to say that to track objects that need to be "finalized," GC maintains a special queues. Those queues hold references to "ready for finalization" objects. Thus, they also constitute roots that should be scanned.

Scanning ready to the finalization queue is straightforward - GC goes through objects in it one by one and starts marking traversal from each of them.

If you would like to investigate scanning finalization roots in CoreCLR source, start from `CFinalize::GcScanRoots` method call from `gc_heap::mark_phase` method (with `GCHeap::Promote` callback).

There is more practical, development related knowledge about finalization in Chapter 12.

GC Internal Roots

As explained in detail in Chapter 5, in case of partial GC there is a need to include references from older-to-younger objects (see Figure 5-8). This step includes traversing through references inside objects stored in cross-generational remembered sets - through the cards mechanism. Card words and bundles described in Chapter 5 help to quickly identify memory regions that may be sources of such references. These are called the GC internal roots because they are originated from the user code.

Having cards information, scanning cards consists of the following, pretty straightforward steps:

- Outer loop finds continuous regions of set cards - those represent memory regions that contain objects with cross-generational references (let's call them set card regions). For each such region:

  - the first object is found (in case of Small Object Heap, with the help of bricks described in Chapter 9),

  - Scanning of object starts inside this region one by one - objects that contain references are checked whether such reference is indeed cross-generational. If yes, it is treated as a root so it starts marking traversal.

During such processing GC calculates also the card's efficiency ratio - it's for detecting how many cards are pointing to the actual generation 0 region versus how many are pointing to ephemeral regions. This ratio is then used during deciding what generation should be collected - if this ratio is too low GC chooses to condemn generation 1 instead of generation 0.

Card roots scanning is done after the previously described stack roots scanning. This means a lot of objects were probably already visited (marked) so card roots may or may not visit many more objects.

Marking through cards is realized by methods gc_heap::mark_through_cards_for_segments (for SOH) and gc_heap::mark_through_cards_for_large_objects (for LOH) called from gc_heap::mark_phase method.

SOH version uses gc_heap::find_card to find 'set' cards regions and gc_heap::find_first_object for such region. For objects found in that way (that contain outgoing references) gc_heap::mark_through_cards_helper is being called, which goes through its reference fields. For target objects that are indeed cross-generational, it calls gc_heap::mark_object_simple callback that starts marking traversal.

LOH version uses very similar logic based on gc_heap::find_card and gc::heap::mark_through_cards_helper methods. The main difference is that dirty regions are scanned object by object due to not having bricks there.

Low cards' efficiency may be a reason for condemning the older generation that initially requested. It was already mentioned in the "Generation to Condemn" section in Chapter 7. Such situations may be observed by PerfView with the help of Condemned reasons for the GCs table from GCStats report - if it occurs, Internal Tuning column will point which generation was tried to be condemned because of this.

Regular Internal Tunings are most probably natural and we should not be worried about them. From the user's perspective, the only effect it has is that it would do a generation 1 GC instead of a generation 0 so it's not a big difference.

GC Handle Roots

The last type of roots are various GC handles. We already seen them in Chapter 4. There are various types of handles, but they are stored in a single global handle table map. That handle table is being scanned for set of handle types and their targets are treated as roots that start marking traversal. Two most important handle types that are searched for are:

- strong handles - strong handles are like normal references. We may create them explicitly via proper `GCHandle.Alloc` call. They are also used by CLR internally, for example to store preallocated exceptions - like `Exception`, `OutOfMemoryException` or `ExecutionEngineException`.

- pinned handles - a subcategory of strong handles. When an object is being pinned via Pinned handle (with the help of proper `GCHandle.Alloc` call), a new handle of type "pinned" is created with that object as a target. During Mark phase those handles are treated as roots and the objects they point to are pinned, which means "pinning bit" is set in the object header. It is later on used by Plan phase (and cleared before GC ends).

There is also an important variation of a pinned handle type - so-called *async pinned handle*. It has the same meaning as regular pinned handle (making an object not movable) but it is used internally by the CLR with asynchronous I/O (like file or sockets reading and writing). Such handle has an additional feature of unpinning an object internally, as soon as the asynchronous I/O operation completes (without waiting for the explicitly releasing such handle from code). It allows it to make pinning related to such popular operations as short as possible, which is always good from its overhead perspective. However, as it is only used for .NET internal needs, we will be rather not interested in such type handle during our everyday work. At least not until our code performs such a tremendous amount of long-running asynchronous I/O operations that the resulting pinning starts to become a problem (i.e., by introducing fragmentation).

Please note that pinning by handle (i.e., using `GCHandle.Alloc(obj, GCHandle Type.Pinned)`) described here is different than pinning via `fixed` keyword (described previously in the Pinned local variables section). Result is the same - object will not be moved during heap compaction. The difference is only the root of such object - handles table in case of `GCHandle` and stack in case of `fixed` keyword.

Please note that handle roots play a much more important role in the current runtime implementation than it may seem at first glance. Two crucial arrays stored in Large Object Heap (per AppDomain) are: an array storing references to interned strings and an array storing references to static objects (see Figure 8-1). Those arrays are pinned by the runtime itself. This is useful because various internal CLR data contains addresses to their elements. For example, in Figure 8-1, a string literal map has been illustrated to clearly show that it is not treated as a root for interned strings - it is only an auxiliary data structure for a fast search (referring to the appropriate elements of the array-storing references to interned strings).

It is interesting to see how some mechanisms are used internally to implement memory management logic!

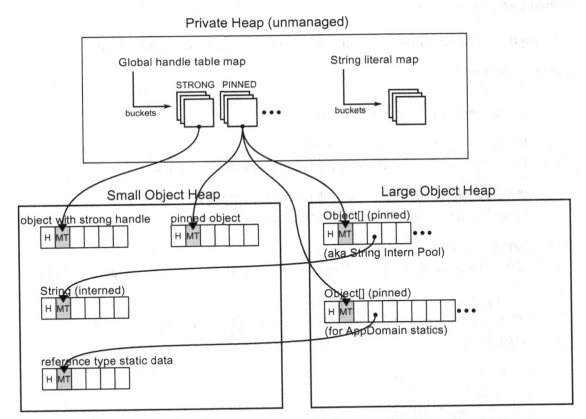

Figure 8-1. *Handle tables as roots for different managed objects*

In CoreCLR source code it starts from GCScan::GcScanHandles (with GCHeap::Promote callback) methods that calls Ref_TracePinningRoots (for types HNDTYPE_PINNED and HNDTYPE_ASYNCPINNED), Ref_TraceNormalRoots (for types HNDTYPE_STRONG, HNDTYPE_SIZEDREF and HNDTYPE_REFCOUNTED) and Ref_ScanDependentHandlesForRelocation.

We can easily see handle roots in actions thanks to WinDbg and SOS extension. Taking very simple code from Listing 8-26 as an example, we will investigate how different objects' roots are reported. This is very useful to know while analyzing various cases of uncontrolled memory growth - we should understand what are the roots of the growing graph of objects.

Listing 8-26. An example program used to show different handle roots

```
public int Run()
{
        Normal normal = new Normal();

        Pinned onlyPinned = new Pinned();
        GCHandle handle = GCHandle.Alloc(onlyPinned, GCHandleType.Pinned);

        ObjectWithStatic obj = new ObjectWithStatic();
        Console.WriteLine(ObjectWithStatic.StaticField);

        Marked strong = new Marked();
        GCHandle strongHandle = GCHandle.Alloc(strong, GCHandleType.Normal);

        string literal = "Hello world!";
        GCHandle literalHandle = GCHandle.Alloc(literal, GCHandleType.
        Normal);

        Console.ReadLine();
        GC.KeepAlive(obj);
        // ... free handles
        return 0;
}
```

```
public class Normal
{
}

[StructLayout(LayoutKind.Sequential)]
public class Pinned
{
    public long F1 = 301;
}

public class Marked
{
    public long F1 = 401;
}

public class ObjectWithStatic
{
    public static Static StaticField = new Static();
}

public class Static
{
    public long F1 = 501;
}
```

By attaching WinDbg to the application running code from Listing 8-26 at the moment of Console.ReadLine, we may investigate various objects roots with the help of the !gcroot command. First, we may confirm that the normal object will be already treated as unreachable because JIT (with eager root collection) should notice that it is no longer used at this moment (see Listing 8-27).

Listing 8-27. Normal object - is not reachable due to eager root collection

```
> !dumpheap -type CoreCLR.CollectScenarios.Scenarios.VariousRoots+Normal
        Address                 MT    Size
000001c6b4dd26a0 00007fff8e84bce0      24

> !gcroot 000001c6b4dd26a0
Found 0 unique roots
```

Next, let's see how roots are reported for an explicitly pinned onlyPinned object (see Listing 8-28). We may notice that the result is in line with Figure 8-1 - the root is said to be handle (of type pinned) from HandleTable that is an unmanaged internal CLR's data structure (see Listing 8-28).

Listing 8-28. Pinned object - is reachable from pinned handle table (unmanaged)

```
> !dumpheap -type CoreCLR.CollectScenarios.Scenarios.VariousRoots+Pinned
        Address                MT        Size
000001c6b4dd26b8 00007fff8e84be80        24


> !gcroot 000001c6b4dd26b8
HandleTable:
    000001c6b0d015d8 (pinned handle)
    -> 000001c6b4dd26b8 CoreCLR.CollectScenarios.Scenarios.
       VariousRoots+Pinned
Found 1 unique roots

> !gcwhere 000001c6b0d015d8
Address 0x1c6b0d015d8 not found in the managed heap.
```

Static reference type data are represented by ObjectWithStatic.StaticField field of type Static. Roots reported for such object instance are also in line with Figure 8-1. The reference to the instance is stored inside LOH allocated (denoted as generation 3 here) array that is kept by a pinned handle from HandleTable (see Listing 8-29).

Listing 8-29. Static object - is reachable from pinned array from LOH (that is reachable from unmanaged pinned handle table)

```
> !dumpheap -type CoreCLR.CollectScenarios.Scenarios.VariousRoots+Static
        Address                MT        Size
000001c6b4dd2700 00007fff8e84c3b0        24

> !gcroot 000001c6b4dd2700
HandleTable:
    000001c6b0d015f8 (pinned handle)
    -> 000001c6c4dc1038 System.Object[]
```

```
   -> 000001c6b4dd2700 CoreCLR.CollectScenarios.Scenarios.VariousRoots+Static
Found 1 unique roots
```

> **!gcwhere 000001c6c4dc1038**

```
Address          Gen   Heap           segment            begin
allocated              size
000001c6c4dc1038  3     0    000001c6c4dc0000   000001c6c4dc1000
000001c6c4dc5480      0x1ff8(8184)
```

You may often see a lot of such System.Object[] arrays being roots of various objects but do not be misled. Most often they are there because such objects are statics or interned strings as in our example.

A strong handle is similar to a pinned case - strong object from Listing 8-26 is said to be referenced from handle (of type string) from HandleTable (see Listing 8-30).

Listing 8-30. Object with strong handle - is reachable from strong handle table (unmanaged)

> **!dumpheap -type CoreCLR.CollectScenarios.Scenarios.VariousRoots+Marked**

```
            Address          MT     Size
000001c6b4dd26d0 00007fff8e84c020     24
```

> **!gcroot 000001c6b4dd26d0**

```
HandleTable:
    000001c6b0d01190 (strong handle)
    -> 000001c6b4dd26d0 CoreCLR.CollectScenarios.Scenarios.
       VariousRoots+Marked
Found 1 unique roots
```

String literal in the example from Listing 8-26 should have two roots. One of them is string intern pool (a pinned array in LOH containing interned string references), and the other is strong handle created explicitly. Output of !gcroot command confirms that (see Listing 8-31).

Listing 8-31. String literal with additional strong handle (instance found by command !dumpheap -mt 00007fffed021400 -min 32 -max 32)

> ! **do 000001c6b4dd2650**

```
Name:        System.String
MethodTable: 00007fffed021400
```

```
EEClass:      00007fffebcdddc0
Size:         50(0x32) bytes
File:         F:\GithubProjects\coreclr\bin\Product\Windows_NT.x64.Debug\
              System.Private.CoreLib.dll
String:       Hello world!
```

> **!gcroot 000001c6b4dd2650**
```
HandleTable:
    000001c6b0d01198 (strong handle)
    -> 000001c6b4dd2650 System.String

    000001c6b0d015e8 (pinned handle)
    -> 000001c6c4dc3050 System.Object[]
    -> 000001c6b4dd2650 System.String
Found 2 unique roots
```

Additionally, we may check that normal ObjectWithStatic instance has no handles roots but only stack roots (see Listing 8-32) - kept in register rsi to be more precise.

Listing 8-32. Instance of normal object - is still reachable from stack root (enregistered into rsi) due to GC.KeepAlive call

> **!dumpheap -type CoreCLR.CollectScenarios.Scenarios.**
VariousRoots+ObjectWithStatic
```
         Address              MT      Size
000001c6b4dd26e8 00007fff8e84c200      24
```

> **!gcroot 000001c6b4dd26e8**
```
Thread 273c:
    000000793097d530 00007fff8e79319d CoreCLR.CollectScenarios.Scenarios.
    VariousRoots.Run()
        rsi:
            -> 000001c6b4dd26e8 CoreCLR.CollectScenarios.Scenarios.
VariousRoots+ObjectWithStatic

Found 1 unique roots
```

It may be also very useful to list all (or specific type) handles in our application with the help of !gchandles command (see Listing 8-33).

Listing 8-33. Convenient !gchandles command to list handles in our application (with filtering possible)

```
> !gchandles
          Handle Type                 Object          Size
Data Type
000001c6b0d013e8 WeakShort     000001c6b4dc1e20       152
System.Buffers.ArrayPoolEventSource
000001c6b0d017a8 WeakLong      000001c6b4dd2740       152
System.RuntimeType+RuntimeTypeCache
000001c6b0d017f8 WeakLong      000001c6b4dc2878       64
Microsoft.Win32.UnsafeNativeMethods+ManifestEtw+EtwEnableCallback
000001c6b0d01190 Strong        000001c6b4dd26d0       24
CoreCLR.CollectScenarios.Scenarios.VariousRoots+Marked
000001c6b0d01198 Strong        000001c6b4dd2650       50
System.String
000001c6b0d011a0 Strong        000001c6b4dc2de0       32
System.Object[]
000001c6b0d011a8 Strong        000001c6b4dc2d78       104
System.Object[]
000001c6b0d011b0 Strong        000001c6b4dc13e0       24
System.SharedStatics
000001c6b0d011b8 Strong        000001c6b4dc1300       144
System.Threading.ThreadAbortException
000001c6b0d011c0 Strong        000001c6b4dc1270       144
System.Threading.ThreadAbortException
000001c6b0d011c8 Strong        000001c6b4dc11e0       144
System.ExecutionEngineException
000001c6b0d011d0 Strong        000001c6b4dc1150       144
System.StackOverflowException
000001c6b0d011d8 Strong        000001c6b4dc10c0       144
System.OutOfMemoryException
```

```
000001c6b0d011e0 Strong        000001c6b4dc1030            144
System.Exception
000001c6b0d011f8 Strong        000001c6b4dc13f8            128
System.AppDomain
000001c6b0d015d8 Pinned        000001c6b4dd26b8             24
CoreCLR.CollectScenarios.Scenarios.VariousRoots+Pinned
000001c6b0d015e0 Pinned        000001c6c4dc3488           8184
System.Object[]
000001c6b0d015e8 Pinned        000001c6c4dc3050           1048
System.Object[]
000001c6b0d015f0 Pinned        000001c6b4dc13a8             24
System.Object
000001c6b0d015f8 Pinned        000001c6c4dc1038           8184
System.Object[]
// ...
// statistical data
```

There are additional types of handles, especially weak handle described in
Chapter 12. However, they do not differ from the perspective of this chapter so
were omitted for brevity.

Handling Memory Leaks

So you have observed that memory usage of your .NET application is growing in time?
Regardless of the complexity of the marking mechanisms, just do not assume that there
are any errors in it. In other words, increasing memory usage and memory leaks in our
application are not caused by bugs in determining the reachability of objects! If there
is a memory leak, most probably it is because in fact something continuously holds a
reference to something else. Thus, the most typical problem in the whole .NET memory
management topic is how to find the source of such memory leak - what are the roots
holding it?

But first of all, you need to find out if you really have a memory leak in the first place, and whether it really comes from managed code. Thus, investigation should be started with the two following steps:

- Check what part of the process memory is growing. It may be that due to some unmanaged library bug or misuse, it is unmanaged memory that is leaking. Such diagnostics are described in Chapter 4.

- If the occurrence of unmanaged memory leak is excluded, only then look at the managed memory, as described below.

The only way to be definitively sure of a managed memory leak is if memory is constantly growing despite the fact that full gen2 GCs are happening. Otherwise it could simply be because GC hasn't gotten around to collecting the full heap yet. They may be such cases that memory is growing in gen2 but full GCs are not triggered because conditions are not met yet - from the GC perspective there is simply no need to do it (like, there is still a lot of memory available). Or there may be only non-compacting background full GCs, so memory simply grows due to fragmentation. Only if compacting full GCs happen without significantly helping in stopping overall memory growth in time, we may suspect a memory leak indeed is happening.

To distinguish those two cases, we should start from general measurements of GCs in time - if and how many GCs of generation 2 are executed? Use the tool of your preference, like Performance Counters or use GCStats view in PerfView. With the knowledge from this book you should be able to figure out why full GCs are not triggered by studying GC Events by Time and Condemned reasons for GCs tables from GCStats view.

After confirming that indeed gen2 GCs are there, we may start investigating the reason behind the memory leak. What are the roots holding more and more objects not becoming dead? This is not an easy question to answer. In simple applications, it is sometimes enough to carefully analyze the committed changes - because the problem most often manifests itself after the deployment of the new version of the application. However, it is difficult to count on such a solution.

In larger applications with tens of thousands or millions of objects, constantly collected and created, it is really difficult to see this real source of the memory leak. Complex maze of connections between objects all tangled up with each other do not make things easier. There are two main ways how one could approach the diagnostics of a memory leak problem:

- The first approach, simpler but requiring a bit more luck, involves the analysis of a single memory dump of our application. We will look for a large number of objects, which in total take up a lot of memory. Preceding the analysis with additional measurements, we can help ourselves by identifying, for example, a particular generation (practically always it will be generation 2 or LOH), which will narrow our search. We can notice the occurrence of many objects from a similar area of our application (specific business logic, specific cross-cutting concern, or specific technology like database access). In this case, the knowledge about the structure and overall source code of the application being researched is very useful. However, this does not change the fact that such analysis requires a lot of intuition. Groups of numerous objects in our application can be many and not all must be a source of the memory leakage. Some of them may simply have to exist in order for the application to function properly. This makes analysis of memory leaks a laborious but rewarding detective challenge. Exactly such approach was presented in scenario 5-2 from Chapter 5 and in scenario 8-1 below. In such cases we may also help ourselves by analyzing several process memory dumps from moments of increasing memory consumption. Analyzing them one by one, we can help our intuition. However, we can also get some help by comparing such snapshots automatically. This leads us to another method of analysis.

- The second approach, which is in fact is the preferred one, involves the analysis of two or more successive memory dumps and focusing on the differences that occur. It makes things easier - now from the whole complicated system of tangled up objects we may notice groups of objects that are increasing in size. The better tool we use, the easier such analysis should be. Still however, such approach requires some intuition and insight into the structure and design of the application because there may be several groups that grow in size (and only one unintentionally). This approach is also presented in scenario 8-1 soon.

As memory leak analysis is tedious and complicated, there is no single work-for-all recipe. Most often the analysis of real-world problems involves mixing all three above-mentioned techniques and scraping the surface of a problem layer by layer.

Finally, one more piece of advice. Regardless of the specifics of our application and the source of the memory leak, in the analyzed memory dumps, strings will almost certainly be the most numerous. This is generally the specifics of the application these days, that they process text - from files, HTTP requests, data from the database, etc. Let's have strings in mind but do not necessarily start with the analysis from them. Strings may, or may not, lead you to the real problem because at the end they may point to the true roots - cumulating objects most probably will have some string data in it.

Scenario 8-1. nopCommerce Memory Leak?

Description: We have a plain installation of nopCommerce - open source e-commerce platform written in ASP.NET. We want to validate nopCommerce performance, including memory usage patterns. We have prepared a simple load test scenario for JMeter 3.2 - popular open source load-testing tool. It executes three steps in a loop - visiting home page, one of the categories (Computers) and one of tags ("awesome"). We have added think times (pauses) between each request to simulate real users. During the test we have noticed increasing memory usage while generation 2 GCs are happening regularly - seems like we have a typical memory leak! This is an alternative approach to the same problem as in scenario 5-2.

Analysis: We know that managed memory is somehow leaking during our load test (see Figure 8-2). Full GCs are happening but apparently, long-living objects are gathering in generation 2. We will try to find the cause using the methods described above for dealing with memory leaks. We will use PerfView as our tool because it provides great capabilities of gathering and analyzing memory snapshots. When Using this tool for this purpose, read beforehand the great and comprehensive help topics Collecting GC Heap Data and Understanding GC Heap Data available from the Collecting Memory Data dialog box.

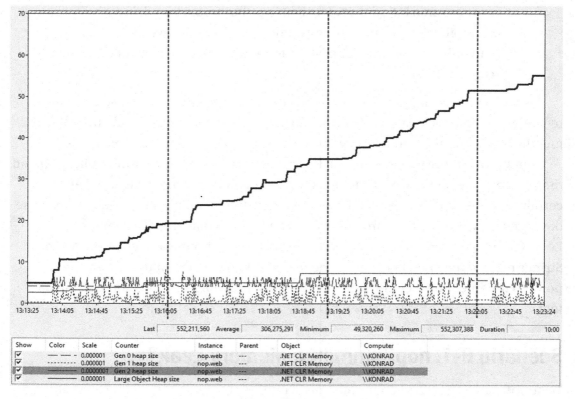

Show	Color	Scale	Counter	Instance	Parent	Object	Computer
☑	— — —	0.000001	Gen 0 heap size	nop.web	---	.NET CLR Memory	\\KONRAD
☑	········	0.000001	Gen 1 heap size	nop.web	---	.NET CLR Memory	\\KONRAD
☑	————	0.000001	Gen 2 heap size	nop.web	---	.NET CLR Memory	\\KONRAD
☑	————	0.000001	Large Object Heap size	nop.web	---	.NET CLR Memory	\\KONRAD

Figure 8-2. *Performance Counters during first 10 minutes of load test - all generation sizes are presented. The moments of performing memory dumps have been marked on the chart.*

Note. Obviously, before jumping into .NET memory analysis, we may also check whether it is indeed managed memory leak. Please refer to scenarios 4-2, 4-3, and 4-4.

Approach 1 - Analyzing single memory snapshot

In the first approach we take a single memory snapshot from PerfView (Memory ➤ Take Heap Snapshot option), the first one marked on Figure 8-2. When looking at objects' statistics, we may notice interesting things. Figure 8-3 shows the overall memory usage of different objects sorted by their inclusive (total) memory space. Obviously, [.NET Roots] reference all data so it takes 100% inclusive space (see Inc column). Most of them are static roots (which is interesting in itself), but nevertheless most of the memory seem to be hold by the Autofac IoC container (it holds 74% of all objects). This still may or may not indicate the root cause - it is not surprising that in an IoC-controlled application, most objects are in control of it. However, it is obviously some trace. Additionally, a lot of "memory cache"-related objects are also noticeably big.

Name	Exc %	Exc	Exc Ct	Inc %	Inc	Inc Ct	Fold	Fold Ct
[.NET Roots]	0.3	407,591	8,736	100.0	144,170,600.0	3,724,871	407,591	8,735
ROOT	0.0	0	0	100.0	144,170,600.0	3,724,871	0	0
[static vars]	5.4	7,779,199	176,526	97.5	140,536,300.0	3,664,079	7,779,199	176,525
[static var Nop.Core.Infrastructure.Singleton.allSingletons]	0.0	0	1	74.0	106,755,100.0	2,792,296	0	0
LIB <<mscorlib!Dictionary<Type,Object>>>	0.0	1,404	46	74.0	106,755,100.0	2,792,295	1,284	43
Nop.Core!Nop.Core.Infrastructure.NopEngine	0.0	12	1	74.0	106,753,700.0	2,792,249	0	0
Autofac.Extensions.DependencyInjection!Autofac.Extensions.DependencyInjection.AutofacServiceProvider	0.0	138	12	74.0	106,753,700.0	2,792,248	0	0
Autofac!Autofac.Core.Container	0.3	476,568	14,590	74.0	106,753,600.0	2,792,237	476,548	14,589
Autofac!Autofac.Core.Lifetime.LifetimeScope	0.0	247	5	73.7	106,276,800.0	2,777,605	0	0
LIB <<mscorlib!Dictionary<Guid,Object>>>	2.7	3,917,683	84,396	73.7	106,276,300.0	2,777,582	3,917,455	84,391
Microsoft.Extensions.Caching.Memory!Microsoft.Extensions.Caching.Memory.MemoryCache	0.0	64	1	48.4	69,808,310.0	1,963,239	0	0
LIB <<mscorlib!ConcurrentDictionary<Object,Microsoft.Extensions.Caching.Memory.CacheEntry>>>	10.7	15,486,060	203,556	48.4	69,808,250.0	1,963,238	15,485,970	203,553
Microsoft.Extensions.Caching.Memory!Microsoft.Extensions.Caching.Memory.CacheEntry	11.1	16,030,910	222,660	38.0	54,777,400.0	1,772,371	1,725,223	114,307
Nop.Core!Nop.Core.Caching.MemoryCacheManager	0.0	16	1	21.3	30,773,610.0	703,282	0	0
LIB <<mscorlib!CancellationTokenSource>>	18.1	26,143,850	477,556	21.3	30,773,590.0	703,281	26,143,160	477,539

Figure 8-3. PerfView's By Name view of the Heap Snapshot (sorted by Inc column in descending order)

We may look at this data with an even clearer view of Flame Graph (see Figure 8-4). The same observations are confirmed, and it seems that via Autofac Container, a lot of `Microsoft.Extensions.Caching.Memory.CacheEntry` entities are held in memory.

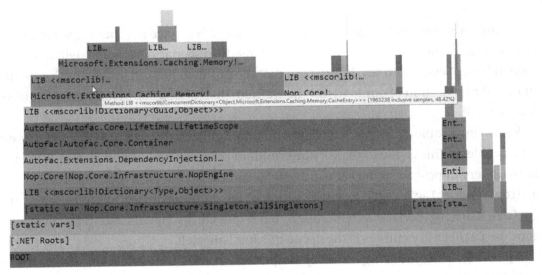

Figure 8-4. PerfView's Flame Graph view of the Heap Snapshot (mousover label is intentionally left)

This still however may be an expected behavior if our application is designed to cache a lot of data. What is worrying is the constant increase of memory usage - maybe we are caching more and more but release nothing? At this stage, without a doubt, it is worth reaching for the application source code and checking the caching mechanisms again. But we may help ourselves a little by looking at application-specific objects referencing `CacheEntry` objects.

By digging into Referred-From view for `CacheEntry` objects, we may find indeed some clues. When looking for nopCommerce-related objects, quite quickly we may find `Nop.Core.Caching.MemoryCacheManager` instances held by `Nop.Services.Catalog.ProductTagService` instances (see Figure 8-5). There are not so many, but it gives some additional tracks to follow.

Name ?	Inc % ?	Inc ?	Inc Ct ?	Exc % ?	Exc ?	Exc Ct ?
☑Microsoft.Extensions.Caching.Memory!Microsoft.Extensions.Caching.Memory.CacheEntry ?	38.0	54,777,400.0	1,772,371	11.1	16,030,910	222,660
+☑LIB <<mscorlib!ConcurrentDictionary<Object,Microsoft.Extensions.Caching.Memory.CacheEntry>>> ?	37.7	54,312,120.0	1,759,621	0.0	0	0
|+☑Microsoft.Extensions.Caching.Memory!Microsoft.Extensions.Caching.Memory.MemoryCache ?	37.7	54,312,120.0	1,759,621	0.0	0	0
||+☐LIB <<mscorlib!Dictionary<Guid,Object>>> ?	37.7	54,312,120.0	1,759,621	0.0	0	0
||+☐[finalization handles] {MinDepth 2} ?	0.0	0.0	0	0.0	0	0
||+☑Nop.Core!Nop.Core.Caching.MemoryCacheManager {MinDepth 10} ?	0.0	0.0	0	0.2	277,008	17,313
|||+☑LIB <<mscorlib!Dictionary<Guid,Object>>> {MinDepth 9} ?	0.0	0.0	0	66.4	95,706,260	17,313
|||+☐Microsoft.Extensions.Caching.Abstractions!Microsoft.Extensions.Caching.Memory.PostEvictionDelegate {MinDepth 15} ?	0.0	0.0	0	372.4	536,870,900	16,777,220
|||+■Nop.Services!Nop.Services.Catalog.ProductTagService {MinDepth 17}	0.0	0.0	0	0.5	761,772	17,313

Figure 8-5. *PerfView's Referred-From view of the Heap Snapshot (for type Microsoft.Extensions.Caching.Memory.CacheEntry)*

At this stage, we can look at the source code how the service `ProductTagService` uses cache and find the real cause presented already in scenario 5-2, so we will not repeat it here. Needless to say, it turns out that the problem lies not in the nopCommerce but in bad preparation of our load test. Be warned, this is not a contrived example. Been there, seen that.

By solving problems in this way, it is sometimes difficult to recognize the real source of the problem. This is due to the very intermittent relations between objects that turn out to be very important at the same time. For example, in our case `Nop.Services.Catalog.ProductTagService` for the duration of the request actually has a reference to `Nop.Core.Caching.MemoryCacheManager,` but it quickly disappears and in fact what keeps the `CacheEntry` entities is the cache mechanism itself.

Approach 2 - Comparing memory snapshots

In the second approach we take two memory snapshots from PerfView (Memory ➤ Take Heap Snapshot option), the second and the third ones marked on Figure 8-2. They are spaced in time by 3 minutes because the memory leak under analysis is quite impressive. Sometimes you will need to compare snapshots taken every few dozen minutes. After taking both snapshots, we can compare them from the Diff menu. The results shown on By Name view seem to speak for themselves (see Figure 8-6). The overwhelming majority of new objects are `CacheEntry` type and other caching related - it is indicated by positive values of the Exc (exclusive size of a given type) and Inc (inclusive size of a given type) columns, which means in between the two snapshots the total size of those types of instances increased.

Name ?	Exc % ?	Exc ?	Exc Ct ?	Inc % ?	Inc ?	Inc Ct ?	Fold ?	Fold Ct ?
ROOT	0.0	0	0	100.0	68,687,080.0	1,700,950	0	0
[.NET Roots]	0.0	-18,380	3,929	100.0	68,687,080.0	1,700,950	-18,380	3,929
[static vars]	1.5	997,758	33,546	93.2	64,034,470.0	1,652,405	997,758	33,546
Microsoft.Extensions.Caching.Memory!Microsoft.Extensions.Caching.Memory.CacheEntry	19.4	13,345,800	102,257	82.4	56,583,260.0	1,518,337	5,019,994	39,201
LIB <<mscorlib!List<IDisposable>>>	43.0	29,524,780	645,303	71.0	48,765,210.0	1,238,704	28,007,190	582,108
LIB <<mscorlib!Action<Microsoft.Extensions.Caching.Memory.CacheEntry>>>	0.0	128	4	15.1	10,366,680.0	386,366	0	0
LIB <<mscorlib!ConcurrentDictionary<Object,Microsoft.Extensions.Caching.Memory.Cach	4.5	3,077,782	74,918	15.1	10,366,560.0	386,362	3,077,781	74,918
Microsoft.Extensions.Caching.Memory!Microsoft.Extensions.Caching.Memory.MemoryCac	0.0	0	0	15.1	10,366,560.0	386,362	0	0
LIB <<mscorlib!List<Microsoft.Extensions.Caching.Memory.PostEvictionCallbackRegistrati	4.8	3,280,897	126,321	9.2	6,308,843.0	252,470	1,768,929	63,187

Figure 8-6. *PerfView's By Name view of two Heap Snapshot difference (sorted by Inc column in descending order)*

In a properly functioning system, the number of new cache entries would be similar to the number of those that have already expired (assuming stable traffic on the page). Thus, inclusive size of CacheEntry instances and other cache-related types should be around zero.[3] This points directly to the problems with the caching mechanism. At this stage, we can take a closer look at the CacheEntry instances in one or both of the snapshots, similar to approach 1 shown above.

Scenario 8-2. Identifying the Most Popular Roots

Description: We would like to analyze the most popular kind of roots in our application. This may be helpful as an additional clue during memory leak analysis. By identifying the most popular roots, as long as they change along the time, we may find interesting patterns that will lead us to some conclusions. It is not realistic to expect that such analysis will lead us directly to the root cause of a problem. However, in the tedious process of reaching the truth, the more tips from different sources, the better.

Analysis: Events emitted by the runtime are great source of knowledge. It is no different if you try to know the statistics of the roots. There is ETW/LTTng event MarkWithType that provides information how many bytes of different root kinds were marked (thus, reachable) during particular GC. There is one event emitted per each root kind, so most typically there are several such events per GC. Types are represented by numbers that comes from _GC_ROOT_KIND enum (see Listing 8-34).

---

[3]Obviously there will be some fluctuations in the traffic on the page, which makes those numbers not equal to zero.

Listing 8-34. Enum representing root kind..

```
namespace ETW
{
typedef  enum _GC_ROOT_KIND {
            GC_ROOT_STACK = 0,
            GC_ROOT_FQ = 1,
            GC_ROOT_HANDLES = 2,
            GC_ROOT_OLDER = 3,
            GC_ROOT_SIZEDREF = 4,
            GC_ROOT_OVERFLOW = 5
     } GC_ROOT_KIND;
};
}
```

MarkWithType will be recorded when using simple GC Collect Only option at Collect dialog box in PerfView. As a result, we will be able to list all events on Events view, filtered to the process that interests us (see Figure 8-7). Unfortunately, currently there is no any summary or any graphical representation of such data inside PerfView, which makes analyzing those events quite difficult.

Figure 8-7. *MarkWithType for a sample process (with columns Promoted, Type, HeapNum and ThreadID displayed)*

However, we can export filtered events as a CSV file (Open View in Excel option from the context menu) and analyze it in any tool understanding it. The most obvious ones are MS Excel or other spreadsheet-like tools. After importing such CSV data, we will be able to analyze in a way we like. For example, Figure 8-8 presents distribution over time of the size of promoted objects due to particular kinds of roots (prepared in MS Excel). Please note that vertical scale is logarithmic.

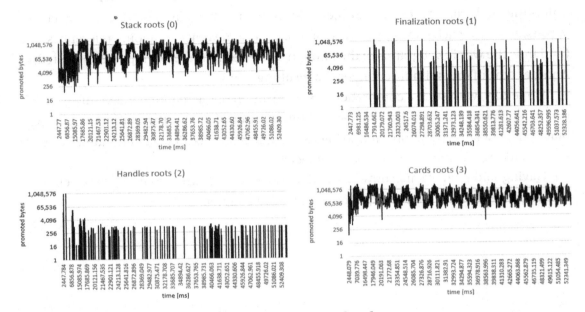

Figure 8-8. *Promoted sized with respect to root kind*

Let's take into account that the values of this events are mostly incremental (excluding the case of rather uncommon GC_ROOT_SIZEDREF), in the order given in Listing 8-34. Each subsequent MarkWithType event during GC indicates how many bytes were additionally promoted due to the given root type. For example, promoted bytes due to the finalization roots will not count in objects already marked due to stack roots. Events for handles roots will not count in objects already promoted due to stacks or finalization, and so on, so forth.

Summary

In this chapter we thoroughly looked at the first crucial part of the GC - Mark phase. Understanding it is crucial in understating which and why objects become dead or stay alive. Thus, it is one of the most important practical parts of the knowledge about .NET memory in general.

The marking mechanism starts from the subsequent types of roots and gradually builds the final graph of reachable objects. Since the marking flag stored in an object is considered for each subsequent type of roots, the same object outgoing references (and thus the whole subgraphs of the entire resulting graph) are not repeatedly visited. Another type of roots simply enlarges the resulting graph.

Hopefully, with such a comprehensive description of the marking mechanisms described in this chapter, you understand much better what it is. Particularly surprising may be the fact that both interned strings and static reference data are operated by the same marking mechanism as for other objects!

Having said that, we may now proceed to description of the next important step in the GC process - Plan phase - explained in the next chapter.

CHAPTER 9

Garbage Collection - Plan Phase

After the mark phase, all objects have been identified as reachable or not. Those reachable are being marked by a dedicated bit. Some of the marked objects may be additionally marked as pinned by another bit. At this moment Garbage Collector has all necessary information to start its job. But the question arises - should it proceed with Sweep or Compact collection?

To answer this question, we can do one of two things. We can make an educated guess, for example - based on the previous memory usage patterns or the previous effects of sweeping and compacting collections. However, this still would be only a guess. And in such dynamic conditions as the continuous creation and removal of objects, it's hard to expect that our guessing will be much more than just a lottery.

Instead of guessing, we can in some way calculate whether in current conditions it pays off to Compact, or whether the resulting fragmentation is not so large and we can do just Sweep. This is a much more promising approach. Depending on the accuracy of our calculations, we are getting closer to the optimal solution. But as we will notice soon, the exact prediction of the resulting fragmentation is not so easy (mainly due to the pinning). We come to a certain paradox - to know if it is worth making compacting, you need to make compacting and see the result.

But how to compact while not doing it? This is exactly what the Plan phase really does. It calculates all information in such a way that they directly correspond to the information about the result of the compacting process. This information is prepared "on the side" - without actually moving objects. In this way we get to know the exact and the actual result of possible compacting.

Moreover, that information is prepared in a way directly used by both Compacting and Sweeping later on. If a compacting result is promising (and we will take a closer look at this decision later in this chapter) - GC performs compacting using directly the

© Konrad Kokosa 2018
K. Kokosa, *Pro .NET Memory Management*, https://doi.org/10.1007/978-1-4842-4027-4_9

collected information. If Sweep is enough, the collected information is also directly used for sweeping. And since compaction is a lot more often than sweeping, especially for ephemeral collections, such simulated compaction results are rarely discarded.

In that way we may see the Plan phase as a main horsepower of the whole GC process. It is doing all heavy, necessary calculations. Sweep or Compact phases are only then consuming results of those calculations in a more or less complicated, but straightforward manner.

So how this magic happens that the Plan phase somehow "executes" both compacting and sweeping at the same time without manipulating objects on the Managed Heap? The answer is very interesting, so I invite you to read further. The description is quite detailed but we are in the heart of the GC here. Understanding the Plan phase gives the best insight what and how GC really works. I believe it pays off to really understand this!

The processes described in this chapter are slightly different in SOH and LOH.

Small Object Heap

Let's start from the SOH planning description first. It is a little more complex than the case of LOH, so after understanding it, we will understand LOH version easily.

Plugs and Gaps

Imagine a fragment of the Managed Heap (inside Small Object Heap) right at the beginning of the GC process (see Figure 9-1). There are some objects located next to each other. Each object obviously consists of a header, Method Table pointer, and at least one pointer-sized field (even if it is not used, as mentioned in Chapter 4). Some objects are bigger, some are smaller.

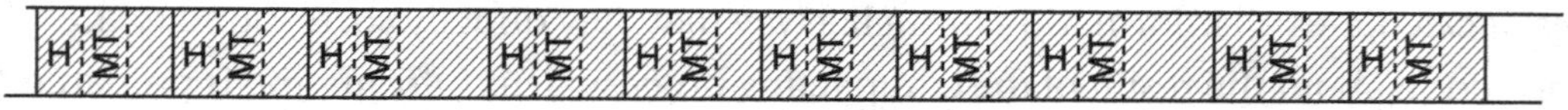

Figure 9-1. *A fragment of the Managed Heap (inside Small Object Heap) right at the beginning of the GC process (H stands for header, MT stands for method table pointer, objects are marked by light gray filling)*

Imagine that after the Mark phase described in the previous point, all reachable objects have been marked (see Figure 9-2). At this point the planning phase comes into action.

Figure 9-2. *A fragment of the Managed Heap right after Mark phase (medium gray objects are marked)*

During the Plan phase whole condemned and younger generations are scanned object by object. This is easy because the size of the current object is easily calculated from the "hot" information inside an object. For arrays this is the base size of an object plus number of components times the size of component. During such scanning a dedicated pointer is simply advanced by the current object size (that's aligned).

The core principle of the planning phase is to group all marked and not-marked objects into groups during such an object-by-object scan (see Figure 9-3). And so a group of two kinds may be created:

- *plug* - represents an adjacent group of marked (reachable) objects

- *gap* - represents an adjacent group of not-marked (unreachable) objects

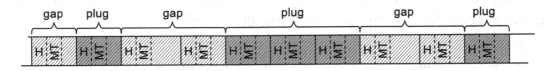

Figure 9-3. *Plugs and gaps on the Managed Heap*

By splitting the whole Managed Heap into a series of plugs and gaps, we can easily calculate important information (see Figure 9-4):

- With each gap its size and location may be remembered. If Sweep collection will be chosen, most of the gaps will become a free space managed by the free-list item.

- With each plug its relocation offset and location are remembered. If Compact collection will be chosen, it will be executed by moving plug by plug using their relocation offsets.

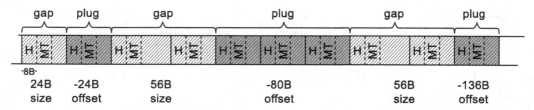

Figure 9-4. *Size and offset information associated with plugs and gaps. Example values have been provided assuming single block (like header) is 8-bytes long*

How to calculate relocation offset? In the simplest scenario we could calculate it as an accumulation of all sizes of previous gaps (as we have done in Figure 9-4). This is however much more complex in a real implementation. It uses its own internal allocator to find a proper address for each successive plug to relocate to, and this address is then recorded instead of actually moving the plugs there.

If you are interested in details and want to study CoreCLR code, all this happens in `gc_heap::plan_phase` method. Inside this method, by scanning successive objects, plugs and gaps are discovered. The new location of each plug is calculated by calling `allocate_in_condemned_generations` or `allocate_in_older_generations`. You can start there with your own investigations.

In case of a simple scenario when we can move plugs, that is, it's not pinned, a bump pointer allocator will lay each plug next to each other. Figure 9-5 illustrates some "virtual space," which is the Managed Heap representation from the internal allocator's point of view (it represents how a heap would look like after compacting). This is an illustration only for our convenience - normally, the allocator simply operates on the pointers updating them accordingly. Plan phase for our small fragment of the heap would consist of the following steps:

- At first allocation pointer is being reset to the beginning of the generation (see Figure 9-5a).

- When first plug is encountered (consisting of one object), the allocator finds a place for it where allocation pointer is located (see Figure 9-5b) and moves the allocation pointer accordingly. The difference between the new and old location of the plug is remembered as its relocation offset.

- When next plug is encountered (consisting of three objects), the allocator finds a new place for it just after the previous one "allocated" plug. Again, the difference between new and old location of the plug is remembered as its relocation offset.

- When last plug is encountered, the same logic happens.

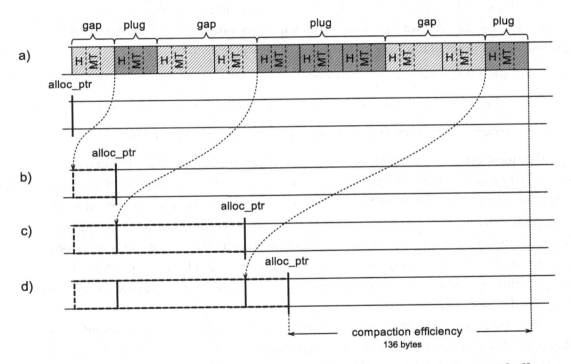

Figure 9-5. *Calculation of plug relocation offsets is based on the internal allocator calculating a new address for each plug – (a) objects layout from Figure 9-4 and resulting view of the allocator on the Managed Heap, (b) internal allocator found a place for the first plug, (c) internal allocator found a plac for the second plug, (d) internal allocator found a place for the last plug*

As a result, all relocation offsets have been calculated so the GC knows exactly when eventually the allocation pointer will be placed if compaction occurs. That gives direct information about compaction efficiency used later during GC's decision on compacting.

In our example from Figure 9-5, we know that after compacting, space taken by objects will shrink by 136 bytes because this is a difference between the current and future location of the allocation pointer.

Our simplified case does not yet show why a more complex internal allocator is needed. This will happen when we go over to discuss pinning of objects.

To summarize what we have learned so far, by organizing objects into plugs and gaps, a complete set of information is obtained very efficiently:

- what is the compaction efficiency,

- where free-list items should be created in case of Sweep collection,

- where to move reachable objects in case of Compact collection.

The question arises, where to store plug- and gap-related data? GC could use a dedicated memory area managed by it for this purpose. However, in case of scenarios where there are many small gaps and plugs interleaved, this area would consume a lot of memory. In addition, intensive access to memory areas of the Managed Heap and separate areas for such information would not be efficient due to the CPU cache usage. Therefore, since GC is already intensively using the Managed Heap memory area, why not just reuse it to store plug- and gap-related information? This is exactly the approach that was decided in the Microsoft .NET.

If we build gaps and plugs appropriately, each plug will have its corresponding gap that precedes it.[1] That is why GC stores interesting information only for every plug - just before where it starts, at the end of the preceding gap (see Figure 9-6). Content of the gap may be safely overwritten - it contains only unreachable objects that will be no longer used. Such plug info takes exactly 24 bytes (on 64-bit runtimes) or 12 bytes (on 32-bit runtimes) - it contains the corresponding gap size, plug relocation offset, and

---

[1]The only exception could be the first plug not preceded by any gap, but we can omit it in our considerations. And as we will see soon, in fact each generation begins with a single empty object so even the first plug is always preceded with a gap.

some additional data explained later (two bits being a part of relocation offset and two additional left/right offsets).

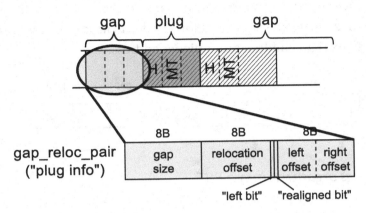

Figure 9-6. *Location of the plug information on the Managed Heap*

Storing plug info on the Managed Heap just before a plug is the main reason why even an empty object must be 24-bytes big (in case of 64-bit runtime). As a gap before a plug contains at least one object, it will be at least 24-bytes long. In this way it is nicely and elegantly assured that there is always enough room to store a plug info!

In that way, each gap and plug pair information is stored on the Managed Heap (see Figure 9-7). It will be used during Sweep or Compact phases later on.

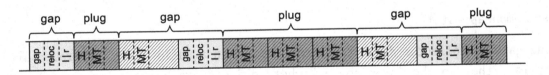

Figure 9-7. *Size and offset information associated with plugs and gaps stored on the Managed Heap itself (based on situation from Figure 9-4)*

If GC decides to perform compacting, it will use plug information very often. Please note that with such information it can answer the most frequent question (used when translating addresses) - what will be the new address of the object at address X? In this case, we only need to check if the address X belongs to some plug and if so, subtract from X the corresponding plug relocation offset. This question may be asked really, really often. All efforts must be made to respond efficiently. This is why plugs are organized into a binary search tree (BST).

Each plug info contains an offset to the left and right child plug info related to the given plug start (we have seen them in Figure 9-6) or 0 if there is no corresponding child. In that way a binary plug tree is build that contains addresses of all plugs (see Figure 9-8). This tree is built in a balanced way so that for a node, all its left children are at smaller addresses, and all its right children are at higher addresses.

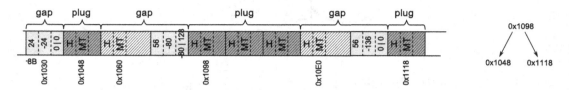

Figure 9-8. *Plugs organized into a BST*

Addresses in a plug tree point to the first object in a plug (their MT field, as usual in CLR). GC knows where to find corresponding plug info by a constant offset related to it.

Scenario 9-1. Memory Dump with Invalid Structures

Description: During some problem investigation, the full memory dump was taken off the .NET application. However, it seems to be unusable because data structures are invalid. For example, when invoking most SOS commands, the following message appears:

```
> !dumpheap -stat
```

The garbage collector data structures are not in a valid state for traversal. It is either in the "plan phase," where objects are being moved around, or we are at the initialization or shutdown of the gc heap. Commands related to displaying, finding or traversing objects as well as gc heap segments may not work properly. !dumpheap and !verifyheap may incorrectly complain of heap consistency errors.

Analysis: Memory dump indeed could be taken during the GC planning phase, when there is no guarantee that objects will be in "normal state" - because the heap is not walkable by the normal means (meaning starting at the beginning of a segment and advancing by the object size as we talked about earlier in this chapter). In fact, if we look at CoreCLR code, we will see the following guard around Plan phase:

```
GCScan::GcRuntimeStructuresValid (FALSE);
plan_phase (n);
GCScan::GcRuntimeStructuresValid (TRUE);
```

It is the only place when such protection is made. Thus we can easily check if indeed our memory dump was taken in a such unfortunate moment by looking for threads executing GC-related code. There are four possible library and namespace combinations we should look for, depending on our environment:

- `coreclr!wks` - .NET Core with Workstation GC

- `coreclr!srv` - .NET Core with Server GC

- `clr!wks` - .NET Framework with Workstation GC

- `clr!srv` - .NET Framework with Server GC

So, for example, if we have a dump of .NET Core application with Workstation GC enabled, we may look for it in the following way:

> **!findstack coreclr!wks**
```
Thread 000, 6 frame(s) match
          * 00 000000a963b7cd30 00007ff903bb0b48 CoreCLR!WKS::gc_heap::
            plan_phase+0xa9
          * 01 000000a963b7ce40 00007ff903bb095a CoreCLR!WKS::gc_heap::
            gc1+0x178
          * 02 000000a963b7ceb0 00007ff903b90d21 CoreCLR!WKS::gc_heap::
            garbage_collect+0x5ca
          * 03 000000a963b7cf20 00007ff903b90e98 CoreCLR!WKS::GCHeap::
            GarbageCollectGeneration+0x191
          * 04 000000a963b7cf60 00007ff903b90b15 CoreCLR!WKS::GCHeap::
            GarbageCollectTry+0xe8
          * 05 000000a963b7cff0 00007ff903670613 CoreCLR!WKS::GCHeap::
            GarbageCollect+0x2a5
```

Obviously, in our case, we are indeed in the middle of Plan phase because there is a thread executing it.

However, from my own experience, this message may be also displayed in case of the generic problem of getting GC data because not the proper SOS was loaded (for example, .NET 2.0 runtime version instead of .NET 4.0 version or opposite).

Brick Table

Root of plug tree needs to be stored somewhere. Creating a single, huge plug tree for the entire Managed Heap would be impractical. While investigating consecutive gaps and plugs, adding a new item to the tree may require rebalancing it. In case of a huge tree covering each and every plug, it could be very costly. Traversing such a tree during lookup would also be expensive because it would involve the need to jump over many levels of the tree.

A much more practical approach is to build plug trees for consecutive address ranges. Such range is called a *brick* in CLR. Brick size is 2,048 B for 32bit and 4,096 B for 64-bit runtimes. In other words, each 2 or 4 kB of the Managed Heap is represented by a single brick that contains information about its plug tree. Bricks are stored in a brick table that covers the whole Managed Heap (see Figure 9-9). Each brick table entry is a 16-bit integer that may take three logically distinct values:

- 0 - brick has no plugs information assigned (there are no plugs in a specified address range).

- >0 - represents an offset of the plug tree root (this value is increased by 1 so that 0 could mean no information, as indicated above) in the corresponding memory region.

- <0 - represents an information that such brick is a continuation of previous bricks (there is a big plug that spans multiple bricks) and we should jump back a given amount of bricks to the start.

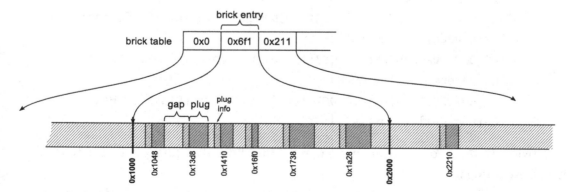

Figure 9-9. *Bricks and brick table*

By combining the brick table entry with the left and right offsets inside plug information of each plug, the plug tree is represented in an efficient way (see Figure 9-10). An example brick table entry contains value 0x6f1 - it represents an offset of plug tree root inside corresponding memory region. Because it is a second brick table entry, it represents a region between addresses 0x1000 and 0x2000. It means that the root is located at the address 0x6f0 (positive values must be reduced by 1 as denoted above) plus 0x1000, which gives address 0x16f0 on the Managed Heap. Starting from this address, we have access to the entire plug tree using the appropriate offsets contained in the plug information.

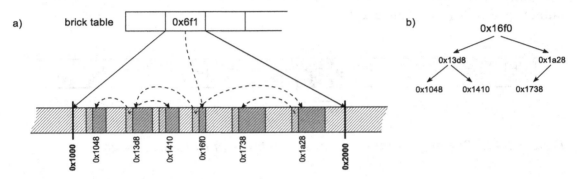

Figure 9-10. *Bricks and brick table example - (a) brick entry as a root of plug tree and plug info entries with child information, (b) logical plug tree representation*

Both brick table entry and left/right offsets are short integers (16-bit) because they allow us to store a value between -32767 to 32767 which is enough to represent offsets inside at most 4-kB address ranges.

When answering the question, "what will be the new address of the object at address X?," the following, simple steps must be taken:

- Calculate the brick table entry based on address X - by simply dividing it by a brick size.

- If brick table entry is <0 - jump into proper brick table entry and repeat.

- If brick table entry is >0 - start to traverse plug tree to find proper plug.

- Get relocation offset from the plug and subtract it from X.

633

At this point, we could conclude the description of the operation of Plan phase. All necessary information has been collected so GC could proceed further. Compaction efficiency could be taken from the relocation offset of the last plug. However, there is still one, very important piece of the puzzle to describe, which makes the whole technique more complex.

Pinning

If an object is pinned, it is most probably because we want to pass its address to the unmanaged code (see Figure 9-11).

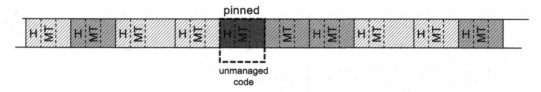

Figure 9-11. *Pinning example. Pinned objects are marked as dark gray*

We cannot simply move a pinned object during compacting because unmanaged code has no chance to be aware of it. It will still refer to the same address, which will now point to a completely different set of data (see Figure 9-12).

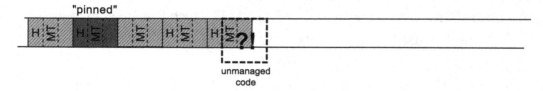

Figure 9-12. *Pinning example - unmanaged code accessing undefined data after pinned object has been moved*

Pinning complicates quite significantly a simple technique described in the previous section. Pinned objects have to be taken into consideration in a special way by internal allocator and when building a plug tree. This section explains how it has been implemented.

Because of pinning, in fact there are three kinds of objects group possible:

- plug - represents a group of marked (reachable) objects,

- pinned plug - represents a group of pinned (and thus marked) objects,

- gap - represents a group of not-marked (unreachable) objects.

Imagine first the simplest scenario - a pinned plug is located just after some gap (see Figure 9-13). In this case we do not change much. We may store plug info as usual, at the end of the corresponding gap. We will store proper left/right offset when building a plug tree. The main difference is that we should zero relocation offset for such plug.

Additionally, with all pinned plugs a size of the free space before it (in case of compacting will be chosen) is stored (see Figure 9-13b).

In that simple manner, during compaction normal plugs will be moved while the pinned plug will not (see Figure 9-13c). This is because the internal allocator described previously simply does not move pinned plugs (it "allocates" a space for them exactly where they are).

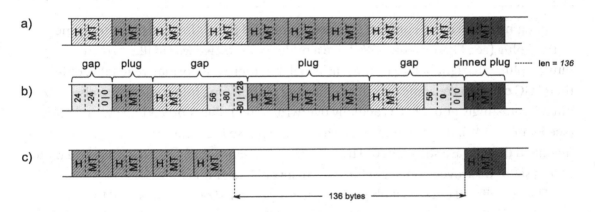

Figure 9-13. *Plug management when pinned plug is located after gap – (a) an example object layout with single pinned plug, (b) organization of plug information, (c) result of compaction*

Please note that in such case as from Figure 9-13c, we may introduce a big free space gap between the normal and pinned plug. Such scenarios will be discussed soon in the section, "Demotion," to not overwhelm you now with all the details.

Data related to all pinned plugs are also remembered on a *pinned plug queue*. As we will soon see, GC often needs to store more information about a pinned plug that will just not fit in standard plug information, hence the necessity to maintain such a separate pinned plug queue.

Interestingly enough, to store pinned plug data already known `mark_stack_array` is being reused. This time, however, it stores pointers to a dedicated mark class instances instead of objects' addresses. Thus, besides its names, when analyzing CoreCLR code you can very often meet `mark_stack_array` (and corresponding `mark_stack_tos` and `mark_stack_bos` pointers) in a code related to the pinned plug handling.

Imagine now a more complex scenario - a pinned plug is located just after some normal plug (see Figure 9-14a). We have a problem here - we would like to store pinned plug info right before it starts, as usual, but there is a normal, reachable object there! GC could make some exceptions, storing pinned plug info somewhere else but... interestingly enough, GC actually overwrites such object preceding pinned plug (see Figure 9-14b). It is possible because the Plan phase is guaranteed to run while all managed threads are suspended. Thus, there is no chance that any .NET code will try to access such "destroyed" object before we "recover" it later on.

The cut-off end of the last object (which is 3-pointer-sized 24 bytes on 64-bit) is stored together with other pinned plug data inside a new pinned plug queue entry. Such object ending is called *pre plug* (because it precedes pinned plug). It would be used later during execution of compacting or sweeping.

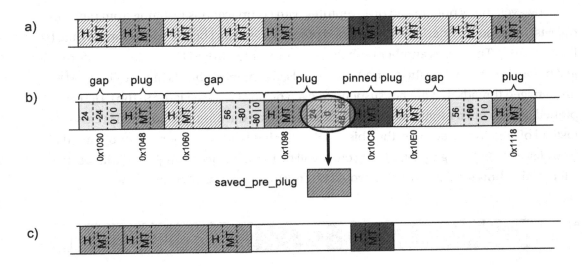

Figure 9-14. Plug management when pinned plug is located after normal plug - (a) an example object layout with single pinned plug after normal object, (b) organization of plug information with end of the object stored as pre plug, (c) possible result of compaction

Please note that again the requirement of an object to be at least 24-bytes long helps here a lot - it is assured that in such scenario there will be enough space for plug information even with the smallest preceding object.

Such an approach allows us to treat pinned plugs in a generic way. Related relocation offset will be 0, gap size will be set artificially to 24 bytes,[2] and such plug info will be incorporated into the plug tree as usual (see Figure 9-15).

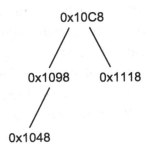

Figure 9-15. Logical representation of plug tree for plugs from Figure 7-43

---

[2]Although there is no real gap here, GC needs to account it for its statistical purposes.

However, this is not the end of adventures with complications resulting from pinning objects. Imagine a scenario when a pinned plug is located just before some normal plug (see Figure 9-16a). This raises another problem – a normal plug would like to store its information just before it starts, where the pinned object ends. But pinned objects may be accessed by unmanaged threads that are not suspended even during GC (see Figure 9-16b). Hence, pinned objects must be guaranteed to be untouched all the time. The solution is easy - instead of creating a new plug, the object right after it is being incorporated into pinned plug (see Figure 9-16c). Single pinned plug entry will be modified accordingly. We will see in a later section how such information would be consumed in case of compacting.

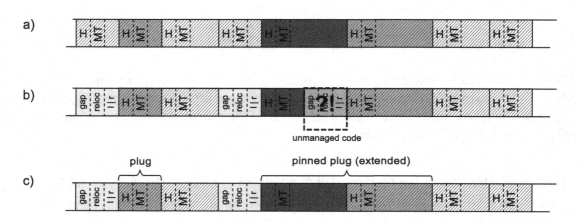

Figure 9-16. *Plug management when pinned plug is located before normal plug - (a) an example object layout with single pinned plug, (b) organization of plug information that needs to be handled properly, (c) organization of plug information*

It is a kind of compromise. From now on both pinned and normal objects are treated as an extended pinned plug so they will count into all pinning-related disadvantages. Pinning should be avoided but what is done here is exactly the opposite - we are aggressively pinning an additional, normal object. The advantage of the still generic treatment of plugs prevails here, however, over the disadvantages. If a normal object located after a pinned object is small, the introduced disturbances will be negligible.

This could be however problematic if a pinned object is followed by a large block of marked objects. Should all of them be included as an extended pinned plug (giving theoretically pinned plugs in size of megabytes or gigabytes)? Obviously not. Extension of pinned plug is done only by a first, single object.

Imagine a pinned object followed by at least two marked objects (see Figure 9-17a). Pinned plug will be extended as described previously. This allows us to create a normal plug from the following marked objects because it is safe to overwrite the last normal object (see Figure 9-17b). Obviously, the ending of such "destroyed" object must be stored elsewhere like it was in case of pre-plug data. Such an object ending is called *post plug*. It would be used later during the execution of compacting or sweeping.

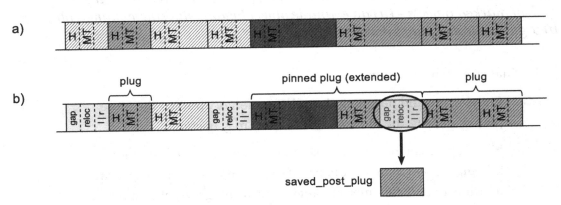

Figure 9-17. *Plug management when pinned plug is located before at least two marked objects – (a) an example object layout with single pinned plug, (b) organization of plug information*

To summarize, the most typical scenario is when a pinned object is lying inside a larger block of marked objects (see Figure 9-18a). In such a case, both pre and post plugs must be saved and three separate plugs (including one pinned and extended) will be created (see Figure 9-18b).

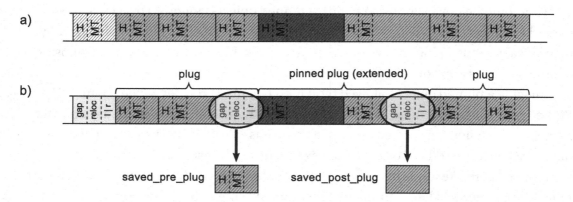

Figure 9-18. *Plug management when pinned plug is located inside larger block of marked objects – (a) an example object layout with single pinned plug, (b) organization of plug information*

This has several implications:

- Copying pre and post plugs introduces memory traffic - the more pinned objects, the more cumbersome it may become.

- Pinned plug can be extended by a single object so more memory is being pinned than it could be - if the normal object is big, we are freezing a significant memory region, disturbing the achievement of small fragmentation.

- During Plan phase some objects on the Managed Heap are "destroyed" making it not "walkable" in a normal way. We may hit this problem when analyzing memory dumps (see Scenario 9-1).

Scenario 9-2. Investigating Pinning

Description: Thanks to \.NET CLR Memory\# of Pinned Objects Performance Counter, a lot of pinning has been observed in our application on the production environment (see Figure 9-19). We would like to investigate whether it is intentional or not.

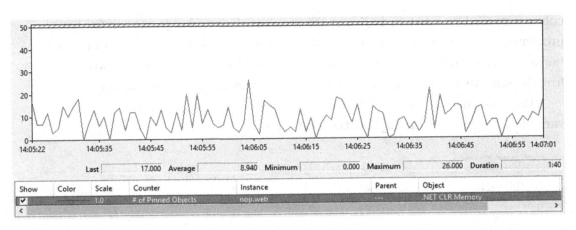

Figure 9-19. \.NET CLR Memory()\# of Pinned Objects

Analysis: As you may remember from previous pinning descriptions, there are in fact two sources of pinning:

- local pinned variables - objects that are local variables, often created implicitly by using `fixed` keyword. Their life is limited to containing method lifetime. Thus, memory dump or Heap Snapshot (from PerfView) will show only a small slice of them based on what is currently executing. However, there is `PinObjectAtGCTime` ETW event emitted for every such object.

- pinned handles - objects that are pinned explicitly by pinned handle reference. Those include some internal objects held by CLR itself, as well as those explicitly created by `GCHandle.Allocate` call. The handle table resides in memory for an entire application lifetime so it may be easily analyzed from memory dump or Heap Snapshot. ETW sessions contain such information also in the form of `PinObjectAtGCTime` event, but only for the generation(s) that the GC is collecting (since handle table is generation aware).

Performance counter \.NET CLR Memory()\# of Pinned Objects also counts both types. At the beginning we do not know which type of pinning is contributing more.

We may start our analysis by recording ETW-based session during periods when # of Pinned Objects is high. Using PerfView, .NET option will be enough (without GC Collect Only selected). After opening GCStats report from Memory Group, we should see confirmation on noticeable number of pinned objects (see Figure 9-20). The last

641

column, named Pinned Obj, indicates the number of pinned objects each GC has promoted. Those values should be the same as observed by Performance Counter. If Performance Counters are not available (in case of .NET Core runtime), you can start from here to check whether there is a noticeable pinning in your application.

Obviously, in our case, # of Pinned Objects value comes mainly from local pinned variables, observed by `PinObjectAtGCTime` event.

All GC Events for Process 20700: nop.web

GC Events by Time

All times are in msec. Hover over columns for help.

GC Index	Pause Start	Trigger Reason	Gen	Suspend Msec	Pause MSec	% Pause Time	% GC	Gen0 Alloc MB	Gen0 Alloc Rate MB/sec	Peak MB	After MB	Ratio Peak/After	Promoted MB	Gen0 MB	Gen0 Survival Rate %	Gen0 Frag %	Gen1 MB	Gen1 Survival Rate %	Gen1 Frag %	Gen2 MB	Gen2 Survival Rate %	Gen2 Frag %	LOH MB	LOH Survival Rate %	LOH Frag %	Finalizable Surv MB	Pinned Obj
1428 Beginning entries truncated, use View in Excel to view all...																											
2326	30,355.591	AllocSmall	0N	0.009	5.089	63.7	31.6	4.082	1,405.13	125.733	125.733	1.00	0.741	3.914	17	99.90	1.019	NaN	0.00	117.470	NaN	0.00	3.330	NaN	0.00	0.00	11
2327	30,367.613	AllocSmall	0N	0.011	10.160	59.4	20.0	4.105	591.57	126.024	125.727	1.00	1.187	2.705	28	99.95	2.222	NaN	0.44	117.470	NaN	0.00	3.330	NaN	0.00	0.00	11
2328	30,387.252	AllocSmall	1N	0.091	9.470	50.0	11.9	6.216	655.31	129.315	128.512	1.01	1.427	7.234	7	99.99	0.477	43	0.00	117.470	NaN	53.97	3.330	NaN	0.13	0.03	8
2329	30,401.142	AllocSmall	1N	0.080	7.653	63.4	17.4	4.138	934.79	128.512	125.504	1.02	0.728	4.403	7	99.99	0.301	89	0.00	117.470	NaN	53.60	3.330	NaN	0.13	0.01	5
2330	30,414.400	AllocSmall	0N	0.055	5.680	50.3	12.8	4.141	737.74	125.504	125.504	1.00	0.213	4.403	5	95.11	0.301	NaN	0.00	117.470	NaN	0.00	3.330	NaN	0.00	0.00	6
2331	30,426.190	AllocSmall	0N	0.057	5.462	47.2	13.3	4.149	678.37	125.511	125.504	1.00	0.494	3.906	11	99.99	0.798	NaN	0.02	117.470	NaN	0.00	3.330	NaN	0.00	0.00	6
2332	30,506.055	AllocSmall	0N	0.009	8.202	9.9	4.1	6.226	83.68	127.891	125.021	1.02	0.698	2.721	11	99.88	1.499	NaN	0.00	117.470	NaN	0.00	3.330	NaN	0.00	0.03	10
2333	30,522.738	AllocSmall	1N	0.010	6.844	44.6	15.2	6.274	739.04	128.594	128.230	1.00	0.904	7.395	0	99.96	0.035	57	0.00	117.470	NaN	52.86	3.330	NaN	0.13	0.00	12
2334	30,534.114	AllocSmall	0N	0.056	5.325	54.0	14.7	4.087	900.15	128.230	124.829	1.03	0.390	3.603	9	99.97	0.426	NaN	0.00	117.470	NaN	0.00	3.330	NaN	0.00	0.00	6

***Figure 9-20.** Pinned Obj column in GC Events by Time table*

As said, there is `PinObjectAtGCTime` event emitted for every pinned object during Mark phase. We can simply investigate those individual events from the Events view - especially interesting there is a TypeName field (see Figure 9-21). Only by looking at it, we can sometimes easily identify the source of pinning, if the pinned type is unique enough.

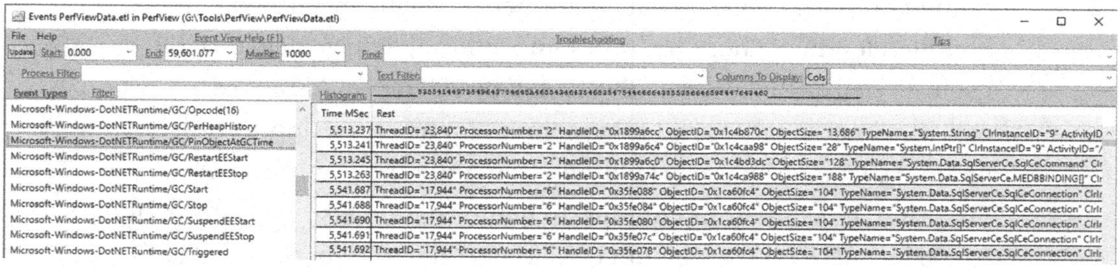

***Figure 9-21.** ETW Microsoft-Windows-DotNETRuntime/GC/PinObjectAtGCTime*

Please note that `PinObjectAtGCTime` have no stack traces attached. We could enable them by using `@StacksEnabled=true` option for .NET ETW provider, but it would not help us at all. The stack trace of such events is always inside the GC code, not at the place where pinned object is being used.

There is however a much better view to analyze this source of pinning - specially dedicated Pinning At GC Time Stacks view from Advanced Group. It does additional analysis and grouping to provide summarized data. The default By Name view will show the main contribution of types that were pinned (see Figure 9-22). We see that all pinned objects are grouped into a NonGen2 source.

By Name ?	Caller-Callee ?	CallTree ?	Callers ?	Callees ?	Flame Graph ?	Notes ?				
Name ?	Exc % ?	Exc ?	Exc Ct ?	Inc % ?	Inc ?	Inc Ct ?	Fold ?	Fold Ct ?
NonGen2	100.0	18,840	18,840	100.0	18,840.0	18,840	0	0
ROOT	0.0	0	0	100.0	18,840.0	18,840	0	0
Type System.String Size: 0x39b8	0.0	0	0	0.0	1.0	1	0	0
Type System.String Size: 0x58	0.0	0	0	0.0	5.0	5	0	0
Type System.String Size: 0x3b8	0.0	0	0	0.0	2.0	2	0	0
Thread (22360) CPU=9350ms (.NET ThreadPool)	0.0	0	0	5.7	1,072.0	1,072	0	0
Type System.String Size: 0x3e	0.0	0	0	0.0	2.0	2	0	0

Figure 9-22. *Pinning At GC Time Stacks - By Name*

By selecting Goto Item in Callers command on it, we will be able to further analyze what types are the main sources of pinning. We may notice that they are in fact mostly "StackPinned" (see Figure 9-23). In our example, clearly, types from the System. Data.SqlServerCe namespace have the largest contribution (namely, SqlCeCommand, SqlCeConnection and MEDBBINDING[] array).

By Name ?	Caller-Callee ?	CallTree ?	Callers ?	Callees ?	Flame Graph ?	Notes ?				

Methods that call NonGen2

Name ?	Inc % ?	Inc ?	Inc Ct ?	Exc % ?	Exc ?	Exc Ct ?	Fold ?	Fold Ct ?
☑ NonGen2	100.0	18,840.0	18,840	100.0	18,840	18,840	0	0
+ ☑ Type System.Data.SqlServerCe.SqlCeCommand Size: 0x80	30.9	5,828.0	5,828	0.0	0	0	0	0
| + ☑ StackPinned	30.9	5,828.0	5,828	0.0	0	0	0	0
| + ☐ Pinning Location	30.9	5,828.0	5,828	0.0	0	0	0	0
+ ☑ Type System.Data.SqlServerCe.SqlCeConnection Size: 0x68	12.7	2,394.0	2,394	0.0	0	0	0	0
| + ☑ StackPinned	12.7	2,394.0	2,394	0.0	0	0	0	0
| + ☐ Pinning Location	12.7	2,394.0	2,394	0.0	0	0	0	0
+ ☑ Type System.Data.SqlServerCe.MEDBBINDING[] Size: 0xe8	6.5	1,216.0	1,216	0.0	0	0	0	0
| + ☑ StackPinned	6.5	1,216.0	1,216	0.0	0	0	0	0
| + ☐ Pinning Location	6.5	1,216.0	1,216	0.0	0	0	0	0
+ ☐ Type System.IntPtr[] Size: 0x20	6.3	1,186.0	1,186	0.0	0	0	0	0
+ ☐ Type System.String Size: 0x119bc	6.2	1,162.0	1,162	0.0	0	0	0	0
+ ☐ Type System.Data.SqlServerCe.MEDBBINDING[] Size: 0x90	5.4	1,014.0	1,014	0.0	0	0	0	0

Figure 9-23. *Pinning At GC Time Stacks - Callers of NonGen2*

At this stage, by searching in source code for those type instances usage (with `fixed` keyword) should be enough to unambiguously identify the root source of such pinning. For example, `System.Data.SqlServerCe.SqlCeCommand.ExecuteCommandText` method contains code shown in Listing 9-1, where `DbBinding` field is of type `MEDBBINDING[]`.

Listing 9-1. An example of local variable pinning from System.Data.SqlServerCe. dll (decompiled by dnSpy)

```
fixed (IntPtr* ptr = this.accessor.DbBinding)
{
    // ...
}
```

There's another way to analyze objects pinned by handles, which is the `!GCHandles` SOS command inside WinDbg. Let's make a memory dump during high \.NET CLR Memory\# of Pinned Objects value. After opening it in WinDbg and loading SOS extension, we may list all pinned handles with the help of `!GCHandles` command (see Listing 9-2). We will see a list of objects pinned due to pinned handles - including CLR internals arrays (remember string intern pool or statics?), various buffers used by Kestrel server, and so on, and so forth. Currently there is no WinDbg extension that would help us listing stack-based pinning sources.

Listing 9-2. !GCHandles command to list all pinned handles

```
> !GCHandles -type Pinned
  Handle Type        Object      Size      Data Type
007f1374 Pinned      04988078    131084    System.Byte[]
007f1378 Pinned      04968058    131084    System.Byte[]
007f137c Pinned      04948038    131084    System.Byte[]
007f1398 Pinned      0490f058    32780     System.Object[]
007f13ac Pinned      04928018    131084    System.Byte[]
007f13b4 Pinned      0490b038    16396     System.Object[]
007f13b8 Pinned      048fb028    65532     System.Object[]
007f13bc Pinned      048f9008    8204      System.Object[]
007f13c0 Pinned      0403dbac    12        Bid+BindingCookie
007f13c4 Pinned      048f7fe8    4108      System.Object[]
007f13c8 Pinned      04918008    65532     System.Object[]
007f13cc Pinned      048e7fd8    65532     System.Object[]
```

007f13d0 Pinned	048e3ff8	16332	System.Object[]
007f13d4 Pinned	048e1ff8	8172	System.Object[]
007f13d8 Pinned	048e17d8	2060	System.Object[]
007f13dc Pinned	048d18b8	65292	System.Object[]
007f13e0 Pinned	048c9918	32652	System.Object[]
007f13e4 Pinned	048c94f8	1036	System.Object[]
007f13e8 Pinned	048c5518	16332	System.Object[]
007f13ec Pinned	048c3518	8172	System.Object[]
007f13f0 Pinned	048c2508	4092	System.Object[]
007f13f4 Pinned	048c22e8	524	System.Object[]
007f13f8 Pinned	038c121c	12	System.Object
007f13fc Pinned	048c1020	4788	System.Object[]

```
Statistics:
      MT    Count    TotalSize Class Name
720dff90        1           12 System.Object
57fbb464        1           12 Bid+BindingCookie
720dffe4       18       417536 System.Object[]
720e419c        4       524336 System.Byte[]
Total 24 objects
```

The conclusion is simple - to have a good overview of pinning, we should look at ETW PinObjectAtGCTime events that take into consideration both pinning sources. Be aware that SOS extensions list only handle-related pinning sources.

As a final remark, the PerfView ability to analyze its Heap Snapshots is slightly more useful here. After opening such snapshot, we may look for [.NET Roots] row and select Goto Item in CallTree command. After removing folding (by clearing out Fold% field), you will be able to list all types of roots - including Pinned local vars (see Figure 9-24). We will see there already known to us the MEDBBINDING[] type as the main source of such kind of pinning. Remember that it is still only the static snapshot so stack-based pinning sources will not be listed exhaustively.

Name ?	Inc % ?	Inc ?	Inc Ct ?	Exc % ?	Exc ?	Exc Ct ?	Fold ?	Fold Ct ?
☑ROOT ?	100.0	477,697,500.0	6,242,025	0.0	0	0	0	0
+☐[not reachable from roots] ?	56.4	269,288,800.0	951,201	0.0	0	0	0	0
+☑[.NET Roots] ?	43.0	205,578,300.0	5,290,824	0.0	0	1	0	0
+☐[static vars] ?	41.8	199,860,700.0	5,206,587	0.0	0	1	0	0
+☐[Pinned handles] ?	0.8	3,606,040.0	51,845	0.0	0	1	0	0
+☐[finalization handles] ?	0.3	1,269,758.0	18,608	0.0	0	1	0	0
+☐[local vars] ?	0.1	581,928.0	13,449	0.0	0	1	0	0
+☐[Strong handles] ?	0.0	34,850.0	303	0.0	0	1	0	0
+☐[AsyncPinned handles] ?	0.0	25,068.0	19	0.0	0	1	0	0
+☑[Pinned local vars] ?	0.0	532.0	8	0.0	0	1	0	0
]+☑System.Data.SqlServerCe!Data.SqlServerCe.MEDBBINDING[] (NoPtrs,ElemSize=44)	0.0	476.0	3	0.0	476	3	0	0
]+☑mscorlib!IntPtr[] (NoPtrs,ElemSize=4) ?	0.0	56.0	2	0.0	56	2	0	0
]+☑UNDEFINED ?	0.0	0.0	2	0.0	0	2	0	0
]+☑mscorlib!String {MinDepth 8} ?	0.0	0.0	0	0.0	32	1	0	0
]+☑mscorlib!String {Bytes > 10K} {MinDepth 10} ?	0.0	0.0	0	0.0	27,372	2	0	0
+☐[COM/WinRT Objects] ?	0.0	232.0	3	0.0	0	1	0	0
+☐[Dependent handles] ?	0.0	0.0	1	0.0	0	1	0	0

Figure 9-24. *RefTree view of [.NET Roots] from PerfView Heap Snapshot analysis*

It is sometimes also good to remove any grouping from GroupPats field and any folding from FoldPats field. This will produce more granular but yet more descriptive results. Figure 9-24 was prepared in such a way.

After identifying sources of pinning, we may decide whether they are avoidable or not. If they are not causing big fragmentation, most probably we may just leave them as they are. In case of being problematic (like causing big fragmentation), we have to find some solution. Approaches to avoid excessive pinning are presented in Chapter 13.

Generation Boundaries

After Sweep or Compact, generation boundaries will be changed accordingly. It is rather simple to do in scenarios without pinned objects. Generation boundaries are aligned in such a way that they contain all accordingly promoted objects.

For example, imagine the layout of objects shown in Figure 9-25a during Full Collection. There are all three generations presented, and some objects are marked (reachable) in each of them. As we already know, during Plan phase the internal allocator calculates new addresses for plugs (see Figure 9-25b). But additionally, new generation boundaries are being calculated. All this is done again only virtually without moving any objects, hence Figure 9-25b shows the resulting view of the internal allocator on the Managed Heap as something abstract.

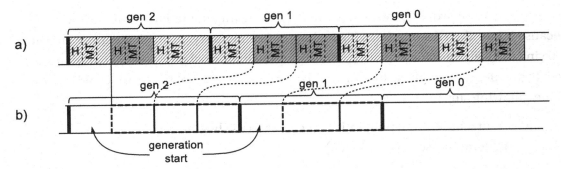

Figure 9-25. *Calculating generation boundaries – (a) object layout, (b) resulting view of the allocator on the Managed Heap (light gray - dead objects, medium gray - live objects that are moved according to the dashed lines)*

New generations' boundaries are located in places that will contain all necessary survived objects. This may be easily calculated during Plan phase. There is however one small remark to mention. Each generation (even empty one) begins with a single Free space with a size of a minimum object. Such a generation start is useful when considering plug info storage for the first plug in the generation. It allows them to be treated in generic way also without worrying about having plugs that span two generations.

Hereinafter such a generation's start is most often omitted to not clutter figures too much. Do not be surprised though when analyzing memory dumps to find out that each generation starts with 24-byte-long free space.

Demotion

Previously in Figures 9-13 and 9-14, possible results of the compacting have been shown. It was not completely clear how the internal allocator will behave around pinned plugs and where generations will start. From the implementation point of view, the simplest solution would be just to reset the accumulated relocation offset after each pinned plug so each following plug will be allocated after it. Then the generation would start in places to cover all survived objects accordingly.

This obviously would be very inefficient from the fragmentation point of view because it introduced sometimes big regions of free memory. Instead, the inner allocator is trying to fill all the gaps between pinned plugs with normal plugs and generation starts (see Figure 9-26). Plan phase for our small example fragment of the heap would consist of the following steps:

- At first allocation, pointer is being reset to the beginning of the generation (see Figure 9-26a).

- The allocator finds a place for the first (see Figure 9-26b) and the second (Figure 9-26c) plugs.

- The allocator "allocates" pinned plug under its original address (see Figure 9-26d).

- The allocator finds a place for the last plug before pinned plug - there is enough room for it (see Figure 9-26e).

One must now decide where generations should begin. At the beginning of our example all objects were in generation 0. If we wanted to promote all survived objects into generation 1 as expected, including a pinned one, generation 0 should start just after the pinned plug - pinned object from generation 0 should be promoted to generation 1 as any other objects. But it would introduce a big fragmentation in generation 1. The better decision is to reuse existing gap and end generation 1 earlier. Generation 0 will be planned to start before pinned object (see Figure 9-26f)!

Thus, because of such decision, the pinned object remained in generation 0 - it was not promoted from generation 0 to generation 1 as usual! In our example, this would happen to all pinned plugs located after our pinned plug (if there were any, and if there's no more non-pinned plugs).

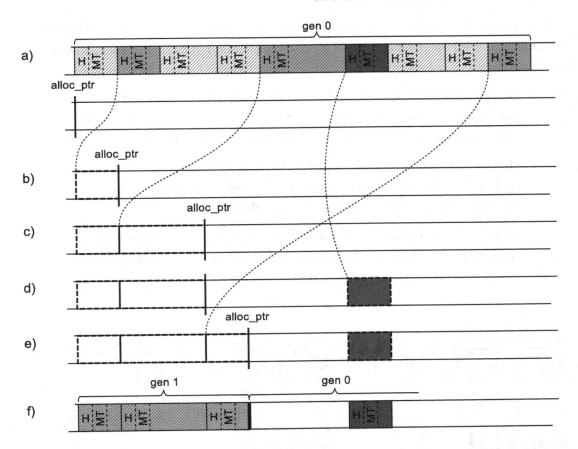

Figure 9-26. *Inner allocator filling gaps created due to pinning – (a) object layout taken from Figure 9-14 and resulting view of the allocator on the Managed Heap, (b) internal allocator found a place for the first plug, (c) internal allocator found a place for the second plug, (d) pinned plug was not moved, (e) internal allocator found a place for the last plug before the pinned plug (there was enough room for it), (f) generation 1 starts before theoretically promoted pinned plug - it was demoted (not promoted).*

Such an event is called *demotion* (as the opposite of promotion) and means that the object does not end up in a generation that it is supposed to be in. Demotion could mean that object is not promoted, but it also could mean that it lands in the lower generation.

So because of pinning, all three possibilities about the object's promotion are possible. Let's analyze it from the perspective of a pinned plug (extended by single object after it) from generation 1. The following three scenarios can happen for such a pinned plug:

- Before it there is a gap big enough to allocate normal plugs and generation starts for both generations 1 and 0 - in such case, a pinned plug would be demoted from generation 1 to 0 (see Figure 9-27).

- Before it there is a gap big enough to allocate normal plugs and generation start for generation 1 - in such case a pinned plug would be demoted, staying in generation 1 (see Figure 9-28).

- Before it there is not enough room for normal plugs - therefore both pinned plug and a normal plug (including large free space gap) must be promoted into older generation (see Figure 9-29).

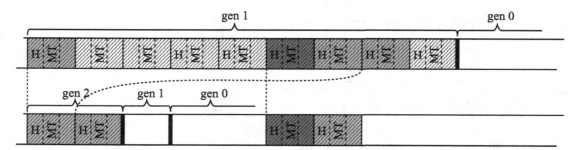

Figure 9-27. *Demotion from generation 1 to 0 – (a) objects layout, (b) result of compaction*

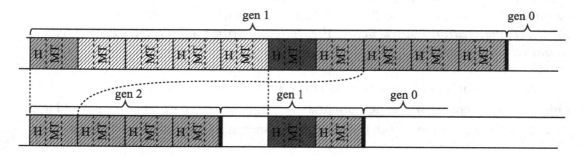

Figure 9-28. *Demotion from generation 1 to 1 – (a) objects layout, (b) result of compaction*

650

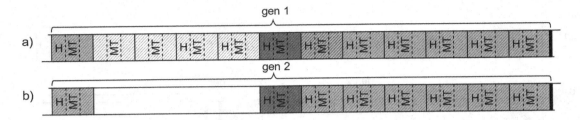

Figure 9-29. *Normal promotion from generation 1 to 2 – (a) objects layout,
(b) result of compaction (introduces unwanted fragmentation)*

Internal allocator operates on plugs, not on single objects. It means that even there was enough place before the pinned object in Figure 9-29, for some objects from the normal plug, it would not be split into smaller plugs to fill such a gap. This is a compromise between inner allocator complexity over the fragmentation overhead it introduces. However, in general, such overhead is rather negligible. Typical pinning either should be short lived or long lived:

- In the former case, it dies in generation 0, which is small and dynamic enough to accommodate that overhead and not introduce fragmentation.

- In the latter case, pinned object lives in generation 2 so the fact of pinning will just be irrelevant most of the time (as long as a compaction in gen2 doesn't happen, whether it's pinned or not or is of no relevance to the GC).

Note   Please note that in the current implementation, only pinned plugs may be demoted (which mean pinned object optionally extended by single non-pinned object following it, if there is one).

Obviously, when there are multiple pinned plugs, only some of them may be demoted. It all depends on the current layout of plugs and gaps. It has been illustrated in Figure 9-30. Normal plugs reused gaps as effectively as possible. It resulted in the first gap being normally promoted white the second demoted from generation 1 to 0.

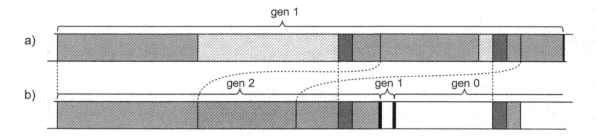

Figure 9-30. *Example of both promotion and demotion*

Demotion is an optimization to make sure that as many gaps have been reused as possible. The remaining free space will be turned into free-list items if they are big enough so they will get a chance to be reused also.

This is probably why there is no diagnostic data about demotion available. We can observe it by thorough memory dump analysis, but it is unlikely you will ever need to. What you should be concerned about is the fragmentation level induced by pinned plugs. Demotion is however an important part of the internal allocator and Plan phase, so describing them without demotion would be not comprehensive. It is good to know that pinned objects may be promoted and demoted. Generational GC concept does not incur any limitations here by design.

In case of previously mentioned ephemeral segment built by reusing already existing gen2-only segment, pinned plugs living there will be demoted from generation 2 to generations 1 and 0.

There is an undocumented !DumpGCData command in WinDBg's SOS extension. In addition to data that can be obtained by other means (e.g., from ETW) - like compacting reasons, a number of different kinds of GCs - it contains also nowhere else available information called "Interesting data points":

```
Interesting data points
        pre short: 0
       post short: 0
      merged pins: 0
   converted pins: 0
```

```
         pre pin: 0
        post pin: 0
 pre and post pin: 0
 pre short padded: 0
post short padded: 0
```

As we see, those include:

- various types of pre and post pin - pinned plugs with both pre and post plug info,

- various types of pre pin - pinned plugs with only pre plug info,

- various types of post pin - pinned plugs with only post plug info,

- converted pin - objects that were converted to pinned because of pinned plug extension.

This method is obviously mostly useful for the GC developers because there is a little practical usage of those data to users. It is even not guaranteed that this command will exist in the future edition of SOS extension. If you would like to investigate more, search for gc_heap::record_interesting_data_point method in CoreCLR's source code.

Large Object Heap

In fact, actually the plan stage in LOH is almost never needed because it is mostly just Sweeping. However, LOH must be organized in a way that allows it to Compact if we explicitly asked the GC to do it.

Plugs and Gaps

Plan phase for Large Object Heap is required only for compacting. The default is to always sweep, which does not use plugs and gaps (as described later). In case of Large Object Heap, compacting must be turned on explicitly and is not executed by default. This means in the vast majority of .NET applications, LOH will never be compacted at all. However, Large Object Heap must be prepared to make compacting possible. Thus, it incorporates the concept of plugs and gaps in a simplified form.

LOH is specific because it is guaranteed that only large objects are living there. This makes some simplifications possible:

- There is no such urgent need to group objects into plugs as separate objects are quite large by itself already. Thus, to simplify LOH Plan phase, each reachable object is treated as a separate plug. First of all, this is enough to provide good address translation efficiency (the object density in LOH is a lot lower than in SOH). Secondly, it helps to avoid fragmentation (it would be much harder to efficiently relocate huge plugs consisting of many large objects).

- To overcome overhead of plug info storage handling (including pre and post plugs around pinned plugs), objects in LOH are allocated with the small padding between them (see Figure 9-31). This padding in current implementation takes 4-pointer-sized words (32 bytes on 64-bit) and is made into a normal Free object.

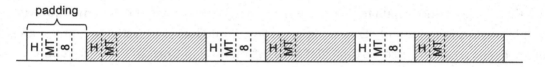

Figure 9-31. *Layout of objects in Large Object heap, including padding between objects in case of a runtime supporting LOH compaction*

Padding in LOH described here is used for all current .NET runtime compilations enabling explicit LOH compaction. However, .NET runtime may be compiled without this feature enabled, which will turn allocations in LOH into "without padding" mode. Because such runtime does not support LOH compaction, there will be no need to Plan phase and to create plugs (storing their info).

During the mark phase, each object may be identified as marked or marked and pinned. From each such object a corresponding plug is created (see Figure 9-32).

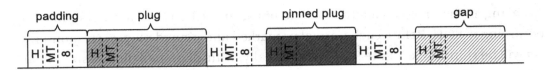

Figure 9-32. *Layout of objects in Large Object heap, after Mark phase*

Before each plug, its information needs to be stored but because of padding, there is always enough space for it (see Figure 9-33). This information is really simple and contains only a relocation offset of the plug.

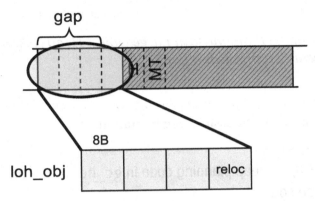

Figure 9-33. *Plug information stored in Large Object Heap (in preceding padding)*

Relocation offset is calculated on the same basis as in case of Small Object Heap. Internal allocator finds a proper place for successive plugs (successive objects). As mentioned, this is why it is good to treat each object as a plug and not to group them into single, huge plugs. Allocator most probably would have a big problem to find a proper place for such huge plugs between pinned plugs.

Because there is no possibility that the plug info will overwrite another object in LOH, there is no need to maintain pre and post plug data.

Because of a relatively small number of objects and big objects sizes, there is no need to manage a plug tree for plugs in LOH. When answering the question, "what will be the new address of the object at address X?," one simple step must be taken - get relocation offset from the plug info of X and subtract it from X. Thus, there is also no need to maintain bricks and a brick table for Large Object Heap.

As there are also no generations inside Large Object Heap, there is no need to recalculate generation boundaries. There is no demotion possibility either.

Taking all that into consideration, Plan phase in LOH is much more simplified comparing to SOH. Before each normal or marked and pinned plug, corresponding info will be stored (see Figure 9-34). Additionally, with all pinned plugs a size of the free space before it, in case of compacting, is stored (in corresponding pinned plug queue entry).

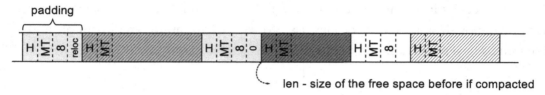

Figure 9-34. *Result of the Plan phase in Large Object Heap (last padding does not have reloc saved because it preceeds a gap)*

As an important side note, pinning in LOH does not differ comparing to SOH. It introduces the same problem of possible fragmentation.

You will find Large Object Heap planning code in `gc_heap::plan_loh` method from CoreCLR source code.

Decide on Compaction

After performing complex calculations in the Plan phase, GC has to decide whether it is worth compaction. There are some objective reasons that can force it. In most cases, however, the decision is based on the level of fragmentation.

The list of reasons why GC might decide to compact is as follows:

- It is a last full GC before throwing `OutOfMemoryException` - GC should do its best trying to reclaim memory.

- Compaction has been induced explicitly - for example, by providing appropriate `GC.Collect` parameter.

- We are running out of space in the ephemeral segment - as mentioned in the section about generation condemnation, GC is aggressively trying to reclaim memory before it decides to expand existing one or create a new ephemeral segment.

- Generation fragmentation is high - if some generation has high fragmentation, collecting that generation with compaction is to be productive - significant memory regions may be reclaimed.

- Physical memory load in the system is high - if possible reclamation of memory due to compaction exceeds certain threshold, GC decides to compact.

In some of the decisions described above, a fragmentation threshold violation takes an important role. One can wonder what its value is. Each generation maintains its own threshold, consisting of two values taken from static generation data (see Tables 7-1 and 7-2):

- Total fragmentation - with the information gathered during Plan phase, it is quite easy to calculate specific generation fragmentation. It is enough to take into account the planned ending allocation's addresses in individual segments and any free space that will be created due to pinning. This value is represented by fragmentation_limit column in Tables 7-1 and 7-2 (see Table 9-1 for a summary).

- Fragmentation ratio - this is the ratio of the above total fragmentation size to the size of the whole collected generation. This value is represented by the fragmentation_burden_limit column in the Tables 7-1 and 7-2 (see Table 9-1 for a summary).

Table 9-1. *Fragmentation Thresholds for Generations*

	Fragmentation size	Fragmentation ratio
Gen0	40000	50%
Gen1	80000	50%
Gen2	200000	25%

For example, generation 2 will be considered as too fragmented if the size of all fragmentation will exceed 200,000 bytes and it will be more than 25% of total generation size.

You will find compaction decision inside gc_heap::decide_on_compacting method from CoreCLR source code.

Summary

Plan phase described in this chapter is often overlooked in simple GC description as consisting of "Mark-Sweep-Compact" phases. However, after reading descriptions in this chapter, hopefully you already understand how crucial and important this phase is. By preparing all necessary data, subsequent phases are just consuming it in a proper way.

Personally, I found it fascinating how clever is the combination of plugs, gaps, and brick tables to proceed with calculating both compacting and sweeping results without actually doing them. This is the part barely documented so far in GC-related materials. Thus, although practical implications of the knowledge from this chapter are not huge (except understanding how pinning may be troublesome to the GC implementation), I believe the curious reader will find all this information very interesting.

This is almost the end of the GC description. The next chapter finishes with the description of the last phases - Compact and Sweep.

CHAPTER 10

Garbage Collection - Sweep and Compact

This last chapter regarding the GC details is the smallest one. Although it describes such crucial GC phases as Sweep or Compact, we already noticed how much is done to this point in the previous phases. After the decision made in the Plan phase (described in the previous chapter), now GC proceeds with one of the steps described here.

Please keep in mind, however, that while most of the calculations are already done at this stage, from a performance overhead perspective, Sweep or Compact phases are still the most contributing - it is the cost of accessing memory while modifying and/or moving plugs that is the most costly. Thus, although from an implementation point of view those stages are less complex than previous ones, from a performance perspective they are the most important ones!

Please also note that the most typical GC combination is to make SOH compaction and LOH sweeping, and then LOH sweeping is done before SOH compaction.

Sweep Phase

If the GC does not decide to compact (or it has not been told explicitly in case of LOH), it proceeds with the Sweep phase. As described in Chapter 1, Sweep collection is easy. All no-longer reachable objects must be turned into a free space. We already know that in .NET GC terminology, it means that it must transform all or some gaps into free-list items.

As mentioned earlier and as you may probably now understand on your own, both Sweep and Compact phases are only a simple consumption of the information gathered during Plan phase. For a person only skimming this book, it may be quite surprising that both Sweep and Compact terms - which are so popular when describing GC in literature - are taking such a small part of the book. This is because all heavy calculations were already done in Plan phase!

659

© Konrad Kokosa 2018
K. Kokosa, *Pro .NET Memory Management*, https://doi.org/10.1007/978-1-4842-4027-4_10

Small Object Heap

In case of Sweep of Small Object Heap, the following steps are taken (see Figure 10-1):

- Create free-list items from gaps - from each gap, bigger than two minimal objects, a new free-list item is created and incorporated into a free list (as described in Chapter 6). Smaller gaps are just treated as unused free space (but counted into fragmentation statistics).

- Recover saved pre and post plugs - all "destroyed" objects are recovered by writing back pre and post plugs.

- Additional tallying work is done to update the finalization queue (to reflect new generations boundaries) and to age (or rejuvenate) survived handles of appropriate type.

- Rearrange segments accordingly, for example, by removing those no longer needed (or storing them in a reusable list in case of VM hoarding).

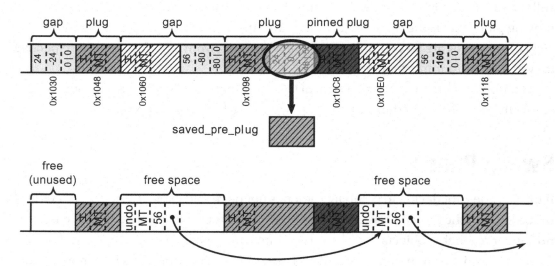

Figure 10-1. *Example of Sweep results in Small Object Heap (based on the information from Plan phase)*

If you would like to make your own investigations about SOH Sweep from CoreCLR code, start from the `gc_heap::plan_phase` method. In the part enclosed by else block of `should_compact` conditional check, the two most important methods are called: `gc_heap::make_free_lists` creates free-list items from gaps and `gc_heap::recover_saved_pinned_info` recovers objects destroyed by pre and post plugs.

Large Object Heap

In case of a Sweep of Large Object Heap, there is no Plan phase involved at all. Sweeping is implemented by scanning object by object (like in SOH Plan phase) and simply creating free-list items between marked objects. Additionally, any no-longer needed LOH segments are deleted (unless VM hoarding is enabled in which case they will be remembered is segment reusage list).

Such simple implementation of LOH Sweep is easy and efficient. It leads only to one disadvantage - fragmentation. Typically, it should not be a big deal. Allocated large objects sizes distribution most probably is quite natural - there are some common sizes and some variations around it. In such case, statistically reusage of free-list items should be good. However, if that's not the case, users can consider asking for LOH to be compacted

Compact Phase

If the GC does decide to compact (or it has been told explicitly to do so), it proceeds with the Compact phase. As mentioned earlier, it means consumption of the information gathered during Plan phase. Compaction phase in general consist of two main phases - moving (copying) objects and updating all references to moved objects wherever they occur. This makes the compact phase significantly more complex compared to Sweep phase. Detailed descriptions for both Small and Large Object Heaps are presented here although they are in principle similar to each other.

Small Object Heap

Compacting of Small Object Heap must be extremely efficient. By default, there are many gaps and plugs interleaved that may span gigabytes of data. Moving all that memory around while keeping all addresses valid is not a trivial task from the performance point of view. Let's dig into proper implementation details.

If you would like to make your own investigations about SOH compaction from CoreCLR code, take a look at `relocate_phase` (which updates addresses to moved objects) and `compact_phase` (which recursively traverses plug tree brick by brick by calling `compact_plug` and `compact_in_brick` methods).

Having information from Plan phase, Compact is a process consisting of the steps described in the following sections.

Getting a New Ephemeral Segment if Necessary

This step is executed if the planning phase has shown a need of expanding the ephemeral segment (there would be not enough space for generations 0 and/or 1 after compaction). This is done either by expanding the current ephemeral segment, by reusing the other one (as described in Chapter 7), or by creating a new one.

Relocate References

This step updates all occurrences of addresses of objects that will be moved later on. Thanks to the data gathered during Plan phase, this is possible before actually moving those objects. Obviously, it requires quite a lot of work because there may be a lot of such references scattered throughout the managed heap. Relocation makes a heavy usage of bricks and plug trees to fast translate current address into a new one. During this step, various memory areas are scanned for addresses to be updated. These include:

- references on the stack - all addresses on the stack are updated by runtime support to scan all managed threads stack frames finding all references to managed objects.

- references inside objects stored in cross-generational remembered set - in case of non-Full GC, all cross-generational references stored through cards (see Chapter 5) must be updated to reflect new addresses (those include both SOH and LOH cross-generational references).

- references inside objects on Small and Large Object Heap - survived objects that contain references to other objects must have their references updated. In case of SOH, bricks and plug trees are used to find survived objects fast (as we know they are grouped into plugs). For full GC, in case of LOH, most typically there are only survived objects at this stage because LOH sweeping is done before SOH compaction. This allows us to scan survived LOH objects one by one quite efficiently without bricks support.

- references inside pre and post plugs - as we know, the ending part of some objects may have been damaged due to overwriting by plug info. Its original memory content is being stored inside pinned plug queue entries. If it contains references, they have to be updated also.

- references inside objects from ready to finalization queue - addresses of objects staying in such queue (see Chapter 12) need to be updated.

- references from handle tables - handles need to update their pointers.

The more reference rich your objects are, the more work you put on GC at this stage. This may not be a problem in typical applications. However, in the case of very complex data structures used on the hot performance path, it is worth considering the avoidance of direct object references.

If you would like to investigate CoreCLR code of the relocation phase, start from `gc_heap::relocate_phase` method. The most important method used by it internally is a `gc_heap::relocate_address` method that utilizes bricks and a plug tree to translate address to a new relocated value. It is used among others by `GCScan::GcScanRoots`, `gc_heap::relocate_in_large_objects` and `gc_heap::relocate_survivors`' methods.

Compact Objects

After all required references have been updated in the previous step, it high time the GC moved all survived objects eventually. It consists of the following steps (see Figure 10-2):

- copying objects - it is done plug by plug using their calculated relocation offsets,

- restoring pre and post plug info - damaged parts of the objects are being restored from the copy stored in pinned plug queue entries.

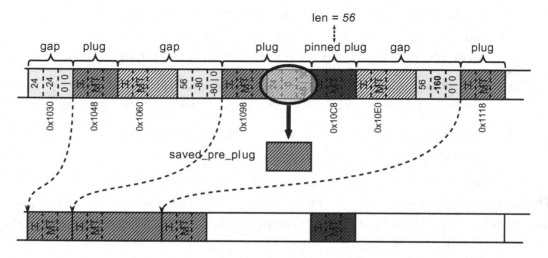

Figure 10-2. *Compacting objects in Small Object Heap by using information calculated during Plan phase*

Although the description of this step is quite short and simple, it is worth realizing how much heavy work may be done here. In case of the full GC, copying all plugs throughout all Managed Heap may introduce quite significant memory traffic. This is in fact the place where the most of the time during compacting GC is spent.

One may wonder how object copying is implemented. Because they are copied one by one in-place as grouped, theoretically quite long plugs, how do they not overwrite each other? (including themselves, see Figure 10-3).

Figure 10-3. *Theoretical problem of copying objects - by copying in-place they may overwrite themselves*

The obvious solution immediately comes to mind - to use some intermediate buffer (see Figure 10-4). However, this would double the memory traffic - now every object would have to be copied twice. Such a solution is obviously unacceptable.

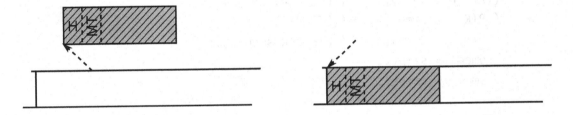

Figure 10-4. *Possible solution to the problem of copying objects - using a temporary buffer*

After a deeper reflection, however, we will come to the conclusion that there is really no problem here. We treat objects unnecessarily as consistent Lego bricks, which must be copied in their entirety. However, these are only continuous areas of memory that can be copied in smaller pieces. That's exactly the approach chosen by CLR. The point of sliding compaction is you always copy earlier addresses first, and you copy in a small enough quantity that naturally makes overlapping impossible (in .NET, as the smallest relocation address is at least one pointer size apart). Thus, object copying is realized by memcopy function that copy memory in groups of four pointer-sized regions at a time, then copying remaining space in two or single pointer-sized regions (see Listing 10-1).

Listing 10-1. Main part of memcopy method used during object copying

```
void memcopy (uint8_t* dmem, uint8_t* smem, size_t size)
{
   const size_t sz4ptr = sizeof(PTR_PTR)*4;
   // ...
   // copy in groups of four pointer sized things at a time
   if (size >= sz4ptr)
   {
      do
      {
         ((PTR_PTR)dmem)[0] = ((PTR_PTR)smem)[0];
         ((PTR_PTR)dmem)[1] = ((PTR_PTR)smem)[1];
         ((PTR_PTR)dmem)[2] = ((PTR_PTR)smem)[2];
         ((PTR_PTR)dmem)[3] = ((PTR_PTR)smem)[3];
           dmem += sz4ptr;
           smem += sz4ptr;
      }
      while ((size -= sz4ptr) >= sz4ptr);
   }
   // copy remaining 16 and/or 8 bytes
}
```

Memory copying lines from Listing 10-1 will be compiled into several mov assembly instructions making those operations extremely efficient.

If you would like to investigate CoreCLR code of compaction phase, start from the gc_heap::compact_phase method. Its main job is to call for each active brick gc_heap::compact_in_brick that underneath calls gc_heap::compact_plug method.

Fix Generation Boundaries

Called after the compact phase to fix all generation boundaries, these steps reset internal allocation pointers, creates free space for planned allocation context, and do other additional necessary corrections.

Delete/Decommit Segments if Necessary

Rearrange segments accordingly, for example by removing those no longer needed (or storing them reusable list in case of VM hording).

Creating Free-List Items

Before each pinned plug, a new free object is created and added to the free list if it is big enough (as we may remember, its length has been calculated and saved during Plan phase in pinned plug queue entry) - see Figure 10-5.

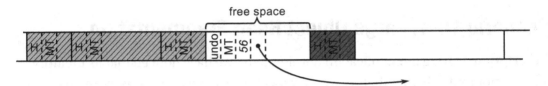

Figure 10-5. *Creating the appropriate free items before pinned plugs (continuation of Figure 10-2)*

Age roots

Additional aging are made to update the finalization queue (to reflect new generations boundaries) and to age (or rejuvenate) survived handles of the appropriate type.

Large Object Heap

Compacting Large Object Heap is based on a similar technique like in case of Small Object Heap. However, due to the lack of generations, complex plugs, bricks and plug tree, its implementation is much simpler.

If enabled, LOH compacting is executed before SOH compacting. It consists of a single loop scanning LOH for marked objects and copying them to the destination one by one (using relocation offset calculated during LOH planning phase). Additionally, for pinned objects, a corresponding free space will be created before them (see Figure 10-6) and threaded into a free list. Padding between objects will obviously remain because it may be needed in the next GC runs.

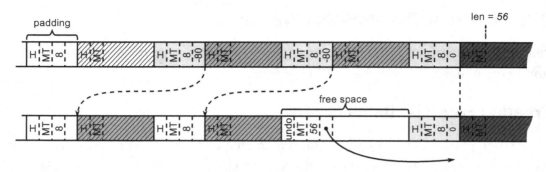

Figure 10-6. *Compacting objects in Large Object Heap by using information calculated during Plan phase*

Scenario 10-1. Large Object Heap Fragmentation

Description: During our application development, we have noticed that its memory usage is noticeable higher that we would expect. The application consists in processing large data packages and producing resulting data packages from them - let's say it is a batch processing of images. The extract of its processing code is presented in Listing 10-2. Notice comments describing sizes of the processed data. Both input and output frames are allocated in LOH because they are bigger than 85,000 bytes. The data we want to store is 100 kilobytes (`largeBlocks`), so they are also created in LOH.

Listing 10-2. An example code that illustrates LOH fragmentation

```
void Main()
{
// ...
List<byte[]> largeBlocks = new List<byte[]>();
while (someCondition)
{
    // ...
    var frame = reader.ReadBytes(size); // input frame is always bigger
                                        than 85,000 bytes
    var output = processor.Process(frame); // output is slightly bigger
                                           than input frame
```

```
    var largeBlock = new byte[102_400];
    // store some data from output in smallBlock
    largeBlocks.Add(largeBlock);
}
// ...
}
```

Please do not be fooled that it is only a contrived example that will never happen. Obviously, you will most probably not write such naïve code as in Listing 10-2. But processing a batch of data that produces some intermediate results that we need to store - that sound much more practical. Using arrays (especially byte arrays) is also not unjustified. It is really hard to introduce LOH fragmentation problems without using arrays and strings because those are the most common types that land in Large Object Heap. It is really hard to create a normal object with so many fields that it will be allocated in LOH. Thus, such code as in this scenario quite realistically reflects the essence of the real source of problems that you may encounter in the real world.

Analysis: Let's assume that from some preliminary analysis, we already checked that indeed LOH is bigger than expected (see Table 10-1). We may have done that by using Performance Counters or ETW-based data.

Table 10-1. *Expected versus Observed Size of Large Object Heap*

# objects	Expected [MB]	Observed [MB]
1,000	102,400,000	152,769,104
2,000	204,800,000	324,972,048
3,000	307,200,000	463,287,752
4,000	409,600,000	686,795,056

By recording the ETW-based session in PerfView (with standard GC Collect Only option), we can quickly spot that the reason is LOH fragmentation (see Figure 10-7). As LOH Frag % column states, the fragmentation is around 48%. A lot of space is wasted!

GC Events by Time

All times are in msec. Hover over columns for help.

GC Index	Pause Start	Trigger Reason	Gen	Suspend Msec	Pause MSec	% Pause Time	% GC	Gen0 Alloc MB	Gen0 Alloc Rate MB/sec	Peak MB	After MB	Ratio Peak/After	Promoted MB
1	3,742.311	AllocLarge	2N	0.004	0.233	0.0	2.7	0.000	0.00	3.264	3.264	1.00	1.271
2	3,877.645	AllocLarge	2B	0.057	0.335	0.2	0.0	0.000	0.00	5.340	5.533	0.97	2.501
3	4,013.101	AllocLarge	2B	0.847	1.010	0.7	7.7	0.000	0.00	7.321	7.513	0.97	3.730
4	4,196.935	AllocLarge	2B	0.092	0.827	0.5	7.1	0.000	0.00	10.342	10.432	0.99	5.368
5	4,495.480	AllocLarge	2B	0.083	0.215	0.1	4.2	0.000	0.00	15.520	15.721	0.99	8.032
6	4,883.850	AllocLarge	2B	0.108	0.230	0.1	3.0	0.104	0.27	22.139	22.229	1.00	11.514
7	5,510.978	AllocLarge	2B	0.007	0.147	0.0	1.8	0.000	0.00	33.560	33.651	1.00	17.238
8	6,359.557	AllocLarge	2B	0.007	0.190	0.0	3.0	0.109	0.13	47.902	48.001	1.00	24.817
9	7,726.891	AllocLarge	2B	0.016	0.255	0.0	2.3	0.000	0.00	71.823	71.921	1.00	36.801
10	9,532.924	AllocLarge	2B	0.257	0.577	0.0	2.9	0.208	0.12	102.471	102.661	1.00	52.984
11	12,415.020	AllocLarge	2B	0.018	0.622	0.0	2.0	0.108	0.04	153.704	153.810	1.00	78.591
12	18,015.951	AllocLarge	2B	0.008	0.651	0.0	1.7	0.212	0.04	218.477	218.679	1.00	112.601
13	24,133.417	AllocLarge	2B	0.013	1.114	0.0	1.9	0.422	0.07	327.169	327.085	1.00	166.779
14	34,280.586	AllocLarge	2B	0.010	1.516	0.0	1.8	0.449	0.04	463.820	463.931	1.00	238.498
15	52,840.287	AllocLarge	2B	0.012	1.551	0.0	1.4	0.747	0.04	690.833	691.048	1.00	350.839

GC Index	Gen0 MB	Gen0 Survival Rate %	Gen0 Frag %	Gen1 MB	Gen1 Survival Rate %	Gen1 Frag %	Gen2 MB	Gen2 Survival Rate %	Gen2 Frag %	LOH MB	LOH Survival Rate %	LOH Frag %	Finalizable Surv MB	Pinned Obj
1	0.000	64	0.00	0.030	0	35.53	0.000	0	0.00	3.234	38	61.29	0.00	5
2	0.008	0	59.04	0.030	0	36.27	0.000	0	0.00	5.495	55	54.85	0.00	0
3	0.010	0	7.41	0.030	0	36.27	0.000	0	0.00	7.473	65	50.36	0.00	0
4	0.011	0	90.17	0.030	0	36.27	0.000	0	0.00	10.390	65	48.52	0.00	0
5	0.019	0	91.30	0.030	0	36.27	0.000	0	0.00	15.672	64	48.88	0.00	0
6	0.023	0	93.02	0.030	0	36.27	0.000	0	0.00	22.176	65	48.17	0.00	0
7	0.039	0	92.75	0.030	0	36.27	0.000	0	0.00	33.581	63	46.73	0.00	0
8	0.058	0	82.05	0.030	0	36.27	0.000	0	0.00	47.912	65	48.24	0.00	0
9	0.099	0	87.37	0.030	0	36.27	0.000	0	0.00	71.793	63	48.77	0.00	0
10	0.129	0	86.80	0.030	0	36.27	0.000	0	0.00	102.502	65	48.33	0.00	0
11	0.170	0	93.10	0.030	0	36.27	0.000	0	0.00	153.810	63	48.85	0.00	0
12	0.251	0	88.80	0.030	0	36.27	0.000	0	0.00	218.397	65	48.36	0.00	0
13	0.367	0	90.70	0.030	0	36.27	0.000	0	0.00	326.687	63	48.95	0.00	0
14	0.510	0	91.31	0.030	0	36.27	0.000	0	0.00	463.391	64	48.54	0.00	0
15	0.744	0	94.09	0.030	0	36.27	0.000	0	0.00	690.273	63	49.18	0.00	0

Figure 10-7. *GC Events by Time table from PerfView's GCStats report for the process under investigation*

Obviously, as always, we can simply analyze our code to find what and when we are allocating LOH objects. Is there any way we could help ourselves? As very often, PerfView to the rescue! LOH fragmentation comes from the dead objects - they are making up fragmentation. Therefore, it would be best to check what objects most often die in Large Object Heap. In the case of such noticeable fragmentation, it is likely that they will be the source of the problem. Fortunately, PerfView can provide us such statistics if we record the ETW session with .NET option enabled (and not GC Collect Only or GC Only). After such recording has ended, we should be able to open Gen 2 Object Deaths (Coarse Sampling) Stacks from Memory Group (see Figure 10-8). Besides its name, this analysis includes also LOH objects. As we can see, a lot of `System.Byte[]` arrays are dying. This may be helpful by itself (if this identifies unambiguously source of such allocations). But we may go further.

Name ?	Exc % ?	Exc ?	Exc Ct ?	Inc % ?	Inc ?
Type System.Byte[]	100.0	627,998,500	3,422	100.0	627,998,500.0
Type System.Char[]	0.0	800	0	0.0	800.0
Type System.String	0.0	800	0	0.0	800.0
Type System.Int32	0.0	200	0	0.0	200.0
Type System.Double	0.0	100	0	0.0	100.0
Type System.Byte[][]	0.0	100	0	0.0	100.0
Type CoreCLR.LOHFragmentation.DataFrame	0.0	100	0	0.0	100.0
GC Occured Gen(2)	0.0	0	15	0.0	0.0
Process64 CoreCLR.LOHFragmentation (32064) Args: 102400	0.0	0	0	100.0	628,000,600.0
Thread (30188) CPU=4528ms (Startup Thread)	0.0	0	0	100.0	628,000,600.0
OTHER <<ntdll!RtlUserThreadStart>>	0.0	0	0	100.0	628,000,600.0
coreclr.lohfragmentation!CoreCLR.LOHFragmentation.Program.Main(class System.String[])	0.0	0	0	100.0	628,000,600.0
coreclr.lohfragmentation!CoreCLR.LOHFragmentation.Processor.Process(class CoreCLR.LOHFragmentation.DataFrame)	0.0	0	0	100.0	627,873,200.0

Figure 10-8. *Gen 2 Object Deaths (Coarse Sampling) - By Name view from PerfView showing objects dying in Gen2+*

After selecting for type System.Byte[] an option Goto Item in Callers from Goto group in the context menu, we will see allocations stack traces of such dying objects (see Figure 10-9). This is now really useful information!

Remember that this is sampling information based on an ETW GCAllocationTick event. However, it is enough for LOH objects, because such an event is generated for each 100k of allocations. In LOH, 100k of memory can't contain two whole objects as they are at least 85,000 bytes big by definition. In case of analyzing fragmentation in SOH, you can get less coarse results by using .NET Alloc or .NET SampAlloc when configuring PerfView's collection.

Methods that call Type System.Byte[]

Name ?	Inc % ?	Inc ?	Inc Ct ?	Exc % ?
☑Type System.Byte[]	100.0	627,998,500.0	3,422	100.0
+☑OTHER <<clrJIT_NewArr1>>	100.0	627,998,500.0	3,422	0.0
+☑ coreclr.lohfragmentation!CoreCLR.LOHFragmentation.Processor.Process(class CoreCLR.LOHFragmentation.DataFrame)	100.0	627,873,200.0	3,421	0.0
+☑coreclr.lohfragmentation!CoreCLR.LOHFragmentation.Program.Main(class System.String[])	100.0	627,873,200.0	3,421	0.0
+☑OTHER <<ntdll!RtlUserThreadStart>>	100.0	627,873,200.0	3,421	0.0
+☑Thread (30188) CPU=4528ms (Startup Thread)	100.0	627,873,200.0	3,421	0.0
+☑Process64 CoreCLR.LOHFragmentation (32064) Args: 102400	100.0	627,873,200.0	3,421	0.0
+☑ ROOT	100.0	627,873,200.0	3,421	0.0
+☑ coreclr.lohfragmentation!CoreCLR.LOHFragmentation.Reader.ReadBytes(int32)	0.0	125,296.0	1	0.0
+☑coreclr.lohfragmentation!CoreCLR.LOHFragmentation.Program.Main(class System.String[])	0.0	125,296.0	1	0.0
+☑OTHER <<ntdll!RtlUserThreadStart>>	0.0	125,296.0	1	0.0
+☑Thread (30188) CPU=4528ms (Startup Thread)	0.0	125,296.0	1	0.0
+☑Process64 CoreCLR.LOHFragmentation (32064) Args: 102400	0.0	125,296.0	1	0.0
+☑ ROOT	0.0	125,296.0	1	0.0

Figure 10-9. Gen 2 Object Deaths (Coarse Sampling) - Callers view from PerfView showing methods that allocate System.Byte[]

We clearly see from the Callers view that there are two sources of dying byte[] allocations. However, Reader.ReadBytes() method allocates only a single dying array. On the other hand, Processor.Process allocates thousands of them.

In many applications, of course, there may be many different types of "often dying" objects. Generally, it is good to search for the cause of the problem from the top of the list of such objects. Thus, in our case, we should look suspiciously at Processor.Process method allocating so many dying byte arrays.

Another way of diagnosing this problem is to use WinDbg and SOS extension, whether by analyzing the memory dump or attaching to the process. By using !heapstat command, we get an overview of the entire Managed Heap (see Listing 10-3). We indeed see big fragmentation of LOH (of 22%). There are also many, not-yet collected but already unreachable objects (of 25%). Altogether it gives an expected fragmentation of 47%, which confirms our previous findings.

Listing 10-3. Analyzing fragmentation - !heapstat command to get the Managed Heap overview

```
> !heapstat -inclUnrooted
Heap            Gen0            Gen1            Gen2            LOH
Heap0        1579192           96024              24      1907001192

Free space:                                                 Percentage
Heap0           7816           11160               0      434527752SOH:  1% LOH: 22%

Unrooted objects:                                           Percentage
Heap0        1567816           65560               0      488427824SOH: 97% LOH: 25%
```

However, we can use the knowledge of how the memory in Large Object Heap is organized and allocated. By using !eeheap command, we get a list of all LOH segments (see Listing 10-4). As memory grows, there are many LOH segments, as expected (as Table 5-3 states, they are 128MB big because our process runs on 64-bit runtime with Workstation GC). We know that typically segments are created one by one when the memory in the current one ends. And we know that Allocator allocates memory inside segments linearly. Thus, simplifing a little, the higher the address, the newest data it contains.

Listing 10-4. Analyzing fragmentation - !eeheap command to list LOH segments

```
> !eeheap -gc
Number of GC Heaps: 1
generation 0 starts at 0x0000013acb3c8730
generation 1 starts at 0x0000013acb3b1018
generation 2 starts at 0x0000013acb3b1000
ephemeral segment allocation context: none
```

segment	begin	allocated	size
0000013acb3b0000	0000013acb3b1000	0000013acb549fe8	0x198fe8(1675240)

Large object heap starts at 0x0000013adb3b1000

segment	begin	allocated	size
0000013adb3b0000	0000013adb3b1000	0000013ae33af528	0x7ffe528(134210856)
0000013ae4a60000	0000013ae4a61000	0000013aeca5fdb0	0x7ffedb0(134213040)
0000013aed130000	0000013aed131000	0000013af512f300	0x7ffe300(134210304)
0000013af5130000	0000013af5131000	0000013afd11c870	0x7feb870(134133872)
0000013a80000000	0000013a80001000	0000013a87fecf10	0x7febf10(134135568)
0000013a8a890000	0000013a8a891000	0000013a9287d0d0	0x7fec0d0(134136016)
0000013a92890000	0000013a92891000	0000013a9a8811c8	0x7ff01c8(134152648)
0000013a9a890000	0000013a9a891000	0000013aa28881a0	0x7ff71a0(134181280)
0000013aa2890000	0000013aa2891000	0000013aaa879090	0x7fe8090(134119568)
0000013aaa890000	0000013aaa891000	0000013ab287d060	0x7fec060(134135904)
0000013ab2890000	0000013ab2891000	0000013aba87bb20	0x7feab20(134130464)
0000013aba890000	0000013aba891000	0000013ac2880680	0x7fef680(134149760)
0000013afd130000	0000013afd131000	0000013b05117f28	0x7fe6f28(134115112)
0000013b05130000	0000013b05131000	0000013b0d118458	0x7fe7458(134116440)
0000013b0d130000	0000013b0d131000	0000013b0ecb6fc8	0x1b85fc8(28860360)

Total Size: Size: 0x71c41750 (1908676432) bytes.

GC Heap Size: Size: 0x71c41750 (1908676432) bytes.

By dumping content of the oldest one segment (first one from Listing 10-4), we will get an insight how old fragmentation looks (see Listing 10-5). Fragmentation is clearly visible indeed - free memory areas of 78,974 bytes are interleaved with 102,424 bytes long objects. We can easily identify them by using !gcroot command (see also Listing 10-5). For example, the only root of the last object (byte array) is the local variable of type List<byte[]> in the Main method, that is - largeBlocks. This is how typical fragmentation looks - a large number of live objects (mostly arrays) interleaved with free blocks of memory.

Listing 10-5. Analyzing fragmentation - !dumpheap command to list object in the first LOH segment (the result trimmed to the last few lines) and !gcroot command to identify roots of sample object

```
> !dumpheap 0000013adb3b1000   0000013ae33af528
...
0000013ae22b4cd8 00007fff857ebe10   102424
0000013ae22cdcf0 0000013ac914e200    78974 Free
0000013ae22e1170 00007fff857ebe10   102424
0000013ae22fa188 0000013ac914e200       30 Free
0000013ae22fa1a8 00007fff857ebe10   102424
0000013ae23131c0 0000013ac914e200    78974 Free
0000013ae2326640 00007fff857ebe10   102424
0000013ae233f658 0000013ac914e200       30 Free
0000013ae233f678 00007fff857ebe10   102424
0000013ae2358690 0000013ac914e200    78974 Free
0000013ae236bb10 00007fff857ebe10   102424
0000013ae2384b28 0000013ac914e200       30 Free
0000013ae2384b48 00007fff857ebe10   102424
0000013ae239db60 0000013ac914e200    78974 Free
0000013ae23b0fe0 00007fff857ebe10   102424
0000013ae23c9ff8 0000013ac914e200       30 Free
0000013ae23ca018 00007fff857ebe10   102424
> !gcroot 0000013ae23ca018
Thread 811c:
    000000233e9feeb0 00007fff28fc0645 CoreCLR.LOHFragmentation.Program.
    Main(System.String[])
        rbp-80: 000000233e9fef20
            -> 0000013acb3b68d0 System.Collections.Generic.List`1
            [[System.Byte[], mscorlib]]
            -> 0000013abaf50a68 System.Byte[][]
            -> 0000013ae23ca018 System.Byte[]

Found 1 unique roots (run '!GCRoot -all' to see all roots).
```

However, knowing that there are holes between still living objects is not very revealing. The real question is, after what object those holes were created! We can search for answers in the latest, just-allocated data. By dumping content of the newest one segment (the last one from Listing 10-4), we will get an insight how the newest fragmentation looks (see Listing 10-6). If we are lucky enough, there should be still some objects instead of future free items. And this is so. The newest LOH region contains small free items for padding (described earlier), 102,424byte-long objects we have seen already but there are also still some objects between them!

Listing 10-6. Analyzing fragmentation - !dumpheap command to list object in the last LOH segment (the result trimmed to the last few lines)

```
> !dumpheap 0000013b0d131000   0000013b0ecb6fc8

0000013b0ec0b4b0 0000013ac914e200       30 Free
0000013b0ec0b4d0 00007fff857ebe10    99634
0000013b0ec23a08 0000013ac914e200       30 Free
0000013b0ec23a28 00007fff857ebe10   102424
0000013b0ec3ca40 0000013ac914e200       30 Free
0000013b0ec3ca60 00007fff857ebe10    99627
0000013b0ec54f90 0000013ac914e200       30 Free
0000013b0ec54fb0 00007fff857ebe10    99635
0000013b0ec6d4e8 0000013ac914e200       30 Free
0000013b0ec6d508 00007fff857ebe10   102424
0000013b0ec86520 0000013ac914e200       30 Free
0000013b0ec86540 00007fff857ebe10    99628
0000013b0ec9ea70 0000013ac914e200       30 Free
0000013b0ec9ea90 00007fff857ebe10    99636
```

By analyzing roots of those objects, we will identify the root cause of fragmentation (see Listing 10-7). Clearly, those are the byte arrays from inside `DataFrame` class created in `Program.Main` and `Processor.Process` methods.

Listing 10-7. Analyzing fragmentation - !gcroot commands to identify roots of objects causing fragmentation

```
0:000> !gcroot 0000013b0ec3ca60
Found 0 unique roots (run '!GCRoot -all' to see all roots).
0:000> !gcroot 0000013b0ec54fb0
Found 0 unique roots (run '!GCRoot -all' to see all roots).
0:000> !gcroot 0000013b0ec86540
Thread 811c:
    000000233e9feeb0 00007fff28fc0645 CoreCLR.LOHFragmentation.Program.
    Main(System.String[])
        r15:
            -> 0000013acb549228 CoreCLR.LOHFragmentation.DataFrame
            -> 0000013b0ec86540 System.Byte[]

Found 1 unique roots (run '!GCRoot -all' to see all roots).
0:000> !gcroot 0000013b0ec9ea90
Thread 811c:
    000000233e9fee50 00007fff28fc0aad CoreCLR.LOHFragmentation.Processor.
    Process(CoreCLR.LOHFragmentation.DataFrame)
        rbx:
            -> 0000013acb549240 CoreCLR.LOHFragmentation.DataFrame
            -> 0000013b0ec9ea90 System.Byte[]
Found 1 unique roots (run '!GCRoot -all' to see all roots).
```

This concludes our investigation. The example was simple, because only a few types are allocated in LOH and because a large objects allocation pattern was prepared to be so unfortunate (each successive input frame is slightly bigger than previous one). It produces free-item holes that might be reused very rarely. In such a scenario the newest objects gather at the end, so we could easily find the place where objects may be still live before collection.

There will be many more different-sized objects in LOH in complex applications. Then, the analysis of the origin of objects, which then become unusable holes is much more tedious. There is no single golden rule of investigation of the fragmentation problems. In fact, this is the most difficult aspect to analyze from various memory-related problems. This is due to its temporal characteristic. There are holes, but there is no easy way to check what was there before. In most cases, those holes are reused thanks to a free-list allocator. It makes investigation even more difficult because new objects are spread over the entire generation 2 or LOH within holes that were reusable. There is no "here is a hole that was used by X object but is not used anymore for long time"-event unfortunately. We only have circumstantial evidence, like shown above.

Please remember that Large Object Heap contains some arrays used by the CLR internally. Arrays including references for statics, created during assembly loading, should not be a problem. However, there are also arrays used for string interning (see Figure 8-1 in Chapter 8 and "String Interning" section in Chapter 4). If you do excessive explicit string interning, creating those tables may also cause LOH fragmentation!

Knowing that LOH fragmentation is a problem, what can we do about it? Since .NET Framework 4.5.1 (and since .NET Core 1.0), there is a possibility to explicitly force compacting Large Object Heap. It can be done by setting GCLargeObjectHeapCompactionMode.CompactOnce to the static GCSettings. LargeObjectHeapCompactionMode property. It will be done only once, during the first blocking GC that occurs. Please note - it influences only blocking collections so any typical non-blocking (background) GC will not take into account this setting. Thus, most often just after setting this property, explicitly blocking full GC is being triggered explicitly.

So, as a solution to our problem, we may trigger LOH compaction explicitly. We can do it periodically or only if the memory usage exceeds a certain limit (as in the example from Listing 10-8). Both solutions are not perfect and should be thoroughly thought out. They simply introduce all the problems already discussed when describing explicit GC calls.

Listing 10-8. An example code that illustrates LOH fragmentation

```
if (GC.GetTotalMemory() > LOH_COMPACTION_THRESHOLD)
{
    GCSettings.LargeObjectHeapCompactionMode =
GCLargeObjectHeapCompactionMode.CompactOnce;
    GC.Collect();
}
```

Additionally, nevertheless since compacting LOH is blocking, it is also simply slow. Pause time scales linearly with the total size of survived objects. Even for small LOH when only a few hundreds of megabytes survived, it will pause your application for something between 100 and 200 milliseconds. The larger the size of the surviving objects, the worse. For the value of several gigabytes, we begin to notice over a second freeze of our application! The graph for both Workstation and Server GC modes is presented in Figure 10-10 (remember that exact values may vary depending on your hardware performance).

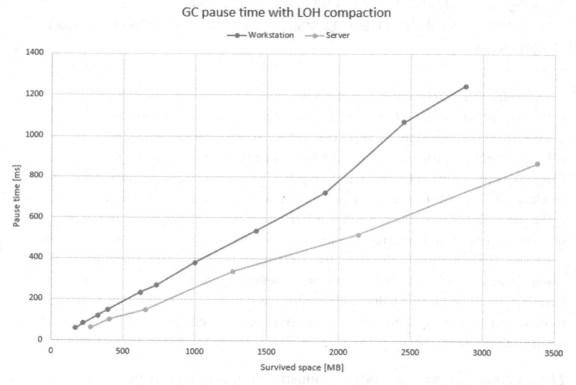

Figure 10-10. *GC pause times with LOH fragmentation for both Workstation GC and Server GC with 8 managed heaps (taken on Intel i7-4770K with 16 GB DDR3-1600 memory)*

Large Object Heap compacting is slightly faster for Server GC because LOH is split into multiple segments that may be compacted concurrently.

There may be times when compacting LOH is the only solution to your problem - for example, when troublesome code is not yours and you cannot do any refactoring toward better management of LOH objects. If you do own source code, a much better solution would be to introduce large objects pooling or arrays pooling (refer to section "Creating Arrays - Use ArrayPool" and "Creating a Lot of Object - Use Object Pool" from Chapter 6).

There are some plans for an undetermined future that LOH compaction may become automatic in some scenarios. The following GitHub issue comment explains it well: "For the near future, please assume that LOH is still not automatically compacted except for this one scenario where we will make it automatic - if you have very little survived on LOH compared to gen2 and LOH's fragmentation ratio is high (eg, say it's 75% fragmented) and/or LOH is full of objects that contain no references (as the relocation is really the expensive part)."

Summary

As you can notice, sweeping may be really fast because it requires small memory traffic. Only some local modifications are required to create free items and restore memory after plug information. On the other hand, compaction is quite complex and may induce quite big memory traffic. It is responsibility of the Plan phase described earlier to choose between them.

This chapter concludes the great amount of knowledge concerning the heart of the memory management in .NET that has been presented - the Garbage Collector itself - presented from Chapters 7 to 10. Everything before those chapters was only an introduction. And everything further is an extension.

To summarize those chapters, they are explained step by step, and all major phases of the GC were thoroughly described:

- mechanisms that triggers garbage collection (Chapter 7),

- how entire runtime cooperates to proceed with the GC suspension, that is - stopping all managed threads (Chapter 7),

- how GC selects which generation should be collected (Chapter 7),

- how GC discovers reachable objects, thanks to marking from various roots (Chapter 8),

- how GC plans both Compact and Sweep collection at the same time and then decides which one is more productive (Chapter 9),

- how compaction and sweeping is executed (this chapter).

Many of those points were interleaved both with theoretical knowledge (how and why it works) and with practical scenarios (how to utilize that knowledge for problem analysis and code development). From now on, if reading all chapters one by one, you should have a really solid foundation about what the GC in .NET really is. Practical scenarios mentioned allows you to investigate common problems and avoid making common mistakes.

Because knowledge from those chapters is tightly coupled, all Rules related to it are gathered and presented here, at the end of Chapter 10.

However, that's not all. GC has still a lot of various nooks to discover. From now on, the book will become even more and more practical. Of course, there is still something to describe about the operation of internal mechanisms - different modes of GC (Chapter 11) and finalization (Chapter 12). I invite you to continue the journey!

Note   Please note that the entire chapter devoted to garbage collection does not mention the IDisposable interface in one place. Sometimes inexperienced programmers seem to be somehow connecting it with the garbage collection mechanism. They tend to think that IDisposable somehow "triggers" collection of an object. This is obviously not true. IDisposable is only an interface, a contract between an object and a developer, saying that its instance's lifetime should be carefully tracked and needs some additional actions when they are no longer needed. In order not to deepen this misunderstanding and not too much clutter in this chapter, the description of IDisposable mechanism was placed in Chapter 10.

Rule 17 - Watch Runtime Suspensions

Applicability: General but rare.

Justification: Runtime suspension is a service that the GC uses to suspend all managed threads in order to make a safe ground for the GC to work. In other words, during a non-concurrent GC, user threads should not modify and access memory that is manipulated by the GC. This process has to be very optimized. Care was taken as much as possible that the process of stopping (and resuming) the threads was as fast as possible. And it really is - it takes fractions of milliseconds to suspend all threads! In rare cases when suspension takes long, something is wrong and should be investigated if it happens consistently.

How to apply: First of all, we can measure EE suspension times in our application. The most convenient mechanism supporting it is ETW events. The easiest way to analyze them is to look at GC suspension times from GC Events by the Timetable in PerfView's GCStat report. Everything near one millisecond and above would be starting to be an interesting fact.

In such an alarming case, we can investigate it by thoughtful debugging or CPU sampling during the suspension period - we may notice that our code is disturbing in giving the control to the runtime (by executing high-priority threads or executing very long IO operations synchronously).

Related scenarios: Scenario 7-4.

Rule 18 - Avoid Mid-Life Crisis

Applicability: General and very popular.

Justification: Generational hypotheses underlie the .NET GC construction that make the assumption that objects either die young or live for a very long time. We already should be fully aware why collecting ephemeral generations introduces much less overhead than collecting the older ones. Mid-life crisis is a failure to comply with the generational hypotheses in our application - many objects are living long enough to be promoted to generation 2 just to die there quickly. This is exactly what generation 2 was not designed for!

How to apply: We know that there are many allocations and that many of them are eventually promoted to generation 2, where they die. Thus, you should be more aware of your object's lifetime. Creating a bunch of temporary data and storing them for too long is a straightforward way to create Mid-life crisis. However, it is often really hard to reason about the lifetime of objects we create in complex applications. Thus, the common way of applying this Rule is the reactive approach - after measuring our application, only after we notice that there is high % Time in GC. Then the diagnostics come in and we start investigation.

We should watch then:

- What is the content of the older generation - by using any dump analysis tool of your preference,

- What is dying in the older generation - for example, by using gen 2 Object Deaths view from PerfView session analysis (see scenario 10-1),

- What are the most common allocations - because Mid-life crisis requires a lot of objects being created and eventually promoted to the oldest generation (see scenario 6-2),

- What are the reasons for condemning the oldest generation (see scenario 7-5).

Related scenarios: Scenarios 5-1, 6-2, 7-5, 10-1.

Rule 19 - Avoid Old Generation and LOH Fragmentation

Applicability: General and very popular.

Justification: Fragmentation, as long as it is used, is not bad at all - allocator reuses created free space for new objects. Fragmentation may be bad, however, if left uncontrolled - if we observe that even GCs of given generation were done, the resulting fragmentation does not drop. The program's memory usage can grow in an unpredictable way, even though we actually use a small number of objects. In Small Object Heap, big fragmentation implies more common, but also more expensive, compacting GCs. In Large Object Heap, fighting with fragmentation is even harder. We need to call for it explicitly, and we may be sure that it will take noticeable time.

How to apply: SOH fragmentation is typically not so painful if it happens only in ephemeral generations. Their compaction is really fast, so we should not be worried about that. More problematic is the fragmentation of generation 2, for at least two reasons:

- Compacting generation 2 is much more costly than ephemeral generations because it typically spans to many segments. This requires a lot bigger memory traffic.

- Fragmentation of gen2 segments may lead to creating more segments. And more segments mean more expensive garbage collection of them.

For similar reasons, we should also take care of Large Object Heap fragmentation. But the main problem there is that LOH is not automatically compacted at all. It exposes LOH to fragmentation problems much more.

For sure, we should observe fragmentation ratios in our applications - for example, by utilizing ETW/LTTng sessions. But knowing that big fragmentation occurs is just the first step. Then we should consider whether it is actually problematic for us - does it cause a large GC overhead or worrying memory usage? If yes, the hardest step takes place - diagnostics of sources of fragmentation. There is no single Golden Rule of Fragmentation Diagnostic. Most common approaches were presented in scenario 10-1.

There isn't a common solution to fragmentation. Commonly its impact may be reduced by pooling the source of fragmentation – namely, various types of arrays.

Related scenarios: Scenario 10-1.

Rule 20 - Avoid Explicit GC

Applicability: General and very popular.

Justification: Explicit Garbage Collection calls are disturbing its work. Regardless of the internal tunings that GC uses, we suddenly make him forget about them and make GC happen at that specific moment. Although there are a few scenarios that calling it may be justified, most often - it is not.

How to apply: Learn about the GC - why, how and when it works (for example, by reading this book!). Then you will understand that very, very often, calling GC explicitly is not the right solution to the problem you experienced. You should think twice or three times before each usage of the GC explicit call in your code. There are really few situations that justify that (listed in "Explicit Trigger" section in Chapter 7).

Related scenarios: Scenario 7-3.

Rule 21 - Avoid Memory Leaks

Applicability: General and very popular.

Justification: This is easy. Memory leaks are bad. Period. They make our programs unusable or so slow over time that we have to restart them. In the worst case, they simply crash. I believe that no one needs to be convinced that memory leak is undesirable. Still, there may be those small and unavoidable memory leaks that are just fine - if the memory growth is so small that it does not hurt us in a practical sense. As in if we have to restart the application process once every few days to deploy a new build, and we know we have memory leaks but they account for such small amounts of memory - we probably should spend effort investigating worse performance problems. Most often such "accepted" memory leaks come from third-party code that we simply cannot fix.

How to apply: In .NET world a memory leak means an uncontrolled memory growth due to the growth of the number of reachable objects. Simply put, something holds a reference to leaking objects, even though we expect those objects are no longer in use and should have died a long time ago.

This is one of the most common problems. There are various types of such "hidden" roots: static variables, events, misconfigured IoC containers, and so on, and so forth.

In this book a few examples of memory leak diagnostics were presented in the form of scenarios. They do not provide any technology-specific leaks (like some memory leaks we may encounter in WCF or WPF). No matter what .NET technologies we use now and will use in the coming years, the GC changes much slower - ds well as such essential tools like WinDbg, SOS, and PerfView. If you have a memory leak problem, investigate it with the knowledge gained in this book!

Related scenarios: Scenarios 5-2, 8-1, 8-2, 9-1, and from 1-1 to 1-5 (to distinguish a managed leak from an unmanaged one).

Rule 22 - Avoid Pinning

Applicability: General - moderately popular. High-performance code - important.

Justification: Pinning is bad because it may cause fragmentation (see Rule 21). It is also a certain overhead for GC itself - it complicates the operation of the internal allocator.

As mentioned in Chapter 9, pinning can either be short lived or long lived - it's the middle ones that cause trouble. In the most commonly used concurrent GC, if a pinned object is in generation 2, it will just be irrelevant most of the time, not causing fragmentation, as most of the time gen2 collections are Background GCs (not compacting and thus ignoring the fact of pinning). Short-living pinned objects also will not have a chance to introduce big fragmentation before dying in generation 0.

Thus, the most problematic are those pinned objects that live enough to be promoted to older generations, causing various unwanted side effects like limiting the freedom of generation planning and necessity of segments reorganization (if ephemeral segment has so many pinned elements that it becomes barely usable).

How to apply: In general, the best rule is just to avoid pinning but obviously sometimes we just need it. In such a case, it is good to remember the fact that the middle-life pinning makes the most trouble. Thus, when using pinning, it is best to:

- Pin for a short period of time, like using `fixed` keyword within a very small amount of code. As described in Chapter 8, it only influences GCInfo of a method, making it a special root during GC. So, if GC does not happen during method execution, `fixed` keyword will have no overhead at all.

- Create pinned buffers that will live long. This has an advantage both of prolonging the lifetime of such reusable pinned objects (thus, making them life in gen2 where their overhead is smaller) and by better locality (making them stay together instead being scattered around the Managed Heap).

As well as observing fragmentation, you should also observe the amount of pinning. It is not that we should get rid of it as soon as we notice it. In a typical application, as long as it does not cause much fragmentation, we have nothing to worry about. On the other hand, in high-performance programs where every millisecond counts, we may want to be fully aware of each pinned object. Your millage may vary here.

Related scenarios: Scenario 9-2.

CHAPTER 11

GC Flavors

The previous four chapters contain a very detailed description of the Garbage Collector in .NET - in the vast majority in its simplest variant. In this chapter, however, we will look at all GC varieties. In addition to the standard knowledge of how and why they are designed, we will consider their pros and cons. We will look at both the GC operating modes and the latency settings.

In terms of the different GC flavors available in .NET, the most common question that arises is - which one to choose? Therefore, after learning how they differ, we will try to answer this important question in this chapter. Additionally, the scenarios contained in this chapter may be interesting in this context - they examine the impact of the selected mode on the performance and behavior of the application.

Modes Overview

A short summary of various modes that .NET GC may operate on has been already provided at the beginning of Chapter 7, in the section "High-Level View." It was necessary to give an overall context of the GC version described there. Let's now take a little, deeper insight into those modes, how they differ, and why.

Workstation vs. Server Mode

The first dividing line is the division into Workstation and Server modes. It has existed since the very beginning of the .NET runtime. The names of both modes come from the typical applications for which they were intended. But let's not take these names dead seriously. Although they represent the typical usage, it may be perfectly fine to use Server mode in your desktop application or Workstation mode in your web application - it all

© Konrad Kokosa 2018
K. Kokosa, *Pro .NET Memory Management*, https://doi.org/10.1007/978-1-4842-4027-4_11

depends on your current needs. It is better to treat Workstation and Server modes as some two, noticeably different sets of GC configurations. However, this does not change the fact that the names of these modes came from the settings adapted for these two main environments.

Workstation Mode

Workstation mode was designed mostly for responsiveness needed in interactive, UI-based applications. Interactivity implies as noticeable pauses in the application as short as possible. We do not want to stall the UI because a long GC was triggered. Longer pauses could impact the smoothness and responsiveness of all actions in general. Therefore:

- GCs will happen more frequently - but thanks to that, they will have less work to do (fewer objects have been created so less can become garbage).

- As a side effect of the above, memory usage will be lower - more often GCs mean memory is reclaimed more aggressively, and there is no large amount of "hanging" garbage.

- There is a single Managed Heap - because desktop applications generally perform one main action related to user actions, there is no need for a special parallelization of their work. Moreover, this mode assumes that many applications are running on the computer. Each of them utilizes some of the CPU cores and memory. Therefore, it is not necessary or especially desirable to multiply GC threads that process several heaps simultaneously. From the beginning, Workstation mode was designed to have one Managed Heap processed by one thread at a time.

- Segments are smaller - to operate on smaller areas of memory.

Please note that although most interactive applications can actually be satisfied with such decisions, this does not necessarily apply to everyone. We can have a desktop application that fits perfectly into, for example, parallel processing in the background.

Server Mode

Server mode was designed for simultaneous, request-based processing applications. It implies that big throughput is desirable - processing as much data in a unit of time as possible. Assuming that the requests are processed relatively shortly, sporadic application stalls will not affect them significantly because statistically GC will happen during processig of at most several requests. Therefore:

- GCs will happen less frequently - but it may mean longer pauses because more objects have been created between GCs.[1] This, however, allows us to improve throughput because we can process in parallel multiple requests during longer no-pause times.

- As a side effect of the above, memory usage will be higher - less often GCs mean more "hanging" garbage will be gathering between them. It implies bigger Working Set than in case of Workstation mode. However, generally understood "servers" are assumed to be equipped with a large amount of memory so it is not such a big problem.

- There are multiple Managed Heaps - this ensures scalability relative to the machine's power. If the GC already happens, we want to do it as fast as possible. Parallel processing of many heaps is faster than of a single, large heap.[2] What's more, server applications are often hosted on dedicated servers so they can quite freely consume all the cores available to them.

- Default segment sizes are larger, especially on 64-bit systems - so if necessary, many more allocations can be accommodated before a GC is triggered.

- Taking the above into consideration, it's often that the Server mode would consume more memory but give you a smaller % time in GC.

---

[1]However, because they are processed by parallel on multiple CPU cores, pauses may be even shorter than in Workstation.

[2]Remember that access to the memory is a bottleneck. Parallel heap processing with four CPU cores will not be four times faster than processing the same memory size by only one CPU core. Undoubtedly, however, it will be faster.

One may wonder how those two various modes are organized in .NET source code and how much code they have in common. Using CoreCLR as an example (while all .NET SKUs share the same GC, as mentioned in Chapter 4), the vast majority is implemented in the same `.\src\gc\gc.cpp` file that contains a lot of portions managed by `#if` preprocessor directives. Then, this file is compiled twice within two different namespaces and set of defines - `.\src\gc\gcsvr.cpp` defines SERVER_GC constant and SVR namespace:

```
#define SERVER_GC 1
namespace SVR {
    #include "gcimpl.h"
    #include "gc.cpp"
}
```

while `.\src\gc\gcwks.cpp` defines WKS namespace:

```
namespace WKS {
    #include "gcimpl.h"
    #include "gc.cpp"
}
```

Thus, when seeing various GC-related types or methods, they will come from either `WKS::` or `SRV::` namespaces. Definition of SERVER_GC implies a few other important defines, especially `MULTIPLE_HEAPS` that many, many regions inside `gc.cpp` rely on.

Non-Concurrent vs. Concurrent Mode

Orthogonally to the mode of operation, the GC can also have two ways of operating in the context of work relative to the user's threads. In general, by non-concurrent, we understand - not happening simultaneously with something else. Concurrent is obviously the opposite.

Non-Concurrent Mode

The non-concurrent GC version has existed since the beginning of .NET, both for Workstation and Server modes. All managed user threads are suspended during a GC. It is conceptually really simple - we have to stop all user threads, do GC, and resume user threads.

Concurrent Mode

Concurrent GC, as one may expect, runs while normal user threads are working. This makes it more complex both in terms of concept as well as implementation. There must by an additional synchronization between user threads and Collector during its work so both have a coherent vision of reality and do not cause serious problems (like modifying collected objects or collecting objects that are still live). Such synchronization is obviously not easy to implement, especially due to the desired high performance of the whole. We will see how such a technique is implemented in .NET soon.

The concurrent flavor of the GC is differently named in different versions of .NET. We can summarize it in the following way:

- In case of Workstation GC, the concurrent flavor was available since .NET 1.0 and was called Concurrent Workstation GC. In .NET 4.0, after introducing important improvements, it has been renamed to Background Workstation GC.

- In case of Server GC, the concurrent flavor was not available until version .NET 4.5. It is called Background Server GC.

In terms of source code organization, again both modes are implemented in the same `.\src\gc\gc.cpp` file. Concurrent version is enclosed by `#if BACKGROUND_GC` preprocessor directive. `BACKGROUND_GC` is however always defined in both SVR and WKS versions. They contain code for both concurrent and non-concurrent flavors that are enabled or disabled during runtime startup.

Modes Configuration

From the previous sections it becomes clear that we have two orthogonal settings with two possible values each. It gives us four possible modes that GC may operate on. This is mostly all we can set in terms of the GC. Those used to very fine-grained settings from JVM world may be surprised. This is of course a design decision made with full awareness. JVM offers a GC-centric approach - we can configure virtually every aspect of a GC operation, but we need to understand it very well and be sure about what and why we change. On the other hand, Microsoft has chosen the application-centric path. Knowing what type of application that we are writing, we set one of the GC operation modes and it is the GC who has to deal with the rest. It is responsible for adjusting properly to the load and the specificity of the provided application mode.

The following sections describe briefly how you may change GC working modes both in .NET Framework and in the newer .NET Core.

You can also set those modes when hosting CLR inside your own process via `ICLRRuntimeHost` interface (including both .NET Framework and .NET Core runtimes) with proper startup flags. CLR Hosting is briefly presented in Chapter 15, altogether with the mentioned flags. This is exactly what a simple hosting CoreRun application does if you built CoreCLR from source code. CoreRun uses its own, very simplified configuration provider that ignores settings described below. Only two environment variables are respected by CoreRun host: `CORECLR_SERVER_GC` and `CORECLR_CONCURRENT_GC` (both can take value of 0 or 1). Use them if you want to play with your own custom-build CoreCLR hosted by CoreRun.

As you may notice, there is no description here how those settings are represented on the level of a project file - for example, in Visual Studio. There may be many tools and project formats along the whole .NET ecosystem. Just refer to the current documentation of your favorite tool. What is presented here are settings consumed by the runtime itself, which will be unlikely changed in the near future.

Be aware that on a machine with only one logic CPU core, Workstation GC is always used, regardless of the `gcServer` setting.

.NET Framework

In case of .NET Framework applications, the main way to change both GC modes is via a standard configuration file (see Listing 11-1):

- ASP.NET web applications - `web.config` file is used in case of web applications hosted in IIS. Please note that in such a case ASP.NET host enables Server GC by default (additionally, on post .NET 4.5+ runtimes, with Background mode enabled).

- Console applications or Windows Services - `[appName].exe.config` file is used by default. If such file does not specify those settings, concurrent Workstation mode is turned on by default. This may be very important especially for Windows Services processing a lot of data in a request-like manner! Such service behaves more like a server application, not an interactive one. Changing to some flavor of a Server GC may significantly improve performance in such a situation.

Listing 11-1. GC-related configuration of .NET Framework applications ([appName].exe.config/Web.config file)

```
<?xml version="1.0" encoding="utf-8" ?>
<configuration>
    <startup>
        <supportedRuntime version="v4.0" sku=".NETFramework,Version=v4.7" />
    </startup>
  <runtime>
    <gcServer enabled="true"/>
    <gcConcurrent enabled="true"/>
  </runtime>
</configuration>
```

.NET Core

In case of .NET Core, slightly better flexibility exists regarding configuration. There are still file-based solutions, but two additional ones exist.

The file configuration is very similar to the one from .NET Framework, only the configuration file format has been changed from XML to JSON (see Listing 11-2).

Listing 11-2. GC-related configuration of .NET Core application

```
SomeApplication.runtimeconfig.json
{
  "runtimeOptions": {
    "tfm": "netcoreapp2.0",
    "framework": {
      "name": "Microsoft.NETCore.App",
      "version": "2.0.0"
    },
    "configProperties": {
      "System.GC.Server": false,
      "System.GC.Concurrent": false
    }
  }
}
```

CoreCLR introduces the concept of so-called *Configuration Knobs*. Their values may be provided in various ways, one of which is the most interesting - via setting an environment variable (and registry in case of Windows). This may be especially useful in strictly isolated environments like docker images. You will find the full list of configuration knobs on the appropriate CoreCLR documentation page.

To set the configuration knob of the name X, you should add the environment variable COMPlus_X with a desired value or HKCU\Software\Microsoft\.NETFramework registry key with the Value of name X. Thus, in case of the GC mode settings, it will be:

- COMPlus_gcServer=0 or 1 environment variable or gcServer registry with value 0 or 1,

- COMPlus_gcConcurrent=0 or 1 environment variable or gcConcurrent registry key with value 0 or 1.

Note   Please remember that COMPlus_ settings will override the JSON version if both are set.

GC Pause and Overhead

The topic of automatic memory management is inherently related to the overhead it introduces. After all, the GC is a code that works as part of our application. It consumes CPU cycles, and it may introduce pauses when the rest of the application is doing nothing. We have not looked at the topic of the GC activity overhead with a special interest so far. It's time to take care of this topic. Different GC operating modes can introduce a different overhead so here is an ideal place for it.

But how to measure such overhead? What overhead are we talking about? In the context of overall .NET application performance, we may look at it from two sides:

- The GC side - as mentioned before, there are two of the most important, unwanted side effects of the GC work:

  - The GC pauses - currently no pauseless GC exists.[3] When application threads are paused by the GC, it is obviously unwanted, especially in interactive applications. We may be interested in measuring GC pauses time (total sum, average, percentiles, and so on, so forth). What is an acceptable threshold of the pause depends on your specific application characteristics. In my personal opinion, single GC pause times above tens of milliseconds should be rather alarming if they occur frequently.

  - The GC CPU overhead - executing GC code, as executing any other code, consumes CPU resources. The longer the GC works or the more CPU cores it uses, the more CPU cycles have been stolen from the execution of regular code of yours and other applications. This is important both in case of concurrent and non-concurrent GCs. Again, what's an acceptable threshold of the GC usage depends on your specific application characteristics. In regular web applications. I've seen constant usage above 10–20% that was rather alarming.

---

[3]Although, you could meet in JVM world a commercial GC named Azul Pauseless GC, it was not truly pauseless because sometimes threads need to stop allocations to "catch up" (e.g., GC is not able to provide free space fast enough for allocations). Such a GC's successor is called Continuously Concurrent Compacting Collector (C4), which is probably a less confusing name.

- Application side - to the topic of measuring application performance, yet another whole book could be dedicated. However, the most obvious metrics should include are the following:

  - Throughput - how fast the application executes. For example, how long it takes to process a single HTTP request of specific user actions.

  - Latency - it's common to look at tail latency, for example, how long your longest x% actions take.

  - Memory consumption - how memory is being consumed, especially in terms of peak memory usage.

Figure 11-1 illustrates the two most popular measurements indicating GC overhead in .NET. It presents two user threads (T1 and T2) and one GC thread (GC1). As you can see, this picture shows the state of the threads over time. When the thread does not take up processor time (it is waiting for something), it is marked with a dashed line. When the thread executes the code associated with GC, it is marked with an arrow. The thread executing the program code is represented by a light gray rectangle. Additionally, the moment of suspending and resuming threads was marked with a dark gray area. We will stick to this convention later in this chapter, illustrating how each GC mode works.

With this approach, it is easy to illustrate the two most popular .NET metrics:

- GC pause times - they are considered non-concurrent phases of the GC, including GC suspension and resumption steps. They are typically obtained from the ETW/LLTNg events - that is, the time between `SuspendEEStart` and `RestartEEStop` events. We may observe them in GC Events by Time table from GCStats report in PerfView (as column Pause MSec).

- Relative GC time spent in CPU - it describes the ratio between the whole time spent in GC (including concurrent part of GC) to the time since the previous GC. We may observe it by % GC column in GC Events by Time from GCStats in PerfView.

Popular % Time in the GC performance counter may be also used to measure GC's CPU overhead. However, it is less accurate and ETW-based measurements are advised by the .NET team (since introduction of background GC they are investing more development in ETW in favor of performance counters in general). Please note that in case of a performance counter, if there is no GC, this counter is not refreshed, and it will indicate the previous value. Thus, do not be surprised about constant 99% time in GC drawn in the Performance Monitor tool - it may just be a last measured value not refreshed due to GC not happening! Always check whether GC happens, for example, by looking also at the # Gen 0 Collections counter.

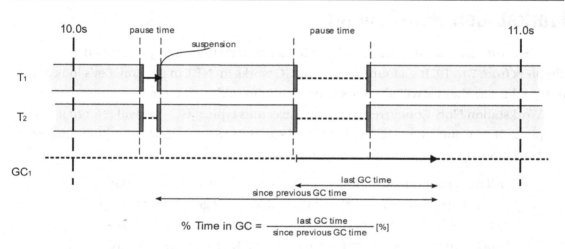

Figure 11-1. *Pause times and % Time in GC as a typical .NET GC measurement*

Obviously, many other free or commercial tools provide their own ways of providing those metrics. It is their implementation detail how exactly they are measured though. Refer to their documentation to get to know the details.

We will come back to those measurements when considering various GC modes. Now, let's move to the comprehensive description of the four possible Garbage Collection flavors we can run in .NET.

Modes Descriptions

The next subsections of this section describe how the four GC modes available in .NET work. They have been illustrated with figures similar to Figure 11-1. For clarity, suspensions blocks were removed from most of them. Just remember they are around each non-concurrent phase of the GC. Additionally, all figures assume that at some point, the Allocator determines the need for GC. The lengths in the charts are only for illustration purposes. How long GC/user threads take should be measured by a proper tool.

Along with the description of the operation, each mode also contains a list of typical situations in which you can consider its use.

Workstation Non-Concurrent

The simplest possible GC mode has been in fact already thoroughly described in chapters from 7 to 10. It's a foundation how GC works in .NET in general. Let's look at it now in the way that we will also look at other modes in this chapter.

Workstation Non-Concurrent GC mode executes typical GC - we will refer to it simply as Non-Concurrent GC (without Workstation or Server annotation) hereinafter. It has the following characteristics (see Figure 11-2):

- All managed threads are suspended for the time of the entire GC, regardless of whether it is garbage collection of generation 0, 1, or 2 (full-GC) - a single ephemeral GC should take very little time so making it non-concurrent is not an issue. But as it is specifically pointed out in the figure, a full-blocking GC (when done in non-concurrent fashion these full-GCs are called full-blocking GCs) can take a lot more time that an ephemeral GC. Full-blocking GCs are thus much more unwanted.

- The GC code is executed on the user thread that triggered collection (from inside Allocator) without changing the user thread's priority, which is usually a normal priority, in which case it must therefore compete with other threads of other applications.

- GC is always executed during the "stop the world" phase; it can be compacting if it decides to.

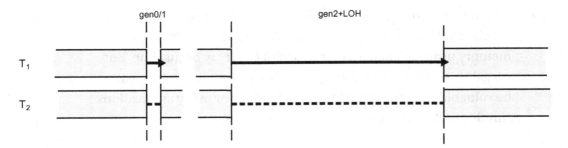

Figure 11-2. *Workstation Non-concurrent GC mode illustration*

If we would like to track such a GC in terms of ETW/LLTNg events, these are generated as in Figure 11-3.

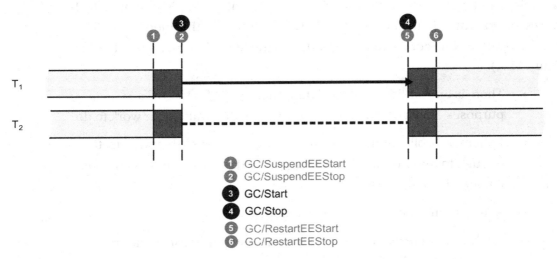

①	GC/SuspendEEStart
②	GC/SuspendEEStop
③	**GC/Start**
④	**GC/Stop**
⑤	GC/RestartEEStart
⑥	GC/RestartEEStop

Figure 11-3. *ETW/LLTNg events emitted during Workstation Non-concurrent GC mode*

Typical usage scenarios:

- A highly saturated environment where many more applications work than the available CPU resources - as there are no additional GC threads, only those regular ones, GCs does not add its own overhead consuming otherwise valuable CPU cores.

- Environment with many lightweight web applications (like "dockerized" microservices) - if they are lightweight and their memory usage is small, non-concurrent GCs may be just fine. But we gain a small amount of threads needed to operate, which can be valuable in terms of CPU cores utilization for many applications running at the same time.

Workstation Concurrent (Before 4.0)

As mentioned before, this was called "Concurrent GC" and was superseded by "Background GC" in 4.0 and beyond. Thus, we will not put a lot of attention to it (for example, omitting the whole section of the Concurrent GC implementation). The successor presented in the next section basically describes this mode as well.

Workstation Non-concurrent GC mode has the following characteristics (see Figure 11-4):

- There is one additional thread dedicated solely for the GC's purposes - most of the time it is just suspended waiting for work to do.

- Ephemeral collections are always Non-concurrent - they are just fast enough to make them non-concurrently. This also allows them to be compacting if they wish.

- A full-GC may be executed in two modes:

  - Non-concurrent GC - because of the "stop the world" nature, such a full-GC may be compacting.

  - Concurrent GC - it executes most of the work while managed threads are normally executed. Because this would complicate the implementation very much, this GC variant is not compacting.

- Concurrent full-GC has the following additional characteristics:

  - User-managed threads may allocate objects during its work – however, such allocations are limited to the size of the ephemeral segment because there is no way to make more space if it runs out (no other GC may be triggered during Concurrent GC). If such situation happens, user threads are suspended until the end of the full-GC.

- It contains two short "stop the world" phases - at the beginning and in the middle.

- Objects allocated since the beginning of the GC and before the second "stop the world" phase will be promoted.

- Everything allocated after the second "stop the world" phase will be promoted.

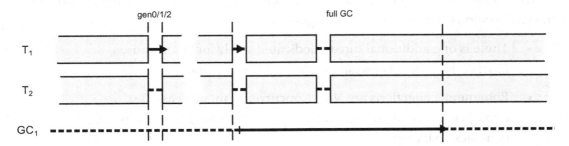

Figure 11-4. *Workstation Concurrent GC mode illustration (available until .NET Framework 4.0)*

Typical usage scenarios:

- Most UI applications before .NET 4.0. Concurrent GC was a big improvement toward smaller pause times, so desirable in interactive applications. Most of the time there were no big stalls due to the GC. Obviously, Concurrent GC were not compacting so from time to time a Non-Concurrent full-GC ought to be triggered to fight with the fragmentation. However, the fact it has to blocking allocating threads when the ephemeral segment is exhausted is a severe limitation. Segment sizes in Workstation mode were not large (especially in 32-bit mode it is only 16 MB!) so even Concurrent GCs can suspend threads more often than desired because the ephemeral segment runs out of space. Overcoming those limitations was the major improvement introduced in the Background Workstation GC mode.

Background Workstation

Background Workstation GC superseded Workstation Concurrent GC since .NET Framework 4.0 and it also exists in .NET Core. The major improvements lie in the fact that even during concurrent GC, ephemeral GCs may be triggered if needed. It removes the allocation limit from the work of normal threads, making them strongly independent of the work of GC operating in the background.

Background Workstation GC mode has the following characteristics, mostly similar to the Workstation Concurrent GC (see Figure 11-5):

- There is one additional thread dedicated solely for GC purposes - most of the time it is just suspended waiting for work to do.

- Ephemeral collections are Non-Concurrent - they are just fast enough to make them non-concurrently. This also allows them to be compacting if they wish.

- A full-GC may be executed in two modes:

  - Non-Concurrent GC - because of the "stop the world" nature, such full-GC may be compacting.

  - Background GC - it executes most of the work while managed threads are normally executed. Exactly as in the case of Concurrent GC, this mode is not compacting.

- Background full-GC has the following additional characteristics:

  - User-managed threads may allocate objects during its work - such allocations may trigger regular ephemeral collections (called *Foreground GCs*, opposite to the Background GC).

  - Foreground GCs may happen many times during Background GC. As .NET documentations says: "The dedicated background garbage collection thread checks at frequent safe points to determine whether there is a request for foreground garbage collection." Foreground GCs are regular Non-Concurrent GCs, during which Background GC is temporarily suspended. They may be compacting (as everything is suspended) and can even expand the heap by creating additional segments.

- It contains two short "stop the world" phases - at the beginning and in the middle; both will be briefly described further.

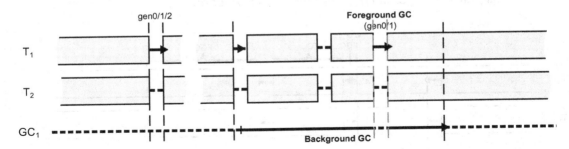

Figure 11-5. *Background Workstation GC mode illustration (available since .NET Framework 4.0)*

Let's now dig into the "anatomy" of Background Workstation mode. Its Non-Concurrent GCs of generation 0, 1, or 2 are trivial. However, how does Background GC work and when exactly may Foreground GCs happen? When considering Background GC, it can be split into several phases (see Figure 11-6):

- Initial "stop the world" phase (**A**) - it is when the allocator triggered regular GC code and it decided to start Background GC. Additionally, likely there is a need to execute a normal ephemeral GC at this stage (for example, some allocation budget has been exceeded). During this phase also, an initial marking of objects is done, later on consumed by Background GC.

- Concurrent mark phase (**B**) - while user threads are resumed, Background GC proceeds with concurrently discovering reachability of objects. How exactly this is solved despite the simultaneous operation of user threads is described later in this chapter. Additionally, during this phase zero or more Foreground GCs may be triggered due to allocations.

- Final mark, "stop the world" phase (**C**) - while user threads are suspended, Background GC determines eventual reachability of objects it will collect in the next phase.

- Concurrent sweep phase (**D**) - while user threads are running, GC may safely sweep not-longer used objects so far discovered. During this phase additional Foreground GCs may happen.

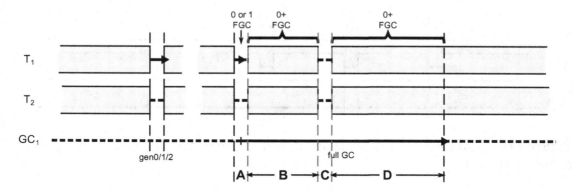

Figure 11-6. *Background Workstation GC mode in-depth view*

If we would like to track such Background and Foreground GCs in terms of ETW/LLTNg events, these are generated as in Figure 11-7. There are much more than in case of a simple Non-Concurrent GC (as seen in Figure 11-3). As we can see, besides the typical GC-related events, there is a bunch of BGC-related events describing the Background GC in details. There are two - BGCRevisit and BGCDrainMark - that will be explained a little further. Other ones are pretty self-descriptive. Please note that Figure 11-7 shows a case with only single Foreground GC during Background GC.

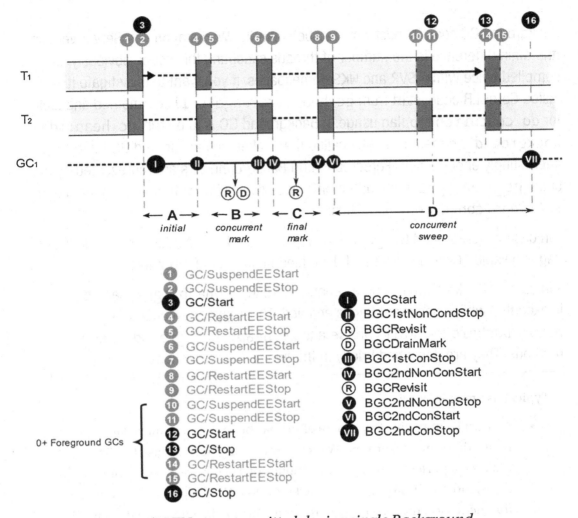

Figure 11-7. *ETW/LLTNg events emitted during single Background Workstation GC*

Background GC code is mostly shared between the Workstation and Server version (the main difference is the number of threads executing this code), obviously compiled twice within SVR and WKS namespaces. If you want to investigate it inside CoreCLR code, start from `gc_heap::garbage_collect` method and look for `do_concurrent_p` flag usage. If Background GC is to be run, `gc_heap::do_background_gc` method will be called that wakes up background GC threads. Interestingly enough, both Foreground and Background GCs are represented by the same `gc_heap::gc1` method; the difference lies inside with respect to the global `settings.concurrent` flag. Thus:

- in case of Foreground GC, `gc_heap::gc1` method is executed while concurrent flag is disabled (which is a variant described in chapters from 7 to 10).

- in case of Background GC, on a separate thread, `gc_heap::gc1` method is executed while concurrent flag is enabled. This triggers executing `gc_heap::background_mark_phase` and `gc_heap::background_sweep` methods. They are described briefly in the two following sections.

Typical usage scenarios:

- In most UI applications, a lot of effort has been put in to make GC pause times in Background Workstation GC as short as possible. This makes it a perfect choice for all varieties of interactive applications (thus, mostly UI-based). Since Background GC still does not compact, fragmentation may become a problem, and so blocking full-GC may be triggered occasionally to fight with fragmentation, but it may ruin low-latency efforts.

Concurrent Mark

One may wonder how it is possible to determine reachability of objects while user threads are running. Obviously, they are constantly modifying objects and creating and deleting references between them. How can reachability be discovered in such dynamic conditions?

As we know, Tracing Collector implemented in .NET discovers reachability of objects starting from various roots and by traversing the whole object graph (see Mark Phase in Chapter 1 and Figure 1-15). Those that it has already visited are marked. At the end of this process, only marked objects are considered live. The rest is treated as garbage and may be collected. This approach, when considering work concurrent with the user threads, leads to two main problems:

- how to mark objects in a way not disturbing normal user threads work?

- how to maintain consistent view of relations between objects from both user threads and the Collector perspective?

Let's consider marking the object problem first. In Chapter 9 it was said that marking an object means setting a single bit in its MethodTable. It was perfectly fine in case of the "stop the world" approach. However, modifying such a crucial pointer as an object's MethodTable while threads may be using it is unacceptable - both for safety and performance reasons (including cache invalidation).

Thus, concurrent marking stores information about marking in a dedicated, separate *mark array*. Its organization is similar to card tables described in Chapter 5. Each single bit in a mark array correspond to 16 bytes region on the Managed Heap (in case of 32-bit runtime it is 8 bytes) as illustrated in Figure 11-8. Mark array is organized into 4-byte-long *mark words*. If GC visited an object and wants to mark it - the corresponding bit in the mark array is being set. As the GC is the only owner of mark array, there are no synchronization problems when accessing it. Moreover, during concurrent marking this bit may be only set, not clear. This makes synchronization much simpler in case of many threads doing parallel, concurrent marking (as is the case with Background Server GC, described later).

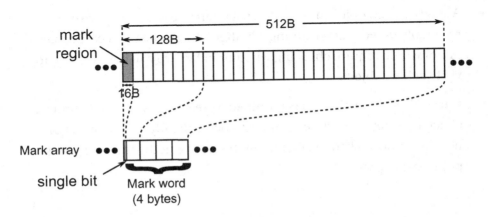

Figure 11-8. *Mark array organization (in case of 64-bit runtime)*

Note that 16-byte granularity is enough because only a single object may lay inside such a region (remember that minimum object size is 24 bytes). Later on, by scanning the mark array for set bits, we get information about the reachability of corresponding objects. This is an easy solution to the first concurrent marking problem.

The second problem requires a little of rethinking. What can go wrong when references between objects are being modified while Collector is traversing objects graph? We may end up then in the following situations:

- Not-yet-visited object has modified (added, removed, or both) references to some other objects - this is fine, however. The object has not been visited yet so those changes will be simply included if GC will visit it.

- Already visited object has removed reference to the otherwise unreachable object (see Figure 11-9a) - this is still fine. We will create so-called *floating garbage* for a moment. Next, GC will discover that such an object is unreachable and will collect it.

- Already visited object has added reference to otherwise unreachable object (see Figure 11-9b), for example, by creating a new one or by reassigning a reference from another object - this is dangerous. It could mean that we will have no chance to visit (mark) an object that after such change is reachable from another object. It is treated as garbage and will be collected while it should still may in use! This is the so-called *"the lost object" problem*. Correct concurrent marking implementation should not allow such situations to happen.

- Already visited object has modified a reference to an otherwise reachable object - determining whether it is "the lost object" problem or not would require checking whether in fact we will have chance to visit such an object.

- Currently visiting object has modified its references - it would require checking whether such reference has been already visited or not. If not, we come back to the first point. If yes, one of the three previous points may apply here.

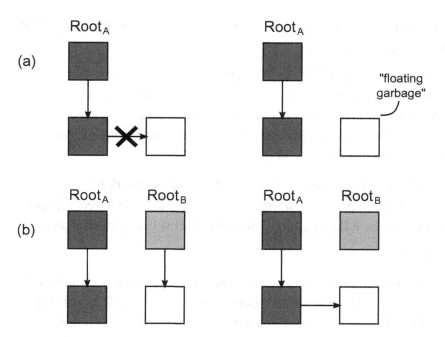

Figure 11-9. *Possible problems during concurrent marking: (a) creating floating garbage, (b) the lost object problem*

The solution to the problems mentioned seems obvious - problematic objects should be revisited! Various concurrent marking techniques exist that introduce different trade-offs between amount of "floating garbage," number of objects to be revisited, and overall synchronization costs between user threads and the Garbage Collector.

In case of .NET, a simple yet effective technique of write barriers was chosen. Every time an already visited (or currently visited) object is being modified, it should be treated as one "to revisit." However, for simplicity, every object modification is treated as such. In case of Windows, the list of modifications is managed by operating system with an already known WriteWatch mechanism (used also by card tables as explained in Chapter 5). This mechanism has page-wide granularity so even a single modified object will invalidate the whole 4kB page. In case of non-Windows runtimes, CLR implements its own Write Watch - with the help of appropriately prepared write barriers injected by JIT that modify corresponding bytes in dedicated arrays. At some moments during the GC, such list of modifications (let's call it *write watch list*) is scanned and marked objects are revisited (treating them as an additional roots). This is quite an easy solution to the second concurrent marking problem.

Thus, coming back to the Background GC phases, as shown in Figures 11-6 or 11-7, they do the following things:

- Initial "stop the world" phase (A) - while threads are suspended, initial list is being prepared. Only stack and finalization queues are scanned to populate "work list" for future, concurrent marking. Such work list contains only discovered objects, and their outgoing references are not followed at this stage.

- Concurrent mark phase (B) - while user threads are working, the main part of concurrent marking is executed. It does an object's graph traversal for the following roots (marking objects in the mark array):

  - Handles.

  - work list prepared in a previous step - so a large graph of objects from the stack is considered here. During this step BGCDrainMark ETW/LLTNg event is emitted with the information about the number of objects in a work list.

  - write watch list - at the end of concurrent marking, all objects modifications that happened during this stage are considered. During this step BGCRevisit ETW/LLTNg event is emitted describing how many pages were initially "dirty" and how many objects have been eventually marked because of that.

- Final mark, "stop the world" phase (C) - this is the "the final truth" point. All threads are suspended and the GC has an opportunity to "catch up." At this moment, a mark array should pretty well reflect the actual state of reachability of objects. However, to be sure, they must be checked again. Note that this is incremental work. Traversing the graph of objects considers the marked flag from the mark array, so many objects will not be visited again. The revisiting of the roots is only to ensure that there are no new reachable objects available. This, of course, will introduce some floating garbage (already marked objects will not be "unmarked"), but as it was mentioned before, this is not a problem in terms of correctness of the result. During such a final marking the following roots are considered:

  - stack, finalization queues, and handles

- write watch list - to include all modifications that the GC cannot keep up with in the previous check

- additionally, all typical marking-related work is done like scanning dependent handles and weak references

---

In case of CoreCLR, the core code responsible for concurrent marking exists in `gc_heap::background_mark_phase` method. The two most important data structures are `mark_array` (realizing array from Figure 11-8) and `c_mark_list` (realizing "work list" populated at the initial phase). `c_mark_list` is populated with `gc_heap::background_promote_callback` method during stack and finalization queue scanning and then consumed by `gc_heap::background_drain_mark_list` method.

The write watch list in case of Windows is managed by the system itself and is consumed in the GC within `gc_heap::revisit_written_pages` method. It gets from the system a current list of dirtied pages (from the Managed Heap memory region) and scans them object by object with the help of `gc_heap::revisit_written_page` method. In case of a non-Windows CoreCLR build, DFEATURE_MANUALLY_MANAGED_CARD_BUNDLES, and DFEATURE_USE_SOFTWARE_WRITE_WATCH_FOR_GC_HEAP are defined and enable the software write watch mechanism. You may see its usage in write barriers like JIT_WriteBarrier_WriteWatch_PreGrow64.

All concurrent marking is done with the help of `gc_heap::background_promote` method that through `gc_heap::background_mark_simple` and `gc_heap::background_mark_simple1` traverses the object's graph (marking corresponding bits in `mark_array` from `gc_heap::background_mark1` method).

In summary, the conclusions from the concurrent marking's operation are as follows:

- It produces some floating garbage so it results in less aggressive garbage collection - more dead objects will occupy space for a longer time than in case of blocking marking.

- Intense modification of the dependencies between objects during Background GC may invalidate many pages, and thus force GC to revisit many objects (remember that the page has 4 KB and may contain many small objects).

Concurrent Sweep

At the moment of concurrent sweep, the mark array already contains information about all live objects. Similar to the non-concurrent Plan and Sweep phases described in Chapters 9 and 10, such information may be used to sweep dead objects. During this phase, objects from the heap are scanned one by one, checked against the mark array, and appropriate free-list items are created (exactly in a way described in Chapter 10, including updating generation allocators). Because SOH allocations may happen during Concurrent Sweep, it is interesting also to see how they interact with each other.

Having said that, we can describe this process as consisting of the following steps:

- Before runtime resumes execution of user threads, free-item lists are cleared in all generations - since then allocators will not be aware of free space for a short period of time (allocating at the end of already consumed segment part).

- Concurrent sweep on ephemeral generations is done - it creates free-list items in generations 0 and 1, operating on a separate list that is published to the allocator at the end (to avoid multithreaded access to the free list both from allocating user threads and concurrent GC). Thus, as soon as this fast step ends, allocators in ephemeral generations are able to consume created free space. Also, during this step Foreground GC is not allowed because it may be compacting - which would conflict with the ongoing object-by-object scanning.

- Concurrent sweep on generation 2 and Large Object Heap - it creates free-list items in generation 2 and LOH, immediately published to its allocators. During this step:

  - user threads, while allocating, are able to consume already published free list in generation 0.

- Foreground GCs are allowed so if objects gets promoted from generation 1 to 2, already created free-list entries in gen2 will be consumed - it is safe because Foreground GCs are regular non-concurrent GCs, during which a Background GC is temporarily suspended so there is no simultaneous access to the list.

- During the entire process, LOH allocations are not allowed. This is because it would require multithreaded access to the free list from LOH allocators while the GC is modifying it. If a user thread wants to allocate a large object during Concurrent Sweep, it is blocked until its end. While such waiting happens, ETW/LLTng events BGCAllocWaitBegin/BGCAllocWaitEnd pair is emitted so we can search for it in our traces to be aware of such unwanted delays (and they are also summarized as a "LOH Allocation Pause (due to background GC) > 200 Msec" section in PerfView's GCStats report).

- During concurrent sweeping, as in non-concurrent version, segments may be deleted if becomes empty (by decommitting its memory).

In case of CoreCLR code, concurrent sweep phase is included in the `gc_heap::background_sweep` method. It calls `gc_heap::background_ephemeral_sweep` method scanning objects from generation 0 and 1) and then scans objects from generation 2 and Large Object Heap (calling `gc_heap::allow_fgc` method at some well-defined safe points, after each of 256 objects has been scanned). During object scanning, already known `gc_heap::thread_gap` or `gc_heap::make_unused_array` methods are used to create a free-list item or small unusable free space respectively.

Mentioned LOH allocations are blocked by global `gc_heap::gc_lh_block_` event which is used in `gc_heap::wait_for_background_planning` by calling `gc_heap::user_thread_wait` on it. This path is used at the beginning of the `gc_heap::a_fit_free_list_large_p` method, which is in fact the begging of the entire LOH allocation path (as described in Chapter 6).

Server Non-Concurrent

Since the beginning of .NET until .NET Framework 4.5, it was the default-only mode dedicated for the server (mainly web) applications. In fact, it is a quite simple extension of Workstation Non-Concurrent described earlier. All GCs are blocking, regardless which generation is collected. As we remember, from a memory management point of view there is an important difference though - by default, there are as many Managed Heaps as logical CPU cores.

Server Non-concurrent GC modes have the following characteristics (see Figure 11-10):

- There are additional threads dedicated solely for the GC's purposes - by default exactly as many as Managed Heaps (they are called simply *Server GC threads*). Most of the time they are suspended waiting for work to do. Each such single thread is dedicated to handle the corresponding Managed Heap.

- All collections are Non-Concurrent GCs - thanks to the parallel collection from many GC threads, introduced pauses are shorter than for corresponding heap sizes in case of Workstation mode. Being "stop the world" collections also allows them to be compacting if they wish.

- Marking is done in parallel from multiple GC threads - it speeds up the blocking phase. Additionally, the *mark stealing* technique is used to balance marking work between multiple threads. Heaps may be unbalanced in terms of required marking jobs because of different distribution of objects containing live outgoing references. Thus, GC threads may occasionally "steal" from each other batches of objects to be visited.

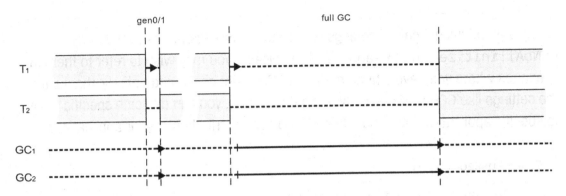

Figure 11-10. *Server Non-concurrent GC mode illustration*

In case of Server GC, the number of GC Heaps, and thus the number of GC threads also do not have to be equal to the number of logical CPU cores on the machine. Since the .NET Framework 4.6+ and .NET Core, an additional configuration has been added - GCHeapCount. It specifies the number of threads and Managed Heaps used by the GC. It may be set only for Server GC mode, via COMPlus_GCHeapCount environment variable or through XML/JSON configuration file (see Listing 11-3). The provided value must be smaller than the number of logical CPUs the process is allowed to run on (as operating systems provide various ways of limiting this number); otherwise it will be cropped to such number.

Listing 11-3. Configuring number of GC-related threads and Managed Heaps

```
<configuration>
    <runtime>
        <gcServer enabled="true"/>
        <GCHeapCount enabled="6"/>
    </runtime>
</configuration>
```

Previously such limitations had to be configured via mentioned operating system techniques - to make the runtime thinking it had less logical cores available than it really had. But it had a severe caveat - the entire runtime had such limitation imposed, not only the GC. It means unwanted limitations on possible concurrency of the entire .NET program, while one would like to limit in that way only the GC configuration. Thus, since the introduction of GCHeapCount setting, this is a preferred way of controlling that GC aspect.

There is an additional pair of settings related to the threads/heaps CPU affinity: `GCNoAffinitize` and `GCHeapAffinitizeMask`. You may wish to refer to them in scenarios where you have a huge number of CPUs not consumed entirely, thanks to the settings like `GCHeapCount`. By using this setting, you can dedicate specific CPUs to specific applications, making a fully CPU-aware distribution of your applications.

Typical usage scenarios:

- In heavily saturated web servers, where there is an intensive CPU cores contention because of many concurrent threads from many applications, this mode may be a better choice than even more resource-heavy Background Server GCs described later. You can additionally limit thread consumption by using `GCHeapCount` setting.

- Because all GCs, including full-GC, may be compacting, this mode fights with fragmentation better than concurrent version. It results in a smaller working set.

- Because all GCs are blocking, no floating garbage is introduced during the concurrent marking state. It reduces the working set further.

Background Server

Since .NET Framework 4.5, this is the default mode for server applications. This is by far the most complex GC available. However, knowing both Non-Concurrent Server and Background Workstation GCs, we will easily notice that it is in fact a combination of them.

Background Server GC mode has the following characteristics (see Figure 11-11) - very similar to the Background Workstation GC:

- There are two threads dedicated solely for the GC purposes per each Managed Heap - most of the time they are suspended waiting for work to do:

  - Server GC threads - as in non-concurrent Server GC, they are responsible for performing all blocking GCs (including Foreground GCs).

  - Background GC threads - an additional per heap thread responsible for performing Background GCs.

- Ephemeral collections are Non-Concurrent GCs - they are fast enough to make them non-concurrently. This also allows them to be compacting if they wish. They are executed by foreground GC threads in parallel - each such thread is responsible for its dedicated Managed Heap.

- A full-GC may be executed in two modes:

    - Non-Concurrent GC - because of the "stop the world" nature, it may be compacting. Like in the ephemeral collection, all Server GC threads are executing such GC in parallel.

    - Background GC - it executes most of the work while managed threads are normally executed. This mode is not compacting. As in Background Workstation case, this GC is executed by dedicated background GC threads (in parallel).

- Background full-GC has the following additional characteristics:

    - User-managed threads can allocate objects during its work - and these allocations can trigger ephemeral collections (Foreground GCs).

    - Foreground GCs may happen many times during a Background GC.

    - It contains two short "stop the world" phases - at the beginning and in the middle of the GC.

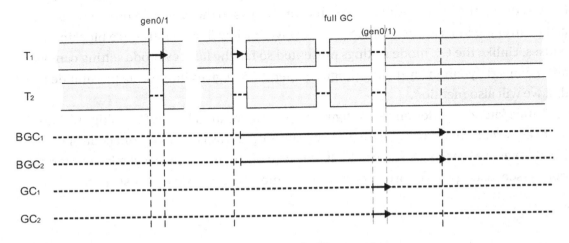

Figure 11-11. *Background Server GC mode illustration*

The exact description of Background Server GC would require repeating most of the content from the description of the Background Workstation GC. The main difference is that instead of a single additional GC thread, there are as many available CPU cores.

This obviously introduces quite a sophisticated solution combining the advantages of both Background Workstation GC (short pauses, weak thread allocation restrictions) and Non-Concurrent Server GC (scalability due to parallel collection). This is the most resource-heavy GC in terms of thread utilization. On an 8-core machine, there will be an additional 16 threads dedicated to the GC.

Typical usage scenarios:

- default GC for most server-based applications. If you have dozens of .NET applications running on the same server instance, you would not want to have them all use Background Server GC.

- Resource heavy desktop application running on dedicated machines. If kind of controlled environment is used (like medical or factory station), running solely your application, you may consider using this mode - this most sophisticated GC should run well, having more resources at its disposal.

Latency Modes

In addition to the four GC modes available, an orthogonal setting is also available that lets us control the latency (or pause) behavior. Thanks to the latency mode settings, we can control the intrusiveness of the GC - how willing it will be to introduce blocking pauses. Unlike the GC mode settings presented so far, the latency mode setting can be also changed dynamically during program operation. It gives interesting possibilities that we will also mention.

While latency mode can be configured via Configuration Knobs (by using COMPlus_ GCLatencyMode environment variable), the supported way is to set it from code via GCSettings.LatencyMode static field. It may take one of the GCLatencyMode enumeration values (see Listing 11-4), corresponding to the modes described in this section.

Listing 11-4. Latency modes enumeration

```
public enum GCLatencyMode
{
        Batch = 0,
        Interactive = 1,
        LowLatency = 2,
        SustainedLowLatency = 3,
        NoGCRegion = 4
}
```

As we will see, the latency mode in fact lets us to control concurrency of the GC also. Let's look at the subsequent sections where all those options are briefly described.

Batch Mode

In Batch mode, we are not concerned about pauses length a lot. This allows to optimize GC in different aspects, for example, throughput or memory usage. Batch mode is a default latency setting for all non-concurrent GCs (meaning, started with the `System.GC.Concurrent` or `gcConcurrent` setting disabled).

What this gives us in practice is the option to disable the possibility of Background GC occurrence. In other words, we can use it to dynamically disable the concurrent GC, even if it was started during runtime as such. But what happens to the background GC threads in such case? The answer differs depending on the GC mode:

- in case of Server GC they are simply infinitely suspended, until one will revert latency mode to the Interactive.

- in case of Workstation GC they will time out after some period of time (currently it is 20 seconds) and will be destroyed, emitting `GCTerminateConcurrentThread` ETW/LLTNg event.

Interactive

In interactive mode, short pauses are most desired, even in cost of memory usage (for example, we are running an interactive UI-based application). It is a default setting for all concurrent GCs - it enables Background GC possibility. Thus, it is a default setting in .NET because both Workstation and Server GC modes are concurrent by default.

Complementary to the Batch mode, we can use it to dynamically enable concurrent GC - in such case, proper background GC threads will be created if they do not exist already, emitting `GCCreateConcurrentThread` ETW/LLTNg event.

Additionally, in case of Workstation GC mode with interactive mode (so default one), GC time tuning is enabled already described in Chapter 7 in the "Generation to Condemn" section.

Low Latency

Low-latency mode should be used when as short as possible pauses are essential, at any cost. It is available only in Workstation GC mode. Low-latency mode disables all regular, both concurrent and non-concurrent generation 2 (full) Garbage Collections - this is quite a strong requirement! Full-GC will be possible only in case of receiving a low-memory system notification or via explicit trigger (like calling `GC.Collect` method).

Needless to say, this mode actually has a very large impact on the operation of the application:

- Overall pause times will be really short because only fast ephemeral collections occur.

- Memory usage will likely grow vastly because all objects gathering in generation 2 or Large Object Heap will not be collected at all.

Such a strong latency mode should be used only for small periods of time, when latency requirements are absolutely essential - for example, during intensive interaction with the user. We should be aware, however, that after operating in this mode, sooner or later there will be intensive garbage collection - most often it is best to call the GC in a controlled moment as soon as possible afterward.

When setting low-latency mode, special care should be taken to make sure it will be soon reverted. Regular try/finally construct may be not enough because there still might be rare situations when finally the block is not executed. To make latency mode setting double-protected, it is best to use so-called *Constrained Execution Regions*. As .NET Documentations says: "A constrained execution region (CER) is part of a mechanism for authoring reliable managed code. A CER defines an area in which the common language runtime (CLR) is constrained from throwing out-of-band exceptions that would prevent the code in the area from executing in its entirety." For example, the CLR delays thread aborts for code that is executing within a CER. Regardless of its internal workings, using them is as easy as preceding try block with the `PrepareConstrainedRegions` method call (see Listing 11-5).

Listing 11-5. Safely setting `LowLatency` mode thanks to the Constrained Execution Regions

```
GCLatencyMode oldMode = GCSettings.LatencyMode;
RuntimeHelpers.PrepareConstrainedRegions();
try
{
    GCSettings.LatencyMode = GCLatencyMode.LowLatency;
    //Perform time-sensitive, short work here
}
finally
{
    GCSettings.LatencyMode = oldMode;
}
```

Sustained Low Latency

Because latency requirements of `LowLatency` mode are so strong and the heap might grow too fast, another version of the low-latency requirement was introduced in .NET Framework 4.5, available both in Workstation and Server GC modes. Sustained low latency is a little compromise between desired short pauses and memory usage - in this mode only non-concurrent full-GCs are disabled. In other words, only ephemeral and Background Garbage Collections are allowed. This mode is available only if runtime has started with the concurrent setting enabled (regardless of changing it later on via Batch and Interactive latency modes). Like in the previous low-latency mode, a full, blocking GC will be possible only in case of receiving a low-memory system notification or via explicit trigger (like calling `GC.Collect` method).

Sustained low-latency mode allows us to stay in low-latency mode for a longer period of time, without such fast heap growth and with still short pauses but not as short as in `LowLatency` mode (due to pauses introduced by ephemeral and Background GCs). It may be a very good compromise in situations of handling user input. While the user makes some UI-based actions, we may enable it to improve interactivity. Exactly this scenario can be found in the source code of the Roslyn parser, used by Visual Studio.

SustainedLowLatency mode is enabled when the user types something in the editor but after a specified timeout, latency is reverted to the original value (see Listing 11-6).

Listing 11-6. Example of setting SustainedLowLatency mode from Roslyn source code

```
/// <summary>
/// This class manages setting the GC mode to SustainedLowLatency.
///
/// It is safe to call from any thread, but is intended to be called from
/// the UI thread whenever user keyboard or mouse input is received.
/// </summary>
internal static class GCManager
{
    /// <summary>
    /// Call this method to suppress expensive blocking Gen 2 garbage GCs in
    /// scenarios where high-latency is unacceptable (e.g. processing
    typing input).
    ///
    /// Blocking GCs will be re-enabled automatically after a short
    duration unless
    /// UseLowLatencyModeForProcessingUserInput is called again.
    /// </summary>
    internal static void UseLowLatencyModeForProcessingUserInput()
    {
        var currentMode = GCSettings.LatencyMode;
        var currentDelay = s_delay;
        if (currentMode != GCLatencyMode.SustainedLowLatency)
        {
            GCSettings.LatencyMode = GCLatencyMode.SustainedLowLatency;
            // Restore the LatencyMode a short duration after the
            // last request to UseLowLatencyModeForProcessingUserInput.
            currentDelay = new ResettableDelay(s_delayMilliseconds);
            currentDelay.Task.SafeContinueWith(_ => RestoreGCLatency
            Mode(currentMode), TaskScheduler.Default);
            s_delay = currentDelay;
        }
```

```
    if (currentDelay != null)
    {
            currentDelay.Reset();
    }
  }
}
```

No GC Region

This is by far the strongest requirement that can be set, added in .NET Framework 4.6. As the MSDN documentations says, this mode: "attempts to disallow garbage collection during the execution of a critical path if a specified amount of memory is available." In other words, it will try to disable GC entirely but it cannot be done indefinitely. Thus, we cannot set no GC mode simply by GCSettings.LatencyMode field (setting it to GCLatencyMode.NoGCRegion will have no effect). Instead, a dedicated method was introduced with several overloads:

- bool GC.TryStartNoGCRegion(long totalSize)

- bool GC.TryStartNoGCRegion(long totalSize, bool disallowFullBlockingGC)

- bool GC.TryStartNoGCRegion(long totalSize, long lohSize)

- bool GC.TryStartNoGCRegion(long totalSize, long lohSize, bool disallowFullBlockingGC)

As we can see, all those methods take the amount of memory (totalSize, in bytes) - it specifies how much memory we would like to be able to allocate without triggering any GC (in other words, how much memory should be already available upfront) per each Managed Heap. TryStartNoGCRegion method returns true if the GC acknowledges that much memory is indeed available and we have just entered no GC latency mode. Additionally, we can specify how much of those allocations may be dedicated to Large Object Heap (lohSize argument). If we do not specify lohSize, totalSize limit will be applied separately for SOH and LOH (thus, in fact, we would be able to allocate twice the totalSize size).

If initially there is less available memory than requested, a full non-concurrent GC will be triggered inside TryStartNoGCRegion method implementation, trying to get it. But we may disallow such behavior by disallowFullBlockingGC parameter.

An important limitation is the fact that a specified size must be less than or equal to the total size of all ephemeral segments (that is, appropriate multiplication of ephemeral segment size in case of Server GC):

- In case of specifying `lohSize`, the `totalSize` minus the `lohSize` value (SOH size) must be less than or equal to the size of an ephemeral segment.

- In case of specifying only `totalSize`, one can't tell if you meant that for SOH, LOH, or some combination of them, so it is assumed to be on the safe side - the whole `totalSize` value must be less than or equal to the size of an ephemeral segment.

This is because GC may be not triggered as long as allocations do not require segment reorganization due to ephemeral segment shortage. If we specify a size exceeding the ephemeral segment sizes, `ArgumentOutOfRangeException` will be thrown.

After entering no GC latency mode, we may proceed normally with our program execution. As long as allocations do not exceed `specified sizes` in SOH and LOH, no GC should be triggered. We should however remember to end no GC latency mode explicitly by calling `GC.EndNoGCRegion()` method! From the GC perspective it is not so important - even if we forget to, it is guaranteed that the latency mode will be reverted to the original one after exceeding `totalSize` allocations.

However, from the no GC API perspective, it is important that each `GC.TryStartNoGCRegion` method has its corresponding `GC.EndNoGCRegion` call - otherwise subsequent `GC.TryStartNoGCRegion` calls will throw `InvalidOperationException` with the message "The NoGCRegion mode was already in progress." It will happen even if the allocations limit were violated and latency mode was reverted to the original one! In such case we still have to call `EndNoGCRegion`, knowing that it will throw `InvalidOperationException` with the message "Allocated memory exceeds specified memory for NoGCRegion mode."

As no GC region is by design limited to certain amount of allocations, disabling it does not have to be as much protected by using Constrained Execution Regions as when setting low-latency modes. In the worst-case scenario, GC will just be triggered. However, it is always good to check whether we should end previous no GC region before calling `TryStartNoGCRegion`, to prevent throwing `InvalidOperationException`.

Taking all that into consideration, using a no GC region may require a few safe checks and will end with a code similar to that in Listing 11-7.

Listing 11-7. An example of no GC region creation

```
// in case of previous finally block not executed
if (GCSettings.LatencyMode == GCLatencyMode.NoGCRegion)
    GC.EndNoGCRegion();
if (GC.TryStartNoGCRegion(1024, true))
{
    try
    {
        // Do some work.
    }
    finally
    {
        try
        {
            GC.EndNoGCRegion();
        }
        catch (InvalidOperationException ex)
        {
            // Log message
        }
    }
}
```

Please note that calling the GC.EndNoGCRegion method without preceding GC.TryStartNoGCRegion call (that succeeds) will throw InvalidOperationException with the message "NoGCRegion mode must be set." Thus, you may see advice to check latency mode in advance, like in code (GCSettings.LatencyMode == GCLatencyMode.NoGCRegion) GC.EndNoGCRegion. This, however, is not useful in the finally block from Listing 11-7. As mentioned, in case of an allocations limit violation, we still need to call GC.EndNoGCRegion, even if GCSettings.LatencyMode will already have reverted a value like Batch or Interactive.

If you would like to investigate no GC latency mode in CoreCLR code, start from `GCHeap::StartNoGCRegion` method, which implements `GC.TryStartNoGCRegion` methods listed before. It may call `GCHeap::GarbageCollect` method and it calls `gc_heap::prepare_for_no_gc_region` - checking ephemeral segment size condition and setting allowed no GC allocation amounts. Afterward, when during normal program execution, the GC would be triggered, `gc_heap::should_proceed_for_no_gc` is called to check allocation limits violations.

Latency Optimization Goals

If you recall section "Static Data" from Chapter 7, an additional level of latency control was presented there - *latency optimization goals (levels)*, affecting the values of static data. As the CoreCLR comment says: "Latency modes required user to have specific GC knowledge (e.g., budget, full-blocking GC). We are trying to move away from them as it makes a lot more sense for users to tell us what's the most important out of the performance aspects that make sense to them" (and those aspects include memory footprint, throughput, and pause predictability). Thus, in the future .NET releases we may expect moving from previously described latency modes into more aspect-oriented latency goals. Currently four such goals (levels) are planned:

- memory footprint (level 1) - where pauses can be long and more frequent but heap size stays small,

- throughput (level 2) - where pauses are unpredictable but not very frequent (and might be long),

- a balance between pauses and throughput (level 3) - where pauses are more predictable and more frequent. The longest pauses are shorter than level 1 pauses,

- short pauses (level 4) - where pauses are more predictable and more frequent. The longest pauses are shorter than level 3 pauses.

As mentioned in Chapter 7, currently (at the time of .NET Framework 4.7 and .NET Core 2.1) only levels 1 and 3 are supported, but their usage along runtime and GC is yet very limited.

Latency level is accessible via GCLatencyLevel Configuration Knob, so it may be set by COMPlus_GCLatencyLevel variable with values 1 or 3.

Choosing GC Flavor

We have already gained a lot of knowledge regarding various modes that GC may operate on as well as its intrusiveness control via latency settings. Although the pros and cons of described modes were already discussed, a clear answer to the question - what is the best GC choice in my case - has not been presented yet.

The simple answer is - use default GC mode! In many cases, this answer is enough and you do not have to tangle your head with alternatives. However, there are various knobs we may turn on and off. There are situations in which it is worth considering their use. The two most common exceptions are:

- Web application hosted on a server with many other applications running - in such case the default Background Server may be just too resource consuming. You can tune it a little by using GCHeapCount setting or change it to other mode.

- Windows Service making a lot of processing - in such case the default Background Workstation may be not scalable enough and you may wish to change it to some Server mode.

A summary of the available modes, taking into account the knowledge presented so far, can be found in Table 11-1.

Table 11-1. Summary of Various GC Modes

	Workstation		Server	
	Non-Concurrent	**Background**	**Non-Concurrent**	**Background**
CPU usage	There are no GC threads	Only single GC thread	Number of GC threads is equal to number of visible logical CPU cores	Number of GC threads is equal to doubled number of visible logical CPU cores)
Batch	yes (default)	yes (disables background GCs)	yes (default)	yes (disables background GCs)
Interactive	yes (enables background GCs)	yes (default)	yes (enables background GCs)	yes (default)
LowLatency	yes	yes	no	No
SustainedLowLatency	no	yes	no	yes
GCHeapCount	no	no	yes	yes
Typical usage	A lot of lightweight applications on a single machine that may accept longer breaks (potentially controlled for short LowLatency periods)	Interactive applications with strict responsiveness requirement (additionally controlled by LowLatency and SustainedLowLatency modes)	Currently quite rare. It can be used as a compromise between a more resource consuming Background Server and Background Workstation, introducing longer GC pauses. Long blocking GCs may be accommodated by GC notifications.	Most applications based on processing requests (IIS hosted web applications, processing windows services)

Scenario 8-1. Checking GC Settings

Description: We are developing or maintaining a .NET application. Due to various reasons, we want to certainly identify its current GC settings on the production environment - let's say that based on the observed behavior, we suspect that it is misconfigured. Obviously, we could check the application's configuration file, but it will not give us one hundred percent certainty. As we know, a file-based configuration may be overridden by environment variables or a registry. Or maybe the file itself configures it in a wrong way (misspelling?). Why not just check what the .NET process itself says about its current settings?

Analysis: The easiest, fastest, and less intrusive way to check process settings is to use ETW/LLTNg mechanism. Every time ETW session starts and stops, .NET runtime sends additional diagnostics events (to be utilized by interpreting tools). We should be interested in the event `Microsoft-Windows-DotNETRuntimeRundown/Runtime/Start`. Although it is emitted when the runtime starts, it is also emitted, as mentioned, when ETW session starts and ends.

So it is as simple as starting and ending the ETW session and looking at this event, which contains the `StartupFlags` field that interests us. We can use for this purpose, for example, PerfView - record a very short standard .NET session and look at this event on the list of events (see Figure 11-12). `StartupFlags` are rather self-descriptive - we will be mostly interested in the following three values:

- `CONCURRENT_GC` - runtime has started with the concurrent GC enabled. If this value is not listed, Non-Concurrent GC is enabled.

- `SERVER_GC` - runtime has starter with the Server GC. If this value is not listed, Workstation GC is enabled.

- `HOARD_GC_VM` - VM hoarding (see Chapter 5) is enabled.

Such values may be combined with each other so. for example, Background Server GC will have both `CONCURRENT_GC` and `SERVER_GC` listed, while Non-Concurrent Workstation GC will have nothing listed.

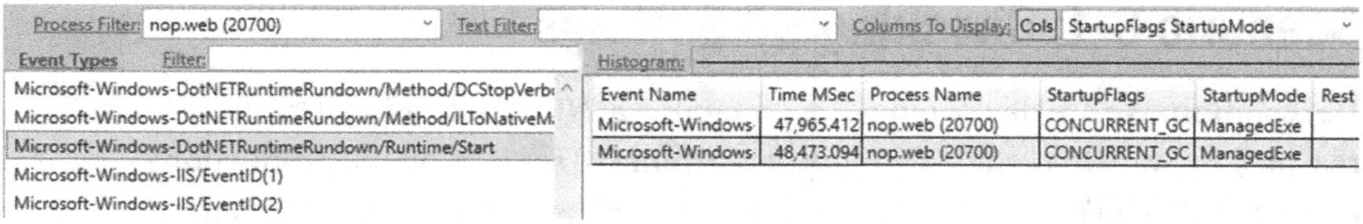

Figure 11-12. *Microsoft-Windows-DotNETRuntimeRundown/Runtime/Start event showing CLR runtime settings*

To make such a check even less invasive, we can use the great *etrace* tool created by Sasha Goldshtein. It allows you to control ETW sessions from the command line, with various filtering features available. In our case we are interested in only a single event of a single process. Because *etrace* starts .NET-related ETW session, mentioned diagnostic events will be emitted, including Runtime/Start. The appropriate command and its result are shown in Listing 11-8.

Listing 11-8. etrace tool to list specific ETW events from given providers and additional filters applied (like process ID)

```
.\etrace.exe --other Microsoft-Windows-DotNETRuntimeRundown --event
Runtime/Start --pid=21316
Processing start time: 30/04/2018 10:21:51
Runtime/Start [PNAME= PID=21316 TID=14648 TIME=30/04/2018 10:21:51]
    ClrInstanceID       = 9
    Sku                 = 1
    BclMajorVersion     = 4
    BclMinorVersion     = 0
    BclBuildNumber      = 0
    BclQfeNumber        = 0
    VMMajorVersion      = 4
    VMMinorVersion      = 0
    VMBuildNumber       = 30319
    VMQfeNumber         = 0
    StartupFlags        = 1
    StartupMode         = 1
    CommandLine         = F:\IIS\nopCommerce\Nop.Web.exe
    ComObjectGuid       = 00000000-0000-0000-0000-000000000000
    RuntimeDllPath      = C:\Windows\Microsoft.NET\Framework\v4.0.30319\clr.dll
```

The only inconvenience of this approach is that the StartupFlags value is given in numerical form, and we have to interpret it ourselves knowing the values of the corresponding enumeration (see Listing 11-9). In case of the result from Listing 11-8, StartupFlags has value 1, which means only CONCURRENT_GC flag is set.

Listing 11-9. Runtime StartupFlags enumeration

```
public enum StartupFlags
{
    None = 0,
    CONCURRENT_GC = 0x000001,
    LOADER_OPTIMIZATION_SINGLE_DOMAIN = 0x000002,
    LOADER_OPTIMIZATION_MULTI_DOMAIN = 0x000004,
    LOADER_SAFEMODE = 0x000010,
    LOADER_SETPREFERENCE = 0x000100,
    SERVER_GC = 0x001000,
    HOARD_GC_VM = 0x002000,
    SINGLE_VERSION_HOSTING_INTERFACE = 0x004000,
    LEGACY_IMPERSONATION = 0x010000,
    DISABLE_COMMITTHREADSTACK = 0x020000,
    ALWAYSFLOW_IMPERSONATION = 0x040000,
    TRIM_GC_COMMIT = 0x080000,
    ETW = 0x100000,
    SERVER_BUILD = 0x200000,
    ARM = 0x400000,
}
```

On the other hand, ASP.NET web application hosted on IIS will have StartupFlags of value 208919 (33017 hexadecimally), which corresponds to flags: CONCURRENT_GC, LOADER_OPTIMIZATION_SINGLE_DOMAIN, LOADER_OPTIMIZATION_MULTI_DOMAIN, LOADER_SAFEMODE, SERVER_GC, HOARD_GC_VM, LEGACY_IMPERSONATION, DISABLE_COMMITTHREADSTACK.

Scenario 8-2. Benchmarking Different GC Modes

Description: The topic of different GC operating modes is inherently related to one question - which one is best for our application? The answer is obvious on the one hand - the default mode is probably good enough in most cases. Web application hosted on server? Background Server GC? Interactive UI-based application? Background Workstation GC? It is rarely justified to disable the concurrent mode. On the other hand, each application is different, and there is no certainty that the default mode best suits it. At this point, there is no answer to our question other than simply measuring the impact of individual options.

But how to measure this influence? What tools? What to look for? This is what the following scenario deals with. We assume in it an analysis of the already known nopCommerce web application. Do not pay too much attention to the results though - they are only significant for this application at its current stage of development. Do not apply the conclusions from the analysis in this scenario directly into your applications. This scenario is to show how to carry out such analyses so that you can apply them in your specific situations. We will also see typical traps that we may come across when analyzing such measurements.

Analysis: First of all, how to measure the effect of different GC settings? It was already discussed in the GC pause and overhead section. nopCommerce application under tests is a Windows-based application. So, in order to have a comprehensive overview of the situation, we will be measuring the following aspects:

- GC overhead using:

    - GC Rollup By Generation data from GCStats report in PerfView,

- Processed CSV data from Individual GC Events file from GCStats report in PerfView -to calculate percentiles of pause times (Pause MSec column) and CPU overhead (% GC column), memory usage using:

    - processed CSV data from Individual GC Events file from GCStats report in PerfView -to calculate the Managed Heap size using After MB column (here we could also use/.NET CLR Memory/# Bytes in all Heaps performance counter with similar accuracy),

    - process private working set as manually measured from the Task Manager (here we could also use /Process/Working Set - Private performance counter).

- Application perspective:

    - response times data from Summary Report in JMeter test.

    - processed CSV data from Response Times Percentiles in JMeter test (to calculate percentiles).

Processing all this data makes such benchmarking quite tedious. The procedure is mainly manual due to the lack of good tools that would automate merging and processing all those results. If you found one, use it! Nevertheless, I strongly encourage you to look at GC settings measurements in a such comprehensive way. Otherwise, the look at the experiment is incomplete and can lead to false conclusions.

Testing scenario consists of the following steps:

- Running load test with the help of JMeter, simulating a typical user's traffic on the site (as always, beware of repeatable starting conditions - restart application pool, warm it up a little, disable any other background applications, and so on, so forth).

- Immediately starting ETW session from PerfView - very simple one, with the lowest overhead possible. Checking only .NET option is just fine.

- Let the load test last for a specified amount of time.

- Stop everything and start analysis - that includes producing graphs similar to those presented below. It may include some Excel (or any other similar tool) manipulations to interpret CSV data, but such trivial aspects were omitted here for brevity.

The main advantage of such approach is its very low invasiveness. We can start tests at any time, even in a production environment. We do not even have to perform any load tests; it's enough that we carry out observations with similar user traffic (time of the day, week, month, ...) if we are sure conditions are repeatable.

There is one more important aspect of this kind of measurements, mentioned in Chapter 3 - beware of averages! The average is a statistical value that gives the illusion of valuable information, but can really obscure many important facts. So while measuring the above values, pay attention to their behavior over time. If, for example, private Working Set does not change significantly, the average may be a sufficient value. But for such key parameters as the response time of the application (or the GC pause in our case), the average is often simply not enough.

For key metrics, the truly valuable information is provided by percentiles. Thus, both for GC pause times and application response times, CSV data is used to produce percentiles graphs. Percentiles directly translate into business requirements - for example, we want 99% of users to have response times below 2 seconds and 99,99% users below 10 seconds. In this scenario percentiles are calculated from observed data - ETW and JMeter samples - with the help of manual work in Microsoft Excel. If we can afford to be more invasive, including changing the application code, we can use an excellent HdrHistogram.NET library (`https://github.com/HdrHistogram/HdrHistogram.NET`) that calculates them from inside the application.

During the scenario, we try to answer the question of which of the four GC configurations seems the most appropriate:

- Workstation Non-Concurrent,

- Background Workstation,

- Server Non-Concurrent,

- Background Server.

Of course, the "appropriateness" should be business-driven - whether it is about response times SLA, resource consumption (CPU, memory) or any other metrics we imagine. Note that the GC overhead itself is not really a business-centric metric. Can you imagine a company management that requires % Time in GC to be less than 10%? In fact, we will see the influence of GC overhead on the whole application also in this scenario.

Before each test, proper runtime settings are set in the configuration file. For each mode, a few tests were conducted to minimize the chance of impact from external factors.

Let's discuss CPU overhead first. As we can see in Figure 11-13, there are some facts that can be noted from such results:

- Ephemeral GCs are a little faster in both Server GC flavors,

- Full-GCs introduce a little less overhead in both concurrent flavors.

This leads us to the conclusion that the best choice here is Background Server GC. However, measured differences are not overwhelming in our scenario so from a CPU's overhead point of view, we can say that every mode behaves similarly. The point is, we had to make detailed measurements to confirm that. Such ETW-based data analysis was done with the help of a data processing tool (like Excel) to get average measurements (while double-checking if histogram does not reveal multimodal distribution).

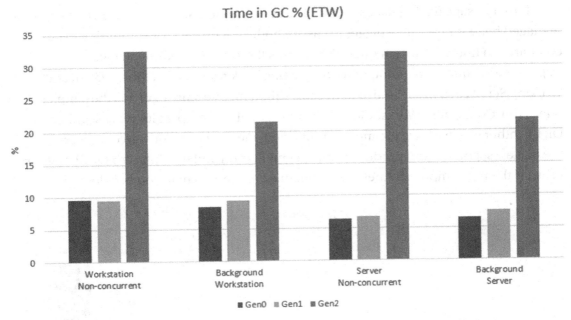

Figure 11-13. % in GC results (for each generation)

If we used % Time in the GC performance counter measure, we would end with quite misleading results where it is much bigger in case of both Workstation modes compared to Server modes. If you recall Figure 11-1, % Time in GC is a time of GC versus time to the previous GC. In case of Server mode, time spent in GC is small but processing is done in parallel for multiple Managed Heaps (on multiple cores). Thus, even the time is shorter, the overall CPU usage is similar, while % Time in GC is not accurately showing this. This is an important observation for us. The % Time in GC counter should be considered together with the GC mode we are in - in Workstation mode we should be more tolerant to higher values than in Server mode. But, as mentioned earlier, it is just much better to use ETW-based data instead of a performance counter in the first place.

Memory usage distinguishes better various GC modes (see Figure 11-14). The managed heap is noticeably bigger in case of both concurrent (background) versions compared to non-concurrent ones - it confirms the already-mentioned bigger fragmentation due to frequent, non-compacting background GCs. Moreover, overall Working Set of each mode is also noticeably different. The smaller one is the simpler one - Non-Concurrent Workstation mode that can often compact its small segments. On the other side we have the most complicated one - Background Server that creates the biggest segments and produces both fragmentation and floating garbage. If memory usage is the most important metric for you, this data should help you decide.

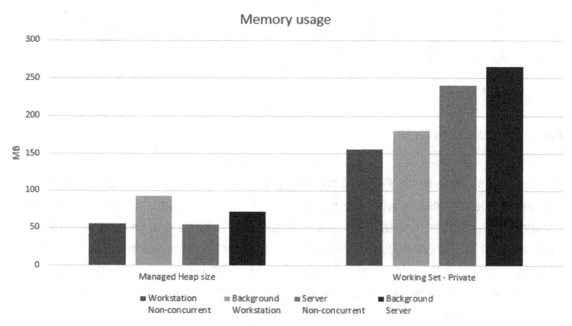

Figure 11-14. *Memory usage results*

More interesting may be information about GC pauses introduced in each GC mode, preferably with respect to each generation condemned. Such data are also in line with expectations (see Figure 11-15). Both ephemeral generations are collected really fast regardless of the GC mode. The real difference is seen for full-GCs. A definite loser here is the Non-Concurrent Workstation mode - one thread in a blocking mode must collect all garbage. The Non-Concurrent Server is faster because it does it in parallel on multiple Managed Heaps. However, it is still noticeably slower than both concurrent versions.

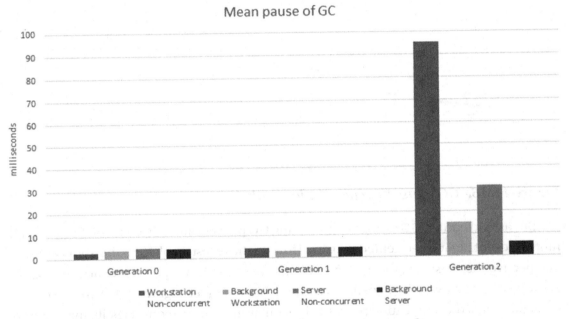

Figure 11-15. *Mean GC pause time for each generation results*

However, as mentioned earlier, the average is not enough precise information for such interesting measurements. Surprisingly enough, when we look at percentiles (see Figure 11-16), Background Workstation looks the best while Workstation Non-Concurrent is clearly the worst one (with a serious degradation for percentiles bigger than 99). This is how we should comprehensively look at pause times in our applications. Measure your own, and maybe you will be surprised by the results!

GC Pauses by Percentile Distribution

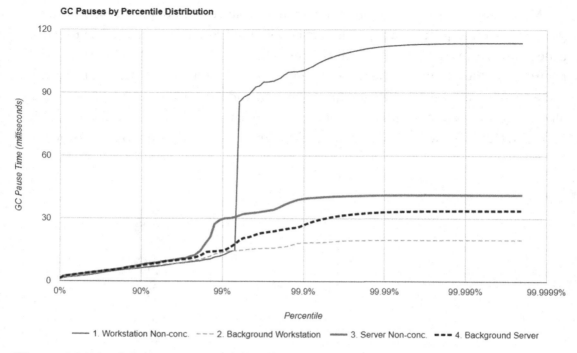

Figure 11-16. GC pause time percentiles results

But as said earlier, GC overhead (including GC pauses) are only contributing to much more relevant business-oriented metrics. How do those tests look from the application perspective? Surprisingly, the average response times of the prepared scenario are big enough to almost overwhelm benefits of the GC settings (see Figure 11-17). In most configurations, the application processed a similar number of requests (still, throughput-driven Concurrent Server GC was able to process a little more). Average response times are smaller with the more "complicated" version of GC we choose, but differences are not huge. These are the specifics of the application being tested. If the response times were generally much shorter, the impact of GC could be much more important.

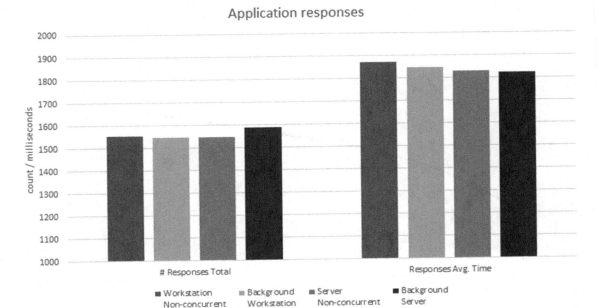

Figure 11-17. *Response count and average response time results*

Averages are not enough though, so let's look at the percentiles of response times (see Figure 11-18). It only confirms a rather negligible influence of the GC settings. However, this does not make this whole scenario senseless. On the contrary! It shows how important it is to measure not only synthetic % Time in GC or pause time, but above all - the resultant impact on the application, on the indicators that will be experienced by real users.

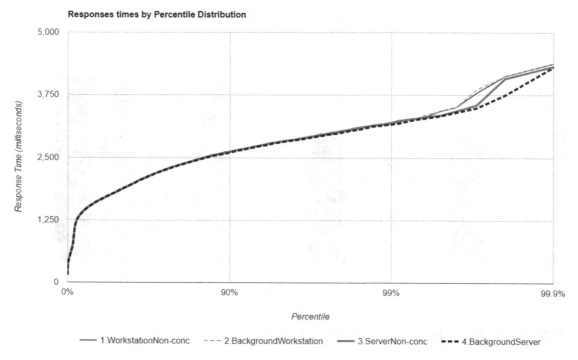

Figure 11-18. *Response time percentiles results*

The conclusion in our case is that it is best to use one of the two concurrent GC versions. Remember that these are conclusions for some assumptions - generated user load, specific environment (number of CPU cores, memory amount, other running applications). That is why it is extremely important to carry out such tests on possibly near-production environments, not your development desktop PC.

The scenario presents a web application in which testing is quite obvious using a load test. However, also desktop or mobile applications can be tested using automated tests. We can also, if our logic is well separated (as in the case of the MVVM approach), test only the logic layer exposed via API. There is no excuse for not performance testing!

For brevity, similar benchmarking of various latency modes was omitted. The procedure would look the same. And the conclusions would be in line with the expectations. Only the measurements of your own application will, however, answer the question whether their use makes sense.

Summary

In this chapter we learned about different ways in which we can configure GC activity in .NET. We have learned about differences between Workstation and Server mode, both from the implementation and practical side. Similarly, we have learned what is Non-Concurrent and Concurrent GC, and that currently the latter are named as Background GC. We also learned briefly how such interesting mechanisms as concurrent marking and sweeping are implemented.

The chapter ended with deliberations on the mode selection - including such an important decision whether it is Workstation or Server GC. On the one hand, knowledge of these different available modes seems quite common. On the other hand, we often do not think about changing the default settings at all. It is a great success of the .NET team that those default settings perform so well, and in fact we do not usually have to bother about changing it.

There will always be a situation where the default settings may not be sufficient. Therefore, the last scenario in the chapter describes in detail how to make an educated decision to choose settings based on careful benchmarks.

The following two rules summarize the knowledge from this chapter. The next one is dedicated to the important mechanism related to the object's lifetime - finalization.

Rule 23 - Choose GC Mode Consciously

Applicability: General - moderately popular. High performance code - very important.

Justification: As we have learned in Chapter 8, there are various GC modes and settings available. We are in control of crucial GC parameters - number of heaps and GC threads, aggressiveness, and so on, so forth. Most of the time the default settings are just fine. However, you should be aware of alternatives and how to make a good, educated decision about them.

How to apply: First of all, you should start with the major flavor that correctly reflects the characteristics of your app. For example, whether it is Server or Workstation app, whether you care about pauses or not. This should be very little work as you should know the general characteristics of you app. On the other hand, each GC mode has its own pros and cons in terms of CPU and memory usage. They may result in different characteristics of the overall application performance. Without measuring them, it is really hard to say which mode best suits your needs. Thus, if you really care about performance, check them and measure. Applying Rules 5 - Measure GC Early and #6 - Measure Your Program may help you in doing that, especially on your pre-production environment (or even on production to some extent). When conducting tests, remember about careful methodology - especially about using percentiles on measurements that matter to you most.

Related scenarios: Scenarios 8-1, 8-2.

Rule 24 - Remember About Latency Modes

Applicability: General - rather uncommon. High performance code - important.

Justification: Besides four .NET Garbage Collector modes, we can also influence GC's aggressiveness by using latency modes. They control how willing GC will be in executing blocking GCs (thus, introducing unwanted pauses). This leads to a clear balance between responsiveness (due to only short blocking pauses) and memory usage (due to most non-compacting background GC). Modes that focus on short latencies is thus most often used in interactive applications when we want to have additional control over UI responsiveness - typically, for short periods of time requiring maximum fluency (e.g., keyboard typing). Some server apps like trading apps also use SustainedLowLatency to indicate they don't want the interruption from full-blocking GCs while making sure they have enough memory during trading hours.

How to apply: Latency modes are changed from within application code. Various ways and related patterns were presented in this chapter. We always set low-latency modes for a certain time, the shorter the stronger our expectations are. On one side is `SustainedLowLatency` mode that may last for a long time as it only disables blocking full-GCs. On the other side we have no GC regions that disable garbage collection all together. Additionally, we can switch between concurrent and non-concurrent GC versions dynamically. If we well understand how users use our application, it can lead to even better-tuned memory and CPU usage. However, such precise tuning is not needed in typical applications. Only when we are approaching the limits of performance requirements we may look at latency mode with interest.

Related scenarios: Scenario 8-2 (to use the same testing methodology).

CHAPTER 12

Object Lifetime

Previous chapters describe the automatic memory management process in .NET quite comprehensively. Chapter 6 contains information about how objects are created, while chapters from 7 to 11 inform in detail how they are collected when no longer needed. However, there are some side mechanisms, without the description of which our knowledge would not be complete. In this chapter we will focus on three such mechanisms. Although they exist separately and can be used independently, they relate to each other conceptually. All of them concern a common topic - the lifetime of the object.

The three mentioned mechanisms include finalization, disposable objects (and very popular Disposable pattern), and weak references. Through this chapter it should become clear how and why they are implemented, as well as how to use them. Typically, some practical scenarios are presented how to diagnose problems related to them. Please note, however, that those mechanisms are presented mainly from a memory management perspective. There are many more comprehensive descriptions available in other books that discuss all possible pros and cons, including common caveats you may face using them. This is not a C# learning book, so no general C#-related discussions happen here.

Both finalization and Disposable patterns are strongly related with interoperability with the unmanaged code (and P/Invoke mechanism), so a lot of this chapter is dedicated to this topic. Keep in mind, however, that both of them, and weak references especially, may be used in a regular managed code not related to unmanaged resources - like for logging or cache purposes. Thus, even if unmanaged code and P/Invoke are not your regular work, please feel invited to read this chapter nevertheless.

© Konrad Kokosa 2018

K. Kokosa, *Pro .NET Memory Management*, https://doi.org/10.1007/978-1-4842-4027-4_12

Object vs. Resource Life Cycle

In the managed world, everything seems to be pretty easy. We create objects, use them, and they are deleted by the GC sometime after we stop needing them. We do not have to worry that garbage collection is non-deterministic - that we do not know exactly when it will happen - as long as the GC will not delete objects too soon, while we are still using it (and this will not happen because it would mean a very severe bug in the GC). Such non-deterministic deallocation of objects is typical for tracing collectors, like the one implemented in .NET.

This is all fine as long as we do not want some action to happen when an object will be no longer needed - a technique called *finalization*. Out of a sudden non-deterministic nature of GC becomes a problem - there is simply no place when a developer could put appropriate code. This is because from the code perspective there is only a well-defined moment of object creation (constructor), but not of object reclamation.

Managed runtimes like .NET provide dedicated finalization mechanisms - including a well-defined place when a programmer can write code to be executed when an object becomes garbage. In fact, most of this chapter is devoted to such a finalization process. Because it is inherently related to the non-deterministic nature of garbage collection, it is often referred to as *non-deterministic finalization* - it will happen, but it is not said when.

Additionally, *deterministic finalization* may be sometimes desired - to take an action explicitly when we know that object becomes unused. .NET provides a contract in the form of `IDisposable` interface that implies using such finalization. We will look at it also later in this chapter.

In addition to the non-deterministic and deterministic finalization names, sometimes also names of *implicit* and *explicit cleanup* are used, respectively.

Please note that conceptually finalization does not relate directly to the mechanisms of garbage collection. It is for sure NOT garbage collection itself, as some developers tend to think. Finalization is just producing a side effect - we may do some action when an object becomes unreachable or simply is no longer needed. But neither finalizers (as we may know it from C#) nor `IDisposable` interface is responsible for reclaiming memory of a no-longer needed object! It happened to me several times during the recruitment interviews to hear such answers that the `Dispose` method frees the memory after the object. I hope after previous chapters, you are fully aware that it is not true.

Why, however, is the finalization mechanism is needed at all? In a completely managed environment, its need is actually negligible. In such cases, all managed objects are referencing each other but the whole resulting objects graphs is properly managed by the GC. If one deletes an object (let's say, by assigning a `null` to its last reference), tracing GC will take care of deleting all other related objects, not reachable from other places. Deleting all those related, owned objects was a typical responsibility of the destructor in an unmanaged world (i.e., C/C++).

In a managed world, finalization is mostly helpful when an object holds resources other than those managed by the GC and the runtime. Such unmanaged resources are typically various types of handles, descriptors, and other data related to the system resources that must be freed explicitly. The more the specific environment relies on such unmanaged cooperation, the more important that finalization is. .NET environment was from the very beginning designed as very "unmanaged-friendly." As mentioned previously, one of the design goals was to take regular C++ code and with very minimal changes be able to compile it as .NET program (which resembles today's C++/CLI language). Many very popular APIs rely on unmanaged resources underneath (like files, sockets, bitmaps, and so on, so forth). Thus, finalization exists in .NET developers' minds since the very beginning - both in the forms of deterministic `IDisposable` contract and non-deterministic finalization.

JVM, as an extremely popular counterpart-managed environment, put much less attention to non-deterministic finalization. They are considered unreliable, problematic, and introducing unnecessary GC overhead. In fact, they are so unpopular that since Java 9 they have received deprecated status. Instead, various methods of deterministic finalization are preferred since many years - by providing an explicit cleanup method and requiring developers to invoke it on object no longer needed (most typically by wrapping its usage within try-finally block). This resembles the well-known `IDisposable` pattern from .NET world.

As a replacement for deprecated `java.lang.Object.finalize` method, a suggested solution for non-deterministic finalization is to use `java.lang.ref.Cleaner` class that manages object references by `java.lang.ref.PhantomReference` and corresponding cleaning actions for them. Phantom references are enqueued after the collector determines that their referents may otherwise be reclaimed (thus making this mechanism also non-deterministic).

Because of managed and unmanaged worlds' coexistence, we should think about two separate issues: management of the object lifetime and management of the resources (unmanaged) that it holds. Object lifetime management is solely the GC responsibility. On the other hand, runtime does not understand well our unmanaged resources so resources management is our responsibility, with the help of features described in this chapter.

Keeping in mind that the finalization is a side effect of removing the object, we will see in this chapter that specific implementations included in .NET do affect the object lifetime.

Finalization

What is most commonly referred to as "finalization" in .NET is generally understood as non-deterministic finalization. As the ECMA-335 standard says: "A class definition that creates an object type can supply an instance method (called a *finalizer*) to be called when an instance of the class is no longer reachable." This is exactly what we will look at in this part of the chapter - how the finalizer method may be declared, used, and how it is implemented in CLR.

Introduction

For declaring a finalizer in a case of C# type, special syntax was introduced, called *destructor* (see Listing 12-1). It represents code called when an object is no longer reachable and is just about to be deleted. In our example it is used to close a handle to the opened file (otherwise, sooner or later we could hit the limit of maximum handles opened in the system). System resources are represented by "handles" in case of Windows, which quite often are represented by IntPtr structure.[1]

Listing 12-1. Simple example of using finalizer in C# (by destructor definition)

```
class FileWrapper
{
    private IntPtr handle;
    public FileWrapper(string filename)
    {
```

---

[1]In the case of Linux resources, they are commonly represented as regular integers.

```
    Unmanaged.OFSTRUCT s;
    handle = Unmanaged.OpenFile(filename, out s, 0x00000000);
}

// Destructor
~FileWrapper()
{
    if (handle != IntPtr.Zero)
        Unmanaged.CloseHandle(handle);
}
```

Destructor in C# is just a wrapper, which will be translated by compiler into a method that overrides System.Object.Finalize method (see Listing 12-2).

Listing 12-2. IL method definition of destructor form

```
.method family hidebysig virtual
instance void Finalize () cil managed
{
    .override method instance void [System.Runtime]System.Object::Finalize()
    // ...
}
```

Overriding the Finalize method is crucial. It is a contract between the type and the GC - objects that have the Finalize method overridden are called *finalizable* and receive special treatment by the GC.

To declare a finalizable type in F# or VB.NET, we simply have to override Finalize method. This is however not possible in case of C#. Trying to do so will result in an error: "Do not override Object.Finalize. Instead, provide a destructor." Thus the only way is to use ~Typename syntax. Its "destructor" name is rather unfortunate because as we know, it has nothing in common with the deconstruction of the managed objects itself but is more related with resource management. Interestingly, because C++ has already used ~Typename() notion for C++ destructor, finalizers are defined by !Typename() in C++/CLI.

Note also that as MSDN states: "every implementation of `Finalize` in a derived type must call its base type's implementation of `Finalize`. This is the only case in which application code is allowed to call `Finalize`." This is done automatically by s destructor wrapper in C# but we should remember about that in other languages.

We can, for example, use finalizers to manage an additional memory pressure (by `GC.AddMemoryPressure` and `GC.RemoveMemoryPressure` methods) introduced by a consumed resource (even if it is managed but we know it uses some resources underneath). A typical example is using `System.Drawing.Bitmap` class that, in fact, is represented as a single handle to a system resource, but obviously it requires some additional memory when bitmap data are used (see Listing 12-3).

Listing 12-3. An example of finalizers usage to maintain additional memory pressure

```
class MemoryAwareBitmap
{
    private System.Drawing.Bitmap bitmap;
    private long memoryPressure;

    public MemoryAwareBitmap(string file, long size)
    {
        bitmap = new System.Drawing.Bitmap(file);
        if (bitmap != null)
        {
            memoryPressure = size;
            GC.AddMemoryPressure(memoryPressure);
        }
    }

    ~MemoryAwareBitmap()
    {
        if (bitmap != null)
        {
```

```
        bitmap.Dispose();
        GC.RemoveMemoryPressure(memoryPressure);
    }
}

...

}
```

However, using finalizers has certain limitations:

- As previously stated, their execution time is non-deterministic – s finalizer will be called (most probably, see below) but it is not defined when. This is bad from s resource management point of view. If an owned resource is limited, it should be released as quickly as possible. Waiting for non-deterministic cleanup is barely optimal. If we really need to make sure that finalizers were executed, we may call the GC.WaitForPendingFinalizers method. We will return to it several times hereinafter.

- Order of execution of finalizers is not defined - even if one finalizable object refers to the other finalizable object, it is not guaranteed their finalizers will run in any logical order (like the e.g., "slave" before the "master" or vice versa). Thus, we should not refer to any other finalizable objects inside a finalizer, even if we "own" them. Unordered execution is a well-thought-out design decision - sometimes it is simply not possible to find a natural order (for example, what about circular references between finalizable objects?). There is, however, some ordering between finalizers possible in the form of critical finalizers, as described later. However, finalizer code may refer to the regular managed objects if the corresponding object holds references to it - it is guaranteed that the whole object graph is collected only after running the finalizer.

- The thread on which the finalizer will be executed is also not defined - although we will see how current implementation defines that, ECMA-335 does not impose any requirements on that field. Thus, relying on any thread context should be avoided (including threads synchronization like locking, which may lead to deadlocks because nothing is guaranteed here).

- It is not guaranteed that finalization code will be executed at all, exactly once, or may be executed only partially - for example, if some finalizer is malfunctioned and blocks its execution indefinitely, or the process is terminated rapidly without giving the GC chance to execute them. Moreover, it is even possible that finalizer will be executed more than once because of a resurrection technique, described later.[2]

- Throwing an exception from the finalizer is very dangerous - by default it simply kills the entire process. Because finalizer code is considered really important (like, for example, releasing system-wide synchronization primitive), being unable to execute it is treated with the highest severity. Thus, you should be extremely careful in not allow throwing any exception from the finalizer.

- Finalizable objects introduce additional overhead to the GC, which may impact overall application performance - as we will see later in the section describing the finalization implementation; this mechanism requires additional handling of such objects that is not without a cost.

All those points lead to one conclusion - implementing finalizers is tricky and using them may be unreliable, thus they should be generally avoided. Treat them as implicit "safety nets" for cases when a developer does not release resources explicitly by a preferred explicit cleanup approach (like Disposable pattern). We will see such typical usage when discussing Disposable patterns later on.

ECMA-335 says that: "it is valid to define a finalizer for a value type. However, that finalizer will only be run for boxed instances of that value type." At least in the case of .NET Core runtime, it is no longer valid. Runtime simply ignores the finalizer defined in value types during boxing.

---

[2]Even worse, due to resurrection and possible timing, there may be multiple simultaneous calls to the same finalizer.

From a programmer's perspective it should be only important that the finalizer is called "at some time" after the object becomes unreachable. And although it is rather an implementation detail, it is good to be aware when in fact finalizers may be called. In general, there are two scenarios when it happens:

- At the end of GC - no matter what triggered GC, at the end of the process, finalizers are called for the object discovered to be unreachable in this particular GC. Please keep in mind that this means only finalizers of objects from condemned (and younger) generations will be called.

- As the CLR internal bookkeeping - when runtime unloads AppDomain and when it is shutting down.

As mentioned earlier, finalizers do not necessarily have to be related to the unmanaged resources only. We may imagine other usages, like the lifetime logging example from Listing 12-4. If for some reason we would like to perform log creation and deletion of an object, its constructor and finalizer seem to be a perfect place - we may need to do it, for example, because such an object represents very crucial or resource-heavy functionality.

Listing 12-4. Simple example of using finalizer in C# (by destructor definition)

```
class LoggedObject
{
    private ILogger logger;
    public LoggedObject(ILogger logger)
    {
        this.logger = logger;
        // ...
        this.logger.Log("Object created.");

    }

    // Destructor
    ~LoggedObject()
    {
        this.logger.Log("Object destroyed.");
    }
```

Please note that even in such a "non-unmanaged" world, implementing a finalizer is not trivial. In case of Listing 12-4, a finalizer could be using a dependency-injected logger via interface. It means we are not guaranteed that an injected, concrete logger instance will not be finalizable and thus we are exposing ourselves to the problem of unordered finalization execution – the logger may be already disposed inside our finalizer. This is a simple yet expressive example of finalization caveats.

How should such danger could be mitigated? Some solutions may be based on code review or automated static analysis - to make sure that ILogger implementations are not finalizable or they are critically finalizable (soon we will understand why it may help). But the preferred solution is always the same - avoid using finalization. If the lifetime of such an object is so important, most probably you will benefit more by incorporating Disposable pattern into it, where the cleanup moment is also well-defined and much safer to include logging facilities.

Eager Root Collection Problem

Separate lifetime management of objects and resources can lead to unusual side effects. We have already seen them in Chapter 8 in Listings from 8-13 to 8-16. Most of them are related to the eager root collection technique. Although in itself it is a great JIT-based optimization that takes care of the shortest possible lifetime of objects, in the context of resource management, it can be sometimes problematic.

The very typical example of such a problem is using a stream to access a file (see Listing 12-5). If we uncomment GC calls inside ProblematicObject.UseMe method (simulating GC that could happen simultaneously during this method execution), such program execution will end with an Unhandled Exception: System. ObjectDisposedException: Cannot access a closed file. This is because due to JIT optimization, inside the UseMe method the whole ProblematicObject instance is treated as unreachable just after the last usage of this.[3] Thus, after stream assignment to a localStream variable, it is perfectly fine to expect ProblematicObject finalizer to be executed. But as we see, such finalizer closes the stream so the following ReadByte call fails. In such a simple case we can quickly correct it by always using Stream from the instance, not from a local variable (so, for example, last line should be return this.stream.ReadByte()). In such a case, the whole ProblematicObject instance is referenced by the last line of UseMe method (by using this reference) so early root collection optimization will not come into play.

---

[3]Refer to the early root collection technique described in Chapter 8.

Listing 12-5. Problem with finalizer releasing resources too early

```
class ProblematicObject
{
    Stream stream;

    public ProblematicObject() => stream = File.OpenRead(@"C:\Temp.txt");

    ~ProblematicObject()
    {
        Console.WriteLine("Finalizing ProblemticObject");
        stream.Close();
    }

    public int UseMe()
    {
        var localStream = this.stream;
        // Normal code, complex enough to make this method not inlineable and
        partialy or fully-interrptible
        ...
        // GC happens here and finalizers had enough time to execute.
        // You can simulate that by the following calls:
        // GC.Collect();
        // GC.WaitForPendingFinalizers();
        return localStream.ReadByte();
    }
}

class Program
{
    static void Main(string[] args)
    {
        var pf = new ProblematicObject();
        Console.WriteLine(pf.UseMe());
        Console.ReadLine();

    }
```

During P/Invoke we may introduce the same problems and because of that, a few ways of improving things have been introduced. Let's start from extending the code from Listing 12-1, by adding corresponding UseMe method but now using P/Invoke calls directly (see Listing 12-6). We have introduced there exactly the same problem - eagerly collected ProblematicFileWrapper instance will trigger its finalizer closing used file handle, while the further code tries to use it. Unmanaged.ReadFile call will fail and UseMe method will return -1. In our example, we can also quickly fix the problem by using this.handle instead of local variable hnd but this is not always possible - quite often IntPtr is not part of the managed object (but only static or local variables).

Listing 12-6. Problem with finalizer releasing resources to0 early (extension from Listing 12-1)

```
public class ProblematicFileWrapper
{
   private IntPtr handle;
   public ProblematicFileWrapper(string filename)
   {
      Unmanaged.OFSTRUCT s;
      handle = Unmanaged.OpenFile(filename, out s, 0x00000000);
   }
   ~ProblematicFileWrapper()
   {
      Console.WriteLine("Finalizing ProblematicFileWrapper");
      if (handle != IntPtr.Zero)
         Unmanaged.CloseHandle(handle);
   }

   public int UseMe()
   {
      var hnd = this.handle;
      // Normal code

      // GC happens here and finalizers had enough time to execute.
      // You can simulate that by the following calls:
      //GC.Collect();
      //GC.WaitForPendingFinalizers();
```

```
    byte[] buffer = new byte[1];
    if (Unmanaged.ReadFile(hnd, buffer, 1, out uint read, IntPtr.Zero))
    {
        return buffer[0];
    }
    return -1;
}
```

The first general solution to this problem is typical to controlling eager root collection - we can add GC.KeepAlive(this) call just before return statement inside the UseMe method. This way we extend the lifetime of the object holding the corresponding handle. But this solution clutters code a lot and is cumbersome.

Such problems lead to introducing a helper structure HandleRef. It is a very simple wrapper that holds both a handle and an object who owns it. It is then specially treated by the interop marshaler, to extend the lifetime of the indicated object during the entire P/Invoke call. APIs of such P/Invoke calls expect HandleRef instead of bare IntPtr (see Listing 12-7).

Listing 12-7. Solving the problem with finalizer with the help of HandleRef struct

```
public int UseMe()
{
    var hnd = this.handle;
    // Normal code

    // GC happens here and finalizers had enough time to execute.
    // You can simulate that by the following calls:
    //GC.Collect();
    //GC.WaitForPendingFinalizers();

    byte[] buffer = new byte[1];
    if (Unmanaged.ReadFile(new HandleRef(this, hnd), buffer, 1, out uint
    read, IntPtr.Zero))
    {
        return buffer[0];
    }
    return -1;
}
```

However, using `HandleRef` does not solve all the problems - especially related to the malicious handle-recycling attack that we will discuss soon. Thus, it is rather an old and deprecated approach, mainly used in legacy code (over 80% of its usage comes from Windows Forms and System.Drawing code).

`HandleCollector` class was introduced at the same time as `HandleRef`, which realizes reference counting semantics for the handles - if a given threshold of handles are created, it triggers GC. It is also considered legacy and its usage is very rare.

Do not use `HandleRef` and its equally old friend `HandleCollector` classes. They are described here to provide a concise view of the resource management topics and give a little historical background that helps to understand the preferred `SafeHandle` approach described later. Even if you encounter those types usage in existing code, do not follow such pattern. Safe handles introduced in .NET Framework 2.0 are much better alternatives, described thoroughly in the next section.

Critical Finalizers

Due to various problems with finalizers mentioned above, in .NET Framework a little firmer counterpart was introduced in the form of *critical finalizers*. They are simply regular finalizers with additional guarantees - designed for a situation where a finalizer code must be executed with certainty, even in case of rude AppDomain or thread abort cases. As MSDN says: "In classes derived from the `CriticalFinalizerObject` class, the common language runtime (CLR) guarantees that all critical finalization code will be given the opportunity to execute, provided the finalizer follows the rules for a *CER* (*Constrained Execution Region*), even in situations where the CLR forcibly unloads an application domain or aborts a thread."

To define a critical finalizer, one must define a finalizer in the `CriticalFinalizerObject`-derived class. The `CriticalFinalizerObject` itself is abstract and has no implementation (see Listing 12-8). It is just yet another contract between type system and the runtime. Runtime makes some precautions to make executing critical finalizers possible in any circumstances. For example, it is JITting critical finalizer code in advance, to avoid a situation when later on there is not enough memory in an out-of-memory exception scenario.

Listing 12-8. Definition of `CriticalFinalizerObject` class (some attributes are omitted for brevity)

```
public abstract class CriticalFinalizerObject
{
    [ReliabilityContract(Consistency.WillNotCorruptState, Cer.MayFail)]
    protected CriticalFinalizerObject()
    {
    }

    [ReliabilityContract(Consistency.WillNotCorruptState, Cer.Success)]
    ~CriticalFinalizerObject()
    {
    }
}
```

Because the undefined order of finalizers execution was sometimes problematic, critical finalizers added some guarantees on that field also. As MSDN says: "the CLR establishes a weak ordering among normal and critical finalizers: for objects reclaimed by garbage collection at the same time, all the noncritical finalizers are called before any of the critical finalizers. For example, a class such as `FileStream`, which holds data in the `SafeHandle` class that is derived from `CriticalFinalizerObject`, can run a standard finalizer to flush out existing buffered data."

You will rarely need to define types derived directly from `CriticalFinalizerObject`. More often, you use them via deriving from `SafeHandle` type (which derive from them). However, because `SafeHandle` type is strictly related both with finalization and Disposable pattern, it is described after both are presented later in this chapter.

Finalization Internals

After learning about the meaning of finalizers, let's now look at how they are currently implemented in the runtime. So far, I put much effort to describe them mostly from the semantic side - what they are designed for, what guarantees they provide, and what limitations they introduce. However, it is also good to understand that their implementation introduces yet another set of disadvantages. Getting to know them is the main purpose of this section.

First of all, as already mentioned in Chapter 6, if a type has a finalizer, a slower allocation path will be used - this is the first important overhead introduced just because a type has Finalize method overridden.

If you would like to investigate slow-allocation path because of finalization in CoreCLR source, start from JIT reaction on CEE_NEWOBJ opcode implemented in JIT importer (importer.cpp:Compiler::impImportBlockCode). It checks inside CEEInfo::getNewHelperStatic whether the type has finalizer defined. If so, CORINFO_HELP_NEWFAST helper is chosen, which is assigned at runtime start to the JIT_New function. Inside it, eventually GCHeap::Alloc or GCHeap::AllocLHeap is called, which at the end contains macro CHECK_ALLOC_AND_POSSIBLY_REGISTER_FOR_FINALIZATION. This macro underneath calls CFinalize::RegisterForFinalization method - responsible for the finalizable objects' bookkeeping described afterward. As mentioned earlier, although ECMA-335 says that finalizers for boxed value types will be called, it is no longer true. When JIT decides what function will represent CORINFO_HELP_BOX helper, finalizer existence is not taken into consideration and most often a fast, assembly-based JIT_BoxFastMP_InlineGetThread helper is used that realizes a simple bump pointer allocation.

The GC must be aware of all finalizable objects, to call their finalizers when they become unreachable. It records these objects on what's called the *finalization queue*. In other words, finalization queue at any moment contains a list of all finalizable objects currently live. If there are many objects in the finalization queue, it does not necessarily mean something bad happened - it means simply that currently there are many objects with a finalizer defined.

During GC, at the end of Mark phase, GC checks the finalization queue to see if any of the finalizable objects are dead. If they are some, they cannot be yet delete because their finalizers will need to be executed. Hence, such object is moved to yet another queue called *fReachable queue*. Its name comes from the fact that it represents *finalization reachable* ([4]) objects - the ones that are now reachable only because of finalization. If there are any such objects found, GC indicates to the dedicated *finalizer thread* there's work to do.

---

[4]Literature calls it "finalizer reachable," but the mentioned name better aligns with the .NET naming.

Finalization thread is yet another thread created by the.NET runtime. It removes objects from the fReachable queue one by one and calls their finalizers. This happens after GC resumes managed threads because finalizer code may need to allocate objects. Since the only root to this object is removed from the fReachable queue, the next GC that condemns the generation this object is in will find it to be unreachable and reclaim it.

Please note, this introduces one of the biggest overhead related to the finalization: a finalizable object by default survives for at least another GC. And if it gets promoted to gen2, it means it would take a gen2 GC to reclaim it instead of a gen1 GC.

Moreover, fReachable queue is treated as a root considered during Mark phase (as mentioned in Chapter 8) because the finalizer thread may not be fast enough to process all objects from it between GCs. This exposes the finalizable objects more to a Mid-life crisis - they may stay in fReachable queue for a while consuming generation 2 just because of pending finalization.

To control such asynchronous nature of finalization processing, the `GC.WaitForPendingFinalizers` method has been exposed. It does exactly what it sounds - it blocks calling thread until all objects have been processed from fReachable queue (that mean, all finalizers have been called). As a side effect, after its call all so-far "finalization reachable" objects have become truly unreachable and thus, subsequent GC will collect them.

This leads us to a very popular, common mantra of "the-ultimate-explicit-garbage-collection" pattern (see Listing 12-9) - commonly used if we want to clean up memory fairly accurately. Seemingly senseless at first glance, those calls have perfect sense:

- first explicit full-blocking GC discovers current set of fReachable objects,

- the thread waits until the GC will process all fReachable objects, making them really unreachable,

- second explicit full-blocking GC reclaims memory after them.

Listing 12-9. Common pattern of explicit GC, taking into account finalization roots

```
GC.Collect();
GC.WaitForPendingFinalizers();
GC.Collect();
```

Obviously, if other threads are allocating finalizable objects during WaitForPendingFinalizers method, at the moment of second GC.Collect call, yet another set of fReachable objects may be discovered. This leads to a paradox - seems we may never be able to fully reclaim memory (at least without aggressively blocking all possibly-allocating threads in the process). This is perfectly visible in the implementation of GC.GetTotalMemory method, returning the total number of bytes currently in use by live objects (see Listing 12-10). If we want to get precise value, we should pass true as its forceFullCollection argument. It then tries to get a true set of currently live objects by triggering full GC and finalization waits multiple times - as long as the result does not stabilize within a 5% change margin (with the maximum iterations limit to not repeat this pattern indefinitely).

Listing 12-10. GC.GetTotalMemory implementation.

```
[System.Security.SecuritySafeCritical]  // auto-generated
public static long GetTotalMemory(bool forceFullCollection) {
   long size = GetTotalMemory();
   if (!forceFullCollection)
      return size;
   // If we force a full collection, we will run the finalizers on all
   // existing objects and do a collection until the value stabilizes.
   // The value is "stable" when either the value is within 5% of the
   // previous call to GetTotalMemory, or if we have been sitting
   // here for more than x times (we don't want to loop forever here).
   int reps = 20;  // Number of iterations
   long newSize = size;
   float diff;
   do {
      GC.WaitForPendingFinalizers();
      GC.Collect();
      size = newSize;
      newSize = GetTotalMemory();
      diff = ((float)(newSize - size)) / size;
   } while (reps-- > 0 && !(-.05 < diff && diff < .05));
   return newSize;
}
```

You can reuse such code from Listing 12-10 as "the-even-more-ultimate-explicit-garbage-collection" pattern (or you may just call GC.GetTotalMemory(true) as long as its implementation does not change). One may be even more aggressive, setting GCSettings.LargeObjectHeapCompactionMode to GCLargeObjectHeapCompactionMode.CompactOnce before first or even each GC.Collect call.

It is thus worth remembering how costly GC.GetTotalMemory call can be in case of forceFullCollection argument being true. In case of very dynamic memory usage pattern, it may call full-blocking GC 20 times! Thus, in large and dynamic applications, be prepared to wait even more than a second for this method result.

There is still one detail not explained so far - as previously said, during GC, finalizable objects only from the condemned and younger generations are considered. To explain it clearly - for example, when generation 1 GC is happening, only finalizable objects from generations 0 and 1 will be considered in the finalization queue and moved to fReachable queue if it becomes unreachable.

It requires a finalization queue to be generation aware - in which generation does the currently considered object live? One could imagine checking each object while finalization queue is being processed - in which generation address boundary it lives within. But remember that generation 2 and LOH may live within multiple segments, thus such check could be costly, consuming precious GC time. So instead, the finalization queue is generational itself - it organizes objects addresses in separate segments, one for each separate generation. Then, only given segments are considered during a particular GC. And yes, it requires promotion or demotion of object addresses between appropriate segments when corresponding objects are promoted or demoted! Do you feel that, yet another one, additional overhead of finalization?

Both finalization and fReachable queues are currently implemented as a single, plain array of object addresses (see Figure 12-1) - I will refer to it herein after as "finalization array." It is logically split into three areas:

- finalization part - further divided into four segments, for the three generations and LOH,

- fReachable part - further divided into segments of object addresses with critical and regular finalizers,

- free part - to be consumed by growing above segment.

Boundaries between segments are managed by yet another, short array of addresses called *fill pointers*. Thus, browsing a finalization queue for a given generations is as easy as accessing subsequent array elements within boundaries designated by appropriate fill pointers. Promotion from finalization to fReachable queue means copying a given address between segments (to the critical or normal part of fReachable area, depending on the finalizer kind). The same as promotion or demotion means copying a given address between source and target generation segments. And because the finalization array is maintained without any gaps, such copying requires in fact shifting all addresses between source and target array elements (and updating fill pointers accordingly).

As said before, a newly created object that contains the finalizer must be added to the finalization queue - this is called *registering for finalization*. From an implementation point of view, such object must be added to the gen0 segment inside finalization array (and yes, this also requires shifting by one element all subsequent elements from Critical and Normal fReachable segments). Because of that, there is a lock around finalization queue access as multiple threads may modify it simultaneously (from its allocators). Additionally, if the finalization array is full, a new 20% bigger copy will be created. This all is obviously yet another overhead of finalization, directly impacting user threads by possibly slowing down allocation - due to the lock usage and copying array elements.

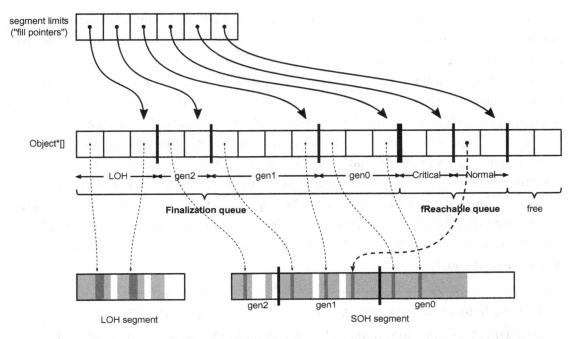

Figure 12-1. *Finalization internals showing finalization and fReachable queues. Only a few object references have been illustrated to not clutter this drawing too much - in reality, all finalization array elements (except the free part) contain a valid address of some object.*

There are two important finalization APIs exposed via GC class. Firstly, there is GC.ReRegisterForFinalize(object) method that allows us to *re-register for finalization* an object that has been already registered. We will see why it may be needed later in this chapter. Underneath GC.ReRegisterForFinalize(object) method call exactly the same runtime methods as used in regular registering for finalization during allocation - thus calling it introduces some overhead similar to described above. However, it is most commonly called from within a finalizer so its overhead is of less importance.

Secondly, in certain scenarios described later, it may be also useful to explicitly disable executing finalizer of finalizable object - a process called *suppressing finalization*. GC.SuppressFinalize(object) method exposes such functionality. Because it is very often called from the user threads (as a part of Disposable pattern), it has been highly optimized. It does not manipulate finalization array at all, as one could expect (for example, by removing such address from it, that would require shifting a lot of subsequent elements). By avoiding synchronized access to the finalization array, it is not exposed to the related overhead. Instead, such method sets a single bit in the object header, which is obviously a very efficient operation. Afterward, `Finalize` method is just not called by finalizer thread for objects with this bit set.

As previously explained, at the end of Mark phase, the GC checks objects for being marked from the appropriate generation's segments of finalization array. If an object is not marked, its address is moved into Critical or Normal fReachable segment.

Later on, finalizer thread reads elements from those segments and updates their fill pointers accordingly (so once read, object lies inside not further scanned "free part" and becomes truly unreachable). With the current implementation, there is a single finalizer thread, and there have been rumors about having multiple finalizer threads but they are not confirmed by the CLR team. From an implementation point of view, it is perfectly possible to have multiple finalizer threads reading and processing fReachable queue items simultaneously.

If you would like to investigate source code of finalization in CoreCLR, start from the `CFinalize` class that realizes the implementation described here. Instances of this class are `gc_heap::finalize_queue` fields so in case of multiple heaps (Server GC), there are in fact multiple finalization arrays (but still single finalization thread). `CFinalize` keeps finalization array as `m_Array` field of `Object**` type (array of `Object` pointers), while fill pointers are managed by `Object**[] m_FillPointers` field (array of pointers to the finalization array elements). At the beginning `m_Array` has 100 elements but is expanded by `CFinalize::GrowArray` method (by creating a 20% bigger array and copying all existing elements) as needed.

`GC.SuppressFinalize` method has very simple implementation, calling `GCHeap::SetFinalizationRun` method that sets `BIT_SBLK_FINALIZER_RUN` bit in the specified object header.

Above-mentioned `GCHeap::RegisterForFinalization` method calls `CFinalize::RegisterForFinalization` method that realizes described logic of shifting appropriate elements (and calling `GrowArray` if needed) to store an object address in the finalize queue.

During Mark phase, `CFinalize::GcScanRoots` method is called that starts marking from objects in both fReachable segments (two last used `m_Array` segments). At the end of Mark phase, `CFinalize::ScanForFinalization` method is called on proper segments (corresponding to condemned and younger generations), that executes finalization promotion - by calling `MoveItem` with appropriate parameters (depending on object having normal or critical finalizer). If there are any fReachable objects found, it signals `hEventFinalizer` event that wakes up the finalizer thread processing. And eventually, at the end of the GC, `CFinalize::UpdatePromotedGenerations` method is called that checks current generation of all objects in the finalization queue and moves them to proper segment accordingly.

The finalizer thread main loop is implemented in `FinalizerThread::FinalizerThreadWorker` method. It indefinitely waits for `hEventFinalizer` event and starts processing if signaled, by calling `FinalizerThread::FinalizeAllObjects` and `FinalizerThread::DoOneFinalization` (that calls `Finalizer` method underneath, if `BIT_SBLK_FINALIZER_RUN` bit is not set).

Careful readers may ask - why are all those queues and dedicated thread used instead of just calling finalizers from within the GC directly? This is a valid question. Remember that finalizer is a user-defined code. Literally everything may be put there by a programmer - including `Thread.Sleep` call for an hour. If the GC called finalizers during its work, it would be blocked for an hour! Even worse, finalizer code could introduce a deadlock and hence, the whole GC would become deadlocked. Executing a user-defined code of finalizers from within the GC would make its pauses completely unpredictable. It is thus much safer to process finalization asynchronously.

Finalization Overhead

What order of magnitude is the finalization overhead? In a general case, it is not so trivial to measure what is the cost of additional object promotion and overall finalization queue handling during GC. We can, however, easily measure the overhead of the slower path of allocation because of finalization handling. It can be done with the help of BenchmarkDotNet simple benchmark of creating multiple finalizable or non-finalizable objects (see Listing 12-11).

Listing 12-11. Simple benchmark to measure overhead of finalizable object allocation

```
public class NonFinalizableClass
{
   public int Value1;
   public int Value2;
   public int Value3;
   public int Value4;
}

public class FinalizableClass
{
   public int Value1;
   public int Value2;
   public int Value3;
   public int Value4;

   ~FinalizableClass()
   {

   }
}

[Benchmark]
public void ConsumeNonFinalizableClass()
{
   for (int i = 0; i < N; ++i)
   {
      var obj = new NonFinalizableClass();
      obj.Value1 = Data;
   }
}

[Benchmark]
public void ConsumeFinalizableClass()
{
```

```
for (int i = 0; i < N; ++i)
{
    var obj = new FinalizableClass();
    obj.Value1 = Data;
}
}
```

Results are eye opening (see Listing 12-12). Allocating the small finalizable object is about 40 times slower than a regular one in such simple scenario (and indeed there are gen1 GCs because of additional promotion)! Underlying JITed assembly code is identical for both methods (with the exception of the allocator function called). This may not be a problem if finalizable object is created rarely, but think twice before adding finalizer to the object with high-allocation rate consumed in the performance-critical path of your application.

Listing 12-12. Results of BenchmarkDotNet benchmarks from Listing 12-11 (Gen 0 and Gen 1 columns show the average number of generation 0 and 1 GCs per single test execution)

Method	N	Mean	Gen 0	Gen 1	Allocated
ConsumeNonFinalizableClass	1	2.777 ns	0.0076	-	32 B
ConsumeFinalizableClass	1	132.138 ns	0.0074	0.0036	32 B
ConsumeNonFinalizableClass	10	30.667 ns	0.0762	-	320 B
ConsumeFinalizableClass	10	1,342.092 ns	0.0744	0.0362	320 B
ConsumeNonFinalizableClass	100	316.633 ns	0.7625	-	3200 B
ConsumeFinalizableClass	100	13,607.436 ns	0.7477	0.3662	3200 B
ConsumeNonFinalizableClass	1000	3,244.837 ns	7.6256	-	32000 B
ConsumeFinalizableClass	1000	131,725.089 ns	7.5684	3.6621	32000 B

Knowing all the implementation details described so far, we can summarize finalization as having the following disadvantages:

- it forces slower allocation by default, including the overhead of manipulating finalization queue during allocation,

- it promotes finalizable object at least once by default, making Mid-life crisis more likely,

- it introduces some overhead of finalizable objects handling even while they are still alive - mostly keeping up-to-date generational finalization list,

- may be dangerous if allocation rate of finalization objects is higher than their finalization rate (see below scenario 12-1).

Scenario 12-1. Finalization Memory Leak

Description: Our application memory usage grows in time constantly. Both \.NET CLR Memory\# Bytes in all Heaps and \.NET CLR Memory\Gen 2 heap size counters are increasing. We would like to investigate such memory leak but nothing obvious is visible. This scenario simulates a rather unusual but yet possible cause of the memory leak.

There is one subtle memory leak possibility. Because finalizers from fReachable queue are executed sequential, it takes longer to process it when some finalizers are slow to execute. If allocation rate of finalizable objects is higher than finalization rate, the fReachable queue will grow, gathering all finalizable objects pending for finalization. This is yet another one reason why finalization code should be as simple as possible.

Let's re-create such an evil finalizers problem with the code from Listing 12-13. Sample application is creating finalizable objects much faster than finalizers are able to run. Simulating a high-traffic scenario, when we already hitting the Mid-life crisis problem, GC is happening very often.[5]

Listing 12-13. Experimental code showing memory leak because of finalization

```
public class LeakyApplication
{
    public void Run()
    {
        while (true)
        {
            Thread.Sleep(100);
            var obj = new EvilFinalizableClass(10, 10000);
            GC.KeepAlive(obj); // prevent optimizing out obj completely
```

[5]For simplicity it happens on each iteration although we could call it, for example, periodically. Such a little contrived example allows us to better illustrate some diagnostic problems.

```
        GC.Collect();
    }
  }
}

public class EvilFinalizableClass
{
    private readonly int finalizationDelay;

    public EvilFinalizableClass(int allocationDelay, int finalizationDelay)
    {
        this.finalizationDelay = finalizationDelay;
        Thread.Sleep(allocationDelay);
    }

    ~EvilFinalizableClass()
    {
        Thread.Sleep(finalizationDelay);
    }
}
```

We already know the reason of the leak but let's see how it looks from the diagnostics point of view. By the way, I hope we already know the solution also - just avoid finalizers and when you really, really need them, take as much care as possible to make it fast and simple.

Analysis: Let's start from the less intrusive and the easiest tool - performance counters. When we look at such application behavior in time, indeed we will notice that generation 2 is growing constantly (see thin line in Figure 12-2). There are also two finalization-related performance counters to look at:

- \.NET CLR Memory \Finalization Survivors - count of objects surviving the last GC because of finalization (to be more precise - the number of objects that were moved from finalization to fReachable queue during last GC).

- \.NET CLR Memory\Promoted Finalization-Memory from Gen 0 - total size of objects surviving the last GC because of finalization (so like above, total sum of objects that were moved from finalization to fReachable queue). Please note an important fact - besides the misleading name of this counter, it considers objects from all collected generations, not only from generation 0.

Remember that in the absence of performance counters, you can gain this information from ETW/LLTng events: GCHeapStats_V1 event contains exactly the same values as FinalizationPromotedCount and FinalizationPromotedSize fields accordingly.

But those two counters in Figure 12-2 are completely stable showing promotion of a single object with a 24bytes size. It would not alarm us for sure during such application monitoring. This is because GC happens after each object allocation, which means each GC only promoted one finalizable object. Please note that those counters are related to the allocation rate of finalization objects - the more such objects will be created, the more will be promoted (because of finalization). Those counters do not depict what is happening to those promoted objects.

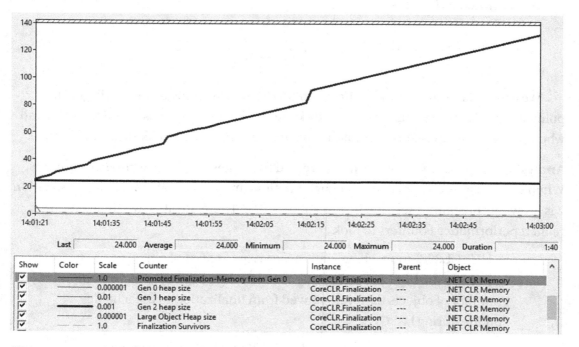

Figure 12-2. *Finalization-related Performance Counters*

Unfortunately, there is no counter for finalization rate nor fReachable queue size. Analyzing such problem as we have is very unpleasant because many tools do not count fReachable queue into memory measurements at all - those objects were already considered dead by user code and the fReachable queue is the only root. Some tools will show `EvilFinalizableClass` instances as unreachable (if at all), which is not alarming and typically we will not look for memory leak reasons there (after all, they are unreachable so they could not be the cause of the problem, right?). Because of that, we move directly into finalization problem analysis. However, a typical way of approaching "gen2 size keeps increasing" problem would be to look to what's holding onto objects in gen2 (for example, by analyzing heap snapshot in PerfView or memory in WinDbg with the help of SOS extension). We will look at such analyses soon also.

We can help ourselves in finalization monitoring with the finalization-related ETW events from `Microsoft-Windows-DotNETRuntime/GC` group (recorded if standard .NET option is used from PerfViews's Collect dialog):

- `FinalizersStart` - emitted when finalizer thread wakes up after GC to start finalization,

- `FinalizeObject` - emitted for each finalizable object processed by finalization thread,

- `FinalizersStop` - emitted at the end of finalization current batch of objects (when all objects from fReachable queue were processed).

Looking at those events in recorded PerfView session quickly reveals our problem (see Figure 12-3). While there is a single and quick finalization run at the beginning of the application, the subsequent one is clearly misbehaving - there is a 10second delay between each finalizer execution! And until new `EvilFinalizableClass` instances will be created, the finalization thread will never be able to catch up (thus, we won't see `FinalizersStop` event any more).

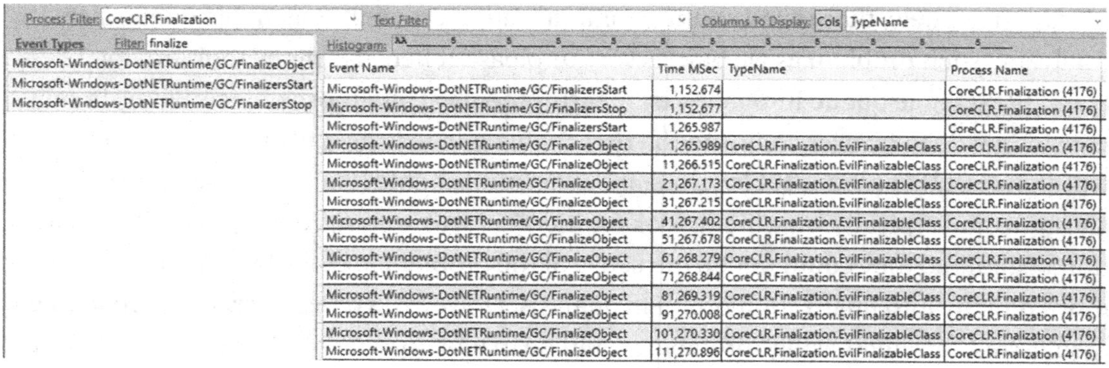

Figure 12-3. *Finalization-related ETW events*

Obviously in a real-world application, such a problem will be more subtle. But generally, long running finalization may be diagnosed in this way.

While observing the long finalization times is a useful clue, it would be much better to observe the root cause - the growing fReachable queue. Unfortunately, currently PerfView heap snapshots do not list fReachable queue roots,[6] but only the finalization queue (see Figure 12-4). Other tools, similarly, most often will list such objects simply as unreachable, without the possibility to investigate fReachable queue directly.

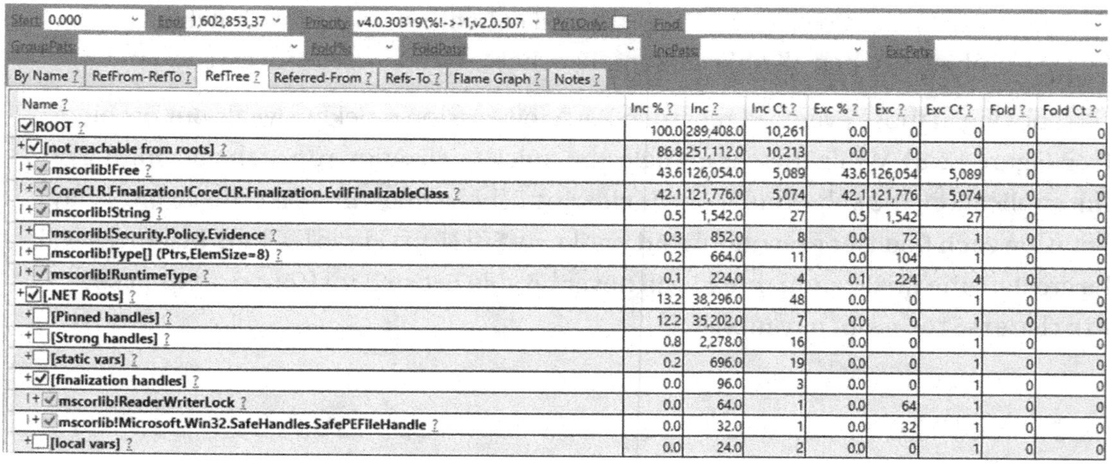

Figure 12-4. *Roots in heap snapshots do not show fReachable queue.*

---

[6]There is an issue `https://github.com/Microsoft/perfview/issues/722` created to fix that, so you can track it whether it has been already fixed at the time of your reading.

However, there is the possibility of a closer look at both the finalization queue and fReachable queue using WinDbg. While during live debugging or memory dump analysis, we may issue !finalizequeue SOS command (see Listing 12-14), which will provide very detailed information. As we can see, it informs both about "finalizable objects" (with respect to generations as finalization queue is generational) and "ready for finalization" objects that are nothing else than objects in fReachable queue. Clearly, we see the problem - there are 5,175 fReachable objects in our case!

Listing 12-14. Using finalizequeue command from SOS to investigate finalization queues

```
> !finalizequeue
SyncBlocks to be cleaned up: 0
Free-Threaded Interfaces to be released: 0
MTA Interfaces to be released: 0
STA Interfaces to be released: 0
-----------------------------------
generation 0 has 1 finalizable objects (000001751fe7e700->000001751fe7e708)
generation 1 has 0 finalizable objects (000001751fe7e700->000001751fe7e700)
generation 2 has 2 finalizable objects (000001751fe7e6f0->000001751fe7e700)
Ready for finalization 5175 objects (000001751fe7e708->000001751fe888c0)
Statistics for all finalizable objects (including all objects ready for
finalization):
              MT      Count    TotalSize Class Name
00007ffcee93c3e0         1           32 Microsoft.Win32.SafeHandles.
SafePEFileHandle
00007ffcee93d680         1           64 System.Threading.ReaderWriterLock
00007ffc93a35c98      5176       124224 CoreCLR.Finalization.
EvilFinalizableClass
Total 5178 objects
```

We may further investigate only fReachable queue by issuing command with an additional -allReady parameter (see Listing 12-15). Now everything is clear and in line with our expectations, there are 5,175 instances of EvilFinalizableClass. Having so many fReachable objects is rather alarming. We could additionally confirm that as a problem by taking further dumps and see whether this number is growing.

Listing 12-15. Using `finalizequeue` command from SOS to investigate only fReachable queue

> **!finalizequeue -allReady**
SyncBlocks to be cleaned up: 0
Free-Threaded Interfaces to be released: 0
MTA Interfaces to be released: 0
STA Interfaces to be released: 0
----
generation 0 has 1 finalizable objects (000001751fe7e700->000001751fe7e708)
generation 1 has 0 finalizable objects (000001751fe7e700->000001751fe7e700)
generation 2 has 2 finalizable objects (000001751fe7e6f0->000001751fe7e700)
Finalizable but not rooted:
Ready for finalization 5175 objects (000001751fe7e708->000001751fe888c0)
Statistics for all finalizable objects that are no longer rooted:
              MT   Count   TotalSize Class Name
00007ffc93a35c98   5175   124200 CoreCLR.Finalization.EvilFinalizableClass
Total 5175 objects

Please also note address ranges of corresponding finalizable objects segments from the underlying finalization array (given in parentheses). We can dump content of this array within given ranges to get concrete finalizable object references (see Listing 12-16 showing the range of fReachable queue).

Listing 12-16. Seeing the content of fReachable queue

> **dq 000001751fe7e708 000001751fe888c0**
. . .
00000175`1fe88888    00000175`21850358 00000175`21850388
00000175`1fe88898    00000175`218503b8 00000175`218503e8
00000175`1fe888a8    00000175`21850418 00000175`21850448
00000175`1fe888b8    00000175`21850478 00000175`2182ae28
> **!do 00000175`2182ae28**
Name: CoreCLR.Finalization.EvilFinalizableClass
MethodTable: 00007ffc93a35c98
EEClass: 00007ffc93b41208
Size: 24(0x18) bytes
. . .

774

Similar analysis may be performed with the help of SOSEX extension, by issuing `finq` and `frq` commands for investigation finalization and fReachable queues accordingly (see Listing 12-17). I'm referring to it here because the output of those commands seems to be a little nicer than from their SOS counterpart.

Listing 12-17. Using `finq` and `frq` commands from SOSEX to investigate both finalization queues

```
> .load g:\Tools\Sosex\64bit\sosex.dll
> !finq -stat
Generation 0:
      Count      Total Size   Type
--------------------------------------------------------------
         1               24   CoreCLR.Finalization.EvilFinalizableClass

1 object, 24 bytes

Generation 1:
0 objects, 0 bytes

Generation 2:
      Count      Total Size   Type
------------------------------------------------------------
         1               32   Microsoft.Win32.SafeHandles.SafePEFileHandle
         1               64   System.Threading.ReaderWriterLock

2 objects, 96 bytes

TOTAL: 3 objects, 120 bytes

> !frq -stat
Freachable Queue:
      Count      Total Size   Type
------------------------------------------------------------
      5175           124200   CoreCLR.Finalization.EvilFinalizableClass

5,175 objects, 124,200 bytes
```

Currently the `!mex.finalizable` command in MEX WinDbg extension seems to be not listing fReachable objects properly in case of .NET Core apps.

Resurrection

There is one very interesting topic related to the finalization. As we already know, the finalizer is called when the only object's root is the fReachable queue. Finalizer thread is calling `Finalize` method and afterward, its reference is removed from the queue. Thus, it becomes unreachable and will be collected in the next GC that collects that generation.

But any user code is allowed in `Finalize` method, which is an instance method (having access to `this`). Thus, nothing can stop us from assigning an object's own reference (`this`) to some globally accessible (like static) root - and of all a sudden our object becomes reachable again (see Listing 12-18)! This is called *resurrection* and is inherently related with the fact that finalizer is an uncontrolled user code.

Listing 12-18. Example of object resurrection (not fully correct)

```
class FinalizableObject
{
    ~FinalizableObject()
    {
        Program.GlobalFinalizableObject = this;
    }
}
```

Object that just was to be collected, becomes a normal reachable object again. Now its global reference (like `Program.GlobalFinalizableObject` in our example) is the only root, but of course it may further expand to other roots if we wish it to.

But what happens if the resurrected object becomes unreachable again? Will it be collected or resurrected again? To answer that question, let's recall that registering for finalization happens during object allocation. After finalizer has been executed, object reference disappears from the fReachable queue. Resurrection does not put it again in finalization queue, so when `FinalizableObject` instance from Listing 12-18 becomes unreachable the second time, its finalizer will not be called - it is simply not in a finalization queue to be discovered!

But when using resurrection, most commonly we would like to resurrect an object always, not only once. Thus, already mentioned `GC.ReRegisterForFinalize` method must be used to register an object for finalization once again (see Listing 12-19). After doing so, we are creating an immortal object - it will never be garbage collected. Please note this is not entirely true for the simplified example from Listing 12-19 because we may create multiple instances of `FinalizableObject` class and there will be a race condition - only the last finalized object will be re-registered for finalization and thus properly resurrected!

Listing 12-19. Example of object resurrection (corrected Listing 12-18)

```
class FinalizableObject
{
    ~FinalizableObject()
    {
        Program.GlobalFinalizableObject = this;
        GC.ReRegisterForFinalize(this);
    }
}
```

Resurrection is not a very popular technique. It is rarely used even in Microsoft's own code. This is because it plays with an object's lifetime in a hidden way. It is a finalization on steroids - taking all its disadvantages and doubling them.

One could imagine an object pooling based on resurrection - finalizer may be responsible for returning an object to some shared pool (resurrecting it), like in Listing 12-20. But the `EvilPool` name and missing implementation details are there not without a reason. There are much better ways how an object pool may be implemented, based on explicit pool management (like in `ArrayPool<T>` showed in Chapter 6). There is no special advantage of making such a pool management implicit. Keeping in mind every caveat of implementing finalizers, not using them is often the best solution (especially if simpler alternatives exist). Please feel invited, however, to implement `EvilPool` on your own as an exercise, regardless of its practical usage - it is a lot of learning fun!

Listing 12-20. Example of practical object resurrection

```
public class EvilPool<T> where T : class
{
    static private List<T> items = new List<T>();
    static public void ReturnToPool(T obj)
```

```
    {
        // ...
        // Add obj to items
        GC.ReRegisterForFinalize(obj);
    }

    static public T GetFromPool() { ... }
}
public class SomeClass
{
    ~SomeClass()
    {
        EvilPool<SomeClass>.ReturnToPool(this);
    }
}
```

Each object defining a finalizer is exposed to calls of `GC.ReRegisterForFinalize` and `GC.SuppressFinalize` methods because they expect just a plain object argument (internally checking whether indeed such object has finalizer defined). It means, we may play with the object resource management, by having some control over how its finalizer is being called. This may be undesirable for some objects. One good example is `System.Threading.Timer` type, which provides a mechanism for period method execution on a thread pool, at specified intervals. Finalization related to `Timer` that tells the thread pool to cancel the timer. So, for example, by calling `GC.SuppressFinalize` on such object, we are controlling the timer behavior in an unusual way - it would be never stopped. This may be or may not be a poor design decision. But in most such scenarios, it is rather unexpected that we control internal behavior of an object in such way.

If we really want to rely on finalization but do not want to expose our type to such problems, we should exclude the possibility to temper with our finalizer. The first step is making our class sealed, to not allow overriding `Finalize` in derived class. The second step is to introduce some helper, or finalizable object, that is responsible for finalization of our main object. Exactly such approach was chosen during `System.Threading.Timer` type implementation. Simplified form of such approach is presented in Listing 12-21. Internal, private class `TimerHolder` holds a reference to our main `Timer` object. When

Timer instance becomes unreachable, so timerHolder field does - triggering its finalizer that is responsible for cleaning parent object (please note that part of Disposable pattern is included in this example).

Listing 12-21. Simplified Timer class implementation (using nested finalizable object)

```
public sealed class Timer : IDisposable
{
    private TimerHolder timerHolder;

    public Timer()
    {
        timerHolder = new TimerHolder(this);
    }

    private sealed class TimerHolder
    {
        internal Timer m_timer;

        public TimerHolder(Timer timer) => m_timer = timer;

        ~TimerHolder() => m_timer?.Close();

        public void Close()
        {
            m_timer.Close();
            GC.SuppressFinalize(this);
        }
    }

    public void Close()
    {
        Console.WriteLine("Finalizing Timer!");
    }

    public void Dispose()
    {
        timerHolder.Close();
    }
```

In that way we are introducing finalization without publicly exposing it - `Timer` is not finalizable by itself! `GC.SuppressFinalize` and `GC.ReRegisterForFinalize` cannot be called on it.

Does it make sense to call `GC.ReRegisterForFinalize` in resurrection scenarios when resurrected object is not assigned to any root (for example, without `Program.GlobalFinalizableObject = this` code in Listing 12-19)? Absolutely! What will happen then? Re-registered object will land in finalization queue to be processed in the next GC. And the whole cycle begins again - it will be promoted to fReachable queue and its finalizer will be eventually called... again resurrecting such object. We may create that way an immortal object that will be ever only referenced by the finalization queues. One example why it may be useful is presented in the Listing 12-37 later in this chapter. However, more often such re-registering for finalization is optional - that way we may trigger finalizer code multiple times (if finalization logic is so complicated or crucial that it makes sense to do it). But please remember - this is absolutely not a design pattern you should follow. Just be aware that this such possibility exists.

Disposable Objects

So far a lot of words have been spoken about non-deterministic finalization. Let's now move to the preferred way of resources cleanup - deterministic, explicit finalization. It is conceptually much simpler than non-deterministic finalization using finalizers - and it makes it one of their strongest advantages. There are no so many finalization caveats and disadvantages. In fact, conceptually there are just only two methods:

- one for initialization - used to create and store resources. In case of .NET this is obviously runtime-supported constructor, called during object allocation.

- one for cleanup - used to release resources. In case of .NET there is no runtime-supported method for it. Your mileage may vary how to name it.

Combing back to the simple FileWrapper class from Listing 12-1, getting rid of finalization and introducing explicit cleanup, we will end in code similar to Listing 12-22. Cleanup method is just a regular method to be called and it releases all relevant resources inside. Additional UseMe method has been added, compared to Listing 12-1, for further the purpose of examples.

Listing 12-22. Simple example of using explicit cleanup

```
class FileWrapper
{
    private IntPtr handle;
    public FileWrapper(string filename)
    {
        Unmanaged.OFSTRUCT s;
        handle = Unmanaged.OpenFile(filename, out s, 0x00000000);
    }

    // Cleanup
    public void Close()
    {
        if (handle != IntPtr.Zero)
            Unmanaged.CloseHandle(handle);
    }

    public int UseMe()
    {
        byte[] buffer = new byte[1];
        if (Unmanaged.ReadFile(this.handle, buffer, 1, out uint read,
        IntPtr.Zero))
        {
            return buffer[0];
        }
        return -1;
    }
}
```

World is so simple when using explicit cleanup (see Listing 12-23). Everything is executed in visible order so there are no surprises here. All object usage is enclosed by its initialization (constructor) and cleanup methods so early root collection will not kick us back here either. We perfectly know when an underlying resource is allocated and released.

Listing 12-23. Usage of `FileWrapper` from Listing 12-22

```
var file = new FileWrapper(@"C:\temp.txt");
Console.WriteLine(file.UseMe());
file.Close();
```

If this approach is so ideal, why did someone even bother to invent an alternative? Obviously, this approach has one huge disadvantage - programmer must remember to call cleanup method. If it fails to do so, we will leak our (probably limited) resource.

To help with that, explicit cleanup has been standardized in C# by introducing IDisposable interface. Its definition is more than trivial (see Listing 12-24). It is a contract that simply says, "I have something that should be cleaned up when I finish my work."

Listing 12-24. IDisposable interface declaration

```
namespace System {
   public interface IDisposable {
      void Dispose();
   }
}
```

Thus, following this design, `FileWrapper` from Listing 12-24 should implement IDisposable interface and its `Dispose` implementation should call `Close` method (or it should replace it as in Listing 12-25).

Listing 12-25. Simple example of using explicit cleanup with IDisposable interface

```
class FileWrapper : IDisposable
{
   private IntPtr handle;
   public FileWrapper(string filename)
```

```
{
    Unmanaged.OFSTRUCT s;
    handle = Unmanaged.OpenFile(filename, out s, 0x00000000);
}

// Cleanup
public void Dispose()
{
    if (handle != IntPtr.Zero)
        Unmanaged.CloseHandle(handle);
}

public int UseMe()
{
    byte[] buffer = new byte[1];
    if (Unmanaged.ReadFile(this.handle, buffer, 1, out uint read,
    IntPtr.Zero))
    {
        return buffer[0];
    }
    return -1;
}
```

Having such a well-established contract helps in various manual and automatic code reviews. If someone creates instance of type implementing IDisposable interface (hereinafter simply called *disposable object*) but never calls its Dispose method, it is a great candidate to be banished. Especially various automatic tools may help here (like ReSharper).

As said in IDisposable interface comment: "This interface could be theoretically used as a marker by a compiler to ensure a disposable object has been cleaned up along all code paths if it's been allocated in that method, though in practice any compiler that draconian may tick off any number of people."

Because language relying on external tools does not sound impressive, C# standardization of explicit cleanup went even further by introducing the *using clause*. It is yet another simple construct that relieves us from the need to manually call Dispose (see Listing 12-26).

Listing 12-26. Example of using clause

```
public static void Main()
{
    using (var file = new FileWrapper())
    {
        Console.WriteLine(file.UseMe());
    }
}
```

Using clause is translated by C# compiler into corresponding try-finally block, in which Dispose method will be called inside finally block (see Listing 12-27). Note that it also gives us confidence that early root collection will not collect an object instance too early, because its Dispose method is called at the end.

Listing 12-27. Resulting code of using clause (from Listing 12-26)

```
public static void Main()
{
    FileWrapper fileWrapper = new FileWrapper();
    try
    {
        Console.WriteLine(file.UseMe());
    }
    finally
    {
        if (fileWrapper != null)
        {
            ((IDisposable)fileWrapper).Dispose();
        }
    }
}
```

However, even having using clause does not guarantee that programmers will be using it. In other words, still nothing stops them from simply instantiating disposable objects and forgetting to call its Dispose method. Using clause is just a good practice.

If from your resource management perspective cleanup code is crucial (and most probably it is), you have namely two possible approaches:

- Be polite and ask your programmers to always call Dispose method of disposable objects - although it sounds a little ridiculous, in fact it is the preferred way. Already-mentioned tools can help you, especially if the requirement is even stronger - that disposable object is always used within using clause. It can be easily discovered and, for example, a pull request may not be accepted if it contains such misbehaving code.

- Create a safety net by utilizing finalizer to call Dispose - this is a quite popular approach. If Dispose was not called explicitly, finalizer will call it on our behalf. There is only one drawback - we are using finalizers while generally it is good to avoid them. Such simple, protecting finalizer code may be really simple so we can assume that there are not so many finalizer-related implementation problems related with it. But still, we are introducing a little overhead of slower allocation and need to maintain one more object in finalization queue. Be sure then that you are using such an approach for something important.

When using the second approach, if the only finalizer's responsibility is to clean up resources by calling Dispose, it not need be called if the well-behaving programmer already called Dispose explicitly. Exactly for that purpose an already-mentioned GC.SuppressFinalize method was introduced - it disables calling finalizer of the object. This leads to very popular pattern, where Dispose method calls GC.SuppressFinalize as a finalizer is no longer needed. Very concise example of such approach may be found inside System.Reflection library in the form of abstract CriticalDisposableObject (see Listing 12-28). It implements critically a finalizable object that uses a finalizer as such a safety net call.

Listing 12-28. `System.Reflection` internal type `CriticalDisposableObject`

```
namespace System.Reflection.Internal
{
    internal abstract class CriticalDisposableObject :
    CriticalFinalizerObject, IDisposable
    {
        protected abstract void Release();

        public void Dispose()
        {
            Release();
            GC.SuppressFinalize(this);
        }

        ~CriticalDisposableObject()
        {
            Release();
        }
    }
}
```

Generally, using both explicit cleanup in the form of `IDisposable` and protecting, implicit cleanup in the form finalization has developed into a form of so-called *Disposable pattern* (or *IDisposable pattern*). It is a little more structured way of combining those both approaches (see Listing 12-29). Disposable pattern may be seen as almost standard in the .NET world. The main difference is the introduction of a virtual `Dispose` method that is both used from finalizer (with its `disposing` argument set to `false`) and from explicit `Dispose` method (with `disposing` parameter set to `true`). Deriving classes are then able to add their own specific cleanup code, while still the whole finalization logic stays. Additionally, a dedicated `disposed` field prevents multiple disposal of such object. Each public method should check this flag and (typically) throw `ObjectDisposedException` to inform that this instance should not be longer used.

Listing 12-29. Simple example of using both implicit and explicit cleanup with IDisposable pattern

```
class FileWrapper : IDisposable
{
   private bool disposed = false;

   private IntPtr handle;
   public FileWrapper(string filename)
   {
      Unmanaged.OFSTRUCT s;
      handle = Unmanaged.OpenFile(filename, out s, 0x00000000);
   }

   // Cleanup
   protected virtual void Dispose(bool disposing)
   {
      if (!disposed)
      {
         if (disposing)
         {
            // Put here code required only in case of explicit Dispose call
         }

         // Common cleanup - including unmanaged resources
         if (handle != IntPtr.Zero)
            Unmanaged.CloseHandle(handle);
         disposed = true;
      }
   }

    ~FileWrapper()
   {
      Dispose(false);
   }
```

```
public void Dispose()
{
   Dispose(true);
   GC.SuppressFinalize(this);
}

public int UseMe()
{
   if (this.disposed) throw new ObjectDisposedException("...");

   byte[] buffer = new byte[1];
   if (Unmanaged.ReadFile(this.handle, buffer, 1, out uint read,
   IntPtr.Zero))
   {
      return buffer[0];
   }
   return -1;
}
}
```

Disposable objects and using a clause may be also used to realize simple reference counting techniques, like in the Listing 7-3 from Chapter 7. Dedicated helper class is introduced, used within a using clause. Its constructor adds a reference counter, while Dispose method decrements it. If it hits zero, target object cleanup is triggered. Obviously, we may be double protected by incorporating whole Disposable pattern to such class, making sure that the cleanup will happen even if the reference counting logic misbehaved.

Generally, giving a voice to IDisposable interface comment from .NET sources, implemented Dispose method should meet the following criteria:

- Be safely callable multiple times,

- Release any resources associated with the instance,

- Call the base class's Dispose method, if necessary,

- Suppress finalization of this class to help the GC by reducing the number of objects on the finalization queue,[7]

- `Dispose` shouldn't generally throw exceptions, except for very serious errors that are particularly unexpected. (i.e., `OutOfMemoryException`).

After all those words said about `IDisposable`, disposable objects and `Disposable` patterns, please, remember - they have nothing directly in common with the GC! `Dispose` method is not reclaiming object's memory, it is not killing them, and so on, so forth. If you were to remember only one thing from this part of the chapter, just remember it. As you noticed, almost nothing about the runtime (besides mentioning finalization) was mentioned here. Disposable objects are implemented purely on the language level.

Safe Handles

Implementing finalizers have many caveats. Most of the time, unmanaged resources are represented simply by some handle or pointer - thus `IntPtr` type. Those two facts lead to introducing a new type helping to deal with unmanaged resources. In .NET Framework 2.0, together with critical finalizers, a `SafeHandle` object was introduced built on top of it. They were introduced as a much better alternative to the previously mentioned approaches of managing system resources (including finalizers, bare `IntPtr`, and `HandleRef`). As said, it comes from the observation that almost all handles may be represented as `IntPtr`, thus it wraps them with an additional default behavior and the support from the runtime itself.

So instead of implementing a finalizer, the preferred and suggested alternative is to create a type that derives from the abstract `System.Runtime.InteropServices.SafeHandle` class (see Listing 12-30) and use it as handle wrapper. Having much of the logic already implemented, we are less exposed to any problem we may introduce implementing our own finalization logic. As we may see, `SafeHandle` is critically finalizable and implements Disposable pattern. Both its `Dispose` and `Finalize` logic is in fact internal (implemented in the runtime itself).

---

[7]As explained earlier, suppressing finalization logic is trivial, based only on setting a single bit in an object header. Thus, we should not be afraid of its overhead (for example, by calling it twice on the same object both from the derived as well as from the base class).

Listing 12-30. Fragments of the SafeHandle class (a lot of code, including members attributes, are omitted for brevity)

```
public abstract class SafeHandle : CriticalFinalizerObject, IDisposable
{
    protected IntPtr handle;    // this must be protected so derived classes
                                  can use out params.
    private int _state;    // Combined ref count and closed/disposed flags
                             (so we can atomically modify them).

    ~SafeHandle()
    {
        Dispose(false);
    }

    public void Dispose() {
        Dispose(true);
    }

    protected virtual void Dispose(bool disposing)
    {
        if (disposing)
            InternalDispose();
        else
            InternalFinalize();
    }

    [MethodImplAttribute(MethodImplOptions.InternalCall)]
    extern void InternalFinalize();

    [MethodImplAttribute(MethodImplOptions.InternalCall)]
    private extern void InternalDispose();

    public abstract bool IsInvalid { get; }

    protected abstract bool ReleaseHandle();
}
```

`InternalDispose` and `InternalFinalize` methods are implemented by `SafeHandle::DisposeNative` and `SafeHandle::Finalize` respectively in CoreCLR code. Both `SafeHandle::DisposeNative` and `SafeHandle::Finalize` calls `SafeHandle::Dispose` that calls `SafeHandle::Release` - the main horse-work method. It calls `IsInvalidHandle` managed method and if it is true, it calls managed `ReleaseHandle` method (via `SafeHandle::RunReleaseMethod`).

Special treatment from the runtime gives `SafeHandle` more than just being a good design practice. What is the most important, CLR treats instances of this class in special way during P/Invoke calls - it is protected from being garbage collected (like `HandleRef`), and for security reasons it implements reference counting semantics. It means each such P/Invoke call has JITed logic to increment an internal reference counter and decrement it at the end of the call. Only instances with a zeroed reference counter will release their handle. And only for zeroed reference counter explicit cleanup will it indeed release the resource. This prevents so-called malicious handle-recycling attack (see note below).

Handle-recycling attack.

There is a subtle security flaw possible with bare usage of system handles (like the most popular `IntPtr` representation used so far in `FileWrapper` examples). In case of Windows, system handles are reused (recycled) aggressively - because they are treated as a very limited, system-wide resource. So-called handle-recycling attack may be used inside a single .NET process to get an elevated privilege from an untrusted thread (with limited security permissions) to the handle otherwise accessible only from fully trusted thread. Such attack may be used when a managed object holding a handle provides some explicit termination method, like in popular Disposable pattern. Attacking, untrusted thread may explicitly clean up such resource (closing underlying handle, but still remembering handle value) while it is being used by other threads. Those other threads will most probably experience some kind of state corruption errors because suddenly their handle was closed. Moreover, simultaneously, other full-trusted thread may have just opened a new resource and received the same, recycled handle value. Attacking thread has now handle value pointing to a new resource, possibly not otherwise accessible to it.

Thus, using SafeHandles provides many advantages over their alternatives:

- They are critically finalizable, making them more reliable than regular finalizers, without the necessity to write custom finalizers code - which removes from the programmer the obligation to avoid multiple finalization code dangers.

- They are minimal wrappers around unmanaged resource (handle) - this eliminates the risk of creating large objects with numerous dependencies that will be promoted due to finalization.

- Our object does not need to be finalizable at all - when an object holding and using SafeHandle-derived object becomes unreachable, such wrapper will become also unreachable. So eventually its finalizer will be called, releasing the handle.

- Better lifetime management - special treatment from the GC during P/Invoke calls keeps them alive, instead of GC.KeepAlive magic or using HandleRef.

- Strongly typing instead of using pure IntPtr because there are multiple SafeHandle-derived types for various resources - so P/Invoke APIs are not cluttered with meaningless IntPtr handles. You will not be able to pass file handle to Mutex API, and so on, so forth.

- Better security by preventing handle-recycling attack.

Unfortunately, besides long existence in .NET ecosystem, SafeHandles seem to be still quite unpopular in regular code (while its usage in framework itself is quite common). Most often people tend to use plain finalization logic, even when wrapping around simple IntPtr handles.

If you are interested how JIT is handling special treatment of SafeHandle, start from the ILSafeHandleMarshaler::ArgumentOverride method. It underneath calls SafeHandle::AddRef and SafeHandle::Release respectively around P/Invoke call.

Meanwhile, defining SafeHandle-based types is trivial. When you inherit from SafeHandle, you must override only two members: IsInvalid and ReleaseHandle. There are even two more specialized abstract classes created for convenience:[8] SafeHandleMinusOneIsInvalid and SafeHandleZeroOrMinusOneIsInvalid that provide trivial IsInvalid implementations (with checks suggested by their names).

In derived class we have access to the protected IntPtr handle, we can also set it via SetHandle method. To improve FileWrapper, we first need to create our custom file SafeHandle (see Listing 12-31). The core logic in SafeHandle-derived class lies in its constructor (allocating handle) and implementation of ReleaseHandle method.

Listing 12-31. Example implementation of SafeHandle-derived class

```
class CustomFileSafeHandle : SafeHandleZeroOrMinusOneIsInvalid {
    // Called by P/Invoke when returning SafeHandles. Valid handle value
    will be set afterwards.
    private CustomFileSafeHandle() : base(true)
    {
    }

    // If and only if you need to support user-supplied handles
    internal CustomFileSafeHandle (IntPtr preexistingHandle, bool
    ownsHandle) : base(ownsHandle)
    {
        SetHandle(preexistingHandle);
    }

    internal CustomFileSafeHandle(string filename) : base(true)
    {
        Unmanaged.OFSTRUCT s;
        IntPtr handle = Unmanaged.OpenFile(filename, out s, 0x00000000);;
        SetHandle(handle);
    }
```

---

[8]They are introduced to provide a standardized way of consuming handles as most often indeed those values are treated as invalid handles.

```
override protected bool ReleaseHandle()
{
    return Unmanaged.CloseHandle(handle);
}
```

Such handle may be then used as a field of our new, improved FileWrapper class (see Listing 12-32). It still implements Disposable pattern like in Listing 12-29. But because now it does not contain unmanaged resources (as unmanaged file handle is hidden inside CustomFileSafeHandle field), finalizer is not necessary. Explicit cleanup will dispose our handle, but in case of forgetting to do it, CustomFileSafeHandle finalizer will do it instead of us.

Listing 12-32. Simple example of using SafeHandle-based resources

```
public class FileWrapper : IDisposable
{
    private bool disposed = false;
    private CustomFileSafeHandle handle;
    public FileWrapper(string filename)
    {
        Unmanaged.OFSTRUCT s;
        handle = Unmanaged.OpenFile(filename, out s, 0x00000000);
    }

    public void Dispose()
    {
        if (!disposed)
        {
            handle?.Dispose();
            disposed = true;
        }
    }

    public int UseMe()
    {
        byte[] buffer = new byte[1];
```

```
    if (Unmanaged.ReadFile(handle, buffer, 1, out uint read, IntPtr.Zero))
    {
        return buffer[0];
    }
    return -1;
  }
}
```

Please note that OpenFile and ReadFile P/Invoke calls visible in Listing 12-32 are returning and accepting CustomFileSafeHandle (see Listing 12-33). It is possible because P/Invoke marshaling mechanism is able to treat SafeHandle-derived class as IntPtr underneath. But it gives us above-mentioned type safety regarding using handles.

Listing 12-33. P/Invoke methods consuming SafeHandle-based handles

```
public static class Unmanaged
{
    [DllImport("kernel32.dll", BestFitMapping = false, ThrowOnUnmappableChar
    = true)]
    public static extern CustomFileSafeHandle OpenFile2([MarshalAs(Unmanaged
    Type.LPStr)]string lpFileName,
        out OFSTRUCT lpReOpenBuff,
        long uStyle);

    [DllImport("kernel32.dll", SetLastError = true)]
    public static extern bool ReadFile(CustomFileSafeHandle hFile,
    [Out] byte[] lpBuffer, uint nNumberOfBytesToRead, out uint
    lpNumberOfBytesRead, IntPtr lpOverlapped);

    ...
}
```

In our example, we even do not need to define custom SafeHandle for file handles. Various predefined safe handles are already implemented for typical resources:

- SafeFileHandle - safe handle for a file handles,

- SafeMemoryMappedFileHandle and SafeMemoryMappedViewHandle - safe handle related to memory-mapped file handles,

- `SafeNCryptKeyHandle`, `SafeNCryptProviderHandle`, and `SafeNCryptSecretHandle` - safe handles for cryptographic resources,

- `SafePipeHandle` - safe handle for named pipes handles,

- `SafeProcessHandle` - safe handle for process,

- `SafeRegistryHandle` - safe handles for registry keys,

- `SafeWaitHandle` - safe wait handle (used for synchronization).

If you are interested in intrinsic (runtime) part of `SafeHandle` implementation, investigate CoreCLR `.\src\vm\safehandle.cpp` file.

If some part of your unmanaged-related code really needs to use `IntPtr` instead of `SafeHandle`, you can get underlying raw handle by `DangerousGetHandle` method. Please note however that it exposes it to the leakage as plain `IntPtr` is not tracked in any way. Thus, you should guard using raw handle from `SafeHandle` by reference counting approach - you inform `SafeHandle` about such usage by calling `DangerousAddRef` and `DangerousRelease` method (implementing reference counting approach).

A large awareness of the existence of finalizers is in fact not so desirable. We should rarely see and even more rarely need to write our custom finalizers. The most use cases may be handled by `SafeHandle` approach.

Weak References

There is one type of handle available but not-yet described that realizes a very interesting type of root - so-called *weak handle*. Conceptually a weak handle is very simple - it stores a reference to an object, but is not treated as a root (it does not make such object reachable). In other words, during Mark phase the GC does not scan weak handles to decide the lifetime of objects. Weak handles are "live" as long as target object is reachable, but they are zeroed when it becomes unreachable.

There are in fact two types of weak handles:

- *short weak handles* - they are zeroed before finalizers run, when GC decides the object is dead. For example, even if finalizer resurrects an object, such handle will remain zeroed.

- *long weak handles* - their target still remains valid when the object is promoted due to finalization. For example, if finalizer resurrects an object, such handle will remain valid (pointing to the same object). Thus, they are said to *track resurrection*.

Let's create a very simple class used in the following examples, with an optional resurrection implemented (see Listing 12-34).

Listing 12-34. A class-implementing resurrection in its finalizer

```
public class LargeClass
{
    private readonly bool ressurect;
    public LargeClass(bool ressurect) => this.ressurect = ressurect;
    ~LargeClass()
    {
        if (ressurect)
        {
            GC.ReRegisterForFinalize(this);
        }
    }
}
```

We create weak handles by using GCHandle.Alloc with GCHandleType.Weak or GCHandleType.WeakTrackResurrection type (see Listings 12-35 and 12-36). Its Target property points to the target object or is null if target was already collected (taking resurrection into consideration or not).

Listing 12-35. Example of short weak handle usage

```
var obj = new LargeClass(ressurect: true);
GCHandle weakHandle = GCHandle.Alloc(obj, GCHandleType.Weak);
GC.Collect();
```

```
GC.WaitForPendingFinalizers();
GC.Collect();
Console.WriteLine(weakHandle.Target ?? "<null>"); // prints <null>
```

Listing 12-36. Example of long weak handle usage

```
var obj = new LargeClass(ressurect: true);
GCHandle weakHandle = GCHandle.Alloc(obj, GCHandleType.
WeakTrackResurrection);
GC.Collect();
GC.WaitForPendingFinalizers();
GC.Collect();
Console.WriteLine(weakHandle.Target ?? "<null>"); // prints CoreCLR.
Finalization.LargeClass
```

We may say that short weak handle is zeroed for the first time an object is to be collected (although it may be resurrected), while long weak handle is zeroed when an object is eventually truly collected.

But why would anyone need something as strange as weak reference? There are two main general situations when they are useful:

- Various types of observers and listeners (like events) - you want to keep reference to an object as long as it is used by someone else. However, we do not want to affect the state of the object by such observation.

- Caching - we may create cache that stores normal references but after some time of no use, they are changed into weak references. So instead of aggressively trimming cache, we will just keep them until the next GC of a given generation (probably generation 2 as objects cached for some time will eventually land there). By controlling the time of such "weak cache eviction," we control the compromise between the memory usage (as we may keep items in cache longer) and the object creation overhead (as they have to be re-created when accessed after cleaning from cache).

There is a very interesting example of the "observer nature" of weak references in the form of Gen2GcCallback class located in the core .NET library (see Listing 12-37). As we should recognize after reading this chapter, it is a critically finalizable object with an optional resurrection. It observes a given target object by holding short weak reference to it. Given callback is executed on each finalization - thus on each GC of the generation where the target object lives. After two GCs it will land in generation 2, thus this is "mostly generation 2 callback" - executed on each gen2 collection and two first ephemeral collections (see the opening comment from Listing 12-37 for possible fixes[9]). Resurrection is terminated when the weak handle become zeroed - thus callbacks on target object will be terminated after target object dies. Without weak reference it would never happen because our callback object would keep the target object alive.

Gen2GcCallback is used inside PinnableBufferCache to TrimFreeListIfNeeded be called on it with every gen 2 GC.

Listing 12-37. Example of interesting weak references and resurrection usage from System library

```
/// <summary>
/// Schedules a callback roughly every gen 2 GC (you may see a Gen 0 an Gen
   1 but only once)
/// (We can fix this by capturing the Gen 2 count at startup and testing,
   but I mostly don't care)
/// </summary>
internal sealed class Gen2GcCallback : CriticalFinalizerObject
{
    private Gen2GcCallback()
    {
    }

    public static void Register(Func<object, bool> callback, object
    targetObj)
    {
        // Create a unreachable object that remembers the callback function
        and target object.
```

---

[9]We are on thin ice here, depending on deep implementation details how objects get promoted. For example, with the current implementation, if the target object is pinned (or becomes a part of extended pinned plug), it may be demoted and we will be calling our callback again for ephemeral GCs also.

```
    Gen2GcCallback gcCallback = new Gen2GcCallback();
    gcCallback.Setup(callback, targetObj);
}

private Func<object, bool> _callback;
private GCHandle _weakTargetObj;

private void Setup(Func<object, bool> callback, object targetObj)
{
    _callback = callback;
    _weakTargetObj = GCHandle.Alloc(targetObj, GCHandleType.Weak);
}

~Gen2GcCallback()
{
    // Check to see if the target object is still alive.
    object targetObj = _weakTargetObj.Target;
    if (targetObj == null)
    {
        // The target object is dead, so this callback object is no longer
        needed.
        _weakTargetObj.Free();
        return;
    }

    // Execute the callback method.
    try
    {
        if (!_callback(targetObj))
        {
            // If the callback returns false, this callback object is no
            longer needed.
            return;
        }
    }
```

```
catch
{
    // Ensure that we still get a chance to resurrect this object,
    // even if the callback throws an exception.
}

// Resurrect ourselves by re-registering for finalization.
if (!Environment.HasShutdownStarted)
{
    GC.ReRegisterForFinalize(this);
}
}
```

Instead of manually creating weak GCHandle, dedicated WeakReference and WeakReference<T> types were introduced (see Listings 12-38 and 12-39). They represent exactly the same logic but as strongly typed representation of weak handles, it is a preferred way to use them. Please note the naming change - as in general weak handles realize weak reference semantics, such a name was chosen to hide its implementation detail (one may not be interested in knowing that weak reference is represented by weak handle underneath).

WeakReference targets object type and provides three important members:

- IsAlive - to check whether target is still alive

- Target - to access target object reference

- TrackResurrection - to check whether weak reference should remain resurrection

There is however a small issue with such API, illustrated in Listing 12-38. Between weakReference.IsAlive and weakReference.Target calls, GC may happen that will collect target object and make such condition check useless. Moreover, losing type information (by keeping reference to plain object type) is far from good design practice and requires further casting to use the target.

Listing 12-38. WeakReference type example usage

```
var obj = new LargeClass(ressurect: true);
WeakReference weakReference = new WeakReference(obj, trackResurrection: false);
if (weakReference.IsAlive)
    Console.WriteLine(weakReference.Target ?? "<null>"); // prints <null>
```

Thus, in .NET Framework 4.5 a new, generic version was introduced. Besides being generic, its API was also revised. Now only one TryGetTarget exists that returns information about target liveness atomically (see Listing 12-39).

Listing 12-39. WeakReference<T> type example usage

```
var obj = new LargeClass(ressurect: true);
WeakReference<LargeClass> weakReference = new
WeakReference<LargeClass>(obj, trackResurrection: false);
if (weakReference.TryGetTarget(out var target))
   Console.WriteLine(target);
```

Please note that we may easily convert a weak reference to a strong reference by assigning its target to some reachable root. Exactly such approach is used in internal System.StrongToWeakReference<T> class (see Listing 12-40). It is a weak reference that optionally keeps strong reference to the target object. Making such pair a weak reference is as easy as setting strong reference to null. We may also try to revert it to a strong reference if weak reference target is still alive. Obviously it may fail if target has been already garbage collected (hence I would prefer to provide bool TryMakeStrong() method instead of MakeStrong used in presented internal class).

Listing 12-40. StrongToWeakReference class as an example of conversion between strong and weak references

```
internal sealed class StrongToWeakReference<T> : WeakReference where T :
class
{
   private T _strongRef;

   public StrongToWeakReference(T obj) : base(obj)
   {
      _strongRef = obj;
   }

   public void MakeWeak() => _strongRef = null;
```

```
public void MakeStrong()
{
    _strongRef = WeakTarget;
}

public new T Target => _strongRef ?? WeakTarget;
private T WeakTarget => base.Target as T;
```

Let's now see briefly the two most typical usages of weak references in the form of caching and event listeners.

Caching

When someone hears or reads about weak references, he will probably associate it with caching immediately. It's tempting to have objects in memory held by such a "weak cache." Objects are used normally but additional weak references exist so we may cache objects without prolonging their life just because of the cache itself. During the time when the target is live, weak reference in cache is also live - but because it is only a weak reference, the object dies as usual, when it becomes unused by the application. In such way we cache objects currently used by the application (for example, to not re-create duplicates if other code needs them). This may be useful by itself.

Most often, however, cache works on a time basis, to keep recently used resources for some time even after they become unused. This may not be achieved with the weak references obviously. In such case, we would probably like to implement regular cache that stores strong references for some absolute time or time related to their last usage. After such threshold time exceeds, such references would be simply removed (*evicted*).

But instead, we may imagine something like *weak eviction cache* where after some time-cached strong references are becoming weak references. This softens caching policy - we certainly keep cached item for some specified amount of time and afterward we keep it cached only if it is still used. In other words, in case of such cache expiration while object is still live, cache is not trimmed prematurely - instead of forced removal from cache after specified amount of time, item is kept there as long as it is used. In case of regular cache, after specified amount of time the item from cache would be simply removed unconditionally, because without weak references there is no way to check whether object is still alive (assuming there is no API provided that informs cache that object is still in use, which is unlikely in generic object cache discussed here).

Let's assume a little extension of StrongToWeakReference class from Listing 12-40 that keeps track of the time when it had become strong (via StrongTime field). Having such helper class, a very simplified design of the weak eviction cache is presented in Listing 12-41. It simply stores a dictionary of cached items as our hybrid strong/weak reference object. Items are saved as strong references at the beginning. At some time, periodically DoWeakEviction method should be called that converts appropriate references from strong to weak (and cleans already dead cache items).

Listing 12-41. Weak eviction cache using weak references after specified amount of time

```
public class WeakEvictionCache<TKey, TValue> where TValue : class
{
    private readonly TimeSpan weakEvictionThreshold;
    private Dictionary<TKey, StrongToWeakReference<TValue>> items;

    WeakEvictionCache(TimeSpan weakEvictionThreshold)
    {
        this.weakEvictionThreshold = weakEvictionThreshold;
        this.items = new Dictionary<TKey, StrongToWeakReference<TValue>>();
    }

    public void Add(TKey key, TValue value)
    {
        items.Add(key, new StrongToWeakReference<TValue>(value));
    }

    public bool TryGet(TKey key, out TValue result)
    {
        result = null;
        if (items.TryGetValue(key, out var value))
        {
            result = value.Target;
            if (result != null)
            {
                // Item was used, try to make it strong again
                value.MakeStrong();
```

```
            return true;
        }
    }
    return false;
}

public void DoWeakEviction()
{
    List<TKey> toRemove = new List<TKey>();
    foreach (var strongToWeakReference in items)
    {
        var reference = strongToWeakReference.Value;
        var target = reference.Target;
        if (target != null)
        {
            if (DateTime.Now.Subtract(reference.StrongTime)
                >= weakEvictionThreshold)
            {
                reference.MakeWeak();
            }
        }
        else
        {
            // Remove already zeroed weak references
            toRemove.Add(strongToWeakReference.Key);
        }
    }

    foreach (var key in toRemove)
    {
        items.Remove(key);
    }
}
```

Please keep in mind that WeakEvictionCache class is trivial and would require a lot of improvement before even thinking about real-world usage (including better API and thread safety to name only two).

Weak Event Pattern

Yet another most typical usage scenario related to weak references are *weak events*. Using events in .NET is not hard but may introduce one of the most typical sources of the memory leak. Let's investigate it now in detail before moving forward to the solution in form of the mentioned weak events.

Let's first introduce two trivial classes simulating windows-based library (whether it would be Windows Forms, WPF, or something else) shown in Listing 12-42. They present overwhelmingly popular hierarchical approach of such libraries - almost every element is in parent-child relationship with some other. It is also quite common to subscribe to events between such elements. Thus, sample SettingsChanged event was prepared for our experiments and RegisterEvents method in the other component that subscribes to it.

Listing 12-42. Two simple classes simulating UI library, used for further experiments

```
public class MainWindow
{
    public delegate void SettingsChangedEventHandler(string message);
    public event SettingsChangedEventHandler SettingsChanged;
}

public class ChildWindow
{
    private MainWindow parent;

    public ChildWindow(MainWindow parent)
    {
        this.parent = parent;
    }

    public void RegisterEvents(MainWindow parent)
    {
        // ChildWindow - target, MainWindow - source
        parent.SettingsChanged += OnParentSettingsChanged;
    }
```

```
private void OnParentSettingsChanged(string message)
{
    Console.WriteLine(message);
}
```

Sample code from Listing 12-43 consumes those types, simulating typical work of an UI-based application - there is a single main window and occasionally created additional child windows doing some work. Child windows subscribe to some of the parent window events. In each iteration GC is triggered to clean up everything aggressively. Additionally, for diagnostic purposes a list of weak references is maintained to track every created child window (note how nicely WeakReference fits into such experimental purposes).

Listing 12-43. Experiment showing memory leak because of unsubscribed events

```
public void Run()
{
    List<WeakReference> observer = new List<WeakReference>();

    MainWindow mainWindow = new MainWindow();
    while (true)
    {
        Thread.Sleep(1000);
        ChildWindow childWindow = new ChildWindow(mainWindow);
        observer.Add(new WeakReference(childWindow));

        childWindow.RegisterEvents(mainWindow); // Leave this line
                                                uncommented to leak child
                                                windows

        childWindow.Show();

        GC.Collect();
        foreach (var weakReference in observer)
        {
            Console.Write(weakReference.IsAlive ? "1" : "0");
        }
        Console.WriteLine();
    }
}
```

Obviously, if RegisterEvents call is commented, child window instance becomes unreachable before GC.Collect call, thanks to the early root collection technique. Thus, the result is in line with expectations (see Listing 12-44). Each child window dies after each iteration.

Listing 12-44. Result of the program from Listing 12-43 (in case of RegisterEvents call is commented)

```
ChildWindows showed
0
ChildWindows showed
00
ChildWindows showed
000
ChildWindows showed
0000
ChildWindows showed
00000
```

However, registering to an event introduces clear memory leak (see Listing 12-45). There are more and more live child windows kept in memory.

Listing 12-45. Result of the program from Listing 12-43 (in case of RegisterEvents call being made)

```
ChildWindows showed
1
ChildWindows showed
11
ChildWindows showed
111
ChildWindows showed
1111
ChildWindows showed
11111
```

Obviously, there is a very simple solution to that problem - at some time UnregisterEvents counterpart should be called that uses -= operator underneath to unsubscribe from the parent window events. This is simple but requires explicit cleanup mindset of a programmer - it needs to remember to unsubscribe from each event subscribed. We will return to that a little later. Let's now dig in a little into the reason of such memory leak.

Registering to an event is a moderately complicated process. When a corresponding delegate is defined in a class, it is internally represented as nested class that derives from System.MulticastDelegate type (see Listing 12-46). As we can see, its constructor expects both an object and a method - because delegate needs to represent information about what should be called (method) and on what target (object instance).

Listing 12-46. SettingsChangedEventHandler internal implementation

```
.class public auto ansi beforefieldinit CoreCLR.Finalization.MainWindow
    extends [System.Runtime]System.Object
{
  // Nested Types
  .class nested public auto ansi sealed SettingsChangedEventHandler
      extends [System.Runtime]System.MulticastDelegate
  {
    // Methods
    .method public hidebysig specialname rtspecialname
        instance void .ctor (
            object 'object',
            native int 'method'
        ) runtime managed
    {
    } // end of method SettingsChangedEventHandler::.ctor

    ...


    .method public hidebysig newslot virtual
        instance void Invoke (
            string message
        ) runtime managed
```

```
    {
    } // end of method SettingsChangedEventHandler::Invoke

} // end of class SettingsChangedEventHandler
```

This is exactly what happens underneath RegisterEvents method (see Listing 12-47). this field (ChildWindow reference) is passed to the SettingsChangedEventHandler constructor and add_SettingsChanged method is called to combine such delegate into current delegate invocation list (see Listing 12-48).

Listing 12-47. RegisterEvents representation in CIL

```
.method public hidebysig
    instance void RegisterEvents (
        class CoreCLR.Finalization.MainWindow parent
    ) cil managed
{
    .maxstack 8

    IL_0000: ldarg.1    // parent
    IL_0001: ldarg.0    // this
    IL_0002: ldftn      instance void ChildWindow::OnParentSettingsChanged
                        (string)
    IL_0008: newobj     instance void MainWindow/
                        SettingsChangedEventHandler::.ctor(object, native int)
    IL_000D: callvirt   instance void MainWindow::add_SettingsChanged
                        (class CoreCLR.Finalization.MainWindow/
                        SettingsChangedEventHandler)
    IL_0012: ret
} // end of method ChildWindow::RegisterEvents
```

Listing 12-48. SettingsChanged event internal implementation (much simplified for brevity, omitting thread safety)

```
public event MainWindow.SettingsChangedEventHandler SettingsChanged
{
    [CompilerGenerated]
    add
    {
```

```
    // value is of type SettingsChangedEventHandler (and contains
    ChildWindows reference in our example)
    this.SettingsChanged = (MainWindow.SettingsChangedEventHandler)
    Delegate.Combine(this.SettingsChanged, value);
}
remove
{
    ...
}
}
```

Thus, `ChildWindow` instances are gathering in the delegate invocation list representing `SettingsChanged` event. In other words, the event becomes the only root of them, keeping them alive even most probably they should be dead. And even more probably those `ChildWindows` instances are no longer interested in the `SettingsChanged` event in the first place. This is simply a bug leading to less or more severe memory leak - depending on how much longer an event source outlives target instances. The worst-case scenario is static events (or events in static classes and so on, and so forth). They live as long as their AppDomain lives (typically, the whole application lifetime) so there is plenty of time to gather a lot of leaked memory.

The longer source outlives targets and the heavier targets are (with respect to memory usage), the more severe such memory leak becomes. I've seen very small objects leaking because of unsubscribed static event in applications running for days, and I've seen also quite large objects killing an application in few hours just because of the same reason.

Please note that our example event is defined intentionally in a little nontypical way. Typically it would be defined with the first argument representing an event source (most often named sender):

```
public delegate void SettingsChangedEventHandler(object
sender, string message);
```

This, however, does not change anything regarding memory leak because sender is taken from the `MulticastDelegate` instance. I'm pointing this out just to ensure your that it is not the presence of this argument that binds source and target so strongly, resulting in a memory leak.

So what is the solution? Knowing about weak references, it should be obvious to you already. The relationship between source and target should be weak reference - there is no need to maintain former if the latter should die, and vice versa.

However, full and correct implementation of such "weak event" pattern is not trivial. It would take too much space to describe it here thoroughly. Instead, let's look briefly how they are implemented in case of Windows Presentation Foundation, which allows to define them explicitly.

Unfortunately, pretty and concise syntax of event handling in C# (represented by += and -= operators) cannot be customized to provide equally pretty weak event syntax. Thus, every weak event pattern implementation uses similar API based on plain method calls. For example, if our dummy UI-based application was written in WPF, we could subscribe a weak event in RegisterEvents method as in Listing 12-49. There are various ways of doing that in WPF, this is however a little more preferred - by using generic WeakEventManager static AddHandler method that ties everything up - it defines that we are interested in SettingsChanged event in parent instance and OnParentSettingsChanged handler should be called (target is taken from underneath delegate implicitly).

Listing 12-49. Usage of weak event pattern in WPF

```
public void RegisterEvents(MainWindow parent)
{
    // ChildWindow - target
    // MainWindow - source
    WeakEventManager<MainWindow, string>.AddHandler(parent,
"SettingsChanged", OnParentSettingsChanged);
}
```

Studying the implementation of WeakEventManager can be very informative. Even the opening comment of the WeakEventManager class contains great details (see Listing 12-50).

Listing 12-50. Opening comment from WeakEventManager.cs source file

```
// Normally, A listens by adding an event handler to B's Foo event:
//    B.Foo += new FooEventHandler(OnFoo);
// but the handler contains a strong reference to A, and thus B now
effectively has a strong reference to A.  (...)
```

812

```
// The solution to this kind of leak is to introduce an intermediate
"proxy" object P with the following properties:
// 1. P does the actual listening to B.
// 2. P maintains a list of "real listeners" such as A, using weak
      references.
// 3. When P receives an event, it forwards it to the real listeners that
      are still alive.
// 4. P's lifetime is expected to be as long as the app (or Dispatcher).
```

If you want to practice weak references, I strongly encourage you to study weak event pattern implementation in WPF. One of the core `WeakEventManager` parts is `WeakEventTable`. Look also at `Listener` struct that contains a weak reference to the target and `EventKey` struct that contains a weak reference to the source.

Why doesn't the default implementation of events in .NET follow a weak event pattern approach? Wouldn't it be helpful and aligned with the spirit of automatic memory management, to not require explicit cleanup of events? The main reason is the ratio of introduced performance cost versus the gained convenience of the API. Using weak events incurs using weak handles and those do not come without performance and memory overhead. Events usage is unbounded - even if typically we expect only a dozen of UI-based events, they have to be designed in a way handling hundreds of instances. Thus, it is much safer to use regular instance member (because in essence, that's what events are) than introduce handles overhead.

In particular, all this would be done just to relieve a little lazy programmer that does not want to think where she or he should unsubscribe an event. In most cases, a desired moment when events should be unsubscribed is well-defined. MSDN says about WPF's weak events: "You typically use the weak event pattern when the event source has an object lifetime that is independent of the event listeners. Using the central event dispatching capability of a `WeakEventManager` allows the listener's handlers to be garbage collected even if the source object persists." Such independent object lifetimes between source and listeners are rather uncommon, thus using explicit cleanup by default was a much better decision. Still, it would be nice to have opt-in possibility to use concise events syntax in C#.

If you would like to investigate weak references CoreCLR source code a little, start from `WeakReferenceNative::Create` method that creates handle of type `HNDTYPE_WEAK_LONG` or `HNDTYPE_WEAK_SHORT` in the regular handle store. During Mark phase, `GCScan::GcShortWeakPtrScan` method nulls out the target of short weak references that were not promoted. Then, after scanning of finalization roots it also nulls out the target of long weak references by calling `GCScan::GcWeakPtrScan`.

Scenario 9-2. Memory Leak Because of Events

Description: Our application memory usage grows in time. After double checking, for example, with the help of performance counters, we are sure that it is the Managed Heap that grows in time. More and more objects are gathering in generation 2, but its fragmentation is stable in time (checked for example via PerfView sessions). Apparently we are dealing with a memory leak, as some objects are continuously reachable because of some not-yet identified root.

Let's use code from Listing 9-43 as a simple simulation of such case. Of course, in this case, we already know the cause of the problem. Let's use it however as a nice and clean playground to see how it could be diagnosed.

Analysis: During memory weak analysis we have always two basic approaches:

- Take a single memory dump when memory usage is huge. We can count on the fact that the leaking objects will somehow stand out - by quantity, total size, numerous presences in the queue of finalization (if we are lucky and it happens that leaking objects are finalizable) and so on, and so forth. This may be sometime the only available approach - for example, if memory leak is extremely rare and we had only a single chance to make a memory dump on production. Analyzing such dumps is tedious though - mainly because memory leak characteristic may be more complex than single leakage of big objects. There may by a whole intricate graph of flyweight objects related to each other kept by some elusive roots that simply hides in the whole big spacious graph of all the objects. Thus, analysis of such single memory shoots requires quite good intuition, at least some level of knowledge about application internals (to quickly identify expected object subgraphs), and a bit of luck also.

- Take two or more successive memory dumps and analyze differences (preferably, automatically). If it is only possible, we should prefer this approach. Comparison of successive application states cleans the analysis from unnecessary noise - the objects that leak should actually stand out from the others, allocated and collected in a stable manner. As already showed in this book, various tools may be used. I prefer low-level analysis from within WinDbg but this requires manual comparison. A much more preferred way is to compare heap snapshots taken from PerfView - with low overhead introduced and good difference analysis support. Of course, all commercial tools support such approach as it is the best way to find a memory leak source.

Let's use the heap snapshots comparison approach from PerfView. While our problematic application runs, we should take two successive heap snapshots (by using Memory ➤ Take Heap Snapshot option), in the time between the process noticeably grows (to have a chance to see leaked objects). I always prefer to take such snapshots after some time the application is running, to give it a chance to warm up and reclaim memory after regular initialization code that often happens at the beginning.

After opening both heap snapshots, compare them by using Diff ➤ With baseline... option from the menu. Your mileage may vary how to analyze such comparison - whether to start from ByName view (and sort by Inc or Exc columns), RefTree view, or simply visually by Flame Graph view. Sometimes indeed looking at the Flame Graphs provides enough of an informative view. In our test application case, it becomes immediately visible that in the snapshots difference the most contributing type is MainWindow, that holds SettingsChangedEventHandler, that then holds ChildWindows instances (see Figure 12-5). We have just identified a very serious suspect!

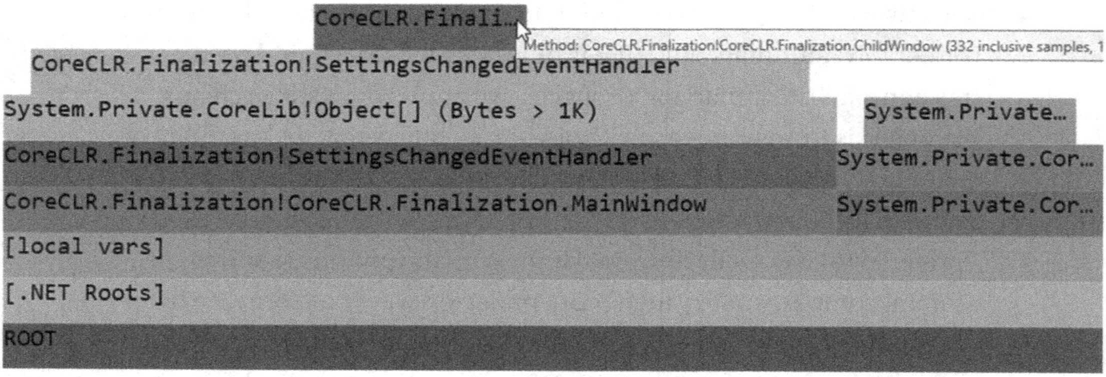

Figure 12-5. *Flame Graph view of two heap snapshots difference in PerfView*

By looking at RefTree view, confirmation immediately stands out - between our snapshots balance shows over three hundred `ChildWindow` and `SettingsChangedEventHandler` instances created (see Figure 12-6).

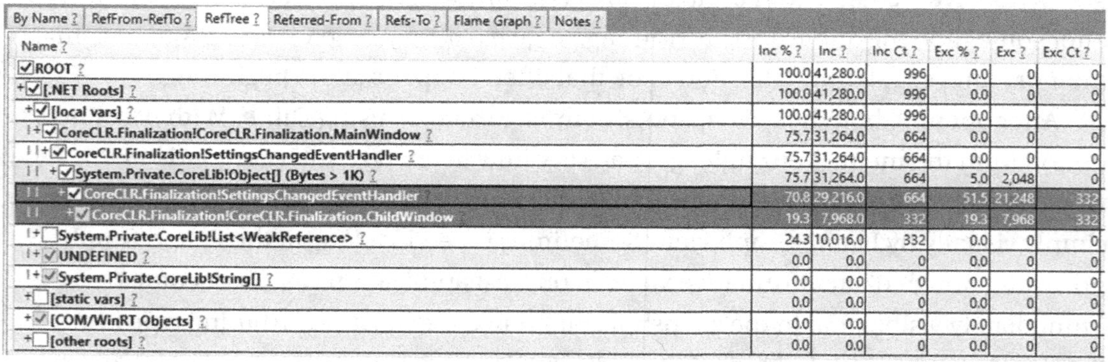

By Name ? | RefFrom-RefTo ? | RefTree ? | Referred-From ? | Refs-To ? | Flame Graph ? | Notes ?

Name ?	Inc % ?	Inc ?	Inc Ct ?	Exc % ?	Exc ?	Exc Ct ?
ROOT ?	100.0	41,280.0	996	0.0	0	0
+[.NET Roots] ?	100.0	41,280.0	996	0.0	0	0
+[local vars] ?	100.0	41,280.0	996	0.0	0	0
+CoreCLR.Finalization!CoreCLR.Finalization.MainWindow ?	75.7	31,264.0	664	0.0	0	0
+CoreCLR.Finalization!SettingsChangedEventHandler ?	75.7	31,264.0	664	0.0	0	0
+System.Private.CoreLib!Object[] (Bytes > 1K) ?	75.7	31,264.0	664	5.0	2,048	0
+CoreCLR.Finalization!SettingsChangedEventHandler	70.8	29,216.0	664	51.5	21,248	332
+CoreCLR.Finalization!CoreCLR.Finalization.ChildWindow	19.3	7,968.0	332	19.3	7,968	332
+System.Private.CoreLib!List<WeakReference> ?	24.3	10,016.0	332	0.0	0	0
+UNDEFINED ?	0.0	0.0	0	0.0	0	0
+System.Private.CoreLib!String[] ?	0.0	0.0	0	0.0	0	0
+[static vars] ?	0.0	0.0	0	0.0	0	0
+[COM/WinRT Objects] ?	0.0	0.0	0	0.0	0	0
+[other roots] ?	0.0	0.0	0	0.0	0	0

Figure 12-6. *RefTree view of two heap snapshots difference in PerfView*

Such analysis will send your directly to the problematic event handler in your application hopefully. Please note also an additional Object[] array used by `SettingsChangedEventHandler` objects. It is nothing else than the invocation list mentioned earlier - because `SettingsChangedEventHandler` is a `MulticastDelegate` (and yes, such kind of delegate holds and array of listening delegates internally, which are delegates also. Look at `MulticastDelegate` .NET source code if you are interested in details).

As an example of how such information is presented in commercial tools, let's see heap snapshots comparison is presented in .NET Memory Profiler (two successive snapshots were taken during live session) in Figure 12-7. Clearly we see the same results, with the same problematic event handlers leaking. We see also increase of GCHandles hold by the weak references but this is expected as they are gathering in our observer list (refer to Listing 12-43).

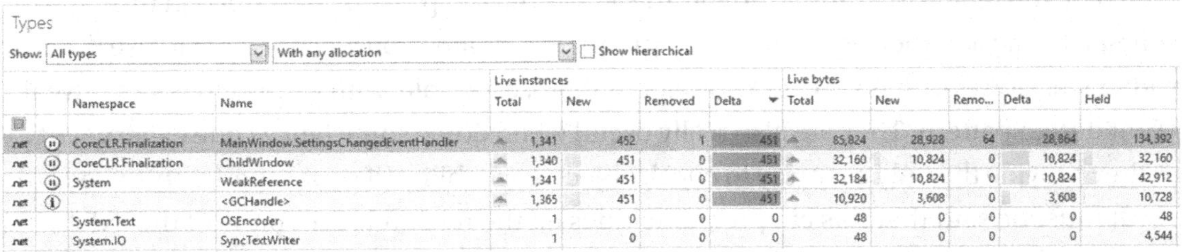

Types

Show: All types | With any allocation | Show hierarchical

Namespace	Name	Live instances Total	New	Removed	Delta	Live bytes Total	New	Remo...	Delta	Held
CoreCLR.Finalization	MainWindow.SettingsChangedEventHandler	1,341	452	1	451	85,824	28,928	64	28,864	134,392
CoreCLR.Finalization	ChildWindow	1,340	451	0	451	32,160	10,824	0	10,824	32,160
System	WeakReference	1,341	451	0	451	32,184	10,824	0	10,824	42,912
	<GCHandle>	1,365	451	0	451	10,920	3,608	0	3,608	10,728
System.Text	OSEncoder	1	0	0	0	48	0	0	0	48
System.IO	SyncTextWriter	1	0	0	0	48	0	0	0	4,544

Figure 12-7. *Overview of two heap snapshots difference in .NET Memory Profiler*

As mentioned earlier, similar reports are available in every other commercial tool available (to not be accused of promoting this particular tool at the moment).

Summary

Finalization and disposable objects are strongly related to the unmanaged world cooperation. They are more related to the resource management than to object lifetime management. However, altogether with weak references, all those topics interleave each other in more or less subtle way.

Disposable objects, introduced by standardization explicit cleanup of resources in the form of `IDisposable` interface and supported by `using` clause in case of C#. This way they tend to replace missing RAII (Resource Acquisition Is Initialization) approach from unmanaged environment when a local variable within its lexical scope is the owner of some resource - it acquires resource at creation (in constructor) and releases it when leaving its scope (in destructor). While `IDisposable` was from the very beginning thought as exactly for that purpose, it gained an additional popularity also in other use cases. Logging, tracing, profiling - those are only a few examples of popular usages not related to unmanaged resources at all. They become popular every time when explicit region of control is required. Besides of this, explicit cleanup stays as a preferred way of managing unmanaged resources.

On the other hand, finalization is quite still popular, especially in case of full Disposable pattern implementation when it is treated as a safety net in case of explicit cleanup omission. But one must be fully aware of all finalization-related caveats and overhead it introduces. I hope all the implementation details, as long as presented benchmarks and scenario 9-1 convinced you about that at least a little. General rule to remember is to avoid finalization if possible.Don't treat them as a fancy feature to add logging or something else to make your code look smart!

Weak references are most probably the less popular type along described in this chapter. Dedicated mostly to only few scenarios, most often you will not need to use them in your code. However, it is good to know about them, especially with respect to popular weak event design pattern. They are also really useful when doing some fancy code experiments, as they provide the only easy way to check object reachability (if your experiments need so).

It must be said that this chapter concludes all the most relevant parts of the .NET memory management internals. We have had a very long journey so far. The next two chapters are much more practical biased, based on the knowledge gained so far. I strongly encourage you to read them!

Rule 25 - Avoid Finalizers

Applicability: General and popular. High performance code - important.

Justification: Finalizers were designed for a very specific purpose - provide implicit cleanup of unmanaged resources, just in case that explicit one is not possible. However, there are not so many cases I can imagine where explicit cleanup could be not possible. By using finalizers. we expose ourselves to many problems. Even implementing a good finalizer is not trivial if we take into consideration each possible edge case (like reentrancy, multithreading, possibility to be executed only partially or not at all, to name a few problems). Moreover, due to required implementation, there are many really considerable overheads - mostly in terms of performance and memory usage.

How to apply: Just try to use some other possible alternatives, namely:

- SafeHandle - as a well-designed finalizable handle representation with the runtime support,

- Disposable pattern - as most probably you may get rid of finalization and manage your resource explicitly,

- Critical finalization - if releasing resource if crucial for you.

In cases when you really do not see a possibility to avoida finalizer, remember about the following good practices:

Write only small wrappers encapsulating only unmanaged resources, without any other managed references - to not promote too much because of finalization.

- Avoid allocating memory in finalizer and critical finalizer - throwing OutOfMemoryException inside of it may be really problematic.

- Always check if you really own expected resources - typical scenario includes throwing an exception from the constructor, which may lead to executing finalizer in not fully initialized object state.

- Avoid any thread context dependency - simply do not assume anything about the thread executing your finalizer. This imposes also avoiding blocking execution by any synchronization techniques.

- Do not throw any exceptions from finalizers - and do not allow it to be thrown by third-party code. Remember to always wrap finalizer code by try-finally block!

- Avoid calling virtual members from finalizers - as they may introduce all unwanted behavior lister above

Related scenarios: Scenario 12-1.

Rule 26 - Prefer Explicit Cleanup

Applicability: General and popular. High performance code - important.

Justification: Deterministic cleanup is a preferred way of managing resources. Cleanup time is well-defined and (if designed well) as early as possible - it helps in limited resources management. Obviously, it is a little more demanding for programmers. They cannot create resources on the fire-and-forget basis. They must take care about proper releasing of all they initialized. Yes, we know. This is a little in opposite what managed environments promise - including automatic memory management at the first place. But unmanaged resources are... unmanaged. We should take a little effort to remember that.

How to apply: Stick to what .NET ecosystem proposes - IDisposable and disposable objects. Most often, when you need to clean up your resources, probably always it is possible to do it in Dispose, not in a dedicated, heavyweight finalizer. It will impose additional care on programmers, but using clause in C# and tools like ReSharper or Visual Studio rules are there to help them.

CHAPTER 13

Miscellaneous Topics

So far, all chapters have focused on how different aspects of memory-management work in .NET (so the vast majority of how Garbage Collector in .NET works). At this point in the book, we have gained most of the knowledge necessary for a profound understanding of how most of this machinery works underneath. I say "most" because of course there are still some more or less minor aspects that we have not touched because of the limited size of the book. I hope, however, that you already feel quite comfortable with the knowledge about partitioning (generations, segments), allocation and deallocation, how garbage collection is proceeded, and so on, and so forth.

All this knowledge was intertwined with some practical tips and various scenarios (usually diagnostic). However, for the sake of clarity and not the excessive growth of individual chapters, not all more advanced practical aspects have been mentioned. Exactly to such things, however, this and the next chapter are dedicated. Let's treat them as the "creme de la creme" of .NET memory management, purely practical (with some internal knowledge still mentioned) and touching more advanced topics. This does not mean that the topics discussed here are not useful in the daily work of the programmer. Quite the opposite, we may see the bigger and bigger adoption of such techniques as more and more performance-aware code is being written in .NET - this especially includes using Span<T> and everything around it.

Due to such a general, complementary nature of this chapter, it a conspectus, and individual subchapters are loosely connected. Choose what you are most interested in or (what I strongly recommend), and read everything in a row!

Dependent Handles

Besides already known kind of handles, there is yet still one more available not mentioned so far - dependent handle, added in .NET Framework 4.0 (and available in .NET Core). It allows us to couple the lifetime of two objects. A dependent handle points to a target, just like what other GC handles do. And it behaves like a weak handle,

821

© Konrad Kokosa 2018
K. Kokosa, *Pro .NET Memory Management*, https://doi.org/10.1007/978-1-4842-4027-4_13

that is, it does not keep the target alive. This is the primary object for the dependent handle. It also carries a secondary object. The behavior of a dependent handle is the following:

- a "weak" handle both to primary and secondary objects (it does not influence their lifetime by itself);

- a strong handle from primary object to secondary object (secondary object will be kept alive as long as primary object is alive).

This makes them a very flexible tool that allows you to something like "adding" fields to objects in a dynamic way. In fact, such "adding fields" usage is exactly the purpose of it, as we will soon see.

Dependent handles are not available via GCHandle API as other types of handles. In fact, they are not directly exposed by any public API. The only way to use it is with the wrapper class ConditionalWeakTable. As its own source code comment says, it provides "compiler support for runtime-generated "object fields," and that it "lets DLR and other language compilers expose the ability to attach arbitrary "properties" to instanced managed objects at runtime."

There is an intrinsic DependentHandle struct (in System.Runtime.CompilerServices namespace) that directly wraps a dependent handle on the runtime level. It has a simple constructor DependentHandle(object primary, object secondary) and methods like GetPrimary and GetPrimaryAndSecondary. But it is internal as it was decided to not expose it directly. DependentHandle is consumed by the mentioned ConditionalWeakTable class.

Additionally, interestingly enough, a dependent handle type is used internally by the runtime to support adding fields during the Edit and Continue debugger features. Since instances of modified type may already exist on the heap, such a feature can't simply change the runtime layout of the object to include the new field. Thus, a dependent handle maintains a lifetime relationship between those two in such a scenario.

ConditionalWeakTable is organized as dictionary, with the key storing primary object and the value storing added "property" (secondary object). Please note that such dictionary keys are weak references and will not keep those objects alive (unlike regular dictionary keys). Once the key dies, the dictionary automatically removes the corresponding dictionary entry.

API of ConditionalWeakTable is intuitive and similar to the regular, generic Dictionary<TKey, TValue> (see Listing 13-1). By using Add method we create a new underlying dependent handle, "adding" a value instance to the key instance. Please note that ConditionalWeakTable is generic, so strong typing is employed (to allow only adding only specific type to other specific type). Because the key must be unique (keys are compared with the help of Object.ReferenceEquals), this class supports attaching only a single value per managed object (you would need to attach as a value yet another dictionary-like object to simulate attaching multiple properties). You can try to get a value represented by a given key using TryGetValue method, as shown in Listing 13-1.

Listing 13-1. Example of ConditionalWeakTable usage

```
class SomeClass
{
   public int Field;
}

class SomeData
{
   public int Data;
}

public static void SimpleConditionalWeakTableUsage()
{
   // Dependent handles between SomeClass (primary) and SomeData
      (secondary)
   ConditionalWeakTable<SomeClass, SomeData> weakTable = new
   ConditionalWeakTable<SomeClass, SomeData>();

   var obj1 = new SomeClass();
   var data1 = new SomeData();
```

```
var obj1weakRef = new WeakReference(obj1);
var data1weakRef = new WeakReference(data1);
weakTable.Add(obj1, data1); // Throws an exception if key already added
weakTable.AddOrUpdate(obj1, data1);

GC.Collect();
Console.WriteLine($"{obj1weakRef.IsAlive} {data1weakRef.IsAlive}");
// Prints True True
if (weakTable.TryGetValue(obj1, out var value))
{
    Console.WriteLine(value.Data);
}
GC.KeepAlive(obj1);
GC.Collect();
Console.WriteLine($"{obj1weakRef.IsAlive} {data1weakRef.IsAlive}");
// Prints False False
}
```

Without a GC.KeepAlive call in Listing 13-1, both obj1 and data1 instances could be already dead after the first GC.Collect (if JIT compiler decided to use early root collection, described in Chapter 8). If, on the other hand, we instead called GC.KeepAlive(data1) to keep alive the secondary object (the value), not the primary object (the key), first Console.WriteLine most probably would print: False True. At this moment the key was collected because nothing holds its reference.

Please note that ConditionalWeakTable is in fact a container maintaining a collection of dependent handles, which are unmanaged resources (like GCHandle-allocated ones). We create them implicitly by using Add or AddOrUpdate, but when they are released (freed) then? With the current implementation, they are released implicitly by the finalizer of the internal container (thus, after ConditionalWeakTable instance becomes unreachable). We can, however, do an explicit cleanup by calling Clear method (which was added in .NET Core 2.0). Even calling Remove method currently does not release underlying handles (due to multithreading issues it could incur).

Of course, we may omit strong typing of the ConditionalWeakTable by using Object type as its generic types (see Listing 13-2). In this way we will be able to add any object to any other object.

Listing 13-2. Example of ConditionalWeakTable usage

```
ConditionalWeakTable<object, object> weakTable = new
ConditionalWeakTable<object, object>();
var obj1 = new SomeClass();
var data1 = new SomeData();
weakTable.Add(obj1, data1);
```

Moreover, keep in mind that the limitation of the single value per managed object (key) comes from the ConditionalWeakTable, not from the dependent handles itself. Thus, nothing can stop us from adding multiple "values" to the same object in that way, by using multiple ConditionalWeakTable instances (see Listing 13-3).

Listing 13-3. Example of ConditionalWeakTable usage

```
var obj1 = new SomeClass();
var weakTable1 = new ConditionalWeakTable<object, object>();
var weakTable2 = new ConditionalWeakTable<object, object>();
var data1 = new SomeData();
var data2 = new SomeData();
weakTable1.Add(obj1, data1);
weakTable2.Add(obj1, data2);
```

Underlying weak references of dependent handle behave as long weak references, so they are maintaining relation between primary and secondary objects even when the primary one is being finalized (see Listing 13-4). It allows us to handle resurrection scenarios properly.

Listing 13-4. Finalization behavior of dependent handles

```
class FinalizableClass : SomeClass
{
   ~FinalizableClass()
   {
   }
}

public static void FinalizationUsage()
{
   ConditionalWeakTable<SomeClass, SomeData> weakTable = new
   ConditionalWeakTable<SomeClass, SomeData>();

   var obj1 = new FinalizableClass();
   var data1 = new SomeData();

   var obj1weakRef = new WeakReference(obj1, trackResurrection: true);
   var data1weakRef = new WeakReference(data1, trackResurrection: true);
   weakTable.Add(obj1, data1);

   GC.Collect();
   Console.WriteLine($"{obj1weakRef.IsAlive} {data1weakRef.IsAlive}");
   // Prints True True
   GC.KeepAlive(obj1);
   GC.Collect();
   Console.WriteLine($"{obj1weakRef.IsAlive} {data1weakRef.IsAlive}");
   // Prints True True
   GC.WaitForPendingFinalizers();
   GC.Collect();
   Console.WriteLine($"{obj1weakRef.IsAlive} {data1weakRef.IsAlive}");
   // Prints False False
}
```

Dependent handles are treated in WinDbg as one of the handles type, so we can use the regular !gchandles SOS command to investigate them (see Listing 13-5). Because internal ConditionalWeakTable container is finalizable, we will also often see it in finalization queues (see Listing 13-6).

Listing 13-5. Result of !gchandles SOS extension command (for code like from Listing 13-3)

> **!gchandles -stat**

...

```
Handles:
    Strong Handles:        10
    Pinned Handles:        4
    Weak Long Handles:     1
    Weak Short Handles:    1
    Dependent Handles:     2
```

> **!gchandles -type Dependent**

```
            Handle Type                 Object       Size                Data
Type
00000292abfe1bf0 Dependent    00000292b034d188        24 00000292b034d448
CoreCLR.DependentHandles.SomeClass
00000292abfe1bf8 Dependent    00000292b034d188        24 00000292b034d430
CoreCLR.DependentHandles.SomeClass

Statistics:
             MT       Count     TotalSize Class Name
00007fff033166b8         2            48 CoreCLR.DependentHandles.SomeClass
Total 2 objects
```

Listing 13-6. Result of !finalizequeue SOS extension command (for code like from Listing 13-3)

> **!finalizequeue**

...

```
Statistics for all finalizable objects (including all objects ready for
finalization):
             MT       Count     TotalSize Class Name
...
00007fff03429678         2           112
System.Runtime.CompilerServices.ConditionalWeakTable`2+Container[[System.
Object, System.Private.CoreLib],[System.Object, System.Private.CoreLib]]
Total 5 objects
```

ConditionalWeakTable is useful in implementing caching or weak event patterns. In the former case, we may cache some data related to an object, as long as such object lives. In the latter case, we may appropriately couple the handler (delegate) lifetime with the target lifetime (see Chapter 12 for a wider weak event pattern description). Listing 13-7 shows fragments of the WeakEventManager class used in Windows Presentation Foundation. To couple delegate the lifetime with its target, ConditionalWeakTable is used (represented here by _cwt field). In this way, a list of delegates is alive as long as the target itself is alive.

Listing 13-7. ListenerList class methods (part of WeakEventManager class from WPF)

```csharp
public void AddHandler(Delegate handler)
{
    object target = handler.Target;
    ...
    // add a record to the main list
    _list.Add(new Listener(target, handler));
    AddHandlerToCWT(target, handler);
}

void AddHandlerToCWT(object target, Delegate handler)
{
    // add the handler to the CWT - this keeps the handler alive throughout
    // the lifetime of the target, without prolonging the lifetime of
    // the target
    object value;
    if (!_cwt.TryGetValue(target, out value))
    {
        // 99% case - the target only listens once
        _cwt.Add(target, handler);
    }
```

```
    else
    {
        // 1% case - the target listens multiple times
        // we store the delegates in a list
        List<Delegate> list = value as List<Delegate>;
        if (list == null)
        {
            // lazily allocate the list, and add the old handler
            Delegate oldHandler = value as Delegate;
            list = new List<Delegate>();
            list.Add(oldHandler);

            // install the list as the CWT value
            _cwt.Remove(target);
            _cwt.Add(target, list);
        }

        // add the new handler to the list
        list.Add(handler);
    }
}
```

During the Mark phase, dependent handles need to be scanned in a special way because they may create complex dependencies and a single scan is simply just not enough. Imagine three dependent handles saved in the handle table in the following order: object C targets object A, B targets C, and A targets B. Assuming that reachability of object A has been already determined (it is marked as reachable), the first scan of such handles will only mark B as reachable. Second scan will mark C as reachable (because now GC knows that B is reachable). Third scan will change nothing (A is already marked) so the whole analysis will be terminated. Such multiple scanning could theoretically introduce some overhead with millions of dependent handles with complex dependencies between them; however, it was assumed there is typically not so many of them.

If you would like to investigate this feature more in CoreCLR code, start from `gc_heap::background_scan_dependent_handles` and `gc_heap::scan_dependent_handles` methods. Both are greatly documented, as well as methods called by them: `GcDhReScan` and `GcDhUnpromotedHandlesExist`. At the beginning of the Mark phase, `GcDhInitialScan` is called whose comments also shed some light on dependent handles implementation.

Thread Local Storage

Normal static variables may be seen as global variables within a single AppDomain. Every thread in our application has access to it. Thus, typically it requires multithreading synchronization techniques to make it thread-safe. However, there is another type of "almost" global data, but which is unique to each thread - *thread local storage* (TLS). In other words, it behaves like a global variable - every thread accesses it by the same name or identifier - but data is stored separately for each thread. It reliefs us from synchronization issues, as each data will be accessible only by its dedicated thread.

Currently in .NET there are three ways to use thread local storage:

- *thread static fields* - available as static fields, additionally marked with `ThreadStatic` attribute,

- class helper that wraps thread static field - available as `ThreadLocal<T>` type,

- *thread data slots* - available with the help of `Thread.SetData` and `Thread.GetData` methods.

.NET documentation clearly states that thread static fields provide much better performance than data slots and should be preferred whenever possible. We will look into both techniques internals to understand the difference. Moreover, static fields are strongly typed (they have type, as any other field in .NET) while data slots always operate on an `Object` type and, in case of named data slots, string-based identifiers that both may lead to problems hard to catch at compile time.

Thread Static Fields

Using thread static fields is as easy as marking a regular static field with a `ThreadStatic` attribute. Both value and reference types may be used as thread static fields (see Listing 13-8). In our example, even the same instance of `SomeClass` is used by two different threads, and its static fields values are separate for both of them. Thus, one thread will print `Worker 1:1` while the other `Worker 2:2`. If both static fields were only regular statics, a multithreaded race condition would occur in writing to them (and as a result, some undetermined combination of 1 and 2 values would be stored).

Listing 13-8. Example of using thread static fields

```
class SomeData
{
   public int Field;
}

class SomeClass
{
   [ThreadStatic]
   private static int threadStaticValueData;
   [ThreadStatic]
   private static SomeData threadStaticReferenceData;

   public void Run(object param)
   {
      int arg = int.Parse(param.ToString());
      threadStaticValueData = arg;
      threadStaticReferenceData = new SomeData() { Field = arg };
      while (true)
      {
         Thread.Sleep(1000);
         Console.WriteLine($"Worker {threadStaticValueData}:{threadStatic
         ReferenceData.Field}.");
      }
   }
}
```

```
static void Main(string[] args)
{
    SomeClass runner = new SomeClass();
    Thread t1 = new Thread(new ParameterizedThreadStart(runner.Run));
    t1.Start(1);
    Thread t2 = new Thread(new ParameterizedThreadStart(runner.Run));
    t2.Start(2);
    Console.ReadLine();
}
```

Plain thread statics have one surprising inconvenience - if a static field has an initializer, it will be invoked only once, on the thread that executed the static constructor. In other words, only the single thread that first used a given type will have a thread static field properly initialized. Others will have such a field initialized to its default value (see Listing 13-9). Quite surprisingly, SomeOtherClass.Run method will print Worker 100 and Worker 0 lines because of such behavior.

Listing 13-9. Example of surprising thread static field initialization

```
class SomeOtherClass
{
    [ThreadStatic]
    private static int threadStaticValueData = 100;

    public void Run()
    {
        while (true)
        {
            Thread.Sleep(1000);
            Console.WriteLine($"Worker {threadStaticValueData}");
            // Will print Worker 100 or Worker 0.
        }
    }
}

static void Main(string[] args)
{
    SomeOtherClass runner = new SomeOtherClass();
```

```
    Thread t1 = new Thread(runner.Run);
    t1.Start();
    Thread t2 = new Thread(runner.Run);
    t2.Start();
}
```

To overcome similar problems, ThreadLocal<T> class is available since .NET Framework 4.0, which provides better, more deterministic initialization behavior. We can provide to its constructor a value factory, which will lazily initialize such class instance when first accessed via Value property (see Listing 13-10).

Listing 13-10. Example of ThreadLocal<T> usage

```
class SomeOtherClass
{
    private ThreadLocal<int> threadValueLocal = new ThreadLocal<int>(() =>
    100, trackAllValues: true);

    public void Run()
    {
        while (true)
        {
            Thread.Sleep(1000);
            Console.WriteLine($"Worker {threadStaticValueData}:{threadValue
            Local.Value}.");
            Console.WriteLine(threadValueLocal.Values.Count);
        }
    }
}
```

Additionally, ThreadLocal<T> provides functionality of tracking all initialized values by passing true to its constructor's trackAllValues argument. We can later on use Values property to iterate all current values. Be careful, however, as it is a straight road to problems - we may start to pass around reference instances between threads that were supposed to be only thread local.

Underneath ThreadLocal<T> still is a thin wrapper around thread static field. With all the additional handling of its internal structures, some performance hit may be observed (see Listing 13-11). However, if performance is not your main concern, ThreadLocal<T> is even more preferred than using plain thread static fields.

Listing 13-11. Results of DotNetBenchmark comparing access to primitive and reference thread local storage - by thread statics and ThreadLocal<T>

```
              Method |      Mean | Allocated |
--------------------- |----------:|----------:|
PrimitiveThreadStatic |   4.072 ns |      0 B |
ReferenceThreadStatic |   5.076 ns |      0 B |
 PrimitiveThreadLocal |   7.866 ns |      0 B |
 ReferenceThreadLocal |  11.762 ns |      0 B |
```

If you really need performance of a plain thread static field, while overcoming an initialization problem, you can use a small trick to wrap around the thread static field with lazy initialization via a regular static field (see Listing 13-12).

Listing 13-12. Solution to problems with thread static data initialization

```
[ThreadStatic]
private static int? threadStaticData;
public static int ThreadStaticData
{
    get
    {
        if (threadStaticData == null)
            threadStaticData = 44;
        return threadStaticData.Value;
    }
}
```

Thread Data Slots

Using a thread data slot is simple and straightforward. There are two different kinds of data slots available (see Listing 13-13):

- *named thread data slot* - they are accessible by string-based name via Thread.GetNamedDataSlot. You can store and reuse LocalDataStoreSlot instance returned by this method or you can call it with an appropriate name whenever you need it.

- *unnamed thread data slot* - they are accessible only by LocalDataStoreSlot instance returned from Thread. AllocateDataSlot method.

Listing 13-13. Example of using thread data slots

```
public void UseDataSlots()
{
   // Named data slots
   Thread.SetData(Thread.GetNamedDataSlot("SlotName"), new SomeData());
   object data = Thread.GetData(Thread.GetNamedDataSlot("SlotName"));
   Console.WriteLine(data);
   Thread.FreeNamedDataSlot("SlotName");

   // Unnamed data slots
   LocalDataStoreSlot slot = Thread.AllocateDataSlot();
   Thread.SetData(slot, new SomeData());
   object data = Thread.GetData(slot);
   Console.WriteLine(data);
}
```

As mentioned later, we lose strong typing because of using thread data slots API - both Thread.SetData and Thread.GetData expect and return Object type. What mostly data slots give in return is flexibility - we may dynamically define thread statics identified by the string. However, such flexibility is rarely required and indeed, thread statics or ThreadLocal<T> should be a preferred approach.

A simple benchmark of accessing both primitive value (an integer) and an integer field of reference type clearly shows a significant performance advantage of plain thread-static variables (see Listing 13-14). I hope such benchmarks conclude why data slots are unpopular - for example, we can find only single usage of it in all .NET-related, open sourced libraries (including WPF and ASP.NET Core).

Listing 13-14. Results of DotNetBenchmark comparing access to primitive and reference thread local storage - by thread statics and data slots

```
                  Method |     Mean | Allocated |
------------------------ |---------:|----------:|
       PrimitiveThreadStatic |  3.938 ns |      0 B |
       ReferenceThreadStatic |  5.061 ns |      0 B |
     PrimitiveThreadDataSlot | 51.843 ns |      0 B |
     ReferenceThreadDataSlot | 48.616 ns |      0 B |
```

To be clearer, you better forget about data slots once and for all.

Thread Local Storage Internals

It is good to understand how thread local storage is implemented because it may be tempting to treat it as some kind of magical, super-fast thread-affinity storage. Thread affinity reminds us of the stack, and the stack is fast, right? So such special thread local storage, kept in some secret thread-related space, probably is even faster, right? The truth is much more complicated and knowing how thread local storage works underneath will help you to remember the pros and cons of this technique.

First of all, indeed there is a special memory region dedicated for each thread's own purposes. It is called *Thread Local Storage* (TLS) in case of Windows, and *Thread-specific data* in case of Linux. However, such a region is rather small, expressed rather in terms of a single memory page. Such a region is organized in terms of single, pointer-sized, so-called *slots*. For example, Windows guarantees only 64 such slots available in each process and that the maximum number of slots will not exceed 1,088. Those are quite tight requirements - guaranteed 64 slots makes only 512 bytes of memory in a 64-bit process!

Thus, let us be careful in saying that such data are kept in TLS. The use of slots kept in TLS means storing in them the address to normally allocated memory. It is a normal technique, used not only in .NET but in any other compiler, including C and C++ ones.

Thread local storage is simply too limited to keep there the data itself. Even so, such storage gives the following performance advantages:

- memory page with TLS is most probably kept in physical memory if we use its data on regular basis,

- access to such page must not be synchronized because only single thread sees it.

CLR uses the regular way of using thread local storage in C++. There is global, thread-static variable defined of type ThreadLocalInfo struct (see Listing 13-15). Single TLS slot is consumed by C++ compiler to store an address of such struct instance (and each underlying system thread keeps an address of its own ThreadLocalInfo copy).

Listing 13-15. Thread local storage definition in CoreCLR

```
#ifndef __llvm__
EXTERN_C __declspec(thread) ThreadLocalInfo gCurrentThreadInfo;
#else // !__llvm__
EXTERN_C __thread ThreadLocalInfo gCurrentThreadInfo;
#endif // !__llvm__
```

ThreadLocalInfo keeps addresses of the three following CLR internal data:

- instance of unmanaged Thread class representing currently running managed thread - this is the crucial part, used overwhelmingly in the whole runtime (for example by GetThread method call);

- instance of AppDomain in which current thread's code is being executed - this is a shortcut for efficiency, as the same pointer could be obtained from the Thread instance;

- instance of ClrTlsInfo structure - this is an array of addresses to many internal, thread-related CLR structures (mostly used for diagnostic and profiling).

So in fact, when we are using any thread local storage technique in .NET, only the pointer to ThreadLocalInfo structure is stored in TLS. The whole other thing lives both in the CLR private heap and on the GC heap, similarly how regular statics are implemented (see Figure 13-1). Thread class instance organizes its thread local storage-related data into two more classes:

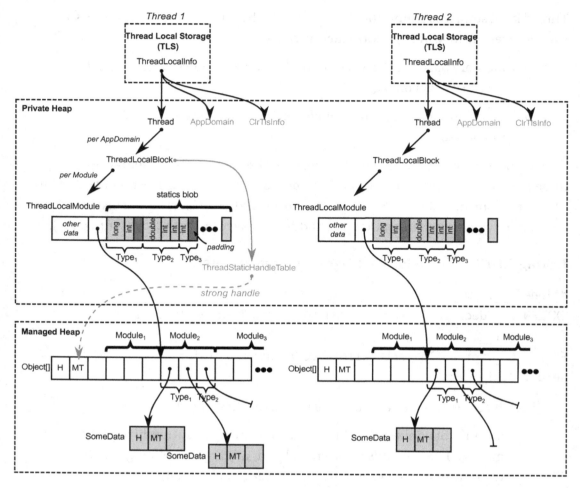

Figure 13-1. *Internals of thread local storage in .NET. Places where thread local data are indeed stored are marked as gray.*

- `ThreadLocalBlock` - it is created for each AppDomain in the application (so there will be only single instance in case of .NET Core apps). It additionally maintains `ThreadStaticHandleTable`, which keeps a strong handle references to dedicated managed arrays, storing references of thread-static field instances (references).

- `ThreadLocalModule` - it is created for each module in each AppDomain. It consists of two crucial data:

- unmanaged statics blob - here all thread-static unmanaged[1] values are stored. For efficient memory access, data in blobs are using padding (to consider memory alignment).

- offset in the managed array where static references of this module begin - here references are also grouped into types.

In other words, thread static data is stored in the following way:

- For fields being reference types - instances are normally heap-allocated and references to them are stored in a dedicated `Object[]` array kept alive by strong handles managed by `ThreadStaticHandleTable`. Please note that it means in particular that:

  - There may be multiple heap-allocated instances of the same type (if those fields are initialized, not nulls) - each for every managed thread running.

  - There will be multiple heap-allocated `Object[]` arrays to store references to the above - each for every AppDomain and managed thread running.

- For fields being unmanaged types - those values are stored in static blobs in unmanaged memory. Again, there will be multiple blobs - each per Thread, per AppDomain, and per Module in it.

- For structs - they are stored on the managed heap in a boxed form and treated the same as above-mentioned reference types.

As the number of types is known at compile time, both dedicated `Object[]` arrays and static blobs have constant, pre-calculated size (we know how many managed and unmanaged thread static fields are out there).

---

[1]Meaning, primitive types or value types that does not contain references.

A careful reader may notice that creating a thread in .NET may incur quite many allocations because of thread static fields. There can be many new `Object[]` arrays created per each AppDomain (most probably in SOH as the number of managed thread static fields is rather small in single AppDomain) as well as even more `ThreadLocalModules` allocated in private CLR data (containing static blobs for each module).

So, for example, in Figure 13-1, the viewpoint of one of the modules is presented - even there would be probably more `ThreadLocalModules`, they are not shown for brevity. In this module a few types are defined. Let's concentrate on `Type1`, which could look like that in Listing 13-16. It contains two primitive thread-static fields (of type `long` and `int`) so its values are stored inside `ThreadLocalModule` statics blob. Additionally, it contains two reference type thread-static fields of type `SomeData`. Like regular statics, such instances are normally heap-allocated and their references are stored in a dedicated, regular object array. In Figure 13-1 both such fields of `Type1` are already initialized for Thread 1, but (for illustrative purposes) only the first field is initialized for Thread 2.

Listing 13-16. Example of simple type showed in Figure 13-1

```
class Type1
{
    [ThreadStatic] private static int static1;
    [ThreadStatic] private static long static2;
    [ThreadStatic] private static SomeData static3;
    [ThreadStatic] private static SomeData static4;
    ...
}
```

Obviously, it may seem pretty uncomfortable at first glance that objects we think of being "thread-only statics" are simply lying somewhere next to each other in a GC heap. Please bear in mind, however, that unless something terrible happens, they are not visible to each other from the managed threads perspective (thus, are still thread-safe). On the other hand, we can unconsciously introduce False Sharing (refer to Chapter 2) between such instances, as they may live inside single cache line boundary.

So again, it is good to keep in mind Figure 13-1 when thinking about TLS as "fast, magic memory." In fact, TLS here is used only as a functional, implementation detail of thread affinity of corresponding data structures. It is not speeding up anything in general.

840

When code is being JITted, appropriate offsets are calculated for thread static fields - in statics blob for unmanaged types and in references array for reference types. Those offsets are stored in MethodTable-related regions so JIT compiler may use them to generate addresses of data access. In fact, data access requires obtaining corresponding ThreadLocalModule of the current thread. Accessing thread-static data introduces additional and noticeable overhead (see Listings 13-17 and 13-18, with comments).

Listing 13-17. Assigning thread-static unmanaged variable (like threadStaticValueData in Listing 13-8)

```
// Assume esi register contains value to store
// Pass info about module and class (type) index into rcx and edx registers
mov     rcx,7FFD3E295690h
mov     edx,2
// Accesses ThreadLocalModule inside (via TLS-stored pointer)
// As a result, rax contains ThreadLocalModule address
call    CoreCLR!JIT_GetSharedNonGCThreadStaticBase
mov     rdi,rax
// Store the value:
// 1Ch is an pre-calculated offset in the statics blob, esi contains value
to storemov     dword ptr [rdi+1Ch],esi
```

Listing 13-18. Assigning thread-static referece variable (like threadStaticReferenceData in Listing 13-8)

```
// Assume rbx contains value (reference) to store
// Pass info about module and class (type) index into rcx and edx registers
mov     rcx,7FFD3E295690h
mov     edx,2
// Accesses ThreadLocalModule inside (via TLS-stored pointer)
// As a result, rax contains reference to an array element where references
of that type begins
call    CoreCLR!JIT_GetSharedGCThreadStaticBase
mov     rcx,rax

// Store the reference (in rbx) under given array element (in rcx) by
calling write barrier
mov     rdx,rbx
call    CoreCLR!JIT_WriteBarrier (00007ffd`9d6c57d0)
```

On the other hand, without fields being statics (regular or thread ones), data access is orders of magnitude faster as it does not require any runtime call (one or two simple mov instructions would be enough in such case).

Both JIT_GetSharedNonGCThreadStaticBase and JIT_GetSharedGCThreadStaticBase are great methods to start of CoreCLR code analysis related to thread local storage. Methods generated by JIT often contain INLINE_GETTHREAD macro that gets gCurrentThreadInfo (thread static ThreadLocalInfo instance) from TLS storage - for example, in case of Windows it uses OFFSET__TEB__ThreadLocalStoragePointer to look for TLS address in current *Thread Environment Block*. As listed before, ThreadLocalInfo contains a pointer to unmanaged Thread instance. AppDomain pointer and m_EETlsData array of pointers are irrelevant for our context. ThreadLocalModule, ThreadLocalBlock and ThreadStatics types from .\src\vm\threadstatics.h file contain main logic related of handling thread local storage.

Regarding the calculation of fields offsets (both regular and thread-static), Module::BuildStaticsOffsets method fills an additional, helper array of all offsets within a module (see fields m_pRegularStaticOffsets and m_pThreadStaticOffsets arrays) that is later on consumed by MethodTable Bulder::PlaceRegularStaticFields and MethodTableBuilder::Place ThreadStaticFields.

One may wonder what about generic types containing thread static fields? It's been said that at compile time a number of thread static fields is known but obviously it is not true in case of generic types - compiler does not know how many various generic types instantiation will happen (and each may require brand new sets of thread static variables). Solution is similar to the regular statics of generic types - ThreadLocalModule maintains an additional, dynamic array of pointers to smaller structures similar to ThreadLocalModule itself (see Figure 13-2 and corresponding Listing 13-19). Each such structure is dedicated for a single generic type instantiation and contains the same data - offset where its reference-type fields begins in ThreadStaticHandleTable (which may be dynamically resized) and static blob fields.

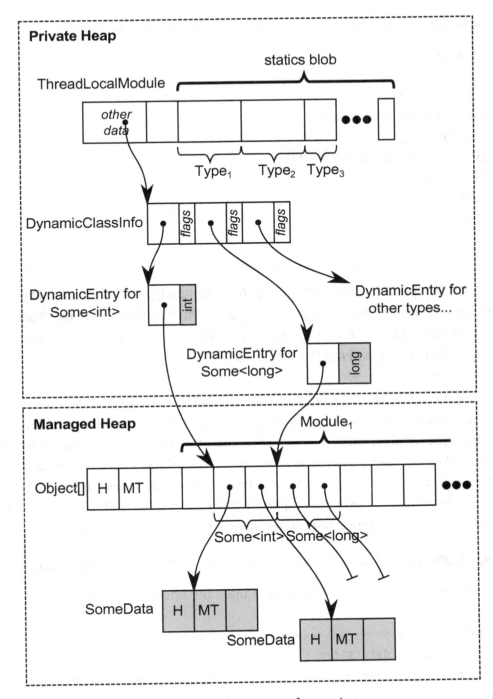

Figure 13-2. *Internals of thread local storage of generic types*

Listing 13-19. Simple Some<T> generic type illustrated in Figure 13-2

```
class Some<T>
{
    [ThreadStatic]
    private static T static1;
    [ThreadStatic]
    private static SomeData static2;
    [ThreadStatic]
    private static SomeData static3;
    ...
}
```

From a GC perspective, thread static data of reference type is a regular object rooted by mentioned, dedicated `Object[]` arrays that are kept alive by strong handles maintained by `ThreadLocalBlock`. Thus, they are alive as long as corresponding Thread and AppDomain are alive.

Using data slots is even slower because its general-purpose mechanism is built on internal, thread-static data store (see Listing 13-20). Thus, it obviously is slower than using a plain thread-static field. It adds some additional bookkeeping of internal dictionary-like structures (to maintain a key-value list of slots) and multithreading synchronization. For unmanaged, primitive types, it also introduces boxing and unboxing overhead. Feel free to investigate further types showed in Listing 13-20 to get a grasp how much is done more than simple access to the static thread variable.

Listing 13-20. Thread data storage-related part of Thread class definition

```
public sealed class Thread : CriticalFinalizerObject, _Thread
{
    /*=====================================================================
    ** Thread-local data store
    =====================================================================*/
    [ThreadStatic]
    static private LocalDataStoreHolder s_LocalDataStore; // stores
    LocalDataStore
```

```
sealed internal class LocalDataStore
{
    private LocalDataStoreElement[] m_DataTable;
    private LocalDataStoreMgr m_Manager;
```

If you conceptually add to Figure 13-1 all managed data structures used by thread data slots, you can probably imagine why data slots are so noticeably slower.

Usage Scenarios

Although the above description of thread data storage clearly shows that it adds some overhead, there is one main advantage of it from a performance perspective - getting rid of multithreading synchronization. Obviously, thread affinity is another, and the main, functional feature that distinguishes it from other data.

In general, thread local storage may be seen as useful in the following scenarios:

- It is required to store and manage thread-aware data - for example, some unmanaged resources may require it to be acquired and released by the same thread,

- It is possible to take advantage of single-thread affinity - for example:

  - Logging or diagnostics - each thread may without synchronization manipulate some local data used for diagnostic purposes, without interfering others (System.Diagnostics. Tracing being an example).

  - Caching - it may be perfectly fine to provide some thread-local cache, although we should be aware that there will be as many possible cache duplicates as running managed threads. StringBuilderCache class showed in Chapter 4 is a perfect example of such approach - there is a cached instance of small StringBuilder for each thread to access it efficiently without thread synchronization from some sort of global pool. Another example is TlsOverPerCoreLockedStacksArrayPool<T> from System.Buffers namespace, an implementation of ArrayPool using a tiered caching scheme, with a small per-thread cache for each array size, followed by a cache per array size shared by all

threads (partitioned into multiple partitions, each with its own
lock, with the goal of minimizing contentions between multiple
CPU cores access) - which is by the way the one returned when
using `ArrayPool<T>.Shared` instance.[2]

Using thread statics is obviously not eligible in async programming because
async method continuations are not guaranteed to be executed on the same
thread - we would lose thread local data after async method is continued. Thus,
complementary to `ThreadLocal<T>`, `AsyncLocal<T>` type is available that
keeps data across all async method execution. From the memory-management
point of view, this class is not so interesting though - it is a class, which instance is
being kept (altogether with the corresponding value) in the dictionary stored in the
execution context (`ExecutionContext` class).

Managed Pointers

So far, the topic of managed pointers was slightly skipped for brevity (although a careful
reader may remember referring to them once or twice). Most of the time a regular
.NET developer uses object references and it is simply enough because this is how a
managed world is constructed - objects are referencing each other via object references.
As explained in Chapter 4, object reference is in fact a type-safe pointer (address) that
always points to an object MethodTable reference field (it is often said it points at the
beginning of an object). Thus, using them may be quite efficient. Having an object
reference, we simply have the whole object address. For example, the GC can quickly
access its header via constant offset. Addresses of fields are also easily computable due
to information stored in MethodTable.

---

[2]This is true in .NET Core 2.1, while in .NET Core 2.0 it was only used for array pools of char and
byte.

There is, however, another pointer type in CLR - a *managed pointer*. It could be defined as a more general type of pointer, which may point to other locations than just the beginning of an object. ECMA-335 says that a managed pointer can point to:

- a local variable - whether it be reference to a heap-allocated object or simply stack-allocated type,

- parameter - like above,

- field of a compound type - meaning a field of other type (whether it is value or reference type),

- element of an array.

Despite this flexibility, managed pointers are still types. There is a managed pointer type that points to System.Int32 objects, regardless of their localization, denoted as System.Int32& in CIL. Or SomeNamespace.SomeClass& type pointing to our custom SomeNamespace.SomeClass instances. Strong typing makes them safer than pure, unmanaged pointers that may be used back and forth for literally everything. This is also why managed pointers do not offer *pointer arithmetic* known from raw pointers - it particularly does not make sense to "add" or "subtract" addresses they represent, pointing to various places inside objects or to local variables.

However, flexibility does not come without a cost. It reveals itself as limitations of a possible place where we can use managed pointers. As ECMA-335 says, managed pointer types are only allowed for:

- local variables

- parameter signatures

It is directly said that "they cannot be used for field signatures, as the element type of an array and boxing a value of managed pointer type is disallowed. Using a managed pointer type for the return type of methods is not verifiable."

Due to those limitations, managed pointers are not directly exposed into C# language. However, they have long been present in the well-known form of ref parameters. Passing parameter by reference is nothing else than using a managed pointer underneath. Thus, managed pointers are also often referred to as *byref types* (or *byref* simply). We have already seen examples of passing by reference in Listings 4-30 and 4-31 from Chapter 4.

Recently, since C# 7.0, managed pointers usage has been widened in the form of ref locals and ref returns. Thus, the last sentence from the above ECMA citation about using a managed pointer type as the return type has been relaxed.

Ref Locals

You can see *ref local* as a local variable to store a managed pointer. Thus, it is a convenient way of creating helper variables that may be later on used for direct access to a given field, array element or other local variable (see Listing 13-21). Please note that both the left and right side of assignment must be marked with the ref keyword to denote operating on managed pointers.

Listing 13-21. Basic usage of ref locals

```
public static void UsingRefLocal(SomeClass data)
{
    ref int refLocal = ref data.Field;
    refLocal = 2;
}
```

A trivial example from Listing 13-21 make only illustrative sense - we are gaining direct access to an int field so the performance gain will be neglectable. More commonly you may want to use ref local to gain direct pointer to some heavyweight instance to make sure copying will not happen (see Listing 13-22) and pass it by reference somewhere or use locally. Ref locals are also commonly used to store the result of ref return method (as we will soon see).

Listing 13-22. Possible usage of ref locals (example from MSDN)

```
ref VeryLargeStruct reflocal = ref veryLargeStruct;
// afterwards, using reflocal we use veryLargeStruct without copying
```

Ref local may be assigned to reference that itself is null (see Listing 13-23). At first glance, it may look strange but makes perfect sense. You can think of ref local as a variable storing an address to a reference, but it does not mean that the reference itself points to anything.

Listing 13-23. Assigning null reference to a ref local

```
SomeClass local = null;
ref SomeClass localRef = ref local;
```

Ref Returns

Ref return allows us to return a managed pointer from a method. Obviously, some limitations must be introduced when using them. As MSDN says: "The return value must have a lifetime that extends beyond the execution of the method. In other words, it cannot be a local variable in the method that returns it. It can be an instance or static field of a class, or it can be an argument passed to the method". Attempting to return a local variable generates compiler error CS8168, "Cannot return local 'obj' by reference because it is not a ref local."

An example of the mentioned local variable limitation is shown in Listing 13-24. Obviously, we cannot return a managed pointer to a stack-allocated (or enregistered) localInt variable because it becomes invalid as soon as ReturnByRefValueTypeInterior method ends.

Listing 13-24. An example of invalid code trying to ref return local variable

```
public static ref int ReturnByRefValueTypeInterior(int index)
{
   int localInt = 7;
   return ref localInt; // Compilation error:  Cannot return local
'localInt' by reference because it is not a ref local
}
```

However, it is perfectly fine to ref return element of the method parameter because from the method perspective, this argument lives longer that the method itself (see Listing 13-25). In our example, GetArrayElementByRef method returns a managed pointer to a given element of the array argument.

Listing 13-25. An example of ref return usage

```
public static ref int GetArrayElementByRef(int[] array, int index)
{
   return ref array[index];
}
```

Consuming ref returning method is easy but may be done in two ways (see Listing 13-26):

- By consuming returned managed pointer - this is by far the most typical way of using ref returning methods because we want to take advantage of the fact that it returns byref. In such case we must call a method with ref keyword and store the result in a local ref variable. The first GetArrayElementByRef call in Listing 13-26 shows such approach. Because we are returning a managed pointer to an array element, we can modify its content directly (423 will be written to the console).

- By consuming a value pointed by the returned managed pointer - it is also possible to fall back to regular method call by omitting both ref keywords (see second GetArrayElementByRef call in Listing 13-26). In that way, the method will return a by value so modifying such result does not modify the original content directly (still 423 will be written to the console, ignoring our try to change first element to 5).

Listing 13-26. Consuming ref return method

```
int[] array = {1, 2, 3};

ref int arrElementRef = ref PassingByref.GetArrayElementByRef(array, 0);
arrElementRef = 4;
Console.WriteLine(string.Join("", array));    // Will write 423

int arrElementVal = PassingByref.GetArrayElementByRef(array, 0);
arrElementVal = 5;
Console.WriteLine(string.Join("", array));    // Will still write 423
```

Please note that like in ref locals, you may ref return a null referencing reference (see Listing 13-27). This example, inspired by .NET samples, provides a very simple book collection type. Its GetBookByTitle method returns by ref a book with the given title if it exists. If it does not exist, it returns a predefined instance reference nobook that is null. It is then perfectly fine to check if GetBookByTitle returns a reference that points to something or not.

Listing 13-27. Ref returning null reference

```
public class BookCollection
{
    private Book[] books =
    {
        new Book { Title = "Call of the Wild, The", Author = "Jack London" },
        new Book { Title = "Tale of Two Cities, A", Author = "Charles
        Dickens" }
    };
    private Book nobook = null;
    public ref Book GetBookByTitle(string title)
    {
        // Book nobook = null; // Would not work
        for (int ctr = 0; ctr < books.Length; ctr++)
        {
            if (title == books[ctr].Title)
                return ref books[ctr];
        }
        return ref nobook;
    }
}

static void Main(string[] args)
{
    var collection = new BookCollection();
    ref var book = ref collection.GetBookByTitle("<Not exists>");
    if (book != null)
    {
        Console.WriteLine(book.Author);
    }
}
```

Please note that we could not simply use local nobook variable (as in commented line inside GetBookByTitle) because it is not possible to ref return local variable value with the lifetime that does not extend beyond the execution of the method.

Readonly Ref Variables and in Parameters

Ref types are quite powerful, because we may change its target. Thus, *readonly refs* were introduced in C# 7.2 that controls the ability to mutate the storage of a ref variable. Please note a subtle difference in such context between a managed pointer to a value type versus a reference type:

- For value type target - it guarantees that the value will not be modified. As the value here is the whole object (memory region), in other words it guarantees that all fields will not be changed.

- For reference type target - it guarantees that the reference value will not be changed. As the value here is the reference itself (pointing to another object), it guarantees that we will not change it to point to another object. But we can still modify the properties of the referenced object.

Let's modify an example from Listing 13-27 to return a readonly ref (see Listing 13-28). The code is in fact identical, the only difference is a signature change of GetBookByTitle method.

Listing 13-28. Example taken from dotnet docs examples

```
public class BookCollection
{
    private Book[] books =
    {
        new Book { Title = "Call of the Wild, The", Author = "Jack London" },
        new Book { Title = "Tale of Two Cities, A", Author = "Charles
        Dickens" }
    };
    private Book nobook = null;
    public ref readonly Book GetBookByTitle(string title)
    {
        // Book nobook = null; // Would not work
        for (int ctr = 0; ctr < books.Length; ctr++)
        {
            if (title == books[ctr].Title)
```

```
            return ref books[ctr];
        }
        return ref nobook;
    }
}
static void Main(string[] args)
{
    var collection = new BookCollection();
    ref readonly var book = ref collection.GetBookByTitle("<Not exists>");
    if (book != null)
    {
        Console.WriteLine(book.Author);
    }
}
```

Our BookCollection may illustrate the difference between readonly reference in case of both value type and reference type. If Book is a class, it is guaranteed that we will not change the reference value, like trying to change it to a new object in commented line in Listing 13-29. However, it is perfectly fine to modify fields of the target referenced instance (like changing the author in Listing 13-29).

Listing 13-29. Using class from Listing 13-28 when Book is a class

```
static void Main(string[] args)
{
    var collection = new BookCollection();
    ref readonly var book = ref collection.GetBookByTitle("Call of the Wild,
    The");
    // book = new Book();            // Not possible. Would be possible
                                                without readonly
    book.Author = "Konrad Kokosa";
}
```

However, if Book is a struct, it is guaranteed that we will not be able to change its value, like trying to change the author in Listing 13-30 (and for the same reason, it is not possible to assign to it a new value in the one line above).

Listing 13-30. Using class from Listing 13-28 when Book is a struct

```
static void Main(string[] args)
{
    var collection = new BookCollection();
    ref readonly var book = ref collection.GetBookByTitle("Call of the Wild,
    The");
    // book = new Book();             // Not possible. Would be possible
                                         without readonly

    // book.Author = "Konrad Kokosa";   // Not possible. Would be possible
                                         without readonly

}
```

These seemingly difficult nuances are easy to remember if we keep in mind what is a protected value - the whole object (for value type) or reference (for reference type).

There is still one important aspect to be mentioned in this context. Let's assume that our Book struct has a method that modifies its field (see Listing 13-31). What happens if we call it on a returned readonly ref? Even in such case it is guaranteed that the original value will not be changed (see Listing 13-32). It is implemented by a *defensive copy* approach - before executing ModifyAuthor method, a copy of the returned value type (a Book struct in our case) is being made and its method is called on it. Compiler does not analyze whether called method modifies state as it really difficult (assuming a lot of possible conditions inside a method, maybe even depending on external data). Thus, any method called on such struct will be treated that way.

So in fact, ModifyAuthor method is still executed but only on temporary instance that becomes unused soon. Any changes applied to such a defensive copy obviously are not performed for the original value.

Listing 13-31. Simple value type method modifying its state

```
public struct Book
{
    ...
    public void ModifyAuthor()
    {
        this.Author = "XXX";
    }
}
```

Listing 13-32. Using class from Listing 13-28 when Book is a struct

```
static void Main(string[] args)
{
    var collection = new BookCollection();
    ref readonly var book = ref collection.GetBookByTitle("Call of the Wild,
    The");
    book.ModifyAuthor();
    Console.WriteLine(collection.GetBookByTitle("Call of the Wild, The")
    .Author);    // Prints Jack London
}
```

Such defensive copy may be both surprising and costly - one may expect the field to be modified if ModifyAuthor method executed successfully. Creating a defensive copy of a struct also is an obvious performance overhead.

Please note in case of a Book being a class, the expected behavior remains - ModifyAuthor would modify the object state even if readonly reference was returned to it. Remember, readonly reference disables reference mutation, not the reference target values.

Please note that readonly refs do not have to be used only in the context of collections. There is a good example of using readonly refs in MSDN to return static value type representing some global, commonly used value (see Listing 13-33). Without readonly ref returned the Origin value would be exposed to modification, which is obviously unacceptable because Origin should be treat as a constant. Before introducing ref returns, such value could be exposed as a regular value type, but it could introduce copying of such structure many times.

Listing 13-33. An example of using readonly ref for public static value (based on MSDN documentation example)

```
struct Point3D
{
    private static Point3D origin = new Point3D();
    public static ref readonly Point3D Origin => ref origin;
    ...
}
```

A form of readonly refs is also available in the form of in parameters. This is a small yet very important addition to passing by reference feature added in C# 7.2. While a passing by reference using ref parameter, the argument may be changed inside such method - exposing the same problems as ref returning. Thus, the in modifier on parameters was added, to specify that an argument is passed by reference but should not be modified by the called method (see Listing 13-34).

Listing 13-34. An example of using in parameter

```
public class BookCollection
{
    ...
    public void CheckBook(in Book book)
    {
        book.Title = "XXX";      // Compilation error: Cannot assign to a
                                 // member of variable 'in Book' because it
                                 // is a readonly variable.

    }
}
```

Please note the same rules apply here as in readonly refs explained before: only a value of the parameter is guaranteed to be not modified. So, in case of in parameter being a reference type, only the reference value is not modifiable - the target reference instance may be changed. So, in Listing 13-34 if Book was a class, it would compile without a problem and Title would be changed. Only an assignment like book = new Book() would not be possible.

Thus, the same defensive copy approach is used when a method is called on in value type parameter (see Listing 13-35). Remember that to avoid such implicit copying overhead that does not make sense in the first place (as any modifications are discarded).

Listing 13-35. An example of using in parameter

```
public class BookCollection
{
    ...
    public void CheckBook(in Book book)
    {
        book.ModifyAuthor(); // Called on book defensive copy, original book
                                Title will not be changed.
    }
}
```

You may also avoid defensive copies by making such struct readonly (if it is applicable) - they will be explained in the next subchapter. Because readonly structs disable any possible modifications on its fields, the compiler may safely omit creating defensive copy and call methods on passed value type arguments directly.

Ref Types Internals

A careful reader may have raised a lot of interesting questions looking at listings from 13-21 to 13-33. For example, how does passing around all those managed pointers cooperate with the GC? What code is generated underneath by the JIT compiler? What are the real performance gains by using all this complicated machinery? If you are interested in answers, read on. You may however feel free to omit this point and go straight into the next one, describing practical usage of ref types in C#.

Let's dig deeper into main use cases that managed pointer usage may be grouped into. Understanding them will reveal reasons behind the mentioned limitations as well as will help us to understand them better. In the following code examples, we will be using two trivial types from Listing 13-36. All three ways how managed pointers appear in C# are utilized in those examples - ref parameters, ref locals, and ref returns.

Listing 13-36. Two trivial types used in the following examples

```
public class SomeClass
{
    public int Field;
}

public struct SomeStruct
{
    public int Field;
}
```

We will start from looking at some details underneath the working of managed pointers. Eventually it will lead us to practical usage considerations.

Managed Pointer Into Stack-Allocated Object

A managed pointer can point to a method's local variable or parameter. From an implementation point of view, as we have seen in Chapter 8, a local variable or parameter may be stack-allocated or enregistered into CPU register (if JIT compiler decides so). How does a managed pointer work in such a case then? Simply put, it is perfectly fine that the managed pointer points to a stack address! This is one of the reasons why a managed pointer may not be the object's field (and may not be boxed). If it appears in this way on the Managed Heap, it could outlive the method within which the indicated stack address is located. It would be very dangerous (pointed stack address would contain undefined data, most probably other's method stack frame). So by limiting a managed pointer's usage to local variables and parameters, their lifetime is limited to the most restrictive lifetime of a possible target they can point to - data on the stack.

What about enregistered local variables and parameters? Remember that such an enregistered target is just an optimization detail; it has to provide at least the same lifetime characteristics as a stack-allocated target. A lot depends on the JIT compiler here. If some target was enregistered, it is even better! Such a register may be simply used as a managed pointer. In other words, using a CPU register instead of a stack address does not change much from the JIT compiler perspective.

But how are managed pointers (or more precisely, objects pointed by them) reported to the GC? They must be, because otherwise GC may not detect reachability of the target object; if it happens that managed pointer is the only root at the moment.

Let's analyze a very simple passing by reference scenario, similar to Listing 4-34 from Chapter 4 (see Listing 13-37). To remove the effects of inlining and make things clearer, NoInlining attribute was used that prevents inlining of Test method (inlined version will be discussed also later on).

Listing 13-37. Simple pass by reference scenario (passing by reference whole reference type object)

```
static void Main(string[] args)
{
    SomeClass someClass = new SomeClass();
    PassingByref.Test(ref someClass);
    Console.WriteLine(someClass.Field); // Prints "11"
}

public class PassingByref
{
    [MethodImpl(MethodImplOptions.NoInlining)]
    public static void Test(ref SomeClass data)
    {
        //data = new SomeClass();
        data.Field = 11; // at least to this line corresponding SomeClass
        instance must be live (not garbage collected)
    }
}
```

What is interesting for us at the moment is to see how such code is represented both on CIL and assembly level after JITting. Corresponding CIL code reveals usage of strongly typed SomeClass& managed pointer (see Listing 13-38). In the Main method ldloca instruction is used that loads the address of the local variable at a specific index (and index 0 corresponds to our someClass variable) onto the evaluation stack, which is then passed to Test method. Then Test method uses ldind.ref instruction to dereference such address and push resulting object reference on the evaluation stack.

Listing 13-38. CIL code from Listing 13-37

```
.method private hidebysig static
    void Main (string[] args) cil managed
{
    .locals init (
        [0] class SomeClass
    )
    IL_0000: newobj instance void SomeClass::.ctor()
    IL_0005: stloc.0
    IL_0006: ldloca.s 0
    IL_0008: call void PassingByref::Test(class SomeClass&)
    IL_000d: ret
}

.method public hidebysig static
    void Test (class SomeClass& data) cil managed noinlining
{
    IL_0000: ldarg.0
    IL_0001: ldind.ref
    IL_0002: ldc.i4.s 11
    IL_0004: stfld int32 SomeClass::Field
    IL_0009: ret
}
```

But while CIL code may be interesting, we already have seen examples that only JITted code reveals the true nature what happens underneath. Looking at the assembly code of both methods, we indeed see that Test method receives an address pointing to the stack where reference to newly created SomeClass instance is stored (see Listing 13-39 with comments).

Listing 13-39. Assembly code of methods from Listing 13-38

```
Program.Main(System.String[])
    L0000: sub rsp, 0x28                    // Growing stack frame
    L0004: xor eax, eax                     // Zeroing EAX register
    L0006: mov [rsp+0x20], rax              // Zeroing the stack under rsp+0x20
                                            //    address (where local variable is
                                            //    stored)

    L000b: mov rcx, 0x7ffa69398840          // Moving MT of SomeClass into RCX
                                            //    register

    L0015: call 0x7ffac3452520              // Calling allocator (as a result,
                                            //    RAX will contain address of the
                                            //    new object)

    L001a: mov [rsp+0x20], rax              // Storing the address of new
                                            //    object onto the stack

    L001f: lea rcx, [rsp+0x20]              // Moving the local variable's stack
                                            //    address into RCX register (which
                                            //    is first Test method argument)

    L0024: call PassingByref.Test(SomeClass ByRef)
    L0029: nop
    L002a: add rsp, 0x28
    L002e: ret

PassingByref.Test(SomeClass ByRef)
    L0000: mov rax, [rcx]                   // Dereferencing the address in
                                            //    RCX into RAX (As a result, RAX
                                            //    contains object instance address)

    L0003: mov dword [rax+0x8], 0xb         // Storing value 11 (0x0B) in the
                                            //    proper field of an object

    L000a: ret
```

From a pure assembly code point of view, similar code as in Listing 13-39 would be generated, for example, if using pointer to a pointer in C++. But how, while Test method is executing, the GC knows that RCX register contains an object address? The answer is interesting for us - Test method from Listing 13-39 contains an empty GCInfo. In other words, Test method is so simple that GC will not interrupt its work. Thus, it does not need to report anything.

In the example from Listing 13-39, SomeClass instance is life because of the Main method. GCInfo of the Main method would reveal that rsp+0x20 stack address is reported to contain live root (Untracked: +sp+20 would be listed by !u -gcinfo command). This, however, does not change anything regarding further passing such instance by reference or not.

If Test method was more complex, it could be JITted into fully- or partially interruptible method (see Chapter 8). For example, in the latter case, we could see various safepoints, some of them listing some CPU registers (or stack addresses) as live slots - see Listing 13-40 as an example, showing an excerpt of !u -gcinfo command from SOS extension in WinDbg (already explained in Chapter 8).

Listing 13-40. Example of JITted code and corresponding GCInfo of more complex Test method variation (its C# source code is not shown as irrelevant)

```
> !u -gcinfo 00007ffc86850d00
Normal JIT generated code
CoreCLR.Unsafe.PassingByref.Test(CoreCLR.Unsafe.SomeClass ByRef)
Begin 00007ffc86850d00, size 44
push    rdi
push    rsi
sub     rsp,28h
mov     rsi,rcx
...
call    00007ffc`86850938
00000029 is a safepoint:
00000028 +rsi(interior)

...
call    00007ffc`868508a0
00000033 is a safepoint:
00000032 +rsi(interior)

...
add     rsp,28h
```

```
pop     rsi
pop     rdi
ret
```

Those life slots would be listed as so-called *interior pointers* because managed pointers in general may point inside objects (it will be explained soon). Thus, managed pointers are always reported as interior roots; besides that in our case they point in fact at the beginning of the object. Interpretation of such pointers is on the GC side, explained later.

As mentioned before, our example was a little contrived by an explicit disabling inlining possibility. If we commented out the NoInlining attribute in Listing 13-37, we would get after JITting the following code:

```
Program.Main(System.String[])
    L0000: sub rsp, 0x28
    L0004: mov rcx, 0x7ffa69398840   // Moving MT of SomeClass
                                         into RCX register
    L000e: call 0x7ffac3452520       // Calling allocator (as a
                                         result, RAX will contain
                                         address of the new object)
    L0013: mov dword [rax+0x8], 0xb  // Directly storing value 11
                                         into proper field of an
                                         object
    L001a: add rsp, 0x28
    L001e: ret
```

Once again, the power of JIT compiler optimizations may be noticed. The whole concept of managed pointers has been reduced into the simplest possible handling of direct object addresses.

Very similar code would be generated in case of using struct instead of class (see Listing 13-41, similar to Listing 4-33 from Chapter 4). What is more interesting, even it is theoretically known that Test method from Listing 13-41 operates only on stack-allocated data (local variable of SomeStruct value type), corresponding GCInfo will still list live slots because of using a managed pointer. It is up to the GC just to ignore them.

Listing 13-41. Simple pass by reference scenario (passing by reference whole value type object)

```
static void Main(string[] args)
{
    SomeStruct someStruct = new SomeStruct();
    PassingByref.Test(ref someStruct);
    Console.WriteLine(someStruct.Field);
}

[MethodImpl(MethodImplOptions.NoInlining)]
public static void Test(ref SomeStruct data)
{
    data.Field = 11;
}
```

Managed Pointer Into Heap-Allocated Object

While stack-pointing managed pointers may seem to be interesting, those that are pointing to objects on the Managed Heap are even more interesting. In contrast to the object reference, a managed pointer can point to the inside of the object - field of a type or element of an array as already cited ECMA standard says (see Figure 13-3). That is why they are in fact "interior pointers," as it is named in the literature. When you think about it a little, it may seem very interesting - how interior pointers pointing inside managed objects may be reported to the GC?

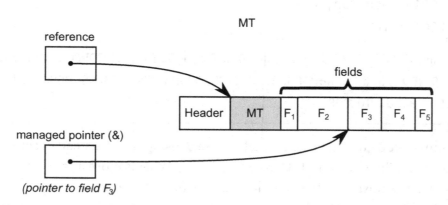

Figure 13-3. *Managed pointer (also known as interior pointer or byref) versus regular object reference*

Let's modify a little code from Listing 13-37, to pass by reference only a field of heap-allocated SomeClass instance (see Listing 13-42). The main method looks straightforward. It instantiates SomeClass object, passes a reference to one of its field to the Test method, and prints the result.

But our modified Test method expects now System.Int32& managed pointer. During execution, Test method operates only on a managed pointer to int. But it is not just a regular pointer to int - it is a field of a heap-allocated object! From where the GC knows that it may not collect corresponding object, to which used managed pointer it belongs? There is absolutely nothing said about from where int& pointer comes from, though.

Listing 13-42. Simple pass by reference scenario (passing by reference object's field)

```
static void Main(string[] args)
{
    SomeClass someClass = new SomeClass();
    PassingByref.Test(ref someClass.Field);
    Console.WriteLine(someClass.Field);   // Prints "11"
}

public class PassingByref
{
    [MethodImpl(MethodImplOptions.NoInlining)]
    public static void Test(ref int data)
    {
        data = 11;   // this should keep containing object life!
    }
}
```

First of all, please note that our Test method contrived example will be JITted into atomic (from the GC point of view) method that the GC will simply not interrupt at all - similarly as in case of code from Listing 13-37 (see Listing 13-43). So the question of proper root reporting is not needed at all for such a simple method.

Listing 13-43. Assembler code after JITting code from Listing 13-42

```
Program.Main(System.String[])
    L0000: sub rsp, 0x28
    L0004: mov rcx, 0x7ffa6d128840
    L000e: call 0x7ffac3452520
    L0013: lea rcx, [rax+0x8]
    L0017: call PassingByref.Test(Int32 ByRef)
    L001c: nop
    L001d: add rsp, 0x28
    L0021: ret

PassingByref.Test(Int32 ByRef)
    L0000: mov dword [rcx], 0xb
    L0006: ret
```

But let's suppose Test method is complex enough to produce interruptible code. Listing 13-44 shows an example of how corresponding JITted code could look then. RSI register, which keeps the value of the integer field address passed as argument in RCX register, is reported as an interior pointer.

Listing 13-44. Fragments of assembler code after JITting code that becomes fully interruptible

```
> !u -gcinfo 00007ffc86fb0ce0
Normal JIT generated code
CoreCLR.Unsafe.PassingByref.Test(Int32 ByRef)
Begin 00007ffc86fb0ce0, size 41
push     rdi
push     rsi
sub      rsp,28h
mov      rsi,rcx
00000009 interruptible
00000009 +rsi(interior)
...
0000003a not interruptible
0000003a -rsi(interior)
add      rsp,28h
```

```
pop    rsi
pop    rdi
ret
```

If GC happens and Test method is suspended when RSI contains such interior pointer, GC must interpret it to find the corresponding object. This is in general not trivial. One could think about simple algorithm that starts from such a pointer's address and then tries to find the beginning of the object by scanning memory to the left byte by byte.[3] This obviously is not efficient and has many drawbacks:

- Interior pointer may point to a distant field of big object (or distant element of very large array) - so a lot of such naïve scans had to be performed.

- It is not trivial to detect beginning of the object - it could be a check if subsequent 8 bytes (or 4 in 32-bit case) forms valid MT address but this only increases such algorithm complexity. One could imagine some "marker" bytes that are allocated at the beginning of each object but this adds unnecessary memory overhead just to support theoretically rare interior pointer's usage (and it would be really hard to define mark bytes unique enough to identify object beginning unambiguously).

- All managed pointers are reported as interior pointers - so they may point to the stack and it makes no sense to find containing object in the first place (as it may point, for example, inside stack-allocated struct).

I hope you get the point that such algorithm is impractical. Some more intelligent support is required to resolve interior pointers efficiently.

We in fact have already seen the mechanism used here. During GC, interior pointers are translated into corresponding objects, thanks to the bricks and plug trees described in Chapter 9. Given a specified address, a proper brick table entry is calculated and a corresponding plug tree traversed to find the plug within which such an address lives

---

[3]It must have been done with a single byte shift because it is not guaranteed in any way how aligned are interior pointers with respect to the object's beginning.

(see Figures 9-9 and 9-10 in Chapter 9). Then, such plug is being scanned object by object to find the one that contains the considered address.[4]

Obviously, such algorithm has its costs also. Plug tree traversal and plug scanning takes some time. Dereferencing interior pointer is not trivial then. This is the second important reason why managed pointers are not allowed to live on the heap (especially as the object's fields) - creating complex graphs of objects referenced by interior pointers would make traversing such a graph quite costly. Giving such flexibility is simply not worth the quite significant overhead it introduces.

Please also note that with such implementation, dereferencing the interior pointer is possible only during GC, after Plan phase. Only then plug and gaps are constructed, altogether with the corresponding plug tree.

If you would like to investigate interior pointers on your own, start from the CoreCLR gc_heap::find_object(uint8_t* interior, ...) method - plug scanning is done in the gc_heap::find_first_object(uint8_t* start, uint8_t* first_object) method.

Interior pointer interpretation allows some magic things to happen, dangerous at the first glance. For example, we are able to return a managed pointer to a locally created class instance or an array (see Listing 13-45). This may seem to be counterintuitive - how one could return from a method reference to single integer array element, while the array object itself seems to become unreachable? Obviously, it is not, because after such method ends, the returned interior pointer becomes the only root of the array.

Listing 13-45. Example of interior pointer becoming the only root

```
public static ref int ReturnByRefReferenceTypeInterior(int index)
{
    int[] localArray = new[] { 1, 2, 3 };
    return ref localArray[index];
}

static void Main(string[] args)
```

---

[4]Plug scanning is possible because the plug starts with an object and then the following objects are easily found because object sizes are known.

```
{
    ref int byRef = ref ReturnByRefReferenceTypeInterior(0);
    // Array created in above method is no longer accessible from code,
        while still alive
    byRef = 4; // using by byRef to prevent eager root collection
}
```

The array itself is then still alive because of the interior pointer; however, we have lost the array object reference (see Figure 13-4). Due to the limitation mentioned previously (bricks and plug tree availability), such a pointer cannot be at runtime "converted back" to the proper reference of the object it points to.

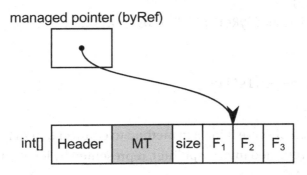

Figure 13-4. *Managed pointer being the only root of the array object (pointing to one of its elements)*

We may play a little with WeakReference type to observe interior pointer behavior (for fun experiments or fancy unit tests). A little modified code in Listing 13-46 uses a class ArrayWrapper instead of plain array, which will turn out to be useful for our experiment soon. Byref is returned to the integer field of ArrayWrapper. Moreover, ObservableReturnByRefReferenceTypeInterior method returns a WeakReference to the created object, to make its liveness observable.

Listing 13-46. Example of interior pointer becoming the only root

```
public static ref int ObservableReturnByRefReferenceTypeInterior(int index,
out WeakReference wr)
{
    ArrayWrapper wrapper = new ArrayWrapper() { Array = new[] {1, 2, 3},
    Field = 0 };
```

```
    wr = new WeakReference(wrapper);
    return ref wrapper.Field;
}

static void Main(string[] args)
{
    ref int byRef = ref ObservableReturnByRefReferenceTypeInterior(2, out
    WeakReference wr);
    byRef = 4;
    for (int i = 0; i < 3; ++i)
    {
      GC.Collect();
      Console.WriteLine(byRef + " " + wr.IsAlive);
    }
    GC.Collect();
    Console.WriteLine(wr.IsAlive);
}
```

In that way we can observe it in Main method to confirm that ArrayWrapper instance is live as long as the returned interior pointer, represented by local ref byRef variable, is used (see Listing 13-47).

Listing 13-47. Results of code from Listing 13-4

```
4 True
4 True
4 True
False
```

If we took a memory dump inside for loop in Main method from Listing 13-46, with the help of WinDbg we could find a root of ArrayWrapper instance to be an interior pointer kept on the stack (see Listing 13-48).

Listing 13-48. Dumpheap and gcroot SOS commands in WinDbg - interior pointer is stored on the stack (RBP is a stack-addressing register)

```
> !dumpheap -type ArrayWrapper
         Address              MT       Size
0000027b00023d20 00007ffdace07220       32

...
> !gcroot 0000027b00023d20
Thread 3f48:
    000000a65857de60 00007ffdacf60598 CoreCLR.Unsafe.Program.Main
    (System.String[])
        rbp-50: 000000a65857dec0 (interior)
            -> 0000027b00023d20 CoreCLR.Unsafe.ArrayWrapper
Found 1 unique roots (run '!GCRoot -all' to see all roots).
```

Other tools, including PerfView, most often list such an object as regular local variable roots ([local vars] root in case of PerfView). This may be sometimes misleading as from code there is no direct connection between Main method and ArrayWrapper type (and such relation could be even more hidden if the interior pointer would point to a more nested type).

What is more interesting, such interior pointer usage may lead to surprising (yet still sensible) behaviors. Let's change code from Listing 13-46 to return byref given element of internal ArrayWrapper array, similarly like in Listing 13-45 (see Listing 13-49).

Listing 13-49. Example of interior pointer becoming the only root

```
public static ref int ObservableReturnByRefReferenceTypeInterior(int index,
out WeakReference wr)
{
    ArrayWrapper wrapper = new ArrayWrapper() {Array = new[] {1, 2, 3},
    Field = 0};
    wr = new WeakReference(wrapper);
    return ref wrapper.Array[index];
}
```

After such a change, Main method produces different results (see Listing 13-50). Apparently, the returned ArrayWrapper instance becomes unreachable (and thus garbage collected) soon after ObservableReturnByRefReferenceTypeInterior method ends. This may be surprising as underlying array is still kept live by byRef interior pointer!

Listing 13-50. Results of code from Listing 13-49

```
4 False
4 False
4 False
False
```

A careful reader probably already catches it. It is easy to explain what happens by illustrating relevant relationships (see Figure 13-5). After `ObservableReturnByRefReferenceTypeInterior` method ends but before first `GC.Collect` call, the situation is as in Figure 13-5a - `ArrayWrapper` instance is still alive, referencing `int[]` array through `Array` field. And there is `byRef` ref local that points into the same array. When GC happens, `int[]` array is still held by interior pointer. But, in fact, nothing points to the `ArrayWrapper` instance, as it is detected as unreachable and garbage collected.

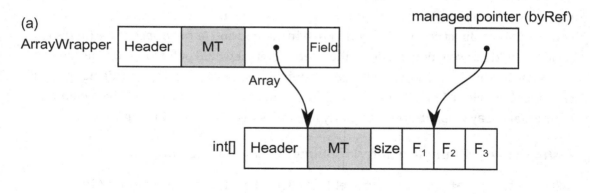

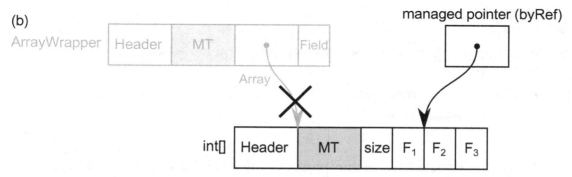

Figure 13-5. *Illustration of objects relationships in Listing 13-49: (a) before the GC run, (b) after the GC run*

I hope you already notice the direction chosen by this description - avoid such ref returns that return interior-only rooted objects. They are fun but may be misleading!

Interior pointers are, of course, also considered during relocation in compacting GC. Their value (address) is accordingly changed according to a corresponding plug offset, just as for regular references.

One may be quite surprised that code from Listing 13-45 is correctly handled by the GC. Similarly, code from Listing 13-51 may be surprising although we should already understand why it works. Even if the array of ints seems to be only temporary, due to the interior pointer to the first element, it will be kept alive as long as such pointer is being used.

Listing 13-51. Ref local with interior pointer to temporary (yet still alive) managed array

```
ref var local = ref (new int[1])[0];
```

We can use such "magical" syntax to create a generic helper of creating interior pointers (see Listing 13-52). Its usage should be limited only for testing and benchmarking scenarios (at least I am not able to imagine any real-world usage of it).

Listing 13-52. Code that creates interior pointer to a given object

```
public class Helpers {
    public static ref T MakeInterior<T>(T obj) => ref (new T[] { obj })[0];
}
```

For flexibility, managed pointers may also point to unmanaged memory regions. They are obviously ignored by the GC during the Mark or Compact phases.

Managed Pointers in C# - ref Variables

As previously said, ref variables (ref parameters, ref locals, and ref return usage) are small wrappers around managed pointers. They should not be treated as pointers obviously. They are variables! Read great "ref returns are not pointers" article by Vladimir Sadov at `http://mustoverride.com/refs-not-ptrs/` for more details.

It is nice to experiment with all those bigger or smaller managed pointers and ref variables usages, but why do we need them at all? Why are all those ref locals, ref returns, and ref parameters were introduced in the first place? There is one single, very important reason behind them:

> to avoid copying data - especially when using large structs - in a type safe manner!

Value types have many advantages and we have seen it already in this book - avoiding heap allocations and better data locality can make code significantly faster. Their value passing semantics (explained in detail in Chapter 4) makes them, however, a little troublesome - JIT compiler is making its best to avoid copying small structures but it is in fact an implementation detail behind our control. Every time we are passing a value type (our custom struct most probably) as a parameter or return it from a method, we should assume that undesired memory copying happens.

Ref variables were introduced to overcome this main disadvantage. They guarantee passing value types by reference, combining the best of two worlds - avoiding heap allocations while still making possible to use them in reference-like manner (because they provide reference semantics).

Let's look at a simple benchmark to let the numbers speak (see Listing 13-53). There are methods defined that are passing value types (structs) both typically by value and also by reference. To measure impact of the passed struct size, three various structs are used - containing 8, 28, and 48 integers (thus, with the sizes of 32, 112, and 192 bytes respectively). Only the smallest struct definition is shown for brevity. Additionally, there is also a single method taking as an argument a similarly sized class.

Listing 13-53. Benchmark to measure by value versus by reference passing

```
public unsafe class ByRef
{
    [GlobalSetup]
    public void Setup()
    {
        this.struct32B = new Struct32B();
        // ...
    }

    [Benchmark]
    public int StructAccess()
    {
        int result = 0;
        result = Helper1(struct32B);
        return result;
    }

    [Benchmark]
    public int ByRefStructAccess()
    {
        int result = 0;
        result = Helper1(ref struct32B);
        return result;
    }

    [Benchmark]
    public int ClassAccess()
    {
        int result = 0;
        result = Helper2(bigClass);
        return result;
    }

    [MethodImpl(MethodImplOptions.NoInlining)]
    private int Helper1(Struct32B data)
    {
```

```
        return data.Value1;
    }

    [MethodImpl(MethodImplOptions.NoInlining)]
    private int Helper1(ref Struct32B data)
    {
        return data.Value1;
    }

    [MethodImpl(MethodImplOptions.NoInlining)]
    private int Helper2(BigClass data)
    {
        return data.Value1;
    }

    public struct Struct32B
    {
        public int Value1;
        public int Value2;
        public int Value3;
        public int Value4;
        public int Value5;
        public int Value6;
        public int Value7;
        public int Value8;
    }
}
```

Results from DotNetBenchmark tool of such a simple benchmark are clearly showing the advantage of passing by reference (see Listing 13-54). Passing by reference shows the same performance regardless of the struct size (and similar to class reference passing, regardless of its size). On the other hand, as regular by value passing (which involves struct copying) becomes the more drastically slower, the bigger the struct size is. The same would apply to the ref returning so a very similar benchmark is omitted for brevity.

Listing 13-54. Results from benchmark in Listing 10-52

Method	Mean	Allocated
Struct32B	1.560 ns	0 B
Struct112B	5.229 ns	0 B
Struct192B	7.457 ns	0 B
ByRefStruc32tB	1.332 ns	0 B
ByRefStruct112B	1.343 ns	0 B
ByRefStruct192B	1.329 ns	0 B
ClassAccess	1.098 ns	0 B

Introducing ref variables is thus especially important when using large value types. Having them, we should be no longer afraid of struct-copying. Moreover, we can control such data mutability with the help of already-mentioned readonly refs and readonly structs that will be explained soon. All this was introduced to make value types more usable in high-performance scenarios.

However, even in trivial cases ref variables may be useful. A good sample from .NET documentation is shown in Listing 13-55. A method that is dedicated to find a value in a given matrix is written in two ways - returning found element by value tuple and by reference. There would be no significant performance difference between those two (as returned value tuple would be rather enregistered and no struct copying would happen). However, the second version allows for very fast modification of the returned value. The first one returns only indexes within a matrix. Modification would require a second matrix access to the element designated by those indexes. This is obviously a matter of the API that we would like to expose to the users of such method. And while the resulting performance difference might not be huge, it may sum up if such method would be called very often.

Listing 13-55. Example of ref return to provide more flexible and faster mutability

```
public static (int i, int j) FindValueReturn(int[,] matrix, Func<int, bool>
predicate)
{
    for (int i = 0; i < matrix.GetLength(0); i++)
        for (int j = 0; j < matrix.GetLength(1); j++)
```

```
            if (predicate(matrix[i, j]))
                return (i, j);
        return (-1, -1); // Not found
}

public static ref int FindRefReturn(int[,] matrix, Func<int, bool>
predicate)
{
    for (int i = 0; i < matrix.GetLength(0); i++)
        for (int j = 0; j < matrix.GetLength(1); j++)
            if (predicate(matrix[i, j]))
                return ref matrix[i, j];
    throw new InvalidOperationException("Not found");
}
```

---

ref structs will be explained soon; this does not change anything with respect to the current context.

Because of ref variables, *ref returning collections* may gain more popularity. They may be especially useful for collections storing big value types, as they allow them to access their elements without copying. An example of such simple collection is presented in Listing 13-56. It exposes an indexer that returns specified element by reference. This allows direct access to the elements without copying as they would regular references (see Main method in Listing 13-56).

Listing 13-56. Simple example of the custom ref returning collection

```
public class SomeStructRefList
{
    private SomeStruct[] items;

    public SomeStructRefList(int count)
    {
        this.items = new SomeStruct[count];
    }
```

```
    public ref SomeStruct this[int index] => ref items[index];
}

static void Main(string[] args)
{
    SomeStructRefList refList = new SomeStructRefList(3);
    for (var i = 0; i < 3; ++i)
        refList[i].Field = i;
    for (var i = 0; i < 3; ++i)
        Console.Write(refList[i].Field); // Prints 012
}
```

Obviously, sometimes one could expose API that does not allow us to modify returned elements (to provide kind of read-only collection). This is perfectly possible with the help of readonly refs explained before (see Listing 13-57). Bear in mind all consequences though - especially about defensive copying of the value when a method is being called on it (see Main method in Listing 13-57).

Listing 13-57. Simple example of the custom read-only ref returning collection

```
public struct SomeStruct
{
    public int Field;

    public void ModifyMe()
    {
        this.Field = 9;
    }
}

public class SomeStructReadOnlyRefList
{
    private SomeStruct[] items;

    public SomeStructReadOnlyRefList(int count)
    {
        this.items = new SomeStruct[count];
    }
```

```
  public ref readonly SomeStruct this[int index] => ref items[index];
}

static void Main(string[] args)
{
  SomeStructReadOnlyRefList readOnlyRefList = new
  SomeStructReadOnlyRefList(3);
  for (var i = 0; i < 3; ++i)
    //readOnlyRefList[i].Field = i; // Error CS8332: Cannot assign to
    a member of property 'SomeStructRefList.this[int]' because it is a
    readonly variable
    readOnlyRefList[i].ModifyMe();   // Called on defensive copy! Does
    not modify orignal value.
  for (var i = 0; i < 3; ++i)
    Console.WriteLine(readOnlyRefList[i].Field);   // Prints 000 instead
                                                        of 999
}
```

If we compare relevant parts of the CIL code of Main method in Listings 13-56 and
13-57, we will notice the mentioned defensive copying. Ref return code just calls
ModifyMe method on the element returned by the indexer:

```
IL_0008: ldc.i4.0
IL_0009: callvirt instance valuetype SomeStruct&
SomeStructRefList::get_Item(int32)
IL_000e: call instance void SomeStruct::ModifyMe()
```

On the other hand, readonly ref value is being copied into an additional, temporary
local variable:

```
IL_0008: ldc.i4.0
IL_0009: callvirt instance valuetype SomeStruct&
modreq(InAttribute)  SomeStructRefList2::get_Item(int32)
IL_000e: ldobj C/SomeStruct      // Load object from the
                                    returned address on the
                                    evaluation stack
```

```
IL_0013: stloc.0           // Store the value from the evaluation
                           // stack into local variable
IL_0014: ldloca.s 0        // Load the address of the local variable
IL_0016: call instance void C/SomeStruct::ModifyMe()
```

After introducing more flexible ref variables in C# 7.2, we may expect more and more public API of common collections to include ref returning semantics. It has been standardized to the method with the ItemRef name. Currently most of the immutable collections from System.Collections.Immutable namespace (like ImmutableArray, ImmutableList, …) include such a change. Ref returning logic may be more complex than single access to the underlying storage. For example, ImmutableSortedSet internal storage is based on Nodes forming binary AVL three. Thus, its ItemRef implementation is based on binary tree traversal (see Listing 13-58).

Listing 13-58. An example of more complex ref returning collection implementation

```
public sealed partial class ImmutableSortedSet<T>
{
    internal sealed class Node : IBinaryTree<T>, IEnumerable<T>
    {
        ...
        internal ref readonly T ItemRef(int index)
        {
            if (index < _left._count)
            {
                return ref _left.ItemRef(index);
            }
            if (index > _left._count)
            {
                return ref _right.ItemRef(index - _left._count - 1);
            }
            return ref _key;
        }
    }
```

```
    ...
}
    ...
}
```

Implementing ref returning behavior is not always trivial because it exposes the collection item. It is sometimes unwanted because such collection may:

- Require special treatment of its items, which is omitted by exposing it via byref - for example, each modification of the collection item should be logged or requires other handling (like versioning).

- Want to reorganize its internal storage, which invalidates returned byref - for example, underlying storage may be based on array, which needs to be recreated when collection growth is needed.

Exactly those two problems make introducing `ItemRef` to popular `List<T>` (or `Dictionary<TKey, TValue>`) problematic:

- It uses internal `_version` counter (used for serialization).

- Tt may reorganize items due to internal array storage.

More on Structs...

Structs were in .NET since the very beginning. It is hard to overlook that they were not so popular since then. Only in the last year or two have we observed the growing popularity and awareness of structs. The times requiring excellent performance pushes more and more limits on the GC and memory usage in overall. Thus, returning to structs is happening - not heap allocated if used carefully, they provide a great performance gain releasing GC from its work. As a performance fan, I am more than happy to see this. Many, many places where allocations were made carelessly are now changed into struct-based types avoiding allocations (often, at all).

This is a great direction I would like to emphasize here. Along with the growing awareness of structs inside .NET-related Microsoft teams, more and more features are released in C# regarding them. Many were already mentioned - ref locals and returns complement ref arguments to make using value types copy-free. Readonly refs and in parameters make easier controlling mutability of used values. And there are two other important new features added in C# 7.2 that need to be carefully described - readonly structs and ref structs. I expect a noticeable growth of their popularity in upcoming years, at least in the code with high-performance requirements. I do not expect that CRUD business layers will all of a sudden be cluttered with all those struct-related features though.

Readonly Structs

We have already seen readonly ref and in parameters that disable modification of the argument in specified context. It may be very helpful in controlling that ref variables used for value types will not allow the programmer to modify its value. One may, however, go even further and create immutable struct - the one that cannot be modified once created. I hope you already see possible C# compiler and JIT compiler optimizations that comes from that fact - like the possibility to safely get rid of defensive copies while methods are called.

We define a readonly struct by adding a readonly modifier to a struct declaration (see Listing 13-59). C# compiler enforces that every field of such struct is also defined as readonly.

Listing 13-59. An example of readonly struct declaration

```
public readonly struct ReadonlyBook
{
    public readonly string Title;
    public readonly string Author;

    public ReadonlyBook(string title, string author)
    {
        this.Title = title;
        this.Author = author;
    }

    public void ModifyAuthor()
    {
        //this.Author = "XXX";   // Compilation error: A readonly field
                                  //                    cannot be assigned to (except in a
                                  //                    constructor or a variable initializer)
        Console.WriteLine(this.Author);
    }
}
```

If your type is (or can be) immutable from business and/or logic requirements point of view, it is always worth it to consider using a readonly struct passed by reference (with the help of in keyword) in high-performance pieces of code.

As MSDN says: "You can use the in modifier at every location where a readonly struct is an argument. In addition, you can return a readonly struct as a ref return when you are returning an object whose lifetime extends beyond the scope of the method returning the object." Thus, using a readonly struct is a very convenient way of manipulating immutable types both in safe and performance-aware manner.

For example, let's modify BookCollection class from Listing 13-28 to contain internally an array of readonly structs instead of regular structs (see Listing 13-60). It is fine that they will be heap allocated inside such an array, because ReadOnlyBookCollection instances are heap-allocated reference types. However, all immutability guarantees remains. Thus, the compiler will omit defensive copy creation in the CheckBook method.

Listing 13-60. Modification of code from Listing 13-28 - storing readonly structs

```
public class ReadOnlyBookCollection
{
    private ReadonlyBook[] books = {
        new ReadonlyBook("Call of the Wild, The", "Jack London" ),
        new ReadonlyBook("Tale of Two Cities, A", "Charles Dickens")
    };
    private ReadonlyBook nobook = default;
    public ref readonly ReadonlyBook GetBookByTitle(string title)
    {
        for (int ctr = 0; ctr < books.Length; ctr++)
        {
            if (title == books[ctr].Title)
                return ref books[ctr];
        }
        return ref nobook;
    }
}
```

```csharp
    public void CheckBook(in ReadonlyBook book)
    {
        //book.Title = "XXX"; // Would generate compiler error.
        book.DoSomething();    // It is guaranteed that DoSomething does not
                               // modify book's fields.

    }
}

public static void Main(string[] args)
{
    var coll = new ReadOnlyBookCollection();
    ref readonly var book = ref coll.GetBookByTitle("Call of the Wild,
    The");
    book.Author = "XXX";    // Compiler error: A readonly field cannot be
                            // assigned to (except in a constructor or a
                            // variable initializer)

}
```

Ref Structs (byref-like types)

As already explained a few times, managed pointers have their well-justified limitations - especially in that they are not allowed to appear on the Managed Heap (as a field of reference type or just by boxing). However, for some scenarios that will be explained later, it would be really nice to have a type that contains a managed pointer. Such type should have similar limitations as the managed pointer itself (to not break limitations of the contained managed pointer). Thus, those kinds of types are commonly called *byref-like types* (as the other name of managed pointer is simply byref).

Since C# 7.3 we can declare our custom byref-like types in the form of *ref structs* by adding a ref modifier to the struct declaration (see Listing 13-61).

Listing 13-61. An example of ref struct declaration

```csharp
public ref struct RefBook
{
    public string Title;
    public string Author;
}
```

C# compiler imposes many limitations on ref structs to make sure that they will only be stack allocated:

- It cannot be declared as a field of a class or normal struct (because it could be boxed).

- It cannot be declared as a static field for the same reasons.

- It cannot be boxed - so it is not possible to assign/cast it to object, dynamic or any interface type. It is also not possible to use them as array elements, as array stores boxed structs.

- It cannot be used as an iterator, generic argument and cannot implement an interface (because it could become boxed then).

- It cannot be used as local variable in async method - as it could be boxed as a part of async state machine.

- It cannot be captured by lambda expressions or local functions - as it would be boxed by the corresponding closure class (see Chapter 6).

Trying to use ref struct in those situations will end with compilation error. Some examples are shown in Listing 13-62.

Listing 13-62. An example of some of not possible ref struct usages

```
public class RefBookTest
{
    private RefBook book;    // Compilation error: Field or auto-implemented
                             //    property cannot be of type 'RefBook' unless
                             //    it is an instance member of a ref struct

    public void Test()
    {
        RefBook localBook = new RefBook();
        object box = (object) localBook;   // Compilation error: Cannot
                                           //    convert type 'CoreCLR.Unsafe
                                           //    Tests.RefBook' to 'object'
        RefBook[] array = new RefBook[4];  // Compilation error: Array
                                           //    elements cannot be of type
                                           //    'RefBook'

    }
}
```

886

Similar to managed pointers, ref structs can be used only as method parameters and local variables. It is also possible to use ref struct as a field type of other ref structs (see Listing 13-63).

Listing 13-63. An example of ref struct as a field of other ref struct

```
public ref struct RefBook
{
    public string Title;
    public string Author;
    public RefPublisher Publisher;
}

public ref struct RefPublisher
{
    public string Name;
}
```

Additionally, we can declare "readonly ref struct" to combine readonly and ref struct features - to declare immutable struct that will exist only on the stack. It helps the C# compiler and JIT compiler to make further optimizations when using them (like ignoring defensive copy creation).

Although we already know what ref structs provide, one could really bother where they can be useful, if anywhere at all? Obviously, if they were not, they would not be introduced. They provide two very important features based on their limitations:

- They will never be heap allocated - this allows to use them in a special way because their lifetime guarantees are quite strong. As mentioned at the beginning of this section, the main advantage is that they may contain a managed pointer as their field (although currently in C#, this is not directly exposed feature, as we will elaborate soon).

- They will be never accessed from multiple threads - as it is illegal to pass stack addresses between threads, it is guaranteed that stack-allocated ref struct is accessed only by its own thread. This eliminates in a trivial way any troublesome synchronization issues without any synchronization costs.

Those two features make ref struct quite interesting on their own. However, the primary motivation of ref structs was Span<T> structure that will be explained in the next chapter.

One could ask why not the stackonly keyword is used instead of ref keyword when declaring "ref structs"? The reason behind that is the fact that "ref structs" provide stronger limitations than a simple "stack-only allocation": as listed above, for example, they can't be used as generic arguments and as pointer types. Thus, naming them "stackonly" would be misleading.

Fixed Size Buffers

When we define an array as a field of a struct, obviously only a reference to such heap-allocated array is a part of such struct (see Listing 13-64 and Figure 13-6a). This may be or may not be suitable for your needs.

Listing 13-64. An example of array as a field of struct

```
public struct StructWithArray
{
    public char[] Text;
    public int F2;
    // other fields...
}

static void Main(string[] args)
{
    StructWithArray data = new StructWithArray();
    data.Text = new char[128];
    ...
}
```

There is, however, s possibility to embed the whole array into the struct itself - it is called *fixed size buffer* then. The only restriction is that the array must have a predefined size and its type must be one of the primitive types only: bool, byte, char, short, int, long, sbyte, ushort, uint, ulong, float, or double. Additionally, struct that uses fixed size buffer must be marked as unsafe (see Listing 13-65 and Figure 13-6b). Fixed array buffers are not allowed in classes. It is clear from Figure 13-6b that it is better to name them as buffers instead of arrays because they are plain, sequential layouts of given elements (without any type or size information).

Listing 13-65. An example of fixed size buffer in struct

```
public unsafe struct StructWithFixedBuffer
{
    public fixed char Text[128];
    public int F2;
    // other fields...
}
```

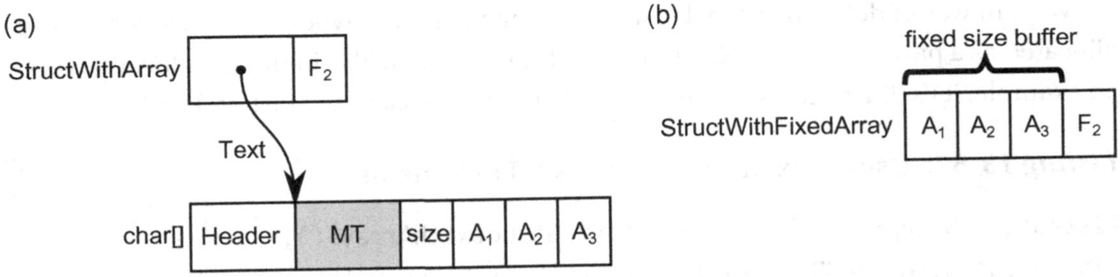

Figure 13-6. *Difference between field of a struct in the form of: (a) typical heap-allocated array, (b) fixed size buffer*

Fixed size buffers are most commonly used in the P/Invoke context to define Interop marshaling structures (see Listing 13-66), typically representing unmanaged array structures of characters or integers (for example, to represent an array of system handles).

Listing 13-66. Examples of fixed buffers from CoreFX repository

```
public unsafe ref partial struct FileSystemEntry
{
    private const int FileNameBufferSize = 256;
    ...
    private fixed char _fileNameBuffer[FileNameBufferSize];

internal unsafe struct WIN32_FIND_DATA
```

```
{
    internal uint dwFileAttributes;
    ...
    private fixed char _cFileName[MAX_PATH];
    private fixed char _cAlternateFileName[14];

    internal ReadOnlySpan<char> cFileName
    {
        get { fixed (char* c = _cFileName) return new ReadOnlySpan<char>
        (c, MAX_PATH); }
    }
}
```

However, one could think about using them for general-purpose code as a convenient way of defining more dense data structures. Even when such structs are heap allocated as a part of generic collection, resulting code provides better data locality. As an example, let's illustrate it in case of generic List<T> usage (see Listing 13-67).

Listing 13-67. Using boxed structs as List<T> elements

```
List<StructWithArray> list = new List<StructWithArray>();
List<StructWithFixedBuffer> list = new List<StructWithFixedBuffer>();
```

The resulting data locality difference is clearly visible in Figure 13-7. In case of using a regular heap-allocated array as a boxed struct field, there are many objects scattered around the Managed Heap (with the obvious advantage that each struct element may have an array of different size). On the other hand, with fixed size buffers, there is only single array with all elements embedded (with the obvious disadvantage that each embedded buffer has the same size). The latter approach provides a much denser data layout, which may be beneficial in high-performance scenarios due to better CPU cache utilization.[5]

---

[5]You can rightly see that this approach is no different from defining in struct many fields of the same type. In this application, it is true, the difference lies in the more convenient (indexed) access to such data.

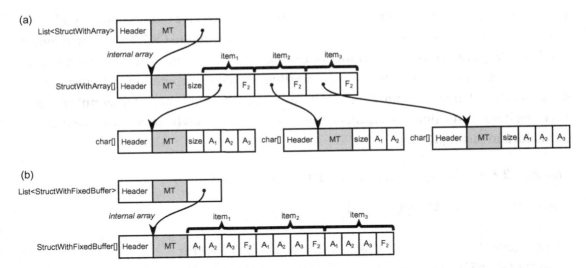

Figure 13-7. *Difference in data locality in case of* List<T> *for boxed structs with: (a) normal arrays, (b) fixed sized buffers*

In case of stack-allocated data, similar results can be gained by using stackalloc operator. Thus, in such scenario it is more a matter of preference if one chooses stackalloc-acted buffer or fixed size buffer of a custom struct (and optionally making it ref struct to make sure it will not be boxed).

C# 7.3 added a feature named *Indexing movable fixed buffers.* A movable fixed buffer is just a fixed size buffer that became part of a heap-allocated object (like in our boxing example of generic List<T>). It is called "movable" because GC may move it while relocating the whole object during Compact phase. Without this feature, in such case it was required to pin the whole buffer before accessing its elements. Let's explain this by using an additional class that wraps around our StructWithFixedArray (see Listing 13-68).

Listing 13-68. Wrapper that boxes struct with fixed size buffer

```
public class StructWithFixedArrayWrapper
{
    public StructWithFixedArray Data = new StructWithFixedArray();
}
```

Accessing fixed size buffer by an index while struct is not boxed is obviously safe because stack-allocated struct will not move, so pinning is not required at all (see first block in Listing 13-69). However, trying to use indexed access to buffer in case of boxed struct would result in compiler error: "You cannot use fixed size buffers contained in unfixed expressions. Try using the fixed statement." Thus, before C# 7.3, the whole buffer needed to be pinned (see second block in Listing 13-69). You can rightly see that pinning here is in fact strange and unnecessary - indexing is a relative operation, with respect to the beginning of the corresponding field, and moving the whole object does not change anything here. Thus, since C# 7.3 this small inconvenience has been removed (see the third block in Listing 13-69).

Listing 13-69. Fixed size buffer indexing changes in C# 7.3

```
static void Main(string[] args)
{
    // Block 1 - accessing stack-allocated fixed buffer
    StructWithFixedBuffer s1 = new StructWithFixedBuffer();
    Console.WriteLine(s1.text[4]);

    // Block 2 - accessing movable buffer before C# 7.3
    StructWithArrayWrapper wrapper1 = new StructWithArrayWrapper();
    fixed (char* buffer = wrapper1.Data.Text)
    {
        Console.WriteLine(buffer[4]);
    }

    // Block 3 - accessing movable buffer after C# 7.3
    StructWithArrayWrapper wrapper2 = new StructWithArrayWrapper();
    Console.WriteLine(wrapper2.Data.text[4]);
}
```

It may be interesting to read the C# Language Designer comment from the discussion of this feature: "One reason why we require pinning of the target when it is movable is the artifact of our code generation strategy - we always convert to unmanaged pointer and thus force the user to pin via fixed statement. However, conversion to unmanaged is unnecessary when doing indexing. The same unsafe pointer math is equally applicable when we have the receiver in the form of managed pointer. If we do that, then the intermediate ref is managed (GC-tracked) and the pinning is unnecessary."

As a last note regarding fixed size buffers usage, keep in mind we can combine them with stackalloc to create stack-allocated arrays of elements that contain other "arrays" (buffers). It would not be possible when using a regular heap-allocated array field, due to limitations described in Chapter 6 (see Listing 13-70).

Listing 13-70. Combining stackalloc with fixed size buffers

```
var data = stackalloc StructWithArray[4]; // Not-possible with compilation
error: Cannot take the address of, get the size of, or declare a pointer to
a managed type ('StructWithArray')
var data = stackalloc StructWithFixedBuffer[4]; // Possible
```

Object/Struct Layout

Did you ever bother to see how a memory layout of instances of classes or structs you create looks? Probably not and this is a good thing. When working with managed code, it should completely not bother you how fields are organized. CLR does a great job in the appropriate layout of the type's fields. Looking at them most probably would be over-engineering things. However, there are always some exceptions when you do like to know such layout or even want to control it. In overwhelmingly popular cases, it is when you pass type instances to unmanaged code, which expect some explicit layout already defined somewhere else (like in system API calls). On the other hand, there may be also rare scenarios when you are so attached to the optimal use of memory and accessing it efficiently, that reliance on automatic field's layout may be not enough.

As this whole book, and this chapter in particular, is focused on such boundary situations so much, let's now dedicate a few words about objects layout in memory. And besides, knowing how things work underneath, and not just that they work, is one of the slogans of this book.

From what we have learned so far, we already know that for reference-type instances there is always an object header and MethodTable reference at the beginning of each instance. On the other hand, value type instances do not have them and contain only their fields values (see Figures 4-17 and 4-18 from Chapter 4). What about fields then?

There is one golden rule of the efficient memory access and field layout relies on it heavily - data alignment (already briefly mentioned in Chapter 2). Each primitive data type (like integers, various floating points and so on, and so forth) has its own preferred alignment - a multiple of what value should be the address (expressed in bytes) under which it is stored. Most often such primitive type alignment is equal to its size. So a 4-byte int32 has 4-byte alignment (its address should be multiplication of 4), 8-byte double has 8-byte alignment, and so on and so forth. The simplest are 1-byte char and byte types because their alignment is 1 byte - they are aligned wherever are stored then. Modern CPUs can use efficient code to access aligned data. Accessing unaligned data, while still possible, requires more instructions and thus is simply slower.

Complex types, containing primitive type fields, should lay out those fields with their alignment requirements in mind. This may introduce *padding* between fields - unused bytes that are there just because the next field needs to be under a specific, aligned address (we will see padding in the examples below). Complex type instances should be aligned by itself also - to make sure that when being a part of other, more complex type (or an array), their fields are still aligned.

All this leads to the following three rules defined by MSDN regarding objects' layout:

- The alignment of the type is the size of its largest element (1, 2, 4, 8, etc., bytes) or the specified packing size, whichever is smaller.[6]

- Each field must align with fields of its own size (1, 2, 4, 8, etc., bytes) or the alignment of the type, whichever is smaller. Because the default alignment of the type is the size of its largest element, which is greater than or equal to all other field lengths, this usually means that fields are aligned by their size. For example, even if the largest field in a type is a 64-bit (8-byte) integer or the Pack field is set to 8, Byte fields align on 1-byte boundaries, Int16 fields align on 2-byte boundaries, and Int32 fields align on 4-byte boundaries.

- Padding is added between fields to satisfy the alignment requirements.

---

[6]Packing will be described a little further but is irrelevant for the current context of automatic fields layout.

Keeping in mind alignment golden rule and resulting three rules presented above, we should be also aware of design decisions regarding a field's layout in both types categories:

- structs - by default have *sequential layout,* so fields are stored in memory in the same order as they are defined. This is mainly because it is assumed they will be passed to unmanaged code and the fields definition order is not accidental but by design. At the beginning of .NET design, it was mostly expected that structs would be used in Interop scenarios so such default behavior was reasonable. This however is only true for "unmanaged types," as defined already in Chapter 6 (we will soon see it again in the context of a new unmanaged constraint). Even fields order is explicitly defined, their layout will still take into account alignment requirements. This may introduce padding and grow the resulting struct size (as a cost of efficient, aligned fields access).

- classes - by default have *automatic layout,* so fields may be reordered freely. Because CLR is the sole owner of such data, it is up to it how to lay out fields. Fields are reordered in the most efficient way both in terms of CPU access time (considering alignment) and memory usage.

Nowadays, with the growing popularity of value types in regular, general-purpose code, default sequential alignment of structs may be not the most optimal one and it is good to know alternatives.

Let's see all this in action. Having a simple struct from Listing 13-71, its field layout will look like that in Figure 13-8a - all three fields are stored in memory in the order of definition. However, because of alignment requirements, fields inside such struct start from the following addresses:

- 0-byte offset - first field is a byte with 1-byte alignment so it can be stored at any address.

- 8-byte offset - second field is a double with 8-byte alignment so it must start at address being multiplication of 8. Unfortunately, it introduces big padding of 7 bytes that are just waste of space.

- 16-byte offset - the last field is an integer with 4-byte alignment so it is fine that it starts at address 16.

Additionally, the alignment of the whole struct must be the size of its largest element - 8 bytes in our case. In other words, the whole struct size must be multiplication of 8. It already occupies 20 bytes so it is rounded up to the 24-bytes size with additional padding at the end.

The whole struct alignment ensures that instances of this struct will have their fields always aligned, for example, in case of being array elements (see Figure 13-8b). If the whole struct was not properly aligned (without additional padding at the end), such scenarios would produce unaligned data (see Figure 13-8c).

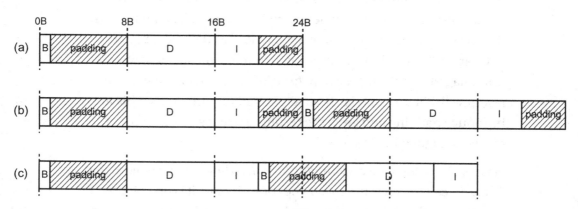

Figure 13-8. *Default fields layout in struct: (a) layout of struct from Listing 13-71, (b) example of using AlignedDouble struct as array element, (c) example of inproper using AlignedDouble struct (if whole struct alignment was not correct)*

As we can see, the sequential layout of struct fields introduced here has quite big memory overhead - 11 bytes are unused, which is almost a half of the whole struct! It most probably will not be a problem if such struct is used occasionally. On the other hand, if your code heavily relies on value types and should process millions of them in performant manner, such waste could make a difference.

Listing 13-71. Example of simple struct (to investigate field's layout)

```
public struct AlignedDouble
{
    public byte B;
    public double D;
    public int I;
}
```

.NET provides a way of controlling a field's layout. While again, it was mainly due to the Interop scenarios, we can utilize this feature to control memory layout that better suits our needs in a general case. Fields layout is controlled by StructLayout attribute, that besides its name may be used both for classes and structs, and may take three values:

- LayoutKind.Sequential - already described layout where proper field's alignment is guaranteed and fields are stored in the order of definition. This is a default value for structs being unmanaged (as explained in Chapter 6 and recalled soon).

- LayoutKind.Auto - layout where field's alignment is guaranteed but fields may be reordered (to utilize memory efficiently). This is a default value for classes and struct not being unmanaged.

- LayoutKind.Explicit - layout where nothing is guaranteed because we explicitly define the layout.

An example struct from Listing 13-71 (that by default uses LayoutKind.Sequential layout) may easily be changed to use automatic layout (see Listing 13-72). As we can see in Figure 13-9, this option indeed produces a much better layout because much less padding of only three bytes was introduced (while still all fields are properly aligned).

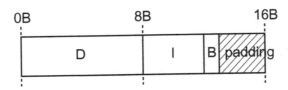

Figure 13-9. *Automatic fields layout in struct from Listing 13-72*

Listing 13-72. Example of simple struct (to investigate automatic field's layout)

```
[StructLayout(LayoutKind.Auto)]
public struct AlignedDoubleAuto
{
    public byte B;
    public double D;
    public int I;
}
```

The main drawback of automatic layout is the fact that we cannot use such struct in Interop. However, I mostly imagine using it in high-performance general code where we do not care at all about this limitation. So when you use value types because of their memory-management advantages (stack allocation, data locality, less space occupancy), you will most probably be interested in using automatic layout instead of the default one!

The more fields and the bigger differences in their sizes, the more unfortunate sequential layout may be introduced. As an exercise, I suggest that you understand why struct from Listing 13-73 will consume:

- 64 bytes bytes with LayoutKind.Sequential (where 28 bytes are wasted because of padding)

- 40 bytes bytes with LayoutKind.Auto (where only 4 bytes are wasted)

Listing 13-73. Example of struct where layout strongly influences its size

```
public struct ManyDoubles
{
    public byte B1;
    public double D1;
    public byte B2;
    public double D2;
    public byte B3;
    public double D3;
    public byte B4;
    public double D5;
}
```

So far presented structs were examples of unmanaged types. To recall – an unmanaged type is a type that is not a reference type and does not contain reference-type fields. However, we may obviously create structs that are not unmanaged - by simply adding a single reference type field to them (see Listing 13-74). As stated before, this changes the default layout to be automatic, like for reference types. As we can see in Figure 13-10, AlignedDoubleWithReference fields are indeed reordered like in LayoutKind.Auto mode.

Listing 13-74. Example of non-unmanaged struct

```
public struct AlignedDoubleWithReference
{
    public byte B;
    public double D;
    public int I;
    public object O;
}
```

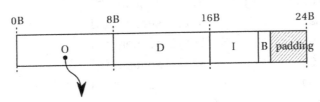

Figure 13-10. *Default fields layout in struct from Listing 13-74*

The default behavior changes for non-unmanaged structs because they are not allowed to be passed via P/Invoke. This is because they contain reference to a managed object that may change during GC. As its unmanaged usage is blocked, it is safe to use automatic layout for such structs.

Please note that automatic layout prefers putting object references as first fields. You should already guess why this is so. It is useful in the Mark phase for more efficient object traversal because of better cache line utilization. Most object references will fall in the same cache line as the already accessed MT field.

The default layout behavior will be changed to automatic also when the struct contains the other struct with LayoutKind.Auto layout. Most of the commonly used built-in structs (Decimal, Guid, Char, Boolean) are sequential so using them will not change the layout behavior. However, surprisingly DateTime has automatic layout so when used as another struct field, it changes its layout also to automatic (see Listing 13-75).

Listing 13-75. Different types of fields and their layout influence

```
public struct StructWithFields
{
    public byte B;
    public double D;
    public int I;
    //public SomeEnum E;       // Still sequential
    //public SomeStruct AD;    // Still sequential
    //public unsafe void* P;   // Still sequential
    //public decimal DE;       // Still sequential
    //public Guid G;           // Still sequential
    //public char C;           // Still sequential
    //public Boolean BL;       // Still sequential
    //public object O;         // Triggers automatic
    //public DateTime DT;      // Triggers automatic because DateTime has
                               //    automatic layout
}
```

If you do really care about memory usage (and probably you do if you decided to use structs), then awareness of its layout should bother you. Imagine those precious bytes of stack space wasted because of padding in your stackallock-ated array! But space utilization is not the only concern - sometimes we should do care about it because of cache utilization (it will be discussed later in the data-oriented design section in the next chapter).

Please note that automatic layout for classes and unmanaged structs cannot be changed - explicitly set LayoutKind.Sequential will be simply ignored.

A not-yet-described explicit layout is especially useful in P/Invoke scenarios as it gives you full control over how the struct storage looks (see Listing 13-76). You may create a layout corresponding to what unmanaged code expects with a 100% guarantee. Obviously, you should remember that with such full control, meeting alignment requirements is on your side so it is really easy to introduce unaligned fields (see Figure 13-11).

In P/Invoke scenarios it is rather irrelevant but be careful when explicitly designing struct for dense, high-performance usage.[7]

Listing 13-76. Example of simple struct (to investigate explicit field's layout)

```
[StructLayout(LayoutKind.Explicit)]
public struct UnalignedDouble
{
    [FieldOffset(0)]
    public byte B;
    [FieldOffset(1)]
    public double D;
    [FieldOffset(9)]
    public int I;
}
```

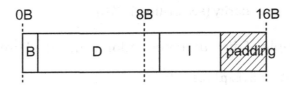

Figure 13-11. *Explicit fields layout in struct from Listing 13-76*

In particular, compiler does not require that fields in our explicit layout do not overlap. Thus, we must be careful when specifying offsets, to not create fields that interfere each other. This is even desirable in one scenario - creating so-called *discriminated unions*. It is a type that is able to represent various set of data. By using explicit layout and setting offsets of differently typed fields to the same value, we are simply simulating such a discriminated union (see Listing 13-77).

---

[7]To be honest, benchmarks conducted by me does not show significant performance change when accessing a double field both from AlignedDouble and UnalignedDouble structs. It seems that underlying Intel® Advanced Vector Extensions (Intel® AVX) instructions used in case of my Intel CPU are really nicely handling unaligned double access. This is, however, implementation detail and aligned memory is still the recommended design.

Listing 13-77. Example of simple discriminated union

```
[StructLayout(LayoutKind.Explicit)]
public struct DiscriminatedUnion
{
    [FieldOffset(0)]
    public bool Bool;
    [FieldOffset(0)]
    public byte Byte;
    [FieldOffset(0)]
    public int Integer;
}
```

This, of course, requires discipline from the programmer, to read the same type as it was written to, unless we want to use this technique to provide memory-based conversion between types. One could think of using a fixed size buffer to access the same memory with different granularity (see Listing 13-78).

Listing 13-78. Example of discriminated union using fixed buffers

```
[StructLayout(LayoutKind.Explicit)]
public struct DiscriminatedUnion
{
    [FieldOffset(0)]
    public bool Bool;
    [FieldOffset(0)]
    public byte Byte;
    [FieldOffset(0)]
    public int Integer;
    [FieldOffset(0)]
    Public fixed byte Buffer[8];
}
```

There is an additional control of object layout in the form of packing. The Pack field of StructLayout attribute controls the alignment of a type's fields in memory. For example, we can define Pack value to be 1 byte:

```
[StructLayout(LayoutKind.Sequential, Pack = 1)]
public struct AlignedDouble
{
public byte B;
public double D;
public int I;
}
```

How will the resulting layout look then? Let's recall the first rule from MSDN documentation presented above: "The alignment of the type is the size of its largest element (1, 2, 4, 8, etc., bytes) or the specified packing size, whichever is smaller." So in our case, instead of 8-byte alignment (double size), type alignment is just 1 byte. The second rule says: "Each field must align with fields of its own size (1, 2, 4, 8, etc., bytes) or the alignment of the type, whichever is smaller." Thus, each field alignment is also just 1 byte. As a result, a very dense 13-byte memory layout will be generated without any padding (but with fields inconsistent with their optimal alignment requirements).

If you would like to investigate your type's layout, there are several ways to do that. There are two great free tools that can be used to do that. The first one is a great ObjectLayoutInspector library (available on GitHub and as a NuGet package) written by Sergey Teplyakov, solely dedicated for inspecting an object's memory layout. It provides a very convenient way of analyzing types with just a single method call (see Listing 13-79). Results are presented then nicely in an ASCII way (see Listing 13-80).

Listing 13-79. Using ObjectLayoutInspector to print layout of structs from Listings 13-71 and 13-74

```
static void Main(string[] args)
{
    TypeLayout.PrintLayout<AlignedDouble>();
    TypeLayout.PrintLayout<AlignedDoubleWithReference>();
}
```

Listing 13-80. Result of the console program from Listing 13-79

```
Type layout for 'AlignedDouble'
Size: 24 bytes. Paddings: 11 bytes (%45 of empty space)
|===========================|
|     0: Byte B (1 byte)    |
|---------------------------|
|   1-7: padding (7 bytes)  |
|---------------------------|
|   8-15: Double D (8 bytes) |
|---------------------------|
| 16-19: Int32 I (4 bytes)  |
|---------------------------|
| 20-23: padding (4 bytes)  |
|===========================|

Type layout for 'AlignedDoubleWithReference'
Size: 24 bytes. Paddings: 3 bytes (%12 of empty space)
|===========================|
|   0-7: Object O (8 bytes) |
|---------------------------|
|   8-15: Double D (8 bytes) |
|---------------------------|
| 16-19: Int32 I (4 bytes)  |
|---------------------------|
|    20: Byte B (1 byte)    |
|---------------------------|
| 21-23: padding (3 bytes)  |
|===========================|
```

If you do not want to use Console application to print object's layout out of the box, you can manually consume an analyzed layout (see Listing 13-81).

Listing 13-81. Using ObjectLayoutInspector to manually analyze layout of structs

```
static void Main(string[] args)
{
    TypeLayout layout = TypeLayout.GetLayout<AlignedDouble>();
    Console.WriteLine($"Total size {layout.FullSize}B with {layout.Paddings}
    B padding.");
    foreach (var fieldBase in layout.Fields)
    {
        switch (fieldBase)
        {
            case FieldLayout field: Console.WriteLine($"{field.Offset}
            {field.Size} {field.FieldInfo.Name}"); break;
            case Padding padding: Console.WriteLine($"{padding.Offset}
            {padding.Size} Padding"); break;
        }
    }
}
```

Obviously, such a tool is more likely to be used during your custom-build step or just offline, during development, than during runtime of your target application.

The second tool is the https://sharplab.io web page that provides great .NET code analysis capabilities. It provides Inspect.Heap and Inspect.Stack static methods that print the layouts of specified types (see Listing 13-82 and Figure 13-12).

Listing 13-82. Sample script used in Sharplab.io to inspect memory layout

```
using System;
using System.Runtime.InteropServices;

public class C {
    public static void Main() {
```

```
        var o = new AlignedDouble();
        Inspect.Heap(new AlignedDouble());
        Inspect.Stack(in o);
    }
}
```

Results	Run	▾																							Release ▾

This is a new feature — might be unstable/too strict. Please report any issues.

AlignedDouble at 0x1FEB1C27E38																									
header								type handle						B									D		
000	000	000	000	000	000	000	000	216	085	038	102	250	127	000	000	000	000	000	000	000	000	000	000	000	000

AlignedDouble																						Decimal ▾	
B							D							I									
000	000	000	000	000	000	000	000	000	000	000	000	000	000	000	000	000	000	000	000	000	000	000	000

Figure 13-12. *The result of script from Listing 13-82 in* `https://sharplab.io` *online tool*

In the presence of those two great tools, I hope you will not need to use low-level tools like WinDbg to inspect object manually. If you decide to do so, I would suggest using SOS !dumpobject (for classes) and !dumpvc (for value types) commands (see Listing 13-83).

Listing 13-83. Inspecting object layout with dumpvc SOS command in WinDbg

```
> !dumpvc 00007ffda2725e18 00007ffda2725e18
Name:        CoreCLR.ObjectLayout.AlignedDouble
MethodTable: 00007ffda2725e18
EEClass:     00007ffda2872110
Size:        40(0x28) bytes
File:        (...)\CoreCLR.ObjectLayout.dll
Fields:
                MT    Field   Offset                 Type VT     Attr
Value Name
00007ffdfd6a8b60  4000001        0        System.Byte  1 instance
0 B
00007ffdfd6b0858  4000002        8      System.Double  1 instance
0.000000 D
00007ffdfd6c66d8  4000003       10       System.Int32  1 instance
-43316160 I
```

Unmanaged Constraint

Unmanaged type was already mentioned in Chapter 6, in context of what type may be used in stackalloc, and in this chapter, in context of unmanaged structs. From C# 7.3 a new generic constraint has been introduced - unmanaged. It allows us to write generic code that operates on unmanaged types and pointers to them.

Let's recall its brief definition from MSDN: "An unmanaged type is a type that is not a reference type and doesn't contain reference type fields at any level of nesting." Stackalloc limitations already mentioned state it a little more precisely: "unmanaged type may contain only primitive types, enum and pointer types and user defined structs satisfying the same criteria."[8]

Listing 13-84 shows an example of two structs, where only the first one meets unmanaged type criteria. Remember that all levels of nesting are checked so if struct A contains struct B, that contains other struct C, that contains struct D with reference type - the whole struct A is treated as not being unmanaged.

Listing 13-84. Example of unmanaged and non-unmanaged type

```
public struct UnmanagedStruct
{
    public int Field;
}

public struct NonUnmanagedStruct
{
    public int Field;
    public object O;
}
```

With the help of the new unmanaged generic constraint, the compiler checks for us unmanaged type criteria. If they are not met, appropriate compilation error will be

---

[8]To be strict, the definition of unmanaged type is listed in ECMA-334 C# Language Specification in paragraph 23.3 Pointer types.

generated. We can use it both for generic methods (see Listing 13-85) and generic struct types (see Listing 13-86).

Listing 13-85. Example of unmanaged generic constraint usage in method

```
public static void UnamanagedContraint<T>(T arg) where T : unmanaged
{
}

static void Main(string[] args)
{
    UnamanagedContraint(new UnmanagedStruct());
    UnamanagedContraint(new NonUnmanagedStruct()); // Compilation error: The
type 'NonUnmanagedStruct' must be a non-nullable value type, along with all
fields at any level of nesting, in order to use it as parameter 'T' in the
generic type or method 'Constraints.UnamanagedContraint<T>(T)'
}
```

Listing 13-86. Example of unmanaged generic constraint usage in type

```
public struct UnmanagedStruct<T> where T : unmanaged
{
    ...
}

static void Main(string[] args)
{
    var obj = new UnmanagedGenericStruct<object>(); // Compilation error:
The type 'object' must be a non-nullable value type, along with all fields
at any level of nesting, in order to use it as parameter 'T' in the generic
type or method 'UnmanagedGenericStruct<T>'
}
```

What does an unmanaged constraint give us? With it the following things are possible:

- We may use pointer of T - if type T satisfies the unmanaged constraint it can also be used as a T* pointer (conversion to void* is also possible).

- We may use sizeof(T).

- We may use stackallock of T.

Without unmanaged constraint, each above operation was not allowed, resulting in the compilation error, "Cannot take the address of, get the size of, or declare a pointer to a managed type ('T')" even when T was constrained to struct. Obviously, those operations require an unsafe context but this is not changed regardless of unmanaged constraint (which by itself does not require unsafe code).

All operations listed above are, of course, quite low level and will be mostly useful in low-level memory-management scenarios like fast serialization of data. Do not expect to see unmanaged constraint in regular business code though!

Listing 13-87 shows an example of a method utilizing possible operations coming from an unmanaged constraint. Please note an interesting fact - in Listing 13-87 we can get the pointer of the argument without pinning. This is because unmanaged constraint implies that T is a value type, thus passed by value. It is safe to take an address in such case (because value is not heap allocated).

Listing 13-87. Simple example of unmanaged constraint usage

```
unsafe public static int UseUnmanagedConstraint<T>(T arg) where T :
unmanaged
{
    T* ptr = &arg;              // Use T* pointer
    T* sa = stackalloc T[16];   // Use stackalloc
    return sizeof(T);           // Use sizeof
}
```

Similar code would work without unmanaged constraint, for simple struct usage (see Listing 13-88).

Listing 13-88. Regular struct usage similar to code from Listing 13-87

```
unsafe static public void UseUnmanagedConstraint2(SomeStruct obj)
{
    SomeStruct* p = &obj;
    ...
}
```

However, if we pass by reference an object with unmanaged constraint, we must explicitly pin it because it may be heap allocated, for example, because of boxing (see Listing 13-89).

Listing 13-89. Simple example of unmanaged constraint usage with object passed by reference

```
unsafe public int UseUnmanagedRefConstraint<T>(ref T arg) where T :
unmanaged
{
    fixed (T* ptr = &arg)
    {
        Console.WriteLine((long) ptr);
        return sizeof(T);
    }
}
```

Because of the same reason, we must explicitly pin fields of the struct when used from within struct instance methods (see Listing 13-90) because method may be called on boxed struct instance.[9]

---

[9]In the current state of C# 7.3, changing StructWithUnmanagedField into ref struct does not change that behavior, although it could, as within Use method context field is guaranteed to be stack allocated.

Listing 13-90. Example of unmanaged constraint usage within a struct method

```
public struct StructWithUnmanagedField<T> where T : unmanaged
{
   private T field;
   unsafe public void Use()
   {
      fixed (T* ptr = &field)
      {
         // ...
      }
   }
}
```

What are practical usage scenarios of unmanaged generic constraints? It is designed to allow handling in generic way types, which otherwise would require many concrete implementations. Perfect examples are various types of serialization. Thanks to `sizeof(T)` availability, we may create, for example, a generic "to byte array" serialization (see Listing 13-91).

Listing 13-91. Example of generic serialization (taken from MSDN documentation)

```
unsafe public static byte[] ToByteArray<T>(this T argument) where T :
unmanaged
{
   var size = sizeof(T);
   var result = new Byte[size];
   Byte* p = (byte*)&argument;
   for (var i = 0; i < size; i++)
      result[i] = *p++;
   return result;
}
```

We can also think of a generic logging mechanism, where the passed argument is consumed in a low-level manner as in Listing 13-92. Here the stackalloc helper structure is a description of logged value (by providing its address and size) passed to some core logging routine. To make such method useful, at least two or three overloads could be necessary that take two and three arguments respectively (and stackalloc bigger arrays respectively).

Listing 13-92. Example of generic, low-level logging (inspired by ETW logging code from .NET code)

```
public unsafe void LogData<T>(T arg) where T : unmanaged
{
    if (IsEnabled())
    {
        EventData* data = stackalloc EventData[1];
        data[0].DataPointer = (IntPtr)(&arg);
        data[0].Size = sizeof(T);
        WriteEventCore(data);
    }
}
```

An unmanaged generic constraint may be also useful in creating types consuming unmanaged memory (especially collections). A very simple example of such type is presented in Listing 13-93. Without a generic constraint, it would not be possible to create such generic type because sizeof would not be accessible (element size should be provided in constructor likely). More importantly, thanks to unmanaged constraint, we can freely use T* pointer - which makes indexing trivial and possible to use ref return T (without constraint we would be forced to use void* and ugly pointer casting to implement indexer's getter and setter).

Listing 13-93. Example of type wrapping unmanaged memory

```
public unsafe class UnmanagedArray<T> : IDisposable
    where T : unmanaged
{
    private T* data;
    public UnmanagedArray(int length)
    {
        data = (T*)Marshal.AllocHGlobal(length * sizeof(T));
    }
```

```
    public ref T this[int index]
    {
        get { return ref data[index]; }
    }

    public void Dispose()
    {
        Marshal.FreeHGlobal((IntPtr)data);
    }
}

static void Main(string[] args)
{
    using (UnmanagedArray<int> array = new UnmanagedArray<int>(20))
    {
        array[10] = 10;
        for (int i = 0; i < 20; i++)
            Console.WriteLine(array[i]); // Will print garbage and only 10 for
                                         // 10th element
    }
}
```

Blittable Types

Besides unmanaged types, there are also so-called *blittable types*, defined as having an identical presentation in memory for both managed and unmanaged code. Blittable types are most often met in the context of Interop marshaling, as they do not require any conversion when using P/Invoke.

Unmanaged and blittable types are almost the same but the latter are a little stricter than the former. This is because some value types are only "sometimes blittable" as they expected representation differs on managed and unmanaged side occasionally:

- decimal - its binary representation is not well-established so unmanaged side format cannot be assumed,

- bool - typically consumes 1 byte on both sides but sometimes is bigger on unmanaged side (for example, C language may use 4 bytes),

- `char` - typically consumes 2 bytes but sometimes is smaller or bigger on unmanaged side (depending on encoding),

- `DateTime` - due to historical reasons, as we have seen, it is a struct with automatic layout, which makes it non-blittable,

- `Guid` - its internal representation depends on machine endianness.

Thus, a struct that contains one of such a special value type field is a valid unmanaged type (so it will meet unmanaged generic constraint) but is no blittable in the Interop marshaling sense. There is a little confusion regarding naming though, as always in computer science.

To make things even a little more complicated, only blittable types may be pinned by `GCHandle.Alloc` call (as it is supposed that pinning is done because of subsequent `AddrOfPinnedObject` call and passing the whole object address into unmanaged code). Thus, an unmanaged generic constraint is not enough to guarantee that such pinning will succeed (see Listing 13-94). `WeirdStruct` struct is non-blittable because it contains fields of non-blittable types (in fact, all kind of them). It is however, still unmanaged type (as it does not break an unmanaged type requirements). Thus, it can be used with unmanaged constraint in `UseUnmanagedConstraint` method, while it will throw appropriate `ArgumentException` when trying to be pinned with `GCHandle.Alloc` call.

Listing 13-94. Blittable vs. managed type difference when pinning with GCHandle

```
public struct WeirdStruct
{
    public decimal DE;
    public DateTime DT;
    public Guid G;
    public char C;
    public Boolean BL;
}

unsafe public static int UseUnmanagedConstraint<T>(T obj) where T : unmanaged
{
    var handle = GCHandle.Alloc(obj, GCHandleType.Pinned); // throws System.
ArgumentException: Object contains non-primitive or non-blittable data.
    ...
}
```

914

```
static void Main(string[] args)
{
    var s = new WeirdStruct();
    UseUnmanagedConstraint(s);
}
```

In summary, we can say that:

- Unmanaged types (along with unmanaged generic constraints) - are used in general-purpose programming, for low-level memory optimization of features like serialization and deserialization, hashing, ... Because they are general purpose in this context, they were more carefully described. As they operate on low-level memory, most often they are used in unsafe context, while an unmanaged constraint does not impose that.

- Blittable types - are used in Interop marshaling scenarios. Because this book does not put a lot of attention on Interop, they were only briefly mentioned here. The only aspect that may be important for us is the blittable requirement of pinning via a GCHandle.

To make things even more fascinatingly complicated, `decimal` is a special except - it is not blittable but structs containing it may be still pinned via GCHandle.

Summary

In this chapter we touched quite a lot of interesting and mostly low-level topics. Starting from a deep explanation of thread static fields, we moved to the managed pointers - which greatly help in understanding passing by reference mechanics in .NET. These are also especially useful nowadays with all the topics related to growing struct usage popularity.

Indeed, a great part of this chapter is taken by everything related to value types - ref structs, byref-like types, byref-like field types, and so on, and so forth. Comprehensive descriptions of managed pointers were also introduced as quite a necessary foundation of understanding all those things. Nowadays, by looking at performance with caution, squeezing every not necessary heap allocation, those topics are gaining more and more attention in the .NET ecosystem. Obviously, one most probably would not need to use them in writing a regular business-driven application. But this chapter is in general not dedicated to such types of programming so it should not be surprising so many words were spoken about that.

Then, interesting information about managed layout has been presented, which is not always so obvious as one could think. The chapter concludes with a description of a generic unmanaged constraint added recently to C# (altogether with slightly related topic of blittable types).

All those topics are useful by itself but also provide a good foundation of the topics introduced in the next chapter - especially about Span<T> usage and implementation.

CHAPTER 14

Advanced Techniques

This chapter is somehow a continuation of the previous one, describing more advanced techniques that are available in .NET. Thus, please note that the knowledge from the previous chapter is really helpful to understand this one (especially regarding ref types, ref returns, and ref structs).

This chapter is aligned with today's trends in .NET programming (at least those heavily performance-oriented) - squeezing all the possible CPU clock cycles and memory usage to make managed frameworks and applications faster. I found it really fascinating. More and more libraries and their APIs are being "spanified" and/or "pipeliefied" by replacing their current code with the code based on efficient Span<T> and/or pipelines usage. I hope that all the descriptions from this chapter will help you to find yourself in this modern .NET world. Speaking of which, this chapter is closed by the section about incoming .NET features that are not yet released (or released in preview).

Span<T> and Memory<T>

We can allocate contiguous memory in a various way in C#, whether it is a regular heap-allocated array, fixed buffer, `stackalloc,` or from unmanaged memory. It would be very convenient to have a single way of representing all such cases, while still in an efficient manner (similar to using plain array). Moreover, quite often such memory needs to be "sliced" - to provide only some part of it to be processed by other methods. And all this ideally should be done without the main enemy of high-performance .NET code - heap allocations. Exactly because of all those dreams, Span<T> was born.

Please keep in mind that in the rest of this chapter, a little simplified stack- and heap-allocation division is used. As we should remember from Chapter 4, whether something is heap or stack allocated is rather an implementation detail, resulting

917

© Konrad Kokosa 2018
K. Kokosa, *Pro .NET Memory Management*, https://doi.org/10.1007/978-1-4842-4027-4_14

from the expected lifetime characteristics of given data. However, repeating all the time in the following sections that stack or heap are in fact implementation details would be both tedious and boring. Span<T> and Memory<T> are somehow leaking underlying abstractions so it is even a little justified.

Span<T>

A new generic Span<T> type was introduced in .NET Core 2.1. It is a value type (ref struct), so it does not incur allocations by itself. It has ref returning indexer so it may be consumed like an array. Moreover, it is designed to provide slicing capabilities so one could use subranges efficiently - subrange is represented by other Span<T> ref struct so yet again, it does not require any allocations.[1]

A few typical Span<T> usage scenarios are presented in Listing 14-1. No matter which span instance we use at the end of UseSpan method (representing various types of memory), it may be consumed in an array-like way by the Length and indexer members exposed from Span<T>. Note that UseSpan is marked as unsafe because of pointer usage, not because of the Span<T>.

Listing 14-1. Typical Span<T> usage scenarios

```
unsafe public static void UseSpan()
{
    var array = new int[64];
    Span<int> span1 = new Span<int>(array);
    Span<int> span2 = new Span<int>(array, start: 8, length: 4);
    Span<int> span3 = span1.Slice(0, 4);

    Span<int> span4 = stackalloc[] { 1, 2, 3, 4, 5 };
    Span<int> span5 = span4.Slice(0, 2);

    IntPtr memory = Marshal.AllocHGlobal(64);
    void* ptr = memory.ToPointer();
    Span<byte> span6 = new Span<byte>(ptr, 64);

    var span = span1; // or span2, span3, ...
```

---

[1]Originally, this type was even supposed to be called Slice, not Span.

```
for (int i = 0; i < span.Length; i++)
    Console.WriteLine(span[i]);

Marshal.FreeHGlobal(memory);
}
```

Obviously, not every memory should be modified. Thus, ReadOnlySpan<T> counterpart is also available, which represent memory that cannot be written to. The typical usage includes representing string data. Strings are immutable and exposing them as Span<char> would break that. Instead, the AsSpan string extension method returns ReadOnlySpan<char>. One could, of course, also be willing to represents regular data (or normal Span<T>) as read-only by using this type (see Listing 14-2).

Listing 14-2. Typical ReadOnlySpan<T> usage scenarios

```
public static void UseReadOnlySpan()
{
    var array = new int[64];
    ReadOnlySpan<int> span1 = new ReadOnlySpan<int>(array);
    ReadOnlySpan<int> span2 = new Span<int>(array);

    string str = "Hello world";
    ReadOnlySpan<char> span3 = str.AsSpan();
    ReadOnlySpan<char> span4 = str.AsSpan(start: 6, length: 5);
}
```

Although it may not sound amazing at first glance, such type is in a way a game changer in many applications. First of all, it can significantly simplify some APIs. Let's imagine an integer parsing routine, which may expect various types of memory (see Listing 14-3). Such an API surface grows very fast to include any possible usage scenario. On the other hand, it can be greatly simplified to a single method by using Span<char> (see Listing 14-4).

Listing 14-3. Problematic int parsing API

```
int Parse(string input);
int Parse(string input, int startIndex, int length);
unsafe int Parse(char* input, int length);
unsafe int Parse(char* input, int startIndex, int length);
```

Listing 14-4. Simplified int parsing API with the help of Span<T>

```
int Parse(Span<int> input);
```

Thanks to Span<T>, the possibility to represent various forms of contiguous collection of values (like arrays, strings, pointers to unmanaged arrays, and so on, and so forth), it may greatly simplify APIs operating on them without creating a bunch of overloads or forcing users to create unnecessary copies (to adapt data to such API expectations).

Secondly, Span<T> greatly simplifies writing high-performance code, for example, by safely using stackalloc like in Listing 14-1. Most important, however, are its slicing abilities, which allow you to operate on smaller blocks of memory (e.g., when parsing) passing them around in your code without overhead. We will soon see how it was implemented to provide efficient slicing though. Moreover, most often all this may be done in a generic way so convenient helper methods or classes are possible.

Compiler is also smart enough to consider the lifetime of data wrapped into Span<T>. So it is perfectly fine to return from a method Span<T> wrapping managed array (because it outlives the method, see method ReturnArrayAsSpan in Listing 14-5), but it is not allowed to return local stack data (as it will be discarded after method ends, see illegal ReturnStackallocAsSpan method in Listing 14-5). Be careful when wrapping around unmanaged memory though, as one needs to remember to explicitly free it afterwards (see ReturnNativeAsSpan method in Listing 14-5 where we've allocated memory but never deallocated it).

Listing 14-5. Three examples of returning Span<T>

```
public Span<int> ReturnArrayAsSpan()
{
    var array = new int[64];
    return new Span<int>(array);
}

public unsafe Span<int> ReturnStackallocAsSpan()
{
    Span<int> span = stackalloc[] { 1, 2, 3, 4, 5 }; // Compilation Error
    CS8352: Cannot use local 'span' in this context because it may expose
    referenced variables outside of their declaration scope
    return span;
}
```

```
public unsafe Span<int> ReturnNativeAsSpan()
{
    IntPtr memory = Marshal.AllocHGlobal(64);
    return new Span<int>(memory.ToPointer(), 8);
}
```

Usage Examples

Let's look at a few examples of Span<T> usage. Please be aware that at the time of writing this book, Span<T> is a quite new beast in the .NET ecosystem so there are not so many well-established design patterns related to it. However, a few nice examples are already there, especially in open sourced .NET-related libraries.

Slicing capabilities of bigger data are nicely utilized in the Kestrel server, used to host ASP.NET Core web applications. Appropriate fragments of HttpParser class from KestrelHttpServer GitHub repository are presented in Listing 14-6. As we can see, line-by-line parsing of an incoming HTTP request is done by using slices of Span<T>. First, each line is passed as separate slice into the ParseRequestLine method. Then, each relevant part of such line (like HTTP path or query) is also sliced into separate Span<T> and passed further to OnStartLine method. This way no memory copying happens, like it would be in case of using string.Substring call. As Span<T> is stack allocated, there are no heap allocations at all.

OnStartLine method further uses passed Span<T> to provide required logic. Similarly, sliced HTTP headers are analyzed in the same HttpParser class.

Listing 14-6. Fragments of HttpParser class from KestrelHttpServer code

```
public unsafe bool ParseRequestLine(TRequestHandler handler, in
ReadOnlySequence<byte> buffer, out SequencePosition consumed, out
SequencePosition examined)
{
    var span = buffer.First.Span;
    var lineIndex = span.IndexOf(ByteLF);
    if (lineIndex >= 0)
    {
        consumed = buffer.GetPosition(lineIndex + 1, consumed);
        span = span.Slice(0, lineIndex + 1);
    }
    ...
```

```
// Fix and parse the span
fixed (byte* data = &MemoryMarshal.GetReference(span))
{
    ParseRequestLine(handler, data, span.Length);
}
}

private unsafe void ParseRequestLine(TRequestHandler handler, byte* data,
int length)
{
    int offset;
    // Get Method and set the offset
    var method = HttpUtilities.GetKnownMethod(data, length, out offset);

    // Find pathStart index
    var pathBuffer = new Span<byte>(data + pathStart, offset - pathStart);
    ...
    // Find queryStart index
    var targetBuffer = new Span<byte>(data + pathStart, offset - pathStart);
    var query = new Span<byte>(data + queryStart, offset - queryStart);

    handler.OnStartLine(method, httpVersion, targetBuffer, pathBuffer,
    query, customMethod, pathEncoded);
}
```

Another great example of using Span<T> is internal ValueStringBuilder ref struct defined in .NET CoreFX library. As its name indicates, its value-typed StringBuilder counterpart provides mutable string functionality.

As a ref struct, it is always stack allocated, getting rid of multithreading problems (because it will be always accessed only from the current thread). As an internal storage it uses Span<char>, which makes it storage agnostic (see Listing 14-7). It can be then initially backed up by stackalloc, native, or heap-allocated array. Ref returning indexer efficiently exposes individual characters.

Listing 14-7. Fragments of internal ValueStringBuilder class

```
internal ref struct ValueStringBuilder
{
    private char[] _arrayToReturnToPool;
```

```
private Span<char> _chars;
private int _pos;

public ValueStringBuilder(Span<char> initialBuffer)
{
    _arrayToReturnToPool = null;
    _chars = initialBuffer;
    _pos = 0;
}

public ref char this[int index]
{
    get
    {
        Debug.Assert(index < _pos);
        return ref _chars[index];
    }
}
...
}
```

As we can see, private _pos field is a cursor indicating how many chars were already consumed. It is then easy to return a current builder content via set of AsSpan methods (see Listing 14-8) using slicing (thus, what is worth repeating yet once again, without any allocations).

Listing 14-8. Fragments of internal ValueStringBuilder class (slicing capability)

```
public ReadOnlySpan<char> AsSpan() => _chars.Slice(0, _pos);
public ReadOnlySpan<char> AsSpan(int start) => _chars.Slice(start, _pos - start);
public ReadOnlySpan<char> AsSpan(int start, int length) => _chars.Slice(start, length);
```

If you really do need string, there is heap-allocating appropriate ToString method (see Listing 14-9). Please note that that it is then assumed that such instance has been consumed so Dispose method is being called (explained later).

Listing 14-9. Fragments of internal `ValueStringBuilder` class (string returning capability)

```
public override string ToString()
{
   var s = new string(_chars.Slice(0, _pos));
   Dispose();
   return s;
}
```

Appending to such a builder is most often as easy as setting the proper character under the current cursor position (or multiple characters in case of appending string) as shown in Listing 14-10. Obviously, there may be a case when initially a used Span<char> runs out of space and there is a need to grow it. In such scenario, an array from ArrayPool<char> is being used to provide bigger storage (see Grow method in Listing 14-10) but yet again, it may be simply assigned to the same internal Span<char> due to its storage-agnostic nature.

Listing 14-10. Fragments of internal ValueStringBuilder class (appending logic)

```
public void Append(char c)
{
   int pos = _pos;
   if (pos < _chars.Length)
   {
      _chars[pos] = c;
      _pos = pos + 1;
   }
   else
   {
      GrowAndAppend(c);
   }
}

[MethodImpl(MethodImplOptions.NoInlining)]
private void GrowAndAppend(char c)
```

```
{
    Grow(1);
    Append(c);
}

[MethodImpl(MethodImplOptions.NoInlining)]
private void Grow(int requiredAdditionalCapacity)
{
    Debug.Assert(requiredAdditionalCapacity > 0);
    char[] poolArray = ArrayPool<char>.Shared.Rent(Math.Max(_pos +
    requiredAdditionalCapacity, _chars.Length * 2));
    _chars.CopyTo(poolArray);
    char[] toReturn = _arrayToReturnToPool;
    _chars = _arrayToReturnToPool = poolArray;
    if (toReturn != null)
    {
        ArrayPool<char>.Shared.Return(toReturn);
    }
}
```

Obviously, an array acquired from the array pool should be returned to it. This is handled in Dispose method (see Listing 14-11). Please note that while such method is named Dispose, ValueStringBuilder does not implement IDisposable interface because ref structs cannot implement interfaces! Thus, it is a sole programmer responsibility to explicitly call Dispose on such a builder instance.

Listing 14-11. Fragments of internal ValueStringBuilder class (dispoe logic)

```
[MethodImpl(MethodImplOptions.AggressiveInlining)]
public void Dispose()
{
    char[] toReturn = _arrayToReturnToPool;
    this = default; // for safety, to avoid using pooled array if this
    instance is erroneously appended to again
    if (toReturn != null)
```

```
    {
        ArrayPool<char>.Shared.Return(toReturn);
    }
}
```

Using ValueStringBuilder is trivial. We just need some initial storage, small stackalloc buffer used most often, and pass it to its constructor (see Listing 14-12).

Listing 14-12. Example usage of ValueStringBuilder

```
public string UseValueStringBuilder()
{
    Span<char> initialBuffer = stackalloc char[40];
    var builder = new ValueStringBuilder(initialBuffer);
    // Logic using builder.Append(...);
    string result = builder.ToString();
    builder.Dispose();
    return result;
}
```

ValueStringBuilder is a very nice example of a type where many various modern techniques are used: ref structs, ref returns, Span<T>, ArrayPool<T>, and (most often) stackalloc. Make sure you understand it well and you are guaranteed that you understand these modern techniques well also. Please, feel invited to read ValueStringBuilder source code in the CoreFX Github repository.

There is also a very similar ValueListBuilder struct in CoreFX code. I invite you to read it also though!

Tempted by Span<T> flexibility, we could think of a concise solution to a small local buffer acquiring as in Listing 14-13. Below some small-size threshold, we are stackalloc-ating our buffer, while using ArrayPool for bigger ones. While it looks nice, is valid and compiles, it has one serious drawback. We have no way to return such an array to the pool (we cannot get back the original array from the Span<T> instance)!

Listing 14-13. Attempt to provide concise conditional local buffer acquiring

```
private const int StackAllocSafeThreshold = 128;
public void UseSpanNotWisely(int size)
{
   Span<int> span = size < StackAllocSafeThreshold ? stackalloc int[size] :
   ArrayPool<int>.Shared.Rent(size);
   for (int i = 0; i < size; ++i)
      Console.WriteLine(span[i]);
   //ArrayPool<int>.Shared.Return(??);
}
```

If we think about it a little, ValueStringBuilder presented before is addressing a similar problem as code from Listing 14-14 (with additional feature of making such a local buffer growable).

If we insist in doing something similar as in Listing 14-13, we will hit some current C# limitations (as far as in current C# 7.3 state). For example, it is not possible to assign stackalloc result to an already defined variable (it may be assigned only in initializer). So this approach requires some additional code and becomes far less concise and pleasant (see Listing 14-14). We may encounter such code in the .NET base library though, as it does what it is supposed to do (unfortunately requiring unsafe, as it uses pointers).

Listing 14-14. Attempt to provide concise conditional local buffer acquiring

```
public unsafe void UseSpanWisely(int size)
{
   int* ptr = default;
   int[] array = null;
   if (size < StackAllocSafeThreshold)
   {
      int* localPtr = stackalloc int[size];
      ptr = localPtr;
   }
   else
   {
      array = ArrayPool<int>.Shared.Rent(size);
   }
```

```
    Span<int> span = array ?? new Span<int>(ptr, size);
    for (int i = 0; i < size; ++i)
        Console.WriteLine(span[i]);
    if (array != null) ArrayPool<int>.Shared.Return(array);
}
```

One more typical usage of Span is a non-allocating substring by using "some string".AsSpan().Slice(...) method calls. This is a great way of string parsing not requiring costly string.Substring calls.

Span<T> Internals

After being saturated with the examples for where you can use Span<T>, let's go over to discuss how it all works. Although maybe not visible at first glance, its implementation is not trivial and reveals some interesting CLR internal issues. Thus, I dedicate quite a lot of words to explain various design decisions behind Span<T> internal workings, step by step. If you are really in a hurry, feel free to skip this section. Although, as always, I invite you to read it thoroughly! Span<T> is really at the heart of current changes in the .NET ecosystem so it is really nice to understand it well.

Knowing what Span<T> should provide, what design decisions come to our minds? To start with:

- As it may represent stack-allocated memory (like stackalloc), it itself should not appear on the heap (as it could outlive what it wraps) - so we have to use stack-allocated struct and somehow ensure it will not be boxed (first difficult challenge).

- Because of performance reasons, it would be nice to use struct anyway (no heap allocations).

- As we need to represent the memory region, we need to somehow represent two items of information: pointer (address) and the size.

- If our Span<T> contains both pointer and size, we are exposed to multithreading issues if multiple threads are using it (so-called *struct tearing*) - both fields should be changed atomically. But such mandatory synchronization is very efficient in a type that we design for high-performance code (second difficult challenge).

- Our Span<T> may represent a subregion of a managed array (for example, because of slicing) so our pointer may point inside a managed object - if it reminds you of an interior pointer, excellent! In fact, ideally our pointer would be a managed pointer (which can point into an object's interior). But we may remember that managed pointers are allowed only for local variables, arguments, and returns, not fields. Even struct fields are disallowed because struct may be boxed (third difficult challenge).

Those points conclude the most relevant design Span<T> considerations. Going further, all three difficult challenges we are facing could be solved if:

- We had type that may be only stack allocated - then it will be safe to store stack address there, and we get rid of threading issues as it is single threaded by default.

- We had the possibility to use a managed pointer as a field of Span<T> - then we can target any interesting memory type in a safe manner.

For sure you have noticed it already. Indeed, we have stack-only types - ref structs! Those *byref-like types* indeed suit our needs perfectly (to be honest - they were introduced mainly because Span<T> needed them). Moreover, byref-like types do not require runtime changes. Most of the work is done on the C# compiler side, and they are back compatible on the CIL level with both current .NET Core and .NET Framework. Thus, we may consider our first requirement fulfilled.

The second requirement is stronger. Having byref-like types, one could think of *byref-like instance fields* - a managed pointer could be a part of byref-like type because their limitations are related. In other words, a managed pointer may be safely a field of stack-only ref struct because it is guaranteed it will not escape to the heap. Unfortunately, currently both C# and CIL does not have support for such byref-like instance fields and runtime changes are required. Specially for Span<T> type, a new intrinsic (implemented in runtime) type has been introduced to represent such byref-like instance field. Thus, the second requirement is fulfilled only in runtimes supporting that change. Currently this is only .NET Core 2.1 (and later ones).

Nothing is lost however. When the second requirement is not met, we can work around it without runtime support (and we will soon see how). This leads to a situation in which we have two versions of Span<T>, referred to as:

- *"slow span"* - it is a back-compatible version running on .NET Framework and .NET Core prior to version 2.1, which does not require runtime changes. Most probably .NET Framework will never include those changes due to backward-compatibility risks it brings.

- *"fast span"* - it is a version running with the support of byref-like instance field added in .NET Core 2.1.

Do not put too much attention to "slow" or "fast" names - both are still quite fast! Slow is simply a little slower than the second version. A corresponding benchmark from Listing 14-15 and results from Listing 14-16 clearly shows that:

- "fast" Span<T> in .NET Core 2.1 achieves performance similar to regular .NET array.

- "slow" Span<T> in .NET Framework is indeed slower by around 25%.

However, keep in mind that such a little contrived benchmark concentrates purely on data access via an indexer. More real-world examples show performance differences on the level of 12–15%.

Listing 14-15. Simple benchmark of access time with the help of Span ("slow" for .NET Framework, "fast" for .NET Core) and regular array, for comparison

```
public class SpanBenchmark
{
    private byte[] array;

    [GlobalSetup]
    public void Setup()
```

```
{
    array = new byte[128];
    for (int i = 0; i < 128; ++i)
        array[i] = (byte)i;
}

[Benchmark]
public int SpanAccess()
{
    var span = new Span<byte>(this.array);
    int result = 0;
    for (int i = 0; i < 128; ++i)
    {
        result += span[i];
    }
    return result;
}

[Benchmark]
public int ArrayAccess()
{
    int result = 0;
    for (int i = 0; i < 128; ++i)
    {
        result += this.array[i];
    }
    return result;
}
}
```

Listing 14-16. Results of BenchmarkDotNet benchmark from Listing 14-1

Method	Job	Mean	Error	Allocated
SpanAccess	.NET 4.7.1	90.35 ns	0.1085 ns	0 B
ArrayAccess	.NET 4.7.1	66.86 ns	0.7334 ns	0 B
SpanAccess	.NET Core 2.1	65.81 ns	0.7035 ns	0 B
ArrayAccess	.NET Core 2.1	66.18 ns	0.0603 ns	0 B

Let's now look how both versions are implemented in detail. We will look only at the most interesting aspects - construction from both managed and unmanaged memory and indexer implementation.

In further code listings, Unsafe class will be quite often used. This is a general-purpose class providing low-level operations on memory and pointers. It is briefly described later in this chapter. Unsafe usage presented here is quite self-explanatory - it is used for casting and simple pointer arithmetic.

"Slow Span"

"Slow Span" has to live without byref-like fields. To simulate an interior pointer as a field, we have to remember both an object reference and offset inside of it (see Listing 14-17). Keeping an object reference avoids creating GC hole - we need to make an object reachable because of wrapping in Span<T>. Obviously, the length is always required.

Listing 14-17. "Slow" Span<T> declaration in CoreFX repository

```
public readonly ref partial struct Span<T>
{
    private readonly Pinnable<T> _pinnable;
    private readonly IntPtr _byteOffset;
    private readonly int _length;

    ...

}
// This class exists solely so that arbitrary objects can be Unsafe-casted
to it to get a ref to the start of the user data.
[StructLayout(LayoutKind.Sequential)]
internal sealed class Pinnable<T>
{
    public T Data;
}
```

So how does construction of Span<T> from both managed and unmanaged data look? Wrapping around the managed array is straightforward (see Listing 14-18). We keep the whole reference to an array (making it discoverable by the GC to avoid collecting it), and we save the offset where the array data begins (this is what ArrayAdjustment really returns), optionally properly shifted in case of array slicing.

Listing 14-18. "Slow" Span<T> construction from managed array

```
public Span(T[] array)
{
    ...
    _length = array.Length;
    _pinnable = Unsafe.As<Pinnable<T>>(array);
    _byteOffset = SpanHelpers.PerTypeValues<T>.ArrayAdjustment;
}

public Span(T[] array, int start, int length)
{
    ...
    _length = length;
    _pinnable = Unsafe.As<Pinnable<T>>(array);
    _byteOffset = SpanHelpers.PerTypeValues<T>.ArrayAdjustment.
    Add<T>(start);    // Add method realizes pointer arithmetic
}
```

Wrapping unmanaged memory is even simpler because there is no object reference that we should be worried about (see Listing 14-19). We only save the length and the address.

Listing 14-19. "Slow" Span<T> construction from unmanaged memory

```
public unsafe Span(void* pointer, int length)
{
    ...
    _length = length;
    _pinnable = null;
    _byteOffset = new IntPtr(pointer);
}
```

The area from which the difference in performance between both Span<T> types is mostly visible is access to the memory elements. Indexer of "slow Span" has to perform more calculations - in case of a managed array, it adds to an object address byte offset where data begins and byte offset of the element under a given index (see Listing 14-20).

Listing 14-20. Indexer implementation in "slow" Span<T>

```
public ref T this[int index]
{
   get
   {
      if (_pinnable == null)
         unsafe { return ref Unsafe.Add<T>(ref Unsafe.AsRef<T>(_byteOffset.
         ToPointer()), index); }
      else
         return ref Unsafe.Add<T>(ref Unsafe.AddByteOffset<T>
         (ref _pinnable.Data, _byteOffset), index);
   }
}
```

If you would like to investigate "slow" Span<T> source code more, look at `.\corefx\src\System.Memory\src\System\Span.Portable.cs` file.

"Fast Span"

"Fast Span" has runtime support of byref-like fields. We could imagine it looks like in Listing 14-21. But C# does not support any syntax to represent byref-like fields so until they will be added (if ever), a dedicated type was introduced to represent such fields.

Listing 14-21. Hypothetical syntax of byref-like fields in "fast" Span<T> declaration

```
public readonly ref partial struct Span<T>
{
   internal readonly ref T _pointer;
```

```
    private readonly int _length;
    ...
}
```

This type is named ByReference<T> so the true declaration of "fast" Span<T> looks like in Listing 14-22. Internal ByReference<T> type is handled by runtime specially to wrap around its managed pointer nature (and currently only Span<T> and ReadOnlySpan<T> types are using it).

Listing 14-22. Fast Span declaration (including ByReference<T> type) in CoreFX repository

```
// ByReference<T> is meant to be used to represent "ref T" fields. It is
// working around lack of first class support for byref fields in C# and IL.
// The JIT and type loader has special handling for it that turns it
// into a thin wrapper around ref T.
[NonVersionable]
internal ref struct ByReference<T>
{
    private IntPtr _value;
    ...
}

public readonly ref partial struct Span<T>
{
    /// <summary>A byref or a native ptr.</summary>
    internal readonly ByReference<T> _pointer;
    /// <summary>The number of elements this Span contains.</summary>
    private readonly int _length;

    ...
}
```

Thanks to the byref-like field, this version of Span<T> has simpler implementation. Both managed and unmanaged data is held by such a byref-like field (see Listing 14-23). As managed (interior) pointer is considered by the GC, no risk exists that the relevant managed object will be collected.

Listing 14-23. "Fast" Span<T> construction from both managed and unmanaged memory

```
public Span(T[] array)
{
    _pointer = new ByReference<T>(ref Unsafe.As<byte, T>(ref array.
    GetRawSzArrayData()));
    _length = array.Length;
}

public Span(T[] array, int start, int length)
{
    _pointer = new ByReference<T>(ref Unsafe.Add(ref Unsafe.As<byte, T>(ref
    array.GetRawSzArrayData()), start));
    _length = length;
}

public unsafe Span(void* pointer, int length)
{
    _pointer = new ByReference<T>(ref Unsafe.As<byte, T>(ref *(byte*)
    pointer));
    _length = length;
}
```

Moreover, access to the memory elements is trivial and requires only very fast pointer arithmetic (see Listing 14-24) - which results in comparable performance to regular arrays.

Listing 14-24. Indexer implementation in "fast" Span<T>f

```
public ref T this[int index]
{
    get
```

```
{
    return ref Unsafe.Add(ref _pointer.Value, index);
}
}
```

The other component of the performance difference comes from JIT compiler improvements in CoreCLR. In particular, it does better bounds check elimination when `for` looping the "fast" span. Another difference is that "fast" span is simply smaller and such a cheaper to pass by value, which shows in some code that passes it a lot.

Interestingly, if you think about it, from the GC overhead point of view, "slow" and "fast" Span<T> are a little opposite. "Slow" version contains direct object reference (in case of wrapping managed object) so it will be faster to traverse. "Fast" version will contain interior pointer, whose dereferencing is slower (requires plugs traversal and scanning). However, this difference is negligible, and it is even hard to imagine application with such a big number of simultaneously living Span<T> that any difference may be noticed.

General byref-like fields? Is there a chance that general-purpose byref fields will be introduced to C#? It is unlikely it will be justified to allow them for classes (which will in fact introduce heap-to-heap interior pointers). As already mentioned, it gives too little compared to the difficulty of implementation.

But what about general-purpose byref-like fields to be allowed in byref-like (ref struct) types? Will code like in Listing 14-21 ever be possible? There are ongoing discussions, and maybe you already know the answer a year or two after reading this book. Besides array slicing already exposed via Span<T>, one could think of other usages of such fields: structs that are interconnected by pointers for faster traversal, returning multiple byref results in a single byref-like struct and so on, and so forth. However, as far as I know, CLR team has no plans to generalize this feature.

Memory<T>

Span<T> is great and fast. But as we've seen, it has many limitations. Many of them are especially painful when considering asynchronous code. For example, Span<T> can't live on the heap, which then means that it can't be boxed so it can't be a field on the async state machine type that might itself be on the heap. Thus, a complementary type was introduced - Memory<T>. It still represents a contiguous region of arbitrary memory similar to Span<T>, but it is not a byref-like type and does not contain a byref-like instance field. So unlike Span<T>, this type can exist on the heap (although it is still struct for performance reasons, it is not ref struct). It can be a field of normal objects, it can be used in async states machines, etc. It is disallowed to wrap stack data with Memory<T> (like returned from stackalloc).

Memory<T> may wrap around the following data (see Listing 14-25):

- array T[] - used as a preallocated buffer reused through asynchronous calls or in APIs for which the limitation to use Span<T> is too strong,

- string - in such case it is represented as ReadOnlyMemory<char>,

- type that implements IMemoryOwner<T> - used in scenarios where more control about Memory<T> instance's lifetime is required (we will look at such scenario soon).

Listing 14-25. Sample Memory<T> usages

```
byte[] array = new byte[] {1, 2, 3};
Memory<byte> memory1 = new Memory<byte>(array);
Memory<byte> memory2 = new Memory<byte>(array, start: 1, length: 2);
ReadOnlyMemory<char> memory3 = "Hello world".AsMemory();
```

You can imagine Memory<T> as a box that can be freely allocated and passed in and out through methods. Mostly its storage is not directly accessible. To utilize it, you have the following options:

- Span<T> may be generated from it for local, efficient use (hence Memory<T> is often described as "Span factory").

- in case of Memory<char> you may generate string from it by calling ToString, in other cases ToArray may be used (remember that both are allocating new reference type!).

- like Span<T>, it can be sliced via Slice methods.

Both slicing and generating Span<T> are efficient operations that do not allocate anything - it is just wrapping around a given memory range into a struct. And as we know it, the whole operation may be sometimes enregistered so even no stack usage may be required.

As mentioned, asynchronous code is the most common use of Memory<T>, as a replacement for Span<T> (see Listing 14-26). Inside the asynchronous code payload of the Memory<T> may be accessed in ways listed before (Listing 14-26 uses direct ToString conversion).

Listing 14-26. Example of using ReadOnlyMemory<T> instead of Span<T> in asynchronous code

```
public static async Task<string> FetchStringAsync(ReadOnlySpan<
char> requestUrl) // Error CS4012  Parameters or locals of type
'ReadOnlySpan<char>' cannot be declared in async methods or lambda
expressions.
{
   HttpClient client = new HttpClient();
   var task = client.GetStringAsync(requestUrl.ToString());
   return await task;
}

public static async Task<string> FetchStringAsync(ReadOnlyMemory<char>
requestUrl)
{
   HttpClient client = new HttpClient();
   var task = client.GetStringAsync(requestUrl.ToString());
   return await task;
}
```

Let's look at a more complex example (see Listing 14-27). BufferedWriter class implements buffered writing to a specified Stream[2]. It uses internally a small array of bytes (writeBuffer) and keeps track of its current utilization by writeOffset field. The only public WriteAsync method is asynchronous so it accepts ReadOnlyMemory<byte> as

---

[2]Although specific Stream implementation may implement its buffering and flushing mechanisms, this is used for example purposes. In fact, such design is used in classes like FileStream where stream is replaced by native OS calls.

a source. This makes it more generic and flexible than various overloads that accept an array, a string, a native memory pointer, and so on, and so forth. Dependency only on ReadOnlyMemory<T> allows us to write much more concise code, as long as the source is compatible with ReadOnlyMemory<T>.

Inside asynchronous WriteAsync method, ReadOnlyMemory<T> is used to get the appropriate span from it and pass it to private, synchronous method WriteToBuffer that consumes it. Inside WriteToBuffer method another Span<T> wraps writeBuffer to use the convenient CopyTo method. Additionally, slicing capabilities help to write simple while loop in the WriteAsync method that consumes sources in chunks. Please note also that BufferedWriter class does not allocate anything besides writeBuffer.

Listing 14-27. Example of ReadOnlyMemory<T> and ReadOnlySpan<T> cooperation

```
public class BufferedWriter : IDisposable
{
    private const int WriteBufferSize = 32;
    private readonly byte[] writeBuffer = new byte[WriteBufferSize];
    private readonly Stream stream;
    private int writeOffset = 0;

    public BufferedWriter(Stream stream)
    {
        this.stream = stream;
    }

    public async Task WriteAsync(ReadOnlyMemory<byte> source)
    {
        int remaining = writeBuffer.Length - writeOffset;
        if (source.Length <= remaining)
        {
            // Fits in current write buffer. Just copy and return.
            WriteToBuffer(source.Span);
            return;
        }
```

```
    while (source.Length > 0)
    {
        // Fit what we can in the current write buffer and flush it.
        remaining = Math.Min(writeBuffer.Length - writeOffset, source.
        Length);
        WriteToBuffer(source.Slice(0, remaining).Span);
        source = source.Slice(remaining);
        await FlushAsync().ConfigureAwait(false);
    }
}
private void WriteToBuffer(ReadOnlySpan<byte> source)
{
    source.CopyTo(new Span<byte>(writeBuffer, writeOffset,
    source.Length));
    writeOffset += source.Length;
}

private Task FlushAsync()
{
    if (writeOffset > 0)
    {
        Task task = stream.WriteAsync(writeBuffer, 0, writeOffset);
        writeOffset = 0;
        return task;
    }
    return default;
}

public void Dispose()
{
    stream?.Dispose();

}
}
```

IMemoryOwner<T>

There is one issue with Memory<T> - lifetime control. In contrary, Span<T> has a very restricted lifetime limited by the method lifetime so it was guaranteed that wrapped memory will not outlive it[3]. Memory<T>, quite oppositely, has less strict lifetime limitations (as it may wrap heap-allocated objects). In other words, the relation between Memory<T> and the memory it wraps is not obvious.

One could think about making Memory<T> to use explicit resource management - because underlying memory can be seen as resource. In .NET words - maybe it should be disposable? However, Memory<T> instances are passed around between various methods, including asynchronous ones. Who and when should be responsible for calling Dispose on such instance would be problematic to determine. We could implement the reference counting approach as the solution but it has its own problems - mostly it imposes the need for multithreaded synchronization when building a general-purpose solution.

Thus, another, more flexible solution was proposed - an additional level of control in the form of *ownership semantic*. If there is a requirement for Memory<T> with a controlled lifetime, we must provide its owner in the form of IMemoryOwner<T> interface implementation (see Listing 14-28). Memory<T> instances are accessible from the owner as the public Memory property. IMemoryOwner<T> implements IDisposable interface so it is clear that the owner itself realizes explicit resource management and controls ownership of the given Memory<T>.

Usage of IMemoryOwner instances is restricted by convention (like always in case of IDisposable) - we have to remember to call Dispose, with the help, for example, of the using clause. Or we may realize ownership semantics - there should be always only one object (or method) that "owns" IMemoryOwner instance, and it is clear it is the one that will have to call Dispose when the job is done.

Listing 14-28. IMemoryOwner<T> interface declaration

```
/// <summary>
/// Owner of Memory<typeparamref name="T"/> that is responsible for
    disposing the underlying memory appropriately.
/// </summary>
```

---

[3]Unless we have passed an unmanaged address, see ReturnNativeAsSpan method in Listing 14-5.

```
public interface IMemoryOwner<T> : IDisposable
{
    Memory<T> Memory { get; }
}
```

IMemoryOwner<T> and ownership semantics are not necessary in cases such as simple as in Listing 14-25. Then, the GC becomes the only one, implicit "owner" of the underlying memory. It will take care of collecting it when all Memory<T> instances using it will be dead.

A typical example when explicit resource management is required is wrapping around an object rented from a pool, like an array from ArrayPool<T> (see Listing 14-29). If we rented an array from a pool and wrapped it in Memory<T>, when it should be returned? Inside Consume method, in our example? Or maybe after await ends? But what if Consume method stored somewhere reference to passed Memory<T> (it is possible because it may be boxed)?

Listing 14-29. Problematic ownership of underlying Memory<T> memory

```
Memory<int> pooledMemory = new Memory<int>(ArrayPool<int>.Shared.
Rent(128));
await Consume(pooledMemory);
```

IMemoryOwner<T> interface helps to organize things a little - only the method or class holding it should be worried about explicit cleanup of resources. IMemoryOwner<T> instance should be very carefully passed - if some method or type's constructor accepts it, such method or type should be treated as the new owner of the underlying memory (it should call Dispose afterwards or pass such instance further). It is assumed that such owner, meaning a given method or a whole type, may safely consume the underlying Memory property.

To see it in action, we can use MemoryPool<T> class already exposed in System.Memory NuGet package that wraps around the array instance returned from ArrayPool<T>. Shared instance. Listing 14-30 shows a simple usage example when ownership is controlled by using a clause inside a single method and Listing 14-31 shows an example when the entire type is the owner of underlying memory. In the latter case, such type should also be disposable to make it clear it has some explicit cleanup to perform.

Listing 14-30. An example of Memory<T> with explicit owner as a method

```
using (IMemoryOwner<int> owner = MemoryPool<int>.Shared.Rent(128))
{
    Memory<int> memory = owner.Memory;
    ConsumeMemory(span);
    ConsumeSpan(memory.Span);
}
```

Listing 14-31. An example of Memory<T> with explicit owner as a type

```
public class Worker : IDisposable
{
    private readonly IMemoryOwner<byte> memoryOwner;

    public Worker(IMemoryOwner<byte> memoryOwner)
    {
        this.memoryOwner = memoryOwner;
    }

    public UseMemory()
    {
        ConsumeMemory(memoryOwner.Memory);
        ConsumeSpan(memoryOwner.Memory.Span);
    }

    public void Dispose()
    {
        this.memoryOwner?.Dispose();
    }
}
```

MemoryPool<T>.Shared uses static ArrayMemoryPool<T> instance whose Rent method returns new ArrayMemoryPoolBuffer<T> instance. It implements IMemoryOwner<T> in a trivial way - its constructor rents a properly sized array from ArrayPool<T>.Shared while Dispose method returns it to the pool. ArrayMemoryPool<T>.Memory property just wraps around a rented array into a new Memory<T> instance. If you would like to investigate this code on your own, read .\corefx\src\System.Memory\src\System\Buffers\ArrayMemoryPool.cs and .\corefx\src\System.Memory\src\System\Buffers\ArrayMemoryPool.ArrayMemoryPoolBuffer.cs files.

For example, we could make BufferedWriter from Listing 14-27 more flexible and let it accept underlying buffer, instead of allocating its own (see Listing 14-32). This allows us to populate it with a rented array or, for example, unmanaged memory.

Listing 14-32. Modification of BufferedWriter class from Listing 14-27 that uses provided buffer

```
public class FlexibleBufferedWriter : IDisposable
{
    private const int WriteBufferSize = 32;
    private readonly IMemoryOwner<byte> memoryOwner;
    private readonly Stream stream;
    private int writeOffset = 0;

    public FlexibleBufferedWriter(Stream stream, IMemoryOwner<byte> memoryOwner)
    {
        Debug.Assert(memoryOwner.Memory.Length > MinimumWriteBufferSize);
        this.stream = stream;
        this.memoryOwner = memoryOwner;
    }

    ...

    public void Dispose()
    {
        stream?.Dispose();
        memoryOwner?.Dispose();
    }
}
```

Thanks to the possibility of getting Span<T> from Memory<T>, most implementation of our changed `FlexibleBufferedWriter` is very similar to previous `BufferedWriter`. For example, `WriteToBuffer` method uses now `CopyTo` method between source `Span<T>` and `Span<T>` representing owned memory (see Listing 14-33). In `WriteAsync` method, all calls to `writeBuffer.Length` may be safely replaced to `memoryOwner.Memory.Length`.

Listing 14-33. `FlexibleBufferedWriter.WriteToBuffer` method implementation

```
private void WriteToBuffer(ReadOnlySpan<byte> source)
{
    source.CopyTo(memoryOwner.Memory.Span.Slice(writeOffset, source.
    Length));
    writeOffset += source.Length;
}
```

Unfortunately, not all APIs will be always aligned to use Span/Memory classes (although hopefully soon most BCL types will cover it). For example, before .NET Core 2.1, `Stream.WriteAsync` method accepted only a byte array parameter. In such a case, we have to convert it accordingly (see Listing 14-34). If we are lucky and the underlying storage is an array, `MemoryMarshal.TryGetArray` will succeed (we will look at `MemoryMarshal` later in this chapter) and we will get an underlying array instance without copying. In other cases, we have to copy the data to a temporary array (so it is better to rent it from the pool to at least avoid allocations). Note that we need now to return optionally rented shared buffer to return the pool by the `FlushAsync` method caller.

Be prepared for the need for this kind of solutions by writing a low-level code. And although code from Listing 14-34 may not be necessary after adjusting Stream API, it serves well as an interesting example of cooperation between various functionalities described in this chapter.

Listing 14-34. `FlexibleBufferedWriter.FlushAsync` method implementation

```
private Task FlushAsync(out byte[] sharedBuffer)
{
    sharedBuffer = null;
    if (writeOffset > 0)
```

```
{
    Task result;
    if (MemoryMarshal.TryGetArray(memoryOwner.Memory, out
    ArraySegment<byte> array))
    {
        result = stream.WriteAsync(array.Array, array.Offset,
        writeOffset);
    }
    else
    {
        sharedBuffer = ArrayPool<byte>.Shared.Rent(writeOffset);
        memoryOwner.Memory.Span.Slice(0, writeOffset).CopyTo(sharedBuffer);
        result = stream.WriteAsync(sharedBuffer, 0, writeOffset);
    }

    writeOffset = 0;
    return result;
    }
    return default;
}
```

General-purpose classes that accept buffers are generally good design patterns that should be followed by libraries creators (at least as opt-in possibility). Especially all kind of serializers or other memory-intensive code is well-behaving if it allows us to specify explicitly provided buffers or pooling mechanism. You can plug in your own machinery then, instead of relying on the internal ones (or no buffering, allocating-all-the-way machinery in the worst case).

Memory<T> may be used in P/Invoke scenarios so it may be necessary to pin underlying memory. For that purpose, Memory<T> exposes Pin method that returns MemoryHandle struct instance (disposable object that represents pinned memory). In case of wrapping string or array, it pins them via GCHandle. In case of Memory<T> returned from IMemoryOwner<T>, it is expected that such owner is an implementation of an abstract class MemoryManager<T>. Such class additionally implements `IPinnable` interface with `Pin` and `Unpin` methods. Its `Pin` method is called from `Memory<T>.Pin` method and `Unpin` method is called from `MemoryHandle.Dispose` method. In that way, the memory owner is responsible for proper pinning and unpinning memory it owns. We will not look thoroughly into `Memory<T>` pinning as it is mostly related to P/Invoke, being not our main interest.

Memory<T> Internals

Unlike `Span<T>`, the implementation of `Memory<T>` is quite obvious and does not contain any puzzles. Of course, this is due to current runtime limitations of managed pointers. When designing `Memory<T>` we should take into account the following aspects:

- it should have reference type lifetime - although it may start as a struct and only be boxed if needed.

- heap-allocated objects are represented only by reference - currently interior pointers cannot live on heap so this is obvious. This simplifies design as the only two types where "interior-like" behavior makes sense are arrays and strings (because they are indexable and may be sliced).

- stack-allocated addresses do not need to be represented.

- unmanaged memory requires explicit resource management - thus it may be backed up by an additional owner class, as explained previously.

Those points lead to simple `Memory<T>` implementation. Listing 14-35 shows an excerpt from the current CoreFX source code. There is simply a managed reference kept (be it an array or `string`), index and the length (used for slicing). Construction is also mostly trivial.

Listing 14-35. `Memory<T>` declaration in CoreFX repository (including example of one constructor)

```
public readonly struct Memory<T>
{
    private readonly object _object;
```

```
    private readonly int _index;
    private readonly int _length;
    ...
}

public Memory(T[] array, int start, int length)
{
    ...
    _object = array;
    _index = start;
    _length = length;
}
```

But because of Memory<T> flexibility, it cannot expose a general-purpose indexer. As previously said, memory may be accessed by slicing and converting to Span<T>. Span property itself has simple implementation also (see Listing 14-36). In case of array or string, appropriate sliced span is returned. If memory is owned, getting a span is delegated to the owner (by calling GetSpan method).

Listing 14-36. Excerpt from Span property implementation in Memory<T>

```
public Span<T> Span
{
    get
    {
        if (_index < 0)
        {
            return ((MemoryManager<T>)_object).GetSpan().Slice(_index &
            RemoveFlagsBitMask, _length);
        }
        else if (typeof(T) == typeof(char) && _object is string s)
        {
            // return string slice as a Span
        }
```

```
    else if (_object != null)
    {
       return new Span<T>((T[])_object, _index, _length &
       RemoveFlagsBitMask);
    }
    ...

  }
}
```

When analyzing Memory<T> code you will notice that both _index and _length are sometimes manipulated by bit flags to indicate the type of memory wrapped. This is due to tight memory usage requirements. While an additional field could be added for that purpose (let's say - an enum), this would obviously noticeably increase the size of the object to store relevantly small information. Thus, for example, the highest order bit of _index is used to discern whether _object is an array/string or an owned memory.

You may wonder how unmanaged memory may be represented by Memory<T> fields shown in Listing 14-35. Because unmanaged memory requires explicit cleanup, in such case _object field would represent appropriate MemoryManager<T> implementation that is responsible for allocating and releasing underlying memory. A very brief outline of such a manager is presented in Listing 14-37, inspired by internal NativeMemoryManager class from System.Buffers namespace.

Listing 14-37. Example of native memory managed

```
class NativeMemoryManager : MemoryManager<byte>
{
   private readonly int _length;
   private IntPtr _ptr;

   public NativeMemoryManager(int length)
   {
      _length = length;
      _ptr = Marshal.AllocHGlobal(length);
   }
```

```
protected override void Dispose(bool disposing)
{
    ...
    Marshal.FreeHGlobal(_ptr);
    ...
}

public override Memory<byte> Memory => CreateMemory(_length);
// Creates Memory<T> instance that sets this as wrapped object
public override unsafe Span<byte> GetSpan() => new Span<byte>((void*)_
ptr, _length);
```

Span<T> and Memory<T> Guidelines

After learning quite a lot about those types, the question arises when to use them and which should be preferred? Please find the following rules regarding their usage:

- use Span<T> or Memory<T> in high-performance, general-purpose code - most probably you do not need to clutter all your business logic with it.

- prefer Span<T> over Memory<T> as a method argument if possible - it is faster (with runtime support) and may represent more memory types. In asynchronous code there is no choice other than Memory<T> though.

- prefer read-only version over mutable ones - to express the intent and make it safer. Do not use regular versions by default. Also, use it because it's more accepting, for example, if you expose a method that accepts a Span<T>, a ReadOnlySpan<T> can't be passed to that method, but if you expose a method that accepts a ReadOnlySpan<T>, then both a Span<T> and a ReadOnlySpan<T> can be passed to it.

- remember that IMemoryOwner<T> instance (or MemoryManager<T>) is... ownership - at some point Dispose method must be called on it. For safety, ideally only a single object at the moment should keep such instance. Types that keep IMemoryOwner<T> (which is a disposable object) should also be disposable (to manage this resource appropriately).

Unsafe

System.Runtime.CompilerServices.Unsafe package provides generic, low-level functionality for manipulating pointers in a safer way than using plain unsafe code (based on pointers and fixed statements) and express some capabilities possible in CIL but not in C# directly. However, what it allows is still really unsafe and dangerous! Thanks to its flexibility, Unsafe class is widely used in modern .NET libraries code (many types like Span<T>, Memory<T>, and others are relying on it underneath).

Describing all capabilities of Unsafe class is by far possible in this book because it is like describing all capabilities of pointer arithmetic or pointer casting - you really can do anything you want. Instead, a short brief of these class methods and a few usage examples are presented to give you an overall grasp of what and how you can do with it.

System.Runtime.CompilerServices.Unsafe provides a rich set of methods (see Listing 14-38). They may be grouped into the following functional groups:

- casting and reinterpretation - you can convert between unmanaged pointer and ref type back and forth. Additionally, you can convert between any two ref types (yes, it is as dangerous as it sounds).

- pointer arithmetic - you can add or subtract ref type instances like regular pointers (and if you remember the managed pointers description, you already imagine all those boundary cases when it is dangerous as hell).

- information - lets you get various information, like size or byte offset between two ref type instances.

- memory access - you can write or read anything from everywhere.

Listing 14-38. Unsafe class API - some overloads removed for brevity, methods are reordered into feature-like groups, comments are my own

```
public static partial class Unsafe
{
    // Casting/reinterpretation
    public unsafe static void* AsPointer<T>(ref T value)
    public unsafe static ref T AsRef<T>(void* source)
    public static ref TTo As<TFrom, TTo>(ref TFrom source)
```

```
// Pointer arithmetic
public static ref T Add<T>(ref T source, int elementOffset)
public static ref T Subtract<T>(ref T source, int elementOffset)

// Informative methods
public static int SizeOf<T>()
public static System.IntPtr ByteOffset<T>(ref T origin, ref T target)
public static bool IsAddressGreaterThan<T>(ref T left, ref T right)
public static bool IsAddressLessThan<T>(ref T left, ref T right)
public static bool AreSame<T>(ref T left, ref T right)

// Memory access methods
public unsafe static T Read<T>(void* source)
public unsafe static void Write<T>(void* destination, T value)
public unsafe static void Copy<T>(void* destination, ref T source)

// Block-based memory access
public static void CopyBlock(ref byte destination, ref byte source, uint
byteCount)
public unsafe static void InitBlock(void* startAddress, byte value, uint
byteCount)
}
```

It is clear that Unsafe is not a general-purpose class. It can be used in only very specific, well-controlled places where the programmer really knows what it wants to do and considered all uncommon, boundary cases. Do not treat this class as a helper to overcome strange type-safety problems, for example, to break a type hierarchy in object-oriented programming!

Let's look at few examples. First of all, we have already seen important Unsafe class usage in Listings 14-18, 14-20, 14-23, and 14-24 where casting and pointer arithmetic were used to implement Span<T>.

Casting is a powerful tool though. For example, we can cast one managed type to another, completely unrelated type (see Listing 14-39). Memory of source instance is reinterpreted with respect to the field's layout of the target instance. In our simple example we are just reinterpreting two successive integers as long, which may even make some sense. Please note that even such low-level pointers operations are used, DangerousPlays method is not marked as unsafe because Unsafe class wraps everything inside.

Listing 14-39. Dangerous but working code - casting with `Unsafe.As`

```
public class SomeClass
{
    public int Field1;
    public int Field2;
}

public class SomeOtherClass
{
    public long Field;
}

public void DangerousPlays(SomeClass obj)
{
    ref SomeOtherClass target = ref Unsafe.As<SomeClass, SomeOtherClass>
    (ref obj);
    Console.WriteLine(target.Field);
}
```

Such powerful casting is used, for example, to break mutability rules and allows them to cast between `Memory<T>` and `ReadOnlyMemory<T>` in both directions. This of course requires that both types have the same memory layout.

Casting is, for example, intensively used in `BitConverter` static class to convert from byte arrays back and forth to various types (see Listing 14-40).

Listing 14-40. Example of `Unsafe` usage in `BitConverter` class

```
public static byte[] GetBytes(double value)
{
    byte[] bytes = new byte[sizeof(double)];
    Unsafe.As<byte, double>(ref bytes[0]) = value;
    return bytes;
}
```

While using all that memory reinterpretation, imagine primitive types reinterpreted into references or the other way around! Obviously, this is extremely dangerous and most probably will lead to the whole runtime crash. As an illustration, see Listing 14-41 as an example of such careless casting. VeryDangerous method will throw AccessViolationException (unless we are so unusual lucky that the value of Long1 had the value of the valid string).

Listing 14-41. Very dangerous code - casting with Unsafe.As

```
public struct UnmanagedStruct
{
    public long Long1;
    public long Long2;
}

public struct ManagedStruct
{
    public string String;
    public long Long2;
}

public void VeryDangerous(ref UnmanagedStruct data)
{
    ref ManagedStruct target = ref Unsafe.As<UnmanagedStruct,
    ManagedStruct>(ref data);
    Console.WriteLine(target.String);   // Value of Long1 is now treated as
                                        //              string reference!
}
```

Pointer arithmetic is the other popular usage of Unsafe. As a good example, consider the may serve Array.Reverse static method implementation (see Listing 14-42). This is nothing else than a reincarnation of regular C or C++-like code manipulating pointers to reverse an array in place.

Listing 14-42. Example of Unsafe usage in Array.Reverse static method

```
public static void Reverse<T>(T[] array, int index, int length)
{
    ...
```

```
ref T first = ref Unsafe.Add(ref Unsafe.As<byte, T>(ref array.
GetRawSzArrayData()), index);
ref T last = ref Unsafe.Add(ref Unsafe.Add(ref first, length), -1);
do
{
    T temp = first;
    first = last;
    last = temp;
    first = ref Unsafe.Add(ref first, 1);
    last = ref Unsafe.Add(ref last, -1);
} while (Unsafe.IsAddressLessThan(ref first, ref last));
}
```

Because many Span<T>, Memory<T>, and Unsafe usages require the same patterns, the MemoryMarshal helper class was introduced with many static methods. To name only a few of them:

- AsBytes - converts any Span<T> of primitive type (struct) to Span<byte>,

- Cast - converts between two Span<T> of primitive types (structs),

- TryGetArray, TryGetMemoryManager, TryGetString - tries to convert from given Memory<T> (or ReadOnlyMemory<T>) to a specific type,

- GetReference - to ref return underlying Span<T> or ReadOnlySpan<T> object.

With the MemoryMarshal class we can even more easily do "magic" things. For example, we can take a part of some struct and reinterpret it as another struct, all without any copying (see Listing 14-43).

Listing 14-43. Example of MemoryMarshal usage

```
public struct SmallStruct
{
    public byte B1;
    public byte B2;
    public byte B3;
    public byte B4;
```

```
    public byte B5;
    public byte B6;
    public byte B7;
    public byte B8;
}

public unsafe void Reinterpretation(ref UnmanagedStruct data)
{
    var span = new Span<UnmanagedStruct>(Unsafe.AsPointer(ref data), 1);
    ref var part = ref MemoryMarshal
                        // cast from Span<byte> to Span<SmallStruct>
                        .Cast<byte, SmallStruct>(
                            // cast from Span<UnmanagedStruct> to Span<byte>
                            MemoryMarshal.AsBytes(span)
                                        // slice accordingly and access
                                        first element
                                        .Slice(0, 8))[0];
    Console.WriteLine(part.B1); // Get the first byte
}
```

One may wonder where all that "magic" may be useful for him. Does a regular
.NET developer need Unsafe at all? To be honest, mostly not. I imagine Unsafe usage
only in low-level operating libraries code - serialization, binary logging, network
communication, and so on, so forth. For example, popular jemalloc.NET library uses it
to provide strong typing over underlying unmanaged memory (see Listing 14-44).

Listing 14-44. Example of Unsafe usage in jemalloc.NET - FixedBuffer.Read
method

```
[MethodImpl(MethodImplOptions.AggressiveInlining)]
public unsafe ref C Read<C>(int index) where C : struct
{
    return ref Unsafe.AsRef<C>(PtrTo(index));
}
```

jemalloc.NET is a great .NET library written by Allister Beharry and hosted on GitHub (`https://github.com/allisterb/jemalloc.NET`). As the author says, it is a wrapper "over the jemalloc native memory allocator and provides .NET applications with efficient data structures backed by native memory for large scale in-memory computation scenarios." jemalloc is indeed a popular and efficient malloc replacement. Feel free to read about its internal implementation at `http://jemalloc.net/` and also feel invited to experiment with jemalloc. NET. Due to the book=size limitations, not without regret, I have to skip a description of this library.

Speaking of unmanaged memory wrappers, there is also ongoing work on the Microsoft side - project Snowflake. Currently its status is a little frozen but expect open sourcing it sooner or later. You can read about it on `https://www.microsoft.com/en-us/research/publication/project-snowflake-non-blocking-safe-manual-memory-management-net/` site.

Unsafe Internals

In fact, what Unsafe class really does is wrap various IL-based possibilities that are otherwise not possible to express in C# - because IL type control is less strict than that incurred by C# compiler. CIL implementation of most Unsafe methods are really trivial (see Listing 14-45).

Listing 14-45. Example of Unsafe method implementation (in Common Intermediate Language)

```
.method public hidebysig static !!TTo& As<TFrom, TTo> (!!TFrom& source) cil
managed
{
   IL_0000: ldarg.0
   IL_0001: ret
}

.method public hidebysig static !!T& Add<T> (!!T& source, int32
elementOffset) cil managed
```

```
{
    IL_0000: ldarg.0
    IL_0001: ldarg.1
    IL_0002: sizeof !!T
    IL_0008: conv.i
    IL_0009: mul
    IL_000A: add
    IL_000B: ret
}
```

There is no magic underneath Unsafe though. What makes it really useful is exposing all those operations, most often consumable even in safe code.

Data-Oriented Design

The discrepancy between CPU performance and memory access times are constantly growing. We have discussed it already in Chapter 2 quite comprehensively - how CPU and memory cooperation are organized into hierarchical cache and how significantly its organization into cache lines and memory internal implementation influences performance of code we write, preferring sequential data access with strong temporal and spatial locality.

Such a low-level view of memory access is not crucial during everyday development of business-driven, regular web, or desktop applications. Those milliseconds of better or worse performance aren't simply noticeable in small volume of processed data, processed HTTP requests, or handled UI interactions. Readability, extensibility, and expressiveness of the source code, as well as the ability to write, deliver, and extend software fast, are the most important factors when designing such applications. Object-oriented programming, with all its design patterns and SOLID principles, are an exact incarnation of such approach.

However, there is a narrow category of applications that can benefit from breaking this universal convention. These are applications that have to process significant amounts of data in the most efficient way and shortest possible time. Where every millisecond counts. To name a few such examples:

- financial software - especially real-time trading and any analytical decisions may require as fast-as-possible answer based on significant amount of various data.

- Big Data - although in general we may associate it more with batch, slow processing, every millisecond per data processing operation can sum up to a difference of hours or days of overall processing. And still, there are applications where fast answer does really count - like search engines.

- games - in a world where FPS (Frames per seconds) decides on game reception and limits possible graphics quality, every millisecond matters.

- machine learning - there is always not enough processing power to execute various, complicated algorithms used in gaining popularity ML.

Please note that although, at first glance, many of those applications could be CPU-bound (i.e., contains complex algorithms to be executed), because of the above-mentioned discrepancy, it may be memory access that introduces a performance bottleneck. Another, not-yet mentioned aspect is parallel processing of the data, to benefit from multiple logical cores installed on our personal or server computers.

This leads us to *data-oriented design* of software - concentrated around designing data representation and architecture that lead to the most efficient memory access. It almost certainly stays in contradiction to the object-oriented design, because techniques like encapsulation or polymorphism are interfering with achieving effective memory utilization.

What data-oriented design is trying to leverage is:

- designing types and data in a way that lead to a sequential memory access wherever possible, taking into consideration cache-line limits (to pack together most frequent used data) and hierarchical cache nature (to keep as much in higher caches as possible).

- designing types and data, as well as algorithms using them, in a way that leads to easy parallelization without costly synchronization.

I would further split data-oriented design into two more categories:

- *tactical data-oriented design* - concentrates on "local" data structures, like most efficient field's layout or accessing data in correct order. Such design is local enough to be incorporated quite easily into already existing object-oriented applications.

- *strategic data-oriented design* - concentrates on high-level view of the application, from architecture perspective. It mostly requires mindset shift from object-oriented structures into more data-oriented ones.

In the two subsequent sections we will look deeper at both mentioned aspects of such design.

Tactical Design

This book is basically steeped with the spirit of tactical data-oriented design since Chapter 2, where we have learned how important cache utilization is - and summarized in *Rule 2 - Random access should be avoided* and *Rule 3 - Improve spatial and temporal data locality*.

Several patterns constitute such tactical design. Let's summarize them here a little, with appropriate references from the rest of the book and additional examples.

Design Types to Fit as Much Relevant Data as Possible in the First Cache Line

We have seen this rule in action when considering the automatic memory layout of managed types - references all laid at the beginning of the object to make them accessible for the GC within already accessed cache line containing MethodTable pointer. This is optimization done by CLR but we should be aware of it.

Such automatic layout may be, or may not be, a desired one when considering the most commonly accessed data. Imagine the class from Listing 14-46. Obviously, the object-oriented programmer will be quite happy with such design[4] - everything is encapsulated within a single object and only behavior (calculating scoring) is publicly exposed.

---

[4]But taking Domain Driven Design into consideration, it would be probably even more complex, with separate types to represent money or other data.

Listing 14-46. Example class used to illustrate cache line utilization

```
class Customer
{
    private double Earnings;
    // ... some other fields ...
    private DateTime DateOfBirth;
    // ... some other fields ...
    private bool IsSmoking;
    // ... some other fields ...
    private double Scoring;
    // ... some other fields ...
    private HealthData Health;
    private AuxiliaryData Auxiliary;

    public void UpdateScoring()
    {
        this.Scoring = this.Earnings * (this.IsSmoking ? 0.8 : 1.0) *
                    ProcessAge(this.DateOfBirth);
    }

    private double ProcessAge(DateTime dateOfBirth) => 1.0;
}
```

Such a programmer will not be completely interested in the resulting automatic layout of the Customer object. On the other hand, imagine that we use Customer class massively, mainly calling UpdateScoring on millions of such instances per second. As UpdateScoring method uses Scoring, Earning, IsSmoking, and DateOfBirth fields, they should be laid out within the range of the first cache line (the one accessed always when Customer instance is used). LayoutKind.Automatic, default one for classes, obviously doesn't care about that. It will put, probably very rarely used, HealthData and AuxiliaryData references at the beginning of the object while the rest will be laid out according to alignment requirements (as explained in Object/struct layout section in the previous chapter).

The solution should be already known to us - we must change `Customer` into unmanaged struct that may use sequential layout (see Listing 14-47). It may be done by:

- changing `HealthData` and `AuxiliaryData` into value-type identifiers, to get rid of references - this helps not only in changing such type into unmanaged type, it will also relieve the GC from marking overhead (as each `Customer` instance will not be a root of two additional objects to be scanned).

- changing `DateTime` to other type as its automatic layout triggers automatic layout of the whole struct, as described in Chapter 13.

Then we may use `LayoutKind.Sequential`, carefully designing the layout of the fields on our own (considering padding introduced due to the alignment, but probably we can sell some space in favor of the speed). Thus, the four most commonly used fields should be placed at the beginning.

Listing 14-47. Struct with layout considering cache-line utilization

```
[StructLayout(LayoutKind.Sequential)]
struct CustomerValue
{
    public double Earnings;
    public double Scoring;
    public long DateOfBirthInTicks;
    public bool IsSmoking;
    // ... some other fields ...
    public int HealthDataId;
    public int AuxiliaryDataId;
}
```

However, not always, we must use sequential layout to achieve good spatial locality. Sometimes it is just enough to make sure that data locality of primitive types is simply taken care of (in other words, it is assured that commonly accessed fields are laid out next to each other).

`FrugalObjectList<T>` and `FrugalStructList<T>` are an example of very interesting internal collections used inside Windows Presentation Library. Their internal storage is an instance of one of the following, specific collections: `SingleItemList<T>`,

ThreeItemList<T>, SixItemList<T>, and ArrayItemList<T>. While adding or removing elements, such storage is converted between those types (while the last one handles storage of seven or more items). What does it give in return? A very concise, trivial, and mostly switch-based implementations of methods like IndexOf, SetAt or EntryAt, used by indexer, for scenarios with less than seven elements (see Listing 14-48, showing fragments of ThreeItemList<T>). So while getting rid of generic array overhead (bounds checking, to name one), such an approach still provides good spatial locality because of three or six fields laid out next to each other.

Listing 14-48. Fragments of ThreeItemList<T> class (one of storages used by FrugalObjectList<T> and FrugalStructList<T> types)

```
/// <summary>
/// A simple class to handle a list with 3 items.  Perf analysis showed
/// that this yielded better memory locality and perf than an object and an
    array.
/// </summary>
internal sealed class ThreeItemList<T> : FrugalListBase<T>
{
    public override T EntryAt(int index)
    {
        switch (index)
        {
            case 0:
                return _entry0;

            case 1:
                return _entry1;

            case 2:
                return _entry2;

            default:
                throw new ArgumentOutOfRangeException("index");
        }
    }
```

```
    private T _entry0;
    private T _entry1;
    private T _entry2;
}
```

As those types comment says: "Performance measurements show that Avalon[5] has many lists that contain a limited number of entries, and frequently zero or a single entry. (…) Therefore these classes are structured to prefer a storage model that starts at zero, and employs a conservative growth strategy to minimize the steady state memory footprint. (…) The code is also structured to perform well from a CPU standpoint. Perf analysis shows that the reduced number of processor cache misses makes FrugalList faster than ArrayList or List<T>, especially for lists of 6 or fewer items."

Design Data to Fit into Higher Cache Levels

Overhead of various cache levels has been already illustrated in Listing 2-5 and corresponding Figure 2-11 in Chapter 2. You should be always aware how big your data is and how it relates to the typical CPU cache sizes.

Design Data That Allows Easy Parallelization

Topic of parallel processing goes out of the scope of this book. However, good data layout and algorithm design may allow some parts of the data to be processed in parallel - whether it be multiple cores and/or SIMD instructions. Remember still about the false-sharing caveat illustrated in Listing 2-6 and corresponding benchmark in Table 2-3.

Avoid Non-sequential, Especially Random Memory Access

This rule has been explained in Chapter 2, starting from explaining how DRAM works and why sequential access is preferred. A simple example of accessing a two-dimensional array by rows versus by columns was shown in Listing 2-1 and corresponding benchmark in Table 2-1, showing several times slower access due to a lot of cache miss.

Accessing the sequentially contiguous memory region of T[ ] is a preferred way over other collections, especially if T is a struct (recall Figure 4-22 from the chapter comparing data locality of arrays). We will make use of this design rule when describing strategic patterns.

---

[5]Avalon is a codename for WPF engine.

Strategic Design

Strategic design pushes forward data-oriented design, leaving far behind typical object-oriented design practices. Code it produces may be surprising to developers used to OOP but become more and more justified if you think about it deeply. Therefore, unlike tactical design, strategic design requires a significant mind-shift of the programmer. Let's now look at some of the most popular techniques.

Moving from Array-of-Structures to Structure-of-Arrays

In object-oriented programming, data is encapsulated. Objects and methods are representing well-crafted, single responsibility behaviors. For example, we can imagine that Customer instances from Listing 14-46 are kept by separate "container." Its UpdateScorings method enumerates all customer instances and ask them to update their scoring (see Listing 14-49). This is a plain and simple code that every developer using OOP would understand.

Listing 14-49. Repository of customers from Listing 14-46

```
class CustomerRepository
{
    List<Customer> customers = new List<Customer>();

    public void UpdateScorings()
    {
        foreach (var customer in customers)
        {
            customer.UpdateScoring();
        }
    }
}
```

Such code introduces a lot of cache-line misses - Customer instances may be scattered all around the GC Heap as there is no guarantee that they are allocated next to each other (see Figure 14-1). Although, as we know, compacting GC eventually may lead to good data locality of objects allocated around the same time. Additionally, a bump-a-pointer allocator may allocate them next to each other in the first place. But those are assumptions, not guarantees. For example, because filled allocation context will be changed into a new one, possibly all around the ephemeral segment, even two successive Customer allocations may land in two completely different places. As a result, we must assume that in case of array of reference types, each cache line consists of only a small part of interesting data and a lot of surrounding garbage.

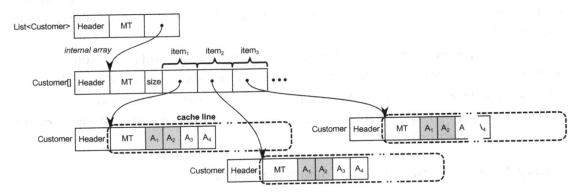

Figure 14-1. *Poor data locality of reference type array leads to many cache lines reading a lot of unnecessary data (necessary data is grayed)*

We know that array of structs provides much better data locality so CustomerRepository instead of Customer instances could store a list of boxed CustomerValue instances, defined in Listing 14-47 (see Figure 14-2). Successive reading of List's underlying array utilizes cache lines much better as CPU's prefetcher will easily recognize such pattern and will prefetch data in advance. There is also much less memory garbage read into each cache line - it consists only of other, currently not needed fields of CustomerValue instance.

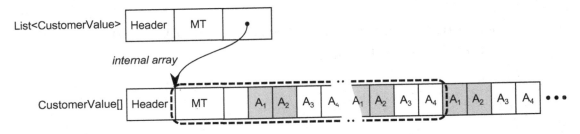

Figure 14-2. *Much better data locality of value-type array leads to cache lines reading a lot less of unnecessary data (necessary data is grayed)*

However, reading those unnecessary data (fields) may be still too costly in performance-critical scenarios. At this moment it's high time we left well-known OOP paradigms and changed things all around. In data-oriented design, the most important are not objects and behaviors they encapsulate, but the data itself. In our case the data consist of a few important attributes of customer (both as input and output).

The first approach would be to split customer data into two separate arrays of value types - one containing "hot data" used in scoring algorithm, the second with the rest, less relevant fields.

But we may go even further. So instead of gathering code around the customer, we may organize them around the data itself - by exposing each relevant data with a separate array (see Listing 14-50). Such approach is one of the most popular in data-oriented design, often referred to as changing the layout from *AoS* (*array-of-structures*) to *SoA* (*structure-of-arrays*).

Listing 14-50. Structure-of-arrays data organization example

```
class CustomerRepository
{
    int NumberOfCustomers;
    double[] Scoring;
    double[] Earnings;
    DateTime[] DateOfBirth;
    bool[] IsSmoking;
    // ...

    public void UpdateScorings()
    {
        for (int i = 0; i < NumberOfCustomers; ++i)
        {
            Scoring[i] = Earnings[i] * (IsSmoking[i] ? 0.8 : 1.0) *
            ProcessAge(DateOfBirth[i]);
        }
    }
    ...
}
```

By directly exposing the data, there is in fact no "customer" entity in such approach. "Customer" is just a bunch of data under a specific index in respective arrays. Those arrays are densely packed with relevant data, accessed sequentially by our hot-path algorithm. Cache-line utilization is optimal (see Figure 14-3). CPU can detect multiple sequential reads simultaneously so prefetcher will be used in each array access.

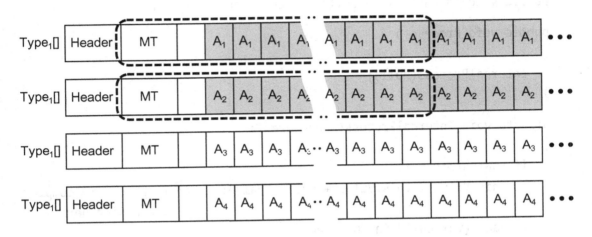

Figure 14-3. Optimal data locality in structure-of-arrays approach (necessary data is grayed)

As an additional advantage, the struct-of-arrays approach provides nice flexibility. If we introduce other high-performance algorithm use at other time, using different fields, such data organization will be beneficial also.

In a similar way we may flatten hierarchical (tree) data. Typically, each node would be storing a list of its children. Obviously, traversal of such tree may be quite costly due to the cache misses while accessing heap-allocated node instances scattered all around the GC Heap.

Let's use a trivial tree example from Listing 14-51, which implements also simple, exemplary algorithm - Process method changes value of each node into a sum of values from its ancestors.[6]

---

[6]Please note that triviality of presented processing is for brevity, but it does not change the overall presented approach.

Listing 14-51. Simple tree with nodes implementation

```
public class Node
{
    public int Value { get; set; }
    public List<Node> Children = new List<Node>();
    public Node(int value) => Value = value;
    public void AddChild(Node child) => Children.Add(child);

    public void Process()
    {
        InternalProcess(null);
    }

    private void InternalProcess(Node parent)
    {
        if (parent != null)
            this.Value = this.Value + parent.Value;    // Imagine more complex
                                                        //   processing here

        foreach (var child in Children)
        {
            child.InternalProcess(this);
        }
    }
}
```

However, such tree may be described quite oppositely by a flat array of nodes - each element being a node, storing a reference (or better, an index) of its parent. Such approach most probably will require preprocessing of an initial, more natural, object-oriented tree into such an array. Processing of such tree may be then linear, if it was appropriately flattened (see Listing 14-52).

Listing 14-52. Example of flattened tree, represented as array of value-type nodes

```
public class Tree
{
    public struct ValueNode
```

```
{
    public int Value;
    public int Parent;
}

private ValueNode[] nodes;

private static Tree PrecalculateFromRoot(OOP.Node root)
{
    // Flatten tree navigating it in pre-order depth-first
        manner...
}
public void Process()
{
    for (int i = 1; i < nodes.Length; ++i)
    {
        ref var node = ref nodes[i];
        node.Value = node.Value + nodes[node.Parent].Value;

    }
}
}
```

Please be careful when designing tree flattening. The particular example from Listing 14-52 works because the used processing algorithm (value adding inside Process method) depends only on parent values so it is perfectly fine to use a pre-order depth-first traversal. After, such flattening elements in the nodes array are always located after the already processed parent. If our algorithm depended on children (like a node value being a sum of all its descendants), post-order depth-first traversal should be used, which guarantees that each element of the flattened array is after all its children.

Entity Component System

In object-oriented programming, inheritance and encapsulation are one of the core features. In complex applications, inheritance tree may be quite complicated, with many objects sharing some part of possible behaviors. Games are perfect example of scenario where there are dozens of various types of differently behaving entities - for example, tanks being armored vehicles while trucks being vehicles not armored but they are containers. Or a regular solider being only movable and having attributes like health, but is not always armored. A sample inheritance tree to illustrate that is presented in Figure 14-4.

In the broader context of software development, such inheritance tree may be cumbersome because adding a new kind of entity that shares only part of possible behaviors is not trivial - it must be added, overriding appropriate methods to include new behavior, and so on, and so forth (like adding `MagicTree` class in Figure 4-4, which is both "positionable" and is a living - but is not movable).

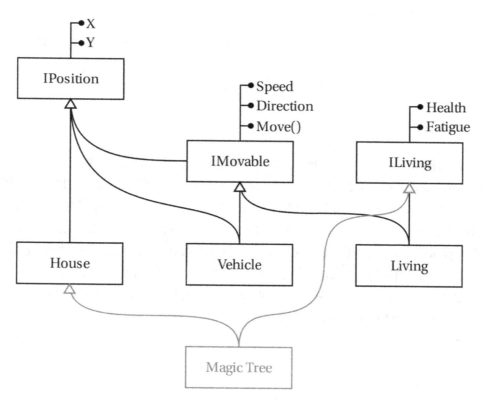

Figure 14-4. *Example of inheritance tree representing some game objects*

In our data-oriented context, caveats of such approach should be immediately visible - data is spread all around such tree hierarchy. It is perfectly OK in regular OOP, where there are few business objects cooperating with each other. But it becomes bottleneck if we have to process thousands or millions similar entities, let's say - vehicles, to update their position.

We could use the structure-of-arrays approach to keep separate list of structs representing houses, vehicles, livings, and so on, so forth. This however is not very practical, and still many algorithms may need to access various set of properties contained in those lists (breaking good data locality benefits).

The solution to this problem is proposed into form of so-called *Entity Component System* that, simply speaking, prefers composition over inheritance. As we will soon see, one of its foundations is good data locality consistent with the idea of structure-of-arrays.

In Entity Component System, there are no types representing house, vehicle, or any other living. Entities are being composed by dynamically adding and removing components, representing capabilities. Such entities are then processed by various systems, representing required logic. In other words, the three main building blocks in ECS are (see Figure 14-5):

- *Entity* - is a simple object with an identity but does not contain any data or logic. By adding or removing specific Components to it, we define capabilities of such Entity. So, for example, when we need something like a vehicle in a game, we create an entity and assign appropriate components to it (Position and Movable component in our simplified example).

- *Component* - simple object only consisting of data but no logic. Those data are needed to represent current state of the capability represented by such component (so position in Position component or speed in Movable component).

- *System* - is where the logic of specific capabilities or features lives. Systems operate on filtered list of entities, one by one. For example, Move System will filter all entities to those that have Position and Movable components assigned (and its logic knows how to transform/process properties of those components).

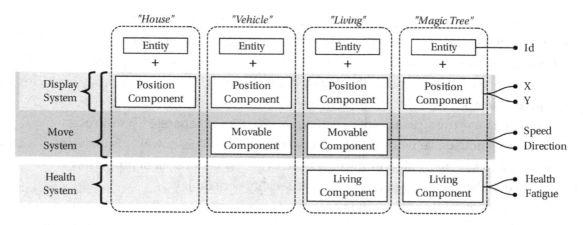

Figure 14-5. *Overview of Entity Component System*

In a main loop of a game, each system executes one after another. I hope it is already visible where the power of such approach is lying. With such design, data of each component are kept sequentially and separately, incorporating structure-of-arrays approach. For example, when Display System iterates through entities, it in fact needs to iterate over sequential collection of Position Component data. Obviously, it requires a very efficient filtering technique of entities (or answering the question whether entity has given component attached). Those are, however, implementation details we will not touch here. Instead, let's implement the simplest possible ECS we can imagine. Hopefully it will allow us to illustrate the whole concept better.

First of all, Entity may be really simple type containing only identifier (see Listing 14-53). It is a readonly struct - to keep it densely in the array of entities and to avoid defensive copies when passing around as in arguments.

Listing 14-53. Entity definition

```
public readonly struct Entity
{
    public readonly long Id;
    public Entity(long id)
    {
        Id = id;
    }
}
```

Components are also only simple containers for data. Again, to make a dense array of component data, they are structs (see Listing 14-54). They are mutable and thanks to ref returns, we will be able to return them from the corresponding storage for modification.

Listing 14-54. Sample components definitions

```
public struct PositionComponent
{
    public double X;
    public double Y;
}

public struct MovableComponent
{
    public double Speed;
    public double Direction;
}

public struct LivingComponent
{
    public double Fatigue;
}
```

To effectively store data of a given component in a data-oriented way, let's introduce ComponentManager<T> class (see Listing 14-55). Its main part is registeredComponents array of a given component type. Registering is as easy as filling the next free slot in the array (and for brevity I've skipped a problem of unregistering and resulting fragmentation). Checking whether given entity (identified by its Id) has component assigned is based on an additional dictionary - this is again by far the most efficient way but it was used for brevity (as well as ignoring any multithreading issues). Its ref returns an array element so no copying is involved.

Listing 14-55. ComponentManager<T> class managing component data

```
public class ComponentManager<T>
{
    private static T Nothing = default;
    private static int registeredComponentsCount = 0;
```

```
private static T[] registeredComponents = ArrayPool<T>.Shared.Rent(128);
private static Dictionary<long, int> entityIdtoComponentIndex = new
Dictionary<long, int>();

public static void Register(in Entity entity, in T initialValue)
{
    registeredComponents[registeredComponentsCount] = initialValue;
    entityIdtoComponentIndex.Add(entity.Id, registeredComponentsCount);
    registeredComponentsCount++;
}

public static ref T TryGetRegistered(in Entity entity)
{
    if (entityIdtoComponentIndex.TryGetValue(entity.Id, out int index))
    {
        //result = true;
        return ref registeredComponents[index];
    }
    //result = false;
    return ref Nothing;
}
}
```

Them we need an abstract representation of the system (see Listing 14-56) and a manager that ties all this together (see Listing 14-57).

Listing 14-56. Definition of simple abstract system base

```
public abstract class SystemBase
{
    public abstract void Update(List<Entity> entities);
}
```

Listing 14-57. Manager storing list of entities and systems

```
public class Manager
{
    private List<Entity> entities = new List<Entity>();
    private List<SystemBase> systems = new List<SystemBase>();
```

```
public void RegisterSystem(SystemBase system)
{
    systems.Add(system);
}

public Entity CreateEntity()
{
    var entity = new Entity(entities.Count);
    entities.Add(entity);
    return entity;
}

public void Update()
{
    foreach (var system in systems)
    {
        system.Update(entities);
    }
}
}
```

Having all those bricks in place, it's high time to write an example system. MoveSystem requires entities with both Position and Movable components, so its Update methods filters them appropriately (see Listing 14-58). The requirement of very efficient entities filtering is clearly visible here. However, if managed properly, data components are accessed sequentially with a high probability, providing great data locality and prefetching possibility.

Listing 14-58. An example of Moving system

```
public class MoveSystem : SystemBase
{
    public override void Update(List<Entity> entities)
    {
        foreach (var entity in entities)
        {
            bool hasPosition = false;
            bool isMovable = false;
```

```
        ref var position = ref ComponentManager<PositionComponent>.
        TryGetRegistered(in entity, out hasPosition);
        ref var movable = ref ComponentManager<MovableComponent>.
        TryGetRegistered(in entity, out isMovable);
        if (hasPosition && isMovable)
        {
            position.X += CalculateDX(movable.Speed, movable.Direction);
            position.Y += CalculateDY(movable.Speed, movable.Direction);
        }
      }
    }
}
```

Please note that provided implementation is oversimplified in many places. As mentioned, it does not include any thread synchronization, and proposed entity-to-component management is also trivialized. Presenting here a full, even closely real-world implementation is by far behind such book capacity. In real-world libraries, like Entitas (`https://github.com/sschmid/Entitas-CSharp` by Simon Schmid) or recently rewritten Entity Component System in Unity, those aspects are much better thought out and implemented. For example, most often System does not filter entities on its own, but receives dynamically managed, already filtered list of entities (appropriately updated underneath when entities are adding or removing components). The presented API is also far from perfect. In addition, a mature ECS implementation must support communication between the systems and the relationships between them (supported by some kind of messaging system), which is completely omitted here.

Entity Component System is overwhelmingly popular in game development, but I believe it may be justified in high-performance scenarios where data-oriented design makes sense. Having a lot of different "entities" with various characteristics, which need to be processes in huge batches? Does not that sound like ECS?

More on Future...

This section contains a list of features that probably could be included in any other part of this chapter (or previous one) because they are quite general. I decided to gather them in a common "future" section because at the time of writing, they are planned for less or more distant future releases of .NET. Probably at the time of your reading some or most of them are already available or even yet already well-established in the .NET ecosystem. On the other hand, seeing absorption of other newer types (like already available Span<T>), at least a few years will pass before they settle in the widespread awareness of programmers.

Nullable Reference Types

Nullable reference types may, but are not guaranteed, to be introduced in C# 8.0. Although they are not directly related to memory management - their usage does not incur better or worse performance or memory consumption - they are such important change related to generally understood memory safety, that a book about memory in .NET just cannot simply ignore it.

In the context of null, everyone must cite British computer scientist Tony Hoare who invented a null reference while designing ALGOL language. In 2009 he apologized for inventing it:

> *I call it my billion-dollar mistake. It was the invention of the null reference in 1965. At that time, I was designing the first comprehensive type system for references in an object oriented language (ALGOL W). My goal was to ensure that all use of references should be absolutely safe, with checking performed automatically by the compiler. But I couldn't resist the temptation to put in a null reference, simply because it was so easy to implement. This has led to innumerable errors, vulnerabilities, and system crashes, which have probably caused a billion dollars of pain and damage in the last forty years.*

Is null billion-dollar really a mistake? Could you imagine a world, C# and .NET world, without null and all those NullReferenceException occurrences in your life? Generally, it is hard to imagine a language that does not have any notion of "nothing." Some values are optional because the domain they come from specifies them as such (being middle name a canonical example). What really null complicates is a lack of clear intent whether it makes sense in a specific context that such "nothing" is allowed (because null is allowed always by default).

Some languages, especially functional ones, replaced nullable types with option types - a polymorphic type that represents an optional value (so it may represent "nothing" or a value). For example, F# uses Option type defined as discriminated union with two cases: Some (containing value) and None. Having such optional type explicitly says that there is possibility a value may be "nothing." Programmer need to use appropriate checks before accessing such type value (or at least it may be checked by a compiler if she does so).

Ideally, reference types in C# should contain such "optionally nullable" reference types to get rid of current "always nullable" reference types. To have clear intent of nullability, two new kinds of safe reference types are planned to be introduced:

- *nullable reference type* - they may have null assigned so dereferencing them always require checking for null value (and such check may be enforced by C# compiler). Please note they differ from current reference types because while being always nullable, dereferencing them now is not guarded by compiler checks. Such types are representing optional value like Option in F#.

- *non-nullable reference type* - they will never have null value so it is always safe to dereference them.

Of course, care should be taken to introduce them in a way that helps to find bugs in existing code without a need to rewrite everything. To make existing code benefit from them, current reference types must take one of these roles (instead of, for example, introducing two new kinds of reference types besides the existing one). It was decided that current, unannotated reference type will be treated as non-nullable reference type. As Mads Torgersen says on behalf of the whole C# language team, this is because:

- They believe reference types actually requiring null values are less common that we may think.

- C# language already has ? syntax of nullable value types so it seems natural to extend it for reference types.

- It seems right to explicitly express a need of nulls and opt-in for them, rather than the other way around.

So in other words, nullable reference types are going to be added in some future C# version (with the ? syntax) while the behavior of already existing reference types will be been changed into non-nullable reference types (see Listing 14-59). This is why this feature is officially called nullable reference types, while we should remember that in fact both new reference types behavior are new.

Listing 14-59. An example of a class with both non-nullable (by default) and nullable (by explicitly stating) reference type fields

```
public class SomeClass
{
    public int Field;
    public OtherClass? NullableReference;     // May be null
    public OtherClass  NonNullableReference;  // May not be null
}

public class OtherClass
{
    public int OtherField;
}
```

Obviously, such a change may generate a lot of errors while compiling existing, pre-nullable reference types code. This is by design, however, as those types are introduced to help us with finding null-related bugs in the first place. Not to paralyze the work, it has decided to treat such null-related issues as warnings, instead of errors (while you may still opt-in to errors though).

With this feature, C# compiler does it best to check for nullability violations, especially with respect to local variables and parameters access (see Listing 14-60). When accessing nullable object instances without any checks (like in first line in Listing 14-60), appropriate warnings are generated. The same happens when compiler discovers null is being accessed (like in the last line in Listing 14-60). Program flow control is considered (like conditions and loops) also, as we may see in Listing 14-60.

Listing 14-60. Compiler behavior with nullable reference type argument

```
public static void UseNullableReference(SomeClass? obj)
{
    Console.WriteLine(obj.Field);   // Warning CS8602: Possible dereference
                                    of a null reference.
    Console.WriteLine(obj?.Field); // Ok, checked
    if (obj == null)
        return;
    Console.WriteLine(obj.Field);   // Ok, checked above
    obj = null;
    Console.WriteLine(obj.Field);   // Warning CS8602: Possible dereference
                                    of a null reference.
}
```

However, there always will be a problem of how deep such a nullability violation check should be. Currently method calls are ignored, as they may contain logic of any complexity you can imagine. So even if `ArgumentsValid` method checks for null internally (in Listing 14-61), a warning still will be generated.

Listing 14-61. Compiler behavior with nullable reference type argument

```
public static void UseChainedNullableReference(SomeClass? obj)
{

    if (!ArgumentsValid(obj))
        return;
    Console.WriteLine(obj.Reference.OtherField);   // Warning or not,
                                                   depending on the
                                                   check used

}
```

On the other hand, accessing non-nullable reference types is much safer so the compiler will generate many less errors (see Listing 14-62).

Listing 14-62. Compiler behavior with non-nullable reference type argument

```
public static void UseNonNullableReference(SomeClass obj)
{
    Console.WriteLine(obj.Field);    // Ok
    Console.WriteLine(obj?.Field);  // Ok, checked
```

```
    if (obj == null)
        return;
    Console.WriteLine(obj.Field);    // Ok, checked above
    obj = null;                      // Warning CS8600: Converting null
                                     //    literal or possible null value to
                                     //    non-nullable type.

    Console.WriteLine(obj.Field);    // Warning CS8602: Possible dereference
                                     //    of a null reference.

}
```

Warning CS8600 may be surprising though, as it seems we may still assign null to a non-nullable reference type! This is because of many scenarios where it is still necessary (and most of them generate an appropriate warning) - like explicitly assigning null like in Listing 14-62 or assigning a nullable reference type to non-nullable reference type. There is still one important exception decided to not generate any warnings - an array creation (see Listing 14-63). In case of an array of non-nullable types, the compiler should require initialization of all its elements but this would break a lot of existing code. Array declarations like in Listing 14-63 are overwhelmingly popular so even emitting a warning would flood our compilation with an unmanageable number of messages.

Listing 14-63. Compiler behavior with the array of non-nullable reference type

```
SomeClass[] array = new SomeClass[4];
UseNonNullableReference(array[1]);       // Ok, warning is not generated.
```

Please note that at the time of writing this book, nullable reference types are in the pre-release version before official release (planned but not yet confirmed for C# 8.0). This section presents possible design and usage of this feature, to give you an overall picture of why and what it does. Please update your knowledge with official .NET documentation regarding the current state of this feature at the time of reading this book.

What is null by the way? In general, it is a representation of an address that should never happen in normal code, to differentiate it from valid pointers (and references in case of .NET). In all popular programming environments, it is an address of value 0 - because at least the first OS memory page is always kept free (unused) so it is always an invalid address. Being a zero is also useful because pointers and references are becoming null by default in zeroed memory regions (like reference type fields in an object).

Any access to an invalid page (like mentioned on the first page) raises an exception by the OS which is then handled by the CLR. The difference is that if the first page was accessed (which is typically, first 64KB), such exception would be turned into a well-known `NullReferenceException`. On the other hand, if any higher address was accessed, `AccessViolationException` will be thrown. So for example, when in C# one tries to access an unmanaged zero pointer, `NullReferenceException` will occur (see Listing 14-64).

Listing 14-64. Example of unsafe code generating `NullReferenceException`

```
unsafe { int read = *((int*)IntPtr.Zero); }
```

On the other hand, if we try to access an address higher than the first 64 KB, `AccessViolationException` will occur (Listing 14-65).

Listing 14-65. Example of unsafe code generating `AccessViolationException`

```
unsafe { int read = *((int*)0x1_0000 + 1); }
```

Most often `NullReferenceException` happens in regular C# code, when we try to access a field of null reference (see Listing 14-66). This is however handled in the same way because accessing an object's field is just dereferencing a given address with a small field's offset (see Listing 14-67). In our example, if the reference argument passed in `rcx` is 0, the corresponding field address will be calculated as 0x8 (assuming `Field` is the first field in `SomeClass`). Trying to access 0x8 address still results in `NullReferenceException` because it fits into the first page.

Listing 14-66. Example of managed code generating `NullReferenceException` (assuming `obj` is null)

```
public static void Test(SomeClass obj)
{
    Console.WriteLine(obj.Field);
}
```

Listing 14-67. Assembly code of Test method from Listing 14-66

```
C.Test(SomeClass)
    L0000: sub rsp, 0x28
    L0004: mov ecx, [rcx+0x8]
    L0007: call System.Console.WriteLine(Int32)
    L000c: nop
    L000d: add rsp, 0x28
    L0011: ret
```

Immediately we may wonder what if an object is bigger than the first page and we are trying to access the end of it (via null reference)? Will it confusingly throw `AccessViolationException` instead of `NullReferenceException`? The answer is, no. Such scenarios are guarded by JIT that generates appropriate code. For example, in case of passing an array, bound-checking code is injected anyway (accessing array's size field) so it will result in `NullReferenceException` even before trying to access given element. And if we imagine an enormous object with thousands of fields (see Listing 14-68), JIT will add null checking of the entire object before accessing a specific field (see Listing 14-69). The second assembly instruction from Listing 14-69 is generated only when higher fields of `SomeClass` instance are accessed (if `rcx` is zero, it will trigger throwing `NullReferenceException`).

Listing 14-68. Example of managed code generating `NullReferenceException` (assuming `obj` is null)

```
public class SomeClass
{
    public long Field0;
    public long Field1;
    public long Field2;
    ...
    public long Field8229;
    public long Field8230;
}
```

```
public static void Test(SomeClass obj)
{
    Console.WriteLine(obj.Field8000);
}
```

Listing 14-69. Assembly code of Test method from Listing 14-68

```
C.Test(SomeClass)
    L0000: sub rsp, 0x28
    L0004: cmp [rcx], ecx
    L0006: mov rcx, [rcx+0xfa08]
    L000d: call System.Console.WriteLine(Int64)
    L0012: nop
    L0013: add rsp, 0x28
    L0017: ret
```

Please note that both 0 and the first page are used here in terms of virtual memory of a given address. This means that physically "null page" is mapped to some arbitrary physical page.

Pipelines

Streams are as old as the entire .NET. They are great and do their job but are not well-suited for high-performance code. They may allocate a lot, requiring copying memory here and there. And they introduce overhead of required synchronization when used in multithreading scenarios. For writing efficient code using buffers, like streams, something new has to be invented. This is exactly how *pipelines* (initially called *channels*) were invented, mostly with network streaming kept in mind, used in a new Kestrel web hosting server. But even Kestrel was one of the main reasons behind them, they will be exposed as a general-purpose library.

Upcoming versions of .NET, at the time of this writing, are expected to include completely new API for pipelines, which may be seen as Stream-like buffers that target a range of problems related to high-performance and high-scalable code. They are designed in a producer-consumer manner, so there is a writer (sending data) and a receiver (reading those data). As its current documentation says: "A pipeline is like a Stream that pushes data to you rather than having you pull. One chunk of code feeds data into a pipeline, and another chunk of code awaits data to pull from the pipeline." As other techniques showed in this chapter, most probably only low-level libraries creators will be interested in them - to be used in networking or serialization code.

Because pipelines are from the ground up designed in high performance and scalability requirements in mind, they have the following characteristics:

- Their memory usage is based on pooling of internal buffers - it allows them to avoid heap allocations.

- They intensively use Span<T> and Memory<T> on API level - it allows them to provide zero-copy usage of the data (data is being provided by slicing internal buffers without a need for copying anything).

- They are asynchronous and thread-safe in an efficient manner.

Regardless of all the complicated machinery underneath, pipeline API is quite straightforward. First of all, we must configure a pipeline instance providing a memory pool that will be used by them (see Listing 14-70). There are other configuration options that are not described in this book, especially related to pipe schedulers. This is because my intent is to only briefly describe pipelines capabilities and usage, without going any further with advanced topics. Although they are interesting, this book can't cover everything in detail.

Listing 14-70. Example of pipeline configuration

```
var pool = MemoryPool<byte>.Shared;
var options = new PipeOptions(pool);
var pipe = new Pipe(options);
```

An instantiated pipeline provides two crucial properties: Writer and Reader. The basic usage of them is presented in Listing 14-71. Keep in mind that write and read side from such example could be split into two different threads in a thread-safe manner. As we may see, when using pipelines, we must explicitly flush the writer buffers with the help of FlushAsyncs method (to make data visible for readers). And the reader must explicitly update the reading position with the help of AdvanceTo method (to inform pipeline that underlying data has been read so corresponding buffers may be released).

Listing 14-71. Basic usage of pipelines

```
static async Task AsynchronousBasicUsage(Pipe pipe)
{
    // Write data
    pipe.Writer.Write(new byte[] { 1, 2, 3 }.AsReadOnlySpan());
    await pipe.Writer.FlushAsync();

    // Read data
    var result = await pipe.Reader.ReadAsync();
    byte[] data = result.Buffer.ToArray();
    pipe.Reader.AdvanceTo(result.Buffer.End);
    data.Print();
}
```

However, while pipelines usage presented in Listing 14-71 is useful for introductory purposes, it is quite an anti-pattern because:

- writer had to heap-allocate byte array before sending data,

- reader had to heap-allocate byte array where read data were copied.

Obviously, it stands in contradiction with the assumptions that were mentioned at the beginning of this section. To make better use of pipelines features, we may get a buffered memory straight from the pipeline itself.

Let's start from improving the write side of our example (see Listing 14-72). As we can see, we may get buffered Span<byte> or Memory<T> from the Writer directly, which does not require any allocations (underneath a slice of required size is returned to use from internal buffers). After accordingly modifying data in the acquired Span<T>, we must explicitly update the writing position with the help of Advance method. It informs the pipeline how many bytes are considered to be written and will be flushed by the following FlushAsync method.

Listing 14-72. Usage of pipelines with buffered memory. Because of Span<byte> usage, method is not async

```
static void SynchronousGetSpanUsage(Pipe pipe)
{
    Span<byte> span = pipe.Writer.GetSpan(minimumLength: 2);
    span[0] = 1;
```

```
span[1] = 2;
pipe.Writer.Advance(2);
pipe.Writer.FlushAsync().GetAwaiter().GetResult();

var readResult = pipe.Reader.ReadAsync().GetAwaiter().GetResult();
byte[] data = readResult.Buffer.ToArray();
pipe.Reader.AdvanceTo(readResult.Buffer.End);
data.Print();
pipe.Reader.Complete();
}
```

We should conceptually treat data returned by GetSpan and GetMemory methods as separate blocks that will be written into the pipeline. Those blocks have a configurable minimum size, which is 2,048 bytes by default. So even if we ask for minimumLength of a few bytes, we will receive 2 kB of memory (this is not a problem as it uses pool internally so no heap allocations are required). Be aware that the returned memory block most probably is reused and may already contain some previously written data. So it is important that Advance method call will truly say how many bytes were indeed modified. Listing 14-73 shows two successive writes of two acquired buffered blocks but more bytes were "advanced" that really modified. As a result, some parts of read data may have undefined values (0 is our example).

Listing 14-73. Usage of pipelines with buffered memory. Thanks to Memory<byte> usage, method may be async.

```
static async Task AsynchronousGetMemoryUsage(Pipe pipe)
{
    Memory<byte> memory = pipe.Writer.GetMemory(minimumLength: 2);
    memory.Span[0] = 1;
    memory.Span[1] = 2;
    Console.WriteLine(memory.Length);   // Prints 2048
    pipe.Writer.Advance(4);
    await pipe.Writer.FlushAsync();

    Memory<byte> memory2 = pipe.Writer.GetMemory(minimumLength: 2);
    memory2.Span[0] = 3;
    memory2.Span[1] = 4;
    pipe.Writer.Advance(4);                     // Prints 2048
```

```
await pipe.Writer.FlushAsync();
//pipe.Writer.Complete(); close the pipeline from writer side (so reader
will not expect more data)

var readResult = await pipe.Reader.ReadAsync();
byte[] data = readResult.Buffer.ToArray();
pipe.Reader.AdvanceTo(readResult.Buffer.End);
data.Print(); // 1,2,0,0,3,4,0,0
//pipe.Reader.Complete(); no more reads possible
}
```

Improving the read side of pipeline usage to use a zero-copy approach requires a little more, yet still quite intuitive changes. Instead of aggressively reading all readResult.Buffer data and copying it to a newly created array, we may investigate it and access data without copying. Reader.Buffer is of type ReadOnlySequence<byte> that provides the following features:

- such sequence (buffer) represents one or more segments received from the producer,

- its IsSingleSegment property tells us whether sequence represents only single segment,

- its First property is of ReadOnlyMemory<byte> type and returns the first segment,

- it is enumerable, providing ReadOnlyMemory<byte> elements in case of representing multiple segments.

This leads us to a common way of consuming a read buffer (see Listing 14-74). Please note that no allocations happen in the presented code - read data is represented by sliced ReadOnlyMemory<byte> and ReadOnlySpan<byte> structs.

Additionally, one more feature of a pipeline is presented in Listing 14-74 - reader's AdvanceTo method may update two different read positions separately:

- consumed position - to inform that memory until such position has been already read (consumed) and we do not need it anymore. Such data will not return to us after successive reader's ReadAsync calls (and may be released by underlying buffering mechanism).

- examined position - to inform that although we read data until such position (we've already seen them) but it was not enough for us – so, for example, we have read only a part of incoming message and we must wait for the rest. Data between consumed and examined position will return to us after successive ReadAsync calls altogether with a new data that arrives.

Listing 14-74. Example of zero-copy read side of pipeline

```
static async Task Process(Pipe pipe)
{
    PipeReader reader = pipe.Reader;
    var readResult = await pipe.Reader.ReadAsync();
    var readBuffer = readResult.Buffer;
    SequencePosition consumed;
    SequencePosition examined;
    try
    {
        ProcessBuffer(in readBuffer, out consumed, out examined);
    }
    finally
    {
        reader.AdvanceTo(consumed, examined);
    }
}

private static void ProcessBuffer(in ReadOnlySequence<byte> sequence, out
SequencePosition consumed, out SequencePosition examined)
{
    consumed = sequence.Start;
    examined = sequence.End;
    if (sequence.IsSingleSegment)
    {
        // Consume buffer as single span
        var span = sequence.First.Span;
        Consume(in span);
    }
```

```
    else
    {
        // Consume buffer as collections of spans
        foreach (var segment in sequence)
        {
            var span = segment.Span;
            Consume(in span);
        }
    }
    // out consumed - to which position we have already consumed the data
        (and do not need them anymore)
    // out examined - to which position we have already analyzed the data
        (data between consumed and examined will be provided again when new
        data arrives)
}

private static void Consume(in ReadOnlySpan<byte> span) // No defensive
copy as ReadOnlySpan is readonly struct
{
    //...
}
```

The way of zero-copy reading from pipelines presented in Listing 14-74 most probably will become a common design pattern. For example, it is already used in HttpParser class in KestrelHttpServer, already presented partially in Listing 14-6 (see Listing 14-75). What such parser needs is to interpret incoming network data line by line. So a design pattern presented in a ProcessBuffer method should be modified to read incoming buffer data, seeking a newline character. If a new line end has been found, the consumed position is set accordingly. But if not, data is mark only as examined so it will be reinterpreted once again when new data comes.

Listing 14-75. Full code of ParseRequestLine from HttpParser class from KestrelHttpServer

```
public unsafe bool ParseRequestLine(TRequestHandler handler, in
ReadOnlySequence<byte> buffer, out SequencePosition consumed, out
SequencePosition examined)
```

```
{
    consumed = buffer.Start;
    examined = buffer.End;

    // Prepare the first span
    var span = buffer.First.Span;
    var lineIndex = span.IndexOf(ByteLF);
    if (lineIndex >= 0)
    {
        consumed = buffer.GetPosition(lineIndex + 1, consumed);
        span = span.Slice(0, lineIndex + 1);
    }
    else if (buffer.IsSingleSegment)
    {
        // No request line end
        return false;
    }
    else if (TryGetNewLine(buffer, out var found))
    {
        span = buffer.Slice(consumed, found).ToSpan();
        consumed = found;
    }
    else
    {
        // No request line end
        return false;
    }
    // Fix and parse the span
    fixed (byte* data = &MemoryMarshal.GetReference(span))
    {
        ParseRequestLine(handler, data, span.Length);
    }
    examined = consumed;
    return true;
}
```

```
private static bool TryGetNewLine(in ReadOnlySequence<byte> buffer, out
SequencePosition found)
{
    var byteLfPosition = buffer.PositionOf(ByteLF);
    if (byteLfPosition != null)
    {
        // Move 1 byte past the \n
        found = buffer.GetPosition(1, byteLfPosition.Value);
        return true;
    }
    found = default;
    return false;
}
```

Interpretation of incoming segments from the read buffer is quite tedious. We need to maintain the interpretation state and correctly handle the interpretation of successive segments (as byte data we interpret most probably will be split into multiple segments). For common scenarios of interpreting underlying segments as stream of bytes, BufferReader helper class is also introduced (see Listing 14-76). Underneath it handles interpreting successive segments while providing single and contiguous stream of bytes accessible by Read method. Obviously, it still does not heap allocate anything as it is also based on zero-copy approach internally.

Listing 14-76. An example of BufferReader helper class usage

```
private static void ProcessWithBufferReader(in ReadOnlySequence<byte>
sequence, out SequencePosition consumed, out SequencePosition examined)
{
    var byteReader = BufferReader.Create(sequence);
    while (!byteReader.End)
    {
        var ch = byteReader.Read();
        // Consume... read more, and so on, so forth.
```

```
    // setting:
    consumed = byteReader.Position;
    examined = byteReader.Position; // or less if Peek was used

    // return if you are done with some part
    }
}
```

Summary

We have covered quite a lot of various topics in this chapter. It is a kind of all-in-one bag where seemingly unrelated techniques and types were discussed. In my opinion, however, they have one important thing in common - they are advanced, highly specialized things required mostly in even-more specialized code with high-performance requirements. This is exactly why this chapter has a title "Advanced Techniques," right?

Many words were spoken here about types like Span<T> or Memory<T>, which allow us to write very efficient, no heap-allocating code as was well as other possibilities, like Unsafe class.

Eventually, we took a little insight into the future of C# and .NET. Of course, predicting the future is always hard. So, I refrained from going too far into the future. Two features that are most important from a memory management perspective were briefly described - nullable reference types and pipelines (one should count here also UTF8 strings that are planned to be introduced).

There are no Rules defined in this chapter. If I were to mention a general one, it would sound: do not over-engineer. I mean, most of the techniques described in this chapter are relevant only on low-level code that should most probably belong to something called Infrastructure Level - preferably generalized and sealed in library or NuGet package. Do not clutter Business Layer with strictly technical types like Span<T> or Memory<T>. They do not belong to the business domain for sure and expressiveness of the domain is one of the most important factors during our application's domain modeling. Span<T> and Memory<T> are the best types for no-copy handling where performance is critical for advanced scenarios.

CHAPTER 15

Programmatical APIs

This is the last chapter of this book. We have seen, so far, many various topics related to .NET memory management - including a comprehensive description of how, in fact, Garbage Collector in .NET works. Other important topics were also described, including resource management with the help of finalization and disposable objects, various types of handles, usage of structs or many diagnostic scenarios, and practical advice related to all of that. At this moment we should feel quite comfortable in the memory management topic, although the amount of knowledge could be a little overwhelming so going back to at least some parts of the book is fully understandable and advisable.

What's left then? Not so much indeed. In this chapter I would like to describe a few programmatical APIs related to the GC. They are available from code on different levels, providing different levels of flexibility. I believe it is a good theme for the end of the book. Already more or less understanding the operation of the GC, we can now look at how it can be controlled and measured from code. We start from reviewing an already well-known GC class, mainly for reference, as most of the available methods were already used here and there throughout the book. Then, the CLR Hosting feature is described. Eventually, two great libraries that provide deep diagnostic capabilities are shown - ClrMD and EventTrace. As the crème de la crème, a few words are dedicated to the possibility of changing the whole GC into our custom one.

GC API

As said, a static GC class with its static methods has been quite intensively already used in the previous chapters. Here, I want to briefly summarize its usage and show those little possibilities not yet mentioned or described with insufficient details. I do not repeat myself, so if examples of a specific method usage were already presented, I just refer back to them. All methods were organized into some functional groups, presented as subsections. Moreover, besides the GC class itself, a few other methods and types are presented that perfectly suit the overall "Programmatical GC API" section.

© Konrad Kokosa 2018
K. Kokosa, *Pro .NET Memory Management*, https://doi.org/10.1007/978-1-4842-4027-4_15

Collection Data and Statistics

The first group contains properties and methods that inform us about the GC status and internal state of memory.

GC.MaxGeneration

This informs about the number of maximum generations currently implemented in the GC. It is mostly useful in a code that would like to iterate over all available generations (to not hard-code its number) - like by successive calls of GC.CollectionCount presented below. Or when you want to check with the help of GC.GetGeneration method whether an object is already in the oldest generation (such usage is shown later as well). Please note, this property currently has a value of 2 because the oldest generation 2 and LOH are treated as one (collected together during full GC).

GC.CollectionCount(Int32)

This informs about the number of GC occurrences of a specific generation since the program's beginning. The generation number we ask for should be not less than 0 and not bigger than a value returned by GC.MaxGeneration. Remember that such count is inclusive, so if generation 1 is condemned, both generations 0 and 1 counters are increased. Thus, Listing 15-1 will produce results as shown in Listing 15-2 (each younger generation collection counter includes collections of older generations).

Listing 15-1. Illustration of GC.CollectionCount method usage

```
GC.Collect(0);
Console.WriteLine($"{GC.CollectionCount(0)} {GC.CollectionCount(1)}
{GC.CollectionCount(2)}");
GC.Collect(1);
Console.WriteLine($"{GC.CollectionCount(0)} {GC.CollectionCount(1)}
{GC.CollectionCount(2)}");
GC.Collect(2);
Console.WriteLine($"{GC.CollectionCount(0)} {GC.CollectionCount(1)}
{GC.CollectionCount(2)}");
```

Listing 15-2. Results of code from Listing 15-1

```
1  0  0
2  1  0
3  2  1
```

We can use this method for diagnostic and logging from inside our application. However, most popular usage is probably implementing a "smart" explicit GC call only if it does not happen by itself (see Listing 15-3). In that way our code that wants to trigger GC will be less aggressive. Recall Chapter 7's elaboration about explicitly calling GC in general. We could also use such code to periodically check each generation counter to notice that the collection of a given generation has happened recently (thus, allowing us to create a sort of "callback" that is executed after each GC, if checking granularity is small enough).

Listing 15-3. Conditional explicit GC call if it didn't happen by itself

```
if (lastGen2CollectionCount == GC.CollectionCount(2))
{
    GC.Collect(2);
}
lastGen2CollectionCount = GC.CollectionCount(2);
```

GC.GetGeneration

This informs about the generation to which the given object belongs. For valid objects on the Managed Heap, it returns value between 0 and GC.MaxGeneration.

It may be used, for example, to create some generation-aware caching policy. Supposing we want to create a pool of objects that are being pinned, it would be good to reuse only objects from the oldest generation, which are most probably living in gen2-only segments. Assuming objects are pinned for a short period of time, pinning in gen2-only segments is less severe because there is much less probability of full GC during that time.

Thanks to the GC.GetGeneration method, we can create such a pool, maintaining a list of already "aged" objects (preferred to be rented from the pool) and another list of younger objects (with the expectation they will become aged at some time). A draft of such pool is presented in Listing 15-4. If someone wants to rent an object from the pool (by calling Rent method), already aged objects are first checked for availability.

999

If there is none, a list of already maintained younger objects is checked in the RentYoungObject method. If again, there is none currently, a new object is being created via a provided factory method. When an object is being returned to the pool (by calling Return method), its "age" is checked with the help of GC.GetGeneration method and depending on the result, added to the appropriate collection for later reuse. Additionally, Gen2GcCallback class (described in Chapter 12) is used to perform an action on every full GC to maintain both lists - moving those objects that already landed in the oldest generation from the young collection to the aged collection.

Listing 15-4. Draft of PinnableObjectPool<T> implementation, preferring to provide objects from the oldest generation

```
public class PinnableObjectPool<T> where T : class
{
   private readonly Func<T> factory;
   private ConcurrentStack<T> agedObjects = new ConcurrentStack<T>();
   private ConcurrentStack<T> notAgedObjects = new ConcurrentStack<T>();

   public PinnableObjectPool(Func<T> factory)
   {
      this.factory = factory;
      Gen2GcCallback.Register(Gen2GcCallbackFunc, this);
   }

   public T Rent()
   {
      if (!agedObjects.TryPop(out T result))
         RentYoungObject(out result);
      return result;
   }

   public void Return(T obj)
   {
      if (GC.GetGeneration(obj) < GC.MaxGeneration)
         notAgedObjects.Push(obj);
      else
         agedObjects.Push(obj);
   }
```

```
private void RentYoungObject(out T result)
{
   if (!notAgedObjects.TryPop(out result))
   {
      result = factory();
   }
}

private static bool Gen2GcCallbackFunc(object targetObj)
{
   ((PinnableObjectPool<T>)(targetObj)).AgeObjects();
   return true;
}

private void AgeObjects()
{
   List<T> notAgedList = new List<T>();
   foreach (var candidateObject in notAgedObjects)
   {
      if (GC.GetGeneration(candidateObject) == GC.MaxGeneration)
      {
         agedObjects.Push(candidateObject);
      }
      else
      {
         notAgedList.Add(candidateObject);
      }
   }
   notAgedObjects.Clear();
   foreach (var notAgedObject in notAgedList)
   {
      notAgedObjects.Push(notAgedObject);
   }
}
}
```

Obviously, `PinnableObjectPool<T>` presented here is simplified for brevity and does not include such important aspects as cache trimming or multithreading synchronization (especially in `AgeObjects` method).

There is already mentioned in Chapter 12, an internal `PinnableBufferCache` class in .NET fundamental libraries (CoreFX) that is a real-world implementation of a pool similar to that presented in Listing 15-4. It includes cache trimming, a lot of care about optimal multithreading access, and another optimization related to managing both objects collections. I strongly recommend that you find a moment to study the code of this class carefully. It is an excellent summary of many of the aspects discussed in this book.

Please note that if we pass an invalid object to `GetGeneration` method, we should treat its result as undefined (see Listing 15-5) - for example, current .NET Core implementation will always return 2 in such a case because it assumes that if an object does not belong to an ephemeral segment, it belongs to one of the LOH or gen2 segments.

Listing 15-5. Passing invalid, stack-allocated object to `GC.GetGeneration` method

```
UnmanagedStruct us = new UnmanagedStruct { Long1 = 1, Long2 = 2 };
int gen = GC.GetGeneration(Unsafe.As<UnmanagedStruct, object>(ref us));
Console.WriteLine(gen);
```

Output:

2

GC.GetTotalMemory

This returns the total number of bytes in use, excluding fragmentation, in all generations. In other words, it is a total size of all managed objects on the Managed Heap. This include the size of already unreachable, dead objects if we do not trigger explicit GC before.[1] As mentioned in Chapter 12, where this method implementation was presented

---

[1]Strictly speaking, since there could be any number of things that happen between explicitly triggering a GC and calling `GetTotalMemory` method, some objects could also have become unreachable, unless there's no other threads running.

(see Listing 12-9), be aware that when passing true as its forceFullCollection argument, this method may be very costly. In the worst scenario, it may trigger full-blocking GC 20 times trying to get a stable result!

GetTotalMemory method may be used obviously for diagnostic and logging purposes. Its usage in various unit tests and experiments is popular. However, for the purpose of tracking allocations during the test, GC.GetAllocatedBytesForCurrentThread, described later, is a better alternative.

Moreover, be cautious when using this method for memory-based limiting processing, like web request throttling. Because of not counting fragmentation and overall overhead of segments management (for example, committing some segment's pages in advance), such measure does not reflect precisely the overall pressure of the memory. For such scenarios, it is better to use overall memory measurements provided by the Process class (or at least relate GC.GetTotalMemory result to them). The simple "Hello world" example in Listing 15-6 illustrates the difference (see Listing 15-7 for results). Objects in the GC Heap are taking around 600 kB of memory. However, private memory usage of the overall process is around 9 MB (while Virtual Memory is obviously bigger, refer to Chapter 2 for memory categorization in a process).

Listing 15-6. Using GC.GetTotalMemory and various Process memory-related measurements

```
static void Main(string[] args)
{
    Console.WriteLine("Hello world!");
    var process = Process.GetCurrentProcess();
    Console.WriteLine($"{process.PrivateMemorySize64:N0}");
    Console.WriteLine($"{process.WorkingSet64:N0}");
    Console.WriteLine($"{process.VirtualMemorySize64:N0}");
    Console.WriteLine($"{GC.GetTotalMemory(true):N0}");
    Console.Readline();
}
```

Listing 15-7. Result of code from Listing 15-6

```
Hello world!
9,162,752
```

146,680,064

2,199,553,761,280

620,496

Even the memory taken by the Managed Heap is noticeably bigger than the total size of objects in it (see Figure 15-1). We can see that memory committed by the GC segments take 1,772 kB while results from Listing 15-7 show only around 600 kB.

And yes, most of this difference lies in fragmentation not being counted in. We may confirm that by using the `heapstat` command from WinDbg's SOS extensions (see Listing 15-8), where total space taken by free space may be easily calculated.

Type	Size	Committed	Private	Total WS	Private WS	Shareable WS	Shared WS	Locked WS
Total	2,148,005,060 K	88,612 K	9,008 K	15,880 K	4,148 K	11,732 K	4,760 K	
Image	41,932 K	41,924 K	3,836 K	11,604 K	796 K	10,808 K	3,892 K	
Mapped File	4,080 K	4,080 K		420 K		420 K	420 K	
Shareable	2,147,509,292 K	37,372 K		552 K	56 K	496 K	440 K	
Heap	3,828 K	2,444 K	2,380 K	1,172 K	1,168 K	4 K	4 K	
Managed Heap	394,624 K	1,148 K	1,148 K	1,104 K	1,104 K			
Stack	9,216 K	160 K	160 K	80 K	80 K			
Private Data	39,248 K	712 K	712 K	176 K	172 K	4 K	4 K	
Page Table	772 K	772 K	772 K	772 K	772 K			
Unusable	2,068 K							
Free	135,290,949,120 K							

Address	Type	Size	Committed	Private	Total WS	Private WS	...	Protection	Details
⊟ 000001A807AC0000	Managed Heap	393,216 K	892 K	892 K	848 K	848 K	4	Read/Write	GC
000001A807AC0000	Managed Heap	4 K	4 K	4 K	4 K	4 K		Read/Write	
000001A807AC1000	Managed Heap	141 K	141 K	141 K	140 K	140 K		Read/Write	Gen2
000001A807AE4780	Managed Heap	24 bytes	24 bytes	24 bytes				Read/Write	Gen1
000001A807AE4798	Managed Heap	55400 bytes	55400 bytes	55400 bytes	12 K	12 K		Read/Write	Gen0
000001A807AF2000	Managed Heap	261,944 K						Reserved	
000001A817AC0000	Managed Heap	692 K	692 K	692 K	692 K	692 K		Read/Write	Large Object Heap
000001A817B6D000	Managed Heap	130,380 K						Reserved	
⊞ 00007FF8BD220000	Managed Heap	64 K	32 K	32 K	32 K	32 K	6	Execute/Read/Write	Shared Domain
⊞ 00007FF8BD230000	Managed Heap	64 K	52 K	52 K	52 K	52 K	2	Read/Write	Domain 1
⊞ 00007FF8BD240000	Managed Heap	576 K	12 K	12 K	12 K	12 K	7	Execute/Read/Write	Domain 1 Virtual Call Stub
⊞ 00007FF8BD2D0000	Managed Heap	448 K	20 K	20 K	20 K	20 K	10	Execute/Read/Write	Shared Domain Virtual Call Stub
⊞ 00007FF8BD340000	Managed Heap	64 K	32 K	32 K	32 K	32 K	2	Read/Write	Shared Domain
⊞ 00007FF8BD3D0000	Managed Heap	64 K	64 K	64 K	64 K	64 K	1	Read/Write	Domain 1 Low Frequency Heap
⊞ 00007FF8BD3E0000	Managed Heap	64 K	24 K	24 K	24 K	24 K	2	Read/Write	Domain 1
⊞ 00007FF8BD3F0000	Managed Heap	64 K	20 K	20 K	20 K	20 K	2	Read/Write	Domain 1

Figure 15-1. *VMMAP view of program from Listing 15-6 (stopped at the last line)*

Listing 15-8. HeapStat SOS command result of program from Listing 15-6

```
> !heapstat -inclUnrooted
Heap            Gen0        Gen1        Gen2        LOH
Heap0           8216          24      145280      701024

Free space:                                     Percentage
Heap0             24           0       94576      131280 SOH: 61% LOH: 18%

Unrooted objects:                               Percentage
Heap0             40           0         184          0 SOH:  0% LOH:  0%
```

1004

Unfortunately, to get the most interesting Working Set - Private value, you would need to use `PerformanceCounter` class and read Performance Counters data of your own process. There is also no way to get programmatically overall Managed Heap size including fragmentation other than using ClrMD or ETW-based TraceEvent library presented later in this chapter. There is also an internal `GC.GetMemoryInfo` method returning such information added in .NET Core 2.1, but at the time of this writing, it was decided to not make it public.

GC.GetAllocatedBytesForCurrentThread

This method returns the total number of bytes allocated so far by the current thread. Please note it is a cumulative value and is always growing. It considers only the number of allocations, and it does not matter for this measure how many objects/bytes were afterwards garbage collected.

As it returns a value only for the current thread, it is not possible to ask about allocations on the other thread. Thanks to that, its implementation is fast and straightforward (see Listing 15-9): it sums the number of bytes so far allocated in the previous allocation contexts plus the already consumed part of the current allocation context (recall Chapter 5 where allocation context was described in detail).

Listing 15-9. Implementation of `GC.GetAllocatedBytesForCurrentThread` method in CoreCLR.

```
FCIMPL0(INT64, GCInterface::GetAllocatedBytesForCurrentThread)
{
    ...
    INT64 currentAllocated = 0;
    Thread *pThread = GetThread();
    gc_alloc_context* ac = pThread->GetAllocContext();
    currentAllocated = ac->alloc_bytes + ac->alloc_bytes_loh -
    (ac->alloc_limit - ac->alloc_ptr);
    return currentAllocated;
}
FCIMPLEND
```

Because the allocation measurement is limited to the only current thread, the `GC.GetAllocatedBytesForCurrentThread` method is much better suited to isolated unit tests or experiments about allocations, instead of using `GC.GetTotalMemory` method (see Listing 15-10). Please note that the latter provides a total memory usage for overall process so other allocating threads will influence the result. On the other hand, thread isolation in case of this method provides clean and reproducible results.

Listing 15-10. Example of using `GC.GetAllocatedBytesForCurrentThread` in unit test

```
[Fact]
public void SampleTest()
{
    string input = "Hello world!";
    var startAllocations = GC.GetAllocatedBytesForCurrentThread();

    ReadOnlySpan<char> span = input.AsSpan().Slice(0, 5);

    var endAllocations = GC.GetAllocatedBytesForCurrentThread();
    Assert.Equal(startAllocations, endAllocations);
    Assert.Equal("Hello", span.ToString());
}
```

Please also note this method was added in .NET Core 2.1 and is not available yet in .NET Framework. On the other hand, .NET Framework exposes yet another way of programmatically measuring memory usage with the help of `AppDomain` class and its two properties[2]:

- `MonitoringTotalAllocatedMemorySize` - it returns total number of bytes allocated so far by an application domain. It is then similar to the `GC.GetAllocatedBytesForCurrentThread` method, but it works on the `AppDomain`, not thread level. Moreover, it is being updated at every allocation context change (which may happen more often than GC). Thus, it has allocation context granularity, which has a few kB accuracies.

---

[2]To use those properties, we have to enable Application Domain Resource Monitoring - refer to MSDN for ways of doing that.

- MonitoringSurvivedMemorySize - it returns total number of bytes
  taken by objects that survived last GC. It is only guaranteed to be
  accurate after a full GC, although it is updated more often but with
  less accuracy.

The current mismatch of the methods of allocations measurements causes difficulty
when writing code compatible with .NET Standard and designed to be used both by
.NET Core and .NET Framework. For example, BenchmarkDotNet library solves this
problem using the best possible (most precise) in each case (see Listing 15-11).

Listing 15-11. Fragments of BenchmarkDotNet's GcStats class used by
MemoryDiagnoser

```
public struct GcStats
{
    private static readonly Func<long>
GetAllocatedBytesForCurrentThreadDelegate =
GetAllocatedBytesForCurrentThread();

    private static Func<long> GetAllocatedBytesForCurrentThread()
    {
        // for some versions of .NET Core this method is internal,
        // for some public and for others public and exposed ;)
        var method = typeof(GC).GetTypeInfo().GetMethod("GetAllocatedBytesFor
        CurrentThread",
                    BindingFlags.Public | BindingFlags.Static)
                ?? typeof(GC).GetTypeInfo().GetMethod("GetAllocatedBytesForCu
                rrentThread",
                    BindingFlags.NonPublic | BindingFlags.Static);
        return () => (long)method.Invoke(null, null);
    }
```

```
    private static long GetAllocatedBytes()
    {
        ...
        // "This instance Int64 property returns the number of bytes that
           have been allocated by a specific
        // AppDomain. The number is accurate as of the last garbage
           collection." - CLR via C#
        // so we enforce GC.Collect here just to make sure we get accurate
           results
        GC.Collect();
#if CLASSIC
        return AppDomain.CurrentDomain.MonitoringTotalAllocatedMemorySize;
#elif NETSTANDARD2_0
        ...
        // https://apisof.net/catalog/System.GC.GetAllocatedBytesForCurrentT
           hread() is not part of the .NET Standard, so we use reflection to
           call it..
        return GetAllocatedBytesForCurrentThreadDelegate.Invoke();
#elif NETCOREAPP2_1
        // but CoreRT does not support the reflection yet, so only because of
           that we have to target .NET Core 2.1
        // to be able to call this method without reflection and get
           MemoryDiagnoser support for CoreRT ;)
        return System.GC.GetAllocatedBytesForCurrentThread();
#endif
    }
    ...
}
```

GC.KeepAlive

GC.KeepAlive is a method that extends the liveness of a stack root, because it makes the passed argument reachable at least to the line when this method is called (influencing generated GC info). The use and significance of this method is discussed in Chapter 8 (see Listings 8-16 and 8-17). It was also used in several other examples throughout the book.

GCSettings.LargeObjectHeapCompactionMode

By setting this property to `GCLargeObjectHeapCompactionMode.CompactOnce` value, we may explicitly ask for compacting LOH when the first-blocking full-GC will occur. The usage and performance impact of this settings was thoroughly described in Scenario 10-1- Large Object Heap Fragmentation in Chapter 10.

GCSettings.LatencyMode

By setting this property, we control the latency mode of the GC, which allows us to control GC's concurrency and enables additional modes like LowLatency or SustainedLowLatency. The usage of various latency modes and elaboration of which one we should choose was presented in Chapter 11.

GCSettings.IsServerGC

This indicates whether CLR was started with Workstation or Server GC mode (see Chapter 11). Please note this is a read-only property as the GC mode cannot be changed after runtime has been started. This field value is also not affected by any other settings, like latency mode. Altogether with the pointer size (designating bitness of a process) and the number of processors, it may provide quite comprehensive diagnostic data that you may wish to log during application startup (see Listing 15-12).

Listing 15-12. Example of getting simple diagnostic data

```
Console.WriteLine("{0} on {1}-bit with {2} CPUs",
                (GCSettings.IsServerGC ? "Server" : "Workstation"),
                ((IntPtr.Size == 8) ? 64 : 32),
                Environment.ProcessorCount);
```

GC Notifications

Part of the GC API are notifications, which allow us to be notified about the possibility of full, blocking GC. Such need comes mainly from pre-.NET 4.5 times where the Server GC had only the non-concurrent, blocking version. Because such GC could take a while, having the possibility to react on it was quite useful. A typical example is to use such notification to tell the load balancer to make this server instance unavailable for the duration of a full-blocking GC. Nowadays GC notifications have lost their importance as most often web applications are running in Background GC mode, with much less noticeable pause times. Moreover, only blocking garbage collections raises such notifications. Thus, if the concurrent configuration is enabled, background garbage collection will not be emitted.

Notifications API consists of the following methods:

- `GC.RegisterForFullGCNotification(int maxGenerationThreshold, int largeObjectHeapThreshold)` - registers GC notification that should be raised if conditions are met to full-blocking GC make this happen. Those conditions are based on generation 2 or LOH allocation budgets utilization It is then important to remember that those notifications are not directly related to the real GC. As MSDN says: "Note that the notification does not guarantee that a full garbage collection will occur, only that conditions have reached the threshold that are favorable for a full garbage collection to occur." If we specify too high of values, we will get a lot of false positive notifications that do not come before real GC. On the other hand, if we specify too low of values, we may miss real GCs that happened.

- `GC.CancelFullGCNotification` - cancels the registration of GC notification.

- `GC.WaitForFullGCApproach` - it is a blocking call that waits indefinitely for GC notification (there is also method overload with a parameter to specify a timeout value).

- `GC.WaitForFullGCComplete` - it is a blocking call that waits indefinitely for full-GC being completed (and again, there is method overload with a parameter to specify a timeout value).

A typical example of GC notifications usage is presented in Listing 15-13. One of the dedicated threads is periodically waiting for GC notification and takes appropriate action if it happens.

Listing 15-13. Example of using GC notifications

```
GC.RegisterForFullGCNotification(10, 10);
Thread startpolling = new Thread(() =>
{
  while (true)
  {
    GCNotificationStatus s = GC.WaitForFullGCApproach(1000);
    if (s == GCNotificationStatus.Succeeded)
    {
      Console.WriteLine("GC is about to begin");
    }
    else if (s == GCNotificationStatus.Timeout)
      continue;

    // ...
    // react to full GC, for example call code disabling current server
       from load balancer
    // ...
    s = GC.WaitForFullGCComplete(10_000);
    if (s == GCNotificationStatus.Succeeded)
    {
      Console.WriteLine("GC has ended");
    }
    else if (s == GCNotificationStatus.Timeout)
      Console.WriteLine("GC took alarming amount of time");
  }
});
startpolling.Start();
GC.CancelFullGCNotification();
```

Remember that this API isn't exact by design because you are asking to predict the future. Therefore, it requires experimentation with your workload to find appropriate values of GC.RegisterForFullGCNotification arguments.

One could complain about necessity of guessing thresholds provided to `RegisterForFullGCNotification`, but there are no good alternatives in fact. The situation changes all the time in a real-world process so if it does not happen to be completely regular, it is hard to expect that we will predict future accurately. Fine-tuning with the help of mentioned thresholds allows us at least to adapt to our typical workload.

Controlling Unmanaged Memory Pressure

By calling the following methods, we may inform GC that some managed objects are holding (or releasing) some amount of unmanaged memory not directly visible to it:

- `GC.AddMemoryPressure(Int64)`
- `GC.RemoveMemoryPressure(Int64)`

If some threshold of such memory is exceeded, GC will be triggered. As mentioned in Chapter 7, altogether with those methods' usage in Scenario 7-3 - Analyzing the Explicit GC Calls, currently this threshold starts at value of 100,000 bytes and is later on dynamically tuned. Listing 12-3 in Chapter 12 is yet another typical example of this method usage.

Note also that you could implement your own similar mechanism, if you want, because the default implementation works poorly for you. Although exposed by GC class, this mechanism is not internal to the GC (while still implemented in runtime).

Explicit Collection

The possibility of explicitly calling GC was thoroughly described already in Chapter 7. Please refer to the "Explicit Trigger" section in Chapter 7 for more details, as well as above-mentioned Scenario 7-3 - Analyzing the Explicit GC Calls.

Just for completeness, please find the list of GC method overloads used to induce such explicit collection:

- `Collect()`

- `Collect(int generation)`

- `Collect(int generation, GCCollectionMode mode)`

- `Collect(int generation, GCCollectionMode mode, bool blocking)`

- `Collect(int generation, GCCollectionMode mode, bool blocking, bool compacting)`

No-GC Regions

Regions of code within which runtime tries to disallow GC may be created with the help of the following methods:

- `GC.TryStartNoGCRegion(long totalSize)`

- `GC.TryStartNoGCRegion(long totalSize, bool disallowFullBlockingGC)`

- `GC.TryStartNoGCRegion(long totalSize, long)`

- `GC.TryStartNoGCRegion(long totalSize, long lohSize, bool disallowFullBlockingGC)`

- `GC.EndNoGCRegion()`

Further discussion, explanation, and examples of those methods' usage were already presented in the "No GC Region" section in Chapter 11.

Finalization Management

Intimately explained in Chapter 12, the set of methods in GC API allow us to control finalization behavior. Such API consists of three methods:

- `GC.ReRegisterForFinalize(object obj)`

- `GC.SuppressFinalize(object obj)`

- `GC.WaitForPendingFinalizers()`

Memory Usage

Handling OutOfMemoryException is cumbersome, especially if it happens in the middle of important processing. To proactively avoid such situations, we may use MemoryFailPoint class that tries to guarantee that there is enough memory available before we start our processing of great importance. Remember that there's no guarantee that you will not get OutOfMemoryException with this API. It's just a best effort to avoid it.

Usage of this class is plain and simple (see Listing 15-14). MemoryFailPoint constructor will throw InsufficientMemoryException if there is less than the required memory available. Due to internal bookkeeping required for multithreaded usage, MemoryFailPoint is a disposable object so we should remember about calling its Dispose method (or use using clause).

Listing 15-14. Simple example of MemoryFailPoint usage

```
try
{
    using (MemoryFailPoint failPoint = new MemoryFailPoint(sizeInMegabytes:
    1024))
    {
        // Do calculations
    }
}
catch (InsufficientMemoryException e)
{
    Console.WriteLine(e);
    throw;
}
```

It is important to note that currently only Windows-based runtimes implement this class functionality. In case of other systems, MemoryFailPoint constructor always succeeds.

In case of current Windows implementation MemoryFailPoint checks for the possibility of allocating a specified amount of managed memory in the following steps:

- Whether there is enough virtual address space in general - this should be always true in case of 64-bit huge address space, as well as it is hard to imagine a need of allocating at once more memory than 32-bit virtual address space.

- It explicitly calls full, blocking, and compacting GC to give it an opportunity to free unused segments and compact managed memory usage as much as possible.

- It checks whether there is enough free virtual memory.

- It checks whether there is a need to grow the OS page file to accommodate required memory size.

- It checks whether there is enough contiguous free virtual memory to create a GC segment, if it is needed.

I strongly encourage you to read MemoryFailPoint class source if you are interested in managing free memory space of a process. Internally it uses Win32 API calls to get currently available memory (in private CheckForAvailableMemory method) and Virtual API's VirtualQuery call to find a contiguous free virtual address region (in private MemFreeAfterAddress method). It has also a private and internal static method GetMemorySettings(out ulong maxGCSegmentSize, out ulong topOfMemory) implemented in runtime that returns the GC segment size and maximum available virtual address of a process. Relying on such implementation detail, we could even use it to gain information about the segment's size by the following Reflection usage:

```
var args = new object[2];

var mi = typeof(MemoryFailPoint).GetMethod("GetMemorySettings",
BindingFlags.Static | BindingFlags.NonPublic); mi.Invoke(null,
args);    // As a result, args[0] contains maxGCSegmentSize
value
```

Internal Calls in the GC Class

Just in case you are curious, static GC class is mainly a thin wrapper around intrinsic, runtime method implementations. Most of its methods are marked as `InternalCall` (see Listing 15-15), which are mapped to appropriate runtime methods in CoreCLR's `.\src\vm\ecalllist.h` file (see Listing 15-16).

Listing 15-15. Fragments of GC class implementation from CoreFX source code

```
public static class GC
{
   [MethodImplAttribute(MethodImplOptions.InternalCall)]
   public static extern int GetGeneration(Object obj);
   [MethodImplAttribute(MethodImplOptions.InternalCall)]
   internal static extern bool IsServerGC();
   ...
}
```

Listing 15-16. Fragments of GC class runtime interface from CoreCLR source code

```
FCFuncStart(gGCInterfaceFuncs)
   FCFuncElement("IsServerGC", SystemNative::IsServerGC)
   FCFuncElement("GetGeneration", GCInterface::GetGeneration)
   ...
FCFuncEnd()
```

Static `GCInterface` methods are calling (mostly) methods defined in `gc.cpp` file (see Listing 15-17).

Listing 15-17. Example runtime implementation of GC method

```
FCIMPL1(int, GCInterface::GetGeneration, Object* objUNSAFE)
{
   FCALL_CONTRACT;
   if (objUNSAFE == NULL)
      FCThrowArgumentNull(W("obj"));
```

```
    int result = (INT32)GCHeapUtilities::GetGCHeap()->WhichGeneration
    (objUNSAFE);
    FC_GC_POLL_RET();
    return result;
}
FCIMPLEND
```

CLR Hosting

Whole CLR runtime may be seen as a set of libraries that are able to load and execute CIL code from compatible .NET assembly. Indeed, every time we use .NET, such runtime must be hosted in some process. In case of a regular .NET Framework, thanks to native Windows support, such a host "bootstrap" is contained in the EXE file itself. In case of .NET Core, there is also already a well-known dotnet host application. If we build CoreCLR on our own, there will be also simplified for testing a CoreRun host available. All those hosts have one thing in common - they load the appropriate CLR runtime into process memory, configure it, and execute loaded assembly code (specified from appropriate assembly file). Such host is also included, for example, in SQL Server instance to allow managed code execution from inside it.

Hosting API is publicly exposed and everyone could write its own CLR hosting process. We can imagine many various use cases, but there at least two common ones:

- Create an internal CLR runtime to be able to call managed code from a native process - which is in fact a use case of SQL Server.

- Create customized CLR runtime to gain control over how the CLR works, including the GC.

Because CLR hosting provides many configuration capabilities, we can somehow craft our "own runtime," suitable for our needs. This is obviously very rarely necessary, so I will not create a full CLR hosting tutorial here. This functionality is pretty well documented. Instead, let's see a few examples for what it can be used for in the context of memory management.

CHAPTER 15   PROGRAMMATICAL APIS

When using CLR Hosting API, we are entering the C++ and COM world - full of well-defined interfaces with well-specified functionality. Every object in CLR Hosting API is represented by some specific interface. The main one, representing the runtime itself, is called ICLRRuntimeHost (in .NET Framework) or ICLRRuntimeHost4 (in .NET Core).[3]

CLR Hosting API is slightly different in .NET Framework and .NET Core. Because currently .NET Core version does not support many features interesting to us, only full .NET Framework examples are shown here. Refer to MSDN documentation to see the current status and API of .NET Core version. Currently .NET Core version of CLR Hosting mainly supports loading runtime and executing code, without the possibility of customizing it via the interfaces described below.

Before moving into examples, let's briefly skim a list of CLR hosting interfaces related to the memory management (including some general, always used ones) to see what is possible in the field of memory management. Although all this information is available on MSDN, I've decided to include here a brief summary because it takes a while to merge all this information (including omitting already obsolete interfaces, and so on, and so forth). Currently, from our perspective, the most interesting interfaces are as follows:

- ICLRControl - interface to get various managers, representing specific functionality (like GC, Debugging, Assembly management, and so on, so forth). With respect to .NET memory management, two managers are interesting: ICLRGCManager2 and ICLRAppDomainResourceMonitor.

- ICLRGCManager2 - interface representing some control over GC. More specifically, it includes the following methods:

    - Collect - triggers GC explicitly.

    - GetStats - gets a set of current statistics about the garbage collection - they are directly based on the same values as represented by corresponding performance counters (thus, in CoreCLR build those stats are not available).

    - SetGCStartupLimitsEx - sets the size of GC segment and the maximum size of the generation 0 used during runtime initialization.

---

[3]We should get used to numbering COM interfaces as it is a canonical way of taking care of backward compatibility. Instead of modifying an existing interface, a new one is added with an increased number.

- `ICLRAppDomainResourceMonitor` - it provides measurements about AppDomain, - the same values as `MonitoringTotalAllocatedMemorySize` and `MonitoringSurvivedMemorySize` properties of `AppDomain` object.

- `IHostControl` - interface allowing to inject various "host managers" into hosted CLR. From a memory management perspective, there are two interesting: `IHostGCManager` and `IHostMemoryManager`. If we want to inject our own manager, we have to override `GetHostManager` method appropriately, returning our custom implementation of those interfaces.

- `IHostGCManager` - interface providing notifications about GC suspensions, with the following methods that we have to implement:

    - `SuspensionStarting` - fired when CLR started to suspend threads because of GC.

    - `SuspensionEnding` - fired when CLR resumed suspended threads because GC of given generation has ended.

    - `ThreadIsBlockingForSuspension` - fired from each running thread before it is being suspended.

- `IHostMemoryManager` - interface providing a range of important methods related to memory management. By implementing it, we gain full control over how CLR is consuming system memory for its purposes. We can, for example, change it completely from using Window's Virtual API to some other libraries (or modify how Virtual API is used). The following methods have to be implemented:

    - `AcquiredVirtualAddressSpace` - informs that CLR has acquired the specified amount of memory from the operating system. It will not be called if we create our custom memory manager if we omit calling it explicitly.

    - `CreateMalloc` - allows to get an `IHostmalloc` interface implementation responsible for requesting heap memory allocations from inside CLR. In this way we can completely change how memory is being allocated for CLR's internal purposes - for example, replacing default `malloc` calls with jemalloc memory allocator (mentioned in Chapter 14). Please note this is the internal runtime's allocator used to allocate memory for private CLR data. It does not replace the GC allocator used to allocate managed objects on the Managed Heap.

- `GetMemoryLoad` - returns the amount of physical memory that is currently being used.

- `NeedsVirtualAddressSpace` - informs the host that CLR will need specified amount of memory.

- `RegisterMemoryNotificationCallback` - allows us to register `ICLRMemoryNotificationCallback` interface implementation, which is used to notify the CLR on the high memory utilization.

- `ReleasedVirtualAddressSpace` - informs the host that CLR will no longer need specified amount of memory.

- `VirtualAlloc` - used to acquire virtual memory from the system. Thanks to this method, we may replace or modify how CLR utilizes Virtual API to get memory pages.

- `VirtualFree` - used to release virtual memory to the system.

- `VirtualProtect` - used to change protection of a given virtual memory region.

- `VirtualQuery` - used to query information about given virtual memory region.

- `IHostMalloc`

  - `Alloc` - called by the runtime, asking the host to allocate the requested amount of memory from the heap.

  - `DebugAlloc` - like above but additionally is should track where the memory was allocated.

  - `Free` - called by the runtime to free memory that was allocated by using the `Alloc` or `DebugAlloc` methods.

An overview of how all those relevant interfaces cooperate is presented in Figure 15-2. Summarizing what is most relevant to us, in our custom CLR host we can override how runtime acquires both memory pages and memory from an unmanaged heap.

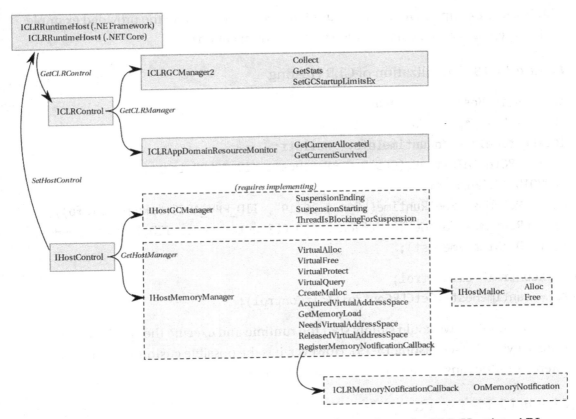

Figure 15-2. *The most relevant memory-related interfaces in CLR Hosting API*

There are many other possibilities when using custom CLR hosting, but only the most relevant to us were presented. For example, it is possible to take an action on StackOverflowException via ICLROnEventManager. Please also note that .NET Framework before version 2.0 used another set of interfaces, starting from ICorRuntimeHost representing runtime and IGCHost used to control GC. Those interfaces are not described here for brevity as they are rather ancient and no longer used.

An example of loading CLR runtime and obtaining ICLRRuntimeHost and ICLRControl interfaces is presented in Listing 15-18[4]. Remember that presented

---

[4]For brevity, only the most relevant parts of code are presented in the subsequent examples. Refer to the accompanying GitHub repository to get full, working examples.

CLR Hosting examples are written in unmanaged C++ code (and the provided example project is created as a regular Windows console application).

Listing 15-18. Initialization of CLR Hosting

```
ICLRRuntimeHost* runtimeHost;
ICLRMetaHost *pMetaHost = nullptr;
ICLRRuntimeInfo *pRuntimeInfo = nullptr;
hr = CLRCreateInstance(CLSID_CLRMetaHost, IID_ICLRMetaHost,
(LPVOID*)&pMetaHost);
hr = pMetaHost->GetRuntime(L"v4.0.30319", IID_PPV_ARGS(&pRuntimeInfo));
hr = pRuntimeInfo->GetInterface(CLSID_CLRRuntimeHost, IID_ICLRRuntimeHost,
(LPVOID*)&runtimeHost);

ICLRControl* clrControl;
hr = runtimeHost->GetCLRControl(&clrControl);
```

From now on, we could simply start the runtime and execute the specified method from a given file (see Listing 15-19). However, it is the possible customization that interests us the most, so let's look at some further examples.

Listing 15-19. Executing code in CLR Hosting

```
DWORD dwReturn;
hr = runtimeHost->Start();
hr = runtimeHost->ExecuteInDefaultAppDomain(targetApp, L"HelloWorld.
Program", L"Test", L"", &dwReturn);
```

From a CLR memory management point of view, we can distinguish possibilities presented by the CLR hosting into two or three groups:

- configuration - besides providing standard CLR flags (GC workstation/server mode and concurrency), we can tune GC a little by using ICLRGCManager2::SetGCStartupLimitsEx that allows us to set default GC segment size and maximum generation 0 size (see Listing 15-20).

- getting diagnostic measurements - thanks to ICLRGCManager2::GetStats or ICLRAppDomainResourceMonitor interface, we may observe memory utilization of hosted CLR instance (see Listing 15-21). This may be especially useful in high environments hosting (like production) to observe if hosted managed code does not violate given memory thresholds.

- customization - thanks to IHostControl interface, we may inject a wide range of managers by providing our custom implementations (see Listing 15-22). This is the most interesting part of this section so let's look at this possibility in detail.

Listing 15-20. Example of setting SetGCStartupLimitsEx in CLR Hosting

```
ICLRGCManager2* clrGCManager;
hr = clrControl->GetCLRManager(IID_ICLRGCManager2, (void**)&clrGCManager);
SIZE_T segmentSize = 4 * 1024 * 1024 * 1024;
SIZE_T maxGen0Size = 4 * 1024 * 1024 * 1024;
hr = clrGCManager->SetGCStartupLimitsEx(segmentSize, maxGen0Size);
```

Listing 15-21. Example of getting CLR memory usage data in CLR Hosting

```
_COR_GC_STATS gcStats;
gcStats.Flags = COR_GC_COUNTS | COR_GC_MEMORYUSAGE;
// Based on perf counters so does not work in CoreCLR
hr = clrGCManager->GetStats(&gcStats);
cout << gcStats.CommittedKBytes << endl
   << gcStats.Gen0HeapSizeKBytes << endl
   << gcStats.Gen1HeapSizeKBytes << endl
   << gcStats.Gen2HeapSizeKBytes << endl
   << gcStats.LargeObjectHeapSizeKBytes << endl
   << gcStats.ExplicitGCCount << endl
   << gcStats.GenCollectionsTaken[0] << endl
   << gcStats.GenCollectionsTaken[1] << endl
   << gcStats.GenCollectionsTaken[2] << endl;
```

Listing 15-22. Setting custom host controller in CLR Hosting

```
CustomHostControl customHostControl;
hr = runtimeHost->SetHostControl(&customHostControl);
```

Custom IHostControl has to implement GetHostManager method called by CLR for obtaining necessary managers (see Listing 15-23). If this method returns E_NOINTERFACE, the default manager will be used. In our case we want to override IHostMemoryManager implementation to return our CustomHostMemoryManager class. Please note that all COM interfaces should implement also common IUnknown methods: AddRef, Release, and QueryInterface. There are presented here but omitted for brevity in subsequent code listings.

Listing 15-23. Example of custom IHostControl implementation

```
class CustomHostControl : public IHostControl
{
    ULONG referenceCounter;

public:
    CustomHostControl()
    {
        referenceCounter = 0;
    }
    // Inherited via IHostControl
    virtual HRESULT GetHostManager(REFIID riid, void ** ppObject) override
    {
        if (riid == IID_IHostMemoryManager)
        {
            IHostMemoryManager *pMemoryManager = new CustomHostMemory
            Manager();
            *ppObject = pMemoryManager;
            return S_OK;
        }
        *ppObject = NULL;
        return E_NOINTERFACE;
    }
    virtual HRESULT QueryInterface(const IID &riid, void **ppvObject)
    {
        if (riid == IID_IUnknown)
        {
```

```
            *ppvObject = static_cast<IUnknown*>(static_cast<IHostControl*>(
            this));
            return S_OK;
        }
        if (riid == IID_IHostControl)
        {
            *ppvObject = static_cast<IHostControl*>(this);
            return S_OK;
        }
        *ppvObject = NULL;
        return E_NOINTERFACE;
    }
    virtual ULONG AddRef()
    {
        return referenceCounter++;
    }
    virtual ULONG Release()
    {
        return referenceCounter--;
    }
};
```

Custom HostMemoryManager has the powerful capability of replacing all virtual memory management and heap-allocation handling. Remember that the whole GC (and its internal allocators) is seen as a black box - memory pages will be obtained for it as for any other necessary regions. There is, in fact, no way to distinguish VirtualAlloc call acquiring pages for the Managed Heap from the other calls.

However, even on such a level of customization, we may implement interesting things. For example, we can override VirtualAlloc method to *lock* all acquired pages in physical memory, so they will not be ever paged to disk (with high probability). In such cases, other methods we may leave as thin wrappers around regular a Virtual API (see Listing 15-24). Aggressive page locking may improve such .NET application performance as its memory most probably will always reside in the physical RAM.

Listing 15-24. Example of custom host memory manager implementing aggressive page locking in physical memory

```
class CustomHostMemoryManager : public IHostMemoryManager
{
    ULONG referenceCounter;

public:
    CustomHostMemoryManager() : referenceCounter(0) { }

    // Inherited via IHostMemoryManager
    virtual HRESULT CreateMalloc(DWORD dwMallocType, IHostMalloc **
    ppMalloc) override
    {
        *ppMalloc = new CustomHostMalloc();
        return S_OK;
    }
    virtual HRESULT VirtualAlloc(void * pAddress, SIZE_T dwSize, DWORD
    flAllocationType, DWORD flProtect, EMemoryCriticalLevel eCriticalLevel,
    void ** ppMem) override
    {
        void* result = ::VirtualAlloc(pAddress, dwSize, flAllocationType,
        flProtect);
        *ppMem = result;
        BOOL locked = false;
        if (flAllocationType & MEM_COMMIT)
        {
            locked = ::VirtualLock(*ppMem, dwSize);
        }
        cout << "VirtualAlloc " << *ppMem << " (" << dwSize << "),
        flags: " << flAllocationType << " " << flProtect << " => "
        << pAddress << " " << locked << endl;
        return S_OK;
    }
    virtual HRESULT VirtualFree(LPVOID lpAddress, SIZE_T dwSize, DWORD
    dwFreeType) override
    {
```

```
    ::VirtualFree(lpAddress, dwSize, dwFreeType);
    return S_OK;
}
virtual HRESULT VirtualQuery(void * lpAddress, void * lpBuffer, SIZE_T
dwLength, SIZE_T * pResult) override
{
    *pResult = ::VirtualQuery(lpAddress, (PMEMORY_BASIC_INFORMATION)
    lpBuffer, dwLength);
    return S_OK;
}
virtual HRESULT VirtualProtect(void * lpAddress, SIZE_T dwSize, DWORD
flNewProtect, DWORD * pflOldProtect) override
{
    ::VirtualProtect(lpAddress, dwSize, flNewProtect, pflOldProtect);
    return S_OK;
}
virtual HRESULT GetMemoryLoad(DWORD * pMemoryLoad, SIZE_T *
pAvailableBytes) override
{
    // Simulate no problems
    *pMemoryLoad = 1;
    *pAvailableBytes = 1024 * 1024 * 1024;
    return S_OK;
}
virtual HRESULT RegisterMemoryNotificationCallback(ICLRMemoryNotificati
onCallback * pCallback) override
{
    return S_OK;
}
virtual HRESULT NeedsVirtualAddressSpace(LPVOID startAddress, SIZE_T
size) override
{
    return S_OK;
}
```

```
    virtual HRESULT AcquiredVirtualAddressSpace(LPVOID startAddress, SIZE_T
    size) override
    {
        return S_OK;
    }
    virtual HRESULT ReleasedVirtualAddressSpace(LPVOID startAddress)
    override
    {
        return S_OK;
    }
    // Inherited via IUnknown
    // ...
};
```

Presented custom IHostMemoryManager overrides also CreateMalloc method, which returns our custom IHostMalloc implementation (see Listing 15-25). It is shown for illustrative purposes, but we can imagine here a whole set of different implementations, including using the already-mentioned jemalloc library instead of malloc and free functions.

Listing 15-25. Example of custom heap-allocation implementation for hosted CLR

```
class CustomHostMalloc : public IHostMalloc
{
    ULONG referenceCounter;

public:
    CustomHostMalloc() : referenceCounter(0) { }

    // Inherited via IHostMalloc
    virtual HRESULT Alloc(SIZE_T cbSize, EMemoryCriticalLevel
    eCriticalLevel, void ** ppMem) override
    {
        *ppMem = ::malloc(cbSize);
        cout << "   Alloc " << *ppMem << " (" << cbSize << ")" << endl;
        return S_OK;
    }
```

```
virtual HRESULT DebugAlloc(SIZE_T cbSize, EMemoryCriticalLevel
eCriticalLevel, char * pszFileName, int iLineNo, void ** ppMem)
override
{
    *ppMem = ::malloc(cbSize);
    return S_OK;
}
virtual HRESULT Free(void * pMem) override
{
    ::free(pMem);
    return S_OK;
}

// Inherited via IUnknown
    // ...
};
```

Such a "non-paged CLR host" as presented here is obviously only a simple draft. Full, much more well-thought-out implementation is already prepared by Sasha Goldshtein and Alon Fliess, currently available at `https://archive.codeplex.com/?p=nonpagedclrhost`. I strongly recommend reading its source code. For example, it takes into consideration limits of possible page locking. Obviously, too aggressive locking could negatively influence overall system performance as other applications will have less physical memory available. As MSDN says: "The maximum number of pages that a process can lock is equal to the number of pages in its minimum working set minus a small overhead." Thus, Sasha and Alon's implementation uses `SetProcessWorkingSetSize` Win32 call to appropriately configure working set limits.

ClrMD

The Microsoft.Diagnostics.Runtime library, also known as ClrMD (or CLR MD) is a set of managed APIs for introspecting managed processes and memory dumps. It is rather designed to build diagnostic tools and small snippets, than to use it as self-monitoring solution of a process (although such possibility also exists as we will soon see). It provides similar capabilities as WinDBG's SOS extensions but in a much more convenient way available from C# code. Microsoft.Diagnostics.Runtime library is available as a NuGet package and may be used both in .NET Framework and .NET Core applications to analyze both .NET Framework and .NET Core targets. Moreover, full source code of ClrMD is publicly available in GitHub so you can investigate how it is implemented!

Please note that describing all possibilities of this library is not possible here due to book space limitations. The following examples are presented to give you an overall grasp of what is possible and how powerful this library is. Do not treat this section neither as a ClrMD tutorial nor as a comprehensive use-case description. Refer to ClrMD's documentation and samples for further knowledge.

The root object required to work with ClrMD is `DataTarget` class instance, which may be obtained by attaching to a running process or loading memory dump, with the help of the following static methods:

- `AttachToProcess` - allows us to attach to existing process of given PID (Process ID). It may be done in three different ways:

    - `Invasive` - the process will be paused and we will be able to control it like we attached from the regular debugger. This is a preferred way in normal circumstances.

    - `NonInvasive` - the process will be paused but we will not be able to control the process. Because in general only a single debugger may control any process, this method is useful if we want to attach to a process with other debugger already attached.

    - `Passive` - the process in not paused and no debugger is attached to it in any mode. We should be aware that many queries about dynamic data, like thread stacks or object references, may be often inconsistent. The overall idea with this mode is that the program using ClrMD is responsible for doing all process control-related work (like suspending the observed process). This gives the developer complete flexibility in how the target process is controlled.

- LoadCrashDump - allows us to load a file of already taken memory dump (e.g., with the help of ProcDump).

Please note that Passive mode theoretically allows us to attach even to our own process, to provide self-monitoring capabilities. This, however, makes many problems if you think about it deeply - like how ClrMD would handle a dynamically changing state of the process, inspecting a heap while GCs and allocations are happening, and so on, and so forth. Thus, the ClrMD maintainer didn't specifically disallow self-inspection, because it was something that could be useful in small corner cases. However, doing this correctly is essentially rocket science, not for the faint of heart, and if you run into issues, treat such a scenario as not supported by the maintainer.

When DataTarget is initialized, we may start investigating underlying data, looking for the runtimes that are (or were) used in it (see Listing 15-26). This includes information about needed underlying DAC (Data Access Component), which is responsible for understanding all of CLR's internal data structures.

Listing 15-26. Example of simple ClrMD usage - attaching to already running process

```
using (DataTarget target = DataTarget.AttachToProcess(pid, 5000,
AttachFlag.Invasive))
{
    foreach (ClrInfo clrInfo in target.ClrVersions)
    {
        Console.WriteLine("Found CLR Version:" + clrInfo.Version.ToString());

        // This is the data needed to request the dac from the symbol server:
        ModuleInfo dacInfo = clrInfo.DacInfo;
        Console.WriteLine($"Filesize:  {dacInfo.FileSize:X}");
```

```
Console.WriteLine($"Timestamp: {dacInfo.TimeStamp:X}");
Console.WriteLine($"Dac File:  {dacInfo.FileName}");

ClrRuntime runtime = clrInfo.CreateRuntime();
...
    }
}
```

Having properly the initialized ClrRuntime instance, we may do a lot of very interesting things. Let's look at only just a few examples. Please note that only a small part of possible methods or attributes of used ClrMD objects is presented here. Refer to documentation to see all of them.

We may inspect all running threads and print their current stacks (see Listing 15-27).

Listing 15-27. Example of ClrMD usage - listing all thread's call stacks

```
foreach (ClrThread thread in runtime.Threads)
{
    if (!thread.IsAlive)
        continue;
    Console.WriteLine("Thread {0:X}:", thread.OSThreadId);
    foreach (ClrStackFrame frame in thread.StackTrace)
        Console.WriteLine("{0,12:X} {1,12:X} {2}", frame.StackPointer, frame.
        InstructionPointer,
            frame.ToString());
    Console.WriteLine();
}
```

We may iterate through all AppDomains and modules loaded by the runtime, as well as every managed type already used by them (see Listing 15-28).

Listing 15-28. Example of ClrMD usage - listing all AppDomains, modules and types loaded

```
foreach (var domain in runtime.AppDomains)
{
    Console.WriteLine($"AppDomain {domain.Name} ({domain.Address:X})");
    foreach (var module in domain.Modules)
```

```
{
    Console.WriteLine($"    Module {module.Name} ({(module.IsFile ?
    module.FileName : "")})");
    foreach (var type in module.EnumerateTypes())
    {
        Console.WriteLine($"{type.Name} Fields: {type.Fields.Count}");
    }
  }
}
```

Please note that ClrMD gives a view into how the runtime sees the process state of the world, and not how things are defined in code. For example, let's say there's a module loaded that defines a type Foo, and Foo is never used by the process. In that case, EnumerateTypes may or may not return Foo... depending on whether the runtime decided to load that type out of the module or not. Having said that, whether it does load Foo is an implementation detail that may change from version to version, in the first place.)

However, from our perspective, the most interesting are obviously all memory-related information. For example, we can investigate all memory regions used by CLR, including the Managed Heap (see Listing 15-29 and sample result in Listing 15-30).

Listing 15-29. Example of ClrMD usage - listing all memory regions of a process

```
foreach (var region in runtime.EnumerateMemoryRegions().OrderBy(r =>
r.Address))
{
    Console.WriteLine($"0x{region.Address:X} (bytes: {region.Size:N0}) -
    {region.Type} " +
                    $"{(region.Type == ClrMemoryRegionType.GCSegment ?
                    "(" + region.GCSegmentType.ToString() + ")" : "")}");
}
```

Listing 15-30. Example results of code from Listing 15-28

```
0x24198CC1000 (bytes: 4,096) - HandleTableChunk
0x24199541000 (bytes: 200,704) - GCSegment (Ephemeral)
0x24199572000 (bytes: 268,230,656) - ReservedGCSegment
0x241A9541000 (bytes: 69,632) - GCSegment (LargeObject)
0x241A9552000 (bytes: 134,144,000) - ReservedGCSegment
0x7FF9F5250000 (bytes: 12,288) - LowFrequencyLoaderHeap
0x7FF9F5250000 (bytes: 12,288) - LowFrequencyLoaderHeap
0x7FF9F5256000 (bytes: 28,672) - HighFrequencyLoaderHeap
0x7FF9F5256000 (bytes: 28,672) - HighFrequencyLoaderHeap
0x7FF9F525D000 (bytes: 12,288) - StubHeap
0x7FF9F525D000 (bytes: 12,288) - StubHeap
0x7FF9F5260000 (bytes: 12,288) - LowFrequencyLoaderHeap
0x7FF9F5263000 (bytes: 40,960) - HighFrequencyLoaderHeap
0x7FF9F5274000 (bytes: 28,672) - CacheEntryHeap
0x7FF9F527D000 (bytes: 192,512) - DispatchHeap
0x7FF9F52AC000 (bytes: 344,064) - ResolveHeap
0x7FF9F5300000 (bytes: 24,576) - IndcellHeap
0x7FF9F5300000 (bytes: 24,576) - IndcellHeap
0x7FF9F5306000 (bytes: 24,576) - CacheEntryHeap
0x7FF9F5306000 (bytes: 24,576) - CacheEntryHeap
0x7FF9F530C000 (bytes: 16,384) - LookupHeap
0x7FF9F530C000 (bytes: 16,384) - LookupHeap
0x7FF9F5310000 (bytes: 155,648) - DispatchHeap
0x7FF9F5310000 (bytes: 155,648) - DispatchHeap
0x7FF9F5336000 (bytes: 237,568) - ResolveHeap
0x7FF9F5336000 (bytes: 237,568) - ResolveHeap
0x7FF9F53B0000 (bytes: 65,536) - LowFrequencyLoaderHeap
```

The Managed Heap may be further investigated through ClrHeap class available as ClrRuntime's Heap property. It allows for iterating over all currently existing managed objects, as well as traversing those object fields and references (see Listings 15-31 and 15-32 for the corresponding result).

Listing 15-31. Example of ClrMD usage - listing references of some managed type instances

```
ClrHeap heap = runtime.Heap;
foreach (var clrObject in heap.EnumerateObjects())
{
    if (clrObject.Type.Name.EndsWith("SampleClass"))
        ShowObject(heap, clrObject, string.Empty);
}

private static void ShowObject(ClrHeap heap, ClrObject clrObject, string
indent)
{
    Console.WriteLine($"{indent}{clrObject.Type.Name} ({clrObject.
    HexAddress}) - gen{heap.GetGeneration(clrObject.Address)}");
    foreach (var reference in clrObject.EnumerateObjectReferences())
    {
        ShowObject(heap, reference, "    ");
    }
}
```

Listing 15-32. Example results of code from Listing 15-31

```
CoreCLR.HelloWorld.SampleClass (24199564fa0) - gen0
    CoreCLR.HelloWorld.AnotherClass (24199564fc0) - gen0
    CoreCLR.HelloWorld.AnotherClass (24199564fd8) - gen0
    CoreCLR.HelloWorld.SomeOtherClass (24199564ff0) - gen0
```

Individual GC segments may be also investigated, thanks to `ClrHeap`'s `Segments` property. Each such `ClrSegment` provides various interesting data, including its internal structure, like generations it contains (see Listing 15-33 and sample result in Listing 15-34).

Listing 15-33. Example of ClrMD usage - listing all GC segments of a process

```
foreach (var segment in heap.Segments)
{
    Console.WriteLine($"{segment.Start:X16} - {segment.End:X16} ({segment.
    CommittedEnd:X16}) Heap#: {segment.ProcessorAffinity}");
```

```
  if (segment.IsEphemeral)
  {
    Console.WriteLine($"   Gen0: {segment.Gen0Start:X16} ({segment.
    Gen0Length})");
    Console.WriteLine($"   Gen1: {segment.Gen1Start:X16} ({segment.
    Gen1Length})");
    if (segment.Gen2Start >= segment.Start &&
        segment.Gen2Start < segment.CommittedEnd)
    {
      Console.WriteLine($"   Gen2: {segment.Gen2Start:X16} ({segment.
      Gen2Length})");
    }
  }
  else if (segment.IsLarge)
  {
    Console.WriteLine($"   LOH: {segment.Start} ({segment.Length})");
  }
  else
  {
    Console.WriteLine($"   Gen2: {segment.Gen2Start:X16} ({segment.
    Gen2Length})");
  }

  foreach (var address in segment.EnumerateObjectAddresses())
  {
    var type = heap.GetObjectType(address);
    if (type == heap.Free)
    {
      Console.WriteLine($"{type.GetSize(address)}");
    }
  }
}
```

Listing 15-34. Example results of code from Listing 15-32

```
000002551B871000 - 000002551B896730 (000002551B8A2000) Heap#: 0
    Gen0: 000002551B871030 (153344)
    Gen1: 000002551B871018 (24)
    Gen2: 000002551B871000 (24)
```

We already know that the GC implementation detail is that segments (representing heaps) are linked to a CPU that handles allocation, marking, and so on. Conceptually, however, `ProcessorAffinity` field is better thought of as which Heap# it lives in. Essentially, it should have been probably named something like `HeapNumber` instead of current `ProcessorAffinity`.

Filling this section with more and more examples seems to be rather redundant. I believe you've already noticed the real power of ClrMD. I will just only mention here a few other interesting possibilities:

- enumerating over all objects in fReachable queue with the help of `runtime.EnumerateFinalizerQueueObjectAddresses()` method,

- enumerating over all handles with the help of `runtime.EnumerateHandles()`,

- enumerating all current GC roots with the help of `heap.EnumerateRoots()`,

- enumerating all current stack roots of a given thread,

- getting an address of JITted method's code (so we may use some disassembler to see its native code).

Quite popular approach to use ClrMD, especially for memory dump analysis, is to use ClrMD from within LINQPad (`https://www.linqpad.net`) application. It provides nice scripting capabilities so we can easily utilize ClrMD without a need of using Visual Studio and creating dedicated projects.

Even though it is so powerful, sometimes we may notice that still ClrMD does not publicly expose some desired properties. One of the examples is investigating the current thread's allocation context. Although such information is known to ClrMD, relevant properties are not directly accessible. We can use Reflection to get them (but remember that there is no guarantee that used properties will not be changed in future versions).

```
foreach (ClrThread thread in runtime.Threads)
{
    var mi = runtime.GetType().GetMethod("GetThread", BindingFlags.Instance
    | BindingFlags.NonPublic);
    var threadData = mi.Invoke(runtime, new object[] {thread.Address});
    var pi = threadData.GetType().GetProperty("AllocPtr", BindingFlags.
    Instance | BindingFlags.Public);
    ulong allocPtr = (ulong) pi.GetValue(threadData);
    pi = threadData.GetType().GetProperty("AllocLimit", BindingFlags.
    Instance | BindingFlags.Public);
    ulong allocLimit = (ulong) pi.GetValue(threadData);
}
```

This is an example that digging into ClrMD source code may be beneficial!

If you are like me, you can see with your eyes all these great diagnostic tools that you can write, thanks to such possibilities. And indeed, there are currently many smaller or bigger initiatives (mostly open sourced) to create such tools, created for various reasons. It is not possible to list them all here, but the two most important should be named: Netext and SOSEX. Those WinDbg extensions are written as wrappers around ClrMD. And yes, it is a little ironic that one of the best WinDbg extensions for .NET diagnostics is written in .NET.

If you want to get a current list of tools based on ClrMD (or integrating with it in some way), please look for Tools built on top of CLRMD online list maintained by Matt Warren available at http://mattwarren.org/2018/06/15/Tools-for-Exploring-.NET-Internals.

TraceEvent Library

Microsoft.Diagnostics.Tracing.TraceEvent is a .NET library providing collecting and processing capabilities of ETW data. It is a relevant part of the main PerfView's machinery, exposed now as a separate Nuget package (but its source code is available also as a part of the PerfView repository).

I would rather like to avoid repeating here basic examples of using TraceEvent to not artificially lengthen the book. You can find comprehensive documentation and examples under the address https://github.com/Microsoft/perfview/blob/master/documentation/TraceEvent/TraceEventProgrammersGuide.md. Let's just briefly summarize it that TraceEvent library allows us to record ETW session to a file (regular ETL file known from PerfView) and analyze such file afterwards, or just to create and consume ETW session in real time. Every ETW provider may be enabled and its events appropriately consumed.

For the convenience of using most common ETW providers, TraceEvent library provides two strongly-typed parsers already built in into it: ClrTraceEventParser and KernelTraceEventParser (represented by Clr and Kernel properties of Source property of the session). As the former knows how to parse all the Common Language Runtime events, it is very useful also in all GC-related scenarios. We are just consuming then strongly-typed callbacks representing the reaction on events of our interest. Listing 15-35 shows an example of creating an ETW session that in real time reacts on the GC start and stop events, printing also the GC statistics.

Listing 15-35. Example of TraceEvent usage - using built-in CLR provider parser

```
using (var session = new TraceEventSession("SampleETWSession"))
{
    Console.CancelKeyPress += (object sender, ConsoleCancelEventArgs
    cancelArgs) =>
    {
        session.Dispose();
        cancelArgs.Cancel = true;
    };

    session.EnableProvider(ClrTraceEventParser.ProviderGuid,
    TraceEventLevel.Verbose, (ulong)ClrTraceEventParser.Keywords.Default);
    session.Source.Clr.GCStart += ClrOnGcStart;
```

```csharp
    session.Source.Clr.GCStop += ClrOnGcStop;
    session.Source.Clr.GCHeapStats += ClrOnGcHeapStats;
    session.Source.Process();
}

private static void ClrOnGcStart(GCStartTraceData data)
{
    Console.WriteLine($"[{data.ProcessName}] GC gen{data.Depth} because
{data.Reason} started {data.Type}.");
}

private static void ClrOnGcStop(GCEndTraceData data)
{
    Console.WriteLine($"[{data.ProcessName}] GC ended.");
}

private static void ClrOnGcHeapStats(GCHeapStatsTraceData data)
{
    Console.WriteLine($"[{data.ProcessName}]     Heapstats -
{data.GenerationSize0:N0}|{data.GenerationSize1:N0}|{data.
GenerationSize2:N0}|{data.GenerationSize3}");
}
```

Using CLR and kernel parsers with appropriate callbacks makes consuming ETW data trivial and very pleasant. Obviously, we can observe events related to our own process by filtering incoming events by the ProcessID field. It allows us to provide quite deep self-monitoring insight into a process with very low overhead (assuming we will carefully choose how many providers and keywords we enabled to not flood us with the incoming events).

Additionally, with the help of TraceEvent, we can use the ETW ability to record the event's stack trace. To make it possible, a "higher-level" type of session interpreter must be used, named TraceLog. If interesting events have stacks registration enabled, we may use CallStack() method on received trace data to obtain a collection of stack frames. Please refer to TraceEvent library code samples to see a working example. Remember also that enabling stack trace capturing significantly increases the session overhead so it should be used carefully.

At this point, we have already described all the possibilities how we can monitor the use of the memory of our application from within a process:

- we can observe allocations of each thread by calling `GC.GetAllocatedBytesForCurrentThread` method (see Listing 15-10 earlier in this chapter). Obviously, we may build some process-wide statistics built on top of that functionality, gathering data from each thread. Please remember this is only information about allocations and does not inform in any way how much of allocated memory survives. Thus, it does not say anything about overall memory usage of a process. In case of .NET Framework, we can also use AppDomain's `MonitoringTotalAllocatedMemorySize` property for the same purpose (see Listing 15-11 shown earlier).

- We can observe the total size occupied by managed objects (excluding fragmentation) in all generations by calling `GC.GetTotalMemory` method (see Listing 15-6). As already explained, this is a very informative measurement but without consideration of fragmentation and overall memory taken by the Managed Heap, it does not relate greatly to the process memory consumption as seen from the operating system point of view. It is, however, a great way of noticing memory leak, when there are more and more reachable objects on the Managed Heap. We can additionally observe overall process memory usage by `Process` properties like `WorkingSet64` or `PrivateMemorySize64`, to support `GC.GetTotalMemory` measurement.

- We can observe .NET CLR Memory Performance Counters of our own process. This provides great insights into a process (generation sizes, virtual memory consumption, and so on, and so forth) provided with at most one-second granularity, which is enough for many use cases. The main drawback is the fact that Performance Counters are supported only on Windows .NET Framework.

- We can observe the GC ETW events with the TraceEvent library. It provides even more precise and deeper insights into a process, because as we have seen many times in this book, ETW provides tremendous amounts of information. The amount of overhead ETW introduces is proportional to the number of events captured. Observing the not so common GC start/end/GCHeapStats events is a reasonable approach to get high-level memory info.

- We can self-attach the ClrMD library to our own process in a passive way, giving ourselves powerful insights into the Managed Heap (including memory organization into segments, objects, and their references, roots, finalization queues, and so on, and so forth). This is a nice diagnostic approach possibility in Debug build, but I would recommend careful consideration before including it in Release builds on production. Remember that self-attaching in passive mode is not supported by the ClrMD maintainers so it is risky and may lead you to strange problems.

Custom GC

Starting from .NET Core 2.1, coupling between Garbage Collector and the Execution Engine itself have been loosened a lot. Prior to this version, the Garbage Collector code was pretty much tangled with the rest of the CoreCLR code. However, .NET Core 2.1 introduces a concept of *Local GC*, which means the runtime can use a GC in its own dll, which means GC is now pluggable. We can plug in our custom GC by setting a single environment variable (see Listing 15-36).

Listing 15-36. Setting proper environment variable to replace GC implementation

```
set COMPlus_GCName=f:\GithubProjects\CoreCLR.ZeroGC\x64\Release\ZeroGC.dll
```

.NET Core, when initializing, notices such an environment variable and will try to load GC code from the specified library instead of default, built-in GC. The custom GC can contain a completely different implementation from the default GC. Concepts like generations, segments, allocators, and finalization may not be available in a custom GC.

The simplest possible implementation of a Local GC is not very complex. It requires including only a few files directly from CoreCLR code to have things compiled: debugmacros.h, gcenv.base.h, and gcinterface.h. Please note that for brevity only most illustrative parts of such code is presented here. Refer to the accompanying book's source repository for the whole, working example.

A custom GC library needs to define only two required exported functions, called by the CoreCLR during initialization: GC_Initialize and GC_VersionInfo (see Listing 15-37). The former should specify custom implementations of two crucial interfaces: IGCHeap and IGCHandleManager. The latter is used to manage backward compatibility, as you can specify which version of runtime (its GC interface, more precisely) is required for our custom GC.

Listing 15-37. Two required exported functions in Local GC library

```
extern "C" DLLEXPORT HRESULT
GC_Initialize(
    /* In */  IGCToCLR* clrToGC,
    /* Out */ IGCHeap** gcHeap,
    /* Out */ IGCHandleManager** gcHandleManager,
    /* Out */ GcDacVars* gcDacVars
)
{
    IGCHeap* heap = new ZeroGCHeap(clrToGC);
    IGCHandleManager* handleManager = new ZeroGCHandleManager();
    *gcHeap = heap;
    *gcHandleManager = handleManager;
    return S_OK;
}

extern "C" DLLEXPORT void
GC_VersionInfo(
    /* Out */ VersionInfo* result
)
{
    result->MajorVersion = GC_INTERFACE_MAJOR_VERSION;
    result->MinorVersion = GC_INTERFACE_MINOR_VERSION;
    result->BuildVersion = 0;
    result->Name = "Zero GC";
}
```

We should additionally store the provided IGCToCLR interface address, used to communicate with CLR from inside our GC code. It contains a lot of methods and some of the most interesting ones are:

- SuspendEE and RestartEE - asks the runtime to suspend and resume managed threads, for a given reason (we can use it to implement not-concurrent parts of our custom GC).

- `GcScanRoots` - performs a stack walk of all managed threads and invokes the given promote_func on all GC roots encountered on the stack (we would need this in our custom Mark phase implementation).

- `GcStartWork` and `GcDone` - inform the runtime that a GC has started and completed.

Custom `IGCHeap` interface implementation is the main interface representing core Garbage Collection functionality (see Listing 15-38). Implementing `IGCHeap` requires implementing about 71 methods! Not all really need to have valid implementation though, as they are declared in built-in current GC design in mind - so we will provide some dummy implementations of methods like `SetGcLatencyMode` or `SetLOHCompactionMode` as our custom GC may does not have the concept of latency mode or LOH at all.

Listing 15-38. Fragment of custom `IGCHeap` implementation

```
class ZeroGCHeap : public IGCHeap
{
private:
    IGCToCLR* gcToCLR;
public:
    ZeroGCHeap(IGCToCLR* gcToCLR)
    {
        this->gcToCLR = gcToCLR;
    }

    // Inherited via IGCHeap
    ...
}
```

Among various `IGCHeap` methods, the top-level methods are for allocations (`IGCHeap::Alloc`) and garbage collection (`IGCHeap::GarbageCollect`). The simplest possible so-called *Zero GC* (only capable of allocating objects but never reclaiming memory) could be implemented as in Listing 15-39. Please note that our custom GC does not have to distinguish "small" or "large" objects (and thus, SOH and LOH). We may allocate our objects as we wish regardless of its size - for example, by always using Heap API with the regular `calloc` function call.

Listing 15-39. Examples of the 2 top-level methods implementation of the custom IGCHeap

```
class ObjHeader
{
private:
#ifdef _WIN64
    DWORD     m_alignpad;
#endif // _WIN64
    DWORD m_SyncBlockValue;
};

Object * ZeroGCHeap::Alloc(gc_alloc_context * acontext, size_t size,
uint32_t flags)
{
    int sizeWithHeader = size + sizeof(ObjHeader);
    ObjHeader* address = (ObjHeader*)calloc(sizeWithHeader, sizeof(char*));
    return (Object*)(address + 1);
}

HRESULT ZeroGCHeap::GarbageCollect(int generation, bool low_memory_p, int
mode)
{
    return NOERROR;
}
```

It is really funny to see a single line of GarbageCollect method - the one that in case of default .NET GC triggers executing several thousand lines of code, described in hundreds of pages in this book. Here is where only our imagination is the limit. Feel free to implement your own GC!

By writing our custom GC, we replace all default GC functionality. Hence, it is not easy to just modify the default behavior "a little." Although, if one takes the whole built-in GC code and will publish it as a Standalone GC library, it will be much easier to complete.

As write barriers are simply specially handled functions written in assembly
code and injected by JIT, currently there is no API to replace them. As we may
remember from Chapter 5, write barriers are responsible for updating card tables
so they are expected to exist, even if our implementation does not need them.
Look for `ZeroGCHeap::Initialize` method in the accompanying example to
see how `IGCToCLR::StompWriteBarrier` is configured to omit its usage by
manipulating the lowest and the highest ephemeral segment address. And even
if in custom GC, distinguishing between Workstation and Server mode should not
make sense, because of write barriers, it still does matter: only in Workstation
mode write barrier checks' ephemeral segment boundaries (as explained in
Chapter 5 in Listing 5-8), so we can use it to omit card table updating. However,
Server GC mode with our custom GC crashes the runtime because `JIT_
WriteBarrier_SVR64` is being used, which requires unconditionally valid card
table address.

Please note that `IGCHandleManager` and `IGCHandleStore` dummy implementations
are omitted for brevity. I invite you to read the Zero GC implementation provided with
this book to see their code.

Summary

This chapter described various ways of controlling and monitoring .NET memory
usage programmatically. Based on the knowledge acquired from previous chapters, we
should feel quite comfortable in writing code utilizing shown capabilities. As we might
notice, knowledge about CLR and GC internals is quite often helpful, if not necessary, to
properly configure and interpret data provided by libraries described in this chapter.

Firstly, comprehensive list of static GC class methods and properties was presented to
summarize its already shown possibilities altogether with things that were not described
well or not at all so far (like GC notifications). GC class usage was quite frequent
throughout the book, so you've probably already noticed how useful it may be in various
scenarios. From all the techniques described in this chapter, GC class (and a few auxiliary
classes) seem to be the most common ones in an everyday's developer work.

Then, CLR Hosting was presented with the most relevant interfaces on the field of memory management, to show what may be achieved with it. I do not expect big popularity of CLR hosting in your development, but I really wanted to present it to widen your toolbox. Maybe your use cases include calling managed code from unmanaged applications (like .NET scripting capabilities in SQL Server), so a possibility to manipulate how hosted CLR uses memory may be beneficial for you (with some monitoring capabilities available).

Presented ClrMD and EventTrace are two great libraries dedicated to deep diagnostic and monitoring of your .NET processes (including your own process in case of a self-monitoring scenario). Used together or alone, they allow us to get very detailed information about .NET runtime and your application's behavior. Even they are overwhelmingly popular in implementing various diagnostic tools, you may also consider using it in self-monitoring scenarios as they provide relatively small overhead (a possibility especially tempting on pre-production environments).

Just in case you might be curious, the last section of this chapter presents a new possibility currently implemented only in .NET Core 2.1, which allows for a complete replacement of the GC implementation. I believe it greatly and ironically concludes the whole book, dedicated solely to the description of the default, built-in GC that may now be removed and replaced with something totally different. I strongly invite you to experiment with the Zero GC included as a sample of such custom GC. With the whole knowledge you've gained in this book, including theoretical introduction in the first chapters, you should now have the solid basics to start writing your own, not-so-trivial GC implementation!

Index

A

AccessViolationException, 1
Accumulator, 5
Address lines, 73
Address windowing extensions
    (AWE), 106
Allocation budget, 355
    AllocSmall, 545
    begin size, 537
    byte[] array, 538, 542
    changes, 543
    C# program, 533–534
    ephemeral generations, 544
    ETW, 535
    GC events table, 535–536, 538
    GCStats report, 535
    generation 0, 539–540
    generation 1, 539–540
    generation 2, 539–540
    generation sizes, 540, 544–545
    gen0 survival rate, 537
    LOH budget, 539–540
    new allocation values, 537, 542–543
    non-concurrent full-GC, 536
    OutOfSpaceSOH, 544–545
    per generation GC events, 535
    promotion size, 539, 541, 543
    SOH allocations, 541, 544
    static GC Data, 535
    subsequent GCs, 545
    survival ratios, 545
    third GC, 541
    Visual Studio, 534
Allocator, 39–40
Amdahl's law, 141
AMD CodeAnalyst Performance
    Analyzer, 207–209
Anscombe's quartet, 135–136
API, GC
    explicit collection, 1013
    finalization management, 1013
    InternalCall, 1016
    MemoryFailPoint usage, 1014–1015
    no GC region, 1013
    notifications, 1009, 1011
    properties and methods
        GC.CollectionCount(Int32), 998–999
        GC.GetAllocatedBytesFor
          CurrentThread, 1005–1008
        GC.GetGeneration, 999–1002
        GC.GetTotalMemory, 1002–1004
        GC.KeepAlive, 1008
        GC.MaxGeneration, 998
        GCSettings.IsServerGC, 1009
        GCSettings.LargeObjectHeap
          CompactionMode, 1009
        GCSettings.LatencyMode, 1009
    unmanaged memory pressure, 1012

Printed in the United States
By Bookmasters